CHRISTMAS
1990

Kitty Armfield

Cheryl Greenhill

Angela Wood

Jim Morrison

John H. Oehm

Carole A. Hoefener

Jack Hill

Bob Kennedy

C. A. Dedevise

Betsy Mayer

David M. Taylor

Randy Sevas

North Carolina Architecture

North Carolina Architecture

Catherine W. Bishir

Photography by Tim Buchman

Published for The Historic Preservation Foundation of North Carolina, Inc.,

by The University of North Carolina Press, Chapel Hill and London

The Historic Preservation Foundation acknowledges with thanks the cooperation and support of the State Historic Preservation Office, Division of Archives and History, North Carolina Department of Cultural Resources.

The paper in this book meets the guidelines for permanence and durability of the Committee on Production Guidelines for Book Longevity of the Council on Library Resources.

Printed and bound in Japan by Dai Nippon Printing Co., Ltd.

94 93 92 91 90   5   4   3   2   1

Library of Congress Cataloging-in-Publication Data
Bishir, Catherine W.
   North Carolina architecture/Catherine W. Bishir; photography
by Tim Buchman.
      p. cm.
   Includes bibliographical references.
   ISBN 0-8078-1923-9
      1. Architecture—North Carolina.   I. Title.
NA730.N8B5 1990
720′.9756—dc20   90-30662
                                                              CIP

Quote, page 363, from *You Can't Go Home Again* by Thomas Wolfe. Copyright 1934, 1937, 1938, 1939, 1940 by Maxwell Perkins as the Executor of the Estate of Thomas Wolfe. Reprinted by permission of Harper and Row, Publishers, Inc.

Photographs: State Capitol, Raleigh, 1833–40, House of Commons (facing p. iii); Bellamy Mansion, Wilmington, 1859–60 (facing p. vii); Hayes Plantation, Chowan County, 1815–17 (facing p. xi)

Contents

Foreword

J. Myrick Howard, Executive Director,
The Historic Preservation Foundation of North Carolina, Inc.

Of the many suggestions for ways to commemorate the fiftieth anniversary of the founding of the Historic Preservation Foundation of North Carolina, Inc., the publication of this book was a natural choice. After all, one catalyst for the founding of the organization, originally named the North Carolina Society for the Preservation of Antiquities, was the publication of *Old Homes and Gardens of North Carolina*, under the auspices of the Garden Club of North Carolina, by the University of North Carolina Press in 1939. That book and the 1941 volume, *Early Architecture of North Carolina*, also published by the University of North Carolina Press, became touchstones for historic preservationists in North Carolina. They influenced which buildings North Carolinians cherished and why.

Almost fifty years later, the need was compelling for a new look at North Carolina's historic buildings: not a replacement for those earlier books nor a new version of them, but a book for our own times. Preservation as a movement is now more inclusive than exclusive, and the preservationist's interest is drawn to the humble as well as the grand.

This new perspective on North Carolina's architectural history is very much in that spirit. Rather than simply identify the most outstanding landmarks in North Carolina's past, this book presents in many cases representative buildings which may evoke images of hundreds more in communities across the state. It is the hope of the Preservation Foundation that this book will stimulate a passion for preserving the whole spectrum of North Carolina's history.

The Historic Preservation Foundation of North Carolina, Inc., is grateful to the following patrons who shared the vision of this book. Through their generous contributions, it can be enjoyed by all those interested in preserving North Carolina's rich heritage for the benefit of present and future generations.

The Cannon Foundation, Inc., Concord (Special Gift)

American Association for State and Local History, Nashville, Tennessee
Newton Duke Angier, Flat Rock and Durham
Anonymous Donors
Charles H. Babcock, Jr., Winston-Salem
The Mary Duke Biddle Foundation, Durham
John and Catherine Bishir, Raleigh
Mr. and Mrs. Ben Mayo Boddie, Rocky Mount
Mr. and Mrs. Nick B. Boddie, Rocky Mount
Dr. and Mrs. Lawrence Kennedy Boggs, Charlotte
Mr. Sion A. Boney, Greensboro
Mr. and Mrs. J. Robert Boykin III, Wilson
Mr. and Mrs. John Bratton, Raleigh
The Brewer Foundation, Rocky Mount
Claudia R. and Gordon L. Brown, Raleigh
George R. Brown/Dennis Cudd, Charlotte
The Broyhill Family Foundation, Inc., Lenoir
Joseph Bryan, Jr., Greensboro
Joseph M. Bryan, Sr., Greensboro
Mrs. Thomas Bullard, Flat Rock
Esther Hatch and C. D. Burnette Family for Southerland-Burnette House, Mount Olive
Robert P. and Norma D. Burns, Raleigh

Mr. Paul F. Callaway, Greensboro
Capital Area Preservation, Inc., Raleigh
Carolista Jewelry Designers, Nags Head
Dr. Gertrude S. Carraway, New Bern
Michael P. Carson/Ronald W. Steigerwalt, Ph.D., Hertford
Dr. and Mrs. Robert Cerwin, Raleigh
Charlotte-Mecklenburg Historic Properties Commission, Charlotte
Mr. and Mrs. Godfrey Cheshire, Jr., Raleigh
E. L. Clark/The Clark Family Trust, Durham
Mr. and Mrs. Edward H. Clement, Salisbury
Elizabeth W. and Benjamin Cone, Jr., Greensboro
Mr. and Mrs. James M. Corcoran, New Bern
Bruce Cotten Fund, North Carolina Collection, Chapel Hill
Mrs. Marion Stedman Covington, Greensboro
James Ruffin Creech, Rocky Mount
Ronald and Sharon Criss, Raleigh
Lillian F. Crosland (Mrs. John), Charlotte
Mrs. Robert Harris Daniel, Greenville
Mr. and Mrs. Frank Daniels, Jr., Raleigh
Davidson County Historical Association, Lexington
Gwendolyn Picklesimer Davis, Raleigh
Ruth Johnston Davis, Wilson
Todd W. and Patricia S. Dickinson, Hillsborough
Mr. G. Wilson Douglas, Jr., Winston-Salem

Mrs. Mary E. Merritt Winstead, Roxboro
Mr. and Mrs. Charles M. Winston, Raleigh
Winston-Salem/Forsyth County/Kernersville Historic Properties
    Commission, Winston-Salem
Mr. and Mrs. Thomas Wright, Jr., Wilmington
Mr. and Mrs. G. Smedes York, Raleigh
Thelma K. and Joseph E. Zaytoun, Cary
Mr. and Mrs. Henry Christian Zenke, Greensboro

In Honor of:

Virginia Storr Atkinson (Mrs. Virginia A. Stevens)
Eleanor Hayes Barnhardt (Mr. and Mrs. James H. Barnhardt)
Mary Louise Haywood Davis (Archie K. Davis)
Todd W. Dickinson (Anonymous)
David and Ethelyne Downs (Donald A. Downs)
Marian Stoudemire Hawkins and Cranford Stoudemire (Sterling
    and Mary Arthur Stoudemire)
J. Myrick Howard (Preservation Colleagues)
Bill McLawhorn (Brinkley Sugg)
Eugene F. and Opal C. Messick (Mr. Gene Messick)
Margaret Hyacinthe Chesson Mizell (Emily Mizell Henson and
    Margaret Mizell Davenport)
Olivia Blount Cowper Moore (R. B. Raney Webb, Jr.)
Clyde Overcash (Wyndham Robertson)
Wyndham Robertson (Nancy B. Faircloth)
C. M. and Helen P. Smith (Mr. James W. M. Smith)
Mr. and Mrs. W. David Stedman (Mrs. Marion S. Covington)
Virginia Atkinson Stevens (Mrs. Virginia S. Atkinson)
Dr. and Mrs. Robert E. Stipe (Marjorie K. N. Salzman, Anne R.
    Williams, and Douglas A. Johnston)
Mrs. Sterling A. Stoudemire (The Rt. Rev. and Mrs. Peter James
    Lee)
Mr. and Mrs. John E. Tyler (Mrs. Marion S. Covington)
Margaret Norris Ward and William Smith Ward (Anonymous)
Anne R. Williams (Mr. and Mrs. Tomme Gamewell,
    J. Myrick Howard, Mr. and Mrs. George F. Kluttz, and
    Mr. and Mrs. Edward P. Norvell)

In Memory of:

Charles H. Babcock, Sr. (Barbara B. Millhouse)
John Blue III (Martha B. Blue)
Mary Lyon Leak Caine (Mrs. Anita C. Schenck)
Mr. Charles A. Cannon (Mr. and Mrs. Robert G. Hayes)
Mrs. Charles A. Cannon (Mr. and Mrs. William C. Cannon)
George Watts Carr and Amy Winston Carr (Robert W. Carr)
Richard Thurmond Chatham (Walter F. Chatham)

Robert Bruce Cooke (Aylene E. Cooke and Robert Cameron
    Cooke)
Nancy-Elisabeth Dill (Dr. Franklin G. Dill)
Mishew R. Edgerton (N. Edward Edgerton)
Walter Clark Erwin (Mrs. Walter Clark Erwin)
Emily Storr Fulford (Mrs. Virginia A. Stevens)
Mildred J. and Lester C. Gifford (Mr. and Mrs. Kenneth
    Millholland)
Bahnson Gray (Anne P. Gray)
James A. and Pauline B. Gray (Mr. and Mrs. John K Gallaher, Sr.)
Susanna Elizabeth Ray Gwyn (Susanna Revelle Gwyn and
    Meyer E. Dworsky)
Mr. and Mrs. Ernest Lauriston Hardin (Mr. and Mrs. Edward
    Tennent Taylor)
Shearon Harris (Mrs. Shearon Harris)
Max Hoffman (Anonymous)
Mr. and Mrs. William Oliver Huske and Dr. Richard Sterling
    Kelly, Jr. (Mrs. Rosalie Huske Kelly)
William E. "Bill" Jackson, and William Raymond Taylor and
    Bertie Yancey Taylor (Eloise Taylor Jackson)
Mr. and Mrs. John A. Kellenberger (The Kellenberger Historical
    Foundation)
Col. Henry E. Kendall (Katharine Kerr Kendall)
Mr. and Mrs. James Edward Latham (The Kellenberger Historical
    Foundation)
Mrs. Lillian Crisp Lawrence (Mrs. Robert C. Cone)
Willie Lee Lumpkin (The Family of Willie Lee Lumpkin)
Jane Williams Lewis and Mary Lewis Williams (Mr. Henry W.
    Lewis)
Mr. and Mrs. Donald Stuart Matheson (Mrs. Esten Matheson
    Bohannon)
Mr. and Mrs. John Flood Matheson (Mary Davidson Matheson)
John Augustus Moore III (Miss Elizabeth V. Moore)
Mrs. Elizabeth L. Moretz (Mrs. Leonard Moretz)
Mrs. Daniel Murray Paul (Mr. Dan M. Paul)
Mr. and Mrs. Elbert Peel, Sr. (Mrs. Elbert Peel, Jr.)
Edward W. Phifer, Jr., M.D. (Mrs. Edward W. Phifer, Jr.)
Mr. and Mrs. Richard Beverly Raney (Dr. R. B. Raney)
Paul Apperson Reid (Mrs. Paul A. Reid)
Richard J. Reynolds, Jr. (Dr. Annemarie S. Reynolds)
Steed Rollins (Mrs. Steed Rollins)
Mr. and Mrs. Ottmar A. (Bill and Sadie) Ruedrich (Mr. Dean A.
    Ruedrich)
C. J. Shoaf and Dale H. Gramley (Wachovia Historical Society)
Mrs. Nancy Blanton Siegel (Mrs. Nancy Dicks Blanton)
Mr. and Mrs. P. D. Snipes and Sarah Snipes Koester (Mr. John D.
    Koester)
Willis Henry Thompson, Jr. (Mrs. Willis H. Thompson, Jr.)
Marion Pittman Troxler (William F. Troxler)
Herbert Clarke Turner (Mrs. Rebecca T. Williams)
Helen E. Vogler (Harold and Elizabeth Vogler)
Ailcie Hairston Glenn Whittle (Mr. Joseph B. C. Kluttz)
Mr. and Mrs. John Gilliam Wood (Mr. and Mrs. Trent Ragland,
    Jr.)
Sterling D. Wooten (Banks C. Talley, Jr.)

Preface

For most of its history, North Carolina has been a rural state without concentrated wealth or great cities. The beauty of its architectural landscape is subtle and at first unprepossessing, seldom magnificent, sometimes untidy, and often utilitarian. It has been a place of rural roads winding through a long-settled, richly storied landscape of small farmsteads and scattered plantations, of hardscrabble farms and hardwon accomplishments, of ambivalence toward opulence, and of hierarchy and distance combined with intimacy and interconnectedness.

Now, in the last decade of the twentieth century, that landscape is being transformed at a dizzying pace. As the nation shifts from a national industrial and agricultural economy to a global service and information economy, the state faces unprecedented change. The family farm, the manufacture of textiles and tobacco and furniture, and the fishing economy are all changing or vanishing. Tourism brings prosperity and change to long-isolated communities, and cities reach out into the landscape and along the highways; yet in other sections, unemployment and poverty are mounting.

What seems to be most threatened is the heritage of North Carolina that seemed most secure when the North Carolina Society for the Preservation of Antiquities was founded in 1939—the heritage of the ordinary people who have made up the state's history and its architecture throughout its three hundred years. In the 1930s, for example, the architecture of the industrial age was new and dominant in the towns. For many observers in that time, the extravagance and overtly industrialized character of Victorian architecture generated distaste rather than admiration, while the architecture of the 1910s and 1920s, if more appealing, was so new as to be considered modern rather than historic. In the countryside, small log dwellings and frame dwellings were thick on the ground, strewn across the countryside, inhabited by tenant families and small landowners. Simple wooden agricultural buildings—barns, privies, chickenhouses, granaries, dairies—stood by the millions, unpainted perhaps, but in daily use. Tobacco barns of log or frame stood in rows; old and young, black and white, men, women, and children clustered around them to work year after year. Covered bridges spanned stream after stream. Crossroads churches and country stores and gristmills bustled with life and were the center of life. Mill villages were crowded with working families. Suburbs lay along the streetcar lines and newly paved avenues, while dense neighborhoods of working people's houses clustered within sight of factories. Small cities and market towns, struggling to recover economic and social stability, centered on their main streets and their factories. Then, it surely seemed unimaginable that within the century all this would be at risk of loss.

As North Carolina has moved into a period of new wealth and postagrarian and postindustrial life, appreciation of the great buildings of the wealthy—from colonial plantation houses to the extravaganzas of the Victorian era to the premier suburbs of the early twentieth century—affirms a sense of continuity with present trends. The traditional, plain farmhouse, the frame country church, the legions of tobacco barns, the rows of mill houses, the houses of rural workers and tenants, and indeed the family farmstead itself—these modest buildings seldom command attention individually. They are, like the people who created and have used them, central to what makes North Carolina itself. I hope that North Carolinians in the twenty-first century will value the modest buildings of our agrarian and industrial past, and that those ordinary buildings built so close to the land will not be lost for the next generation.

Two earlier works that inspired this volume, *Old Homes and Gardens of North Carolina* by Archibald Henderson and Bayard Wootten (1939) and *The Early Architecture of North Carolina* by

Frances Benjamin Johnston and Thomas Tileston Waterman (1941), are revered as classics. The architectural patterns their authors discerned, and the images of buildings their photographers recorded, have become the canons for subsequent generations. Amid the rapid growth and widespread destruction of the 1950s and 1960s, the places singled out in these two volumes often survived by dint of their representation there, and in the late 1960s and early 1970s, when historic preservation activities began to expand throughout the country, North Carolinians turned first to these two books and to another great product of that time—the WPA-sponsored *North Carolina Guide*—as references both for local preservation efforts and to begin the statewide architectural survey and National Register of Historic Places program in the North Carolina Department of Archives and History. Today, for the most part, the buildings shown in deshabille in the images of the 1930s are no longer standing at the threshold of disappearance: they have either been lost from the landscape or, in the majority of cases, have been maintained by their owners or restored as local or state museums. Those landmarks have maintained their importance to us today, as the pages of this volume suggest, and they will and should play a prominent role in our future.

Still, this is ultimately a book of the 1980s. The writer and the photographer are part of a generation that was born after the Great Depression and grew up in times of economic growth and social change. For us it has been urbanization, rural abandonment, and new construction that have most altered the historic landscape. So, too, new currents have shaped our view of architectural and cultural history. The late twentieth century has seen a renewal of interest in the architecture not only of the antebellum and colonial periods but also of the Victorian era and the early twentieth century. Paralleling this has been an expansion of concern from the oldest and most ambitious architecture toward ordinary buildings, urban and rural.

In choosing from the expanse of North Carolina's architecture the places to photograph for this book, we have continued to praise famous landmarks, but we have also dwelt on the quieter beauty of the simple buildings. These examples cannot form a canon of individual landmarks. They may, we hope, suggest the importance of the whole. In the narrative that accompanies the photographs, and the drawings and older images that supplement them, I have tried to tell a story that looks to the larger world and what was happening in it while also focusing on the particular realities and individual sagas—where they are known—of the people whose choices, needs, ideals, and problems shaped and were shaped by the buildings.

It is impossible in a single volume on the state's architecture to survey the topic comprehensively, or to include all significant buildings or even types of buildings. This work is necessarily selective rather than comprehensive. By highlighting through photographs a few examples, we want to call attention to the thousands more that compose our rural and urban landscapes. By tracing the stories of a few local, state, and national patterns of development and by looking closely at a few communities, congregations, families, and individuals and their hopes, purposes, and endeavors, I hope to hint at the complexity of the stories that are part of each building and each place.

Several factors have affected the selection of buildings. We envisioned from the outset a book with principal emphasis on photographs made by Tim Buchman. Hence selection was guided by the visual impact of a building or buildings along with architectural and historical significance. Could the essential character and important elements of a place be revealed in a photograph? This consideration was important in choosing among well-known landmarks, and it was even more critical in our quest for the ideal examples of important types of buildings and places where one or two must evoke hundreds more. In some unexpected cases, trees and bushes or extensive additions shielded key buildings from photography. In other cases, recent changes and lighting conditions redirected our search: an exemplary small-town Queen Anne–style house had been vinyl sided; a perfect small country church had gained a new front deck; and a handsome bungalow with a porch of rich, dark-stained woodwork faced north into deep shadows. One classic mill village had grown up in tall hedges, another was far gone in decay, and still another had front yards filled with animal sculptures by a local artist. Hence the process of selection resulted from a continuing and mutually enlightening interplay between aesthetic and historical values.

The choice to stress Tim Buchman's photographs also means that other images are used sparingly. Site plans and floor plans indicate a few principal types of arrangement rather than depicting the many variations of plan from building to building. Documentary photographs are restricted to a few lost landmarks and outstanding examples that cannot be satisfactorily photographed today because of foliage or condition. Original architectural drawings and plates from architectural books merely suggest the kinds of sources from which people drew architectural ideas in various periods.

Choice of examples has also been shaped by the status of research by many students of North Carolina architecture. I have relied on the work of the dozens of architectural historians who have conducted county and town architectural surveys for localities in coordination with the North Carolina State Historic Preservation Office and on the in-depth research and description contained in the hundreds of nominations to the National Register of Historic Places. Over thirty published survey books provide ready access to this invaluable material. Also crucial to any broad study are the intensive studies of specific buildings and types of buildings, ranging from the Cupola House to the Capitol to the courthouses of all one hundred counties. These are cited in the notes and bibliography. Recent and valuable broader studies of the state's architecture include *Carolina Dwelling*, edited by Douglas Swaim, *The Architecture of the Old South: North Carolina*, by Mills Lane, and "Architecture in North Carolina, 1700–1900," by Lawrence Wodehouse. Research conducted for *Architects and Builders in North Carolina: A History of the Practice of Building* has been important in establishing patterns of patronage and building; I am grateful to my colleagues Charlotte Brown, Carl Lounsbury, and Ernest Wood, and to Marshall Bullock and William Bushong for their knowledge and generous help. Finally, the process of selection has also naturally reflected my experiences, interests, and values, and my own interpretation of patterns at work in the state's architectural development.

We decided to limit the span of the book to the period from about 1700 to about 1940—from the first surviving buildings to the onset of World War II and the sweeping changes that followed it. Chapter divisions reflect conventional periodization marked by major wars and the turn of the twentieth century. For the most part, this arrangement accords reasonably well with the patterns of architectural and social development in the state. But as human affairs seldom fit perfectly into arbitrary divisions, some architectural trends reach across chronological sections. The situation is complicated when the examples that are best for photography date from the latter phases of a long period of development. This is especially true for the slow-changing patterns of traditional construction and building forms of small houses and farm outbuildings and for generations of industrial buildings. These cases are addressed directly in captions and text.

Crucial to any project such as this are the scores of individuals who generously allowed us to photograph their houses and farm buildings and who opened up churches, public buildings, museums, and other buildings. Unfailingly, people have been helpful, patient, and gracious even when we disrupted their buildings and lives for hours on end. We are grateful for their help, and our memories of their kindnesses remain strong, though it is not possible to mention them all here individually.

Many other people have given us special assistance in gaining access to buildings, by offering hospitality and logistical help, and by providing information or documentary pictures. Among them are Jean Anderson, Millie Barbee, Richard Barentine, Brad Barker, Ray Beck, John Bivins, Martha Boxley, Jack Boyte, Tom Butchko, Robert Cain, Jerry Cashion, John Compton, Dennis Cudd, Randy Davis, Todd Dickinson, Donna Dodenhoff, Linda Eure, Elva Gheen, John Green, Catherine Hoffman, Richard Hunter, John Wesley Jones, Roger Jones, Rosalie Kelly, John Larson, William McCrea, Linda McCurdy, Ken McFarland, Timothy Mattimoe, Richard Mattson, Elizabeth V. Moore, Elizabeth Morgan, William Murphy, Sylvia Nash, Joe and Langdon Oppermann, Richard Parsons, Laura Phillips, Suzanne Pickens, Joe and Bernice Pitt, Dean Ruedrich, Janet Seapker, Robert Stern, George Stevenson, Jim Sumner, Gwynne Taylor, Neville Thompson, Edward Turberg, William Turpin, Sarah Williamson, and Jo Ann Williford. Vital support has been given freely by many individuals, including Norma Burns and Elizabeth Matheson; Rick Alexander of Rick Alexander and Associates for his extensive technical and professional support; and David Brook, William Price, Michael Southern, and Sondra Ward at Archives and History.

In addition, I am indebted to the architectural historians and the staff of the State Historic Preservation Office who have shared insights and interpretations over the years, including Allison Black, David Black, John Clauser, Brent Glass, Renée Gledhill-Earley, Al Honeycutt, Davyd Foard Hood, Peter Kaplan, Ruth Little, Keith Morgan, Peter Sandbeck, McKelden Smith, Michael Southern, Doug Swaim, Mitch Wilds, and Drucilla York. Thanks for inspiring particular angles of vision for places in this book go to Greer Suttlemyre for Many Pines, Davyd Foard Hood for Cleveland Presbyterian Church, Ruth Little for Old Bluff Presbyterian Church, and Doug Swaim for the Matthews House. I am also grateful to other friends and colleagues who have expanded my view of North Carolina architecture, including Robert Burns, Tom Carter, Edward Chappell, Paul Groth, Bernard Herman, Orlando Ridout V, Dell Upton, and Camille Wells. My thanks to the Henry Francis du Pont Winterthur Museum for a 1987 H. F. du Pont research fellowship and the use of the museum's excellent library.

For readings of all or part of the manuscript and for encouragement along the way, thanks to Charlotte Brown, Claudia Roberts Brown, Al Chambers, Kate Hutchins, John Larson, Ruth Little, Carl Lounsbury, John Sanders, Margaret Supplee Smith, Michael Southern, and Harry Watson. At the University of North Carolina Press, I am grateful for the steady encouragement and expert assistance from our excellent editors, David Perry and Pamela Upton, designer Ed King, and the fine staff of the Press throughout the editing, design, production, and marketing of this book.

Special thanks go to individuals central to this endeavor: Carl Lounsbury, for the many drawings he prepared for this book, and for continuing encouragement; to Sandra Webbere, who coordinated photography visits and provided unstinting enthusiasm, patience, and attention to detail; and to Paul Murphy of Image Plus, who printed the photographs with skill and care. My thanks to John Bishir for help beyond measure.

Finally, I want to thank the Historic Preservation Foundation of North Carolina for creating and sustaining this project and Myrick Howard for his vision, determination, and unfailing support. For both Tim and me, the chance to participate in this undertaking has been an extraordinary privilege.

Catherine W. Bishir
Raleigh, December, 1989

North Carolina Architecture

CHAPTER I

The Colonial Period, 1680–1776

The country . . . must be imagined as a continuous, measureless forest, an ocean of trees, in which only here and there cultivated spots, what are called plantations, of more or less extent are to be seen. In the midst of the fields stands commonly a house, better or worse; the kitchen and other mean out-buildings are at a distance. . . . There is nothing to see but a few cabins for negroes and store-houses, which in outward appearance are seldom much inferior to the dwelling-house of the master. One comes upon such plantations scattered about in these woods at various distances, 3–6 miles, and often as much as 10–15–20 miles apart. . . . It is the forests which supply the present inhabitants of North Carolina not merely an occupation and a support, but the means of an easier life and often considerable estates. For the products of these pine-woods as such, the convenience and small expence of keeping numerous cattle in them, and the pretty abundant stock of game even now, these have for long formed the most important items in the export trade of the province, carried on chiefly with the West Indies, where there is a near and ready market.
—Johann Schoepf, *Travels in the Confederation*

The Architecture of a Forest Society

For a century and more after Europeans and Africans began to build in North Carolina, their architecture, like their economy, was that of a forest society.[1] As in New England and the Chesapeake region, settlers entered a landscape at once enticing and threatening, where the endless forests and vast distances, the scarcity of workers, and the absence of urban centers demanded that they adapt quickly to survive and flourish. As in the Chesapeake and other southern colonies, too, the fecund land, the forests and streams bountiful with game and fish, and, especially, the warm climate and long growing season promised a life of leisure and plenty. The daytime sky darkened with flocks of birds and mockingbirds trilled, and at night lightning bugs glowed "like so many burning candles" in the forest, to the accompanying roar of bullfrogs and the screams of panthers.[2] North Carolina's early architectural development was part of the process by which settlers adapted old customs to a new life in a subtropical coastal forest.[3]

The sponsors of the colonies in Virginia, South Carolina, and the Caribbean islands successfully encouraged development of a plantation economy. In those areas with broad rivers leading into natural harbors, planters who survived the heat and diseases had easy access to markets for their exports. They reinvested their profits in land and slaves. On this basis, a colonial elite soon emerged at the top of a stratified plantation culture.

By contrast, North Carolina's dangerous coastline and lack of good ports or long inland rivers slowed settlement and discouraged commercial agriculture. A trickle of settlers entered North Carolina in the 1650s and 1660s as fur traders, planters looking for cheaper land, and

Figure 1.1. Chowan County Courthouse, Edenton, begun 1767. The courtroom presents a richly layered history of its central role in the county's political and cultural life, from the original judge's chair and benches in the apse to the early 19th-century columns, late-19th-century benches, 20th-century jury chairs, and memorial plaques from the late 19th and early 20th centuries.

runaway servants began to move from Virginia into the region along the Albemarle Sound, or "the land to the Southward" as they termed it. Through the seventeenth century and into the first decades of the eighteenth, the colony remained small, numbering only about 5,000 settlers in 1700 and 11,000 in 1715. These people were mainly of British stock but also included a few African slaves and a colony of Swiss and Germans at New Bern. They occupied a narrow fringe along the Albemarle and Pamlico sounds, on the edge of a country dominated until after 1712 by the Tuscarora and other powerful Indian nations.

In the second quarter of the eighteenth century, however, conditions gradually became more stable. Wars with the Tuscarora had ended with their defeat in eastern North Carolina. Government of the colony shifted from the various Lords Proprietors to the British Crown, and immigration rose dramatically. Land-hungry settlers continued to migrate south from Virginia and north from South Carolina. Other newcomers arrived from New England, the mid-Atlantic colonies, and the Caribbean, and still others from England, Scotland, Ireland, Wales, France, and Africa. These settlers pushed the frontier westward as they traveled up the rivers into the coastal plain and toward the fall line. By 1730 there were about 30,000 colonists. Then, beginning in the 1740s, the population soared—to 100,000 by 1752, 200,000 by 1765, and 350,000 by 1786—as immigration continued in the east and, especially, as land opened up in the west and settlers moved down the Valley of Virginia into the Piedmont. The principal towns along the coast, all very small, were Edenton, Bath, Beaufort, New Bern, Wilmington, and Brunswick; prominent inland river ports and crossroads villages were Halifax, Campbelltown (later Fayetteville), Corbinton (later Hillsborough), and Salisbury. By midcentury North Carolina had become, as a minister in Brunswick put it, "a country inhabited by many sorts of people, of various nations and different opinions, customs and manners."[4]

Despite this rapid population growth, the difficulties of navigation still limited trade and hampered the development of commercial agriculture and staple-crop production, city growth, and a stratified social structure. But the warm climate and bountiful forest provided a "coarse Subsistence" to thousands of small farmers, and with it a full and heady measure of independence. More than two-thirds of the white men owned land, most of them holding tracts of a hundred to five hundred acres. Social and economic patterns varied greatly from one region to another, ranging from the clique of South Carolina planters that dominated the Lower Cape Fear region to the small and middling planters who were numerous in most of the coastal plain and the yeoman farmers who settled the Piedmont.[5]

The settlers soon learned forest agriculture. They followed Indian custom and girdled a few trees, let them decay, and hoed their crops of corn, beans, and tobacco around them. They fenced in their crops with branches and rails and set their pigs and cattle to forage and multiply in the woods. And they tapped and burned the longleaf pine for turpentine, pitch, and tar or felled the towering trees for lumber and shingles, for which the British market paid well.[6]

The small farmer, the tenant, and the squatter could obtain the necessities of life from the common woods and streams. They could decide for themselves how much time they would spend working, and they could remain independent of the patronage of large landowners. These possibilities were highly attractive to the ordinary folk arriving from Great Britain and Europe, where few could call their land or their time their own. Some observers condemned the "Lubberland" character of Carolina, while others praised the colony as "the Best poor mans Cuntry I Ever heard of."[7]

The forest society created a landscape and architecture of its own. Carolinians built small farmsteads, each located some distance from the others and each consisting of small, separate buildings for the main dwelling, the storage of crops, and the housing of servants. Large barns were unnecessary when livestock ranged free in the woods. The pattern of building farmsteads of small individual structures had developed in the seventeenth-century Chesapeake; this idea paralleled building patterns traditional among both the Indians, who remained a strong presence into the eighteenth century, and many Africans, who were becoming more numerous in the mid-eighteenth century.[8]

To European and northern visitors, the landscape of the forest society was bewildering and threatening. It seemed a wilderness, where the disorderly farmsteads, crude buildings, unchecked livestock roaming through the woods or streets, and the absence of the trappings of authority bore no resemblance to civilization. For residents, however, the paths and interfamilial connections among farms and settlements created a complex network of knowledge, kinship, and community that extended through the forest in a series of overlapping circles centering on home, meetinghouse, courthouse, mill, and ferry crossing.

Amidst this informal and seemingly atomistic settlement landscape, some colonial leaders strove to establish a more centralized, profitable, and orderly society and to bolster the production of goods for the British mercantile system. This was a slow and difficult process. The vastness of the forest, the numerousness of the small farmers essentially outside the reach of central authority, and the overwhelming difficulties of transportation and trade were tremendous obstacles. However, as ambitious newcomers continued to arrive in the colony, and as settlements grew and matured in the 1750s and 1760s, a trend had begun toward greater concentration of property among the wealthiest residents. Efforts to create order and a degree of gentility grew stronger.

Focusing on the improvement and expansion of towns, civic leaders in the mid-eighteenth century repeatedly passed laws aimed at the "better regulation" of town life. Standard measures included straightening out surveys; ridding streets of "misplaced" houses that encroached on them (these were allowed to remain until they decayed or fell into ruin, but if repaired they must be moved back from the street); and eliminating such fire hazards as wooden chimneys and rubbish in the streets. Funds were authorized to repair rundown public buildings and to build new ones. To encourage growth and substantial construction, towns set minimum standards for houses that had to be built to establish ownership of a lot—typically a frame or masonry house of 15 or 16 feet by 20 feet, though particulars varied. In these jumbled, busy little towns, with their mud streets and decaying frame buildings, the words "regular," "proper," and "substantial," the construction of a well-built market here or a brick courthouse there, and a row of sturdy dwellings or a brick parish church represented important advances.[9]

Early Construction Methods in the Coastal Plain

Though time has swept the North Carolina landscape clean of nearly all its first generation of buildings, the patterns established by the colonial forest society served for many years to come. Most buildings were constructed in ways that took full advantage of the abundant timber supply while minimizing the need for skilled workmanship and costly imported items such as glass, hardware, and paint. This course enabled the farmer to erect buildings without undue expenditures of time or money. Even those who sought to build substantial and elaborate structures found that the availability of land had led so many artisans to "turn farmer" that workmen were scarce and labor costs high, while trading difficulties made all imported goods extremely expensive and hard to obtain. Within this setting, eastern North Carolina artisans demonstrated a variety of construction techniques that encompassed log, plank, frame, and brick buildings.

Log construction appeared in coastal North Carolina in the late seventeenth century. As early as 1676, amid political disturbances, Gov. Thomas Miller was captured by his opponents and "enclosed in a Logghouse about 10 or 11 foot square purposely built for him." In the 1680s, Gov. Seth Sothel had a house built for him, which English colonial surveyor John Lawson described in 1709 as "a House made of Logs (such as the Swedes in America very often make, and are very strong)." Log buildings were commonplace by the early eighteenth century, as William Byrd found in 1728 near Edenton: "Most of the Houses . . . are Log-houses, covered with Pine or Cypress Shingles, 3 feet long, and one broad. They are hung upon Laths with Peggs, and their doors too turn upon Wooden Hinges and have wooden Locks to Secure them, so that the

Building is finisht without Nails or other Iron-Work." Other travelers provided similar descriptions. The antecedents of log construction in America are complex and much debated, but whatever the Old World origins, in North Carolina log building appeared first in the coastal plain in houses built for and by British settlers.[10]

The simplest log structures could be built quickly—in a day or two—and without highly specialized skills, with logs left round, sometimes with the bark on, and the ends overlapping at the corners. Such houses were never intended to last long, but as a type they had great longevity, as farmers handed down the knowledge of how to build efficiently and independently. Generation after generation, the rudimentary log house flourished, not as an ancient tree withstanding the decades, but like grasses reseeding themselves year after year.[11]

Log construction was used in the coastal plain from early settlement into the twentieth century. By about 1800, however, the method was considered old-fashioned, and by the 1850s, observers commented on the disappearance of the "primeval style of log cabin buildings." Only a few remnants still stand—principally early log buildings encapsulated as thick-walled rooms in larger houses or later examples that survive in remote areas. These buildings are part of a tradition of lowland or eastern log construction that reached along the Atlantic coastal plain.[12] The O'Quinn House (fig. 1.2) in the Sandhills of Moore County is a remarkable and exemplary survival. Although the house probably dates from the mid-nineteenth century, it provides our best illustration of an approach to building that once prevailed in much of eastern North Carolina. The sturdy, one-room house, measuring 22 by 17 feet, is built of saddle-notched logs—a type of notching common in the coastal plain in which the logs are left round and their ends cut

Figure 1.2. O'Quinn House, Moore County, mid-19th century. A rare surviving example of a tradition of simple log construction with wood chimneys and foundations employed by the earliest settlers in coastal North Carolina.

Figure 1.3. O'Quinn House. Lightwood-block foundation.

out to allow them to overlap closely. Sometimes the gaps are chinked with mud, but in the O'Quinn House the interstices are covered with wooden strips. The house also exhibits the widely used forest technique that employed wood for foundations and chimneys, and it has a little wooden bench projecting from between the logs to make a seat beside the chimney.[13]

Forest-wise builders possessed a well-developed understanding of the properties of wood, selecting different varieties for different purposes. When they chose resin-filled lightwood for foundation piers in both log and frame buildings, they used a material that could last a century and more. When a pine tree is girdled and the sap left in the tree, the resulting lightwood is a resinous, rock-hard wood that resists water and insects. Spectacularly flammable, split lightwood is often used as kindling. Building committees sometimes required structures to be set on "good lightwood blocks," and, to take best advantage of the wood grain, some specified that the blocks were to be set on their sides. The trapezoidal blocks at the O'Quinn House (fig. 1.3) exemplify the best lightwood-block foundations.[14]

Wooden chimneys were likewise common in eastern North Carolina in both frame and log buildings. A visitor in the Albemarle in 1745 commented that the "common peoples houses . . . all have Wooden Chimneys which I admire do not catch fire oftener than they do."[15] This ancient technique was used frequently in the colonies and continued to serve thousands of families in the South into the early twentieth century. Only a few examples still stand. There were various methods for building chimneys of wood and clay using either logs or small splints to form a structure that was then daubed with clay. At the O'Quinn House, the builder raised the chimney of V-notched logs with a stack of small splints and daubed it with clay inside. He joined the

Figure 1.4. Boyette Slave House, Johnston County, mid-19th century.

chimney to the house with a tenon that projected through the house wall and was pegged inside. He extended the roof out over the chimney to protect the daubing from dissolving in the rain, supported the roof with braces and an extended roof plate, and cut a hole in the roof to accommodate the stack. Another type of wooden chimney construction can be seen at the mid-nineteenth-century Boyette Slave House (fig. 1.4), located in Johnston County in the central coastal plain. In this case, the chimney of the dovetailed plank house is formed from dozens of pine splints solidified by a thick clay mortar and tenoned to the house wall.[16]

Tightly dovetailed buildings made of squared logs or thick planks also appeared early in the coastal building repertoire. These followed a tradition known in New England and the mid-Atlantic colonies in the late seventeenth and early eighteenth centuries. There were various methods of joining hewn logs at the corners with notches that lock them together; the full dovetail, with angles flaring to top and bottom, was especially prevalent in early eastern North Carolina buildings. Squared—hewn or sawn—and dovetailed log construction was considered a superior method to round-log building, as town ordinances and building specifications reveal. From the mid-eighteenth century onward, building committees frequently specified dovetailed log construction for local jails. In 1759 officials in Johnston County, for example, laid plans to build a frame courthouse and a prison 16 by 12 feet, "made of Hewn or Sawn Loggs four Inshes thick Duf deald. To be seeld or lined with Plank of Insh & quarter from the saw and sleepers ye same." Such specifications typically addressed the matter of security in determined tones—seeking every possible method of preventing prisoners from cutting, drilling, or burrowing out of the building—indicating that dovetailed log and plank construction was seen as the most secure method of building in wood.[17]

Small dovetailed log or plank buildings appear occasionally throughout the coastal plain, even in areas where other types of log buildings are not prevalent. Typically, the timbers are hewn or sawn to a size that shows a clear difference between thickness and height, ranging from 1 ½ to 6 or more inches thick and from 6 to 20 or more inches high. Often these planks are cut to fit so precisely that there is no need for chinking between them. The tightness of dovetailed construction particularly recommended it for smokehouses. Dovetailed plank smokehouses, beautifully crafted little cubes of buildings, stand on many eastern North Carolina farms. Most are square in plan, 10 or 12 feet on a side, and many stand alongside frame dairies.

One of the oldest surviving examples is the Joseph Evans Smokehouse (fig. 1.5), a mid- to late-eighteenth-century structure in Perquimans County. It measures about 12½ feet square. The planks, sawn 1½ to 2 inches thick and 6 to 7 inches high, are joined with full dovetails and, using a standard technique, are further stabilized by means of vertical pegs inserted between the planks during construction. Also typifying eighteenth-century carpentry techniques, the roof rafters are pegged to the false plate (a board set atop the joists) and down through the joists, and the wood shingles are likewise pegged to the rafters. The batten door is hung on wooden hinges and wooden pintles. Clapboards covering the gable are riven (split) and have feathered edges.[18]

Dovetailed plank construction took various forms and appeared in buildings of various purposes. The Pasquotank Log House (fig. 1.6), for example, was about 22 by 18 feet, built of planks about 3 by 10 inches and reinforced at the corners with an interior locking post to which

Figure 1.5. Evans Smokehouse, Perquimans County, middle to late 18th century.

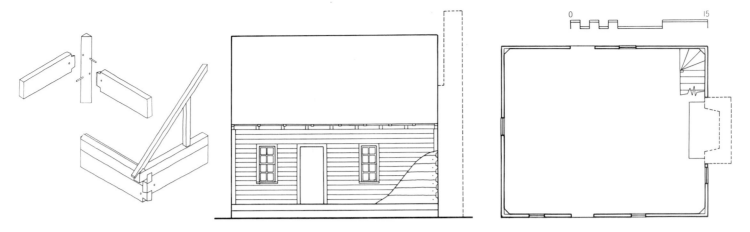

Figure 1.6. Pasquotank Log House, Pasquotank County, ca. 1760. Elevation, plan, and construction details by Carl R., Lounsbury.

the planks were pegged. In this carefully finished little house, the walls were covered on the outside with beaded, feather-edged clapboards and on the inside with beaded board sheathing, and the ceiling joists were planed and beaded.[19] Coastal Carolina carpenters also knew a method of plank building akin to the French *pièce sur pièce* construction, sometimes called "hog-trough" construction. The small Bear Swamp House in Perquimans County (fig. 1.7) is made of 3-by-15-inch sawn planks set into vertically slotted cornerposts rather than dovetailed together.[20] Such small, rare survivors depict a rich and varied carpentry tradition that offered many techniques for the construction of wooden buildings.

The dominant legacy of early North Carolina builders, however, consisted of small frame structures. Carpenters continued to use frame construction methods that had evolved in the Chesapeake in the seventeenth century as builders adapted from English precedents those techniques suited to a labor-short society. Traditional massive English frames were stout boxes of heavy timbers, in which many skill-demanding mortise-and-tenon joints made the walls and roof into a complicated, integral, and interdependent unit. Conditions in the southern colonies encouraged carpenters to employ simplified framing techniques. Relatively small framing members were joined into front and back walls, which were linked by the side walls and ceiling joists. A roof of slender common rafters was built to be structurally independent of the walls: rather than being joined into the wall structure, the roof rafters rested on a false plate (a board or timber) that sat atop the joists, which in turn rested on the uppermost timber—the plate—of the wall. Clapboards or weatherboards further stiffened the walls, and collar beams, boards, and shingles helped stabilize the roof.[21]

This simplified framing method required less skilled craftwork than did the traditional English frame. It also accommodated—and is believed to have developed because of—southern builders' reliance on "post-in-the-ground" frame construction. In this type of building, the principal vertical structural members—cornerposts and other posts—were set directly into the

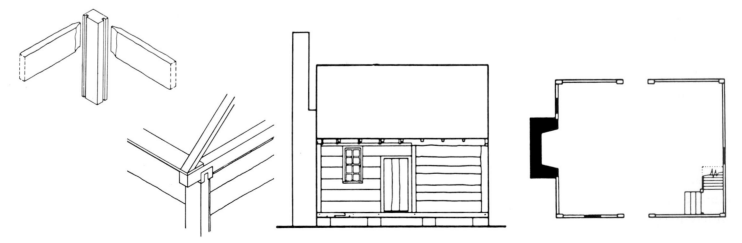

Figure 1.7. Bear Swamp House, Perquimans County, late 18th to early 19th century. Elevation, plan, and construction details by Carl R. Lounsbury.

ground, and the rest of the frame was built around them. An Anglican church built in Chowan County, near present-day Edenton, in 1701, for example, was a frame building 25 feet long with "posts in the ground." It had "neither floor nor seats only a few loose benches upon the sand." Its door usually hung ajar, and "all the Hoggs & Cattle flee thither for shade in the summer and warmth in the Winter." Describing the properties of various tree species, John Lawson singled out the durable red cedar as "much used in Posts for Houses and Sills" as well as for boats, coffins, and fences. No early examples of post-in-the-ground buildings are known to survive in North Carolina.[22]

The building of light frame structures, whether earthfast with posts in the ground or set on masonry or wood foundations, developed into the predominant construction method in the southern colonies. Only a few large buildings boasted massive frames or the complex roof structures of principal rafters, purlins, and secondary common rafters characteristic of New England, English, and European frame buildings. Within the southern tradition of light frame construction, however, there were various levels of quality. Thus in 1741, when new chapels were needed in Chowan County to supplement the raw old post-in-the-ground church, the vestry specified that each of the new buildings was to have "a Good fraim Gott out of Good Timber and covered with Good Siprus Shingles and weatherboarded with feather Edged plank." The roof was to be "workmanlike," the windows and doors "Suitable for such a house," and the chapels were to be fitted with a pulpit and "all things Suitable." And, in contrast to earlier disorder, the pews inside were to be laid out in "a Regular form all alike."[23]

Early Colonial Houses of the Coastal Plain: Landmarks of Survival

It was within this evolving tradition of small wooden buildings that the earliest surviving buildings in North Carolina were constructed. Only a few unusually substantial houses remain from the first half of the eighteenth century. Durable brick construction, usually employing locally made brick and oystershell mortar, was an indication of great ambition and prosperity. Even a stout framed house with a brick chimney and foundations was a notable accomplishment. Such projects thus represented tremendous efforts and investments by a few exceptionally wealthy or determined members of the emerging gentry. In 1722, Thomas Pollock of Chowan Precinct, one of the colony's richest men and biggest landowners, was living in a house he valued at £20. He struggled for several years and spent £300 to build a good house for his son Cullen, including payments to the carpenter to frame and cover the house and to the bricklayer to make and lay bricks in the cellar, underpinning, and chimney. Even for as wealthy a man as Pollock, such a seemingly modest undertaking was so onerous that he cursed it as "the plague of building."[24]

Well-finished buildings of frame or brick required the skills of carpenters, sawyers, joiners, and bricklayers, who became more numerous as communities developed. Towns and prosperous rural neighborhoods usually possessed artisans in the building trades, the most successful of whom were often also landowners and planters. Others were landless workmen, often itinerants, and many were slaves. As early as 1711, a resident commented on Carolinians' dependence on "slaves who understand most handycrafts." Usually the client worked directly with artisans to plan his building and hired each tradesman separately to transform timber or clay into construction materials and assemble them into a building.[25]

Surviving buildings from the first half of the eighteenth century are so few, their histories so uncertain, and their architectural character so diverse that significant patterns remain elusive. The evidence suggests, however, that the individuals who had the wherewithal to build well also had access to a remarkably rich and flexible set of possibilities. That variety also recalls the diverse culture of the colony, which was composed of "many sorts of people, of various nations and different opinions, customs and manners," and where most of the wealthiest residents were newcomers. It is not clear whether the builders of these early houses imported their ideas directly

Figure 1.8. Newbold-White House, Perquimans County, ca. 1680–1730.

from other traditions, or whether North Carolina had developed a multifaceted local craft tradition whose other examples have been lost.

In any case, the character of these early survivors is rooted in broader Anglo-American patterns of planning and craftsmanship that were shared throughout the colonies and that shaped building practices throughout the eighteenth and early nineteenth centuries. These houses combine straightforward expression of construction elements with variations on a few basic plans, a preference for general but not strict symmetry, and an established hierarchy of materials and craftsmanship, whereby the expenditure of skilled labor denoted the social status of the building and its owner or sponsors and the relative importance of the spaces within it.[26]

The oldest building in North Carolina is believed to be the Newbold-White House (figs. 1.8, 1.9), for which various construction dates have been estimated, ranging from the 1680s through the 1720s or 1730s. In form, plan, and the use of materials, the house represents a constellation of important features. It is oriented toward the water, facing the Perquimans River, a common arrangement in an era when waterways directed the course of transportation and settlement. The simple, rectangular house, measuring 20 by 40 feet, has a steep gabled roof, framed of common rafters, and chimneys rising within the brick walls. The water and land fronts both accommodate a central doorway and small, segmental-arched windows, though the water front has five openings and the land side only three. Two rooms of unequal size—the hall into which one enters and the smaller parlor beside it—follow a plan common in the Atlantic seaboard region from the seventeenth century onward.[27]

The hall-parlor plan evolved in the Chesapeake from English antecedents and continued into the nineteenth century. In such dwellings the larger room, the hall, was the heart of the house—a lively, multipurpose room. Family, servants, and visitors entered the hall directly through the outside door, and around its hearth they cooked, ate, and visited. From the hall one might enter the parlor, a more private room usually reserved for formal entertaining, and which often contained the main bed. Also from the hall, a stair led to the bedchambers above. In the Newbold-White House, the stair originally rose beside the fireplace, a typical configuration. Later in the eighteenth century, carpenters installed a partition to create a central passage through the house and built a new stair, which was entered from the passage and deflected traffic away from the hall, thus making that room a more protected and potentially private space.[28]

Though the house was small, it was by no means modest. It grew out of a tradition of craft-intensive architecture, rooted in England, that extended throughout the seaboard colonies from New York to South Carolina and was especially prevalent in the mid-Atlantic colonies and Virginia. A display of bricklayers' skill amid the small wooden houses of the region offered a proud statement of exceptional success and status for the family and the artisans who built it. The walls of the Newbold-White House are of Flemish bond with glazed headers—the dark, glassy ends of bricks nearest the fire in the kiln. The vivacious pattern of glittering header bricks alternating with plain red stretchers transforms the clean, simple form into a sparkling checkerboard in the sunlight. Each decorative detail emphasizes the quality of form and construction. A course of molded brick marks the water table, suggesting the interior floor level, beneath which bricks are laid in the strong, utilitarian English-bond pattern of alternating rows of headers and stretchers. A narrow belt course across the gable end indicates the upper floor level. Corbeled or

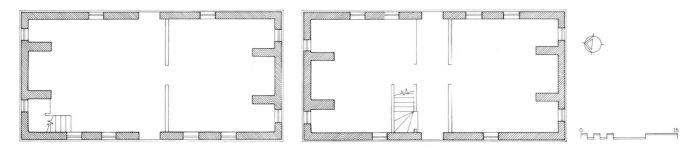

Figure 1.9. Newbold-White House. Plans by Carl R. Lounsbury. These show the arrangement of the house in the early 18th century (left) and the middle to late 18th century (right).

Figure 1.10. Charlton-Jordan House, Bertie County, ca. 1738.

Figure 1.11. Charlton-Jordan House.
Plan by Carl R. Lounsbury.

stepped bricks project to form the base of the parapeted roofline, and a row of glazed headers outlines the rake of the roof.[29]

The Charlton-Jordan House (figs. 1.10, 1.11) in Bertie County was probably new or underway in 1738, when William Charlton sold Joseph Jordan a tract of three hundred acres "on which I now liveth," together with "the plank and brick that was got or procured for the use and furnishing of the Dwelling house." At his death in 1776, Jordan owned five hundred acres and thirty-three slaves, characteristic of the dominant planter class in the region. Though the house is similar in many respects to the Newbold-White House—the orientation to a waterway (the Roanoke River), the compact form, the resplendent Flemish-bond brickwork—there are differences that illustrate the range of possibilities in the regional building tradition. The 25-by-45-foot house is raised on a cellar. Shallow arches surmount windows somewhat larger than those in the Newbold-White House, and the execution of the brickwork is more refined. Interior end chimneys are built with T-shaped stacks, a type characteristic of the late seventeenth and early eighteenth centuries.[30]

Figure 1.12. Walton House, Gates County, 1755. Destroyed. (Historic American Buildings Survey)

The house follows another plan widely used in the colonial period—the three-room plan. As in a hall-parlor house, the central entry opens into a large, multipurpose hall, but the remaining space is divided into two small rooms heated by corner fireplaces. Such rooms were commonly used as a parlor and a bedchamber. This plan, described in a late-seventeenth-century promotional pamphlet for Pennsylvania as a good plan for a beginner house, continued to be built in the mid-Atlantic and Upper South well into the nineteenth century.[31]

Other early colonial houses in northeastern North Carolina also exhibit vivid decorative masonry work, their walls and chimneys emblazoned with glazed headers forming chevrons, diamonds, hearts, and even dates and initials. Such techniques are prevalent in Quaker regions of the Delaware Valley, with Salem County, New Jersey, being the best-known center. Quaker influence was likewise strong in Perquimans, Pasquotank, and neighboring counties in the Albemarle. Links between families and artisans that may explain the shared patterns have not yet been made, and, unfortunately, many of the best North Carolina examples of these buildings have been lost in recent decades. The Walton House (1755) (fig. 1.12) in Gates County had brick ends with lozenge decorations in dark headers, which, like details of its woodwork, strongly resembled Delaware Valley work.[32] Surviving examples of frame dwellings with chevron-patterned brick ends are the Sutton-Newby House (ca. 1730) in Perquimans County and the Sumner-Winslow House (1748) in Gates County.[33]

Other distinctive Delaware Valley–type masonry appears in Camden County at Milford (fig. 1.13), a great two-story brick house, overlooking the Pasquotank River, which is believed to have been built in 1746. The walls, laid in glazed-header Flemish bond, are accentuated with belt courses at the story levels. Hallmarks of Delaware Valley work include the great coved and plastered cornice that dramatizes the eaves and the "tumbled" bricks finishing the rake of the gable (fig. 1.14), though these are set vertically rather than in the more common pattern of aligning them at right angles to the slope.[34]

Figure 1.13. Milford, Camden County, ca. 1746.

Figure 1.14. Milford. Gable detail showing coved plaster cornice and vertically aligned tumbled bricks.

Figure 1.15. Palmer-Marsh House, Bath, ca. 1740.

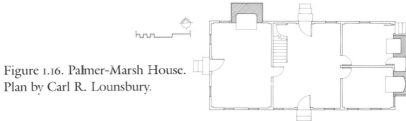

Figure 1.16. Palmer-Marsh House.
Plan by Carl R. Lounsbury.

Figure 1.17. Palmer-Marsh House. Second-story chamber showing
exposed and finished framing members.

Two important frame houses, believed to date from the first half of the eighteenth century, likewise reflect the diversity of colonial building techniques, although the uncertainty of their histories and the absence of comparable buildings make them appear as unique and isolated examples. Both were built for wealthy newcomers in emerging port towns.

The Palmer-Marsh House (figs. 1.15, 1.16) in Bath is thought to have been built around 1740 for Michael Coutanche, a recent arrival from the Isle of Jersey off the coast of Normandy who became a merchant, justice, and assemblyman. It occupies a large town lot and presents a gable end to the business street. Just as brickwork could be elaborated to emphasize the quality and status of a building and its owner and maker, so too, in frame construction, direct expression of structure and craftsmanship could serve a similar purpose. A massive frame required great skill to plan and assemble, particularly for such a large structure as the Palmer-Marsh House, which is 25 by 51 feet and two stories tall plus an attic. Substantial frame houses in North Carolina frequently had large exterior chimneys of masonry, but few rival the mammoth double brick chimney of English bond—more than 16 feet wide and 4 feet deep, composed of two chimneys joined by a two-story brick pent—that rises on the east gable end of Coutanche's house. Windows in both stories light small closets between the chimney stacks. On the northwest, at the back of the house, stands a Flemish-bond chimney that serves a big cooking fireplace in the basement. The main entrance opens into a large, central room with a handsome turned stair at the rear and doorways into the pair of chambers on one end and a large room on the other. The latter, with a separate gable-end doorway to the street, may have served as a business office. Inside the house, the heavy frame is displayed: the cornerposts and plates project into the rooms and are neatly planed and beaded, as are the lesser posts that frame the doors and windows (fig. 1.17). The great summer beam runs the 50-foot length of the building, its mass asserting—like the decorated summer beams of New England and English houses—the well-crafted solidity of the dwelling.[35]

A diverse set of influences combined in the Cupola House (fig. 1.18) in Edenton. The 2½-story frame house stands on a spacious lot that once reached to the wharves in Edenton Bay. Its date of construction remains uncertain. Between 1724 and 1767, the property was owned by a series of merchants and political appointees—beginning with Richard Sanderson, a rich land-owner, shipowner, and merchant in the West Indies and New England trade, and ending with Francis Corbin, the controversial land agent who bought the property in 1756—but no certain evidence establishes which of these men commissioned construction of a residence of such ambition and assertive individuality.[36]

The Cupola House shares some elements with other substantial eighteenth-century houses. The heavy frame is covered with weatherboards and has a wood-shingled, gabled roof and massive double-shouldered brick chimneys at the ends. The plan (fig. 1.20) has a central passage with two rooms on each side; the front rooms are much larger than the rear ones and originally were the only ones with fireplaces. Although houses with central-passage plans, with their possibilities of formality and privacy, apparently were not numerous in early and mid-eighteenth-century North Carolina, they were familiar enough in colonial America.

At the same time, the Cupola House presents elements that appear to be unique in combination: the overhanging, or jettied, upper story of the front facade; the massive cupola; and the lavish carved decoration. Houses with jettied upper stories were common in England and northern Europe from the late medieval period onward, and the form was repeated in seventeenth- and eighteenth-century New England buildings. Nor was the feature unknown in the early Albemarle region: in 1725, a 35-by-18-foot courthouse planned in Currituck County was to have "a fashionable overjet framed Worke Standing on Cedar Blocks the roof to be Shingled with Cypress Shingles the sides & ends with Boards."[37] The big, octagonal cupola, sheathed in wood cut to resemble stone, dominates the house. It rises above a central cross-gable and emphasizes the deviations from symmetry that enliven the facade. The front gable and the cupola, like the jetty, recall New England precedents; but in New England, a cupola and a jetty together are unusual.

Figure 1.18. Cupola House, Edenton, early to mid-18th century.

Figure 1.19. Cupola House. Stair detail.

The structure supporting these elements is likewise unorthodox. New England carpenters constructed jetties either by cantilevering the second story out beyond the first or by hewing the girt (the horizontal timber between stories) into an L shape; but at the Cupola House the carpenter attached a false girt to the front girt of the house with massive spikes, supported it further with brackets spiked to the main posts of the frame, and raised the second-story wall on this false girt. The roof frame is also unusual. It combines a heavy principal rafter-and-purlin system—which carries the cupola and rests on the front-to-back bearing walls and the main posts of the building—with a common rafter roof that, laid atop the principal rafters and purlins in a different plane, extends out to the eaves over the jettied front wall.[38]

Inside the house, elaborate classical trim with carved decoration exemplifies the use of finish work to denote the social hierarchy of rooms. This ornamentation complements the stout frame,

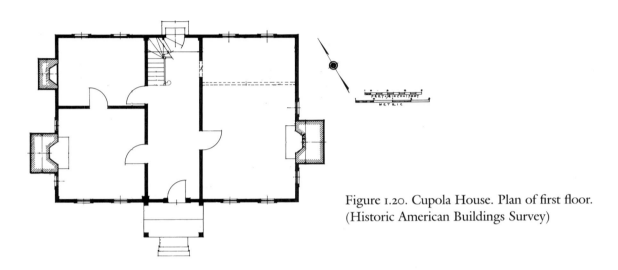

Figure 1.20. Cupola House. Plan of first floor. (Historic American Buildings Survey)

Figures 1.21, 1.22, 1.23. Cupola House. Above: Principal room, fireplace wall. Above right: Principal room, partition wall, doorway, and cupboard. Right: Front west parlor. The woodwork of the first-story rooms was removed in 1918 and installed in the Brooklyn Museum. Beginning in 1965, in cooperation with the Brooklyn Museum, the first-floor interiors were copied and installed in the Cupola House. (Photos in situ, 1918, Brooklyn Museum, Woodward Memorial Funds)

which is expressed within the house: where plates, girts, and posts project into the rooms they are faced with beaded boards, and moldings project around them. Upon entering the passage, the visitor confronts a formal space packed with bold and vibrant woodwork. Ceiling-high, pedimented doorways open into the two main rooms, while a compact and heavy stair rich with turned balusters, a molded and ramped railing, and floral carved brackets dominates the opposite end of the passage (fig. 1.19). The largest room, the hall to the right of the passage, is fully paneled, enriched with carved moldings, and features a pedimented doorway, an elaborate chimneypiece, and an arched, built-in cupboard for additional displays of silver, glass, and ceramics (figs. 1.21, 1.22). To the left of the passage, the parlor (fig. 1.23) also has an ornate mantel and moldings, but the walls are plastered rather than paneled. The rear rooms are plainly finished and are entered through simple doorways. The second story shows a similar arrangement, with the large room paneled and the smaller one plastered; both are treated more simply, each having a pedimented chimneypiece with flat acanthus consoles.

For the most elaborate classical motifs, the artisan may have drawn upon William Salmon's *Palladio Londinensis* (1734, 1738), an English architectural book widely used in the colonies. It contains plates (figs. 1.25, 1.26) akin to the pedimented doorways, astral-paneled doors, and mantels in the main first-floor rooms. The compression of these designs, intended for lofty mansions, into the compact, low-ceilinged rooms of the Cupola House gives them an energy and eccentricity quite at odds with their classical origins. In addition, carved leaf and floral patterns enrich the mantels, moldings, and stairs. The distinctive thick-stemmed acanthus motif seen in the upstairs mantels (fig. 1.24) recurs on the rafter ends of the cupola and the exposed purlin tips of the main roof. Though the carving is bold and carefully executed, it exhibits a shallow surface treatment and limited range of techniques that distinguish it from the work of accomplished carvers in urban areas. In sum, the Cupola House is a rich, sometimes contradictory amalgam of seemingly disparate traditions, its extraordinary individuality suggesting a client who conceived a house that lay outside the tradition of the local area—or, indeed, any single locale—and thus challenged the resourcefulness and skill of the artisans he employed.[39]

Figure 1.24. Cupola House.
Second-story mantel.

Figure 1.25. Design for chimneypiece, from William Salmon, *Palladio Londinensis*, 2d ed., 1738. Plates from this book may have been a source for the first-story woodwork of the Cupola House. (Henry Francis du Pont Winterthur Museum Library, Collection of Printed Books)

Figure 1.26. Design for doorway, from William Salmon, *Palladio Londinensis*. (Henry Francis du Pont Winterthur Museum Library, Collection of Printed Books)

Late Colonial Houses of the Coastal Plain: Emerging Plans and Forms

By the 1750s and 1760s, North Carolina's economy and social system had become more complex and its political situation more stable. Its population was large enough and its agricultural and forest profits sufficient to encourage more families to invest in substantial construction. The emerging planter and merchant classes and the growing population of artisans in the building trades produced handsome if modest dwellings that survive today in greater numbers than those from earlier periods. For the most part, these men built from a shared understanding of a workable range of plans and forms, materials and techniques—often citing in their written agreements existing buildings as models for whole structures or for specific elements of them.

Most houses were small. Like the Newbold-White House and the Charlton-Jordan House, they were usually one or one-and-a-half stories tall. A limited family of plans predominated: the house with one main room, the hall-parlor plan, and the three-room plan. Only a few houses had a passage through the middle or along the side. A shed or lean-to often provided secondary chambers, sometimes divided by a passage or open porch. From these basic choices, artisans and clients built many variations to suit clients' needs and pocketbooks.

Workmanship also fell within a well-established range, from the cheapest and most expedient methods to costly displays of labor, skill, and fine materials. The simplified framing system and common rafter roof continued to be the standard method of construction. But in communities where the wealthy planter and the middling farmer both occupied small wooden houses with only a few rooms, subtle but well-understood differentiations in workmanship were of great significance in denoting quality and status. In an economy still cash poor and labor short, the display of high-quality workmanship might make a small dwelling a fine house indeed.[40]

Old Town Plantation House (fig. 1.27) in Edgecombe County typifies the scale, plan, and finishing of well-built houses of the mid-eighteenth-century planter class. It has a hall-parlor plan, with two front doors providing separate entrances into the hall and parlor. The living space is expanded by chambers in the rear shed and front piazza and a half-story beneath the gambrel roof. The double-slope gambrel roof, which allowed more room in the upper chambers than did a gable roof, was an especially prevalent form among substantial town and plantation dwellings of the middle and late eighteenth century. In an often-used arrangement, the rear shed is integral to the plan: the central shed room gives access both to the flanking shed rooms and to the stair rising to the upper chambers. The front porch was also enclosed at each end to form small rooms

Figure 1.27. Old Town Plantation House, Edgecombe County, 1742. During restoration of the house in the mid-1980s, the front piazza rooms were reconstructed.

Figure 1.28. King House, Bertie County, 1763.

that were accessible only from the porch, a practice common in eastern Carolina.[41] Characteristic of top-quality workmanship are such features as Flemish-bond brick chimneys and English-bond foundations, heavy paneled doors, beaded weatherboards, and beaded flush sheathing in the sheltered porch areas. In the hall, a large, paneled mantel and wainscoting with two rows of paneling assert the primacy of that room, whereas the wainscot in the parlor is simpler, and the upper chambers are sheathed with flush beaded boards.

The King House in Bertie County (fig. 1.28), built in 1763 for William and Elizabeth King, exhibits variations and elaborations on a similar theme. The great-grandson of an indentured servant in Virginia, William King acquired more than a thousand acres and ten slaves, which made him one of the wealthiest men and largest slaveholders in Bertie County. He and his wife built a house of unmistakable substance. Although it is a frame dwelling, the ends of the house are built of brick—a combination not uncommon in the mid-eighteenth-century Albemarle. The brick ends contain the chimneys, which repeat the T-stack form of the Charlton-Jordan House (ca. 1738) in the same county. The hall-parlor-plan house (fig. 1.29) is 18 by 42 feet; when the Kings required additional rooms, they enclosed chambers in the rear shed porch but left the

Figure 1.29. King House. Plan by Carl R. Lounsbury.

Figure 1.30. King House. Hall.

center bay open. Although there is no elaborate turning, carving, or classical embellishment, the disposition of paneling and moldings denotes the social hierarchy of the rooms within the house and its owners' status in the community. The handsomely wainscoted hall (fig. 1.30) focuses on a paneled fireplace wall with a broad, arched fire opening flanked by built-in, glazed cupboards to display the Kings' pewter dishes, china cups and saucers, tea pots, and silver spoons.[42] The smaller parlor has a paneled fireplace wall, simple closets beside the chimney, and plastered walls, while the upper chambers are finished with plain base and chair boards.

The Old Town Plantation House and the King House are part of a sphere of substantial, traditional architecture built for the wealthiest citizens, an architecture that encompassed myriad combinations within a narrow range of materials, workmanship, form, and plan. Most mid-eighteenth-century houses stood one or one-and-a-half stories beneath their gable or gambrel roofs. The majority, such as the Theophilus White House in Perquimans County, were frame buildings. Like the King House, several of the finest such houses had brick ends: the Old Brick House in Pasquotank County, the Myers-White House (ca. 1750) and the Davenport House (ca. 1750) in Perquimans County, and the Shoulars House (ca. 1760) in Northampton County. Only a few houses, such as the Gregory House in Camden County, were built entirely of brick, though references to brick houses appear more frequently in records than do surviving buildings in the landscape.[43]

The interiors of these houses covered a spectrum from the spectacular paneled room in the Old Brick House (fig. 1.31)—which had a fireplace wall adorned with full-height Ionic pilasters, arched niches, and an extraordinary chimneypiece adapted from a design for a doorway (fig. 1.32) illustrated in Batty Langley's *Ancient Masonry* (1736) and *Builder's Jewel* (1741)—to the more standard application of a paneled mantel and wainscoting, to planed board sheathing. Enclosed staircases were the norm, and the presence of an open staircase with a heavy turned railing was an indication of high status. So indeed was the presence of paneling, carving, and other handsome workmanship in an architectural setting dominated by simple and crude dwellings.

Although hall-parlor and three-room plans continued to dominate, central passages became more common in the 1760s and 1770s, either built initially into the house or formed later by a new partition wall. At Belvidere in Perquimans County and the Joel Lane House (1760s) in Wake County, for example, two unequal front rooms are separated by a passage, as are the rear shed rooms.

In a few houses, builders integrated secondary rear rooms under the main roofline. The Clear Springs Plantation House near New Bern (fig. 1.33), built around 1760, has a steep gable roof that shelters a hall and parlor plus small rear chambers that flank an off-center passage. The full-width piazza, raised cellar of local marl (shell rock), and the interior end chimneys with their lower faces exposed are early examples of important local usages. The Patrick Gordon House (ca.

Figure 1.31. Old Brick House, Pasquotank County, mid-18th century. The unusually elaborate woodwork, including this fireplace wall, was removed from the house, a brick-ended frame dwelling that stands near the Pasquotank River. (Private collection)

Figure 1.32. Design for door pediment, from Batty Langley, *Builder's Jewel*. (Henry Francis du Pont Winterthur Museum Library, Collection of Printed Books)

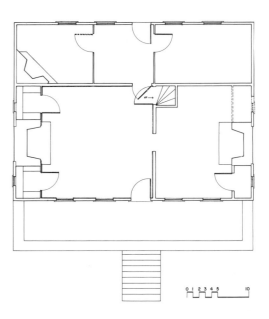

Figure 1.33. Clear Springs Plantation House, Craven County, ca. 1760. Plan and elevation by Bernard Herman and William MacIntire.

1771) in New Bern also has a hall-parlor arrangement plus small rear rooms, divided by a stair passage, beneath its broad gambrel roof.[44]

Houses with only one main room also constituted respectable dwellings when built in a good and workmanlike manner. Two late-eighteenth-century dwellings are especially well-built examples of the many small houses of the period. About 1759 Edenton carpenter Gilbert Leigh built himself a frame house (fig. 1.35), 14 feet wide and 20 feet deep, with a single, carefully finished lower room served by a brick chimney and a chamber in the gambrel half-story above. In time the house was expanded, with shed rooms to the rear and a two-story addition built to one side.[45] In 1775 Wake County planter Joseph Lane—brother of Joel Lane—likewise erected a good frame house with one main room (fig. 1.36). A steep gable roof slopes down to rear shed rooms and a front piazza, which is neatly embellished with slim, tapered posts and a scalloped cornice board. The main room was finished with wainscoted and plastered walls, planed and beaded ceiling joists, and a fireplace wall treated with boards arranged to frame the fire opening, a tiny door to a closet containing a bake oven, and a stair that winds up beside the interior chimney to a snug chamber above (fig. 1.34). As at the Leigh House, a later generation extended the dwelling by building on to one side. Countless other one-room houses stand as rooms that have been enclosed by many years of expansion around them.[46]

Figure 1.34. Lane House. Hall. Wainscoting was removed during a long period of vacancy.

Figure 1.35. Leigh House, Edenton, ca. 1759. Attributed to Gilbert Leigh, carpenter.

Figure 1.36. Lane House, Wake County, 1775.

Piazzas

By the mid-eighteenth century, visitors to North Carolina towns commented on the distinctive coastal architecture that had developed. Though not large, such towns as Wilmington, New Bern, and Edenton had their small public buildings and enough comfortable houses to warrant mention. Especially did the visitors from other climes remark on the prevalence of piazzas. In 1757 a visitor to Wilmington noted that the houses were "in General very Good. Many of Brick, two & three stor[i]es High with double Piazas w[hi]ch make a good appera[nce]." By 1771 town commissioners were struggling to prevent the encroachment of piazzas and other structures into the city streets.[47]

Although porches appear in much of European and African architecture, it is believed that the distinctive porches of the Atlantic coast—whether called galleries, verandas, porches, or piazzas—developed from French, Indian, and perhaps African influences in the Caribbean islands. Broad, functional porches were usually called "piazzas" in eighteenth-century North Carolina and pronounced with a short *a*: one eighteenth-century Edenton builder put it down phonetically as *peasor*.[48] It was along the Lower Cape Fear River, first settled by Barbadians and South Carolinians, and especially in the port towns of Brunswick and Wilmington, with their continuing Caribbean trade, that the North Carolina piazza emerged earliest and strongest.

Although frequent fires left little of Wilmington's early architecture standing, the Smith-Anderson House (fig. 1.37) probably typifies the city's first generation of brick townhouses organized around piazza living. Initially it had a two-story piazza inset at the rear, as marks in the brickwork indicate. Subsequently a double piazza was built across the rear, while tall second-story windows on the front and side opened onto balconies overlooking the street.[49] Near Brunswick, down the Cape Fear from Wilmington, a house called Russellborough, built before 1758, was spruced up in 1765 to serve as the residence of Lt. Gov. William Tryon. It was a two-story house over a full cellar, 45 by 35 feet, with four rooms on each floor, and, reported Tryon, "there is a Piaza Runs Round the House both Stories of ten feet Wide with a Ballustrade of four feet high, which is a great Security for my little girl."[50]

The Burgwin-Wright House (fig. 1.38) was built about 1770 as a Wilmington townhouse for John Burgwin, an immigrant from England who had lived first in Charleston, then had come to Wilmington and established himself as one of the Cape Fear's richest merchants and planters. His house displays a characteristic regional form in its dramatic roofline, whose double slope breaks from a steep to a shallow pitch to shelter broad double piazzas front and back. The high ballast-stone basement opens onto a shaded subporch. Within the house, Burgwin created rooms of a style universally familiar to the mercantile elite throughout the colonies. A broad central stair passage with an elegant stair of turned balusters is flanked by a large parlor on one side and two smaller rooms on the other. In stylish urban fashion, the principal room is located on the second floor—a fully paneled drawing room (fig. 1.39) embellished with fluted pilasters, heavy molded cornices, and domed niches.[51]

Residents of North Carolina ports from Wilmington northward to Edenton used piazzas as important social spaces. In contrast to Charleston's side galleries secluded behind their gated walls, piazzas in North Carolina towns overlooked and often projected into the street, making them a part of a shared community life. The diary of James Iredell provides a rare glimpse of colonial town life among the gentry, which in Edenton included planter and lawyer Samuel Johnston, Samuel's sister Hannah, and Joseph Hewes, a leading merchant:

August 22, 1770. Just stept over to Mr Jones's piazza—chatted a little with Mrs. Jones & Mrs Hall.

August 29, 1770. Just after Breakfast yesterday, walked up Town with Mr. Johnston—called at the Barber's to have my Hair drest—walked over to Mr. Hewes's Piazza & chatted for some time with three or four Gentlemen there,—had not intended to go, if Mr. Johnston had not been there, *as he was*, I thought, going immediately to his office from the Barber's would have had too much the Appearance of Affectation—went soon after to his Office & staid there most of the morning.

Figure 1.37. Smith-Anderson House, Wilmington, ca. 1740.

November 13, 1772. Dinner not being ready immediately as I came in I was going to walk in the Piazza, & Charles Ackly said, I might as well look out of the Window as from there.— How easily is my Attachment perceived? I should abhor myself if I was capable of Disguise, & am pleased, all the World see how affectionately, how fondly I love Miss Hannah Johnston.

November 23, 1772. Talking with our Folks in the Piazza 'till dinner.

January 3, 1773. Nothing to remark of this morning than that I went up Town, and went to Mrs. Blair's from whence I accompanied the young Ladies to the Boat, which was lying at her Wharf. Came home, spoke to Mr. Jones in his Piazza, walked with him in his Garden, *but was not asked in to his house*—This is very different from former times, and I know I have done nothing to deserve this Shyness—Him I do not *blame*—but *pity*—he is under a Government that is very capricious.

January 13, 1773. While I was in the Piazza, I had the happiness to see Hannah at her Sister's but my time was too limited to admit my going to see her. Mr. Johnston and Mr. Jones came up soon after, and as I was talking with the former, his Sister [Hannah] came down Street with his little Daughter.

January 23, 1773. After Dinner till Sunset writing in my Office. Then came home and drank tea. Being by accident in the Piazza I heard Mrs. Jones in hers, and called to her. She answered me very kindly, and I went over and staid an hour with them very agreeably. Oh! how I hate coldness, and love a cordiality of acquaintance.[52]

The piazzas lining the streets of North Carolina towns formed a middle social zone essential to the subtle rituals of urban genteel society, which by this time had begun to take form in the ports of North Carolina.

Figure 1.38. Burgwin-Wright House, Wilmington, ca. 1770.

Figure 1.39. Burgwin-Wright House. Drawing room, second floor.

The Backcountry

As plantation and town life developed in the east, the Piedmont region opened up into a rapidly expanding frontier. Thousands of families and individuals moved from Pennsylvania and Maryland down the Great Wagon Road that led from Philadelphia through the Valley of Virginia and into the rolling red-clay country of North Carolina. One observer asserted, "There is scarce any history, either antient or modern, which affords an account of such a rapid and sudden increase of inhabitants in a back frontier country, as that of North Carolina."[53]

Like the coastal plain, the Piedmont offered plentiful game, abundant timber, cheap virgin land, and, in contrast to much of the steamy coastal lowlands, a temperate and healthy climate. Streams coursing through the rolling hills provided unlimited fish, created broad and fertile alluvial valleys, and promised power for gristmills and sawmills. But the lay of the land made transportation and trade even more difficult than in eastern Carolina, for no rivers were navigable far past the fall line, and only the Cape Fear and its tributaries offered transport from the Piedmont to a North Carolina seaport.

Settlers came to this region from many different backgrounds. English Quakers settled in present-day Orange, Chatham, Randolph, and Guilford counties on the Eno, Haw, and Deep rivers. Germans established communities in the central and western Piedmont along the Yadkin and Catawba rivers. Highland Scots settled along the Cape Fear above Wilmington, upriver at the site where Fayetteville is located today, and elsewhere on the Upper Cape Fear, along the South Carolina border, and in the Sandhills region. Lowland Scots, English, Irish, and, especially, Scotch-Irish settlers—descendants of Lowland Scots who had moved to Ulster (Northern Ireland) in the seventeenth century—penetrated every region; some traveled up the Cape Fear from the coast, but many came down the Valley of Virginia, then pushed the edge of settlement westward to the Blue Ridge. Gaelic and German resounded through the woods and fields, along with English and many African and Indian languages.

These men and women held a wide range of cultural, social, and economic expectations. Thousands hungered simply for enough land to live independently, to hunt freely, to raise their own food, and to set their own terms for work, play, and worship. The streams, forests, and cheap land provided ample subsistence and nurtured a small-scale agrarian culture focused on family and neighborhood. Other settlers aimed to take up large tracts in the river bottoms and to engage profitably in commercial agriculture, to acquire slaves, and to establish their position in a new landed gentry. Although the problems of transportation continually frustrated these entrepreneurs by reducing their potential profits, nevertheless, as settlement thickened in the third quarter of the eighteenth century, a class of lawyers, merchants, and large planters gradually emerged.

Whatever their national or religious origins, most Piedmont settlers initially built small log dwellings and sheds and fenced their fields with split rails to keep out free-ranging pigs and cattle. On these farmsteads as on those in the east, farmers planted corn among the rotting stumps of trees. English Quakers, Scots and Scotch-Irish Presbyterians, German Lutherans, Calvinists, Moravians, and a scattering of Baptists built log meetinghouses, while county officials erected the first rudimentary courthouses and jails.[54]

German Architecture

An important minority among North Carolina's Piedmont settlers were German. Their architecture composes the chief example of an identifiable, non-British building tradition. Beginning in the late seventeenth century, thousands of Rhinelanders left a homeland wracked by war and religious strife and emigrated, often via Holland and England, to the American colonies. An early contingent of these immigrants, including Swiss and German Palatines or Rhinelanders, had settled New Bern in 1710. Their ranks included a mason, four carpenters, and a potter and roof tile maker, who set to work immediately: in 1711 a New Bern resident boasted, "We have much stronger houses than the English." However superior these dwellings were, they vanished during or after the Tuscarora attack that laid waste to New Bern in 1711.[55]

Within the next few decades, growing numbers of German and Swiss immigrants arrived in Philadelphia and fanned out into the mid-Atlantic zone, and, as land filled up, they began to move southward. By the 1750s German-speaking families were moving into the western North Carolina Piedmont, where they established farming communities distinct from the Scotch-Irish and other British farmers. One eighteenth-century writer admonished his fellow Germans against marrying with the English or the "lazy, dissipated and poor" Irish who lived in "wretched huts."[56] The tenacity of German culture varied from community to community, family to family, and one aspect of life to another. In general, their architecture—like such other indicators as language, pottery making, and tombstones—depicts a pattern of strongly held Germanic traditions maintained through the eighteenth century, a transitional or bilingual era in the late eighteenth and early nineteenth centuries, and acceptance or accommodation of American popular culture by the mid-nineteenth century.[57]

The largest single German settlement in North Carolina was the 98,985-acre Wachovia tract, purchased by the Unitas Fratrum (Unity of Brethren), or Moravians, in 1752. The Moravians, a Protestant group that included people from all over northern and central Europe, shared many traits of language and culture with their other German neighbors, but their theocratic community life was quite different.[58] They had previously established a community in Bethlehem, Pennsylvania, and from there Moravian leaders sent eleven strong and multiskilled men to establish a communal settlement in Wachovia. After spending the winter of 1753–54 in an abandoned settler's cabin in a place they named Bethabara, meaning "House of Passage," they began erecting buildings that represented a spectrum of traditional German methods adapted to their needs and the available materials.

They built a cabin for visitors, made of wide rails laid up like logs; log outbuildings, including a stable, corncribs, and thatched fodder huts; a sturdier log house; and in 1755 a mill constructed of *Fachwerk* (fig. 1.40). Such timber framing infilled with wattle and daub or brick, sometimes plastered over, was a standard construction method in Germany and much of northern Europe. Although the Moravians preferred masonry construction, fachwerk was suitable to building in an area where lime for mortar was hard to obtain. (There were few limestone deposits, and oyster shells had to be shipped long distances.) At first they used wood-shingle roofs, but the arrival of potter Gottfried Aust in 1755 enabled them to produce traditional German roof tiles and tile stoves. Wachovia's master artisans in this period—mason Melchior Rasp, carpenter Christian Triebel, and others—had all learned in their trades in Europe and built from them readily as they established a community.[59]

In 1766, when the Moravians began to build Salem, their main congregational town, these craftsmen, along with administrator Frederic William Marshall and surveyor Christian Reuter, directed the efforts of Moravian and "stranger" workmen. Salem was to be the center of trade, government, and religion for Wachovia. Practicality demanded that the town plan, originally designed as a grandiose, baroque, circular city in the style of the Roman architect Vitruvius, be modified to a grid plan with the principal buildings located near the central square. In contrast to the "common housekeeping" of Bethabara's frontier days, once Salem was completed its operation shifted to a system of individual family households and shops that leased lots from the congregation. The community was divided into "choirs" by gender and marital status, and congregational councils guided spiritual and material affairs.[60]

From 1766 until after 1780, the builders of Salem used log, fachwerk, and stone construction, with logs restricted usually to secondary buildings. The first small family dwellings were planned by surveyor Reuter and built in a row during 1766–68 (fig. 1.41). In 1768 administrator Marshall reported with pleasure on the three family houses then finished, all made of framework covered with clay or filled with brick and clay; he was pleased with their proportions, and "with their regular placing and their tile roofs they make a not unpleasing appearance," but he feared that,

Figure 1.40. Drawing of Bethabara by Christian Gottlieb Reuter, ca. 1759–60, showing fachwerk mill and log dwelling. (Old Salem Restoration, Winston-Salem, and Moravian Church Archives, Herrnhut, East Germany)

lacking lime to plaster them, they might need to be covered with weatherboards. These one-story fachwerk dwellings stood over stone cellars and followed a traditional Germanic plan common in mid-Atlantic and Virginia settlements. Rooms were organized around a center chimney, and the main entrance gave into a large hall-kitchen, the *Kuche* or hearth-room, where the family cooked, ate, and entertained around the large open hearth. The adjacent *Stube*, or stove-room, was a more private room, usually heated by a stove connected to the chimney. (In some houses a small room, the *Kammer* or chamber, was behind the *Stube*, and in some cases a vestibule separated the entrance from the *Kuche*.) Such plans were used in house after house in Salem, including the log Miksch House and the frame dwelling built for Reuter and his wife Anna Catharina in 1772.[61]

Salem's large community buildings also embodied German traditions. The Single Brothers House (fig. 1.42), built in 1768–69, is a fachwerk building 50 by 38 feet. Its heavy timbers are joined in bracing patterns typical of Germanic framing and are infilled with soft bricks. Other Germanic building techniques characteristic of Salem's early buildings are the herringbone-patterned doors and the tile roof with a distinctive "kick" at the eaves, created by inserting shims beneath the lower tiles. The building takes advantage of the sloping terrain so that the rear is a full three stories tall, making the basement into a ground-level story. The single brothers—the unmarried men of the community—lived here, as did apprentices to all tradesmen, and the town's male artisans practiced their trades here. The building contains small individual work-

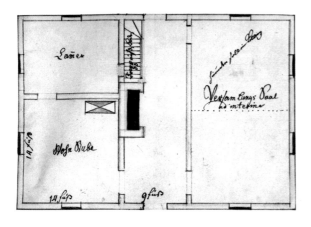

Figure 1.41. First House, Salem, 1768. Plan by Christian Gottlieb Reuter. (Old Salem Restoration, Winston-Salem, and Moravian Church Archives, Herrnhut, East Germany)

Figure 1.42. Single Brothers House, Salem, 1768–69; brick addition, 1786.

Figure 1.43. Single Brothers House. Kitchen in basement of 1786 addition.

shops as well as communal rooms for worship, sleeping, eating, and cooking, including the large basement kitchen with its great hooded hearth and stove (fig. 1.43).

Other large buildings in Salem included a log workshop (1767), a stone-and-fachwerk Gemein Haus (1771), a fachwerk tavern (1772), and the first all-stone building, the community store, begun in 1774. Because of the persistent shortage of lime, the Moravian masons laid stone walls in clay mortar and covered (parged) the walls with a thin layer of plaster marked to resemble stone blocks.[62]

Late Colonial Houses of the Piedmont: German and Scotch-Irish

Beyond Wachovia, there are few remnants of the houses built for the thousands of original settlers in the Piedmont. By all accounts, most of these were rudimentary log structures built on newly established farms and lining the streets of tiny new towns. In some cases, however, Piedmont farmers built substantial and spacious dwellings that continued traditional methods and plans seen elsewhere in the mid-Atlantic and Virginia settlement areas. The Spach House (fig. 1.44) was built of fieldstone by Bethabara masons for Adam Spach and his wife, Moravian converts who had come from Pennsylvania and settled at the edge of the Wachovia tract in 1754. The house was begun on May 16, 1774, and the masons' work was completed on October 31. In accord with German preference, the Spachs sited the house to take advantage of a hillside and a spring, so that the basement opened at ground level at the rear and good water was convenient within the house. Rather than a center chimney, the masons built two interior end chimneys, with corner fireplaces in the four nearly equal rooms of the 30-by-36-foot dwelling. A herringbone-patterned Dutch door, located slightly off-center, opened into the front room on the left.[63]

Outside the Moravian settlement, Valentin Leonardt emigrated from Katzenbach, Germany, to present-day Davidson County, where he reportedly built in the mid-eighteenth century a house two stories tall, 30 by 40 feet, and made of "immense logs." The massive ceiling beams, measuring 12 by 14 inches, were "hewn with a 'broad axe' almost to perfect smoothness, and the lower edges nicely chamfered. . . . Under the west end of the house was the great cellar, walled with large rough stones. This cellar was entered by a heavy slanting door on the south side of the house. The immense chimney stood near the middle of the house with a fireplace on either side below, but with none on the upper floor. The chimney was wide enough to receive wood eight feet long."[64] Such was the classic German-American house as built in Virginia and Pennsylvania—massively constructed, with a center chimney and south-facing hillside cellar. Whether other German settlers built on similar lines throughout the Carolina Piedmont remains an open question.

The principal surviving example of early Germanic architecture outside of Salem is the Braun House (fig. 1.46) in Rowan County. It was built in 1766 for Michael and Margareta Braun; he was a native of Hesse who came as a boy to Philadelphia in 1737, learned the wheelwright and

Figure 1.44. Spach House, Davidson County, 1774. Rear elevation. Destroyed. (Old Salem Restoration, Winston-Salem)

printing trades, prospered, and moved with his wife and children to Rowan County about 1758. He entered into the business and political life of Salisbury and the surrounding county, acquired slaves (fifteen by 1790), and, at his death in 1807, held over two thousand acres. The Brauns built a massive, two-story stone house, 29 by 40 feet, which like the Spach House has four main rooms heated by end chimneys and is situated on a gentle incline, with the basement opening to ground level at the rear. It is an imposing statement of strength, substance, and craft. The stone walls are some two feet thick, with the front stonework composed of neatly coursed blocks. The heavy roof structure is a classic example of a Germanic underframe system (fig. 1.45). Principal rafters linked by purlins are truncated at the height of the collar beams; this sturdy truss supports a common rafter roof with its own collar beams, and the whole is mortised and tenoned and pegged together.[65]

The off-center entrance opens into the main room, which is heated by a corner fireplace, as is the smaller room behind (fig. 1.47). To the right, the smaller front room is, like the traditional *Stube*, heated by a stove plugged into the righthand chimney; a tiny, unheated chamber lies behind it. On the outside face of this chimney is an eight-foot-wide cooking fireplace serving an attached frame kitchen. The Brauns' house thus contains many familiar Germanic elements, but rearranged: perhaps to accommodate the climate by eliminating a center chimney and putting the cooking area outside the stone core of the house; perhaps to make the dwelling more like those of Braun's British associates among Rowan County's business and political leaders; perhaps to separate the functions of the traditional hall and kitchen and thus allow the family's slaves to cook meals in a room apart from the principal living room. Braun commemorated his accomplishment in a stone slab on the front of the house, inscribed "10-Pe-Me-Be-Mi-Ch-Da-1766" for "Pensum Meines Bendigem Mit Christim Dank," which translates as "My undertaking completed thanks to Christ, October 1766."[66]

Figure 1.45. Braun House. Detail showing Germanic underframe roof structure.

Figure 1.46. Braun House, Rowan County, 1766.

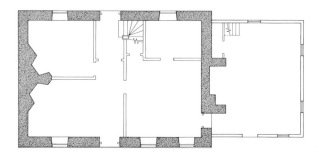

Figure 1.47. Braun House. Plan by Carl R. Lounsbury.

The same straightforward grandeur appears in the Alexander House (fig. 1.48) in Mecklenburg County, built for an equally successful entrepreneurial settler of Scotch-Irish descent. Hezekiah Alexander's grandfather had come from Ireland to Cecil County, Maryland. Hezekiah, one of fifteen children, learned the blacksmith's trade, married Mary Sample in 1752, and, after several years in western Pennsylvania's developing frontier, the couple and their five children moved to Mecklenburg County in 1767, as did Mary's parents and several of Hezekiah's brothers and sisters. Alexander bought two 300-acre tracts, became a leading member of the county's emerging Presbyterian planter class, and by 1774 had built an imposing stone house, in which the couple's tenth child was born in 1775.[67]

The Alexanders' rock house strongly resembles those of successful farmers in Cecil County, Maryland. It avoids opulence or ornateness but expresses wealth and success with the same direct simplicity as the Braun House. Nearly square in plan—about 36 by 32 feet—the stone mass rises from a high basement. The slightly asymmetrical facade is unadorned except for simple keystoned arches spanning the door and windows. There are four nearly equal-sized rooms on the first floor; a stair vestibule occupies the right quadrant, and the three other rooms are heated by corner fireplaces. The upstairs arrangement is similar, but without fireplaces. The finish is fine and plain: the walls are plastered with a glassy-smooth, troweled finish; the interior partition walls are made of heavy, carefully finished boards; and the ceiling joists are planed smooth and neatly beaded. In such a house the Alexanders, like the Brauns, asserted their success in a new land through powerful architecture combining substance, plenty, and workmanship.[68]

Figure 1.48. Alexander House, Mecklenburg County, completed 1774.

Genteel Classicism

Amid the growing prosperity of the late colonial period, North Carolinians, like their compatriots throughout the seaboard colonies, began to participate more fully in the international world of classical taste. In the early and mid-eighteenth century, English architects and builders had increased their output of architectural treatises. Large, handsome volumes containing beautiful plates of Roman and Renaissance buildings and their ideal components were joined by more and more handbooks aimed at the provincial builder. They presented schemes for entire buildings and complexes; dozens of examples of mantels, entrances, stairs, railings, and other architectural details; careful depictions of Roman orders and variations upon them; instructions for particularly difficult feats of construction; and mathematical formulas for "proportioning" each element of a building. Architectural books varied in cost and elaborateness, but nearly all of them claimed descent from the models of ancient Rome and the Renaissance classicism of the Italian architect Andrea Palladio.[69]

Merchants, planters, and political appointees owned a few such volumes, as did some builders who catered to wealthy and fashion-conscious clients. As the gentry class grew with the influx of educated and ambitious newcomers in the late colonial period, participation in the growing genteel culture of classicism grew stronger. An international language and code of social behavior displayed itself in such ways as the drinking of tea with proper ceremony and accoutrements, acquisition of stylish furniture, china, and silver, and wearing fashionable clothing and powdered wigs. Visitors from other colonies or from Britain commonly evaluated the level of civilization in a community by how fully the people they met participated in this culture.[70]

Buildings that referred to the norms of Palladian classicism provided strong and universally understood statements of genteel taste. In North Carolina domestic architecture until the 1760s, elaborate paneling and classical ornament were restricted to a few singular examples such as the Cupola House and the Old Brick House, and even those were joiners' adaptations of English patternbook motifs installed in houses of traditional form. It was in government buildings and parish churches that the eighteenth-century taste for classicism appeared most prominently.

Churches

Whereas members of dissenting denominations had to rely on their own resources to build their meetinghouses, the vestries of the Church of England could levy taxes on all taxpayers in the parish to pay for churches. Parish churches were public buildings in every sense, and their sponsors planned their scale, materials, and style accordingly. Virginia and South Carolina built opulent parish churches, but in North Carolina, the Church of England was weak, and such buildings came into being slowly and with great difficulty. The populace as a whole was notoriously resistant to taxes, wary of centralized authority, and generally unwilling to pay for more than minimal court and prison facilities. Moreover, dissenting denominations, including Quakers, Presbyterians, and Baptists, were strongly entrenched. Some Piedmont Presbyterians, in fact, saw themselves not as dissenters but as members of the Church of Scotland. Even after laws in the 1760s strengthened the Anglican church in North Carolina, many citizens openly refused to pay church rates. Hence most of the colony's religious buildings, like its courthouses, were small, expediently built wooden structures that followed the same standard, laborsaving, inexpensive building methods used for dwellings and farm buildings.[71]

In the 1730s, interest in parish church building stirred. Building campaigns began that sorely tried their sponsors, sometimes for years on end. Though these picturesque colonial landmarks now stand on venerated and carefully tended grounds, they were built amid continual delays and difficulties and frequent controversy, the accomplishments of a small minority who sought monuments of order in a disorderly landscape. In the village of Bath, the churchwardens and

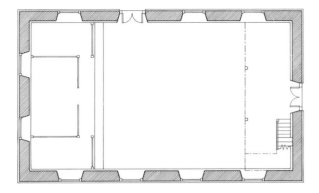

Figure 1.49. St. Thomas Episcopal Church, Bath, 1734–35. Plan by Carl R. Lounsbury.

vestry of St. Thomas Parish reported in 1734 that they were building a small church at their own expense, the only one in the whole province, they claimed. Though they feared their abilities would be "far short of compleating and adorning the same as becomes a temple of God," the modest brick church (fig. 1.49) was finished the next year, and the priest requested a Bible, two Books of Common Prayer, a font, a pulpit cloth and cushion, and a carpet for the communion table, with which to conduct the liturgy of the church.[72]

When parish leaders set their sights on more elaborate buildings, however, progress was slow. Construction of St. Paul's Episcopal Church in Edenton (fig. 1.50) took more than thirty years. As early as 1723, as Edenton grew more populous and the governor established residency there, talk began of a "large and beautiful church" to be built, but it was not until 1736 that several "well disposed Persons" began a "large, handsome Brick Church, with a steeple" to assert the community as the "metropolis" of the colony. The group collected and spent some £1,200, including £561 to a bricklayer to build the walls.[73]

Soon, however, leading members of the committee died, money ran out, and the vestry of the parish refused to assist in the completion of the church. By 1740 it appeared that the building might fall into ruin and the investment be lost, "to the great Discouragement of Religion and much good and pious intention." Time and time again the assembly authorized taxes on every tithable in the parish to support sporadic efforts to complete the project. In 1746 the roof was raised, but disagreements once again brought the work to a standstill. In 1750 money was collected to enclose the church, but not until 1760 was it ready for use. In 1762 the interior was finished in some fashion. In 1769 architect John Hawks designed a cupola for the tower, but it was never erected. In 1774 interior woodwork was installed to complete the church in a "good decent workmanlike manner," and the next year a pulpit was built.[74]

St. Paul's is a beautiful eighteenth-century parish church, akin in form, function, and workmanship to its predecessors and contemporaries in England and Virginia. It is oriented in characteristic fashion, with a stout, square entrance tower on the west; a long nave with an arched ceiling, tall "compass" arched windows, and opposing side entries; and a semicircular apse on the east end containing the chancel (figs. 1.51, 1.52). In medieval church architecture, the chancel (the area containing the altar) was likely to be a deep, clearly separated structure reflecting the prominence of the priest and the communion in the liturgy, but eighteenth-century Anglicans in America accommodated Low Church practices by building churches that were essentially rectangular preaching halls, with only a low railing and the arrangement of doors and windows to define the chancel with its simple communion table. The apse at St. Paul's gives unusual architectural emphasis to the chancel area. The materials and craftsmanship in the church emphasize its kinship with the finest houses and other public buildings of the era. The bricklayer laid the walls in Flemish bond and used an all-header bond to form the apse. Projecting brick courses delineate the stories of the tower and form quoined door enframements of a classical type standard in architectural books of the era.[75]

The most ambitious of the colony's churches was St. Philip's in Brunswick (fig. 1.53). It was begun early in the 1750s, by which time the governor had moved his residence to Brunswick, making it the de facto capital. In 1754 Gov. Arthur Dobbs reported that "the Planters about being

Figure 1.50. St. Paul's Episcopal Church, Edenton, 1736–74.

Figure 1.51. St. Paul's Episcopal Church. Apse.

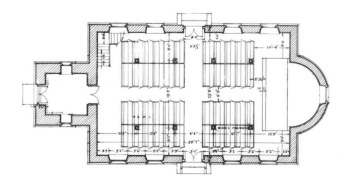

Figure 1.52. St. Paul's Episcopal Church.
Plan. (Historic American Buildings Survey)

Figure 1.53. St. Philip's Church, Brunswick, ca. 1750–68. The church burned during the American Revolution and is now stabilized as a ruin.

opulent they are building a large brick church 76 feet long by 56 feet wide, which they have raised this season so as to cover the windows." In 1760, with the walls built and the roof up, Dobbs promised to provide pews for himself and the council, the pulpit and reading desk, and plate, linens, and a carpet for the communion table. But when Dobbs died in 1765, the church was still unfinished. In 1767 his successor, Gov. William Tryon, donated the windows to spur other donations. A belfry was made, doors hung, and arches for the ceiling built. Finally, in 1768, the church, the largest in the colony, was ready for services.[76] It is rectangular in plan, with entries at the end and the sides and compass-arched windows as at St. Paul's. A new and fashionable architectural element dominates the church: the broad Palladian chancel window. The Palladian motif, with its central arched opening flanked by lower rectangular ones, was an important theme in the classical vocabulary of the time and an indicator of elegant and up-to-date taste.

Gov. Arthur Dobbs, who may have taken a hand in planning St. Philip's, strove to improve the colony by bettering its trade, strengthening the Church of England, and promoting handsome public architecture. He was unusually well equipped for the latter task, for, as engineer and surveyor-general of Ireland, he had supervised construction of the Parliament House in Dublin and other public buildings. He brought to North Carolina an excellent library that included architectural books by Palladio and Scamozzi and Colen Campbell's *Vitruvius Britannicus*. In 1758 Dobbs promoted a scheme to establish a permanent capital, George City, at Tower Hill midway along the coast near the Neuse River, and it may have been he who developed the detailed specifications for its formal, axial plan and its proposed buildings: a two-story statehouse; a secretary's office; and a governor's residence, a Palladian composition with central block and colonnades leading to projecting "offices," which were to contain a kitchen and a stables. Although George City was never to be, it represented the period's ideal vision of a classical, orderly capital, and it indicates that the notion of a Palladian governor's palace was put into the public mind some ten years before Dobbs's successor, William Tryon, actually erected such a building.[77]

After assuming office in 1765, the young and ambitious Governor Tryon moved quickly to expand the established church. He found that the colony had only five Anglican clergymen, and of the church buildings he reported: "At Brunswick, only outside Walls built, and roofed. At Wilmington, Walls only. At Newbern, in good repair. Bath, wanting considerable Repairs.

Edenton, wanting as much." Tryon pushed the long-unfinished churches to completion, established new ministers in parishes, and encouraged construction of new parish churches, giving special attention to expanding the church into the populous backcountry.[78]

Establishment of the church in the backcountry proved difficult, for dissenting denominations were especially strong there and the western farmers were resistant to taxation. The situation was exacerbated by the protests and eventually the violence of the Regulator movement. This organized resistance by Piedmont farmers against official abuses of tax policies began in 1766, intensified in 1768–70, and culminated in May 1771, when Tryon's militia put down the movement in an armed conflict with some 6,000 Regulators. In Hillsborough, epicenter of the conflict, the vestry of the newly established parish began construction of a church in 1768, and it had scarcely been completed when the Regulators entered Hillsborough, broke up the court, dragged officials through the streets, and headed for the church where they "split to pieces" the new church bell. They "were at the point of pulling down the church, but their leaders, thinking it would betray their religious principles, restrained them."[79]

St. John's Church (fig. 1.54) in Williamsboro, the only standing colonial church outside the coastal towns, was built on the heels of the Regulator crisis in the Nutbush community, also a hotbed of Regulator activity. Controversy was still in the air in the fall of 1771, when the vestry of Granville Parish moved to erect two churches and levied taxes to provide the £1,200 needed. Prominent among the parish leaders was Richard Henderson, a powerful planter and the judge who had been the butt of Regulator violence and who had condemned defeated Regulator leaders to death. Inhabitants of the county, led by Regulator spokesman Thomas Person, petitioned the legislature to halt the projects, because, they asserted, the vestry had acted "without

Figure 1.54. St. John's Episcopal Church, Williamsboro, begun 1771.

Figure 1.55. St. John's Episcopal Church. Interior. Altered during the 19th century, the church was restored in the 20th century to recreate its late-18th-century character. The pulpit and altar fittings are reconstructions.

duly Considering" the "Heavy & Burthensome" tax already imposed to pay for Tryon's military expedition against the Regulators. But the petition failed and, despite local objections, work on the Nutbush church proceeded.[80]

In their agreement with builder John Linch, the building committee carefully defined a "strong and substantial" frame structure, 60 by 34 feet, which was not only to be "good and workmanlike" but also to adhere to the "Rules of Architecture." Touches of elegance were specified in a circular pediment or shell over the door and "a good mondillion Cornish." Here was no frank expression of sturdy frame, but a smooth and elegant room: doorposts were to be "worked off" and the cornerposts "Rabited out so as to make flush walls with the other framing." Characteristic of Anglican churches, the ceiling was to be coved, a rear gallery was to sit on "elegant" posts, and boxed pews were to flank a central aisle. Fittings for the Anglican service included a "good Communion Table . . . neatly Bannistered & Railed" and a "good Reading Desk with a Genteel Pulpit." This bright and orderly space (fig. 1.55) conveys an aura of formality, an ordered service, and the place of the established church—hard-won qualities in a community dominated by dissenters and in which the Regulator conflict had so recently raged.[81]

Tryon Palace and Palladian Classicism

Even before he assumed office in 1765, Gov. William Tryon had given thought to construction of an official "Edifice" as a combination governor's residence and assembly meeting place. In 1764 Tryon had brought with him from England architect John Hawks, who was fully qualified to design and supervise the construction of such a building. During 1766 and early 1767,

Tryon and Hawks worked through a sequence of ideas that began with a simple, hip-roofed mansion adorned with a Palladian window and ended with an imposing complex that included a main building of 82 by 59 feet and curved colonnades leading to "offices" containing a kitchen and a stable.[82]

In December 1766, the assembly authorized Tryon to spend £5,000 proclamation money on land and construction. The governor estimated that the sum allotted for the house and offices would be "short of the expense of erecting them." He reported that, with the cost of finishing the building "in the plainest manner" estimated at £10,000 sterling, he planned to begin work on the body of the house and defer construction of the flanking secondary buildings. Hawks agreed to manage all aspects of the work and to complete the job in three years' time. Tryon sent Hawks to Philadelphia "to hire able workmen, as this province affords none capable of such an undertaking."[83] Despite opposition from many, including the Regulators, Tryon obtained additional taxes to pay for the complex, work went quickly, and, late in 1770, Tryon moved into the completed residence (fig. 1.56).

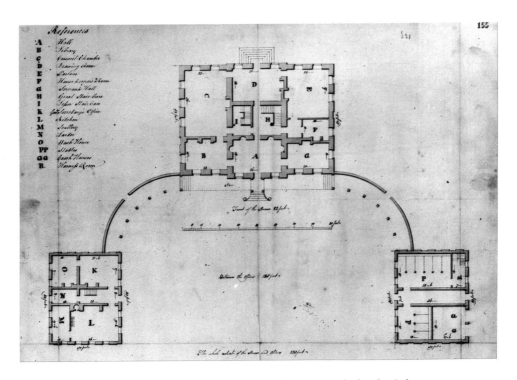

Figure 1.56. Tryon Palace, New Bern, 1767–70. Elevation and plan by John Hawks, 1767. This set of drawings, which was sent to England for approval, is believed to be the version from which Hawks built the palace. Tryon Palace burned in 1798 and was reconstructed in 1950–59. (North Carolina Division of Archives and History, from British Public Record Office)

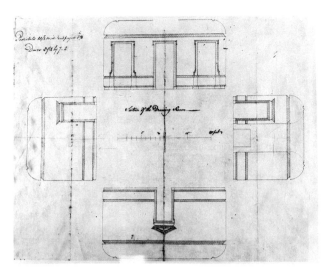

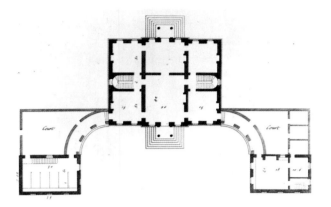

Figure 1.58. Tryon Palace. Section of drawing room, drawing by John Hawks, 1767. (New-York Historical Society)

Figure 1.57. Tripartite villa design, from James Gibbs, *A Book of Architecture*. Hawks and Tryon probably referred to Gibbs's and other English architectural books in planning the palace. (Henry Francis du Pont Winterthur Museum Library, Collection of Printed Books)

The composition of the palace, with its pedimented central pavilion and simple pedimented entry and its forecourt formed by curved colonnades and projecting flankers, partook of themes well established in mid-eighteenth-century British architecture. Hawks and Tryon were doubtless acquainted with Palladian residences in England, and tripartite Palladian villa designs (fig. 1.57) had also appeared in such architectural books as James Gibbs's *A Book of Architecture* (1728), Isaac Ware's *A Complete Body of Architecture* (1756), and Robert Morris's *Select Architecture* (1757).

Though simple by English standards, Tryon Palace was a monument of opulence and elegance extraordinary in the American colonies. The pediment of the main facade featured the royal coat of arms. Niches for statuary graced the entrance hall, which led to a skylit stair hall. Tryon was especially pleased with the "great elegance both in the Taste and workmanship" of the council chamber's "large statuary Ionic chimney piece" of sienna and black marble richly carved and with inlaid medals of the king and queen. The finishing of the principal rooms, as indicated in Hawks's drawing for a section of the drawing room (fig. 1.58), resembled plates in Abraham Swan's popular *Collection of Designs in Architecture* with its pedimented and crossetted doorways and window frames integrated into the wainscoting.[84]

Tryon had ensured that the colony he governed at last had an "elegant and noble structure." The grandeur of the building, like its cost and the taxes required to support its construction, generated complaints, particularly from the backcountry Regulators already disgruntled over tax issues and abuses of Crown authority, but visitors found it the most admirable building in the colony. One traveler predicted that the palace would "excel for Magnificence & architecture any edifice on the continent," while another praised it as an elegant building "in the pure English taste," with "all the ornamentation extremely simple and placed with considerable taste and intelligence."[85]

The palace had a marked influence on architecture in New Bern and beyond. Several buildings of the era indicate the "sudden appearance in the town . . . of a school of sophisticated

Figure 1.59. Coor-Gaston House, New Bern, ca. 1770.

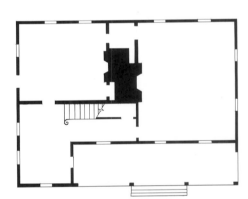

Figure 1.60. Coor-Gaston House.
Plan by Richard Parsons.

academic Georgian interior woodwork of a decidedly Philadelphia character." The Coor-Gaston House (fig. 1.59) in New Bern, built about 1770, illustrates how builders incorporated stylish Georgian motifs into houses of regional form. The large frame house sits with its gable end to the street, a two-story piazza set beneath the broad gable roofline. A stair passage and two large rooms bend around the inset porch (fig. 1.60). Touches of fashionable taste appear in the classical motif of the Diocletian gable window and stylish Chinese lattice balustrade of the piazza—a type of railing commonly illustrated in English builders' guides. The principal rooms are adorned with woodwork akin to Hawks's plan for the drawing room of the palace and illustrations in Swan's *Designs in Architecture*.[86] Similar motifs appear in the best room at Bellair (fig. 1.61), a plantation house near New Bern that was probably built in the early 1770s for Richard Dobbs Spaight. In a dramatic departure from the forms of houses previously built in the region, this residence has a Palladian three-part facade in the spirit of the palace, behind which lies a floor plan only one room deep.[87]

At the same time, whether as a direct influence of the palace, its architect, and its artisans or merely as a result of the developing taste for Palladian classicism, the penchant for fine building found expression among the gentry beyond New Bern. About 1770 young English baronet Nathaniel Duckenfield began construction of a tripartite brick villa in Bertie County, but only the wings were completed before he ran out of money and returned to England in 1772.[88] It was likewise about 1770 that John Burgwin built his fine mansion in Wilmington, which, like the Coor-Gaston House in New Bern, blended regional form with handsome Georgian interiors.

The most important building erected in the Palladian spirit of the palace is the Chowan County Courthouse (fig. 1.62). Standing at the head of the town green overlooking Edenton Bay, the courthouse is among the finest and most beautifully sited public buildings of colonial America. Circumstantial evidence and certain similarities to the palace point to John Hawks as architect. In 1767 commissioners advertised for contractors to build a brick courthouse 68 by 45 feet, for which they would supply the plan on the day of bidding. (In fact the structure as built was 69 by 48 feet.) In 1773 John Hawks provided a plan and specifications for an accompanying prison, which had been authorized at the same time as the courthouse. In that year, Hawks also wrote to Joseph Hewes, a member of the courthouse building committee, enclosing drawings and raising questions concerning a building that was nearing completion. Hawks discussed a proposed colonnade that would "make the Job more complete" but would be expensive and might place the columns "quite close to the first Step of the Court, which may be thought an obstruction to the passing and repassing." He may well have been referring to the courthouse

Figure 1.61. Bellair, Craven County, ca. 1770. (Collection of Mrs. G. Tull Richardson)

Figure 1.62. Chowan County Courthouse, Edenton, begun 1767.

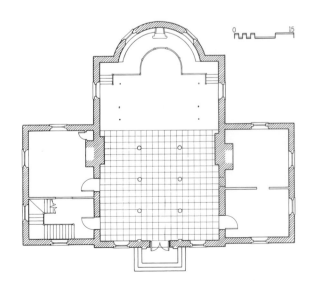

Figure 1.63. Chowan County Courthouse.
Plan by Carl R. Lounsbury.

Figure 1.64. Chowan
County Courthouse.
Assembly Room.

and to the addition of supporting columns in the courtroom; apparently not built initially, columns were required in the early nineteenth century.[89]

The courthouse shares the assurance and balance of Tryon's palace, but it is executed on a smaller scale and with greater simplicity. Fine craftsmanship and restrained detail stress the solidity, quality, and carefully controlled proportions of the building. The walls are of Flemish bond, with a molded water table and belt course defining the stories. Windows are set cleanly into the walls, and a modillion cornice accentuates the roofline and the broad pediment. Atop the hip roof rises a tall cupola, which was originally glazed rather than louvered.

The exterior expresses the interior spaces with clarity and directness (fig. 1.63). The simple pedimented entrance opens into a large courtroom that fills the central pavilion (see fig. 1.1). The room has a floor paved with stone; the area in which the public stood during court sessions was plainly finished and whitewashed. Opposite the entrance, paneling and turned railings define the small formal area for the court. In a small apse—similar to the chancel of nearby St. Paul's—a semicircular platform upholds the chief justice's tall chair and the flanking benches of the associate justices. Clerks' offices, jury rooms, and the stair occupy the flanking spaces.[90] On the upper floor, the central pavilion is likewise occupied by a single grand space (fig. 1.64) for public meetings and social events—a 30-by-45-foot room that was one of the largest fully paneled rooms in the colonies. Fine, tall paneling carries around the projecting chimney breasts with their simple crossetted fire openings and frames the generous windows that flood the room with light.

The new courthouse soon became the setting for meetings that led up to the American Revolution, as Edenton's politicians, including Samuel Johnston, Joseph Hewes, and James Iredell, took a prominent role in the colony's movement toward independence. And in 1789, Edenton's leaders of the Federalist campaign for the U.S. Constitution illuminated the courthouse cupola to celebrate North Carolina's ratification of the document.[91] Throughout the colonies, in buildings that likewise presented the image of British classicism rendered in local materials and with local skill, the unified genteel culture of the colonial leadership expressed a deeper set of shared philosophical, economic, and political values that served them well during the years of war and the building of a new nation.

CHAPTER 2

The Federal Period, 1780–1830

Lexington has increased rapidly for the past few years, they distinguish it by the old and new towns, in the latter are very many pretty houses, a very handsome courthouse, built in the modern style (I do not know what order of architecture) and a portico supported by pillars: they are always the most prominent building in town and are usually placed in the middle of the main street. We left at 7 o'clock a.m. . . . and arrived at the far famed town of Salem about 11 o'clock, having rode 20 miles. We saw on the road many houses which would have answered to the description of those which lie in the region of Sleepy Hollow which Mr. Irving so admirably describes, this country is almost peopled with dutch and their fashions neither vary with age or clime.
—*Diary of Juliana Margaret Conner*

    The American Revolution caused a hiatus in construction in most communities. Wartime inflation and the scarcity of materials and workmen were followed in the immediate postwar years by economic and political uncertainties that likewise slowed building. In the late 1780s, however, and especially in the 1790s, a resurgence of building began throughout the state and the nation. In North Carolina, several factors combined to support this broad-based building boom: growth in population from about 350,000 in 1786 to 478,000 in 1800; the need to effect repairs and replacements delayed by wartime shortages; the development of frontier settlements into more complex communities; and the accompanying desire for handsome and substantial buildings. In the 1790s, the new nation took its first steps to protect shipping along its coastline. The new state established a capital in Raleigh and a university at Chapel Hill, both of them laid out in formal, axial plans on rural, inland sites far from established coastal towns. Towns replaced worn market houses and counties their old jails and courthouses, and newly formed counties built their first public buildings. Established congregations replaced log meetinghouses with frame ones, and new congregations built their first churches. Farmers built new houses and outbuildings. And as small port and crossroads towns grew, townspeople erected larger and more stylish houses and stores than ever before.[1]

    In the early years of the nineteenth century, however, the old difficulties of transportation, conservative political and fiscal policies, and a slow-growing and predominantly agricultural economy earned North Carolina a reputation as a poor and backward state in a nation bent on economic expansion and cultural assertiveness. The state's population grew to 555,000 in 1810 and 738,000 in 1830, but immigration tapered off and outmigration mounted as national expansion drew thousands to the west. At the same time—especially in the east, and in many areas of the Piedmont—agricultural wealth became more concentrated as planters assembled greater holdings in land and slaves, swallowing up small farms and establishing larger plantations. Within the

Figure 2.1. Mendenhall House, Jamestown, early 19th century. Enclosed stairs continued to be prevalent in houses of the Federal period.

state, there was tension between those who sought to participate more fully in the national and international market economy through commercial agriculture, trade, and internal improvements and those who preferred a life of economic independence from taxation and government.

Overall, most North Carolinians regarded their architecture with a coolly realistic eye, commenting that their buildings were "snug" and "comfortable" but included few imposing "edifices."[2] Most public buildings shared a few common forms and fell within an established range of size, materials, and workmanship according to their cost, status, and purpose. Only extraordinary structures stood more than two stories tall. Gable roofs prevailed, though a few fashionable buildings had hip roofs. In the period from 1780 to 1830, architecture was dominated by artisans working in established craft traditions. Two overlapping trends predominated: the persistence of classicism and the development of traditional regional patterns.

Classicism maintained its appeal in the culture of the expanding gentry. As the young United States sought to establish its identity as an ideal republic in the midst of debate over slavery, social and religious turmoil, European revolutions, and Napoleonic wars, the classic virtues of ancient Rome and Greece offered Americans a myth that suffused their architecture as well as their literature and rhetoric. Within this classical vision, there was tension between the ideals of republican simplicity and the agrarian life and the emerging social reality of urban opulence and the trappings of aristocracy.

In leading towns and on a few plantations, the classical, primarily Palladian tradition established shortly before the Revolution continued to develop. At first it proceeded along familiar lines in the spirit of Batty Langley and Abraham Swan, whose books continued to be reissued by English and American publishers.[3] After about 1800, North Carolinians gradually responded to the national and international taste, promoted by the brothers Robert and James Adam, for light, delicate, Roman-inspired neoclassical motifs, which were popularized by English and then American builders' guides.

In his *American Builder's Companion* (1806), which presented the new style in a form intended for "the American workman," Asher Benjamin acknowledged that "old-fashioned workmen, who have for many years followed the footsteps of Palladio and Langley, will no doubt leave their old path with reluctance." But the new books, especially those of Benjamin, Englishman William Pain, and Philadelphian Owen Biddle, found a ready audience among American artisans and their clients. Like earlier builders' guides, they demonstrated the proper proportioning of the classical orders and other elements of a building and included a few plans and elevations. They also offered details that artisans could adapt to customary building forms—a wealth of delicate moldings, mantels, and doorways, which inspired improvisation as craftsmen translated the line drawings into exuberant carved, gouged, and molded sunbursts, urns, swags, and garlands. After 1810 there began to appear in a few adventurous buildings hints of the new taste for Grecian and even Gothic Revival motifs, part of national and international trends that had just begun to appear in the American countryside.[4]

At the same time, the rural, conservative society nurtured the full and rich development of a traditional architecture that continued forms, plans, and techniques introduced in the mideighteenth century.[5] Diverse forms that appear only in scattered examples from the colonial period evolved into strong regional patterns, within which artisans displayed considerable flexibility in planning and virtuosity in craftsmanship. This trend was especially strong in the years from 1780 to 1810. Although a few residences and public buildings replicated the formal plans of classical style, the familiar open house plans continued to dominate until the 1820s and 1830s. Indeed, the persistence of traditional building patterns among the planter elite as well as yeoman farmers is particularly striking. Many large houses from this period are characterized by room arrangements that provided entrance directly into the main room. Tokens of changing fashion appeared in subtle adjustments of proportion, a trend toward symmetry, and artisans' individualized embellishments from builders' guides. Examples of traditional architecture's potential for variation within an established framework appear in such diverse forms as the coastal piazza houses, the brick houses of the Piedmont, log architecture throughout the state, and domestic and agricultural outbuildings. In the early national period, clients and builders brought together many crosscurrents from local, regional, national, and international sources, as French engineers, English architects, and hundreds of black and white carpenters and masons, natives and immigrants, met the needs of a diverse rural state.

Public Works and Public Buildings

Federal Building Projects

Construction of public works ranked high on the national agenda in the years after the Revolution. Government leaders saw the improvement and protection of interstate travel and overseas trade routes as critical to the survival of the new nation. Works of engineering, designed in many cases by French and British immigrants, were landmarks in promoting the general welfare and providing for the common defense. In North Carolina, the most compelling need was the protection of shipping along the coast.

In 1783, as soon as the Revolution ended, the state planned improvements for the coast, beginning with authorization of a lighthouse on Bald Head Island near the mouth of the Cape Fear River. Six years later, with the Bald Head lighthouse not yet complete, the state planned another lighthouse for the important inlet at Ocracoke. In that year, however, the first U.S. Congress met and authorized a national system of lighthouses and other maritime aids. The federal government took over existing lighthouses, funded completion of the Bald Head Island Lighthouse and other unfinished state beacons, and authorized the Lighthouse Service to build more. Implementing a system that laid the groundwork for many generations of federal building projects, the U.S. Treasury Department published specifications, received bids, and awarded contracts. Uniform federal standards were established with the aim of producing plain, strong, permanent structures. Soon a system of lighthouses along the coast gave evidence of the new federal presence at work.[6]

The early lighthouse prototype was still in effect when the beacon at Bald Head required replacement in 1816. The Treasury Department issued specifications for an octagonal brick lighthouse 90 feet tall plus lantern. The customary language of construction specified the materials and workmanship: hard-fired brick, walls of diminishing thickness from 5 to 2 feet, floors and stairs of Carolina yellow pine, and a "complete iron lanthorn" with glass "of the first quality Boston manufacture." The keeper's house was to be built of brick in "plain workmanlike manner." In keeping with local practice, the 35-by-17-foot dwelling was to have two main rooms divided by a passage, a front piazza, and two rear shed rooms "divided by a piazza." The lighthouse, a stout, tapering shaft of brick trimmed with brown sandstone, was completed by contractor D. S. Way in 1817 and became one of fifty-five lighthouses built by that time. In 1823 it was joined by another simple brick shaft at Ocracoke.[7] Bald Head Island Lighthouse (fig. 2.2), like many of this first generation of American lighthouses, stands weathered, plain, and strong, a remote outpost of a new nation.

To provide for the common defense, the U.S. government built a series of forts along the strategically vulnerable North Carolina coast. Two phases of construction produced modest individual forts along the Atlantic coastline, but after the War of 1812, the nation moved to strengthen its defenses with a unified and permanent system of masonry fortifications, professionally planned by French and American engineers.

Fort Macon, which guards the harbor at Beaufort, is part of this "third system" of magnificent French-influenced military architecture. After the fall of Napoleon, the United States employed French émigré officers in many positions, the most important of which was the appointment in 1816 of Napoleon's military engineer Gen. Simon Bernard (along with American Joseph Totten) to head a board charged with creating a system of national defense.[8] Bernard, accompa-

Figure 2.2. Bald Head Island Lighthouse, Brunswick County, 1817. D. S. Way, contractor.

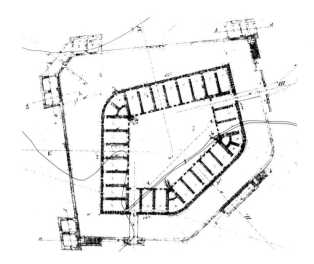

Figure 2.3. Plan of fortification for Beaufort Harbor by William Tell Poussin, 1821. Drawn by Poussin and planned by General Simon Bernard, this was the basis of the design for Fort Macon. (National Archives)

nied by his assistant, Capt. William Tell Poussin, traveled along the coast and planned forts in the French tradition of masonry fortifications—some were set below ground level, while others rose several stories above ground, depending on the situation. Poussin's survey of the Beaufort Harbor site and his 1821 drawings for what was later known as Fort Macon (fig. 2.3) were among the results of this campaign.

Although the actual construction, under the direction of Lt. William A. Eliason, did not begin until 1826, the fort followed the Bernard-Poussin scheme. It is a recessed pentagon, set into the dunes so as to be invisible from the sea, with a series of barriers and a moat or ditch arranged to protect the fort from attack by sea (fig. 2.4). The structure presents a subtle and powerful

Figure 2.4. Fort Macon, Carteret County, 1826–34. View from the outer fortification (covertway) across the ditch or moat to the citadel, with its cannon embrasures and rifle loopholes arranged to provide full fire coverage of the ditch.

Figure 2.5. Fort Macon. View from sally port into parade ground surrounded by barracks in vaulted casemates.

blend of formidable strength and fine craftsmanship. It was built of brick manufactured locally, but the masons came from Philadelphia and Alexandria. Within the fort, the parade ground is surrounded by quarters located in the thick-walled casemates (fig. 2.5). The masonry work in the round-arched openings and handsome brickwork compares with other public buildings of the period. Graceful staircases with stone steps and stylish iron railings mount to the ramparts overlooking the sea.[9]

State Buildings

As North Carolina set out to house its new government institutions, the need for economy and a sense of republican virtue precluded the construction of opulent monuments—there were to be no new palaces to rival Tryon's. Substantial, neat, and convenient public "houses" were the order of a new day.

Remarkable unity informed the scale and form of nearly all buildings, with only some slight adjustments in plan, symbolic trappings, or orientation to accommodate specific purposes. Raleigh, the new state capital, was laid out with axial streets, four public squares, and a large central square for the State House—an orderly and formal urban plan, similar to Philadelphia's, hacked out from the forest. In its plans authorizing construction of the State House (fig. 2.6) in 1792, the financially strapped legislature set a maximum of $10,000 for construction. The building committee planned a hip-roofed brick "house" that, though measuring some 110 by 52 feet, was conceived in familiar domestic terms. The specifications addressed issues of sturdy workmanship and materials and included a customary hierarchy of finishing details, from the "elegant staircase" and modillion cornices and wainscoting in the passages and principal rooms to the smaller rooms with "chair & wash boards only." The roof of heart cypress was to be painted "some lively

in appearance — It is built of Brick with a stone foundation & has four ——
on each Side —

Figure 2.6. State House, Raleigh, 1793–95. Rhodham Atkins, contractor. Watercolor
by J. S. Glennie, 1811. (Princeton University Library)

colours." After the plan was completed, the legislature decided that the structure demanded
additional "elegance" and ordered "a brake in the center of the East and West front walls
projecting two feet by twenty feet . . . so as to have a Frontispiece East and West, something
similar to the front of the public buildings in New Bern"—thus continuing the Palladian influence of the palace, where the assembly was meeting.[10]

Similarly, in 1793, when trustees of the University of North Carolina contracted for the first
major building (now called Old East), the specifications called for a two-story brick "House"
measuring 96′7″ by 40′1½″, its finish to be "neat but plain." The plan was a simple doubling of a
central-passage house, two rooms deep. Completed in 1795, the building housed the first state
university to open its doors. Standing in the rural village of Chapel Hill, it was part of an axial
mall-plan campus designed to permit long-term growth along a "Grand Avenue."[11] In 1795 the
next major building, the present South Building, was planned for the head of the mall; it was to
be "a house about 120 feet long, fifty feet wide, and three stories tall" and thus the largest
building in the state aside from the governor's palace. Its pedimented, pavilioned facade was
familiar from the palace and statehouse and resembled other major collegiate buildings, including Nassau Hall at Princeton, which greatly influenced North Carolina's university. Political
rivalries plagued the project, as opponents objected to building a costly "palace" that smacked of
the "aristocratic principles" of its Federalist sponsors. Construction money ran out, and the
building stood unfinished for several years before finally being completed in 1814.[12]

Meetinghouses

Meetinghouses, like the first state buildings, took an essentially domestic form. They were
central landmarks in the rural culture that flourished in North Carolina. In contrast to the
colonial period, from which only a few Anglican churches survive, the early national period saw
the construction of sturdy meetinghouses for Presbyterians, Quakers, Methodists, Moravians,
and Lutherans. Whereas the Anglican church collapsed in postwar North Carolina, leaving
isolated congregations to maintain their buildings and hold services as best they could, other

Protestant denominations flourished and grew. A wave of evangelical Protestantism swept the countryside, and ministers preached to hundreds and thousands at countless revivals. Rural congregations grew more numerous and more prosperous.

The meetinghouse was usually a gable-roofed building similar to dwellings in the neighborhood, with the main entrance on the long side (opposite the pulpit) and secondary entrances on the gable ends. Benches, or pews, and sometimes galleries clustered around the pulpit, which usually stood near the north wall. This arrangement contrasted with that of Anglican churches, which were entered on the gable end, with a long aisle leading to a communion table at the opposite end and a pulpit to one side. The meetinghouse form was shared by most Protestant denominations.

Figure 2.7. Grace Reformed Church, Rowan County, 1795.

Figure 2.8. St. Paul's Lutheran Church, Catawba County, 1818. Attributed to Henry Cline, carpenter.

Figure 2.9. St. Paul's Lutheran Church. Interior.

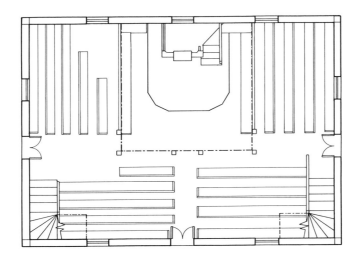

Figure 2.10. St. Paul's Lutheran Church.
Plan by Carl R. Lounsbury.

The most impressive examples of the form in North Carolina are the great stone meeting-houses built after the Revolution by the German farmers along the Yadkin River. The German settlers who came to Rowan County in the mid-eighteenth century had built a log meetinghouse shared by Lutheran and Reformed (Calvinist) congregations. As the congregations prospered and grew, first the Lutherans, then the Reformed members erected separate, nearly identical stone meetinghouses, each measuring 40 by 50 feet. The Lutherans began Zion Church in 1792 and completed it in 1795. Soon afterward, the Reformed congregation began Grace Church (fig. 2.7), and, like Michael Braun at his stone house not far away, they installed a tablet of thanks inscribed in German and dated 1795, and another bearing a clock face with hands set at 9:30.[13]

St. Paul's Lutheran Church (figs. 2.8, 2.9), built several years later for the Germans of the Catawba River valley, epitomizes the simplicity and intimacy of the meetinghouse form. It, too, replaced a log meetinghouse built by settlers in the eighteenth century for both the Reformed and Lutheran denominations. In 1818, it is believed, Henry Cline, a carpenter and member of the congregation, built a new, two-story log meetinghouse, covered with weatherboards and mea-suring about 27 by 37 feet (fig. 2.10). A narrow double doorway on the long southwest side and single doors at the gable ends open into a perfectly preserved meetinghouse interior. The snug pews and steep galleries filled with as many as 250 worshipers, as men and women entered the church from opposite sites and sat separately. In contrast to the austere dignity of the exterior, the room is far from stark. Like fine houses of the region, it has planed board sheathing, fluted pillars, and paneled wainscot. Touches of stylish regional ornamentation emphasize the central importance of the pulpit: consoles adorn the tall triple window behind the pulpit, and urns and guilloches enrich the sounding board suspended from scrolled ironwork.[14]

Far more typical of rural meetinghouses is the utterly plain Brown Marsh Presbyterian Church (figs. 2.11, 2.12) in Bladen County, in the heart of the Cape Fear Scots region. Thomas Sheridan, a local, free black carpenter, is believed to have built the church in 1828.[15] He weatherboarded the walls, shuttered the windows with board shutters, and finished the inside with fine, planed boards. The congregation sat on simple wooden benches facing one another and the pulpit, and a sounding board suspended from the ceiling spread the word through the room.

Industrial and Commercial Buildings

Industrial and commercial architecture also shared in the dominant domestic scale and traditional workmanship. The finest early nineteenth-century industrial building still standing in the state is the Kerr Mill (fig. 2.13), located in the plantation community once called "Kerrsville" in the Scotch-Irish section of Rowan County. A mill was a landmark in any rural community—the main secular gathering place outside the courthouse town—where farmers came to exchange

Figure 2.11. Brown Marsh Presbyterian Church, Bladen County, 1828. Attributed to Thomas Sheridan, carpenter.

Figure 2.12. Brown Marsh Presbyterian Church. Interior.

Figure 2.13. Kerr Mill, Rowan County, ca. 1822–23.

Figure 2.14. Union Tavern, Milton, ca. 1819.

old gossip for new and whole corn for meal, and thus it was as much a public building as a private one. Built about 1822–23, the Kerr Mill is comparable to the most substantial houses and public buildings in its stone foundation, well-laid brick walls, flat arches over the windows and doors, and corbeled cornice. "Plain" and "good" workmanship, suitable to the building's function, appear in the lamb's-tongue chamfers on its heavy timbers, the sturdy batten shutters, and the Dutch door.

Like many rural mills, the Kerr Mill was built for a wealthy planter family that diversified its enterprises by damming a stream, building a mill, and hiring a miller to grind local farmers' corn into meal and wheat into flour. Joseph Kerr's father had been among the small landholders who established the "Irish" settlement in Rowan County; Joseph emerged as a leader among the second generation who accumulated land and slaves and transformed the neighborhood into a plantation culture. In 1822 Joseph's son Samuel, soon to outstrip his father as a planter, had just returned from college, and the construction of the mill may have been one of his first undertakings.[16] The Kerrs' brick mill, unusual among the plain wooden mills common in the region, rivaled in its workmanship the mansions of the area's wealthiest planters and even the county courthouse and gave clear evidence of the family's position in the local economy.

Domestic form and scale also predominated in public hostelries, the rural and small-town inns that served travelers. Indeed, many inns were homes whose owners took in travelers, such as Sherrill's Inn near Asheville, Walker's Inn in Cherokee County, and Brummel's Inn in Davidson County. The Lafayette Hotel in Fayetteville was admired for its fine accommodations and private chambers, but it was the exception. In many instances, owners of inns and taverns expanded or adapted domestic forms to provide suitable public spaces and guest chambers. At the Yellow

Figure 2.15. Wright Tavern, Wentworth, ca. 1810–30.

Figure 2.16. Wright Tavern. Passage.

House in Pittsboro, a paneled wall between the passage and the parlor can be slid up against the ceiling to open two spaces into one great room. In Milton, a tobacco-trading town established to compete with Virginia markets, innkeeper Richard Ogilby advertised in 1819 his newly built Union Tavern (fig. 2.14).[17] The building took the form of a standard gable-roof house, two rooms deep, but with some adjustments to suit its purpose: three street entrances opened into a central passage and into two pairs of parlors, where open archways in the partition walls created public rooms extending the full depth of the house.[18]

In building the Wright Tavern (fig. 2.15), which catered to customers attending court in the county seat of Wentworth, the Wright family manipulated the plan in another fashion. Several stages of construction produced an elongated, two-story house. At one end are a spacious parlor, a rear dining room wing, and, above the parlor, tiny but well-appointed bedchambers. On the other end there are two rooms below and a single chamber above, probably family quarters. The two sections are separated by an open stair passage (fig. 2.16) that provides a dual indoor-outdoor, public-private space. Visually, this passage is treated as an interior room, framed by a molded arch and finished with wainscoting and an elaborately carved stair, yet spatially it is a continuation of the porch, from which customers and family could proceed through the house or mount the stairs to separate chambers.[19]

Urban Architecture in New Bern: The Vortex of Fashion

New Bern was the largest town in the state throughout most of the Federal period, and it is there that Federal architecture appears at its most elegant and consistent. Travelers who had wended their way through the endless pine forests and swamps of the coastal plain fell upon New Bern with relief. The little city had regular streets, neat houses generously spaced with their private gardens, and a refined social life among the mercantile elite. Typical of many visitors was Francisco de Miranda, who in 1783 admired Tryon's palace and the city's small and well-kept wooden houses, which, he noted, "correspond to the classes." In the post-Revolutionary era, New Bern absorbed several blows, including the loss of British trade, the removal of the capital to Raleigh, and several major fires, one of which destroyed the palace in 1798. Nevertheless, the community maintained its status as a thriving and stylish little city. Its business rebounded by means of a triangular trade route that circulated goods, people, and ideas among the Caribbean islands, coastal North Carolina, and northern ports in New England, New York, and Philadelphia. By 1802 a visitor adjudged it "a growing, trading town" with 700 to 1,000 houses, "among which are some respectable brick edifices." Population growth continued, and the number of inhabitants rose from 2,500 in 1800 to 3,600 in 1815.[20]

New Bern's merchant gentry came from diverse origins—many were newcomers from England, Scotland, the Caribbean, and Philadelphia or other American port cities—but they shared a taste for fashion and a lively social season. One participant found New Bern "full of extravagance and fine dressing, the poorest people make a show," while her planter husband believed he was "among a set of sharpers." Dances, dinners, and tea parties, as well as politics, horse racing, and billiards, were favorite pastimes and opportunities for the display of wealth and taste: "Last evening Ma and myself were at Mrs McKinleys, her house is like a palace she has the most splendid drawing room I ever beheld, quite new and the latest fashion, she told us the furniture of that room cost 1500 dolls it almost surpasses description." The trend reached its extreme in the person of "a certain old Lady [who] plunges deep into the vortex of fashion."[21]

With the palace gone but growth and prosperity mounting, and with new people and new money arriving, New Bernians almost built a new town. As they erected new townhouses, banks, civic buildings, and churches, the town's artisans, black and white, created an architecture of remarkable quality, sophistication, and unity.[22] Interweaving local precedent and new ideas, they established a clear hierarchy among and within buildings, all the while adhering to a domestic scale and variations on a narrow range of plans. For their principal civic monuments, they drew on the Georgian and Palladian ideal epitomized by the palace, but they also adjusted to neoclassical themes just coming to the fore. In their domestic buildings they incorporated influences from Philadelphia, New England, and New York and elements from old and new builders' guides.

Domestic Architecture

The John Wright Stanly House (fig. 2.17) demonstrates the culture of genteel fashion and display that began its resurgence soon after the Revolution. Stanly had traded in exports in Jamaica and had run into trouble that led to a jail term in Philadelphia. He arrived in New Bern in 1772, prospered as a privateer during the Revolution, acquired a plantation, slaves, and wharves, and in 1779 bought a large town lot on which he built the grandest private residence in New Bern. In 1787 visiting Philadelphia merchant William Attmore dined with Stanly and labeled his success an "instance of the vicissitudes of human affairs. . . . This Man of whom the first knowledge I had, was, his being confined a prisoner in the Gaol of Philadelphia for debt, upon his liberation removed to this Country, where by a Series of fortunate events in Trade during the War he acquired a great property, and has built a house in Newbern where he resides, that is truly elegant and convenient; at an expense of near 20,000 Dollars."[23]

Stanly's house, which may have been designed by John Hawks, who had remained in New Bern, is a sophisticated if conservative late-Georgian house, which shows continuing use of Abraham Swan's *British Architect* and *Designs in Architecture*. Flush-boarded walls create a sleek background for a presentation of classical themes: quoined corners, a modillion cornice, pedimented windows, and an open pedimented entrance, a popular motif in eighteenth-century English books.[24]

The central-passage plan (fig. 2.18), two rooms deep, displays the eighteenth century's careful modulation of spaces. The off-center entry passage opens into a wider stair passage at the rear, and the flanking rooms thus vary in size. A secondary service stair permitted discreet movement of servants through the house.

The finish is likewise artfully deployed to emphasize the relative importance of the rooms. In the passage, a simple transverse arch focuses attention on the splendid stair (fig. 2.19) with turned balusters and a molded handrail that rises from a scrolled base to ramped curves at the landings. Scrolled, leafy brackets in the spirit of Swan's plates are expertly carved, their luxuriant exuberance the work of a Philadelphia carver who either came to New Bern or sent the work out from his city shop.[25] The largest room (fig. 2.20), to the left of the passage, is fully paneled and treated with crossetted moldings and pediments in the style of Hawks's drawings for the palace drawing room and such pre-Revolutionary houses as Bellair and the Coor-Gaston House. Horizontal bands of Greek fret, Wall of Troy, dentils, and modillions, from baseboard to ceiling cornice, unify the ensemble. In the slightly smaller dining room across the passage, the scheme is similar but uses simpler details and has wainscoting rather than full paneling.

Such rooms were part of the presentation of self through the code of gentility. Contemporary documents provide a glimpse of the possessions and social rituals that filled Stanly's house. Portraits of Stanly and his family hung prominently on the walls, including one by Charles Willson Peale. The rooms were rich with color and pattern, the furniture covered and the windows hung with vivid fabrics—red-and-white or blue-and-white check, green-and-white stripes, or purple and yellow. Carpets covered the floors, and a canvas floor cloth lay in the passage. On such occasions as the small afternoon dinner party that visitor William Attmore attended in 1787, the mahogany dining table in Stanly's dining room would be set with one of several sets of blue-and-white, red-and-white, or queensware dishes and adorned with silver-handled knives and forks, silver salts, and silver mustard pots. After dinner the group moved into the "tea room," where they took tea from Stanly's black-penciled china tea set, arranged on a mahogany tea table and poured from a japanned teapot on a japanned tea board.[26]

As New Bern prospered after the war, Stanly's house was joined by other elegant town-

Figure 2.17. Stanly House, New Bern, ca. 1779–83.

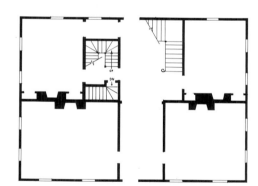

Figure 2.18. Stanly House. Plan by Richard Parsons.

houses. Most were freestanding two- or three-story dwellings, many of them built with a side-passage plan. They usually stood on spacious lots, and several overlooked their owners' wharves on the Neuse or the Trent rivers. The earliest example is the Isaac Taylor House (fig. 2.21) on Craven Street, built about 1792 for a Scots-born merchant. The severely handsome, three-story house abuts the street. The Flemish-bond brick walls have fine flat arches above the windows; the clean-cut windows, parapeted roofline, and slate roof suggest urban precedents.[27] The Diocletian window is a classical motif used in New Bern before the Revolution, and the pedimented entrance with sunburst ornament exhibits the coming influence of the Adam taste. Simple Adamesque work continues inside the house, which features a side-passage plan and interior chimney. Like many city businessmen, Taylor had his office in the front first-story room, which

Figure 2.19. Stanly House. Passage.

Figure 2.20. Stanly House. Drawing room.

Figure 2.21. Taylor House, New Bern, ca. 1792.

originally had a separate entrance. A more elaborate arrangement appeared in the nearby town-house and office of English-born merchant John Harvey, who, in about 1798, built a three-story edifice that contained his offices on the first floor, an arched driveway running through the house from street to wharf, and family chambers, including a large drawing room, above.[28]

After the turn of the century, New Bern artisans erected a series of similar two-story brick townhouses, including the James Bryan House (1803–5), the Jones-Jarvis and Smallwood houses (ca. 1805–10), and the John Donnell House (1815–19). In their proportions, they are broader than the Taylor House, and they have pairs of chimneys on the gable end opposite the passage rather

Figure 2.22. Smallwood House, New Bern, ca. 1810–15. Asa King, carpenter.

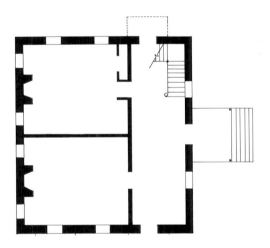

Figure 2.23. Smallwood House.
Plan by Richard Parsons.

Figure 2.24. Smallwood House. Portico.

Figure 2.25. Smallwood House. Second-story drawing room.

than central chimneys between the rooms. In such houses it was fashionable to place the dining room on the first story, convenient to the kitchen, while locating the formal drawing room on the second floor. By this time, the terms *dining room* and *drawing room* were routinely used to describe the formal and specialized uses of rooms, while the older terms *passage*, *parlor*, and *chamber* were still common.[29] John Donnell's accounts for his house (which is now lost) depict a construction process that was probably typical of the time. He employed leading members of the city's building trades—bricklayer Wallace Moore, plasterer Bennett Flanner, painter William Charlotte, and carpenter Asa King—and paid each separately for his work. And he ordered many specialty items such as stone steps, fanlight, and portico columns from New York suppliers.[30]

Figure 2.26. Smallwood House. Passage.

The epitome of Federal elegance in New Bern is represented by the Smallwood House (figs. 2.22, 2.23). In this residence, carpenter Asa King executed a carefully ordered procession of intricate detail from outside to inside, from street to roofline, and in each room from floor to ceiling.[31] The entrance portico (fig. 2.24) shows a Palladian motif in its vaulted pediment flanked by pairs of attenuated columns. The typical New Bern door has a six-panel scheme with the lower two panels flush, and the transom is filled with fan tracery. A distinctive cornice of modillions, cable molding, and dentils appears here and elsewhere throughout the house.

Inside, elements carried over from the Stanly House blend with lighter, neoclassical motifs—columns and pilasters and sunbursts, fluting and gougework. In the stair passage (fig. 2.26), a transverse arch frames a ramped stair with scroll newel, but, typical of late Federal-period work, the railing is slim and rounded, the balusters are thin, and the treads are adorned with a wave pattern copied from William Pain's *Practical House Carpenter*. The first-floor counting room and rear dining room are handsomely finished, but the most elaborate work is reserved for the second-story drawing room (fig. 2.25). This room reverberates with intricately wrought classicism: columns frame the mantel and overmantel; paneled pilasters define the doorways and windows; and all culminate in a series of broken pediments. Carpenter Asa King wove these elements together with horizontal bands of ornamental moldings that carry around the room and grow richer as the eye moves upward, from the Wall of Troy baseboard to the cabled modillion cornice at ceiling level.[32]

Such luxurious establishments were but one facet of New Bern's architecture. Far more numerous were the workaday buildings of trade and industry, the wharves and open sheds, and tradesmen's small houses, most of which have vanished. Several modest, well-crafted dwellings of artisan families do survive, constituting the state's best collection of small urban houses from the Federal era. The houses of white and free black tradesmen often stood on the same streets as the great houses or on small streets tucked between the broader avenues.[33]

Figure 2.27. McLin House, New Bern, ca. 1810–15.

Figure 2.28. McLin House. Center partition wall.

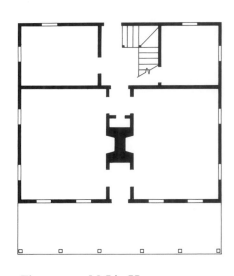

Figure 2.29. McLin House. Plan by Peter Sandbeck.

An excellent example of the middling class of houses in New Bern is the McLin House (fig. 2.27), built about 1810–15 for coppersmith and merchant Thomas McLin. The house is a remarkable blend of influences. It has a center-chimney plan (fig. 2.29) of a type common in New England but seldom seen in North Carolina outside New Bern. There is a small vestibule in front of the chimney, opening into the two main rooms at either side (fig. 2.28). Across the front stretches a broad piazza of the southern coastal type, and the gable roof that shelters the inset porch extends to the rear over secondary rooms separated by a snug stair passage. Carefully scaled woodwork partakes of the taste of the period: a small fanlight at the entrance; mantels adorned with sunbursts, gougework, and tiny beads; and a small archway framing the stair.[34]

Center-chimney plans also appeared in other small houses of various forms, including the artisan houses on Pollock Street. The John Jones House, probably built for a blacksmith, is a two-story house with two rooms flanking the chimney and the long side of the house facing the street. In the house of silversmith Nathan Tisdale (fig. 2.30), this plan is reoriented so that the gable end faces the street. The Tisdale House has two rooms on each floor, with the stair rising from the front room alongside the chimney (fig. 2.31). The front room, with its paneled wainscot and neat mantel, displays simple versions of New Bern finish carpentry.[35]

Figure 2.30. Tisdale House, New Bern, ca. 1810.

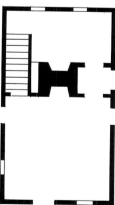

Figure 2.31. Tisdale House. Plan by Richard Parsons.

As was true elsewhere in the state, New Bern's Federal-period commercial and public buildings had much in common with the townhouses in which their sponsors resided. Both the State Bank (ca. 1818) and the Bank of New Bern (ca. 1819) resembled five-bay brick houses with hip roofs and stylish trim. Even the Craven County Jail (1821–25) took a similar form and was built with Philadelphia brick, brownstone trim, and a slate roof.[36] In these handsome buildings, New Bern leaders demonstrated both their fashion-consciousness and their sense of community. As they moved from counting room to banking house to wharf to courtroom, from drawing room to dining room to ballroom to lodge meetings, New Bern's elite proceeded from building to building as if through one great, harmonious suite of rooms that extended from the Trent to the Neuse.

The Masons of St. John's Lodge (fig. 2.32) had met in the palace during the 1790s, but after it burned they bought a lot and had lodge member and carpenter John Dewey draw up plans in 1799 for a new building; construction began in 1801 and continued through 1809. The facade has a Palladian format similar to the central block of the palace, but its designer created an adventurous new neoclassical version of the familiar idea: projecting bays at either end of the pavilion frame an elliptical blind arch set into the pediment. The lodge room (fig. 2.33) is an imposing space with a tall coved ceiling and woodwork that repeats the motifs—paneled pilasters, cabled modillions, and guilloches—of the Smallwood House and other related residences. Whether Asa King executed this carpentry, too, or was one of several who participated in a single school of work, remains an open question.

Figure 2.32. St. John's Masonic Lodge and Theater, 1801–9. John Dewey, builder. In 1904 and 1947 the exterior and first-story interior were remodeled. (Photo ca. 1863, Tryon Palace Restoration)

Figure 2.33. St. John's Masonic Lodge. Second-story lodge room. The decorative paint scheme dates from 1859–60.

New Bern's academy had also occupied the palace for a time, and, after the fire, its sponsors also built a brick building with pedimented facade. The New Bern Academy (fig. 2.34) was authorized in 1801, and money for construction was raised through a lottery and donations. The work was carried out between about 1806 and 1810. New motifs appear in the small, curved portico, the wide fanlight, and the paired cornice modillions—elements that may link the building with the later work of English-born and trained architect-builder William Nichols, who lived in New Bern from about 1800 to 1806.[37]

In the 1810s and early 1820s, New Bern congregations erected substantial new churches. In 1800 the old Anglican parish church was the only church in New Bern, but soon the Baptists and the Methodists had also built plain and capacious meetinghouses. The newly organized Presbyterians and the recently reorganized Episcopalians erected more fashionable buildings. Both of the latter churches were built by leading local artisans, but their innovative designs raise the possibility that William Nichols, who by this time was designing churches and public buildings elsewhere in the state, may have had a role in their planning.

The Presbyterians organized in 1817, and two years later they embarked on the construction of a large church, a 70-by-52-foot building designed to seat eight hundred people (a quarter of the city's population). The principal contractor was a young New Bern–trained carpenter, Uriah Sandy, who contracted to erect the frame building for $2,000 and was paid in four equal installments between November 5, 1819, and October 22, 1821. Completed in 1822, the First Presbyterian Church (fig. 2.35) is the finest Federal-period church in the state.[38]

Though it fits harmoniously among the city's other Federal-period buildings, the Presbyterian Church introduces new architectural themes into the community. It resembles the classic New England meetinghouse with its pedimented portico and tall tower ascending in three square stages to an ogee-roofed belfry. Small urns once topped the corners of the tower. Arched

Figure 2.34. New Bern Academy, New Bern, ca. 1806–10.

Figure 2.35. First Presbyterian Church, New Bern, 1819–22. Uriah Sandy, builder.

Figure 2.36. First Presbyterian Church. Interior.

openings, each one subtly different from the next, proceed in six stages up the vertical axis of the facade, from the fanlight to the cupola. Dominating the facade, the heroic Ionic-order portico marks a dramatic departure from anything seen in New Bern before.

Throughout the church, in contrast to the intricacy of earlier work, the detail is simple and geometric, from the flat, plain modillion blocks to the effective use of circular and elliptical forms (fig. 2.36). At each end of the bright vestibule, an arch frames a spiral stair, a change from New

Bern's usual ramped stairs. The sanctuary is a graceful version of a new church plan that had recently been introduced in New England churches, in which the raised pulpit is set against the front wall and worshipers enter from either side of the pulpit. Galleries with slender, turned columns line the sides of the sanctuary and, in yet another innovation, curve across the rear. The columns support an elliptical ceiling vault over the nave, making the whole space into an airy Palladian form.[39]

As the Presbyterian church neared completion, the city's Episcopalians moved to replace their old church. In 1820 the building committee advertised for proposals to build a brick church of about 70 by 55 feet, with shingled or slate roof, side and end galleries, two aisles with 50 to 60 pews, and "high arched windows." Although the new Christ Church (fig. 2.37) shared the tall, pedimented portico and staged tower of the Presbyterian church, it introduced another new element into the city—the Gothic Revival style then beginning to influence American church architecture. The "high arched windows" were tall, pointed ones, and the tower had a spire rather than a cupola and pinnacles rather than urns at the corners. The church was built by New Bern artisans—carpenters Martin Stevenson and Thomas S. Gooding were identified as "architects" and Bennett Flanner and Wallace Moore were the master masons—but, with this building as with the Presbyterian church, design innovations raise the possibility of William Nichols's hand in the planning.[40]

In the late 1820s, New Bern's trade with the West Indies declined, and the economy of the town began to stagnate. Some merchants went heavily into debt, and fortunes were lost. A visitor commented in 1830: "The continued show & dash of those who are insolvants, may be compaired to a candle in the socket. Just before it sinks it brims up with more brilincy, sinks and is no more seen. There will be a dash with the sums perloined from creditors until it is extinguished, and then they will sink to be seen no more."[41] The pace of construction slowed, and many of the city's leading builders quit their trades or moved away. No major buildings were erected for nearly twenty years, when prosperity began to return in the 1840s.

Figure 2.37. Christ Episcopal Church, New Bern, 1821–24. Martin Stevenson and Thomas S. Gooding, carpenter-architects; Bennett Flanner and Wallace Moore, brickmasons. The church burned in 1871 and was rebuilt using the existing walls. (North Carolina Division of Archives and History)

Stylish Architecture beyond New Bern

As plantation and town culture developed between 1780 and 1830, families in the wealthiest plantation neighborhoods built far more elaborate residences than ever before. For the first time, significant numbers of rural houses followed formal plans and presented prominent exterior ornament in the classical style.

The most formal of these rural residences concentrated in eastern North Carolina, where the plantation culture developed most fully. There, especially among the northern tier of counties, the slave-based, tobacco-and-corn-producing plantation economy supported a luxurious way of life. Planter families enjoyed the pleasures of horse racing, frequent entertaining, travels to northern cities, and well-stocked larders and libraries. They built and furnished their houses with a fashion-conscious blend of regional and urban elements. Architectural patterns express the complex, overlapping networks of kinship, politics, and trade that bound one rural neighborhood to another and to national and international markets. Working with local or regional artisans, including many who traveled from one area to another, planters incorporated into their houses a dynamic blend of stylish models, imported items, customary forms, and various craftsmen's personal styles. In some cases these houses were conceived and executed with confidence and unity; others suggest the complications that resulted when artisans dealt with themes and plans outside the local pool of knowledge.

In the country as in New Bern, the Palladian ideal persisted and provided a basic structure that could accommodate new stylistic devices. Perennially popular architectural books and the well-known architectural projects of Thomas Jefferson in Virginia carried forward Palladian themes, while other examples presented the delicate novelties of Adamesque neoclassicism.

At Hope Plantation (fig. 2.39) near Windsor in Bertie County, planter David Stone used the Palladian model of a square, hip-roofed block with pedimented, two-tier portico, as depicted in Palladio's *Four Books of Architecture* and exemplified in the Miles Brewton House in Charleston. In Stone's house the porticoes have turned Tuscan-inspired posts and a railing of Chinese latticework, the latter a typical accent motif in otherwise classically finished buildings of the late eighteenth century.

Educated at Princeton and widely traveled, Stone owned over 8,000 acres and 100 slaves, kept up with agricultural advances, and prided himself on his impressive library of 1,499 books. He was a prominent Federalist who, between 1798 and 1812, served as congressman, senator, and governor. To plan his house, which he began about 1796 and completed in 1803, he drew upon

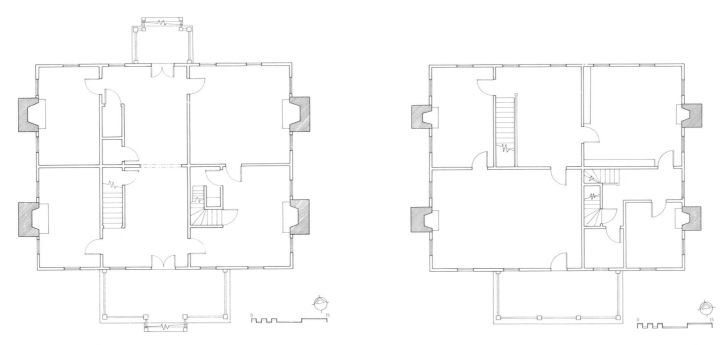

Figure 2.38. Hope Plantation. Plans of first and second floors by Carl R. Lounsbury.

Figure 2.39. Hope Plantation, Bertie County, ca. 1796–1803.

William Pain's *Practical House Carpenter* for many of the details, but he adapted the plan of the main floor (fig. 2.38) from plate 61 of Abraham Swan's *British Architect* (fig. 2.40).[42]

Departing dramatically from the open plans and multifunctional rooms favored by his father's generation and by most of his contemporaries, Stone created an elaborate and studied sequence of access. The visitor approached the house and mounted the steps to the portico, then crossed the threshold into a broad, semipublic passage and reception room filled with chairs. Family chambers and the dining room occupied the first floor, convenient to kitchens in the basement and in the yard. Emulating stylish English and American practice, Stone placed his most formal rooms in the upper stories. Invited guests continued their progress from the passage up a long, surprisingly unpretentious, enclosed stair and into a 20-by-30-foot drawing room that occupied most of front of the mansion. A compact service stair allowed servants to move unob-

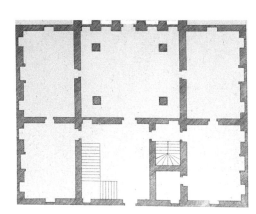

Figure 2.40. Plan, from Abraham Swan, *The British Architect*. (Historic Hope Foundation, Inc.)

trusively from the basement kitchen to the upper stories. Also on the upper floor was Stone's private library (fig. 2.41). Glass-fronted bookcases held law books and agricultural treatises, histories and novels, works of Machiavelli, Bacon, Swift, and Pope, and classics from Euripedes to Cicero and Caesar—the prized possessions of "a gentleman of great erudition and learning."[43]

Figure 2.41. Hope Plantation. Library.

At Hayes Plantation (figs. 2.42, 2.43) near Edenton, architect and builder William Nichols combined Palladian planning with elements of Adamesque and Greek neoclassicism to create a villa of great individuality and presence. In 1814 James C. Johnston was deeded the plantation by his father Samuel, a wealthy Scots-born planter and former governor of the state, who also provided money for James to build a house for himself and his sisters. Samuel cautioned his son not to "admit of profusion or any great degree of elegance in your establishment. . . . I hope you will always prefer a plain and simple stile of living to a gaudy and tinsel appearance, a passion to which there are no bounds and which too often leads to the want of solid comforts and a wretched state of dependence."[44]

Figure 2.42. Hayes Plantation, Chowan County, 1815–17. Land front. William Nichols, architect.

Figure 2.43. Hayes Plantation. Plan.
(Historic American Buildings Survey)

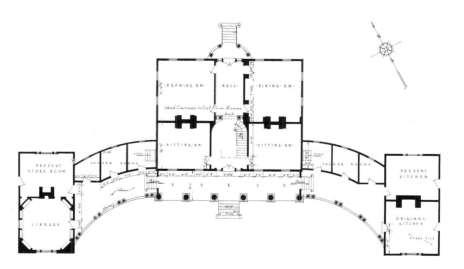

James began buying timber and hiring slave sawyers to cut his lumber in the spring and summer of 1814. He obtained brick locally but ordered tools, hardware, and other goods from New York. When he began construction in the fall of 1815, Johnston hired artisans from the area, again mostly slaves, who included bricklayers Joe Welcome and Jim Millen, carpenters Cato, Dave, Elijah, and Daniel, and a painter, Jack. He engaged William Nichols for $60 a month to superintend construction, and Nichols began work on October 3, 1815.[45]

In Nichols, Johnston had found a talented and ambitious architect and builder with an eye for fashion, opportunity, and economy. A native of Bath, England, Nichols had come to New Bern about 1800, and in 1806 he arrived in Edenton to restore and remodel St. Paul's Episcopal Church in neoclassical style. At Hayes, his earliest major construction project thus far documented, several motifs seen in New Bern buildings appear in combination, as Nichols designed freely from a full range of Palladian, Adamesque, Grecian, and even Gothic themes.[46]

For Johnston's house, Nichols used a Palladian layout—central main block, curved colonnades, and pedimented flankers—to striking effect.[47] From the land side, the approach leads through urn-topped gates to a tall, hip-roofed house, its windows shadowed by two-tier blinds and its roof surmounted by a broad louvered cupola. The facade is centered on a delicate portico, semicircular in form, with slim columns and an abstracted entablature in stylized Grecian taste. By contrast, the water side of the house (fig. 2.44) "dazzles the unsuspecting eye" with a treatment as bold and expansive as the land facade is restrained. A full-width, two-story piazza is treated as a monumental portico, and curved, colonnaded hyphens and pedimented wings create a forecourt that commands the view toward the Albemarle Sound. Nichols adapted the order of the portico from a plate in Stuart and Revett's *Antiquities of Athens*, a book that became more

Figure 2.44. Hayes Plantation. Water front.

Figure 2.45. Hayes Plantation. Passage.

influential in America in the 1820s and 1830s. He treated the wings with Adamesque blind arches similar to some New Bern work. The flat block modillions precede those at the New Bern Presbyterian Church, while the paired modillions and the curved entry portico recall the New Bern Academy.[48]

In the main house, a central passage is flanked by pairs of rooms. The larger land-front rooms were designated as drawing room and dining room, the latter having arched niches for sideboards. A column screen forming a Palladian motif divides the passage, and the walls of the rear passage, which contains the stair, are gently curved (fig. 2.45). The ceiling cornice design and Greek fret details suggest the influence of Benjamin's *American Builder's Companion*. Nichols also obtained finish items in New York, including delicate ironwork for the porches, fine stone steps, and a "simple and pleasing" mahogany handrail. He rejected the city's offerings in marble mantels, preferring to make his own of wood "with the assistance of a few composition ornaments."[49] The wings contain the kitchen on the east side nearest the dining room and, on the opposite side, an extraordinary Gothic Revival library (fig. 2.46) for a collection of nearly a thousand volumes. The notion of a Gothic room, particularly a library, in an otherwise classical building was fashionable; for its decor, Johnston and Nichols could have turned to many books, including Horace Walpole's *Works* (of which Johnston owned a copy) or Batty Langley's *Ancient Architecture*. Johnston filled his library with busts of heroes, including likenesses of Washington and Hamilton purchased by Nichols in New York in 1817.[50]

Elsewhere along the Virginia border, another Palladian-inspired form became popular: a two-story, pedimented central block flanked by one-story wings that created a small but emphatically stylish villa with a T-shaped plan. This arrangement had appeared in English architectural books beginning in the mid-eighteenth century, and it was especially popular in late-eighteenth- and early nineteenth-century Virginia. The form also appealed to North Carolina's Roanoke River planters.

An early example of the T-plan appeared at the Grove, the late-eighteenth-century residence, now lost, of Willie Jones of Halifax, a leading planter and anti-Federalist politician.[51] Another

Figure 2.46.
Hayes Plantation.
Library.

Halifax County plantation house known as the Hermitage (figs. 2.47, 2.48) is among the best-preserved T-plan villas of the Roanoke. Built around the turn of the century, it was the home of Thomas Blount Hill and Rebecca Norfleet, members of a close-knit local planter elite whose kin networks stretched along the Roanoke and into the Albemarle region. Dentil and modillion cornices (fig. 2.49) emphasize the pediment, wings, and portico, while a vigorous, crossetted frame defines the doorway. The craftsmanship displayed in the house includes the customary labor-intensive finishing work of molded weatherboards, molded door and window frames and sills, and paneled doors and wainscot. The entry room, like that of the Grove, is a large, heated space that in some respects parallels the traditional role of the hall. To the rear are a secondary stair passage across the waist of the T and a single, formal parlor. The mantel in the parlor was a

Figure 2.47. The Hermitage, Halifax County, ca. 1790–1810.

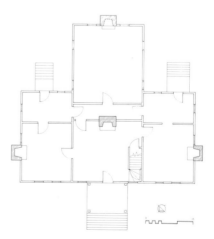

Figure 2.48. The Hermitage. Plan by Carl R. Lounsbury.

Figure 2.49. The Hermitage.
Detail showing workmanship of
molded weatherboards, molded
window frame, and modillion and
dentil cornice, characteristic of
first-quality carpentry of the
period.

fine Adamesque composition, its pilasters and frieze enriched with reeding, fans, and leaf motifs. A different hand is suggested by the other finishing work, which features bold and eccentric cushion friezes, dentils, and fretwork.[52]

Planters and artisans of the Roanoke region created many versions of the T-plan villa in the early nineteenth century. It was a form well suited to tobacco planters whose engagement in the market economy whetted their taste for fashion but produced only modest fortunes, for it provided a formal and obviously stylish house on economical terms. The plan featured two main rooms on each floor in the main block, plus two wing rooms on the first floor. This was roughly the same amount of living space offered by a hall-parlor house with rear shed rooms, but the T-plan created an imposing and formal facade with prominent pediments for the display of classical ornamentation, and it made the two central rooms into a formal sequence of spaces. Often the entry room was reduced to a small, unheated stair vestibule that led directly into the parlor or drawing room.[53]

The Smith family in Halifax County reduced the villa to its minimum without giving up any of the richness: at the Sally-Billy House, the compression of the main block to a single-bay width only intensifies the effect of the lavish ornamentation inside and out, including a Chinese lattice stair in the tiny entry vestibule. At Shady Oaks in Warren County, extravagant decorative work is concentrated in the entry vestibule, with its intricately carved three-run stair, and in the parlor, with its elaborately framed windows and an ornate mantel that features floral vines swarming up the reeded pilasters. Farther west, a few central Piedmont planters and lawyers built other small T-plan villas: the simply finished, late-eighteenth-century Graves House near Yanceyville, for example, and Moorefields (ca. 1785) near Hillsborough, which has a side-passage plan in the main block and a handsome Chinese lattice stair. The Hasell-Nash House, built in Hillsborough about 1820, is a more elaborate tripartite villa, but it repeats the side-passage plan in the center block.

The villa concept could also be expanded into a very large house. The grandest of the Roanoke's pedimented villas was surely Little Manor at Littleton, now a ruin. It consisted of a broad, pedimented five-bay block containing a central passage and two large rooms, plus one-story wings; to the rear, a cross passage containing the stair led to an eighteenth-century hall-parlor house that formed the stem of the T. The finish of Little Manor was as remarkable as its size. Sophisticated Adamesque mantels featured composition figures from the Wellford firm of Philadelphia, and the elaborate plaster cornices and medallions of acanthus and egg-and-dart patterns probably came from molds obtained from the same city. Other woodwork, probably carved locally, carried incised sunburst and gougework motifs throughout the rooms.[54]

Mulberry Hill (fig. 2.50), near Edenton, embodies another stylish form: the side-passage plan usually seen in urban settings, but here standing on open farmland beside the Albemarle Sound. It was built about 1810 for planter Clement Blount, who was probably inspired by New Bern precedent; his brother Frederick had recently married a New Bern widow, Rachel Bryan, and was residing in a new side-passage brick townhouse built (1803–5) for James Bryan. Though similar to New Bern houses in form and plan, in its detailing Mulberry Hill boasts a freer spirit of decorative inventiveness. An intricate cornice of tapered modillions and fretwork outlines the roof and pedimented gable, and the broad pediment lunette is richly carved. The elegant

Figure 2.50. Mulberry Hill, Chowan County, ca. 1810.

Figure 2.51. Mulberry Hill. Mantel in front parlor.

Figure 2.52. Mulberry Hill. Detail of stair.

Adamesque mantel in the parlor (fig. 2.51), similar to one at the Hermitage, is adorned with reeding, sunburst, fan, and leaf motifs. The stair, framed by a transverse arch in New Bern style, likewise represents typical urban work. The other woodwork, however, suggests that another hand took the mantel themes as inspiration for lavish carved ornament (fig. 2.52) from the parlor chair rail to the passage arch to the wainscot rising along the stair.[55]

In the 1810s and especially the 1820s, builders erected pedimented houses that, in contrast to the tripartite villa, gave principal emphasis to the main block. Beneath a broad, pedimented gable roof, these houses followed a plan that was essentially a 90-degree reorientation of the side-passage plan: a transverse stair passage ran across the front and opened into two rooms to the rear. A graceful and well-detailed example of this plan is the Hinton-Morgan House (fig. 2.53), built in 1826 in Pasquotank County.

During this same period, a cluster of prominent Roanoke planter families in Warren and Halifax counties built a group of houses that represented the full flowering of a regional school of work. The plans of these houses included transverse-passage, pediment-front arrangements as well as central-passage plans, one or two rooms deep with porches, ells, and porticoes arranged in many ways. All share in a distinctive vocabulary of individualized neoclassical decoration. Each house displays the artisan's resolution of familiar and novel elements of form and plan, together with a selective, additive approach to ornament. Together, these buildings form an intricate architectural and family network among a sociable rural oligarchy.[56]

The most spectacular monuments within the regional group were Montmorenci (fig. 2.54) and Prospect Hill, both now lost. Montmorenci was built about 1820 for Warren County planter William Williams. Owner of nearly six thousand acres and more than sixty slaves, Williams kept in touch with current fashion on frequent trips to Philadelphia and New York. He and his third wife, Melissa Burgess, built a great, T-shaped mansion with a towering portico and an extraordinary freestanding spiral stair (fig. 2.55). A Palladian doorway, false Palladian windows, a cornice

Figure 2.53. Hinton-Morgan House, Pasquotank County, 1826.

of triglyphs tipped with little fans, and a distinctive spool molding adorned the exterior. Principal mantels were adorned with composition ornament, probably made by the Robert Wellford firm of Philadelphia, but complementary woodwork featured an array of reeding, flowers, swags, guilloches, and fretwork (fig. 2.56). The stair was adorned with a delicate and distinctive scalloped bracket.[57]

Prospect Hill, built in 1825–28 for Williams's nephew William Williams Thorne, had a different center-passage plan, a small front portico, and a graceful, full-height rear loggia. Instead of the imported Philadelphia work, an extravaganza of carving and gougework repeated themes from Montmorenci. The exterior was graced with hallmark Palladian motifs, and the stair was a beautiful curve with scalloped brackets and a guilloche band. But in the rest of the house, decorative carpentry was laid on with an almost obsessive exuberance, so that mantels, chair rails, and window and door frames teemed with ornament.[58]

Surviving examples of the Montmorenci–Prospect Hill school of work, most of which date from the 1820s, present a collective sampling of the hallmark elements. These include a Palladian window and doorway at the Coleman-White House in Warrenton; a small scalloped stair at White Rock in Halifax County, remodeled for William Williams's nephew, Joseph John Williams; related work at Dalkeith, a temple-front house built for William Williams's brother-in-law, and at Tusculum nearby; and a full range of distinctive carpentry at two more temple-front houses—Oakland, built for Joseph's sister Elizabeth Williams Thorne, and Elgin near Warrenton.

Figure 2.54. Montmorenci, Warren County, ca. 1820. Destroyed. Photographs of Montmorenci were made before the wooden and plaster decorations and the stair were removed to the Winterthur Museum in Delaware in 1935. (North Carolina Division of Archives and History)

Figure 2.55. Montmorenci. Stair in situ. (Henry Francis du Pont Winterthur Museum Library)

Figure 2.56. Montmorenci. Interior in situ. (Henry Francis du Pont Winterthur Museum Library)

Elgin (fig. 2.57) was built in 1827–32 for Elizabeth Person, the daughter of a local planter, and her husband, Peter Mitchel, a Scots-born merchant. The main house has a transverse front passage (fig. 2.59) and two large rooms to the rear. The ebullient individualism of the regional school appears in the Palladian entrance, with its spool moldings and fan-tipped triglyphs, and continues in the passage and main rooms (fig. 2.58), where expertly carved sunbursts, flowers, reeding, and gougework luxuriate on mantels, door and window entablatures, and wainscoting. The stair features Biddle's delicate bud spiral rather than the Montmorenci scallop, and the symmetrical moldings and cornerblocks at the doorways are new Greek Revival themes. The rear wing of Elgin was added soon after the front section was completed. Yet the form of the addition—perhaps in emulation of such nearby houses as Little Manor that began with a smaller

Figure 2.57. Elgin, Warren County, 1827–32.

Figure 2.58.
Elgin. Parlor.

Figure 2.59. Elgin.
Transverse passage.

dwelling and received large formal front sections—is that of a traditional, one-and-a-half-story, dormered dwelling.[59]

By the late Federal period, Adamesque neoclassicism had permeated stylish buildings throughout the state. Artisans had become expert in rendering motifs from books and examples, and planters and merchants delighted in parlors ever more ornately adorned with columns, sunbursts, and reeding. Often, such work was further embellished with vibrant colors and patterns. The parlor at Rose Hill (plate 1), built in about 1829 as a new wing for the house of Caswell County planter and politician Bedford Brown, exemplifies such finery. Its mantel and other woodwork are carved in high relief, then painted to imitate marble; the walls are covered with French wallpaper in deep colors, with floral medallions and dark flowered borders.[60]

The Early Greek and Gothic Revivals

Although increasingly ornate Adamesque work dominated fashionable architecture into the 1820s, a few buildings presented unusually early and sophisticated examples of the Greek Revival style, with its compelling aura of chaste simplicity and pure forms associated with the virtues of the ideal democracy. In early applications of the "Grecian taste," the Greek orders depicted in Stuart and Revett's *Antiquities of Athens* were adapted to buildings of familiar Renaissance and Adam-inspired form. In such North Carolina examples as Hayes Plantation, the Oval Ballroom in Fayetteville, and the Mordecai House in Raleigh, these "touches of Greek feeling at an unusually early date" appeared not as literal copies of published plates but in fresh and original designs. Most, if not all, of this work was the accomplishment of William Nichols.[61]

After completing Hayes in 1817, Nichols circulated successfully among the mercantile elite of the coast and the central Piedmont. He moved from Edenton to Fayetteville, a progressive and flourishing port, and in 1818 became the state architect for various works in Raleigh and at the university. Taking additional commissions as far west as Hillsborough, Greensboro, and Lexington, he left a trail of elegant architecture that was stylistically advanced on the national as well as the local scene. While he was in Fayetteville, Nichols may have designed the Oval Ballroom (fig. 2.60), a 20-by-30-foot octagonal structure built as an addition to the Halliday residence, probably in 1818. It contains a splendidly appointed oval chamber—the state's only surviving example of the curved rooms favored in Adamesque planning. Ionic pilasters flank six oversized windows and carry a fine wreathed entablature of molded plaster, a scheme that opens up the space dramatically and creates a room of extraordinary richness and grace.[62]

Nichols persuaded the legislature to fund a complete remodeling of the State House in Raleigh (1820–24), during which he transformed the old Georgian structure into a domed, cruciform building glamorized with Ionic pseudo porticoes (fig. 2.61). He planned a new rotunda to hold the celebrated Antonio Canova statue of George Washington, which North Carolina had commissioned in a grand and costly gesture of patriotic and artistic enthusiasm. He made the legislative chambers similar to those in the U.S. Capitol: the Senate had a circular form and a gallery carried by "pillars of the Greek Ionic order"; and the semielliptical House of Commons had a vaulted ceiling supported by columns of the same order. The remodeled State House impressed every visitor; New York architect Ithiel Town said it was "a more elegant

Figure 2.60. Oval Ballroom, Fayetteville, ca. 1818.

Figure 2.61. State House, Raleigh, remodeled 1820–24. William Nichols, architect. Drawing by W. Goodacre. (North Carolina Division of Archives and History)

building than any other State has yet erected, it is convenient, appropriate and in good taste." Also in his role as state architect, Nichols repeated the Greek Ionic order in the portico of Gerrard Hall at the University of North Carolina. In 1823 Nichols provided the design for Eagle Lodge in nearby Hillsborough (fig. 2.62). Constructed by local bricklayers Samuel Hancock and John Berry, the Masonic lodge is a severely elegant 40-foot cube with a small Greek Ionic portico.[63]

Nichols continued his neoclassical remodeling for the Mordecai family of Raleigh in 1826, when he expanded a hall-parlor dwelling by means of a large front addition (fig. 2.63). The form of the new section is familiar enough—a central-passage plan beneath a shallow hipped roof—but the two-story pedimented portico of Palladian type exhibits a fresh and sophisticated Greek Revival spirit. The lower columns are adapted from Stuart and Revett's plate of the Temple of

Figure 2.62. Eagle Lodge, Hillsborough, ca. 1823. Attributed to William Nichols, architect; John Berry and Samuel Hancock, builders.

Figure 2.63. Mordecai House, Raleigh, enlarged 1826. William Nichols, architect and builder.

Figure 2.64. Mordecai House. Parlor.

Figure 2.65. St. Matthew's Episcopal Church, Hillsborough, 1825–26. William Nichols, architect; John Berry and Samuel Hancock, builders.

Apollo at Delos and carry a plain, three-band architrave, while the upper columns follow a Greek Ionic order beneath a simple entablature. The interior work (fig. 2.64) is similarly advanced, as evidenced by the Ionic pilaster mantels, the absence of wainscoting or chair rails, and the symmetrical cornerblock moldings.[64]

During this same time, Nichols also introduced elements of the Gothic Revival style. Prominent among his clients were families active in the resuscitation of the Episcopal church and the repair and construction of churches in Edenton and Raleigh. It is not known whether he had a hand in planning St. John's Church in Fayetteville (1817) or Christ Church in New Bern (1821–24), the state's first Gothic Revival churches. He did, however, design St. Matthew's Church in Hillsborough (fig. 2.65). A parishioner reported in 1825, "Mr. Nichols has made a farther alteration in the plan of our church, making it 35 by 45, saying that a less width would not be proportionate to the length."[65] Built in 1825–26 by John Berry, the quietly picturesque church stands on a hill overlooking the town. Consistent with early versions of the Gothic Revival, it is a simple rectangular building of Flemish-bond brick with slim, lancet-arched windows; later generations continued the style in the tower and interior enrichment.

Developments in Regional Traditions

Throughout the Federal period, there was a fluid continuity among all levels of building, for almost every building was the product of local craft knowledge and direct interaction between the client and the craftsmen who planned the structure and, with minor exceptions, fabricated all its components. While some wealthy residents indulged in a taste for classicism, most prosperous North Carolinians continued to build along traditional lines established before the Revolution.

Examples of a few regional building patterns illustrate broader trends of unity, local and individual variation, and accommodation to change over time. During this period, there appeared across the state scores of conservative, handsome houses that adhered to the same family of plans seen earlier, though now more of them stood two stories tall. Most of these were built as part of regional clusters of houses linked by artisans and family connections. In the coastal zone, builders continued to develop their inventive and practical variations on the use of the piazza and the interplay between outdoor and indoor living space. In the Piedmont, handsome brick buildings, displaying a high level of expertise in traditional techniques, were built for the first time. Throughout the state, log houses presented the manifold forms of this prevalent construction method. And in each region there were various methods for building and arranging domestic and agricultural outbuildings. These regional patterns flourished from 1780 to 1830, and they continued in many communities throughout the 1830s, 1840s, and 1850s.

In most rural areas, even the richest planters built along conservative lines. They continued to use a range of traditional house forms and an approach to ornament established before the Revolution. One-and-a-half-story gable-roofed houses were built for many large planters in the 1780s and 1790s. After about 1800, however, wealthy residents increasingly chose to build two-story houses. The gambrel roof, widely used in one-and-a-half-story houses in the eighteenth century, gradually disappeared from new construction as two-story houses became more common. By the early nineteenth century, the two-story gable-roofed house, usually with exterior end chimneys, became a proud and predominant house form for leading residents of town and plantation. Holly Bend, a plantation house in Mecklenburg County, where cotton crops and gold discoveries brought unusual prosperity, characterizes many such houses. Built around 1800 for Robert Davidson, it is a tall, slim house with end chimneys rising high above the gable roof (fig. 2.66). The plan in this case has an off-center passage between two flanking rooms, plus a shed porch and a rear ell.[66]

Generally, houses like this presented little external display of ornament and fashion. They communicated their owners' status through their size and the familiar language of good materials and craftsmanship, which they shared with more elaborate buildings. The exterior trim

Figure 2.66. Holly Bend, Mecklenburg County, ca. 1800.

Figure 2.67. Holly Bend. Fireplace wall.

Figure 2.68. Holly Bend. Passage.

seldom exceeded a simple molded cornice, occasionally enriched with dentils or modillions, molded and tapered porch posts, and a touch of carved trim or a fanlight at the door. The principal evidence of changing styles was reserved for those who entered the house. A Georgian influence in paneling, stairs, mantels, and door and window treatment continued as late as 1810 or 1815 in some areas, while in others, beginning around 1800, some artisans adopted Adamesque themes, often blending elements of old and new.

At Holly Bend, sturdy backcountry workmanship is embellished with exuberant ornament, probably derived from William Pain's plates. Front and back doors are paneled on the outside but backed with stout, diagonal boards and hung on massive strap hinges. Walls are flush sheathed, and the passage has a heavy stair with short balusters and large wave brackets at the tread ends (fig. 2.68). In the main parlor, the carpenter applied to the wood-sheathed walls an ambitious composition of volutes and swags, consoles, rosettes, and fans on the mantel; a wiry, scrolled pediment overmantel; and consoles and entablatures over the doors and windows (fig. 2.67). Similar motifs are carved on the front doorframe and narrow cornice.

Within a general rectilinear format, builders in this period experimented with various floor plans. Although the central-passage plan, one or occasionally two rooms deep, was built, it was still far from dominant. Some well-finished two-story houses had only one main room per floor. The Freeman House (fig. 2.69), for example, built for a Gates County farmer and cabinetmaker in 1820, has a main first-floor room and a rear shed, and, in the second story, a side passage and two small, unheated chambers.

At the other extreme was the four-room house with a central passage—a plan still restricted to the grandest dwellings. The Grove (fig. 2.70) was built near Tarboro for Gen. Thomas Blount, a rich planter, politician, and land speculator. He was reported in 1810 to have "lately built a very good house, the best that is in the county."[67] The Grove has two full stories plus an attic set high atop a raised basement, with four end chimneys emphasizing its size and eight heated rooms. Typically for the period, the rooms were of different sizes, with the passage being narrow between the large front rooms and then broadening to form a wider stair passage between the smaller rear rooms. Stylish regional workmanship appears in its double-molded weatherboards and molded windowsills, a modillion cornice, and fanlights in the gables.

Especially striking in this period is the continued use of traditional open plans—the hall-parlor, three-room, and various four-room plans—in large as well as small houses. While some wealthy families built houses with passages, many still preferred to have the main entrance directly into the principal room. Three-room plans continued in common use, both in the coastal plain and especially in the Piedmont. The Edwards-Franklin House (fig. 2.71), the home of leading planter and political families in Surry County in the northwestern Piedmont, is a large version of such a plan. Its strong vertical form is reinforced by tall end chimneys. In a variation common in the Piedmont, two front doors open into the two front rooms. Inside, the house is a dazzling example of the inward concentration of display. The standard paneling, mantels, and staircase are transfigured by a spectacular decorative painting program (plate 2) that extends throughout the house.[68]

During the early nineteenth century, decorative painting proliferated in the work of resident and itinerant artists in many parts of the state.[69] These painters usually adhered to certain conventions, such as marbleizing baseboards and stair risers and using woodgrain patterns for wainscoting and doors. Mantels might resemble either marble or wood. Some artists created realistic imitations, as in the parlor at Rose Hill in Caswell County, but many went past imitation into bold stylization. The swirling, featherlike painting on the doors at the Bynum-Sugg House (plate 3) in Edgecombe County resembles work at the Edwards-Franklin House but removes the woodgraining theme still further from literal copying. At the Savage House (plate 4) in Edgecombe County, the wainscot is painted in brilliant red and yellow spotted with black, part of a house-wide embellishment.

An unusual outward display of adornment appears at White Oak (fig. 2.72), built for Johnston County planter Reubin Sanders, probably in the late eighteenth century. Tall end chimneys, a steep gable roof, and a shed porch across the subtly asymmetrical five-bay facade form a familiar whole, to which the artisan applied a wealth of classical ornament: the fluted porch posts and dentil-trimmed rail, modillion cornices, and windows adorned with keystones and pediments. The house follows an enlarged variation of a three-room plan, with the entrance into an elaborately finished principal room, and with a small back room carved out of this space. Tall wainscoting features double ranges of paneling, and the main room has a formal mantel with overmantel and pilasters (fig. 2.73).

Many large plantation houses were part of regional clusters. Throughout the coastal plain and Piedmont such groups appeared, typically displaying a pattern of variation on certain plan types and sets of details. One such group appears in Franklin and neighboring counties in the northeastern Piedmont. The Patty Person Taylor House (fig. 2.74) in Franklin County, probably built late in the eighteenth century for the wealthy sister of political leader Thomas Person, is similar in form to Holly Bend: it is a tall, weatherboarded dwelling house five bays wide, with double-shouldered chimneys of Flemish-bond brickwork and a rear ell. The exterior finish is

Figure 2.69. Freeman House, Gates County, 1820.

Figure 2.70. The Grove (Blount-Bridgers House), Tarboro, ca. 1810.

Figure 2.71. Edwards-Franklin House, Surry County, ca. 1799.

Figure 2.72. White Oak, Johnston County, ca. 1790s.

Figure 2.73. White Oak. Hall.

Figure 2.74. Patty Person Taylor House, Franklin County, late 18th century.

Figure 2.75. Taylor House. Passage.

Figure 2.76. Taylor House. Mantel in left-hand parlor.

neat and plain, consisting of molded window surrounds and sills, raised, paneled double doors, and a simple molded cornice. This house, too, follows the pattern of inward concentration of display; stepping into the central passage, the visitor enters a narrow space crowded with craftsmanship (fig. 2.75). The turned stair nearly fills the passage, which is finished with a paneled wainscot and four paneled doors in heavy molded frames. Heavy cornices, wainscoting, and robust mantels in a distinctive late-Georgian style enrich the principal rooms (fig. 2.76).

Several other substantial houses in Franklin and the adjoining counties—all residences of leading planters, built between 1780 and 1810—display similar motifs. These include distinctive mantels related to those in the Taylor House and, in several houses, a Chinese lattice stair rail. These elements suggest the work of a single carpenter or school of artisans. Especially remarkable is the variety of plans within the group. Only the Taylor House has a central-passage plan. In the other houses, the two front rooms are arranged in a hall-parlor plan, and the smaller rear rooms take various configurations. Elmwood in Granville County, built in 1805, for example, is a two-story house two rooms deep, with the smaller rear rooms flanking a small stair passage in a layout akin to the familiar trio of shed rooms. The McLemore House (fig. 2.77), on the other hand, has a hall-parlor plan plus a rear ell and stair passage—a form repeated many times among the middle-sized plantation houses of the state.[70]

In some cases, interregional family and political connections gave artisans a clientele beyond a single neighborhood. A group of fine houses in the central Piedmont exhibits the distinctive carpentry of Raleigh artisans Elhannon Nutt and John J. Briggs, who were employed by leading politicians, planters, and merchants centering in Raleigh and Hillsborough. Two of these houses, Fairntosh and Ayr Mount, present felicitous blends of traditional and stylish elements in an architecture of selective conservatism.

Duncan Cameron, the son of a Scots-born minister, moved from Virginia to Hillsborough as a young attorney, acquired land and money, and in 1803 married Rebecca Bennehan, daughter

Figure 2.77. McLemore House, Franklin County, ca. 1800–1810.

Figure 2.78. Fairntosh, Durham County, 1810–11, 1818–21. Elias Fort, John Fort, and John J. Briggs, carpenters; Elhannon Nutt, joiner; William Collier, bricklayer; Henry Gorman, plasterer.

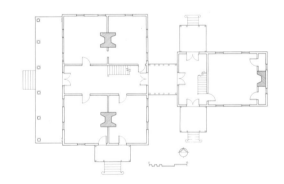

Figure 2.79. Fairntosh. Plan by Carl R. Lounsbury after drawing by Historic American Buildings Survey.

of Richard Bennehan, a Piedmont merchant turned planter. By 1810 Cameron, owner of sixty-seven slaves and more than six thousand acres, was on his way to becoming one of the richest and most influential men in North Carolina. In that year he and Rebecca began construction of Fairntosh (fig. 2.78), named after the Cameron family home in Scotland. The front block was built in 1810–11 by Wake County carpenters Elias and John Fort; William Collier laid the brick foundations and chimneys. For the finish work, Cameron hired Raleigh plasterer Henry Gorman, joiner Elhannon Nutt, who made the mantels, and carpenter John J. Briggs, who built the stairs. The house is an early Piedmont example of the central-passage plan, two rooms deep (fig. 2.79), but rather than having formal dining and drawing rooms on the first floor, the Camerons designated the main rooms as passage, hall, breakfast room, chamber, and nursery, with additional chambers above. In 1818–21 the Camerons employed most of the same men to build a two-story rear addition.[71]

Figure 2.80. Fairntosh. Mantel in front left-hand room. Elhannon Nutt, joiner.

The house is finished in conservative fashion, with some elements suggesting a New Bern influence. A modillion cornice is the principal exterior ornament, along with pedimented gables containing Diocletian windows reminiscent of New Bern work. (The Doric-order porch was added in 1827.)[72] The interior has tall wainscoting, with double ranges of panels similar to the work at White Rock, and a stair with ramped and voluted handrail and wave brackets of New Bern cast. The principal mantels (fig. 2.80) proclaim Elhannon Nutt's free and confident hand with familiar Georgian elements—cushion friezes, consoles, and paneled overmantels—rendered in a flattened, stylized fashion and adorned with guilloches of interlocking circles and sunbursts and gougework in the Adamesque spirit.

Nutt billed Cameron $196.47 for eight chimneypieces in May 1811. The next month, he advertised from Raleigh that he was "now at leisure, and . . . ready to make an engagement in my line of business . . . of House Carpenter and Joiner." Assuring the public that his work was done in "a superiour manner to what has been customary in this place," he referred customers to Cameron, Capt. William Jones, John Haywood, Esq., and "other gentlemen." At the residence of state treasurer John Haywood, Nutt had executed mantels similar to those at Fairntosh, and Gov. Benjamin Williams apparently employed Nutt to fashion a mantel for his Moore County plantation house.[73]

A few years later, about 1814–17, many of the same artisans built Ayr Mount (fig. 2.81) near Hillsborough. This substantial, stylistically conservative house has a self-possessed unity that exceeds all but the best examples of fashionable neoclassicism of the time. William Kirkland had left his native Ayr, Scotland, and by 1789 he had come to Warrenton. He became a merchant, married his partner's sister, Margaret Scott, and moved to Hillsborough. The couple began a large family, and as Kirkland prospered he bought a plantation, where, after a visit back to Scotland, he employed bricklayer William Collier to erect a great brick house overlooking the Eno River. The massing of the two-story center block with lower wings recalls the tripartite villa idea, but, in contrast to the pedimented T-plan villas of the Roanoke, the main block of Ayr Mount is a spacious, two-story, gable-sided house, 40 feet square, with a small central entrance portico. The impact of the house derives from its scale and proportions and its air of quality and substance.[74]

The plan (fig. 2.82) likewise shows kinship with Palladian houses: a lateral stair passage stretches across the front and gives access to two unequal rear rooms and a room in each wing.

Figure 2.81. Ayr Mount, Hillsborough, ca. 1814–17.
William Collier, bricklayer; John J. Briggs, carpenter.

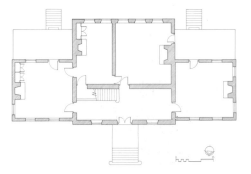

Figure 2.82. Ayr Mount. Plan by Carl R. Lounsbury after
drawing by Historic American Buildings Survey.

The workmanship of the interior, however, is similar to that at Fairntosh. Mantels in Nutt's "superiour manner" repeat motifs from Fairntosh, in somewhat flatter and more stylized fashion (fig. 2.83). Briggs's voluted and ramped stair dominates the front passage, and double ranges of raised and flat paneling compose the tall wainscoting in the passage and rooms.

These elements in common reflect not merely the work of the same artisans, but clients' and artisans' participation in a social network of building. A revealing glimpse of the complex relationships and values that underlay such projects appears in a letter from another of Briggs's employers, Thomas Littlejohn of Oxford, who wrote to Duncan Cameron in 1817:

> I fear I shall not be able to settle with Mr. Briggs for running my staircase without getting from you or Mr. Kirkland the sums you paid for having your work done—my bargain with him was to pay the same price you and Mr. K. paid for the same kind of work—my passage is 12 feet wide—12 feet pitch, and the staircase (executed exactly like yours as Mr. Briggs informs me) has 23 steps—I think your passage is of the same width & pitch, and probably has the same number of steps—will you have the goodness to state to me the price you gave for running the stair case, making wainscot, & the price of plain wainscot from the foot of the stair to your parlour door, mentioning also the number of yards or feet in this last item. I hope you will pardon me giving you this trouble, but I fear I shall be unable to settle with Mr. Brigs [*sic*] without it—I understand you to say that your bargain was made with Mr. Fort, and the work executed by Mr. Brigs; but I understood Mr. Kirkland's bill was settled upon the same terms your work was done, and Mr. Briggs agreed with me to do my work upon the same terms.

For the gentlemen of the Piedmont, these handsome and well-crafted houses presented their success and taste in terms shared within their class; at the same time, they were sites of continual negotiation between ambitious and accomplished artisans such as Briggs and their wealthy but cost-conscious clientele.[75]

Figure 2.83. Ayr Mount. Mantel in right rear room. Attributed to Elhannon Nutt.

For men like Kirkland and Cameron, building within a regional framework was a choice based on personal values as well as practical convenience. These men had traveled widely and knew trends in architectural fashion, and both were very wealthy. Yet like their fellow Scot, Samuel Johnston, who was cautioning his son James about expenditure at Hayes at about this same time, these men eschewed extravagance. They preferred the established practice of building well but with restraint, in a manner that bespoke substance and plenty but not opulence. Inside their houses, rooms and passages were arranged according to urban standards but exhibited the fine—if stylistically conservative—handiwork of artisans from their own region.

Piazzas

In 1790 Wilmingtonians rallied in defense of their piazzas. Ninety-one inhabitants petitioned the state House of Representatives to revoke sections of a law, passed six years earlier, that was intended to rid Wilmington of "the many incroachments made on the streets . . . by erecting piazzas, porches, platforms and other buildings thereon." The residents objected to being "restrained from building or repairing coverd Piazzas or Balconies, to their houses, situate on the Streets, in the said town, under an idea that the same may communicate Fire from street to street." They insisted that "such Buildings are not only really useful and greatly contribute to prevent and extinguish Fire, but in this hot Climate, are essentially necessary to the Health and convenience of the Inhabitants." The petitioners thus attested to the continued vitality of the piazza in the region's architecture. In New Bern, a visitor was struck by the same pattern: "There are to many of the houses Balconies or Piazzas in front and sometimes back of the house, this Method of Building is found convenient on account of the great Summer Heats here."[76]

North Carolina artisans up and down the coast and deep into the coastal plain used the piazza in many ways, displaying another facet of the traditional builder's capacity for variation

Figure 2.84. Church Street House, Wilmington, late 18th century.

within a familiar range. Houses with piazzas spanned the usual range of height from one to two-and-a-half stories and followed common plan types. The porch might be joined to the house in one of three main ways: as an attached structure, engaged under a double-sloped roof, or inset beneath a single broad roof slope.[77]

Many piazzas were attached as structurally discrete units. A handsome house on Church Street in Wilmington (fig. 2.84) is one of the few late-eighteenth-century frame houses to escape the city's recurrent fires; it stands above a brick cellar and has a broad, attached piazza set on pillars above a subporch paved in brick. The house, which resembles examples in Nassau and mid-eighteenth-century Brunswick, probably typifies much of early Wilmington architecture. The plan has a central passage—fitted with hammock hooks in opposing doorways—that extends between a pair of large parlors and very small secondary rooms.[78]

Other roof forms that integrate the piazza structurally and visually into the house appear throughout the North Carolina coastal plain and elsewhere in the Atlantic trading sphere, especially the Caribbean islands. One type adds a second set of rafters midway down the main common rafters of the house to create a double-slope or broken-pitch roof that shelters an engaged porch or shed rooms. This roof type—seen in the circa 1770 Burgwin-Wright House in Wilmington (see Chapter 1)—was extremely common in the Federal period. The Everitt House (fig. 2.85) in Edgecombe County is a classic example. It is a modest hall-parlor house with a broken-pitch gable roof extending in the front to cover an engaged porch and at the rear to shelter a pair of shed rooms flanking an open bay. Built about 1810 for Silas and Rebecca Everitt, the small house is finished in a manner comparable to larger houses of the neighborhood, including tapered porch posts with molded caps, intricate dentil cornices, and decoratively painted interior paneling and mantels. Such small houses with balancing engaged porches and shed rooms dot the landscape of the coastal plain—houses of convenient and graceful form built for middling and small farmers throughout most of the nineteenth century.[79]

Figure 2.85. Everitt House, Tarboro, ca. 1810.

Figure 2.86. Sloop Point, Pender County, middle and late 18th century.

Another equally distinctive way of building a piazza is to build a single broad roof of long rafters that integrates the piazza into the main roof structure of the house. Sloop Point (fig. 2.86), overlooking Topsail Sound, began as a mid-eighteenth-century house with a three-room plan and probably with small attic rooms and porches. Late in the eighteenth century, a major remodeling effaced the upper rooms and most of the old porch and shed. The new roof has long common rafters extending unbroken to create a triangle that measures fifty feet from front to back. It provides spacious rooms in the second story and shelters an eleven-foot-deep porch in front and shed chambers flanking an open stair passage in the rear. An inventive system of wooden chutes running up from the porch ceiling gave added ventilation to the upper chambers.[80]

The Blue House (fig. 2.87) in Scotland County presents the same roof type in a small house built about 1836 for John Blue and his wife Margaret McGoogan. It illustrates the long popularity of the piazza house and its reach throughout the coastal plain, especially among the Scottish settlements along the Upper Cape Fear River and the South Carolina border.[81] The house has paired entrances into the hall-parlor front rooms. The roof extends unbroken to shelter the inset front porch and the rear rooms that flank the enclosed stair passage. The facade is a subtle accommodation of evenly spaced posts to the asymmetrical doors and windows. Simple mantels and natural board sheathing finish the interior (fig. 2.88). A breezeway leads to a freestanding dining room and kitchen structure, which was probably built slightly later in the nineteenth century; such side kitchens were common elements in southeastern North Carolina.

Figure 2.87. Blue House, Scotland County, ca. 1836

Figure 2.88. Blue House. Hall. Flush-sheathed walls and ceilings were a common alternative to plastering.

Figure 2.89. China Grove, Pamlico County, ca. 1803.

China Grove (fig. 2.89), overlooking the Neuse River from Pamlico County, provides a dramatic example of a large house with a two-story piazza inset within the principal structure. Built about 1803, the house has an off-center passage and two main rooms on each floor, with the front porch occupying the front bay of the structure; a full dormered attic reaches out over the double piazza. A few large houses, such as Mowfield in Northampton County, were built with hip roofs that created broad, umbrellalike forms encompassing the porch, but in North Carolina, in contrast to the Deep South, such expansive roof structures were rare.

All of these piazza types—attached, engaged, and inset—could appear in one- or two-tier arrangements and in various positions. In some cases, front and rear porches took different forms. The two-story Hogg-Anderson House in Wilmington and the one-and-a-half-story Nimocks House in Fayetteville, for example, both have small porticoes facing the street and wide piazzas across the back.

Piazzas occasionally surrounded a house on all four sides. This was the pattern at Russellborough, the mid-eighteenth-century house on the Lower Cape Fear at Brunswick. At Ellerslie (figs. 2.90, 2.91), the Cumberland County residence of Scots-born planter William Elliott, the three-room-plan house was surrounded by attached porches that formed a continuous outdoor room, an airy space with a gently vaulted plastered ceiling.[82] In Edenton, the Homestead (fig. 2.92), overlooking Edenton Bay, may have been standing in 1786 when the lot was purchased by English-born merchant and planter Josiah Collins, who developed the huge Somerset plantation across the Albemarle Sound and ran a multitude of commercial enterprises. The hall-parlor plan opens out onto two-tier porches graced by scalloped cornice boards, which carry around all four sides of the house in characteristic Caribbean fashion. Both Ellerslie and the Homestead remained in the hands of descendants, who gradually enclosed all but the front porch to create additional rooms and built large additions during the nineteenth century.[83]

Figure 2.90. Ellerslie, Cumberland County, ca. 1790.

Figure 2.91. Ellerslie. Porch.

Figure 2.92. The Homestead, Edenton, ca. 1770–80.

Figure 2.93. Oakland, Bladen County, late 18th century. Land front.

Commonly, both engaged and integral porches appeared as balancing extensions on the front and rear of a house, creating a bold, generally symmetrical side elevation. This arrangement was well suited to the plantation houses along the Lower Cape Fear River, most of which had a dual orientation to land and river. Although most of the river plantation houses are long gone, a few still remain in Bladen County. Oakland (fig. 2.93), built in the late eighteenth century for planter Thomas Brown, has deep double piazzas on either side of a large Flemish-bond brick house some 60 feet long and 20 feet deep. Standing high above the steep southwestern bluff of the Cape Fear, approached by a mile-long drive from the road, Oakland by its imposing scale and orientation epitomizes river plantation life. The unusual plan has a formally appointed parlor to one side of an off-center passage, and, on the other side, a narrow lateral passage along the land front opens into two small rooms overlooking the river.[84]

Often the piazza contained porch stairs that made it a conduit between stories. Harmony Hall, an eighteenth-century frame house on the Cape Fear in Bladen County, has a hall-parlor plan, and the sole stair rises on the two-story porch. At the nearby Purdie House (fig. 2.94), built 1803–9, the stair in the double porch of the river front may once have been the only connection between floors. The well-detailed brick house of Flemish-bond brickwork has a three-room plan divided by a passage that apparently was widened to accommodate a later stair.[85]

At the Bryan Lavender House (fig. 2.95) in Jones County near New Bern, a builder used the piazza to expand a hall-parlor dwelling in the early nineteenth century. He removed an indoor stair, built a partially enclosed stair at the end of the porch, and fitted the end of the upper porch with weatherboards and windows to create a porch room. Such enclosures were familiar in the region; observing the prevalence of the two-story piazza in New Bern, William Attmore noted in 1787 that "sometimes one or both ends of it are boarded up, and made into a room."[86] Other Jones County houses such as the Shine Inn and Eagle Nest likewise have partly enclosed piazzas, both showing handsome detail of the New Bern school.

Figure 2.94. Purdie House, Bladen County, 1803–9. Land front.

Figure 2.95. Lavender House, Jones County, early 19th century.

Northward in the coastal plain, in Edgecombe County, planter Peter Evans used the enclosed piazza in strikingly inventive fashion. In the early nineteenth century he expanded an existing house at Piney Prospect (fig. 2.96) by building a large ell containing a formal stair passage and parlor. To unify the whole, he built a broad gable roof that covered the new rooms as well as a deep porch set into the angle of the ell. He treated the gable end toward the road with a pedimented facade, its northern windows lighting the rooms, the southern ones lighting the porch. Free classical decorations adorn both the gable end and the porch, which is treated as a richly ambiguous indoor-outdoor space, complete with wainscoting, a chair rail, and built-in benches.

The piazza also offered a capacity for phased growth that permitted a building to develop through a sequence in which each stage was a complete house.[87] It was commonplace to build a house with porch and shed rooms as a single unit. But the construction of piazzas and shed rooms offered a familiar, convenient, and thrifty way to expand an existing house—either by adding an attached shed or by building a broken-pitch roof with its second set of rafters springing from the main roof of the house. Front and rear porches, once built, might be left alone or enclosed later to yield more rooms, still within a structurally and visually acceptable scheme. The Jacob Henry House (fig. 2.97), begun in the late eighteenth century, epitomizes this potential for growth within a coherent form, for it was expanded several times with porches and enclosures. The slope of the roof breaks near its apex to reach over the front porch and rear rooms, then continues out to cover the lowest rear shed.[88] The Henry House stands in Beaufort, an old maritime village in which porches have created a powerful architectural identity. In this community of porches, the unity and infinite variations of a local vernacular are eloquently expressed. The picture is enriched by the accretiveness of Beaufort's architecture. Residents continually expanded their houses, adding a room or a story, building a porch and then enclosing it a few years later—all within a continuum of building in a form deemed "essentially necessary."

Figure 2.96. Piney Prospect, Edgecombe County, early 19th century.

Figure 2.97. Henry House, Beaufort, late 18th and early 19th centuries.

Brick Buildings of the Piedmont

In the central and western Piedmont, where the second generation of settlers had come to maturity during the Revolution, another sturdy strain of traditional artisan building dominated construction in the Federal period. In contrast to the paucity of Piedmont buildings dating from the colonial period, a substantial number survive from the period 1780–1830.

The buildings of the 1780s and 1790s show strong continuity with and variations on familiar plan types, including hall-parlor and three-room plans and four-room plans of various forms in large houses—as seen earlier in the Braun and Alexander houses (Chapter 1). In these same years, an efflorescence of the bricklayer's art produced the Piedmont's first generation of brick buildings and an important body of decoratively patterned brickwork. Then around the turn of the century and especially after about 1815, paralleling developments in the east, buildings began to demonstrate a growing accommodation of popular taste and neoclassicism. Builders adopted central-passage plans, put a greater emphasis on symmetry and quieter workmanship as a background to classical details, and incorporated Adam-inspired patternbook motifs.

Wachovia

In the Wachovia settlement, a sequence of well-documented buildings exemplifies this general pattern of development. Although the theocratic community leaders sought to regulate outside influences, Wachovia was neither provincial nor isolated: such cosmopolitan leaders as Frederic William Marshall kept abreast of international trends; trade and travel to and from

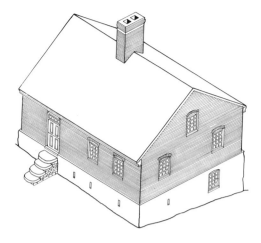
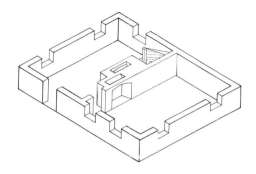

Figure 2.98. Dyer's and Potter's House, Bethabara, 1782. Isometric view and plan by Carl R. Lounsbury.

distant cities was frequent; and, especially among the young people, national cultural, political, and social trends began to challenge the old ways.

In the village of Bethabara, houses continued to be built with the traditional Germanic central-chimney plans, sited to take advantage of sloping terrain. In the 25-by-31-foot brick house built in 1782 for Johannes Schaub, for example, the entry opened into the hearth room, while a more private room lay on the opposite side of the chimney (fig. 2.98). Inside, the plastered walls, exposed ceiling joists, and heavy beams—planed, beaded, and chamfered in the best rooms— illustrate the continued use of sturdy framing (fig. 2.99). In the basement, which opened at the rear ground level, and in adjoining frame structures, dyer Schaub operated his business. This is probably the oldest brick building in North Carolina's western Piedmont and was the first of several brick structures erected in Wachovia. Typical of early Moravian brick buildings, because

Figure 2.99. Dyer's and Potter's House. Hall-kitchen showing exposed and finished framing and projecting chimney breast.

of the scarcity of lime, masons used clay mortar for the stone foundation and Flemish-bond brick walls, then pointed the joints on the outside with lime.[89] Across the road from Schaub's house, a stone and brick house was built for the brewer in 1803, perhaps reusing elements from the 1777–78 brewer's house, which had burned. It too is fitted into the hillside, which slopes down to the road, and the rooms fit around a massive central chimney.[90]

In Salem, beginning in the mid-1780s, several big brick buildings were erected. Johann Gottlob Krause, who had trained in Bethabara as a potter, entered the bricklayer's trade after a brief stint with the old German master, Melchior Rasp. In 1784 Krause was employed to erect the first all-brick building in Salem, the Tavern. It, like the Single Sisters House (1786) and the 1786 addition to the Single Brothers House, is a large, plainly finished building with the traditional tile roofs and eave kick, but built of Flemish-bond brick instead of fachwerk or stone. Windows and doors are surmounted by shallow, arched openings, and roof plate locks are set into the eaves. With these three large brick buildings finished, Krause resigned the position of mason to Abraham Loesch and returned to the potter's trade in Bethabara.[91]

The same aesthetic of simplicity and direct expression of materials and function appears in the beautiful Gemein Haus (fig. 2.100), built in Bethabara in 1788. For the small congregation, Wachovia administrator Frederic William Marshall planned a building that would contain the *Saal* (meeting room) and residence for the minister. His design gracefully expresses the two functions through different window treatments and the shift in the roofline, where a narrow window set deftly into the rake of the higher roof sheds light into the organ loft of the saal. The building was erected by Loesch and other Moravian and "stranger" workmen. Above an exposed stone foundation, walls are parged to the flaring eaves and brick gables. From the roof of the saal rises a delicate, arcaded tower—designed by Marshall in an echo of church towers throughout

Figure 2.100. Gemein Haus, Bethabara, 1788. Frederic William Marshall, designer; Abraham Loesch, master mason. The pastor's residence is on the left, the saal on the right.

Figure 2.101. Gemein Haus, Bethabara. Saal.

central Europe—from which the music of trombones resounded through the village. The pastor's residence contains rooms arranged around a center chimney, with a cooking hearth in a second chimney at the gable end. The full eloquence of Moravian simplicity culminates in the saal (fig. 2.101), where light pours in through the tall arched windows.[92]

By 1793, when he returned to the mason's trade to build the Salem Boys' School, Johann Krause had developed a newly vivid, even flashy style of masonry work. He executed the Flemish-bond brickwork with dark headers, adorned one gable with a molded belt course and the other with a diamond pattern in dark brick, and finished the eaves with a coved cornice. Krause displayed the same techniques in confident style in the Christoph Vogler House (fig. 2.102), built in 1797 as both dwelling and shop for the gunsmith. Above the parged stone foundation he laid a course of molded brick accentuating the Flemish bond walls, and beneath the eaves he ran a coved and beaded plaster cornice. And on the gable end he proclaimed his authorship with large initials, "I[J] G K," set in dark brick beneath bold chevrons outlining the gable.

These decorative techniques were familiar in the mid-Atlantic region along the Delaware River and in the mid-eighteenth-century Albemarle region in North Carolina, but they were new to the North Carolina Piedmont. In Salem they represented an Anglo-American strain woven into a Germanic building tradition. It is not known whether Krause was involved in work outside Wachovia, or what "stranger" workmen may have taught him. One intriguing figure is William Craig, a non-Moravian Stokes County bricklayer whom Krause employed to help on the Boys' School; Craig subsequently worked on the Vorsteher's House in 1797 and Home Church in 1800. It is clear that Krause's adoption of patterned brickwork about 1793 coincided with the efflorescence of brick building in the Piedmont. There are no known examples of brick houses dating from the pre-Revolutionary era in the central and western Piedmont, but they became numerous in the late 1780s and 1790s and many display a full-blown, expert use of decorative motifs.[93]

At the turn of the nineteenth century, Krause continued to develop Salem's brick building tradition. Home Church (fig. 2.103), completed in 1800 from a plan developed by Marshall,

Figure 2.102. Christoph Vogler House (left), Salem, 1797. Johann Gottlob Krause, mason. John Vogler House (right), 1818.

Figure 2.103. Home Moravian Church, Salem, completed 1800. Frederic William Marshall, designer; Johann Gottlob Krause, mason.

blends Salem craftsmanship—stone foundation, tile roof with coved cornice, double-leaf door—with broader classical influences such as the symmetrical facade, elliptical arched window and door openings, and a baroque Germanic steeple. The familiar eave kick has vanished, and new elements appear in the arched hood over the door—a design probably introduced by Marshall and soon popular throughout Salem—and the painted brick that imitates rubbed brick around doors and windows and at the corners. Krause used similar motifs in his last project, the 1802 residence of Dr. Samuel Vierling, a big, symmetrical house that exceeded any private dwelling previously erected under Salem's building rules.

By 1818, when John Vogler sought to built a large house next door to Christoph Vogler's, the community's rules had been amended to permit greater individual investment in building. (Under the lease system, the community owned the land and, if a leaseholder left Salem or had his lease canceled, would purchase his house if he could not sell it otherwise. When first adopted in 1788, Salem's building rules set limits on the cost and elaborateness of all houses to assure that the building could be sold to the next leaseholder for a reasonable sum. As individuals began to chafe under this restriction, the rules were altered to permit the establishment of a maximum price an owner expected to receive if his building exceeded community standards.) The John Vogler House (see fig. 2.102), built under a ruling of a maximum buy-back price of $2,000, continues the shift away from Germanic traditions. The brickwork lacks the quality of Krause's work, and though the Dutch door and eave kick recall local customs, the rectangular-headed windows, gabled entry hood, Federal-style interior woodwork, and, not least, the symmetrical facade and central-passage plan reveal Salem's growing acceptance of national architectural trends.[94]

Beyond Wachovia

Similar developments in brick building took place among German, Scotch-Irish, and Quaker families throughout the Piedmont. The Haley House (fig. 2.104) in Guilford County, built in 1786 for the Quaker family of John and Phoebe Haley, is a compact, three-room-plan house executed in Flemish-bond brickwork with dark headers. It shares in the tradition seen earlier in the mid-eighteenth-century Albemarle and Delaware Valley. A circular stone plaque in the gable, inscribed with the couple's initials and the year 1786, is like one at the contemporary Single Sisters House in Salem and raises the idea of a common craftsman.[95]

Several major houses built in the late 1780s and 1790s display the apparently sudden regional development of patterned brickwork in initials, dates, and decorations. The owners of these residences were both Scotch-Irish and German families. One splendid, firmly dated example is the Loretz House in Lincoln County (figs. 2.105, 2.106). A German-Swiss farmer and Reformed minister, Andrew Loretz had lived for a time near Philadelphia before coming to Lincoln County about 1788 and may have been influenced by work he saw there. His 1793 house is co-

Figure 2.104. Haley House, High Point, 1786.

Figure 2.105. Loretz House,
Lincoln County, 1793.

Figure 2.106. Loretz House.
Plan by Carl R. Lounsbury.

eval with the first such work in Salem. The front and back walls are laid in Flemish bond with all glazed headers. On the west gable end, lozenges stream down the center; on the east, Loretz's initials and the date 1793 stretch across the top, beneath which are hearts and an X reaching down the wall. Loretz chose a plan that had four main rooms, with the main room entered directly from the outside.[96]

The great double chimney of Alexander and Elizabeth Long's large frame house (fig. 2.107) in Rowan County features similar work. The couple's initials, A L and E L, each topped by a heart, appear on the paired Flemish-bond chimneys joined by a brick closet. Long, a Scotch-Irish ferry owner whose parents came from Lancaster County, Pennsylvania, married his second wife, Elizabeth Chapman, in 1786. Their house was built on Long's 500-acre farm probably within a few years of their marriage. Like several other large houses of the Piedmont, the 29-by-40-foot frame house has four main rooms, with the stair rising from a corner entry room; the depth of the house is spanned by a heavy kingpost and principal-rafter roof truss.[97]

The John Stigerwalt House (figs. 2.108, 2.110) in Rowan County, featuring a plaque dated 1811, is a late example of the region's patterned brick houses, with lozenge patterns on the

Figure 2.107. Long House, Rowan County, late 1780s.

Figure 2.108. Stigerwalt House, Rowan County, 1811.

Figure 2.109. Stigerwalt House. Plaque in front wall.

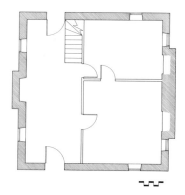

Figure 2.110. Stigerwalt House.
Plan by Bernard Herman.

chimneys and the front facade. The plan appears to be an adaptation of the Germanic hall-kitchen plan, but with end chimneys rather than a central chimney. The hall in this house is narrower than the usual main room of a three-room-plan house, yet unlike a normal side passage, it is dominated by a broad fireplace. The stone date plaque (fig. 2.109) serves as a small icon of acculturation: the presence of a plaque with name and date and a clock with hands is traditionally Germanic, but the words are in English and the stone is adorned with an American eagle.[98]

By the 1810s and 1820s, the use of patterned brickwork had subsided. Throughout the Piedmont in these two decades, tall, handsomely finished brick houses became the standard for the most substantial residences. Exterior decoration was usually restricted to fine, flat arches over openings or a molded or corbeled cornice. In contrast to the variety of plans used in the late eighteenth century, these houses nearly always had a hall-parlor or three-room plan with end chimneys.[99] In Jamestown, a Quaker settlement up the road from the Haley House, a cluster of early nineteenth-century brick buildings includes a meetinghouse, a three-room-plan store, and Richard Mendenhall's plantation house. All three share the features of Flemish-bond brickwork, compact forms, shallow-arched windows, and round gable openings. The Mendenhall House (fig. 2.111) has broad porches and a rear wing that expands the space beyond the original two rooms. The house possesses a quality of straightforward simplicity that prevailed in Piedmont building well into the nineteenth century. The thick brick walls with deep, splayed window openings, the simple geometry of an enclosed corner stair (see fig. 2.1), and the stout batten doors are all part of an architecture of plain prosperity.

Other brick houses of the Piedmont reveal a customary contrast between exterior simplicity, direct-access plans, and the interior display of fashionable woodwork—chiefly in the form of exuberant, individualized renditions of Adam-inspired patternbook motifs. This pattern is especially notable in the large brick houses built for the growing planter class along the Catawba

Figure 2.111. Mendenhall House, Jamestown, early 19th century.

Figure 2.112. Perkins House, Catawba County. Mantel, 1811. Now installed at the Museum of Early Southern Decorative Arts in Old Salem, the woodwork from the Perkins House combines decorative painting and elaborate carved ornament. (Museum of Early Southern Decorative Arts, Winston-Salem)

River. One of the most spectacular examples is the Perkins House, built on a prominent site in present-day Catawba County. The three-room-plan, two-story brick house was built either about 1790 for John Perkins or about 1810 for his son Eli. During Eli's ownership, woodwork was installed that gave full rein to the carpenter's boldest and most imaginative work. A big, magnificently carved mantel and overmantel (fig. 2.112), dated 1811, combines paneling and deep consoles with neoclassical urns, fans, swags, and flowers in the spirit of Owen Biddle's *Young Carpenter's Assistant*. Urns and scrolls adorn the ceiling cornice, and the carving is enlivened by a vivid paint scheme. Similar motifs, presumably by the same hand, also appear at Rosedale, a frame plantation house built about 1805 in Mecklenburg County.[100]

Farther up the Catawba, river-bottom planters in Burke County followed similar patterns in their big brick houses. Quaker Meadows (fig. 2.113), built for the marriage of Charles and Ann McDowell in 1813, features twin entrances into the three-room plan, a common variation in the Catawba Valley; bold carpentry work includes a massive, reeded Federal-type mantel that dominates the main room. Local variations on this plan sometimes included a recessed porch behind the principal room. This feature appears at Bellevue (fig. 2.114), built in 1823–26 for planter James Erwin, not far from Quaker Meadows. Carpenter Jonas Bost executed the woodwork, which is concentrated in the principal room—paneled wainscoting and a mantel with sturdy pilasters, sunbursts, and fans (fig. 2.115), typical of many rural artisans' renditions of Adamesque themes.[101]

A more conventional accommodation of neoclassicism appears in the fine brick houses of Lincoln County. Their emphasis on symmetry, introduction of a central passage, and subdued brickwork to complement neoclassical details were all departures from the plan and craftsmanship of the 1793 Loretz House in the same county.

Figure 2.113. Quaker Meadows, Burke County, 1813.

Figure 2.114. Bellevue, Burke County, 1823–26. Jonas Bost, carpenter.
Elevation by Tom McGimsey. (Historic Burke Foundation)

Figure 2.115. Bellevue. Mantel. Jonas Bost, carpenter.

Ingleside (fig. 2.116) was built for Daniel and Harriet Brevard Forney, supposedly about the time of their marriage in 1817. The couple were descendants of French Huguenots who had come to the area in the mid-eighteenth century and prospered as planters, iron manufacturers, and political leaders. Daniel served in the U.S. Congress from 1815 to 1818; he succeeded his father, Peter Forney, who had served in 1813–15. Among the region's restrained brick houses, Ingleside makes an imposing statement of fashionable taste. The quiet Flemish-bond brickwork, fine flat arches, and simple windows form a background for a full-height Ionic portico—a remarkably early use of a heroic order—and the modillion cornice of the portico extends to outline pediments at the gable ends.[102]

Stylish opulence continues within the house (fig. 2.117). Three large rooms recall the customary regional plan, but a broad center passage separates the two right-hand rooms from the

Figure 2.116. Ingleside, Lincoln County, ca. 1817.

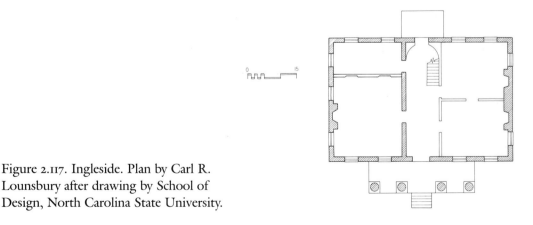

Figure 2.117. Ingleside. Plan by Carl R. Lounsbury after drawing by School of Design, North Carolina State University.

Figure 2.118. Ingleside. Parlor.

large parlor on the left (fig. 2.118); to the rear of the parlor is a narrow service room, which recalls recessed loggias of upper Catawba Valley houses. The passage contains a beautiful curving stair (fig. 2.119), a graceful swirl of slender balusters, with a bud-and-spiral bracket decorating each tread and a slim handrail descending to a volute. Owen Biddle's *Young Carpenter's Assistant*

Figure 2.119. Ingleside. Stair.

provided the model for this widely popular stair design (fig. 2.120). The rear wall of the house is curved to allow the stair to complete its gentle spiral. The spacious parlor culminates the presentation of fashionable elegance. Pilasters and entablatures enframe the windows; a fine three-part mantel, decorated with sunbursts and fluted colonnettes, frames the fireplace; and the ceiling blooms with a cornice of swags and acanthus and a center medallion of bellflowers and acanthus, probably made from molds obtained in Philadelphia. The elaborate stair from Biddle, the elegant plasterwork, and the enriched woodwork were features that appeared repeatedly in the western Piedmont.[103]

Other big brick houses in Lincoln County accommodated new styles in more subtle ways. At Magnolia Grove, David Smith and Elizabeth Arends, the children of German settlers, built in

Figure 2.120. Design for stair, from Owen Biddle, *Young Carpenter's Assistant*. (Henry Francis du Pont Winterthur Museum Library, Collection of Printed Books)

1824 a handsome brick plantation house with a symmetrical, five-bay facade, behind which lies a customary three-room plan.[104] Two years later, Smith's sister Ann and her husband, Paul Kistler, also built a fine brick house in Lincolnton (fig. 2.121), likewise with a symmetrical, five-bay facade. Here, however, the three-room plan has a passage similar to the one at Ingleside. Such details as a molded water table, string course, and cornice emphasize the formality and horizontal lines of the house.[105]

Throughout the western Piedmont, from Mecklenburg County in the south up through Cabarrus, Rowan, Davie, Lincoln, Catawba, and Iredell counties, the emerging gentry of growing towns and river-valley plantations built handsome residences along similar lines. Some built their houses of brick, others of frame, but nearly all shared in the confident retention of familiar forms and plans into which stylish elements were incorporated.

Figure 2.121. Shadow Lawn, Lincolnton, 1826.

Log Houses

While the emerging Piedmont elite were building tall brick and frame houses touched with currents of neoclassicism, the predominant domestic architecture of the rural Piedmont and mountain regions was built of logs. In the frontier period, nearly every family had lived first in a log house. Then, as economic and social distinctions grew more pronounced, architecture developed accordingly.

There was a recognized range in the quality of log construction. A traveler in the mountains observed in 1805: "The temporary buildings of the first settlers in the wilds are called *Cabins*. They are built with unhewn logs, the interstices between which are stopped with rails, calked with moss or straw, and daubed with mud. The roof is covered with a sort of thin staves split out of oak or ash, about four feet long and five inches wide, fastened on by heavy poles being laid upon them. 'If the logs be hewed; if the interstices be stopped with stone and neatly plastered; and the roof composed of shingles nicely laid on, it is called a *log-house*.'" Many North Carolinians viewed well-built log houses as economical, practical, and warm.[106]

In the period from the 1780s through the 1830s, when traditional building flourished at all levels of society, log architecture in North Carolina apparently attained its greatest variety and highest quality. By the late eighteenth and early nineteenth centuries, North Carolinians from every ethnic background—English, Scottish, Scotch-Irish, German, African, and American Indian—were competent in log construction.[107] Log houses, churches, schools, and farm buildings were commonplace throughout the Piedmont, especially in areas where a yeoman culture flourished, and they dominated the landscape in the mountains' coves and valleys. In many sections, this building tradition continued into the antebellum period and beyond. Although most of these structures have been lost, nevertheless the diversity and richness of North Carolina log architecture are striking.

There are several patterns of regional variation and gradual change through time. Notching techniques are one obvious example. Whereas the saddle and dovetail notches are most common among the scattered log buildings of the coastal plain, two other notching types predominate in the many handsome log buildings of the Piedmont: the V-notch, with the top of each log cut to a triangular form; and the half-dovetail, in which one side of the squared log is flared out at an angle. Uses of the diamond and the full-dovetail notches are rare and scattered. Although patterns vary locally, in general, the greatest diversity of notching types appears in the eastern and central Piedmont, and as one moves west, the half-dovetail becomes increasingly prevalent and finally dominates in the mountain region.

Many well-built log houses have a single main room, sometimes square but more often rectangular. Substantial one-room log houses usually range from 16 to 24 feet on a side; most also have a loft chamber and many a rear shed.[108] The Robert J. Hill House (figs. 2.122, 2.123) in Surry County characterizes many well-finished, one-room log houses. Measuring 18 by 22 feet, it is built of V-notched logs and is sheathed inside with planed boards. Built-in cupboards flank the interior chimney of stone, and a dovetailed ladder stair rises to a loft, where floorboards are pegged into the heavy joists. An early nineteenth-century shed addition combines a log rear wall of half-dovetailing with side walls of slotted hog-trough construction.[109]

Especially in the late eighteenth and early nineteenth centuries, a good number of log houses were partitioned into two- or three-room plans similar to those used in contemporary frame and brick houses. Their walls often incorporated logs 24 to 30 feet long in one direction and 15 or 20 feet long in the other. One example of such a house is located in Sampson County—a rare survivor of a log construction tradition that once extended into the Cape Fear region. The Bannerman House (fig. 2.124) was supposedly built for a Scottish settler in the late eighteenth century. Like many log dwellings, it was covered at an early date with weatherboards. It is a single pen, about 16 by 28 feet, partitioned into a three-room plan. Wide, beaded wall sheathing and planed and beaded ceiling joists finish the rooms neatly. There were shed rooms across the rear, and the stair to the loft rose from the central shed room.[110]

Figure 2.122. Hill House, Surry County, late 18th to early 19th century.

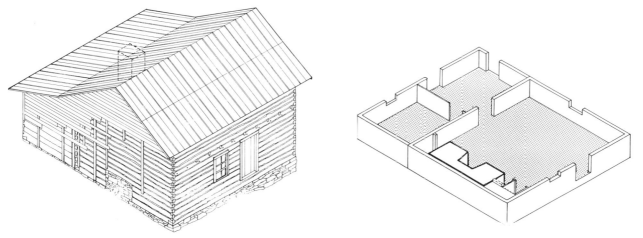

Figure 2.123. Hill House. Isometric and plan by Carl R. Lounsbury.

Other well-finished log houses with three-room plans appear throughout the Piedmont, as for example the A. N. Sink House (fig. 2.125), which was built in Davidson County in the early nineteenth century. Hall-parlor plans were also common, exemplified by the Duke House in Franklin County, the Mullican House in Forsyth County, and the two-story Shrum-Keener House in Lincoln County, built respectively for English, Scotch-Irish, and German farmers. Typically such houses were, like the Bannerman House, fitted out with beaded joists, hand-planed sheathing, good batten doors, and other careful workmanship, and many were also covered with weatherboards, rendering them nearly identical in appearance to their frame contemporaries.[111] Houses like these were most common in the period from the 1780s through the 1820s, and most were found in communities in which substantial houses of all materials shared similar plans and workmanship.

Figure 2.124. Bannerman House, Sampson County, late 18th century.

Figure 2.125. Sink House, Davidson County, early 19th century. (Davidson County Historical Association)

Less common were houses of dovetailed plank construction. A tour-de-force example of this type is the Daniel Stone House (figs. 2.126, 2.127) in Vance County. It seems to be a unique occurrence of a plank house in which the upper story has been cantilevered out on all four sides to give the house the form of early New England "block houses." The 22-by-23-foot house is made of planks sawn 2 inches thick and about 11 inches wide; the top planks extend out an additional 2½ feet on three sides and 4 feet on the chimney end. The planks are internally pegged together, and the narrow gaps between them are covered with split strips. A partition of hog-trough construction divides the house into a large main room and a narrow back chamber, which subsequently was itself subdivided. The house was probably built in the late eighteenth century for a small planter, possibly Gideon Johnson, who died in 1797 owning a hundred acres, four slaves, and modest farm and household goods.[112]

Gradually during the nineteenth century, changes began to appear in choices made about log houses. After about 1820 or 1830—the timing varied from region to region—fewer families built large, single-pen log houses that were divided into hall-parlor or three-room plans. Families who wanted and could afford spacious and well-finished houses increasingly chose to build them of frame or brick. Single-pen log houses tended more and more to be small, plain, one-room dwellings. Such sturdy, straightforward houses were built by small farmers from the eighteenth century through the early twentieth. Typical of many is the Mast House (fig. 2.128), built about 1812 on a mountain valley farmstead near the Blue Ridge for David and Mary Mast. The Swiss Mennonite Mast family had come from Pennsylvania to Piedmont North Carolina and thence west. Their small house stands two stories high with a tall fieldstone chimney. The dovetailed logs are exposed in the single room on each floor. Log outbuildings cluster around it in the small cove.[113]

Increasingly, too, families who built log houses with more than one main room arranged them in plans that differed from the plans of multiroom frame and brick houses. Rather than partitioning one large log pen into rooms, some families built separate log pens side by side: some had the two pens adjoining and chimneys at both ends; others had pens flanking a central chimney (the "saddlebag" plan); still others had two pens with end chimneys separated by an

Figure 2.126. Stone House, Vance County, late 18th century.

Figure 2.127. Stone House. Detail of dovetailed plank construction.

open passage (the "dogtrot"). Such houses could be built of smaller logs than those required for a large, single-pen house. Moreover, a family could build both units at once or build one section first and add the second unit as need or opportunity arose. This capacity for building in stages—in which a modest initial structure is conceived of as a complete building yet permits easy expansion without waste of materials or time—is well suited to the needs of small farm families.

A saddlebag house that was built in stages is the Roberts House (fig. 2.129) in Buncombe County. Probably dating from the early nineteenth century, the house is composed of two half-dovetailed sections (one about 18 by 20 feet, the other about 19 by 22), each containing a single room and a loft, flanking a massive fieldstone chimney. One section is said to have been an old slave house moved down the mountain. The Gragg House (fig. 2.130) in Watauga County is magnificently built of half-dovetailed planks, 16 to 22 inches wide, and joined with such tight precision as to need no chinking. It was apparently erected in a single phase as a saddlebag house with two 16-by-20-foot pens flanking a stone chimney. Two-pen log houses became increasingly common in the mid-nineteenth century, at the same time that the plans of frame and brick houses were shifting from two- and three-room plans toward central-passage plans.

Figure 2.128. Mast House, Watauga County, ca. 1812. The farmstead developed around the original house, encompassing several log and frame outbuildings; the 19th-century frame house was expanded to become a mountain inn.

Figure 2.129. Roberts House, Buncombe County, early to mid-19th century.

Figure 2.130. Gragg House, Watauga County, mid-19th century.

Outbuildings and Farm Complexes

Whether on a coastal plain plantation or a Piedmont farmstead, the house was only one part of the complex of domestic and agricultural life. However large or small it might be, the dwelling stood among a cluster of outbuildings. In contrast to European and English farmsteads that often collected many different functions into an extended complex under one roof, farmers and planters throughout the South erected numerous small buildings, each with its own specific purpose. Various explanations for this practice have been offered. A Virginian observed in 1705 that "all their Drudgeries of Cookery, Washing, Daries, etc. are performed in Offices detacht from the Dwelling-House, which by this means are kept more cool and Sweet." The ease of constructing several small buildings rather a large building provided another reason. Free-ranging livestock did not require large stables or feed-storage barns. And the desire of planters to house their servants in separate quarters rather than within the family home supplied an additional motive.[114] Visitors continually remarked on the appearance of such farmsteads, comparing a plantation to a sow with piglets or, more often, to a village. Although few outbuildings from the eighteenth century remain standing, evidence suggests that the basic forms of outbuildings established in the eighteenth century persisted through much of the nineteenth.

An unusually complete example of a large plantation's domestic complex survives at Fairntosh (fig. 2.131) in Durham County. Here, in 1814, carpenters Elias and John Fort erected for Duncan and Rebecca Cameron a series of domestic outbuildings in two neat rows around the house. At the front, an office, schoolhouse, and teacher's dwelling align in an extension of the front facade of the main house (fig. 2.132). To the rear, along the side of the yard, a perpendicular row places the kitchen nearest the house, followed by the dairy, smokehouse, commissary, and a slave house (fig. 2.133). An overseer's house occupies a back corner of the house yard. The carpenters surrounded the yard with a wooden fence, which they finished and painted at the same time as the other structures. Beyond, at a distance on the plantation, stood barns and storage buildings, rows of slave dwellings, and other structures.[115]

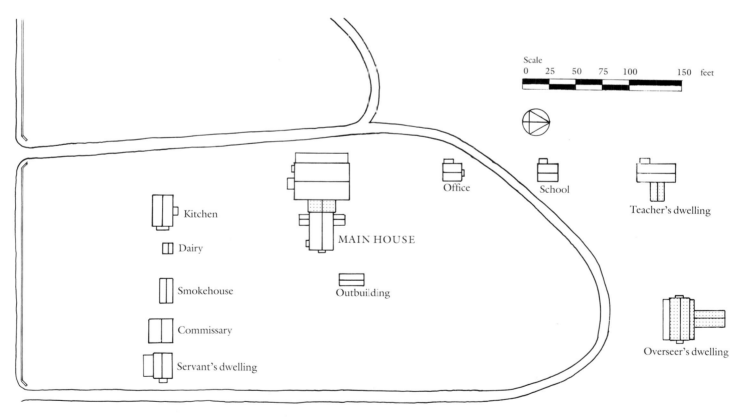

Figure 2.131. Fairntosh. Plan of plantation complex by Carl R. Lounsbury.

Figure 2.132. Fairntosh, Durham County, 1814. Elias Fort and John Fort, carpenters. The front row of outbuildings consists of schoolhouse, office, and a teacher's dwelling (not shown).

Figure 2.133. Fairntosh. Domestic outbuildings at rear of main house are, from left: kitchen, dairy, smokehouse, commissary, and slave dwelling.

The Fairntosh complex, while atypical in the size of the plantation it served, illustrates important patterns. Although the complex stood in the midst of broad fields and woodlands, it was arranged in a neat, compact, rectilinear form that defined and extended the position of the house. Each structure had its own form and placement in accord with its function, though with time those uses might change. The front buildings were treated more formally, as they were of the highest status and public involvement—a plantation or law office, a schoolhouse, and the schoolmaster's residence.

Outbuildings connected with food production and storage stood to the rear and were neatly but less formally treated. All were modest frame structures, and each assumed a customary, functional form. The kitchen, convenient to the residence, has a big chimney for cooking and, as was common, upper chambers for a cook or house servants. This particular example was especially large and sturdily built, but freestanding kitchens were standard elements on many farms. The adjacent dairy typifies the use of ventilated storage buildings for milk, butter, and other goods, with eave vents in a decorative pattern. (Some dairies also had double walls filled with sawdust for insulation.) The smokehouse, commissary, and a servants' dwelling were also one-story frame buildings, each with a simple plan and the necessary fittings. A fence protected the area from ranging livestock and defined a domain of domesticity and order. Cameron's fence of painted boards filled the same role as the unpainted board fences and snaking rail fences of many of his neighbors.[116]

Throughout North Carolina, farmers built their outbuildings in more or less formal patterns of courtyards, rows, or casually arranged clusters. Domestic outbuildings frequently stood near houses on town lots as well. Planters, lawyers, and doctors often erected small office buildings near their dwellings, which often matched the house in finish. Usually they placed these in prominent front locations, whether the front house yard of a farmstead or a front lot line in town. A handsomely detailed frame law office in Salisbury (fig. 2.134), built by Archibald

Figure 2.134. Henderson Law Office, Salisbury, early 19th century.

Figure 2.135. Gatling Dairy and Smokehouse, Gates County, early 19th century.

Henderson or his son-in-law Nathaniel Boyden, stood on the owner's house lot on a prominent corner, enabling the attorney to receive clients without having them enter his dwelling.[117]

Dairies and smokehouses were often placed in pairs convenient to the kitchen. In eastern North Carolina they typically were square or rectangular buildings, often about 10 by 10 or 12 by 12 feet. Whereas smokehouses might be of plank or frame construction, dairies were usually built of frame. The frame duo at the Gatling Farm (fig. 2.135) in Gates County is set into the house yard fence.[118] The smokehouse has a gabled roof, while the dairy takes a characteristic and distinctive form, with a pyramidal roof above wide eaves that shade a typical vented frieze with decoratively scrolled slats (fig. 2.136).

Sheds and barns in eastern counties were also likely to be modest. One common type is a simple gable-end structure, with a central entry in the gable end and, often, sheds along the sides. Some farmers built barns in a form called the English barn—a rectangular, gable-roofed structure with the entry on the long side, like a house. Barns and stables sometimes stood in pairs. At the Morris-Meades Farm in Pasquotank County, for example, there is a fine, late-eighteenth-century frame storage barn and a six-stall stable of dovetail plank construction, subsequently surrounded by sheds.[119] Such barns, along with a variety of small sheds, stood on many farmsteads, composing agricultural complexes at a distance from the domestic outbuildings.[120]

Slave dwellings were an integral part of the larger plantations. Typical of many is a small, crudely built log slave house in Cumberland County (fig. 2.137), covered at some time with weatherboards and containing a single room with a loft, a fireplace, and whitewashed walls. Nineteenth-century reports commonly described slave houses that were "huts . . . built of round pine or cypress logs, with dirt floors, and dirt in the interstices between the logs"; these were "small, crowded, and smoky." Others reported "log huts with sand floors and stick and dirt

Figure 2.136. Gatling Dairy. Detail of frieze.

Figure 2.137. Slave house, Cumberland County, mid-19th century.

Figure 2.138. Slave house, Franklin County, probably early 19th century.

Figure 2.139. Slave house, Gates County, mid-19th century.

chimneys."[121] Such houses were physically similar to the small dwellings of workers and small farmers that dotted fields and forests.

A rare example of a stone slave dwelling (fig. 2.138) survives in Franklin County; it contains a single 12-by-15-foot room, heated by a big fireplace and lit by the front door and tiny windows. It obviously represented an effort to build in unusually durable fashion, its walls being 18 inches thick and the roof timbers massive. Another common plan for slave dwellings featured two rooms side by side and flanking a single chimney. Some of these were of logs, others of frame, such as the 16-by-34-foot dwelling (fig. 2.139) in Gates County. Probably a similar arrangement was envisioned when planter William Shepard directed his slaves to erect on his Pasquotank County plantation "five negro houses about 36 feet long and 18 feet wide."[122]

In the central and western Piedmont, the domestic and agricultural outbuildings, like the houses, suggest connections with farms in the Valley of Virginia and the mid-Atlantic region. Quaker farmer Richard Mendenhall built a cluster of farm buildings around his two-story brick house in Jamestown, including a big frame barn (fig. 2.140) that was set into the hillside. The hayloft was accessible from the top of the slope, and the stalls, recessed into the hillside, opened at ground level below an overhanging shelter. Mendenhall, who apprenticed as a potter in his ancestors' home of Chester County, Pennsylvania, may have admired the barns he saw there. Such hillside bank barns, common among Pennsylvania and western Virginia farmers, are rare in Piedmont North Carolina.[123]

Among the farm buildings of the Piedmont and mountain counties, log construction dominated at every economic level, from the late eighteenth century through the mid-nineteenth century. These buildings repeat types seen throughout the mid-Atlantic region and the Upland South. To build log smokehouses, farmers used tightly chinked construction, often with a front gabled shelter cantilevered out over the door, as in the half-dovetailed smokehouse at Bellevue Plantation (fig. 2.141) in Burke County. Corncribs, which needed ventilation, were commonly built of unchinked, well-spaced logs, as seen in the Bunker Corncrib (fig. 2.142) in Surry County, which also has a cantilevered entry shelter. Some corncribs were larger, consisting of two structures flanking a wagon passage.

Figure 2.140. Mendenhall Barn, Jamestown, early 19th century.

Figure 2.141. Bellevue Smokehouse, Burke County, early 19th century.

Figure 2.142. Bunker Corncrib, Surry County, mid-19th century.

The most imposing agricultural landmarks of the western Piedmont and mountains are the great double-crib log barns. In these structures, two cribs flank a runway that is entered on the long side. Doors into the cribs may open either from the front or from the runway. This barn form was found in Pennsylvania in the eighteenth and early nineteenth centuries, but there, as in Piedmont Virginia, it was often supplanted by other types. In Piedmont and western North Carolina, the double-crib log barn continued as the dominant large barn form throughout the nineteenth century.

The barn at the Sink Farm in Davidson County (figs. 2.143, 2.144, 2.145) is a fine example of this construction, probably dating from the early nineteenth century. It is built of large logs joined with V-notches; the upper logs run the full 48-foot length of the barn, and the topmost plates extend another 5 feet on each side to support the cantilevered roof pent that diverts rain away from the walls and foundation. This big barn and others like it have haylofts above and stalls below. A feed trough hewn from a single huge log extends between the stalls on the right and is built through the end wall. A barn on the Sowers farm in the same county (fig. 2.146), built in the mid-nineteenth century, shows other possibilities in this type of structure in its half-dovetail notches and the entries opening to the front rather than to the runway. Double-crib log barns still stand on farms throughout the western Piedmont and in many areas of the mountains. Though they are especially common in German areas and on German farms, they became part of the region's architectural repertoire for both German and Scotch-Irish farmers.[124]

Perhaps more than any other single kind of building, these sturdy, serviceable, and handsome farm buildings represent the development of a strong regional tradition based on a variety of cultural practices. Both the small farmer and the river-bottom planter stored their corn, smoked their hams, and sheltered their horses and cows in buildings whose forms were shared across regional, class, and cultural lines. This continuity persisted amid the widespread changes that reshaped fashionable houses and public buildings in the years after 1830.

Figure 2.143. Sink Barn, Davidson County, early 19th century.

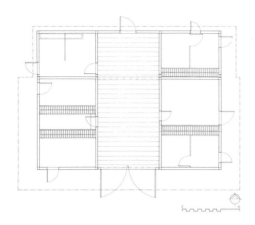

Figure 2.144. Sink Barn. Plan by Carl R. Lounsbury.

Figure 2.145. Sink Barn. Detail.

Figure 2.146. Sowers Barn, Davidson County, mid-19th century.

CHAPTER 3

The Antebellum Period, 1830–1861

From my room at the hotel at Fayetteville . . . I walked out, about eleven o'clock . . . and found, upon the edge of an old-field, near the town, a camp of wagoners, with half-a-dozen fires, around which were clustered groups of white men and women and negroes cooking and eating their suppers (black and white from the same kettle, in many cases), some singing Methodist songs, and some listening to a banjo or fiddle-player. . . . I could easily imagine myself to be on the Oregon or California trail, a thousand miles from the realm of civilization—not readily realize that I was within the limits of one of the oldest towns of the American continent. Those were the farmers of the distant highland districts, and their slaves, come to market with their produce. Next morning I counted sixty of their great wagons in the main street of the little town. . . . The merchants stood in the doors of their stores, or walked out into the street to observe their contents—generally of corn, meal, flour or cotton—and to traffic for them. . . . Several of the wagons had come, I found, from a hundred miles distant; and one of them from beyond the Blue Ridge, nearly two hundred miles distant. In this tedious way, until lately, nearly all the commerce between the back country and the river towns and sea-ports of Virginia and North Carolina has been carried on, strong teams of horses toiling on, less than a score of miles a day, with the lumbering wagons, the roads running through a sparsely settled district of clay soil.
—Frederick Law Olmsted, *Journey in the Seaboard Slave States*

In 1853 Frederick Law Olmsted traversed North Carolina on his tour of the South, traveling by rail from Virginia to Raleigh, by stagecoach to Fayetteville, and thence by river to Wilmington, where he boarded a train for Charleston. As he moved through a landscape remarkably like the one encountered by German traveler Johann Schoepf, yet also changed in important ways, the observant writer put broad themes in North Carolina's antebellum society and architecture into concrete terms.

Olmsted found that much of the country was still "almost all pine forest, or cypress swamp; and on the little land that is cultivated, I saw no indication of any other crop than maize." Along the Roanoke, "we passed several cotton fields, and substantial planters' mansions," but south of Raleigh, "the road was a mere opening through a forest of the long-leaf pine," along which "I do not think I passed, in ten miles, more than half a dozen homesteads, and of these but one was above the character of a hut or cabin." Repeatedly he commented on thin crops of corn on worn-out land, primitive living conditions, and an absence of trade due to poor transportation. He described unruly "vagabond" families dwelling in the pine woods, small farmers living in log dwellings and modest frame houses, slaves working in fisheries and turpentine forests as well as cotton fields, white girls employed in a cotton factory, and plantation owners, "gentlemen of good estate—intelligent, cultivated, and hospital. The number of these, however, is extremely few."[1]

Like many of his contemporaries, Olmsted saw this isolated, subsistence way of life as being out of step with modern America. The forest economy had begun to recede in the agricultural society, outmoded farming methods had depleted the once fertile soil, landowners were consoli-

Figure 3.1. Coolmore, Edgecombe County, 1859–60. Rotunda. E. G. Lind, architect; Mr. Dreyer, fresco painter.

dating their holdings, and emphasis on commercial agriculture and the market economy was growing. Olmsted reported that the state's "proverbial reputation for the ignorance and torpidity of her people" arose not from inherent flaws in the people themselves but from the problems of transportation and a lack of "concert of action among the small and scattered proprietors of capital." In the first half of the nineteenth century, conservatism and poverty, combined with westward outmigration, slowed economic development, and the state once known as "the best poor man's cuntry" was ridiculed as the "Rip Van Winkle State."[2]

Yet Olmsted also described signs of progress. He admired the "excellent" new rails of the Raleigh and Gaston Railroad that he rode to the capital, and he predicted that completion of the North Carolina Railroad from Raleigh to Charlotte would "stimulate a greatly increased production" in the Piedmont. He praised the miles of new plank roads so well suited to "all the circumstances of the country," including farmers' preference for hauling their crops to market rather than entrusting them to strangers.[3] And he found Raleigh, a city of 2,500 people amidst the pine forests, "a pleasing town—the streets wide and lined with trees, and many white wooden mansions, all having little courtyards of flowers and shrubbery around them." He praised its "public buildings and institutions of charity and education, honorable to the State," including churches and a lunatic asylum. The State House was "in every way, a noble building, constructed of brownish-grey granite, in Grecian style." He also praised a nearby church under construction as "very beautiful; cruciform in ground plan, the walls of stone."[4]

The contrasts Olmsted saw revealed that North Carolina was going through a complex period of growth and change. The state remained intensely rural, its people conservative and isolated and its commercial agriculture backward. Yet, motivated by a conscious determination to break this pattern, some North Carolinians in the 1830s had begun a campaign for change that produced the public works Olmsted so admired. Men who shared his views of progress pressed for rail and plank roads to extend the plantation system into the Piedmont; they demanded expansion of public education, social institutions, and the university; and they strove to elevate culture and overcome the state's self-image of inferiority and backwardness. However poor North Carolina appeared to Olmsted, by 1853 Rip Van Winkle had been aroused, and progress and prosperity were on the rise.[5]

Architectural change was intimately entwined with economic progress. State leaders saw the creation of modern and refined architecture as an essential step in pulling North Carolina into the national mainstream of commerce and culture. It only seems paradoxical that in this period North Carolina commissioned an extraordinary number of designs from leading national architects, resulting in a body of architecture that includes major works by America's foremost antebellum practitioners. The American architectural profession had just begun to develop in the 1830s and 1840s, and although its leading members concentrated their efforts in New York and Philadelphia, they needed jobs from distant clients as well. Local builders acquainted with traditional construction methods quickly adapted elements of new styles from a growing supply of builders' guides, but, to design the buildings that would redefine the state's image in national terms, ambitious clients often looked to urban architects. Only in the late 1850s and afterward did the architectural profession develop the regional strength that literally and readily transferred national styles across the landscape.[6]

Although continuity dominated the state's architecture, as most farm and small-town dwellers built the same kinds of traditional houses, barns, and churches they had erected in the early nineteenth century, it was changes in architecture that captured the most attention. Two overlapping patterns influenced the development of monumental and popular architecture: the widely popular Greek Revival and the more restricted picturesque styles of the Gothic Revival and Italian modes.

The very landmarks Olmsted admired in Raleigh epitomized these new trends, which will be discussed in this chapter. The white wooden mansions with their neat gardens represented a sequential movement from the traditional dwellings of the Federal period to local builders' columned Greek Revival houses and towered Italianate villas. The North Carolina Hospital for the Insane was a vast and modern complex in the Tuscan mode, designed by New York architect

Alexander Jackson Davis. The unfinished stone church, Christ Church, was designed by New York architect Richard Upjohn, the leading proponent of the American Gothic Revival style. And the "noble" State House at the city center—a major project of New York's principal firm of the 1830s, Ithiel Town and A. J. Davis—stood as the state's principal symbol of hard-won progress and pride.[7]

The Greek Revival

Neoclassicism on a grand scale, and in particular the Greek Revival, gained broad popularity in the period from the 1830s through the 1850s. The international taste for monumental neoclassicism, coupled with the special associations that ancient Greece evoked both for the new American democracy and for the slave South, gave the Greek Revival style powerful and universal appeal. James Stuart and Nicholas Revett's eighteenth-century study, *The Antiquities of Athens*, was a prime source of inspiration for the details and proportions of Greek orders and for the terms of classical "correctness" promoted as the ideal for modern architecture. The Greek Revival style fit comfortably into familiar classically derived and traditional formats. The authors of builders' guides updated their old books with new plates and issued new volumes—Asher Benjamin's 1830 edition of the *Practical House Carpenter* was especially popular—that depicted Greek as well as Roman orders and supplied simple but stylish designs for porches, mantels, doorways, and occasional buildings, plus readily understood instructions to enable local artisans to incorporate the new style into customary building patterns.

The Capitol

The North Carolina State Capitol (fig. 3.2) is a neoclassical building of a scale and sophistication that surpassed anything built in the state before. Despite the serene unity of its composition, its design involved at least three different currents of neoclassicism and five different architects, as well as the views of the commissioners appointed to manage the project. From the start of planning in 1833 to its completion in 1840, the character of the building evolved as a sequence of individuals put their stamp on the design. Throughout the years, in spite of controversy, rising costs, and resignations of commission members, successive commissioners maintained the vision of a monument of "durability and splendor, that will vie with the proudest specimens of European architecture." By erecting "one of the finest specimens of classic taste," built in accord with "the principles of Architecture, and rules of Architectural taste," the state asserted a new sense of North Carolina's cultural, political, and economic place in the Union.[8]

On June 21, 1831, William Nichols's handsomely remodeled State House had burned, ignited by a spark dropped by a workman replacing the roof. Citizens struggled to remove the revered Canova statue of George Washington from the burning building, but it was too heavy and was damaged beyond repair. Charred ruins blighted Union Square as Raleigh entered a "gloomy winter of discontent" that lasted for eighteen long months while debate continued over the idea of moving the capital to Fayetteville. Not until December 20, 1832, did the legislature agree to rebuild on the old site. The legislature established a board of commissioners and directed it to plan a building similar in arrangement to the old State House, but larger and also fireproof.[9]

Early January 1833, the commissioners decided that the new capitol should be "entirely of stone." In February and March they reviewed "several" plans—including a temple-form design by the New York architectural firm of Ithiel Town and A. J. Davis. After considerable politicking, they employed William Nichols, Jr., to draw up a plan and specifications for a building that complied with the legislature's instructions. By May, he had essentially completed plans for a building similar to his father's earlier State House and recently completed Alabama State Capitol: a cruciform structure three stories tall, with a rusticated stone base pierced by arched openings, pseudo porticoes of engaged columns fronting the east and west wings, and a domed

Figure 3.2. State Capitol, Raleigh, 1833–40. William Nichols, Jr., Ithiel Town and A. J. Davis, and David Paton, architects.

Figure 3.3. State Capitol. Right, plan of second floor by A. J. Davis, as originally designed by Town and Davis. (The Metropolitan Museum of Art, Harris Brisbane Dick Fund, 24.66.1771.) Far right, longitudinal section looking west, showing the spaces as revised and executed under David Paton. (William Tate Doggett, School of Design, North Carolina State University)

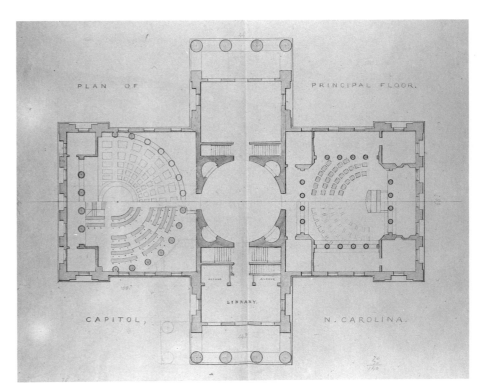

rotunda. After Nichols finished the plans in July 1833, his connection with the project was terminated.[10]

Early in the year, the commissioners had employed William Drummond, recently of Fayetteville, to superintend construction, and he had begun work. A state stone quarry was opened a mile and a quarter from the site, from which a railway was laid to carry horse-drawn cartloads of stone—a fine-grained, warm-hued, extremely hard gneiss. Workmen were hired, including slave and free laborers, local and immigrant carpenters, and stonecutters who, because North Carolina had no tradition of monumental stonework, were primarily northern and British artisans. Construction was begun and the cornerstone was laid on July 4, 1833.

Thus matters stood when Ithiel Town reentered the picture a few weeks later. Town had influential friends in North Carolina, both in Fayetteville, where he had resided for a time and built a toll bridge, and in the person of prominent lawyer William Gaston, who had earlier encouraged the adoption of Town's temple-form design. Through these connections, Town succeeded in gaining the commission.[11] Because the stone walls were already begun, the cruciform plan was set, but Town proposed changes to shift the design toward the monumental Greek Revival style characteristic of his firm: "To dispense with the rustick work on the north and south ends, to change the situation of the windows in the sides of the east and west projections, and to add porticoes to the same," "to dispense with the arches in the basement story windows [which] violate true architectural taste," and so forth. The commissioners accepted Town's proposals in August 1833.[12]

Challenged by an existing plan, Town and Davis created one of the most beautiful and original neoclassical buildings in America (fig. 3.3). They drew upon the principal sourcebook of the Greek Revival, Stuart and Revett's *Antiquities of Athens*, but by necessity they adapted its elements to a building whose cruciform plan and dome were based on Roman and Renaissance rather than Grecian precedents. For the exterior, Town and Davis adopted the powerful Doric order of the Parthenon and used its massiveness and simplicity to give the building its chaste and gracious dignity. They designed full porticoes for the east and west wings and redefined the north and south fronts with the pilastrades, or rows of bold antas, that were the firm's hallmark. Inside the building, their plans also developed from Nichols's layout. On the ground level, passages flanked by offices crossed at a rotunda, the intended location for the fire-damaged Canova statue, for which hopes of restoration had not yet died.[13] On the main floor above, the two-story amphitheatrical House of Commons and fully domed Senate flanked an upper rotunda

Figure 3.4. State Capitol. Dome.

that rose to a tall dome; the library and supreme court were to occupy the east and west wings (fig. 3.4).

Town visited the site but could not provide daily supervision. That was the responsibility of Drummond and the commissioners. In mid-1834 problems arose that led to important alterations in the design. After tangling with the commissioners over the hiring of an assistant, Drummond left the project. To replace him, Town recommended a young Scot, David Paton, who had come to New York from Edinburgh to seek work. Paton had learned architecture and stone construction under his father in Edinburgh and had worked in London as an assistant to the great English neoclassicist John Soane.[14] Hired specifically to superintend the stonework on the Capitol building, Paton came to Raleigh in September 1834 and soon assumed the responsibilities of clerk of the works and supervising architect. As he produced working drawings, Paton at first consulted Town about every detail, but gradually he began to assert more independence. In 1835 tensions arose between Paton and Town and climaxed over Paton's alteration of Town's roof-truss system—a touchy matter, considering Town's fame as the inventor of a patented truss. Town threatened Paton with dismissal. But the commissioners decided to retain Paton and end their relations with Town. The young Scotsman thus became the architect in charge of a project that Town regarded as one of the greatest stone buildings then underway in the nation.[15]

With Paton, a third current of neoclassicism entered the design. He brought to the building the abstract and geometricized neoclassical ideas of Soane and the Edinburgh school—and the confidence to put them into effect (fig. 3.5). He not only directed the execution of the work to

Figure 3.5. State Capitol. Rotunda.

the highest technical standards; he also pushed the design toward greater purity and boldness and created a series of adventurous spaces within the Town and Davis design. He moved the supreme court and state library from the second floor to the third and planned their decoration in Gothic Revival style. He simplified and strengthened the treatment of the legislative chambers and added public galleries in each. In a strong reference to Soane's themes, he lit the third-floor vestibules with top-lighted elliptical domes (fig. 3.6). His most dramatic revision, though, was in the rotunda. Drawing upon Edinburgh precedents in cantilevered stonework to support the second floor around a circular opening, he created a daringly beautiful core of light that reaches from the top of the dome to the ground ninety-nine feet below. This superb central space

Figure 3.6. State Capitol. Dome in third-story passage.

Figure 3.7. State Capitol. House of Commons.

Figure 3.8. State Capitol. Senate Chamber.

enhances the building's uniquely satisfying blend of intimacy and monumentality: from the center of the building are revealed its full height and depth, its reach in each direction, and the relationships among its magnificent spaces.[16]

As Paton's role expanded, the commissioners sought to assure themselves that his changes were "correct" in terms of scholarly precedent. These commissioners came from a tradition of active lay management of building projects, and they had a well-developed awareness of correct taste. In 1836, when Paton sought to keep the stairs out of the rotunda and to move the supreme court and library to the third floor, and again in 1837, when he designed the final details for the legislative chambers, Paton and the commissioners sought the opinion of noted Philadelphia architect William Strickland. On the latter occasion, Paton visited the architect in his offices, bringing with him a list of queries from the commission chairman. Strickland ruled decisively on each matter. In the House of Commons, for example, he stated that there should be six columns, not eight, supporting the semicircular ceiling and four behind the speaker, carefully spaced "in strict conformity with the Grecian rule." Finally, when queried about the capping of the dome, Strickland recommended "a plain blocking course, supporting a honey *suckle* or *fret* ornament as a corona and ultimate finish:—A balustrade is Roman and inadmissible." Once these matters were settled, Paton gave drawings for the capitals to the Philadelphia carver and returned to Raleigh.[17]

The acceptance of Paton's changes was the last stage in the evolution of the two chambers whose form had progressed from Nichols's 1819–22 State House remodeling based on Latrobe's U.S. Capitol, through the 1833 design by William Nichols, Jr., for the Capitol, to Town and Davis's revisions and Paton's refinements. In the House (fig. 3.7), a semicircular grove of towering columns rises to the coffered half-dome ceiling, dwarfing the arcs of legislators' desks and sloping spectators' galleries that focus on the speaker's desk. The Senate (fig. 3.8) has a symmetrical Greek cross plan surmounted by a central dome resting on pendentives that spring from the angle walls. On each side opens a broad, semicircular arch above a screen of Ionic columns. Paton's simplification of forms intensified the similarity of the chamber to major rooms in Soane's Bank of England. In these two chambers, as everywhere in the building, the superb craftsmanship of each detail reveals Paton's unrelenting standards of excellence.[18]

During the seven years of construction, the building commissioners saw the costs escalate beyond their wildest expectations. Labor costs, especially for stonecutters, were higher than anticipated, and the costs of manufactured items were also high—glass from New York, the roof copper from Baltimore, and iron and brass railings, fine hardware, and marble mantels from Philadelphia. By 1835 the state had spent $200,000 and the commissioners predicted the project would take two more years and $100,000 more. By 1836 the commissioners had abandoned any attempt at "any thing like accuracy in estimating the time it will take to complete the building, or the amount of its final cost." Grumbling mounted. More than once, the commissioners ran out of money between legislative sessions and had to borrow funds to continue work, on faith that the legislature would agree to repay it. Yet through it all, the commissioners remained adamantly committed to the original vision. "In the construction of an Edifice designed to last for ages," they insisted, "any petty attempts at economy in labor or materials could but defeat the true intent of the work, or display a ludicrous contrast of meanness or magnificence."[19]

In 1838, a legislative report intended to bolster public confidence included a grand architectural tour of the Capitol, doubtless provided by Paton in the spirit of *Antiquities of Athens*. It was full of sonorous references to the "models of Grecian Architecture, from which it was taken": the exterior "copied from the Temple of Minerva, commonly called the Parthenon, which was erected in Athens about 500 years before Christ"; the vestibule columns like "the Ionic Temple on the Ilissus near the Acropolis of Athens"; the House of Commons with its order from the Tower of Andronicus Cyrrhestes, in a plan derived from a Greek theater; and the Senate, modeled after the "Temple of Erechtheus, Minerva, Polias, and Pandrosus in the Acropolis of Athens."[20] Work continued and money was found. When the Capitol was completed in 1840 it had cost nearly $533,000, not including the stone. After disagreements with the commissioners over his pay rate, Paton left the project in the spring of 1840.

The completion of the Capitol brought North Carolinians boundless satisfaction. A magnificent celebration on June 10–12, 1840, marked the completion of the Capitol—"the pride and ornament of the state"—and the simultaneous finishing of the Raleigh and Gaston Railroad. Dinners, train rides, dances, and parades brought crowds from throughout the state and beyond, and the rhetoric of the day stressed the symbolic linkage of classicism and progress.[21] The sheer scale of the building had a tremendous impact. Every visitor to the city, claimed the *Raleigh Rasp*, "'goes up,' in order 'to see what he can see.' A few days ago, a gentleman from the backwoods, ascended to the top, and took a peep over the precipice, and immediately threw himself back on the house, exclaiming that it was so far down, that it drew his toe nail off, and, had he not fallen back, would have drawn his neck out of his shoulders."[22]

Even those who viewed such a costly building as "incompatible with the true principles of republican simplicity" agreed with a legislator who said, "much as we have complained of expense, I hope we will be satisfied, as we can say we have the best State House in the United States." State pride lifted with the sense that "this Political Temple, the Capitol of North Carolina, will vie with any legislative building in the Union, if not the world, and presents one of the finest specimens extant of classic taste in Architecture."[23]

Classic Halls and Temples of Justice

The Greek Revival style also permeated public architecture elsewhere in the state. The increasing desire and ability to erect handsome civic buildings joined with the rising interest in "correct"—primarily Greek—neoclassical taste to produce many new public buildings. Many of these buildings, like the Capitol, were also influenced by local precedents, which supplied a strong sense of continuity amid changing tastes.

Such was the case at the Market House and Town Hall (fig. 3.9) in Fayetteville, where another landmark lost to fire shaped the design of its successor. On May 27, 1831, less than a month before the State House burned, a fire destroyed most of Fayetteville. Among the losses was the Town House, the principal civic building, which stood at the centerpoint of two axial thoroughfares. That building, known originally as the State House, had been erected for the Constitutional Convention in 1789 and had housed the legislature when it met during the convention. It repeated a form common throughout America, England, and Europe, with civic chambers on the upper floor and an arcade at ground level for a city-regulated public market.[24]

After the fire, Fayetteville leaders quickly decided to rebuild the Town House on the old site, probably reusing the old foundations. In May 1832, the local newspaper proudly announced completion of "a Market House surmounted by a Town Hall and belfry, a beautiful ornament to the town."[25] The builder recast familiar elements in a bold mix of Greek and Gothic Revival styles. He retained the full length of the market arcade and emphasized its openings with alternating round and pointed arches; on the second floor, he reduced the former bicameral meeting rooms to a central municipal hall, flanked by platforms for public ceremonies. He graced the Town Hall with arched windows framed by Ionic pilasters and topped it with a belfry adorned with Ionic colonnettes and pinnacles.[26] The emphasis on the belfry befitted the importance of a town bell, which announced celebrations and disasters. The bell also rang at regular intervals—sunrise, breakfast, dinner, and sunset—by which the residents set their work day, and at curfew to signal that slaves must be in their quarters.[27] From ground to top, the Market House and Town Hall regulated Fayetteville's trade, its government, and the pace of daily life.

During the 1840s and 1850s, a wave of courthouse building swept the state as one county government after another invested in a proud new "temple of justice." Local papers promoted the idea that a county's pride depended on the character of its courthouse. The dignity and modernity of the Greek Revival style, enhanced by the symbolic linkages with Greek democracy, exerted a powerful appeal. Some counties employed architects to design their courthouses, but most turned to established builders who adapted classical orders and motifs from builders' guides and fit them to the county's requirements.

Figure 3.9. Market House and Town Hall, Fayetteville, 1831–32.

The functional demands of a courthouse were straightforward: a large and well-lighted courtroom with some aura of dignity; a jury room; judge's chamber; and a few offices for court and county officials. Colonial- and Federal-period courthouses commonly had the courtroom on the ground floor.[28] But antebellum courthouses in North Carolina typically had the courtroom on the upper floor and often treated the ground level as a raised basement containing offices. The example of the Capitol may have influenced local leaders in this direction. The Camden County Courthouse (fig. 3.10), built in 1847, displays this arrangement in a small but monumental brick structure. The courtroom occupies the upper story, which is treated as a piano nobile or principal upper story, emphasized by large windows and a portico set high on brick piers.

A similar arrangement prevailed when the courthouse took the literal form of a temple of justice. The temple form, which required that all the functions of a building be fitted into a rectangular form, was extraordinarily popular at the height of the Greek Revival in America. North Carolinians, though, tended to adopt it only when the restrictions of the form suited the function. The temple form could handsomely accommodate a large and well-lighted courtroom and a portico to shelter citizens who were attending court. Most builders favored the solemnity and economy of the Doric and Ionic orders. The porticoes took various forms: in some, the columns rose the full two-story height of the building, in which case the stairs were usually located inside the building or within the portico; others had exterior stairs rising to a second-level portico that sat atop a raised base.

The Orange County Courthouse (fig. 3.11), designed and built by Hillsborough brickmason John Berry in 1845, is a chaste and beautifully composed example of builders' Greek Revival at its

Figure 3.10. Camden County Courthouse, Camden, 1847.

Figure 3.11. Orange County Courthouse, Hillsborough, 1845. John Berry, builder.

Figure 3.12. Northampton County Courthouse, Jackson, 1858.

finest. Berry combined a carefully honed sense of proportion with a demanding standard of craftsmanship in the Flemish-bond brick walls and wooden trim. From the works of Minard Lafever and Asher Benjamin, he drew the Doric order and the domed cupola, and in the entry hall he repeated a stair design from Biddle. He designed the building with a sure hand, unifying the whole with a full Doric entablature and pilaster strips suggestive of antas. The building meets the ground with simple directness, so that the pilasters and portico columns rise from ground to entablature, strengthening the sense of dignity, stability, and accessibility.[29]

A contrasting temple scheme appears in the Northampton County Courthouse of 1858 (fig. 3.12), which has its courtroom and Ionic portico set high upon a base. The facade was probably modeled after the Temple on the Ilissus depicted in *Antiquities of Athens* and featured in various popular builders' guides such as Benjamin's and Lafever's. Unsigned specifications for the building describe each element in detail, including the columns of brick, covered with wood fluted and sanded, with Ionic capitals and bases and window lintels of iron.[30]

In the 1850s, leaders in blossoming Piedmont towns along the new North Carolina Railroad engaged in spirited competition in courthouse building. Rowan County initiated the joust in 1854 by displaying plans and specifications, and Davidson County builders John W. Conrad and John W. Williams began construction the next year.[31] The soberly monumental structure (fig. 3.13) features a tall, hexastyle Doric portico; the entablature continues along the sides, above windows cut simply into the side walls without antas. Meanwhile, the Salisbury newspaper reported, "No sooner had Rowan proceeded to build a new Court House than her daughter Davidson began to talk of the same thing." The Davidson County Courthouse (fig. 3.14) was

Figure 3.13. Rowan County Courthouse, Salisbury, 1855. John W. Conrad and John W. Williams, builders.

Figure 3.14. Davidson County Courthouse, Lexington, 1856–58. George Dudley and William Ashley, builders.

begun in 1856 and completed in 1858 by two builders from Raleigh, George Dudley and William Ashley.[32] In contrast to the courthouse in Rowan County, it follows the light and opulent Corinthian order, with paired antas at the corners and an enriched cornice. Typical of the 1850s, the ornate order is combined with arched windows in the Italianate mode. In 1858 a newspaperman visited Lexington from Greensboro, where yet another courthouse (now lost) was underway. He reported that Lexington's new "Temple of Justice" was so splendid that strangers "involuntarily stop to gaze on its beautiful proportions, its majestic columns." And he noted that other counties, "stirred up by the example of Davidson and Guilford, have entered the lists and are determined to compete with them for the honor of having the finest and most magnificent Court House in the State."[33]

Temples of Faith

Simultaneously with the building of new courthouses and other public buildings, a surge of church building spread across the countryside as dozens of Methodist, Baptist, and Presbyterian congregations erected newly imposing churches. Although a few urban churches rivaled the courthouses in their scale and stylishness, most were simpler wooden structures built for country congregations. In these, regional builders accommodated local custom, current standards for evangelical churches, and, where style was a concern, the Greek Revival temple form.

The roots of the antebellum church-building campaign reach back to the revival movements of the late eighteenth and early nineteenth centuries. Until the nineteenth century, churches in North Carolina had been few and small, and religious affiliations tended to parallel ethnic and cultural patterns; there were Presbyterians in the Scottish and Scotch-Irish settlements, Anglicans and Quakers in English-dominated areas, and Lutheran, Moravian, and Reformed congregations in German sections. Among these, a scattering of Baptists and Methodists reflected the efforts of early evangelists. Around 1800, however, evangelization by Baptists, Methodists, and New Light Presbyterians had brought North Carolina full force into the Great Revival, an emotional, salvation-oriented movement that cut across lines of class and race to bring thousands of people, literate and illiterate, slave and free, rich and poor, into the fold. The wave of evangelism that surged through the state climaxed around 1804. "A religious distemper," some called it, while the Raleigh newspaper claimed, "There was never so great a stir of Religion since the day of Penticost." The first great surge was only the beginning, for another wave of revivalism came in 1829–35 and yet another in 1857. "We don't remember ever hearing of as many religious revivals at one time as at the present," reported the Charlotte newspaper.[34] The revival movement transformed the configuration of church membership. Evangelical Protestants—mostly Methodists and Baptists and some Presbyterians, though that traditionally Calvinist denomination was divided on evangelicalism—had been a minority of the state's religious population in 1800. By the antebellum period they had become the mainstream majority among churchgoing people. By 1860 in North Carolina, Methodists and Baptists composed about 80 percent of some 2,000 congregations and 157,000 church members; about 10 percent more were Presbyterians; and all others, including Episcopalians, Lutherans, and Quakers, composed the remaining 10 percent.[35]

Camp Meetings

The most direct architectural expression of the revival movement appears in the Methodist camp-meeting grounds of the Piedmont. Camping at religious meetings was common from the eighteenth century onward, but the Great Revival increased the size and frequency of camp meetings and originated the idea of the annual camp meeting. At certain times of the year, usually in late summer, hundreds of people left the isolation and daily routine of the farm and gathered for a week or more in a great forest encampment. There, in a world away from the world, all ranks of people focused on the preached word and the emotional experience of individual conversion. Although Presbyterians had begun the practice, both they and the Baptists tapered off their involvement in camp meetings in the antebellum years. It was principally among Methodists that camp meetings took a lasting form in the 1830s through the construction of permanent buildings.[36]

Rock Springs Camp Meeting Ground (figs. 3.15, 3.16), in Lincoln County, is one of the oldest and most nearly intact meeting grounds in the Piedmont. Like many, it traces its origins to the eighteenth century—a 1794 camp meeting that won more than three hundred converts in a few days. In 1830 the trustees obtained a site of forty acres and began the sale of lots to individual owners. A central arbor was built for $255 in 1832, and after a time, instead of pitching temporary tents, lot holders began to build wooden "tents" around the arbor.[37]

Figure 3.15. Rock Springs Camp Meeting
Ground, Lincoln County,
established 1832.

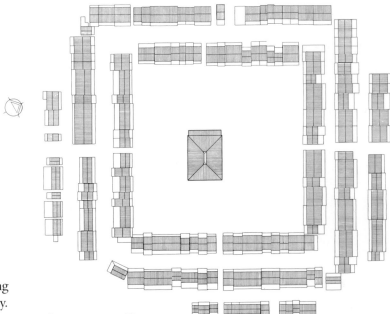

Figure 3.16. Rock Springs Camp Meeting
Ground. Site plan by Carl R. Lounsbury.

Figure 3.17. Rock Springs Camp Meeting Ground. Arbor, 1832.

The arbor, 94 by 64 feet, consists of a broad, sheltering hip roof of massive timbers resting on timber posts (fig. 3.17). Beneath it, rows of benches for as many as a thousand people face the platform and pulpit. At nineteenth-century camp meetings, there were typically separate sections for men and women and for whites and blacks. Around the arbor plaza, some three hundred numbered wooden "tents" (fig. 3.18) form two and part of a third concentric squares. They create narrow streets, each side shaded by a continuous row of porches. A typical tent is about 14 feet wide and has one main room with a sawdust-sprinkled earthen floor, plus a partial sleeping loft, a rear shed room, and a front entrance that is sheltered by a porch and has a bench bracketed out from the front wall. The rear shed is fitted out as an eating area with benches and shelves. Although their basic forms were established before the Civil War, these structures reflect continuous rebuilding throughout the late nineteenth and twentieth centuries. Rock Springs continues to grow and rebuild to suit the worshipers who still gather each August.[38]

The origins of camp-meeting architecture remain unclear. The tight rows of adjoining individual structures clustered around a central communal building differ from the prevalent southern preference for dispersed small buildings. Possibly the form had its origins in military encampments, a model easily transferred to religious campsites. Possibly, too, the participation of blacks in the revival movement had an influence. According to one interpretation, the hymns, preaching style, and conversion experiences of southern evangelical religion embodied traits shared between African and English religious traditions. Did this interaction have architectural dimensions as well? Certainly African traditions included models for concentric rows of small buildings around a plaza or main building.[39] Whatever its origins, the architecture of the camp-meeting ground powerfully evokes the revival experience of emotional, individual salvation.

Churches

The growth and, especially, the changing status and self-image of evangelical Protestant denominations in the antebellum period supported the transformation of their church architecture. Evangelicalism had begun as a movement of separation and alienation that often challenged institutions of privilege and slavery. Evangelicals focused on personal salvation and self-discipline and rejected the opinions of the world. Their construction of rudimentary log or frame meetinghouses was based not only on economic necessity but also on doctrines that eschewed elaborate buildings and symbolic trappings. But in the antebellum period, as revival cycles continued and as Baptists and Methodists attracted more and more wealthy members, evangelical Protestants gradually shifted their stance on social issues, including slavery, and consciously assumed a new role as a mainstream majority. Presbyterians, whose growth had waned along with their early revivalism, began after 1850 to press forward the work of evangelism and church expansion. Church leaders displayed new concern for an image of refinement and respectability to undergird their positions as moral leaders within southern society.[40]

These changing attitudes and rising numbers were translated into architecture. To be sure, many congregations continued to build small, simple structures. A now rare example of a typical country church is Walker Top Baptist Church (fig. 3.19) on Walker Mountain in Burke County. Built in the 1840s by Joseph Walker, the small log church was little different in form from the dwellings of families who worshiped there. At the time Walker Top Church was built, however, denominational leaders had begun to urge congregations to follow improved models of church design in order to assure maximum seating, good acoustics for preaching, and a respectable image.

An 1834 circular encouraged Methodists in one Piedmont circuit to abandon their "former mode of building" and to build churches that were "neat and comfortable and in every way worthy of enlightened, honorable, and liberal people." Following what was "said to be the proper model of church building by the General Conference," the writer offered plans for two plain, gable-end churches measuring 36 by 50 feet (fig. 3.20). One had two front doors and a pair

Figure 3.18. Rock Springs Camp Meeting Ground. Tents.

Figure 3.19. Walker Top Baptist Church, Burke County, 1840s.

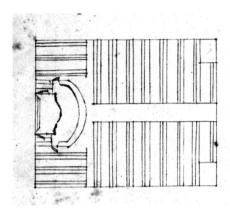

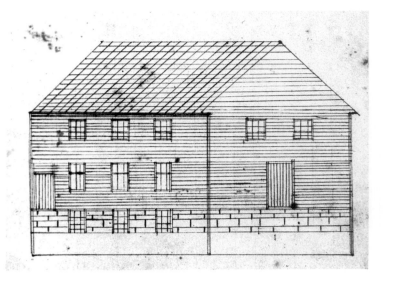

Figure 3.20. Model Methodist church.
Plan and perspective drawing, 1834.
(Duke University Archives)

Figure 3.21. Bethesda Presbyterian Church, Moore County, 1860.
Archie McLeod and Norman McCaskill, builders.

Figure 3.22. Bear Grass Primitive Baptist Church, Martin County, begun 1829.

of aisles, the other a single door and aisle. Both had galleries on three sides. At the gable end opposite the entrance stood the altar on a platform, and behind and above it rose the pulpit. (This contrasted with the meetinghouse, which had the main entrance and the pulpit on opposing long sides, and with the Anglican pattern, which placed the communion table at the gable end opposite the entrance and the pulpit to one side.) The writer of the circular cited the "science of church building" in such matters as the height, length, and width of the sanctuary and the precise measurements and arrangement of doors, windows, seats, galleries, and pulpit to assure good hearing—"which have become objects of great importance to us as a people."[41]

The simple aisled, gable-end church became a standard form for Protestant congregations. Depending on the size of the congregation, it might be built one or two stories tall, with or without a gallery, and with one or two front doors and corresponding aisles dividing the pews; either aisle arrangement could be used for seating by gender or by family unit. When Bethesda Presbyterian Church (fig. 3.21) was built in Moore County in 1860 for a Highland Scots congregation, the contract with builders Archie McLeod and Norman McCaskill focused on the same "objects" that engaged the Methodists. Specifications for the 35-by-45-foot frame church carefully described the heart pine frame and weatherboards and the rock pillars and paid close attention to the placement of doors and windows and the precise arrangement, height, and depth of the seats flanking the two aisles and in the galleries. The plain, hip-roofed, weatherboarded church on its high stone piers stands outside the stylistic currents of 1860 but epitomizes the continuing mainstream of interest in a sturdy and spacious hall for preaching.[42]

Paradoxically, Primitive Baptist churches continue the architectural patterns that once in-

Figure 3.23. Bear Grass Primitive Baptist Church. Interior.

formed the buildings of their evangelical brothers and sisters; their predestinarian doctrines support a conservative architecture that remains untouched by stylistic devices or symbolic motifs. Baptists had long experienced tensions between those who promoted evangelism and missionary work and those who held to strict interpretations of predestination theology. After 1827 several congregations in eastern North Carolina separated from the General Baptists and became known as Primitive Baptists—primitive in the sense of maintaining ancient apostolic beliefs. Bear Grass Primitive Baptist Church (figs. 3.22, 3.23) in Martin County, established in 1829, epitomizes this architecture of uncompromising simplicity. The broad gable end has two doors, one for men and one for women. Large, plain windows along the sides light the worship space. Two aisles lead to the pulpit on its raised platform, from which elders direct their extemporaneous sermons on predestination and salvation to church leaders in the "Amen corner" on either side and to the rows of the faithful seated in plain, slatted benches divided midway along their length by a narrow board rail.[43]

The gable-end, linear church plan was also well suited to more elaborate churches, most of which were temple-form structures in some version of the Greek Revival style. The temple image, seen in such public landmarks as the county courthouse, conveyed a powerful aura of respectability and community presence to antebellum evangelical congregations who were beginning to assume a new role in their community. Popular builders' guides, including those of Benjamin and Lafever, illustrated church designs with porticoes, pediments, and pilasters. These churches followed three principal arrangements: a projecting (prostyle) portico; a recessed (in antis) portico; and a simple pedimented facade without portico. Some builders used pilasters and entablatures along the sides and rear to knit the entire building into a temple-like whole, while others frankly concentrated on the facade. Whatever the form, most congregations chose the sober and economical Grecian Doric order or the simplest of the Roman orders, the Tuscan.

The most literal versions of the temple idea tended to be urban churches. Among the first and most imposing temple-form churches was Front Street Methodist Church in Wilmington (which burned in 1886). The congregation was established by an eighteenth-century missionary to the city's blacks: their contributions bought a lot and built a church. By the 1840s revivals had expanded the membership to some nine hundred blacks and two hundred whites. After a city-wide fire destroyed their newly rebuilt church in 1844, the congregation contracted with local builders John C. and Robert B. Wood and Bradford Sherman to erect "a plain, substantial and commodious brick house" for $7,100. They built the church as a Doric temple on the order of the Parthenon, with a prostyle portico and tall windows.[44] Ten years later, when Goldsboro's Presbyterians planned their own stylish brick church (fig. 3.24), they chose a popular design with a portico in antis. The entry porch is set behind stately columns and antas, while matching pilasters mark the corners and adorn the heavy, rectangular rooftop belfry.[45]

Rural churches display their builders' myriad accommodations of the Greek temple idea, through simplification, abstraction, and exaggeration of key elements. The Piedmont Scotch-Irish Presbyterians had built brick churches as early as the 1820s, when Buffalo Presbyterian Church in Guilford County erected a two-story brick church with two gable-end doors. In 1833 the congregation of Third Creek Church built a similar one in Rowan County, a "house to be completed in a plain but workman like manner, with a sufficient number of doors and windows for such a house." In the 1850s, the renewed vitality among Presbyterians spurred construction of several handsome brick churches in a simplified temple form. These include Hawfields in Alamance County, Poplar Tent in Cabarrus County, Centre in Iredell County, and Back Creek

Figure 3.24. First Presbyterian Church, Goldsboro, 1855.

Figure 3.25. Back Creek Presbyterian Church, Rowan County, 1856–57.

Figure 3.26. Rehoboth Methodist Church, Washington County, 1850–53.

Church in Rowan County. Back Creek Church (fig. 3.25), built in 1856–57 for a congregation born of the Great Revival, displays the builder's bold and well-proportioned handling of classical elements.[46] The pediment dominates the facade, while broad, plain pilasters frame the entrance and the windows beneath a wide brick frieze. The tall windows rise through the gallery level, so that with the blinds thrown open, the church evokes a sense of an open temple.

The pedimented country church at its simplest is Rehoboth Methodist Church (fig. 3.26), built in Washington County between 1850 and 1853.[47] The carpenters, said to have been slaves of a church member who sold the land to the congregation, finished the small frame structure with a pediment, narrow corner pilasters, and simple Greek Revival moldings, but the eloquence of the building depends less on these classical motifs than on the sense of scale and proportion and on the broad, clear windows that flood the quiet interior with light and, from the outside, make the building almost translucent.

Carpenters building churches for rural Highland Scots Presbyterians in southeastern North Carolina created their own variations on the neoclassical church model. In this region, too, the Great Revival had spurred growth among old congregations; and, though growth had lagged in the 1830s and 1840s, in a second renewal after 1850 leaders strove to rekindle the energies of the denomination.[48] One congregation after another proudly replaced its old log or frame "meeting house" with a new "church." Most were big, plain, weatherboarded frame buildings, conservative in form but with carpenters' inventive classical enrichment concentrating on the facade.

At Long Street Presbyterian Church (fig. 3.27), built in 1845–48, the frame building measuring 58 by 38 feet is starkly simple except for the dramatic portico set beneath its broad hip roof.[49] Slim, widely spaced Doric-type columns, grooved to suggest fluting, rise two stories high. They frame a flush-boarded facade with stylized Greek Revival trim accenting the twin doors, windows, and a large, Palladian-inspired window. Inside, smooth-planed boards and simple mold-

Figure 3.27. Long Street Presbyterian Church, Hoke County, 1845–48.

Figure 3.28. Long Street Presbyterian Church. Interior.

ings continue the theme of spare, stylized classicism (fig. 3.28). The plan follows the arrangement of New Bern's First Presbyterian Church (1819), with the pulpit rising at the front wall beneath the Palladian window, between the two main entrances.

At Philadelphus Presbyterian Church (fig. 3.29) in Robeson County, carpenter Gilbert Higley, a native of Connecticut, built a handsome church in 1859, with an in antis portico similar to that of the Presbyterian church in Goldsboro but with more vertical proportions to accommodate a two-story sanctuary with gallery. At Old Bluff Presbyterian Church (fig. 3.30) in Cumberland County, the builder took another approach to the recessed portico. He built a plain, weatherboarded church with two front doors in the gable end and two tiers of plain windows. He gave it a stylish, pedimented facade and tucked a portico in antis into the first story, thereby leaving room for the gallery and flanking stairs. He finished the entry porch with the customary flush boarding and wainscoting. And he used meticulous cutout and drilled work to suggest neoclassical moldings—triglyphs, dentils, and egg and dart—on the frieze and pediment. In the airy sanctuary (fig. 3.31), square pillars like those in the porch support the galleries on three sides. The building was dedicated in 1858 as a "new and beautiful church" for an old Scots congregation.[50]

Whether they were stylish neoclassical temples, plain preaching halls, or a carpenter's amalgamation of the two, such "new and beautiful" churches bore witness to antebellum congregations' growing attention to architecture. Although by the 1850s the Gothic Revival style had gained popularity in some urban and advanced rural areas, in most areas the "modern country church" employed themes of classicism to create an architecture of stability and respectability as well as of moral authority.

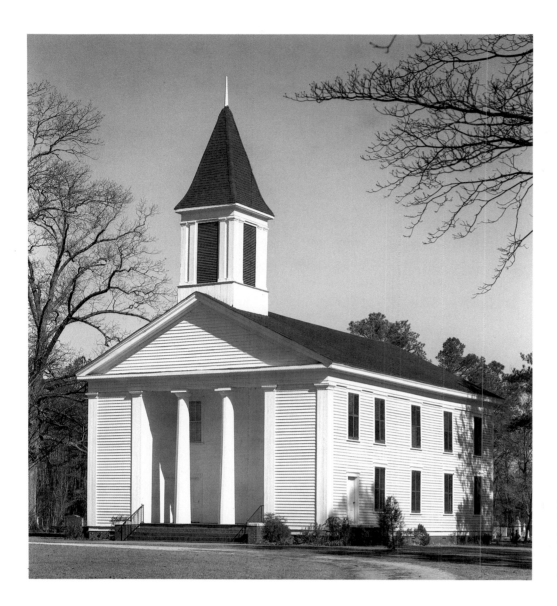

Figure 3.29. Philadelphus Presbyterian Church, Robeson County, 1859. Attributed to Gilbert Higley, carpenter.

Figure 3.30. Old Bluff Presbyterian Church, Cumberland County, 1858.

Figure 3.31. Old Bluff Presbyterian Church. Interior.

Temples of Learning

The Greek Revival also took a strong hold in collegiate architecture. It embodied the classical curriculum and Greco-Roman tradition to which most colleges and academies aspired, lent an air of authority and venerability to many newly established institutions, and evoked the spirit of democracy and the broadening of higher education. Growing prosperity and emphasis on education spurred the establishment of more than twenty colleges in North Carolina between 1830 and 1860; many of these were denominational colleges that reflected the new role of religion in society, particularly the efforts of Protestant evangelical denominations to assert their respectability and elevate general morality and learning.[51] The infant institutions usually met for a time in temporary quarters, but as soon as possible, school leaders strove to erect large and handsome, multipurpose main buildings, generally classical in style and designed to become proud community landmarks. Besides asserting the stature and permanence of its institution, the college building needed to accommodate offices, classrooms, dormitories, and formal reception areas and to fit within a budget for which donations were often slow in coming.

Such college buildings represented some of the largest construction projects of the antebellum building boom. The Main Building at the Baptist-affiliated Wake Forest Institute, erected in 1835–37 by John Berry of Hillsborough, took a conservative Palladian form, with a pedimented center pavilion and a cupola similar to South Building at the university.[52] At the Episcopal School in Raleigh in 1835, builder William Drummond (late of the Capitol) erected a brick main building that was an enlarged version of a central-passage house, with Greek Revival detail and a modest portico.[53] Full-blown neoclassicism appeared in North Carolina college buildings around 1850. Most such buildings followed a symmetrical plan, often with a central passage intersecting a lateral one. At Louisburg Female College, Warren County builder Albert Gamaliel Jones erected a four-story structure with a Doric entrance portico. At Wesleyan Female College in Murfreesboro, Jones built from architect Thomas Fentress's design a massive structure, nine bays wide, with a Corinthian portico and a big cupola; and at the Baptist-affiliated Chowan College in the same town, he stretched a Doric colonnade across an eleven-bay facade and topped the whole with a cupola.[54]

Among the most ambitious denominational college buildings was the Concord Female College in Statesville (fig. 3.32). It was established in 1852 by the Presbyterians of western North Carolina, who had founded Davidson College for men in Mecklenburg County in 1837. The school obtained from South Carolina architect Jacob Graves a design for a four-story, thirteen-bay building with a Corinthian portico atop an arcaded base. Builder J. W. Conrad of Davidson County contracted in 1854 to complete the building for $25,000 and pushed the work ahead swiftly. Then, just before the last bricks were to be laid on June 9, 1855, a windstorm leveled the building. After recovering from "this stroke from the hand of our Heavenly Father," the trustees signed a new contract with Conrad for $19,000. Salvaging what they could, they built on the old foundations but reduced the height to three stories and changed the portico to the Doric order, which was recommended by its simplicity and lower proportions. Builder and trustees confronted their changed circumstances pragmatically by moving from one classical order to another, while still realizing the initial vision of an institution where "from its classic halls may go forth year after year the daughters of the church refined and polished by science, literature and piety."[55]

North Carolinians generally restricted temple-form collegiate structures to buildings with special purposes. Temples were especially popular on American campuses for the housing of Greek-named "debating societies," which dominated student life. These societies were run by the students themselves and usually divided the student population between them.[56] In 1849 and 1850, at Davidson College near Charlotte, the Eumenean and Philanthropic societies built a facing pair of small but forceful brick temples. Behind its portico, each hall contains a handsomely appointed debating room in the main upper story.

Smith Hall (fig. 3.33), which graces the campus at the University of North Carolina, shows the temple form at its most elegant. In 1848, the student debating societies—the Dialectic and

Figure 3.32. Concord Female College (Mitchell Community College), Statesville, 1854–57. John W. Conrad, builder.

Figure 3.33. Smith Hall (Playmakers Theater), University of North Carolina at Chapel Hill, 1850–52.
A. J. Davis, architect; John Berry, builder.

Philanthropic—proposed construction of a campus ballroom. In 1849 university leaders expanded the concept to include a library and meeting hall and commissioned a design from architect A. J. Davis, who had already designed other improvements to the campus. He planned first an 80-foot structure with a recessed portico. But in May 1850, after visiting the campus and consulting university president David Swain, he enlarged the plan to make a building of 122 feet "with a portico of 4 columns detached. . . . I was obliged to redraw the whole, but the result has been to improve the plan, so as to make it such as would be creditable to any University, as a specimen of Classical taste." Influenced by Latrobe's American order used in the U.S. Capitol, Davis designed an order of wheat and corn and had the "corn capitals" carved in New York. The rich, individualized portico complements the simplicity of the long pilastraded sides, a hallmark of Davis's style. The building was completed by John Berry of Hillsborough in time for the commencement ball of 1852.[57]

Temples of Commerce

The classical imagery that appealed to educational leaders also struck a chord with businessmen. Although very few antebellum commercial buildings still stand, it appears that the pedimented bank or shop was popular in North Carolina towns, as it was in larger American cities. The design suited a narrow commercial lot and presented an impressive street front. Small porticoed facades offered a wide range of interpretation. In 1854, when directors of the new Bank of Washington (fig. 3.34) advertised for the construction of a "banking house" in Washington, they explained that the building was to be of brick stuccoed to resemble stone, with a fireproof roof, and they wanted "the front gable . . . to extend so as to form a Portico supported by four columns."[58] The bank's strong proportions and boldly treated Ionic portico give it a confident and unmistakably fashionable stance.

Figure 3.34. Bank of Washington, Washington, 1854.

A lively interpretation of the form appears in the Darden Hotel (fig. 3.35), in the river town of Hamilton. Unconstrained by bookish correctness, the carpenter extracted the essence of the double portico, the grooves of fluting, and the spiral curves of the Ionic volute and then restated them in stylized fashion.[59] The simplest version of the store as temple can be found in brick commercial buildings in Caswell County. The Graves Store in Yanceyville has a simple pediment front, whereas the Warren Store (fig. 3.36), built at Prospect Hill about 1858, adds a plain double portico suitable to a trading house in a thriving plantation community.[60]

Figure 3.35. Darden Hotel, Hamilton, probably 1850s.

Figure 3.36. Warren Store, Caswell County, ca. 1858.

Houses

The mainstream Greek Revival style entered North Carolina domestic architecture in dramatic form in large houses of the 1830s. For many Carolinians, the 1830s were years of economic decline and outmigration; the decade was also a time of greater economic stratification, as planter families continued to consolidate property and the plantation system expanded into the Piedmont. Most members of the planter class had grown up in houses like those of their neighbors in form and plan. In the antebellum period, as their fortunes and positions rose, they began to build houses far larger and more splendid than anything seen in their neighborhoods before. Yet they did not depart entirely from familiar standards; even as they adopted the new taste for monumentality, new styles, and newly prominent exterior display of fashion, North Carolinians demonstrated their continuing preference for established precedents of craftsmanship, plan, and form.

Remarkably few North Carolinians adopted the notion of building houses to resemble temples. Orton Plantation House (fig. 3.37), on a huge estate overlooking the Cape Fear River near Brunswick, was expanded in the 1840s from a mid-eighteenth-century dwelling into a Doric temple form; the deep, broad portico, set low to the ground, gives a powerful impression of leisured repose. Wills Forest, a plantation house built by Dabney Cosby near Raleigh in 1840, was fronted by an Ionic portico high atop a raised base. Stockton (ca. 1848), in Perquimans County, has a tripartite facade adapted from Lafever's *Modern Builder's Guide*.[61] But such houses were rare exceptions in a domestic architecture that by and large remained faithful to proven forms. At the height of the Greek Revival, popular writers satirized Americans' unthinking use of the temple for every conceivable purpose. Most North Carolinians, however, had made their own distinctions about the form, which they found convenient and expressive for public buildings but seldom suitable for dwellings.

Almost universally, the principal Greek Revival houses followed a format established in the eighteenth century: a symmetrical house with a low hip or gable roof and a central-passage plan, one or two rooms deep. Chimneys rose either on the ends or between the front and rear rooms. The central-passage plan, used in only a few Georgian and Federal houses, supplanted all others among the principal houses of the antebellum period. In many examples, two adjoining parlors were linked by sliding doors, which opened to form a large formal room. The long-favored hall-parlor plan and three- and four-room open plans all but vanished from major new construction.

Figure 3.37. Orton Plantation House, Brunswick County, enlarged 1840s.
(North Carolina Division of Archives and History)

This standardization of plan paralleled a growing standardization of stylistic elements. The influence of nationally popular patternbooks expanded as builders accommodated the new style in broader proportions of every element and copied or adapted published designs for porticoes, columns, doors, windows, cornices, and pilasters, and the impact of individual artisans' styles and local traditions gradually ebbed.

Major houses from the 1830s illustrate the stylistic transition from the Adamesque to the Greek Revival. Stonewall (fig. 3.38), built about 1830 on the vast Tar River plantation of Bennett Bunn, is a big brick house that, in scale and materials, exceeds anything in its neighborhood. The elaborate interior woodwork—a wishbone stair and pilastered overmantels (fig. 3.39)—features regional Adamesque motifs in the spirit of William Pain and Benjamin's *Country Builder's Assistant*, giving little hint of Greek Revival influence. In contrast, the Homestead (fig. 3.40), built in Lexington in 1834 for progressive planter and physician William R. Holt, incorporates such Federal motifs as Palladian windows and a stair with brackets copied from Biddle's *Young Carpenter's Assistant*, but these are commingled with Greek Ionic pilasters, Greek key and anthemion decorations, and an entrance from Benjamin's new *Practice of Architecture* (1833).[62]

Figure 3.38. Stonewall, Nash County, ca. 1830.

Figure 3.39. Stonewall. Mantel in parlor.

Figure 3.40. The Homestead, Lexington, 1834.

Cedar Grove (figs. 3.41, 3.42) in Mecklenburg County is an especially fine and well-documented example of builders' ready adoption of the Greek Revival style. The massive brick house was constructed in 1831–33 for James Torrence, a second-generation Scotch-Irish merchant who had become a large planter. Like many other plantation owners, Torrence had the timber for the house sawed in his own mill, and, according to family tradition, his slaves made the brick. He hired local or regional artisans: brickmason James Huston, carpenters David Hampton and Jacob Shuman, plasterer H. S. Gorman, and painter J. W. Thompson. He obtained his hardware and other manufactured items from New York and Philadelphia, usually by way of Charleston. In 1831 he sold to carpenter Hampton "1 Nicholson Architecture," and in 1832, "1 Benjamin Architecture," from which to complete the house.[63]

Figure 3.41. Cedar Grove, Mecklenburg County, 1831–33. James Huston, bricklayer; David Hampton and Jacob Shuman, carpenters; H. S. Gorman, plasterer.

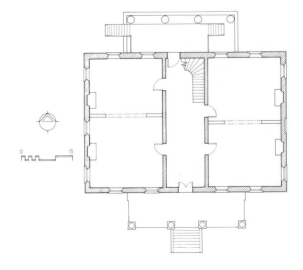

Figure 3.42. Cedar Grove. Plan by Carl R. Lounsbury after drawing by School of Design, North Carolina State University.

Figure 3.43. Cedar Grove. Double parlors.

Figure 3.44. Cedar Grove. Stair.

With its straightforward, gable-roof form, as well as its Flemish-bond brickwork, corbeled cornices, and flat arches over the windows, Cedar Grove stands within the Piedmont tradition. But its sheer mass—60 by 40 feet in extent, rising two-and-a-half stories atop a tall basement— sets it apart from its predecessors, and its impact is heightened by the stepped gables that mount to the chimney tops. The airy grandeur of the interior exemplifies builders' Greek Revival at its finest. The new elements—simple Doric columned mantels, wide moldings with bull's-eye cornerblocks, and massive plaster cornices —possess the largeness in scale that the building demands. Oversized windows, expanded by splayed jambs in the thick brick walls, flood the large, high rooms with light, including the pair of parlors that open into a single great space (fig. 3.43). The stair (fig. 3.44) is a grand expansion of the regionally favored design from Biddle, spiraling up to the third story.[64]

About 1837 near Morganton, planter Thomas George Walton also erected his mansion, Creekside (fig. 3.45), within the tradition of brick plantation houses along the Catawba River, but he too set a new standard of monumentality—supposedly inspired by houses he had seen in Virginia. Creekside is dominated by a towering portico, and its mass is emphasized by brick pilasters and a bold, original frieze of carved blocks. The mantels, doors, and windows run the gamut of designs from Benjamin's *Practical House Carpenter*, and trompe l'oeil niches with classical nymphs flanking the parlor fireplace complete the ensemble.[65]

Two plantation houses at the opposite end of the state in Perquimans County exemplify the integration of monumental neoclassicism into coastal North Carolina's double-piazza form. Cove Grove and Land's End are linked by architectural form and family, though their dates are not certain. Their construction is credited to James Leigh, a builder who rose from the middling class—he was the orphaned son of carpenter Gilbert Leigh—to become a rich planter and one of the county's largest slaveowners. Grand, unorthodox blends of regional forms and patternbook neoclassicism, built on a scale unprecedented in the county and rivaling the houses of the greatest planters of the Albemarle, Cove Grove and Land's End were powerful assertions of attainment and intent.[66]

Figure 3.45. Creekside, Burke County, ca. 1837.

Figure 3.46. Cove Grove, Perquimans County, ca. 1830. Attributed to James Leigh, builder.

Figure 3.47. Land's End, Perquimans County, 1830s. Attributed to James Leigh, builder.

Cove Grove (fig. 3.46) is said to have been built by Leigh in about 1830 for his daughter Elizabeth and her husband, Benjamin Skinner, a member of an established local plantation family. It is a house of extraordinary presence and individuality. The regional engaged porches take the form of colossal Ionic porticoes front and rear. The use of a heroic Greek Ionic order, as well as other elements, suggests a connection with William Nichols, who had left North Carolina for Alabama in 1827, but any connection remains undocumented. The columns of the front portico rise uninterrupted from an arcaded brick base, sheltering a fanlit main entrance and a delicate iron balcony at an upper doorway of Greek Revival type. At the rear, a two-tiered porch is set within the columns. The house measures 36 by 55 feet, with the porches expanding its depth to 58 feet. The rooms are finished with late-Federal woodwork. A molded keystone arch frames the sliding doors between the parlors on the right, and a similar arch in the passage frames the graceful Federal stair, which terminates in a curious scallop-form newel.[67]

For his own residence, Land's End (figs. 3.47, 3.48), Leigh followed the same format, but he built bigger, of brick, and in a different spirit. The house measures 38 by 60 feet, plus porches that are 10 feet deep; it stands high on a raised basement, commanding a broad, flat landscape that once included a large barn and rows of slave dwellings. Materially, the house is the statement of an artisan who knew and could afford the best work—Flemish-bond brick walls, brick partition walls 18 inches thick, and fine stone steps and iron railings. Powerful horizontals emphasize the building's mass. The porticoes, engaged beneath the broad, multisloped gable roof, feature tall, unfluted Doric columns, second-level galleries, and a heavy Doric entablature. Leigh treated the porch, in customary fashion, as a wainscoted outdoor room. He applied a full range of motifs

Figure 3.48. Land's End. Front doorway.

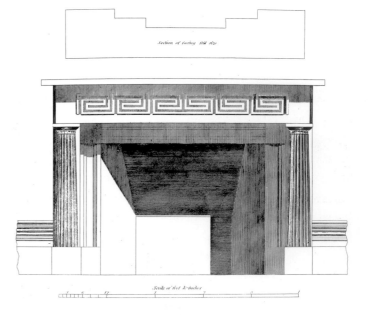

Figure 3.49. Design for chimneypiece, from Asher Benjamin, *Practical House Carpenter*. (Henry Francis du Pont Winterthur Museum Library, Collection of Printed Books)

Figure 3.50. Land's End. Mantel.

from Benjamin's *Practical House Carpenter* (fig. 3.49): bold forms adorned with Greek key motifs appear at the front and back doors and stout columned mantels (fig. 3.50), doors, and windows. Broad archways link the parlors and frame the stair, which repeats the signature scallop newel (fig. 3.51).[68]

These first Greek Revival mansions introduced themes that became dominant in the 1840s and persisted throughout the antebellum period. The general broadening of proportions found expression in the use of simple, wide moldings, large windows, and double doors with broad transoms and sidelights. Carpenters rendered interior woodwork in similar style, adapting columnar mantels and cornerblock door and window frames from Benjamin's and other popular volumes in a fashion akin to their contemporaries throughout the nation. The greatest individuality and variation appears in the classicized treatments of the porch, principally in the forms seen in these early examples—a pedimented central portico, a columned shed porch, or a colonnaded piazza.

The columned piazza offered an especially rich amalgam of regional custom and classical taste. On the Collins family's vast Somerset Plantation (fig. 3.52), Josiah Collins III built a double-piazza house in about 1838–39 in a much simpler Greek Revival style. Harvard-educated, well traveled, and married to a New Jersey lady of fashionable tastes, Collins nevertheless built within the local idiom. Standing at the center of a plantation of some four thousand acres of laboriously drained swampland beside Lake Phelps, the T-shaped dwelling has two-tiered piazzas across the front and along the rear ell. The multisloped roofline stretches the pedimented gables out over the deep porches with their simple turned columns. Characteristically heavy woodwork appears throughout the interior, including the columned archway in the passage (fig. 3.53), which frames the stair in the ell's transverse hall.[69]

Figure 3.51. Land's End. Stair detail.

Figure 3.52. Somerset Plantation, Washington County, late 1830s.

Figure 3.53. Somerset
Plantation. Passage.

Across the Albemarle Sound, on Collins property in Edenton, Josiah's sister Henrietta and her husband, Dr. Matthew Page (widower of her sister, Mary Matilda Collins), built a more elaborate residence about 1849–50. Their townhouse, Pembroke Hall, is an elegant frame house whose broad hip roof encompasses double porticoes on both land and water fronts. The columns of the upper tier display an invented waterleaf order presented in Lafever's *Beauties of Modern Architecture*, and the roofline was topped by an elegant paneled balustrade and tablet.[70] The plan of the house accommodates the dual frontage by recessing the stair in a side passage so that the broad central passage runs from land to water side, accentuated by a column screen in the waterleaf order.

During the 1840s and 1850s, builders throughout the plantation regions and growing towns erected their own versions of the broad, symmetrical forms and classical porches of the Greek Revival. A characteristically restrained example is Midway Plantation in Wake County (fig. 3.54), with its generous proportions and unpretentious entrance portico of square pillars. The house has four rooms flanking the passage on the first floor, but only the front half of the house is two stories tall—an updated rendition of the shallow two-story house with rear shed rooms. Built in 1848 for David Hinton and Mary Carr, the house was one of many Greek Revival houses of moderate size built for the interlocking rural gentry; indeed, a few years before the Hintons built Midway, Mary's father Jonas Carr of Edgecombe County had remodeled his own plantation house, Bracebridge Hall, with a new Greek Revival front and Doric portico.[71]

Regional clusters of Greek Revival houses display distinctive touches within their overall unity of plan and aesthetic. The tobacco-planting counties along the Virginia line produced

Figure 3.54. Midway Plantation, Wake County, 1848.

Figure 3.55. Eaton House, Warrenton, 1843. Attributed to Jacob W. Holt, carpenter.

several large, forcefully designed brick mansions, including Dongola in Yanceyville and High Rock Ford in Rockingham. The Eaton House in Warrenton (fig. 3.55) is one of several border county houses that suggest a Virginia influence. The tall brick house, only one room deep, was built in 1843 as the summer townhouse of planter William Eaton, reputedly the richest man on the Roanoke. Tradition claims it was the work of artisans from Prince Edward County, Virginia, and it shares with southern Virginia houses such details as panels embedded in the Flemish-bond brick walls and offset windowblocks. The boldly carved, arched entrances, the blend of Federal and Greek Revival elements, and the easy manner in which the second-story fanlight projects into the Doric entablature suggest a freewheeling approach to neoclassicism. Inside, the shallow hallway is filled with a spiral stair from Biddle (fig. 3.56), while the heavy doorways and original mantels were adapted from Benjamin's *Practical House Carpenter*.[72]

Prominent among the Prince Edward County artisans who came to Warrenton was builder Jacob Holt, to whom local tradition ascribes construction of the Eaton House. Holt settled in Warrenton in the mid-1840s and erected a series of sturdy Greek Revival dwellings. Like many of his generation, he adapted elements from various popular books to develop his own style. At the Somerville House in Warrenton (fig. 3.57), for example, the columned entry (fig. 3.58) recalls a plate from Lafever, the porch suggests Benjamin's *Practice of Architecture*, and the Greek fret and burly, columned mantels (fig. 3.59) suggest models in *The Practical House Carpenter*. Holt modified the period's standard central-passage plan with a louvered door that screens the front and back halls with their public and private stairs—an arrangement that, like his ornament, became part of his shop's standard work.[73]

The most vividly personal style of antebellum artisanry appears in another group of houses along the Virginia border, in the interior work of cabinetmaker Thomas Day of Milton.[74] Day

Figure 3.56.
Eaton House. Passage.

was a free black whose cabinet shop produced sophisticated furniture—beds, case pieces, tables, and chairs—in his own neoclassical and Empire styles. He apparently worked closely with local builders and fabricated finishing woodwork for the same planters who prided themselves on possessing his furniture. Like many of the houses that contain work attributed to Day, Burleigh Plantation in Person County, with its conventional Greek Revival exterior, gives no hint of the extraordinary artisanry inside: three-dimensional columned mantels with sinuous friezes and a sculpted newel coiled at the base of the stair (fig. 3.60). For the Long family in Caswell County, Day stylized the stair newel (fig. 3.61) into a lean and abstract form in which rounded posts emerge subtly from a squared base and playfully deny the ideas of rail and support. His expressiveness within a classical framework is also demonstrated in the extraordinary parlor mantel (fig. 3.62) of the Long House. Into its pilasters he carved two forcefully realized male heads, their solemn young faces capped by tiny Gothic arcades evoking jesters' caps (fig. 3.63). Apparently unique in Day's work, these heads draw upon the classical tradition of the herm—a column or pilaster crowned by a human torso or head—that appeared in patternbooks, and also, perhaps, upon the distant tradition of African figurative sculptures and masks.[75]

Figure 3.57. Somerville House, Warrenton, ca. 1850. Attributed to Jacob W. Holt, builder.

Figure 3.58. Somerville House. Porch and entrance.

Figure 3.59. Somerville House. Mantel.

Figure 3.60. Burleigh Plantation, Person County, ca. 1850.
Stair. Attributed to Thomas Day, cabinetmaker.

Figure 3.61. Long House, Caswell County, 1856–60.
Stair. Attributed to Thomas Day, cabinetmaker.

Figure 3.62. Long House. Parlor. Attributed to Thomas Day, cabinetmaker.

Figure 3.63. Long House. Detail of mantel. Attributed to Thomas Day, cabinetmaker.

Figure 3.64. Gillespie House, Kenansville, 1850s.

There were clusters of builders' Greek Revival work in many regions, from the columned plantation houses of the coastal plain to the straightforward, handsomely proportioned farmhouses of the western Piedmont and a few opulent residences in the river valleys between the mountains. In the southern coastal plain, for example, cotton and forest products supported the construction of several broadly detailed houses in Duplin and Sampson counties. Typical of these is the Gillespie House in Kenansville (fig. 3.64), which has a portico made up of square pillars, broad pilasters and frieze boards outlining the elevations and defining the pedimented gable ends, and windows and doors with peaked and crossetted frames. These same elements were also used effectively in one-story dwellings like the house of Dr. David Dickson Sloan (fig. 3.65), built in 1849 in Sampson County, a spacious, high-ceilinged house set atop tall piers.

Also in southeastern North Carolina, several dwellings, such as the Humphrey-Williams House near Raft Swamp in Robeson County (fig. 3.66), integrate stylish motifs into houses that continue the regional emphasis on the porch as an outdoor room. In this plantation house, built in 1845–46 for Richard and Charity Humphrey, the wall sheltered by the porch is finished with paneled wainscoting, and simple Greek Revival moldings embellish the doorways opening into the central passage and flanking rooms. In addition, the passage was partitioned midway along its length to leave the rear part open as a porch at both stories. Another regional theme appears in the treatment of the front porch posts, which address the problem of moisture and decay with a technique typical of South Carolina border counties: the turned porch posts sit on piers that stand forward of the porch floor, which rests on its own separate piers.[76]

Figure 3.65. Sloan House, Sampson County, 1849.

Figure 3.66. Humphrey-Williams House, Robeson County, 1845–46.

Farm Buildings

Houses were, of course, but part of a large unit—either an in-town establishment or, most often, a farm complex made up of domestic and agricultural buildings. In constructing their outbuildings, farmers of the antebellum period continued to use many general patterns from earlier years while updating stylistic details for domestic buildings near the house and adopting functional innovations for farm buildings. Such changes were most evident on the larger plantations, whose owners were interested in and capable of creating an imposing image and incorporating progressive agricultural theories.

On such large plantations as Somerset Place—as at Fairntosh earlier—outbuildings typically displayed the greatest formality and hierarchy of planning. The row of slave houses—some thirty-seven of them in 1860, according to the census—is gone, as are the barns that once stood at a distance. But behind the house stands a dense cluster of domestic buildings (figs. 3.67, 3.68) arranged in a fenced, rectilinear courtyard. The laundry-kitchen is nearest the house, with the dairy beside it; a bathhouse and storehouse stand perpendicular to these; and beyond them are the smokehouse and ice house.[77] These domestic structures are tidily finished, in keeping with the main house. Although handsome domestic outbuildings were part of many plantation complexes, few matched the attention to detail evident at Burleigh Plantation in Person County, where the epitome of a stylish outbuilding appears in a frame privy adorned with trim Ionic pilasters (fig. 3.69).

Some planters also introduced practical innovations in their agricultural buildings. Large barns became increasingly common in eastern North Carolina, indicating both an attention to

Figure 3.67. Somerset Plantation, Washington County. Domestic outbuildings.

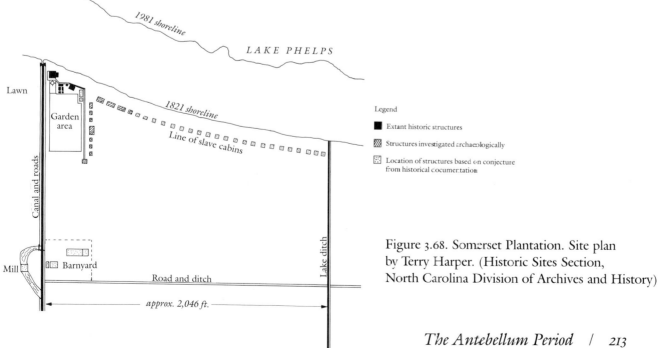

Figure 3.68. Somerset Plantation. Site plan by Terry Harper. (Historic Sites Section, North Carolina Division of Archives and History)

Figure 3.69. Burleigh Plantation. Privy.

Figure 3.70. Elliott Barn and Stable, Chowan County, 1850s.

current agricultural literature and, probably, the planters' desire for greater control over both their livestock and the landscape. The Collins family once had a vast barn at Somerset Place, and James Leigh's big barn was a landmark at Land's End. In Chowan County, William Elliott, a planter who owned a mill, worked as a builder, and rapidly accumulated property in the antebellum period, erected in the 1850s a pair of gable-roofed frame barns (fig. 3.70) that were innovative in form and structure, though the basic idea of a stable and a storage building set at right angles was a familiar one. Elliott built his stable in a form then new in his area: a transverse crib plan with the runway opening on the gable ends and flanked by stalls. He oriented his big storage barn in the opposite direction, with the main runway perpendicular to the roof ridge. Heavy posts form four cribs and crossing runways. In both buildings, Elliott employed ingenious systems of adjustable partitions, with planks slotted into the posts to allow flexible use of the stalls and storage spaces and to provide maximum ventilation.[78]

A complex probably typical of good-sized plantations is preserved at Walnut Grove Plantation (figs. 3.71, 3.72) in Bladen County. James and Eliza Ann Robeson ran a plantation that in 1850 included more than 2,000 acres and twenty-four slaves (fig. 3.73). They cultivated 240 acres that produced corn, oats, peas, and potatoes; they raised swine, cattle, and sheep; and from the

Figure 3.71. Walnut Grove Plantation, Bladen County, 1850s.

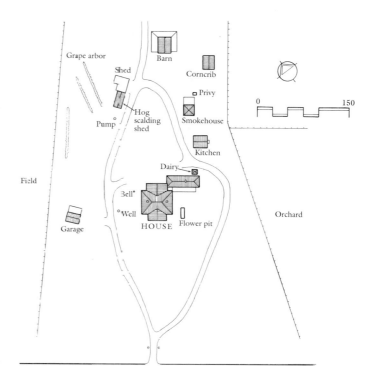

Figure 3.72. Walnut Grove.
Site plan by Carl R. Lounsbury.

woodlands they produced staves and turpentine. By 1860 the family plantation had doubled in size and slaveholdings. The plantation complex was built in the 1850s, during this period of expansion. Approached through wooden gateposts and a formal yard, the main house is a substantial, straightforward plantation house with simple Greek Revival detail and a two-tiered porch. In the back, a two-tiered porch with exterior stair opens onto an informal courtyard that shows a subtle hierarchy of construction types.[79]

At the rear corner of the house, a breezeway leads to a dining room finished to match the house. Next to it stands a tiny, hip-roofed dairy or milk house on stilts (fig. 3.74)—almost an

Figure 3.73. Walnut Grove. Farmyard.

Figure 3.74. Walnut Grove. Dairy. The dairy originally stood near the well but has been moved nearer the house.

outdoor cupboard. The kitchen, several feet back from the dining room, has a wide chimney for cooking, weatherboarded walls, sash windows, and a sheathed interior. Next is the smokehouse, which stands on lightwood piers and has horizontal flush boards and vertical battens nailed tight over a frame that is exposed inside. To the rear of the complex stands a single-crib, saddle-notched log barn with flanking sheds, a type long familiar in the region. The ensemble typifies many farmsteads in its concurrent use of different forms and techniques to suit various purposes. From the formal approach and portico of the house to the farmyard and log barn, the whole embodies a common sense of appropriate usage.

The small farm and the simple house, however, remained the basic unit of the state's architectural landscape. Among yeoman farmers like the German-descended Seagle family in Lincoln County, a strong continuity prevailed throughout the antebellum era. Andrew and

Annie Heavner Seagle, who married in 1856, acquired their farm in the mid-1850s from his father and another landowner. Cultivating about 20 out of some 180 acres, they raised their crops of wheat, corn, oats, and potatoes, husbanded livestock, and produced their own wool and flax. Small log structures form a loose courtyard that extends from the house to a double-pen log and frame barn at the back (figs. 3.75, 3.78). A rare survival of a specialized domestic structure is the little freestanding "beehive" domed oven covered with a gable roof (fig. 3.77), once a common feature on Germanic farmsteads in the region. Yet the Seagles, too, followed the period's modernizing trends on their own terms, for in about 1860 they moved their old log house back to become a farmyard building and erected in its stead a new dwelling (fig. 3.76), thus fronting their farmstead with a new, weatherboarded house of simple form and broad proportions, in keeping with the times.[80]

Figure 3.75. Seagle Farm, Lincoln County, 1850s.

Figure 3.76. Seagle Farm. House, ca. 1860.

Figure 3.77. Seagle Farm. Bake oven.

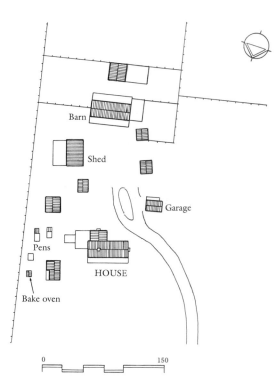

Figure 3.78. Seagle Farm. Site plan by Carl R. Lounsbury.

Transformations

New construction within existing traditions was only one way in which builders reconciled new and old. Many individuals also altered existing buildings to accommodate new standards. The Carson House in McDowell County (figs. 3.79, 3.80) is a dramatic example. It began as a one-room-plan log house built by Scotch-Irish immigrant John Carson, the personification of frontier entrepreneurship. Through land speculation in western North Carolina after the Revolution, Carson owned thousands of acres when, in 1793, he built his house on Buck Creek on the Catawba River. He soon added a second, similar structure joined to the first by an open dogtrot. By 1803, when a traveler described "old man Carson" as "very rich," his house had become a well-known stage stop on the road to Asheville.[81] When Jonathan Logan Carson inherited the place in 1841, he enhanced its business as a mountain inn and expanded his father's log house into a grand landmark. He built a two-story addition across the back and created a central-passage plan two rooms deep. He erected a deep, two-tiered piazza across the 60-foot frontage, raised a

Figure 3.79. Carson House, McDowell County, ca. 1793–95, ca. 1800, 1840–50.

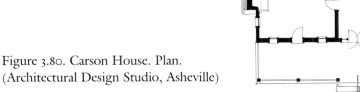

Figure 3.80. Carson House. Plan.
(Architectural Design Studio, Asheville)

high gable roof that spanned the whole 40-foot depth, and treated the broad gable as a pediment. Yet with all these changes, Carson left the old dogtrot passage open—transforming his dwelling to meet new needs and styles while retaining familiar spaces at its heart.[82]

New influences also permeated the long-conservative culture of Wachovia, as mid-nineteenth-century Moravians responded to changes in mainstream popular culture. Architectural transformations in the village of Bethania show a pattern opposite to that of the Carson House; there, families radically reordered their old log houses from the inside out. The Reich-Strupe-Butner House (figs. 3.81, 3.82) is a two-story, weatherboarded dwelling that, like its neighbors in the village, is built of logs and has a heavy German roof frame. The main rooms are heated by chimneys at the gable ends, and a kitchen wing extends to the rear. Yet this simple plan conceals a complex history.

Figure 3.81. Reich-Strupe-Butner House, Bethania, late 18th to early 19th century, remodeled ca. 1850.

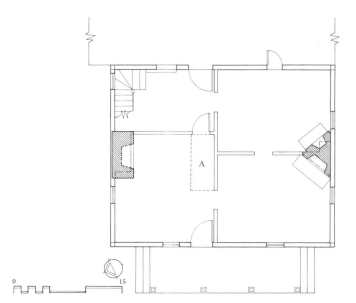

Figure 3.82. Reich-Strupe-Butner House. Plan by Carl R. Lounsbury. "A" marks approximate location of the original chimney.

Bethania, founded in 1759 as a farming village, was laid out as a traditional Germanic linear village with a double row of houses facing the road, nearby garden and orchard lots, and outlying fields—the only village in Wachovia to follow this plan. Soon after the Revolution, Bethanians replaced their initial log dwellings with two-story log houses that had Germanic plans focused around massive center chimneys.[83]

In the late 1840s, families began making drastic changes that must have reflected patterns of household life that no longer suited the old plan. One Bethabara resident, Emma Lehman, remembered the change in her own family's residence, the Shore-Lehman House: originally, "you entered a sort of passage, used for a kitchen; only one chimney in the middle, a mass of brick, one long fireplace in this kitchen, and another on the opposite side opening into the large sitting or living room." But then, "just before my sister's birth in 1849—it may even have been the year before—my father had changes made. The house was modernized. The large chimney with two fire places was torn out of the middle, and two chimneys . . . were built at each end of the house." Thus, "instead of one long passage or room we had a room just to the right as you entered; back of this was kitchen and dining-room combined." The family soon moved the kitchen, a grandmother's bedroom, and the shoemaking shop out of the center of the house into wings or separate structures. These alterations brought the household into conformity with broader trends that were separating domestic spaces and segregating household and trade life throughout America.[84]

In Bethania, Lehman remembered, various households "all remodeled their home about the same time." In Naaman Reich's house (plate 5), across the street from the Lehmans', the same process took place, leaving traces only in the attic and cellar of the great chimney that once filled the heart of the dwelling. Reich, a painter, took a further step to incorporate national culture into his house. He painted the walls of his parlor with a classical composition of trompe l'oeil stone blocks, dentiled cornices, and arched niches framing figurative paintings. These took the form of a genteel bouquet over the mantel and imaginary landscapes flanking the window on the street—one of a water-powered mill, the other of a peaceable kingdom scene, both evoking the popular image of an ideal America.

In Salem at this same time, Edward Belo undertook the first of two architectural transformations that displayed the metamorphosis of Salem from congregation town to modern business community (fig. 3.83). In 1849 Belo, a cabinetmaker turned merchant, sought permission from the Salem Board of Overseers to build a huge, three-part structure on two adjoining lots on Main Street, where his and his brother's store buildings stood. He planned two new brick buildings, each 20 feet wide and 50 feet deep, to be connected by a 110-foot-long frame structure recessed 6 feet and incorporating the existing stores. He planned to locate his store on the first story, his residence above. Although the concept far exceeded community precedents, the board approved it because there was "no question" that Belo could afford the estimated cost of $3,000, and, most important, because he absolved the community of any obligation to purchase the building if his lot lease were terminated.[85]

The decision reflected the shift in Salem from community control to the predominance of individual wealth and responsibility. Earlier in the century, rules had been modified to allow individuals some latitude in erecting buildings as long as they set a maximum value expected from purchase by the community if their lease was terminated. But Belo's case moved beyond this, for by voluntarily assuming all financial risk, he cut the cord of the lease system.

Belo was one of several energetic Moravian entrepreneurs who pressed for the modernization of Salem. His friend Francis Fries, for example, established local textile mills, helped found Winston as the county seat of newly created Forsyth County, and erected its Greek Revival courthouse; in 1854–56 Fries built for Salem College a main building with a great Doric portico that created a striking new presence opposite Home Church on the town square.[86] So, too, in 1856 Moravian leaders including Fries acknowledged that the lease system and the old rules that undergirded the congregation town had lasted past their time, particularly those that interfered with "that free & untrammeled action so necessary to the successful pursuit of business." In that

Figure 3.83. Belo House, Old Salem, Winston-Salem, 1849, 1859.

year, the lease system was dismantled and lots were sold in fee simple; other rules were amended "to conform to the new state of things," as Salem officially entered a new era of individualism and private entrepreneurship.[87]

In this new atmosphere, Belo's own "pursuit of business" thrived, including his establishment of an iron foundry. He expressed his success and the new "state of things" in a second transformation of his building into a monumental Greek Revival composition. In 1859 he proposed to add a third story with a central portion "supported by four Iron Pillars between which to place steps which would extend some 32 inches on the sidewalk"—an extension into the public street that still required permission.[88] The towering, three-story Corinthian portico dominates the Main Street facade, and the brick wings are pedimented flankers, linked by a 110-foot colonnade of the same order beneath a gallery of iron grillwork. Another portico dramatizes the family entrance on Bank Street, and a decorative iron fence, iron hitching posts on Main Street, and a recumbent iron dog and lion mark the Belo domain. Belo's complex, like the plantation houses and courthouses from Edenton to Morganton and beyond, expressed a new vision of progress, of popular neoclassicism, and of the modern individual's attainment of that vision through success in the market economy.

The Modern Picturesque

Although neoclassicism was the most universally popular architectural style of the antebellum period, by the 1840s and 1850s it was by no means the only possibility. The romantic movement's interest in the legendary virtues of the Middle Ages competed with the classic ideal of ancient Greece and Rome. Especially for English idealists, the Middle Ages represented an era superior to the irreligion and materialism of the mid-nineteenth century, and some saw the revival of medieval architectural forms as a force for reforming modern society.

Popular architectural literature promoted the "picturesque" as the ideal American architecture. Proponents of the picturesque asserted that its pleasing irregularity of form stirred the emotions, while the associations it stimulated in the knowledgeable viewer (or demonstrated to the less erudite) would uplift the morality of both the building's resident and society at large. Others simply enjoyed the prospect of new and varied fashions from which to choose. The models for the picturesque ideal included Gothic cathedrals, English parish churches, rustic cottages, and early Tudor mansions (an attractive source for Anglophile Americans) and also Italian villas, Swiss chalets, and myriad combinations of these.

In contrast to the Greek Revival's presentation in builders' guides, the picturesque style appeared mainly in patternbooks aimed at America's growing class of taste-conscious clients. Andrew Jackson Downing's *Treatise on Landscape Gardening* (1841) and *Cottage Residences* (1842) —which followed in the footsteps of Englishman J. C. Loudon's 1833 *Encyclopaedia of Cottage, Farm, and Villa Architecture and Furniture*—inaugurated a long series of American picturesque stylebooks. These were soon followed by Downing's *Architecture of Country Houses* (1850) and works by William Ranlett, Samuel Sloan, Calvert Vaux, and others. Defining the new styles as the special product and purview of the professional architect, these volumes did not show details for local builders to adapt; instead, they presented beguiling views of buildings as picturesque ensembles, complete with landscaping and even furnishings, to inspire the culturally alert client.[89]

In North Carolina, the picturesque movement concentrated in cities and along the new transportation routes that were extending the market economy across the state. Far from supplanting neoclassicism in popular taste, the picturesque mode was restricted to an urban and progressive rural clientele, for whom it remained one among many stylistic alternatives. Examples of the Gothic Revival and the Italianate style appeared alongside Greek Revival and traditional structures. Not until after the Civil War and the widespread industrialization of popular architecture did the picturesque mode penetrate ordinary building.

Wilmington: Urban Eclecticism

Antebellum Wilmington provides a vivid introduction to the architectural eclecticism of the era, for the interweaving of styles and influences in the city's architecture summarizes trends that had begun to reach across the state. With 3,000 people in 1830, the Cape Fear port had surpassed New Bern and Fayetteville in population to become the state's largest city, but from all accounts it was a sleepy place where trade was sluggish and the buildings old and unimpressive. Late in the 1830s, however, a new spirit entered the town as construction began on the Wilmington and Raleigh Railroad, which was completed to Weldon in 1840 and later renamed the Wilmington and Weldon. This and additional rail lines reaching west and south expanded trade. Lumber, turpentine and naval stores, and cotton left Wilmington's wharves, as ships brought in northern manufactured goods and guano, rum, and molasses from the West Indies bound for inland markets. The burgeoning trade attracted ambitious immigrants, and the population grew to 7,100 by 1850 and nearly 10,000 by 1860. Both the mercantile elite of established Cape Fear families and the working classes gained energy from northern and immigrant newcomers. Like New Bern in the Federal period, antebellum Wilmington underwent a full-scale transformation and by the late 1850s had rebuilt itself into the "most 'City-like' town in the State."[90]

Fires in the 1830s and 1840s destroyed great swaths of the city and stimulated construction of new buildings with an emphasis on fireproof materials and elegant styles. Local newspaper writers, quick to promote the city's ambitions, predicted that "a better order of buildings than those now in ruins will be put up," while another claimed that newly rebuilt stores on Market Street would "compare favorably in their fitting up with those of Broadway or Chestnut street [in New York and Philadelphia]." In 1846 a northern correspondent described the results: "Formerly the town had a rather shabby appearance, and reminded one of a certain yankee town, in which it was said, the people built old homes. But it has been almost destroyed by the numerous fires that have occurred here in the last thirty years, and the buildings erected during that period, and particularly within the last seven years, are of a much better character than those that have passed away; and many of them are elegant." Evaluating the city's architecture from a northern perspective, this writer singled out the "new and elegant" Custom House and "fine" Methodist and Episcopal churches for special praise, blasted the "apology for a Market House," and noted with approval the Presbyterian and Baptist churches and a Roman Catholic church then under construction. He ended by asserting, "Of all the places in the State, Wilmington has the most of go-a-headity of the yankees."[91]

It was not only the "go-a-headity of the yankees" that inspirited the new architecture, but also "yankee" architects and builders who had designed and erected the landmarks the visitor admired. Contact with northern cities was constant, and building materials, like other goods, arrived regularly from the North, along with a steady stream of architects and artisans from northern cities. Indeed, with few exceptions, antebellum Wilmington's leading architects and builders were northern men.[92]

Prime among the new monuments of progress was St. James Episcopal Church (fig. 3.85), which set a new tone and introduced men who redefined the city's architectural direction. In 1837, when the parish decided to replace its colonial church, the local paper advocated "a grand building—the most costly that the means of the congregation and its friends could possibly erect." The parish obtained a design from the noted Philadelphia architect Thomas U. Walter and hired New York architect and builder John S. Norris to execute the project in 1839–40. Chief carpenter C. H. Dahl came with Norris from New York; the masons were John Coffin Wood and Robert Barclay Wood, brothers from Nantucket, Massachusetts, for whom this was the first of many large construction projects in Wilmington.[93] St. James Church, completed in 1840, was the city's first example of the Gothic Revival style, and a bold and prominent statement it was, with its tall, crenellated tower and its roofline bristling with Gothic decorations.

Norris found patrons in Wilmington who brought him commissions for the city's first examples of the Italianate and academic Greek Revival styles. After the fire of 1840, which spared St. James but damaged the Bank of the Cape Fear, the bank directors (who included prominent parishioners from St. James) hired Norris to repair the building. By 1841 he had remodeled the bank (fig. 3.84) as a stuccoed Italianate building with elaborate cast-iron porches approached by

Figure 3.84. Cape Fear Bank, Wilmington, ca. 1841. John Norris, architect. (New Hanover County Museum)

Figure 3.85. St. James Episcopal Church, Wilmington, 1839–40. Thomas U. Walter, architect; John Norris, superintending architect; John C. Wood and Robert B. Wood, masons; C. H. Dahl, carpenter.

iron-balustraded stairs and a deep, bracketed cornice beneath a shallow hip roof.[94] In 1843 he gained the commission for designing and superintending the U.S. Custom House (fig. 3.86), a federal project that reflected the port's rising stature. Norris had already returned to New York, but his Wilmington friends won him the job over a distinguished competitor, Robert Mills of Washington. Norris designed a temple-form structure in a dignified Greek Revival style suited to its public purpose. Probably recalling a conversation with Norris, a newspaper writer displayed typical relish for modernity and classical terms in his description of the fireproof building of "celebrated Baltimore pressed brick," trimmed with Connecticut River red sandstone and featuring a "pedimented front" with "two antaes, and two columns, with capitals, after the manner of the Temple [*sic*] of the Winds at Athens."[95] Soon Norris left the city to take on another federal project in Savannah.

In Wilmington, builders continued to work in the new styles. In 1844 the Wood brothers built the Greek Revival–style Front Street Methodist Church and followed that project with St. Thomas the Apostle Church (fig. 3.88), built in 1845–47 for the city's small Roman Catholic congregation. Here they incorporated themes from St. James—crenellated roofline, prominent buttresses, generous lancet windows—into a small but boldly composed Gothic Revival church.[96]

The city's air of urbanity was enhanced in the 1840s by highly original essays in the Greek Revival style. Benjamin Gardner, a local builder-architect influenced by Norris, constructed and may have designed two prominent examples that possess a freshness and vigor extraordinary in the state's architecture. The Market House (fig. 3.87), which Gardner built at the foot of Market Street in 1847–48, repeated an established type of colonnaded, open-air market house but presented it in adventurously stylized terms. A cast-iron colonnade 187 feet long and 25 feet wide

Figure 3.86. U.S. Custom House, Wilmington, 1843. John Norris, architect. Destroyed. Drawing by John Norris. (New Hanover County Museum)

Figure 3.87. Market House, Wilmington, 1847–48. Benjamin Gardner, builder. Destroyed. (New Hanover County Museum)

Figure 3.88. St. Thomas the Apostle Catholic Church, Wilmington, 1845–47. John C. Wood and Robert B. Wood, builders.

Figure 3.89. John A. Taylor House, Wilmington, late 1840s. Attributed to Benjamin Gardner, builder.

carried a galvanized iron roof, and the east front presented a classical facade topped by a severely elegant, rectilinear belfry with an oversized anthemion cresting.[97] Abstracted neoclassicism went still further in the splendid residence of John A. Taylor (fig. 3.89), also built by Gardner in the late 1840s. Taylor, a native of New York, had investments in ferry, steamboat, and railroad enterprises. Built when granite-fronted commercial buildings were the pride of many American cities, his house of pressed brick, fronted in marble and reputed to have cost $30,000, represented the height of urban opulence. The facade is a sophisticated composition whose geometric severity emphasizes the luxuriousness of the material. Blocky pilaster strips rise through a broad frieze, framing an entrance bay set deeply in antis.[98]

By the 1850s, Wilmington builders had begun to weave a stylish architectural fabric well adapted to the city's preferences. Prominent among them were the Wood brothers, who were joined by James F. Post, a New Jersey carpenter who arrived about 1848 via railroad work in Petersburg, Virginia. Like many of their contemporaries, these builders could work from architects' designs, copy from architectural books available from Wilmington booksellers, and devise their own compositions, frequently repeating themes introduced by Norris in the 1840s.[99]

The Italianate style dominated domestic architecture among the mercantile elite and the middling merchants and leading tradesmen. Wilmington builders favored a set of distinctive motifs that included decorative vents in the bracketed frieze, canopylike porches made of steamed and fitted wood, and lavish cast-iron decoration. At the 1852 Eilers House (fig. 3.90), an array of iron filigree embellishes an otherwise simple brick house from the fence and gate to the posts and cresting of the porch.

Figure 3.90. Eilers House, Wilmington, 1852.

Two houses built side by side in 1851–53 by the Wood brothers, with carpentry by James Post, present two different faces of Wilmington's Italianate style. For the simple and elegant townhouse of Edward Savage (fig. 3.91), the Woods probably drew on the design for a "Cubical Cottage in the Tuscan Style" in Downing's new *Architecture of Country Houses*. Plain stuccoed walls, "simple and bold" Italian window dressings, and wide eaves on plain rafter extensions typify Downing's economical Tuscan mode. Wilmingtonians translated Downing's suggestion for a romantic, trellised veranda overgrown with vines into permanent cast-iron work that casts intricate shadows on the smooth wall behind.[100]

A more eclectic approach appears in the neighboring residence of Savage's sister Elizabeth and her husband, Connecticut-born merchant Zebulon Latimer (fig. 3.92). The Woods' $7,000 contract called for a brick house, stuccoed and jointed in imitation of stone and trimmed in Connecticut brownstone or granite. The builders applied a variety of stylistic devices, including quoins, an exaggerated, dentiled corbel course, and "Grecian wreaths" of concrete between the brackets of the frieze. Especially revealing are the contract's references to other local buildings—the veranda and the window frames to be like Dr. Dixon's, the piazza like Mr. Kidder's, and the inside carpentry like Dr. DeRosset's house—which demonstrate that by this time Wilmington builders had created a body of architecture that had become a local standard for good and stylish work. Client and builder also maintained a certain flexibility as construction proceeded; although the side porch was of iron filigree, bills for extra costs cited a "difference in front Portico" and "Wooden columns from Philadelphia" that produced a classical porch with the same Tower of the Winds order used in Norris's Custom House and other Wilmington buildings.[101]

Figure 3.91. Savage House, Wilmington, 1851–53. John C. Wood and Robert B. Wood, contractors; James F. Post, carpenter.

Figure 3.92. Latimer House, Wilmington, 1851–53. John C. Wood and Robert B. Wood, contractors; James F. Post, carpenter.

Creative and eclectic negotiation between local preferences and northern models continued as the scale and richness of Wilmington's buildings grew. The principal civic monument constructed during this period was the City Hall-Thalian Hall (fig. 3.93) of 1854–58. The L-shaped structure, 100 by 170 feet, has municipal offices in front and a theater behind, for which the city commissioned plans from New York's leading theater architect, John M. Trimble. The Woods and carpenter G. W. Rose were the contractors, and Post was the superintending architect. As the local paper reported in 1858: "The original plans were drawn, we believe, by Mr. Trimble of New York, but subsequently modified in some of their details. The pediment and portico on the Western or Town Hall front, for instance." In fact, Robert Wood replaced Trimble's small entry porch with a towering Corinthian portico, adjudged to "add elevation and dignity to the principal front." And although the theater plan remained generally faithful to Trimble's design, here, too, certain "details" were adapted "to circumstances" by Post and the officers of the Thalian Association. The result was a magnificent space with Trimble's characteristically fine acoustics and opulent fittings (plate 6). Galleries sweep in great curves, supported by iron columns decorated with spiraling grapevines. The proscenium arch was painted and gilded, and all was brilliantly lit with gas.[102]

In the late 1850s, in Wilmington as in much of the state, major architectural commissions proliferated. In 1857–59, a handsome new U.S. Marine Hospital was built from a design by Treasury Department architect Ammi B. Young. In 1857, too, Wilmington's Baptists sent their minister and a deacon north to examine buildings and consult architects, "with the view of

Figure 3.93. City Hall-Thalian Hall, Wilmington, 1854–58. John M. Trimble, architect; James F. Post, superintending architect; John C. Wood and Robert B. Wood, masonry contractors; G. W. Rose, carpenter.

securing the best plan for their new edifice." The building committee chose as architect Samuel Sloan of Philadelphia, who designed a church in the "Early English Gothic" style with two towers, the taller rising to a height of 197 feet. After Wilmington Presbyterians saw their early nineteenth-century church destroyed by fire, they too hired Sloan to design a large Gothic Revival church.[103]

Within sight of the big new city hall and churches rose a spectacular house that culminated the city's antebellum building boom—the Bellamy Mansion. Begun in 1859 for physician and turpentine plantation owner John D. Bellamy, the 45-by-51-foot house (figs. 3.94, 3.96) is surrounded on three sides by a 10-foot-wide, full-height colonnade. An air of opulence established by the Corinthian order is carried through the detail of the richly worked doorway, arched windows, and ornate classical cornices of the roofline and large cupola. Within, a simple, central-passage plan with flanking parlors is executed on a grand scale. The double porch at the rear is recessed behind a tall arcade, which shelters an outside stair. A full basement opens onto a paved subgallery—a familiar Wilmington usage—from which paths originally led to supporting buildings that included a slave quarter and laundry, a brick building in simple Italianate style (fig. 3.95).

According to family accounts, the idea for the design came from Bellamy's daughter Mary and was given to James Post, who had become a prominent local architect as well as contractor. Post provided plans and specifications in October 1859 and entrusted much of the work to Elvin Artis, a free black carpenter, and Rufus Bunnell, a Connecticut-born architect whom Post had

Figure 3.94. Bellamy Mansion, Wilmington, 1859–60. James F. Post, architect and builder; Rufus Bunnell, draftsman and architect; Elvin Artis, carpenter.

Figure 3.95. Bellamy Mansion. Slave quarter and laundry.

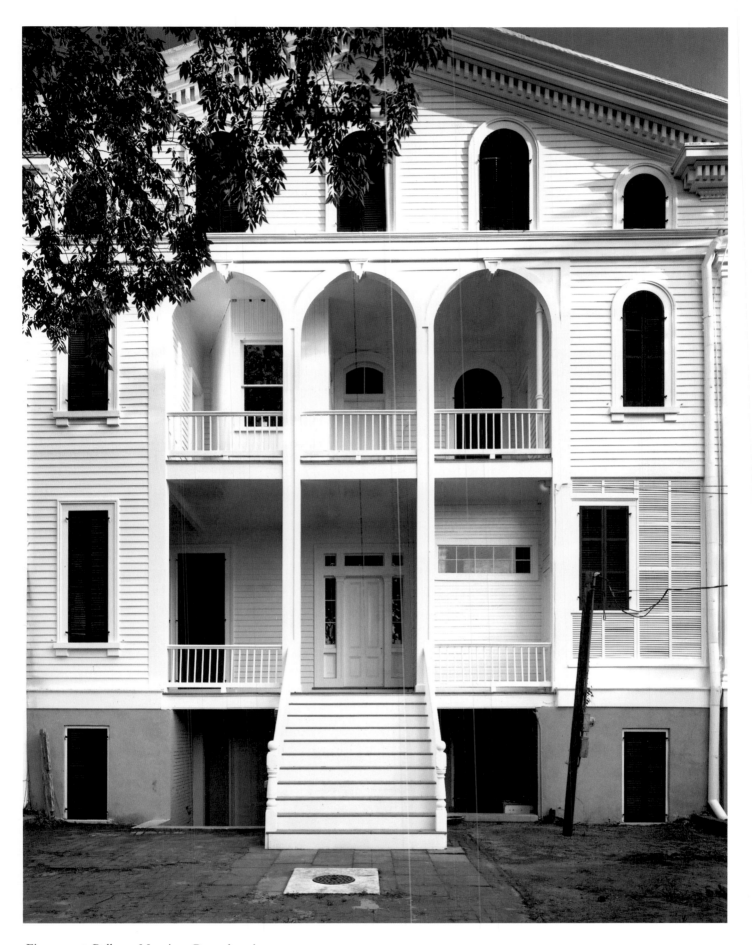

Figure 3.96. Bellamy Mansion. Rear elevation.

employed to help in his office. Bunnell recalled that the rich doctor was "a free trader" who "notwithstanding all the feeling that had sprung up against the northern people, still put the principle in practice and ordered from the North *every thing that could be cheaper [than] in Wilmington.* 'For,' he said 'that really carries out the good old democratic teachings to purchase in the lowest market.'" Post and Bunnell were "quite pleased at such a decision and so went on to make out all the bills and orders to be filled *in New York.*" Early in 1860, Bunnell sent drawings for window sashes, inside trim, and the 25-foot Corinthian columns for the "colonade" to the factory of Jenkins and Porter, on Canal Street in New York.[104]

By February, Artis had the heavy pine frame nearly completed and Bunnell drew up the roof framing; in March Artis finished the roof and "observatory." As summer came, Bunnell found that "Southern politics" and "Secession talk" were "fast growing hotter than the weather." During July Bunnell sent plans to New York for thirteen kinds of blinds and "was getting the residence pretty well off my hands, while hoping for a clear chance to go North." On August 5, 1860, he packed up his drawing equipment and "taking a seat on the moonlit piazza . . . waited the arrival of a baggage man who was to take our trunks . . . for the 2:30 morning train for the North."[105]

As the young architect headed north, he left behind a community whose new "city-like" character reflected the rich complexities of the period's architectural development. Such neoclassical buildings as the Bellamy Mansion and Custom House were interspersed with Gothic churches and Italianate residences. Ambitious clients took advantage of northern architectural sources through books, manufactured goods, architects, and builders. Through their participation in the newly eclectic marketplace of architectural styles, they gave physical expression of their ever-tightening connections with the national network of trade and profit.

Gothic Revival Church Architecture

In communities beyond Wilmington, groups and individuals who had strong ties to national ideological or business networks were the principal patrons of the picturesque. As in Wilmington, the Gothic Revival was introduced in Episcopal church architecture and spread into other denominations.

Within the Protestant Episcopal church, Gothic Revival architecture was part of an effort by High Church leaders to reform and strengthen the denomination in a society increasingly dominated by mainstream evangelical Protestantism. Evangelical Protestants emphasized religious feelings, the personal salvation experience, a service focused more on preaching than on ritual, and rejection of worldly indulgences. Critics accused Episcopalians of lacking piety and religious feeling and being altogether too fond of "fashionable amusements." Some Episcopalians shared these beliefs. High Church leaders, however, stressed the distinctiveness of their church by arguing for its exclusive claim to unbroken apostolic succession from the early Christian church and thus the validity of its sacraments. Through sacraments administered by duly ordained priests and a reasoned acceptance of Christian doctrine, they believed, one attained grace. At the same time, seeking to attract new members in an age of religious emotion, some churchmen embellished the traditional prayer book service with ritual and music designed to appeal to religious feelings. A few, influenced by the Oxford tractarian movement in England, also looked to devotional ritualism to elevate piety and reverence among communicants.[106]

Gothic Revival architecture provided an ideal means to attain these ends. It symbolized continuity with the medieval and ancient church, and it was believed to inspire religious feeling—"embellishments that delight the eye" might also "enlighten the understanding and elevate the heart." In these beliefs American churchmen also adopted views put forward by English idealists such as A. W. Pugin, who sought to reform society with a renewal of medieval virtues.[107]

North Carolina Episcopalians had used touches of the Gothic Revival in the first churches built after the 1817 organization of the diocese. In the 1830s, Bishop Levi Silliman Ives made the diocese a focus of High Church Gothic Revivalism. When Ives took office in 1831, the diocese had only sixteen clergy and about four hundred communicants. Convinced that High Church reforms would draw new members, and hoping to improve piety among lay members who had a reputation for worldly show rather than religious zeal, he encouraged the use of organ music, ritual, and symbolism—and of Gothic Revival architecture.[108]

The completion of St. James Church in 1840 for the state's largest and richest parish gave North Carolina a prominent model of High Church Gothic Revival architecture in the spirit of Bishop John Henry Hopkins's *Essay on Gothic Architecture* (1836), the first American book on the style. Architect Thomas U. Walter's design for St. James was a stronger composition than Hopkins's example, but it shared the symmetrical towered form, rectangular nave, and Gothic decorations. And, as the parish priest explained at the laying of the cornerstone, "the style of the building (which is Gothic), was peculiarly adapted to sacred uses . . . better calculated than any other to fill men with awe and reverence, to repress the tumult of unreflecting gaiety, and to render the mind sedate and solemn." When the diocesan convention met at St. James in 1841, Bishop Ives cited it as "a model of Church Architecture." Thus inspired, in 1842 William Mercer Green, chaplain at the state university, obtained a similar but simpler plan from Walter for the Chapel of the Cross (fig. 3.97) in Chapel Hill, which was completed in 1848.[109]

Meanwhile, a rarefied strain of churchmanship and Gothic Revival architecture was gaining attention. Influenced by the Oxford tractarians' emphasis on devotional ritual, first the Cambridge Ecclesiologists and then the New York Ecclesiologists (the term *ecclesiology* refers to the study of churches) argued that true religion required adherence to "correct principles" of medieval ritual and architecture, best exemplified by the English parish church. Rejecting the simple rectangular church with Gothic tower and trimmings, ecclesiologists advocated a return to scholarly medieval forms, honest expression of materials, the use of religious symbols including the cross, and—especially important to authentic ritual—an east-oriented and well-defined chancel that emphasized the priestly role and the eucharist.[110] Ives's growing interest in the tractarian movement as a way of elevating lay piety was paralleled by his advocacy of ecclesiology. He believed that architecture worked through the senses to move the spirit, and that the proper arrangement of chancel and altar, together with the "'dim religious light' of an ancient Gothic church," helped the worshiper feel the presence of God.[111]

Figure 3.97. Chapel of the Cross, Chapel Hill, 1842–48. Elevation drawing by Thomas U. Walter. (The Athenaeum of Philadelphia)

Figure 3.98. Christ Church, Raleigh, 1848–52; tower, ca. 1859–61. Richard Upjohn, architect; James Puttick and Robert Findlater, stonemasons; Justin Martindale, carpenter; John Whitelaw, tower stonemason.

It was through Ives's efforts that Christ Church (fig. 3.98) in Raleigh became the first of several important southern commissions for Richard Upjohn, the English-born architect who defined the High Church Gothic Revival in America. Although Upjohn had his differences with the Ecclesiological Society, his work embodied its principles, especially the revival of early English parish church architecture at its most eloquent. In December 1842, Richard Sharp Mason, the rector of Christ Church, opened correspondence with Upjohn, whose Trinity Church in New York was then under construction. Mason explained the congregation's need for a larger church, preferably of local stone and "Gothick in design. if the cost be comparatively with some other order not to great."[112] Upjohn responded quickly, but his fees exceeded the vestry's expectations, and the project was laid aside.

Three years later, in January 1846, Ives reopened the correspondence with Upjohn, inquiring on behalf of the vestry "whether a neat Gothic Church edifice could be built for 12,000 dollars, and what you would ask to furnish for them the necessary drawings." This time the project went forward. In October 1846 Upjohn sent Mason plans and specifications (fig. 3.99).

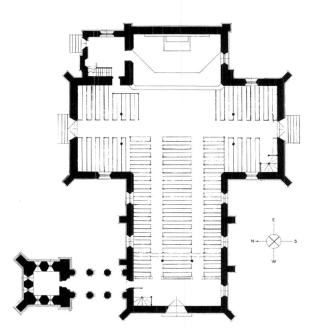

Figure 3.99. Christ Church. Plan. (Historic American Buildings Survey)

More than a year elapsed before a contract was let for construction, and at one point Mason feared he might have to settle for a brick instead of a stone building. Finally, in 1848, James Puttick and Robert Findlater, stonemasons who had come to Raleigh to work on the Capitol, and Justin Martindale, a carpenter, contracted to build the walls and complete the roof for $11,250. After further delays for lack of money, the body of the church was completed in 1852. Because Upjohn had designed the bell tower as a freestanding element, the parish could let it wait until money was available. A bequest permitted John Whitelaw, another Scots stonemason, to begin the soaring stone tower in about 1859, and Upjohn's 1846 design was finally completed in 1861.[113]

Christ Church was a magnificent accomplishment, revealing Upjohn's unique mastery of the English parish church mode and the skill of the artisans who built it. The lancet openings, cut cleanly into the weighty, rough walls, are emphasized by bands of darker stone, and the broach spire rises in a subtle display of the stonemason's art. In the cruciform sanctuary, the dark pine pews and massive roof truss lead the eye to the deep chancel (fig. 3.100). A local writer saw the church as "rather antique and striking in its general appearance than elegant or beautiful," but Frederick Law Olmsted, who found it "very beautiful." also noticed that it had "none of the irreligious falsities in stucco and paint that so generally disenchant all expression of worship in our city meeting-houses."[114]

Figure 3.100. Christ Church. Interior.

As the stone walls of Christ Church rose in the late 1840s, however, controversy was mounting within the diocese. To the dismay of diocesan leaders, Ives was moving closer to Roman Catholicism. Ives's theological statements, his tractarian ritualism, and, not least, his espousal of ecclesiology came under attack.[115]

In 1848 the growth of the church in western North Carolina prompted the construction in Wilkesboro of St. Paul's Episcopal Church (fig. 3.101), a small brick building that epitomized ecclesiological tenets in its steep roof topped with crosses and its deep, well-defined chancel. Designed by its minister, a student at the nearby Valle Crucis seminary established by Ives, St. Paul's gained praise in 1851 for its "very satisfactory liturgical arrangement" from the *New York*

Figure 3.101. St. Paul's Episcopal Church, Wilkesboro, 1848–49. William Grier, designer; D. Dameron, builder.

Ecclesiologist (which had in 1849 blasted the Chapel of the Cross for its painted and marbled woodwork, superficial decorations, and absence of a chancel).[116]

Also in 1851, William H. Battle, a member of the Chapel of the Cross, visited St. Paul's and saw it from a different perspective. The minister, he thought, was "too fond of the novelties which have of late caused so much agitation and confusion in our Church," which encouraged "enemies of the Episcopal Church to charge it with [being] . . . little else than Roman Catholicism in disguise." Battle added that "the style even of the church edifice is pointed to as proof of the allegations. It is indeed quite a quaint looking building, being the extreme of the Gothic style with quite a sufficiency of crosses on the outside as well as within. Its site too is romantic, and to an unprejudiced eye its appearance, though picturesque, is very pleasant."[117] For Battle, as for the *New York Ecclesiologist*, differences between the two small Gothic Revival churches took on great meaning in the climate of the times. The Ives controversy racked the diocese from 1848 to 1852. The matter culminated in 1852 when Ives traveled to Rome and converted to Roman Catholicism.[118]

Despite the furor over Ives's "apostasy," North Carolina Episcopalians continued to favor the Gothic Revival architecture he had encouraged. Among the churches that drew upon *Upjohn's Rural Architecture* (1852), which featured designs for an inexpensive church and chapel, were St. Mark's in Halifax (1854) and St. Paul's in Beaufort (1857). In 1856 the principal of St. Mary's, an Episcopal girls' school in Raleigh, obtained from Upjohn a customized rendition for the school's chapel. Upjohn also provided original designs for parish churches, including Grace Church in Plymouth, a brick church with side tower, which was begun in 1859.[119]

For the new Trinity Church in Halifax County, rector Joseph Blount Cheshire obtained from leading ecclesiologist architect Frank Wills a design for a towered, symmetrical brick structure with chancel. In 1858 Ives's successor, Thomas Atkinson, rejoiced over Trinity's fulfillment of the High Church Gothic Revival ideal: "The beauty of our ritual is made to appear. Aliens from the church come from curiosity . . . are struck by a service so different from, and so much more solemn and attractive than, any to which they have become accustomed, and resolve to come again."[120]

By the mid-1850s, however, the special associations of the Gothic Revival had begun to dissipate. As early as 1846, the central-tower, decorated Gothic church type had been adopted by other denominations: New Bern's First Baptist Church, designed by New York architects T. Thomas and Son, was a prominent example, built in 1846–48 by New Bern contractor Hardy B. Lane in the town's favored Flemish-bond brickwork and brownstone trim. In the late 1850s, Baptists and Presbyterians in Wilmington, Raleigh, and Rowan County, among others, were building Gothic Revival churches. A few congregations adopted an alternative medieval style— the early Romanesque Revival. Although some architects argued that the round-arched Romanesque style was best suited for nonliturgical churches, Baltimore architect L. L. Long used it for St. Anne's Catholic Church in Edenton in 1858. He repeated the popular central-tower facade and crenellated roofline but employed round-arched rather than lancet openings. By this time, both the Gothic and Romanesque styles had become stylistic choices within the religious as well as the architectural mainstream.[121]

Pioneers of the Picturesque

Paradoxically, in North Carolina's secular architecture, the prime sponsors of the picturesque mode—the romantic revival of the architecture of the Middle Ages initiated by idealists seeking antidotes to the ills of modern industrial society—were the individuals most active in bringing the industrial revolution, new transportation routes, and the expansion of commercial agriculture to the rural state. While generally avoiding the extremes of fashion, both for reasons of economy and from a preference for simplicity and symmetry, these leaders consistently favored the cottage, villa, and Tuscan modes as the architecture of modernity and material progress.

Foremost among this group were the Piedmont progressives who led the campaigns to improve the university and to build the east-west North Carolina Railroad to expand commerce in the Piedmont. They included John Motley Morehead of Greensboro, governor, textile developer, and railroad president; Edwin M. Holt, Alamance County textile pioneer; William A. Graham of Hillsborough, governor, railroad sponsor, and secretary of the navy; and David L. Swain, governor, university president, and spokesman for railroad development and social reforms. These men combined a state orientation with a broad outlook and an awareness of national trends as they strove to bring North Carolina into the mainstream of modern America.

The man who helped them realize their vision in architectural terms was A. J. Davis.[122] Davis, partner of Ithiel Town during the firm's work on the Capitol, had begun to practice on his own in 1836. Already proficient in the neoclassical style, he soon became a leading proponent of the picturesque. In 1838 he entered into collaboration with Andrew Jackson Downing, a landscape designer and writer devoted to realizing the picturesque ideal in America. Davis designed cottages and villas—first "English Collegiate," "American Swiss," and "Gothic or Pointed," and then "Bracketed," "Italian," and "Tuscan"—which Downing published in his books and in his journal, *The Horticulturalist*. This fruitful relationship established the two as tastemakers for mid-nineteenth-century America and boosted Davis's patronage.[123]

Davis's work in North Carolina came about through the efforts of Robert Donaldson, a native of Fayetteville who had become a successful businessman and patron of the arts in New York. Donaldson commissioned Davis to design Blithewood, his estate on the Hudson, and he also introduced Davis to Downing and encouraged their collaboration.[124] Donaldson, who maintained close ties with North Carolina and with his alma mater, the University of North Carolina, took every opportunity to get Davis commissions in his home state. In 1832 Donaldson had Davis design a library for the university, and in 1834 Davis planned a Gothic Revival church for the Catholic parish in New Bern to which Donaldson's father-in-law, William Gaston, belonged, but both proved too expensive to build. It was probably the Donaldson-Gaston connection that got Town and Davis the commission for the Capitol. Then, in 1843, Donaldson persuaded university president David L. Swain to consider Davis as the architect for a campus improvement plan.[125]

In late January 1844, Davis left New York on his "Trip South to Chapel Hill." In Raleigh he saw for the first time the Capitol he and Town had designed a decade before, and he dined with Gov. John Motley Morehead—a university schoolmate of Donaldson's. In Chapel Hill, he met Swain and various professors and began plans to improve the campus and remodel two existing buildings. Then he drove with Morehead to Greensboro, where he began designs for an expansion of the governor's residence, Blandwood. Before his trip, Donaldson had cautioned Davis, "You must take into consideration the materials and mechanics there—my opinion decidedly is to build the society halls of brick & to stucco them."[126] Davis heeded this advice. Beginning with Blandwood and the expansions of Old East and Old West at the university, he relied on roughcast stuccoed brick construction and the style he called Vitruvian Tuscan, which he recommended for its simplicity and economy.

At Blandwood (fig. 3.102), Davis presented a prototype that he and others would use for years to come: the symmetrical villa with front tower—an "Italian tower residence," as he called

Figure 3.102. Blandwood, Greensboro, 1844. A. J. Davis, architect; Joseph Conrad and William Conrad, builders. The wings were reconstructed in the early 1980s along the lines of the original ones, which were destroyed.

it—which he promptly published in the second edition of Downing's *Treatise on Landscape Gardening*. For Morehead, Davis thriftily retained an existing frame dwelling and added a front section of stuccoed brick; it was built by Davidson County contractors Joseph and William Conrad in one of the first of their many large projects in the Piedmont. Davis's clean-cut forms combine with simple door and window openings, deep eaves, and plain rafter-brackets to create a sleek modern villa. Arcades and wings create a horizontal ensemble that roots the house solidly in the landscape.[127]

Davis employed similar strategies in updating the university's Old East and Old West (fig. 3.103). He remodeled the plain, rectangular buildings to accommodate dormitory rooms and elegant quarters for the campus debating societies, Dialectic and Philanthropic, and gave both buildings low-pitched, bracketed roofs. Transforming the public aspect of the buildings with a bold and original gesture, Davis dramatized the twin ends that faced the open end of the quadrangle. Beneath low, bracketed pediments he raised pilasters flanking a tall, unbroken central opening and full-height blind panels. These "Davisean windows," with their unbraced vertical spaces, were architecturally exciting but, as Swain and builder Dabney Cosby saw them, structurally risky. When Swain suggested that masonry ties be placed across the opening, Davis responded, "We would give a *common place character* by inserting ordinary factory-like windows, wholly at variance with the other features of this front, which I wish to preserve in a grave, or *august* character, even at the hazard of a *contrast* with the sides of the building." In any case, he wrote, "it will be better (in my mind) that the building have one redeeming, characteristic feature, *one* good eye altho' that be Cyclopean in its character." Ever the romantic, he urged, "Let us look sometimes with the *heart* as well as the head, and more eagerly for beauties than for defects."[128]

Having satisfied Morehead and Swain, Davis attracted additional inquiries from them and their friends, to which he responded with a balanced awareness of national trends and local circumstances. In 1847, when he designed a church for Chapel Hill's Presbyterians, he discouraged an initial proposal for a Gothic church with a spire, explaining that the spire alone would exceed their budget, whereas the Vitruvian Tuscan mode was much cheaper and more expressive of Protestant worship, and its portico would be more "convenient, airy and pleasant than a lobby in a tower."[129] Additional work at the university included the ballroom and library, Smith Hall, for which Davis persuaded Swain to adopt a Greek Revival style rather than repeating the Tuscan mode of the church. In 1850 William A. Graham, former governor and secretary of the navy, asked Davis to redesign his house near Hillsborough, but after considering the architect's sketches in the English and Italian styles, Graham decided on a plainer scheme more in keeping with local architecture.[130]

Figure 3.103. Old West, University of North Carolina at Chapel Hill, remodeled 1844–45. A. J. Davis, architect; Isaac J. Collier and Kendall B. Waitt, contractors, Dabney Cosby, masonry subcontractor. (North Carolina Division of Archives and History)

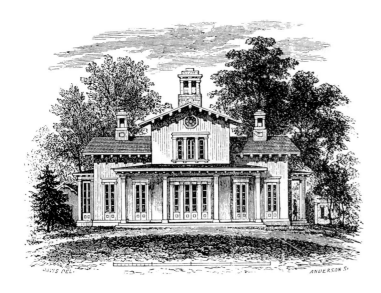

Figure 3.104. "Small Classical Villa," from A. J. Downing, *Architecture of Country Houses.* This plan was the model for E. M. Holt's Locust Grove, Alamance County, 1849.

In March 1849, Edwin M. Holt, the hard-driving and pragmatic entrepreneur of the Piedmont textile industry, wrote to Davis: "My attention has lately be[en] called to a design in the January No. of the Horticulturist, though that design does not suit me, yet a friend [probably Morehead] insists on my calling on you for a design." He asked Davis for a preliminary design and cost estimates but cautioned, "I would here remark that all the designs I have seen are better calculated for a Northern than a Southern climate you must recollect that we of the South never have the kitchen, the wash & wood house in our dwellings, our Kitchen is always in a separate building. I would also remark that our climate requires our sleeping apartments to be more roomy & better ventilated than the North." The busy industrialist advised, "I desire an immediate answer and should your sketch meet my views will immediately order the drawing plans—my workmen are to commence (on this plan) on the 20th Inst. and the time is short to correspond on the subject."[131]

Davis evidently responded quickly, for Holt's builder "came to work on house" on March 19 and finished the frame on March 31. After the masons laid the foundations, on April 20, Holt noted, "Raised my new house, fine day," and by summer he had his own version of Davis's "Small Classical Villa" (fig. 3.104), which still stands in rural Alamance County.[132] For his part, Davis must have taken note of Holt's remarks, because Downing's *Architecture of Country Houses*, published the next year, included a plan for a "Small Country House for the Southern States" with a commentary on the detached kitchen—a "peculiar feature in all Southern country houses."[133]

While Holt pressed Davis for adaptations to local domestic needs, Morehead encouraged him to design the North Carolina Hospital for the Insane in the forefront of national trends. This huge project allowed Davis to execute ideas for large-scale institutional architecture that he had developed in the 1830s based on English models.[134] In December 1849, Morehead wrote to Davis, directing him to "examine several of the crack, and most recently constructed institutions" and "give us the best plan in the United States." Davis was first to "run up some evening to Providence and see the Butler Institution" and also to visit asylums in Worcester and Springfield, Massachusetts, and Hartford, Connecticut. On his way south in 1850, Davis was to confer in Philadelphia with Dr. Thomas S. Kirkbride, a leading influence in American asylum planning, and tour the Trenton, New Jersey, asylum built under Kirkbride's direction. Then Davis was to inspect the Western State Hospital in Staunton, Virginia, and to consult with its director, Dr. Francis Stribling, who was "acquainted with our climate, and our habits." Thus, under Morehead's instructions and at state expense, Davis absorbed the latest advances in asylum design.[135]

The North Carolina asylum (fig. 3.105), which exemplified Kirkbride's theories of treatment, was a handsome public monument erected on a prominent site just outside the city of Raleigh, with spacious grounds for therapeutic gardening and farming. Rooms were arranged to de-emphasize the aura of constraint and to encourage recovery. From a central administration pavilion extended two long wings containing corridors lined by patients' rooms, each with its

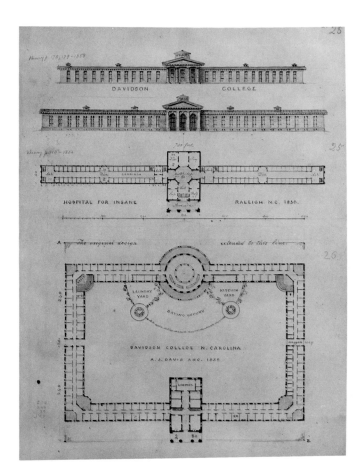

Figure 3.105. Drawing of the North Carolina Hospital for the Insane and Davidson College, by A. J. Davis. (Metropolitan Museum of Art, Harris Brisbane Dick Fund, 24.66.1403.)

own large window. Davis executed the 726-foot-long building in a bold version of his Tuscan style, with a powerful portico dominating the pavilion and pilastrades and tall windows punctuating the wings. The stuccoed brick building was equipped with advanced systems of running water, indoor plumbing, air and heat flues, and, after 1857, gaslights.[136] Contracts were let to established builders: carpentry to William and Joseph Conrad, who had built Blandwood; stonework to Eleazar Colbourn, quarryman for the Capitol; and brickwork to Dabney Cosby, who had executed Davis's designs for the Presbyterian church and campus buildings in Chapel Hill. Completed in 1856, the asylum was the largest building yet erected in North Carolina—"a great work," Davis later called it.[137]

In his last major project in North Carolina, Davidson College (fig. 3.106), Davis planned a 600-foot quadrangle that carried his institutional plan to its fullest form. Davis had emerged as the nation's leading college architect during a time of rapid expansion in the scale of American campus planning. Davidson College had just received a $250,000 bequest from Salisbury businessman Maxwell Chambers, which suddenly made the small Presbyterian school the richest

Figure 3.106. Chambers Hall, Davidson College, 1858–60. A. J. Davis, architect. Destroyed. (Davidson College)

private college in the South. School leaders promptly commissioned a campus plan that proved to be the grandest of all Davis's college designs. Davis bent his linear institutional plan into a Vitruvian Tuscan rendition of the traditional English quadrangle. Two great temple-form pavilions, one rectangular, one circular, were to face one another across the quadrangle. The college began by erecting one colossal pedimented pavilion with attached wings. This building, magnificent in itself, was completed on the eve of the Civil War, at which point construction stopped. Davis's concept of a great Tuscan quadrangle surrounded by villas dotting an ideal landscape was a vision never to be realized.[138]

Yet Davis had given the Carolina Piedmont a body of architecture vital to the state's changing self-image and to the American picturesque movement as a whole. In his North Carolina work, Davis displayed an inspired blend of informed taste and respect for his clients' needs and budgets. At the same time, his Carolina patrons offered Davis admiration and encouragement and, most important, commissions that enabled him actually to construct his developing ideas, so that his North Carolina projects constitute an important component of his work in America.

Patternbooks, Builders, and Regional Architects

During the 1850s, the picturesque styles spread quickly. A new generation of merchant and planter families had the example of existing buildings before them, and builders had incorporated new motifs into their repertoires. Architectural books proliferated. Downing's *Cottage Residences* alone ran through nine printings and sold over sixteen thousand copies by 1861. Popular magazines such as *Godey's Lady's Book* and, closer to home, the *Carolina Cultivator* also published villa and cottage designs. North Carolina newspaper articles and popular speeches urged residents to reject old-fashioned building forms and improve their rural architecture by adopting Downing's ideals—and thereby to elevate public morality, stability, and prosperity. While most North Carolinians paid little attention to such messages, the picturesque style gained increasing popularity among the planter and merchant class that resided along the arteries of trade.[139]

A few clients had their builders copy directly from published plates. For Cooleemee, their plantation house on the Yadkin River, Peter and Columbia Stuart Hairston chose an "Anglo-Grecian villa" from William Ranlett's *The Architect* (figs. 3.107, 3.108). At Cooleemee, Hairston had over three thousand acres and nearly two hundred slaves who raised corn, tobacco, and cotton. After a visit from surveyors for the plank road and the North Carolina Railroad in 1850, he observed, "If these improvements are carried out it may make this part of the Country worth living in. As it is, it is almost a misfortune to have any produce to send to market, the expense and trouble of getting it there is so great." In 1852 the Hairstons had begun to think of building a new house, and Columbia Hairston's brother, J. E. B. Stuart, then a cadet at West Point, wrote, "I have been looking for a Plan for Cousin P. but find nothing new or odd except some Gothic coops. I would send him a plan of these but am afraid he would be insulted."[140]

By 1853, when work began on Cooleemee, the plank road had been completed from Fayetteville to Bethania—"the Appian Way of North Carolina"—which improved Hairston's economic outlook and facilitated construction of the house. For although Hairston contracted with the experienced Davidson County contractors Conrad and Williams to build the house and employed his own slaves to dig clay for bricks, he obtained many of the materials from distant sources. The elaborate woodwork, including the mahogany handrail, columns, and carved trim, are said to have been made in Philadelphia, shipped to Fayetteville via Wilmington, then hauled up the plank road by oxcart.[141] The resulting house brought patternbook model to reality in splendidly expressive form. The house based on Ranlett's "Anglo-Grecian" plan, which had been illustrated in *Godey's Lady's Book*, was a far cry from a "Gothic coop." It was a symmetrical, classically detailed, cruciform villa perfectly suited to its location atop a knoll, with four equal wings radiating from a central stair hall (fig. 3.109) that was capped by a glazed cupola overlook-

Figure 3.107. Cooleemee, Davie County, 1853–55. John W. Conrad and John W. Williams, builders.

Figure 3.108. "Anglo-Grecian Villa," from William Ranlett, *The Architect*. (Henry Francis du Pont Winterthur Museum Library, Collection of Printed Books)

Figure 3.109. Cooleemee. Stair hall.

Figure 3.110. Henderson House, Lincoln County, ca. 1855.

ing the family domain. Within the skylit stairwell, the spectacular cantilevered stair sweeps grandly from floor to floor.

A more modest residence characteristic of the Downingesque "cottage" style was built by Lincoln County landowner Charles C. Henderson, probably for his son Lawson in about 1855 (fig. 3.110). The deep roof overhang, peaked front roofline, and broad, deep porch link the dwelling with such models as the "Small Country House for the Southern States" (fig. 3.111) in Downing's *Architecture of Country Houses*. The board-and-batten sheathing and light latticework posts typical of the Downingesque mode were not only stylish but suited to economical mass production. Such an unpretentious cottage might have appeared tame in some communities, but it represented a bold departure from Lincoln County's traditional and neoclassical architecture. Henderson, a typical patron of the picturesque, was one of the most important merchants in

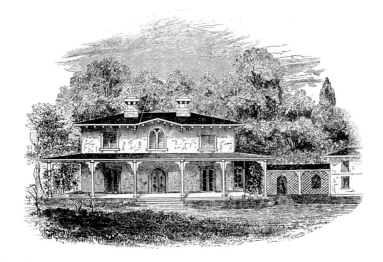

Figure 3.111. "Small Country House for the Southern States," from A. J. Downing, *Architecture of Country Houses*.

western North Carolina, proprietor of a tannery, president of the Charlotte-Lincolnton plank road, and a major contractor for the railroad from Charlotte to Columbia.[142]

In the port town of Edenton, physician Thomas Warren also selected a plate from Ranlett's *The Architect* as the model for his house, Wessington (fig. 3.112), but he adapted the design to local precedents by adding a double porch in front and two tiers of iron balconies on the sides. In Tarboro, the Tar River port serving burgeoning cotton plantations, builder Thomas Coates erected in about 1860 a brick cottage (figs. 3.113, 3.114) with a peaked roofline and center cupola, which was adapted from Lafever's *Architectural Instructor* (1858). A sale advertisement subsequently described it as a "new brick English Cottage" with a "nicely laid out yard," convenient to the railroad depot.[143]

An important thread of picturesque architecture ran along the Buncombe Turnpike that led from South Carolina to Asheville. Completed in 1827, the road wrought change along its route, and development quickened in the 1840s and 1850s. At Flat Rock near Hendersonville, the turnpike ran through a summer colony established by Charlestonians in the early nineteenth century. Charleston architect E. C. Jones inaugurated a stylish era when he provided his fellow Charlestonians with designs for summer pleasure as well as city elegance. In 1852 he designed St. John in the Wilderness (fig. 3.115), a summer parish church that was built by Ephraim Clayton, Asheville's leading contractor.[144] On the steep, verdant hillside site, approached through terraced family burial plots, Jones created a quietly picturesque church in a round-arched style evocative

Figure 3.112. Wessington, Edenton, ca. 1850.

Figure 3.113. Coates-Walston House, Tarboro, ca. 1860. Attributed to Thomas Coates, builder.

Figure 3.114. Cottage with cupola, from Minard Lafever, *Architectural Instructor*. (Henry Francis du Pont Winterthur Museum Library, Collection of Printed Books)

Figure 3.115. St. John in the Wilderness, Flat Rock, 1852. E. C. Jones, architect; Ephraim Clayton, builder.

of Italian hill churches. The facade combines a broad gable with a corner tower, while along the buttressed sides round-arched windows shadowed with blinds impart a lowcountry air. In the simply finished sanctuary, a handsome roof truss repeats the round-arched theme.

While the church was under construction, Jones designed a different picturesque effect for the Flat Rock Hotel, also known as the Woodfield Inn (fig. 3.116), which Flat Rock stockholders erected beside the turnpike. It was constructed by Henry T. Farmer, who soon bought the inn and ran it for nearly thirty years. The hotel blends the deep-porched, high-ceilinged informality of many nineteenth-century resorts with economical but stylish ornament. The broad rooflines drip with sawnwork, and artfully arranged latticework transforms the porch into an airy Gothic arcade.[145]

The picturesque mode suited the life of fashionable informality in a mountain setting where summer "cottages" stood on spacious estates, and driveways and plantings created a careful balance of privacy and sociability. Henry Farmer took a prominent role in Flat Rock's antebellum building boom, during which old houses were remodeled and new ones erected, some as Downingesque cottages, others as square residences with deep, bracketed roofs. Many Pines (fig. 3.117), with its remarkable group of outbuildings, dates from about 1859 and is among the least changed of the nineteenth-century houses in the area. Bracketed and latticed millwork adorns the house and gives the porch (fig. 3.118) the aura of a Gothic gazebo.[146]

Figure 3.116. Flat Rock Hotel (Woodfield Inn), Flat Rock, 1852. E. C. Jones, architect; Henry T. Farmer, builder.

Figure 3.117. Many Pines, Flat Rock, ca. 1859 and later.

Figure 3.118. Many Pines. Porch.

Figure 3.119. Jacob W. Holt House, Warrenton, ca. 1855. Jacob W. Holt, builder.
(North Carolina Division of Archives and History)

The taste for cottages and villas continued along the turnpike to Asheville. The Meadows and Rugby Grange, near Fletcher, are big, bracketed stone houses that resemble the Flat Rock work and may also have been inspired by Downing's "Suburban Cottage" in *The Architecture of Country Houses*. Newington, near Asheville, is a stone house with a peaked roof, bargeboards, and porch akin to the "Ornamental Farmhouse" in *Cottage Residences*. And Asheville merchant Joseph Osborne's towered brick villa (later the Ravenscroft School) probably derives from a "Cottage in the Italian, or Tuscan style" in the same book.[147]

Although replication of patternbook plates was the course urged by their authors, most builders used their motifs in the same selective way in which they had employed previous builders' guides, choosing and adapting certain elements into established building types and local preferences. Warrenton contractor Jacob Holt exemplifies this pragmatic and flexible approach to the picturesque mode. Holt had established his basic method in the 1840s: he used a few basic floor plans and house forms and applied to them various elements from Biddle, Benjamin, and Lafever, as illustrated in the Somerville House in Warrenton (see above). In the 1850s, Holt added new motifs to his repertoire. For his own house in Warrenton (fig. 3.119), he adapted a towered villa from Downing's *Cottage Residences*, and in remodeling Emmanuel Episcopal Church in Warrenton, he copied a "village church" from Sloan's *Model Architect*.[148]

But such copies were the exception, not the rule, in Holt's work. As he built for the wealthy planters and merchants along the Roanoke River and the Raleigh and Gaston and the Wilmington and Weldon railroads, he continued to employ the rectilinear form and central-passage plan common to his earlier work, including the characteristic pair of stairs separated by a louvered doorway. He adapted from Sloan's and Ranlett's plates such Italianate and Gothic details as brackets, round and lancet arches, quatrefoils, and trefoils as well as door and window designs, porch railings, and mantelpieces.

Figure 3.120. Cherry Hill. Mantel.

Figure 3.121. Cherry Hill, Warren County, 1859. John A. Waddell, builder, school of Jacob W. Holt.

Cherry Hill in Warren County (fig. 3.121), built by Holt's associate John A. Waddell, exemplifies the Holt school at its most graceful. Brackets emphasize the eaves and the porch and reappear in miniature on the pilaster caps. The sawnwork of the porch forms ogee arches with a bud or trefoil theme. The interior work is typical of the Holt shop (fig. 3.120), characterized by heavy moldings, a divided stair passage, and mantels in which the columned design from Benjamin is modified with brackets, trefoils, and arches after plates from Ranlett.[149]

Holt's contracts for his large workshop often included "painting the entire house in fashionable and best manner." In many cases, this included enrichment of carpentry work with stylish graining and marbling techniques. At Cherry Hill, doors are beautifully painted to resemble rosewood and other fine woods, and baseboards were treated to imitate black or gray marble (plate 7). The Watson House near Warrenton exhibits characteristic marbleizing of the stair risers (plate 8). And at the Taylor House in Franklin County, the front passage presents a dazzling display of painting, from the multicolor marble-block walls to the trompe l'oeil ceiling medallions and bracket cornices (plate 9).[150]

Throughout the plantation areas of the state, from the tobacco-raising counties of the north to the cotton-growing areas of the south, builders adapted picturesque decorations into standard house forms. The Warren House in Caswell County (fig. 3.122) exemplifies the grace with which carpenters applied the airy and inexpensive latticework porch and bracketed cornices to houses that were basically Greek Revival in form and finish. At the Buckner Hill House (fig. 3.123), built

Figure 3.123. Buckner Hill House, Duplin County, 1850s.

Figure 3.124. Buckner Hill House. Passage crossing.

in the 1850s within earshot of the Wilmington and Weldon Railroad in Duplin County, a bracketed cornice gives an Italianate flavor to a massive frame residence with square porch posts and
heavy corner pilasters executed in the region's Greek Revival idiom. The plan takes to its extreme
the interplay between interior and exterior space. When the wide double doors on all four sides
of the house are thrown open, the broad passages that meet at the center of the dwelling become
a vast interior porch, from which transomed doors and interior windows open into the four large
corner rooms (fig. 3.124). The eccentric and eclectic woodwork, Wilmingtonian in spirit, has a
boldness suited to the scale of the house.

Agricultural, Commercial, and Industrial Buildings

Progressive commercial planters also incorporated innovations, including elements of the
picturesque styles, into their agricultural buildings. They organized agricultural societies and
subscribed to such periodicals as Edmund Ruffin's *Farmer's Journal* and the *Carolina Cultivator*,
from which they gained ideas for renewing the soil, improving their crops and livestock, and
enhancing rural architecture. Some planters superficially updated familiar outbuilding types
with stylish new finish. At his Hermitage Plantation, located near the Roanoke River and the
Wilmington and Weldon Railroad, cotton planter John Tillery built a smokehouse, two-room

Figure 3.125. The Hermitage, Halifax County. Domestic outbuildings, 1850s.

kitchen, and dairy (fig. 3.125), all finished in modern board-and-batten sheathing, with the familiar eave vents of the dairy rendered in modern latticework.[151]

The plantation buildings erected by Paul Cameron exemplified most fully the philosophy of the modern antebellum planter. Cameron, said to have been the richest man in the state, delighted in managing family holdings of some thirty thousand acres that included the Stagville and Fairntosh plantations established by his grandfather Richard Bennehan and his father Duncan Cameron. Paul Cameron was a powerful and energetic proponent of internal improvements, an investor in factories and rail lines, a contractor for several sections of the North Carolina Railroad, and a strong supporter of the University of North Carolina, but his consuming interest was agriculture. A great admirer of Downing's works, he engaged endlessly in innovations on his plantation.[152]

In the 1850s Cameron began a construction campaign that put into effect his ideas of modern plantation architecture. For the plans of slave houses at the various plantation centers on the vast estate, he probably drew upon advice in southern agricultural journals, which often recommended brick construction as well as two-room plans with center chimneys. At Eno Quarter, Cameron built one-story quarters using this plan; the buildings were of heavy frame construction nogged with brick. At Horton Grove (fig. 3.126), another Stagville plantation center, he built larger houses, two stories tall, with end chimneys. The brick nogging provided an unusual measure of stability and warmth. He covered these sturdy structures with the latest modern walling of board and batten.

The barn at Horton Grove (fig. 3.127) capped the building campaign. In 1860 Cameron wrote to his father-in-law, Thomas Ruffin, who shared his interest in progressive farming, "I have a great wish to show you the 'best stables' ever built in Orange (at Stagville) 135 feet long

Figure 3.126. Horton Grove, Durham County. Slave house, 1850s.

Figure 3.127. Horton Grove. Barn and stable, 1860.

Figure 3.128. Engine house, McCulloch's Gold Mill, Guilford County, probably 1830s.

covered with cypress shingles at a cost of $6 per thousand."[153] The size of the barn alone was a major statement, and its formal composition relates it more closely to mansions and public buildings than to the standard gable-roofed barn forms. A massive, hip-roofed central block with a central entry is flanked by lower, hip-roofed wings. The central runway intersects a transverse aisle that extends the length of the building. The roof structure is a magnificent display of heavy framing in a modified queenpost truss. For the exterior covering, Cameron again chose board and batten, and he had the "V. [vertical] w/boarding" and "strips" milled locally at a Durham mill, thus giving his barn, like his slave houses, an exterior in keeping with current "rural architecture."[154]

The combination of picturesque motifs and functional forms also appeared in buildings erected in the direct service of commercial development. Most antebellum industrial buildings were straightforward, functional buildings, such as Edwin Holt's and others' Piedmont textile mills with their gable roofs, rows of simple windows, and clerestory roofs adapted from New England precedents; these were substantially altered or replaced as the industry expanded in the later nineteenth century. Only a few surviving industrial and commercial structures exhibit their owners' efforts at greater elaboration. One of the most splendid is the massive stone engine house at McCulloch's Gold Mill near Jamestown (fig. 3.128), in which the scale of the building is emphasized by the 20-foot-tall Gothic-arched entrance and a 70-foot smokestack that once served steam engines that ran the gold-crushing mills. The building's monumental form links the Gothic image with the era's twin magnets of steam power and gold.[155]

The main buildings at Company Shops, now Burlington, included Italianate railroad repair buildings and a hotel; top employees were housed in Downingesque cottages.[156] In New Bern, where the 1858 completion of the Atlantic and North Carolina Railroad linked the North Carolina Railroad to the coast and boosted the town's economy, a railroad officer built a row of Downingesque rental cottages opposite the company shops and depot. In Salisbury, the arrival of the North Carolina Railroad signaled rapid improvements in building.[157] The Purcell-Kluttz Drugstore (fig. 3.129), built in 1858 and probably designed by A. B. Hendren, was "more noticed and talked of than any put up in this place for some time," reported the local paper. "Its most striking feature is the extraordinary beauty of the brick work. No stuccoed building we ever saw approaches it; and with this pattern before our citizens, we shall be very much surprised if Salisbury has not done with outside plastering."[158] The dark red brick building, with its Italianate and Gothic corbeling and arched windows, presents a bold example of the commercial style that was to dominate the next generation's architecture.

By the late 1850s, modern picturesque landmarks stood in many leading towns. Castellated

Figure 3.129. Purcell-Kluttz Drugstore, Salisbury, 1858. Attributed to A. B. Hendren, architect.

Gothic styles were employed for some school buildings, such as the School for the Deaf in Raleigh, St. John's College, a Masonic institution in Oxford, and the Hillsborough Military Academy. Newspaper writers eagerly called attention to new examples of the cottage and villa styles. In 1859, when a Raleigh newspaperman took one of the period's characteristic booster tours to promote "Improvement in Architecture" in the city, he singled out an "imposing and effective" Baptist church in the Gothic Revival style, a bank in the Italianate mode, and three "striking and handsomely arranged" suburban villas.[159]

These stylish new buildings in Raleigh all happened to be the work of William Percival, an architect whose brief and flashy career in North Carolina (1857–60) capped off the antebellum picturesque movement with a flourish. In many respects Percival's work provides a pendant to that of A. J. Davis, for he served some of the same clients and used some of Davis's motifs in a manner that illustrates both individual differences and changing times.[160]

Percival, who claimed an English background in engineering, came to North Carolina from Virginia, where he had worked in railroad construction and had an architectural office in Richmond. He found his principal clientele among those who were enjoying the improvements brought by the progressive pioneers of the 1840s. Percival had imbibed the rhetoric of the picturesque, and he spouted it magnificently. To the Raleigh newspaperman touring city improvements, he explained the special genius of the architect: "The beautiful structure which towers up is the creation of *his* mind, no matter what hands wrought among the timber and stones of which it is composed. It stands out like a picture in the air, for the contemplation and admiration of all."[161] Percival's creations began with concepts that, by the 1850s, had become familiar elements in American popular architecture, but he reordered massing and plan as well as details to produce a body of freewheeling, theatrically eclectic architecture unique in the state.

The commission that brought him to Raleigh was the 1857 design of the First Baptist Church. The church demonstrated the broadening appeal of the Gothic Revival style and asserted the congregation's recent transition from a "struggling institution" to a position of stability and civic prominence. Executed in the "decorated English style of architecture," the church has an entrance tower dramatized by tall pinnacles and a "lofty spire" 160 feet tall. Facing across the capitol square toward Upjohn's Christ Church (which in 1857–59 still lacked its tower), the building was praised as "highly creditable to the respectable denomination which erected it, and to the architect who designed it."[162]

As the Baptist church went up, Percival gained so many commissions that he established a Raleigh office. Some of these put him in charge of jobs that might previously have gone to Davis—prominent churches, villas for planters and industrialists, renovations to the Capitol, and new buildings at the University of North Carolina.

University president David L. Swain had been corresponding with Davis about plans to accommodate a growing student body, but Davis was busy at this time, and his 1856 trip to North Carolina focused mainly on the big job at Davidson College. He did offer Swain suggestions for

Figure 3.130. New West, University of North Carolina at Chapel Hill, 1858; altered, 1920s. William Percival, architect; Thomas Coates, builder. (North Carolina Division of Archives and History)

remodeling some existing buildings, which the faculty rejected. The trustees pressed for two large new buildings. In 1858 Percival was hired to design New East and New West (fig. 3.130) to flank Davis's Old East and Old West.[163] He took his cue from Davis's precedents—being "in a measure governed by . . . the old buildings" so that "hereafter the university buildings may present an effective and harmonious appearance"—but restated the Tuscan idiom with his own flair for drama. He persuaded the building committee to place his buildings perpendicular rather than parallel to Davis's pair. He broke up the massing of the new buildings with raised central pavilions and articulated the walls with pilasters and strong cornice lines. And he made New East a story higher than New West to compensate for the sloping terrain, so that the bold cornices form a level horizontal line across the sky. This strong counterpoint to the verticals of the Davisean windows at Old East and Old West unified the ensemble and gave an "effective and harmonious" aspect to the main north view of the campus.[164]

For the Caswell County Courthouse, in the tobacco plantation town of Yanceyville (fig. 3.131), Percival began with the familiar symmetrical, pavilioned facades and a piano nobile but rendered these in new terms—round arched openings and large arched pavilions accented by corbeling and acanthus modillions. The loggia of the entrance pavilion is at once romantically Italian and reminiscent of the upper portico of the Capitol. Its pilasters feature capitals of corn and tobacco, evocative both of Caswell's tobacco-based wealth and of the agricultural orders at

Figure 3.131. Caswell County Courthouse, Yanceyville, 1858. William Percival, architect.

Figure 3.132. Caswell County Courthouse. Courtroom.

Davis's Smith Hall in Chapel Hill and the U.S. Capitol. The courtroom (fig. 3.132), lit by tall, arched windows beneath a molded and coffered ceiling, provides an opulent setting for the drama of the law.

Percival employed similarly rich themes in his suburban villas. He designed the Barracks (fig. 3.133) in Tarboro for William S. Battle, who in 1854 had inherited from his father the land, slaves, and cotton mills along the Wilmington and Weldon Railroad that made him Edgecombe County's richest man.[165] For Battle's suburban residence, one of several on the outskirts of Tarboro, Percival endowed an Italian villa with the symbolic dignity of a Corinthian portico. The symmetrical plan features a ceremonial rotunda with a cantilevered gallery and cupola skylight that Percival evidently copied from the Capitol. He created a similar effect at Montfort Hall,

Figure 3.133. The Barracks, Tarboro, 1858. William Percival, architect.

located on a suburban estate alongside the North Carolina Railroad near Raleigh and built for William Montfort Boylan, another free-spending heir of an energetic railroad man and planter. For Carter Braxton Harrison's suburban mansion (fig. 3.134) beside the Raleigh and Gaston line, Percival reassembled his bracketed cupola, round-arched windows, and pavilions in a new and restlessly unorthodox form, shifting the cupola to one side, setting the entry at a corner, adding balconies, and projecting the front pavilion between jutting, angled towers.[166]

Percival took a more restrained approach in designing Calvary Church (fig. 3.135) in Tarboro. The rector, Joseph Blount Cheshire, had previously built a Gothic Revival church at Scotland Neck's Trinity Parish from Frank Wills's designs, and as an amateur landscape gardener he had a well-developed taste for the picturesque. Cheshire worked out the design with Percival late in 1859, and, with the aid of a handsome watercolor rendering, he obtained approval from the building committee in January 1860. In a variation of the English parish church idea, Percival designed a simple nave-plan church with two unequal towers, their spires 60 and 120 feet high. In the spring of 1860, contractor Thomas Coates began work on the brick walls. At that point, Percival vanished. He left North Carolina with several major projects underway and was last heard from in Richmond in June 1860.[167]

Just outside Tarboro, while the walls of Calvary Church rose, work was also nearing completion on a plantation complex that seemed to incorporate all the threads of change that had by 1860 wound their way into the countryside. At Coolmore (fig. 3.136), Baltimore architect E. G. Lind designed a splendid Italianate villa for J. J. W. and Martha Powell; Powell was a physician and one of the county's largest cotton planters. Lind sent a builder, N. A. Sherman, down from Baltimore and ordered most of the building materials from that city as well—not only the usual glass, hardware, and paint, but also lumber, brackets, ornaments, and the stair rail. He also had a framed lithograph of the residence (fig. 3.137) printed in Baltimore. Steamboats churning up the

Tar River brought most of these goods, though the Wilmington and Weldon Railroad also linked the Powells with national markets.[168]

Around the house, the domestic outbuildings stand in a neat courtyard, each one a miniature villa fitted out with cross-gabled or hipped roof and a cupola to match the residence: the dairy, the smokehouse, a servants' dwelling, the gas house that provided light for the dwelling, and the stable (figs. 3.138, 3.139, 3.140, 3.141, 3.142, 3.143).

The spacious house has a central-passage plan, with the passage divided into a vestibule, a skylit stair hall, and a back hall. A full array of goods from Baltimore—sets of furniture, carpets and oil floorcloths, wallpaper and curtains, pictures and decorations, and a large set of imported dishes—fills the rooms with exuberant pattern and color. To cap off his creation, Lind sent a fresco painter named Mr. Dreyer to enrich the principal rooms. The entry vestibule (plate 10) is a small, spectacular chamber painted in cream and chalky blue and crowned with gilded moldings.

Figure 3.135. Calvary Church, Tarboro, 1860–67. William Percival, architect; Thomas Coates, builder.

Figure 3.134. Harrison House, Raleigh, 1859. William Percival, architect. Destroyed.
(North Carolina Division of Archives and History)

Figure 3.136. Coolmore, Edgecombe County, 1859–60. E. G. Lind, architect; N. A. Sherman, builder;
Mr. Dreyer, fresco painter.

Figure 3.137. Coolmore.
Lithograph by E. G. Lind.

The flanking parlors are rich with floral painting and paper, gilding, and molding—the ladies' parlor in pastels, the gentlemen's (plate 12) in darker hues. The pièce de résistance is the stair hall rising to the cupola (plate 11): the spiraling stair and the curving walls are frescoed in a grandly conceived and subtly rendered program of trompe l'oeil paneling and niches, creating an effect that transports the visitor to thoughts of the Po rather than the Tar.

Coolmore was completed late in 1860 as predictions of war intensified. In December Lind sent Powell a few last bills. The Baltimore workmen finished their tasks and returned home. Within a few months, the builders in Tarboro boarded up the windows of Percival's Calvary Church, leaving it to stand unfinished until 1867. And in Wilmington, the minister watched anxiously as work proceeded on Samuel Sloan's First Baptist Church: in August 1860, "went to the new church—it has grown some. But O, I feel so sad at the thought of the troublous times. Lord shall the work cease?"; in December, "at work on the west side, turning arches over the windows. . . . Heard cannon firing at the news of the secession of South Carolina"; on April 16, 1861, "Fort Sumter bombarded all night! . . . The windows on towers of our church raised to-day. So glad"; on July 30, "The doors and windows are being closed and the lumber piled."[169]

In Wilmington, Tarboro, and elsewhere along the tracks of steam-propelled progress, North Carolinians had created a new architecture, an architecture of full participation in the national mainstream of trade and taste. For the modern merchant or planter, regional forms and traditional methods were subsumed by an emphasis on the national, the historical, the romantic image. Ironically, that hard-won interconnectedness had come just as the nation was about to be torn apart by war.

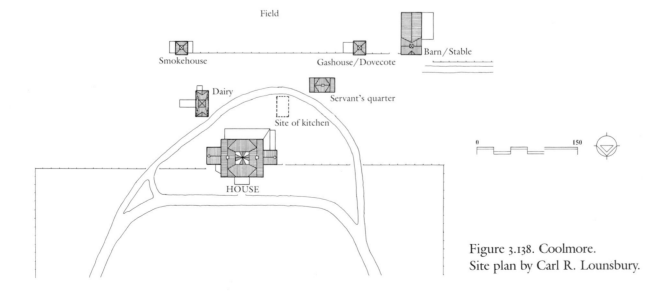

Figure 3.138. Coolmore.
Site plan by Carl R. Lounsbury.

Figure 3.139. Coolmore. Dairy.

Figure 3.140. Coolmore. Smokehouse.

Figure 3.141. Coolmore. Servants' house.

Figure 3.142. Coolmore. Gas house.

Figure 3.143. Coolmore. Barn.

CHAPTER 4

The Late Nineteenth Century, 1865–1900

Until after the close of the war 1861–65 . . . town people visit[ed] in the country on holidays and Sundays . . . for
social enjoyment and festive occasions. The reverse is the rule now. Everybody who can, has left the country
and lives in the towns and cities; and the people of the country districts enjoy few of the real comforts, and
scarcely any of the luxuries of life.
—Lizzie Wilson Montgomery, *Sketches of Old Warrenton*

After the Civil War, sweeping changes in the economic and social structure of North Carolina pulled waves of people into the towns and cities. The war had left thousands of farmers in
debt, and with emancipation, thousands of newly free but landless blacks sought work on new
terms. The tenant system developed, and with it the crop-lien system. Workers and landowners,
small and large, were drawn into a spiral of debt and cash-crop production that increased
dependence on a single money crop—most often cotton or tobacco—and reduced diversified,
self-sufficient agriculture. Farm families found their livelihoods increasingly at the mercy of the
erratic national and international markets and the costs of seed and fertilizer, railroad transportation, and credit. New fence laws eliminated the customary open range throughout most of the
state, and the old forest society retreated to the margins of the economy and the landscape.
Although the state remained overwhelmingly rural and agricultural, and although country stores
and local mills continued as the familiar centers of rural neighborhoods (fig. 4.2), the balance of
power and wealth had shifted from the plantation to the city, and North Carolinians streamed off
the farms and into the burgeoning towns and factories.

In town, change was palpable in the air. Politically, there was turmoil and tension as North
Carolina's Republicans and Conservatives struggled for ascendancy, renegotiated relations with
the federal government, and established new roles for black and white citizens and their leaders.
Amid the chaos, high hopes, bitter rivalries, violence, and excitement, there was a continuing
focus on economic recuperation. Although some would never recover from the war and the
changes it had wrought, many others were eager to put the war behind them and create new lives
in the new day. Fortunes were made and lost. Newspapers were full of hopeful boosterism,
praising new investments and singling out every sign of renewal.[1]

In the press and among business leaders, the recurrent theme was modernization and industrialization. "Property here cannot advance," wrote one North Carolinian, "unless interests other
than selling goods to the farmer are developed. . . . The solution is not difficult. We want
factories."[2] Textile manufacturing was reborn on the streams of the Piedmont, and soon the
industry spread across the state. Tobacco factories started small but quickly expanded in many
Piedmont towns; Durham and Winston mushroomed into tobacco manufacturing cities. Dozens
of small mercantile communities blossomed along the railroad lines. By the end of the century,

Figure 4.1. Biltmore House, Asheville, 1890–95. Richard Morris Hunt, architect. Swimming pool.

Figure 4.2. Webb's Mill, Nash County. This water-power site on the Tar River has had a gristmill operation for as long as 200 years. The present building, which dates from the turn of the century, is typical of many late-19th-century and early 20th-century mills in its traditional form and heavy timber construction.

Charlotte, the cotton-manufacturing center of the South, was pushing past Wilmington to become the state's largest city.

Architectural and economic developments of the late nineteenth century fall into two principal phases: a period of recovery and renewal lasting from the end of the war in 1865 to the mid-1880s, and a period of expansion from the mid-1880s to the end of the century. During the fifteen or twenty years immediately following the war, architectural innovations seen only occasionally before the war entered the popular mainstream. The cottage and villa styles were translated into myriad forms, brightening the recovery period, gracing the industrial revolution, and permeating the newly industrialized popular architecture from lavish town mansions to simple farmhouses. Churches and public buildings continued familiar forms, though, like houses, many displayed newly ornate renditions of established styles. Many houses and agricultural buildings, whether of frame or log construction, also retained familiar patterns or changed in response to functional rather than stylistic developments. These general trends, emerging in the late 1860s and early 1870s, created types and styles of buildings that continued into the early twentieth century.

In the 1880s, paralleling the rapid expansion of industry and burgeoning city growth, construction took off as well. In 1885 one Winston builder averaged a house every two weeks, and two years later, another city firm was building a house every ten days. The local newspaper termed it a "building boom," estimating the construction in 1885 at about $200,000 and the next year's work at $250,000.[3] Architecture grew more complex, eclectic, and monumental. Suburban neighborhoods developed as cities expanded and installed trolley lines. Public architecture, especially that of courthouses and federal post offices, became more ornate. Protestant churches adopted dramatically new plans. Increasingly elaborate architectural expression included new versions of the Gothic and Romanesque modes and, most spectacular of all, the Queen Anne style, whose restless massing and ebullient exploitation of the glories of mass-produced ornament captured the spirit of the age.

The Industrial Picturesque

In describing the building that accompanied North Carolina's economic rebirth, such watchwords as "artistic," "tasty," "modern," and "city-like" were ready on the pens of newspaper editors, who were continually on the lookout for signs of progress. Pride in renewal and rebuilding was interwoven with the knowledge and fear that the South was far behind northern cities. This was expressed both in a frank emulation of northern models and in a recurrent local and sectional defensiveness. New architectural styles, like new factories, new railroad lines, and simply the construction of new buildings, gave cause to celebrate, and the more "ornate" and "modern" the new buildings the better.[4]

"Artistic" and "modern" architecture expressed a frank and exuberant delight in the changes made possible by the new industrial age. Mass production of lumber and nails encouraged carpenters to abandon the familiar mortise-and-tenon frame in favor of the lighter, faster balloon frame made of small framing members nailed together. This new frame made building cheaper and accommodated ever more complex forms and plans, which correlated with the popular domestic ideal of many specialized rooms for formal entertaining, family life, and individual privacy. Steam-powered factories churned out millions of turned balusters, paneled doors, and sawn brackets, as well as mile after mile of sized planks, framing lumber, and weatherboards. They produced millwork in any shape, size, or finish, fast and cheap and in endless supply. New buildings sported a wealth of sawn, turned, and incised decorations across porches, around windows, and along rooflines. Factories also stamped out millions of bricks cheaper than ever before, and they were loaded onto railroad cars that sped them to the booming towns throughout the state. Brick buildings went up in every growing town. In three months during 1885 alone, it was said, a single building firm in Winston bought and laid one-and-a-quarter million bricks.[5]

Interiors also displayed mass-produced components. At a minimum, builders commonly "ceiled" walls and ceilings with narrow tongue-and-groove sheathing. Simple mantelpieces, paneled doors, and windows streamed out of sash-and-blind factories and into all but the cheapest houses. The middle range of homes usually had stairs with turned balusters and a decorated newel and, atop the doorway that separated entry hall from stair hall, a grillwork of fancy spindles. Mantels ranged from simple post-and-lintel models, usually with a slightly peaked fire opening, to elaborate compositions of wood or marble-painted slate, with columns, turnings, decorative incised patterns, and applied ornament. In the costliest houses, fire openings were outlined with brilliant tiles, mirrors glittered in overmantels, and rooms gleamed with dark paneling and stairs with polished turnings, and rich colors glowed on the walls (plate 13).

Thus form followed not only function but fabrication: just as the best-quality buildings of an earlier age had displayed the hours of skilled artisanry, so these new buildings exhibited the accomplishments of the machine age. A national architecture, child of the patternbook, the factory, and the railroad, made its way throughout the upper and middle levels of building. Local and regional builders quickly incorporated the new themes into their repertoires. Only a few architects operated in the state, some of whom had established practices before the war, while others arrived afterward in search of work. Many clients commissioned work from distant urban professionals, but, in contrast to the patronage patterns of the antebellum era, North Carolinians no longer employed the foremost architects in the country but instead commissioned designs from the middle rank of a greatly expanded profession.

Figure 4.3. Cape Hatteras Lighthouse, Dare County, 1869–70. Dexter Stetson, builder.

Recovery-Era Beginnings and Continuing Patterns

The picturesque modes that A. J. Downing and other romantic modernizers had promoted during the antebellum period as the expression of individuality provided the universal language for a standardized, mass-produced national architecture in the postwar years. Prominent examples are the lighthouses and lifesaving stations built by the federal government along the coastline in the 1860s and 1870s, as the nation recovered from war and assumed a new role in international trade. Federal lighthouses had been built along the Outer Banks of North Carolina from the early national period onward, but the lighthouses of the later nineteenth century took on a new scale and grandeur.

The Cape Hatteras Lighthouse (fig. 4.3) was built in 1869–70 as a part of the Light House Board's ambitious plan for a comprehensive system of markers from Cape Hatteras to Cape Henry. Towering structures equipped with first-order (the largest and most powerful) Fresnel lenses were planned to enable ships to "pick up sight of the light ahead before losing sight of the one astern." The board took as prototype the 150-foot-tall Cape Lookout Lighthouse, which had been built in 1857–59. Top priority was placed on the Hatteras light, and in 1867 Congress authorized $75,000 to replace the old lighthouse there with a new structure standing 180 feet high—"the most imposing and substantial brick lighthouse on this continent, if not in the world." The design, though patterned after that of Cape Lookout, was much taller and thus more massive. Dexter Stetson directed the construction, which required a tramway from the wharf to carry the brick and stone arriving from Baltimore and Philadelphia. When a base of pilings proved impracticable, Stetson devised a foundation of yellow pine timbers set in the dense sand below water level. Above ground, the base of the tower is a granite pedestal, from which rises the tapering brick shaft. The boldly bracketed cap of iron and glass has a balustraded balcony and catwalk and a cupola in which the large flashing lens was installed. In 1873, to help sailors distinguish among the nearly identical lighthouses lining the coast, the Light House Board ordered them to be painted in distinctive patterns, and Hatteras received its spiral bands of black and white.[6]

Currituck Beach Lighthouse (fig. 4.5), built in 1874–75, was the last of the great first-order lighthouses to be erected on the Outer Banks; it rises 150 feet from its base to the lantern.[7] It follows the standard design, and it, too, combines fine masonry work—beautifully laid dark-red brick with stone trim, left unpainted—with an elegantly bracketed iron and glass cap. At the base is a small entry building in the cottage style, its doorway sheltered by a kingpost gabled hood.

Figure 4.4. Currituck Beach Lighthouse. Keeper's House, 1876.

As a domestic complement to the lighthouse, the Light House Board published plans for a "Keepers Dwelling for a First Order Light House"—a customized version of the Downingesque cottage. The frame, weatherboarded cottage built near the Currituck Lighthouse (fig. 4.4) was prefabricated, complete with decorative battens and kingpost ornament, and the components were marked for assembly on location—"Main Building, A," "Left Wing, Top Plate," and so forth. It was completed in 1876. The cruciform plan is divided into a duplex, for two men were required to operate the light around the clock. There are two separate front porches, and, in back, two parallel paths (once divided by a fence) lead from the dwelling to the lighthouse. On

Figure 4.5. Currituck Beach Lighthouse, Currituck County, 1874–76.

either side of the divided yard, each family had its own matching outhouse and storage build-ings—an outpost of picturesque domesticity in which two families lived in intimate isolation.[8]

A similar style emanated from the U.S. Life-Saving Service, which, like the Light House Board, embarked on a building campaign after the war. In 1874 twenty-two new lifesaving stations were built, including seven in North Carolina.[9] The small wooden building at the Chicamacomico Life-Saving Station, subsequently converted to a boathouse, was one of that vanguard generation of functional, multiuse stations. Each one was a steep-gabled, two-story house, measuring 18 to 20 feet wide by 40 to 45 feet long. On a windswept barrier island, the crews cooked and ate and stored their boats on the first story and slept in quarters above. They climbed to the observation deck to scan the horizon and, on a moment's notice, dragged their boats through the big doors and pushed off into wild seas. Pine weatherboards, cypress or cedar shingles, foundations of cypress or locust foundation posts, and strong shutters suited the build-ings to the rigors of their environment. In contrast to the plain, barnlike buildings that had preceded them, the lifesaving stations of the 1870s displayed a new attention to architectural image, a trend that would continue in subsequent generations of stations. "Their architecture is of the pointed order, somewhat in the chalet style. . . . The appearance of the houses is tasty and picturesque."[10] Decorative board and batten and kingpost ornaments adorned the 1874 stations, and variations appeared in subsequent models. A model station displayed at the 1876 Centennial Exposition in Philadelphia was similar to that built in 1878 at Big Kinnakeet in Buxton, North Carolina (fig. 4.6), which had shingled walls, sawtooth batten trim, a stylized gable ornament, and hipped dormers.[11]

Similar themes of standardized picturesque architecture also appeared in railroad depots of the period. The great urban railroad depots combined engineering feats and ornate decoration in magnificent Gothic and Romanesque piles; in small railroad towns, modest brick and wooden depots such as the Thomasville Depot (fig. 4.7), built about 1871 for the North Carolina Rail-road, presented their own versions of a modern image. Its standard, functional form is neatly trimmed with millwork—wide eaves carried on deep brackets, the ticket bay and waiting room finished with narrow beaded sheathing, and the fanciful sawnwork frieze beneath the eaves giving an unmistakably stylish note.[12]

Figure 4.6. Big Kinnakeet Life-Saving Station, Dare County, 1878. J. L. Parkinson, architect. (North Carolina Division of Archives and History)

Figure 4.7. Thomasville Depot, Thomasville, ca. 1871.

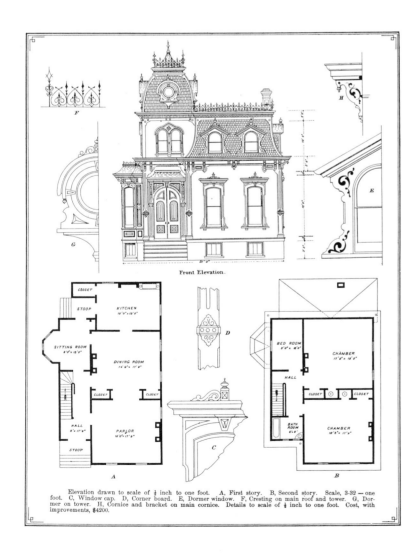

Elevation drawn to scale of ⅛ inch to one foot. A, First story. B, Second story. Scale, 3-32 = one foot. C, Window cap. D, Corner board. E, Dormer window. F, Cresting on main roof and tower. G, Dormer on tower. H, Cornice and bracket on main cornice. Details to scale of ½ inch to one foot. Cost, with improvements, $4200.

Figure 4.8. Typical plate from A. J. Bicknell, *Bicknell's Village Builder*. (North Carolina State University Library)

Houses

The industrialized picturesque found its widest expression in the houses built for a changing society. Thousands of small dwellings were needed for tenant farmers, for small landowners as farm sizes shrank and the number of small farms increased, and for the families who moved to isolated waterpower sites to work in textile mills. Those who moved into the towns all needed a room to rent, a little house, or a handsome residence on a fashionable street.

The house designs promoted in patternbooks took full advantage of mass-produced, standardized building materials (fig. 4.8). Popular works of the 1860s and 1870s—including those of George Woodward and A. J. Bicknell in *Woodward's Cottages and Farm Houses*, *Bicknell's Village Builder*, and *Cottage and Constructive Architecture*—offered designs for houses of moderate size and elaboration.[13] Like earlier builders' guides, these books also provided endless drawings of windows and doors, porch posts, gable ornaments, chimney tops, friezes and cornices, stairs, mantels, and storefronts that gave manufacturers and builders models to copy; they also imparted a heady sense of the possibilities of the industrial age.

Both in books and in actual construction, three principal styles dominated popular domestic construction in the immediate postwar years: the Second Empire or "French" style, with its distinctive mansard roof; the Gothic cottage mode; and the newly ornate and vertical Italianate. A profound and widespread change appeared in form and plan, as, for the first time, North Carolinians generally accepted the asymmetrical massing and crosswing plans promoted by mid-nineteenth-century patternbooks. Some houses were composed of intersecting wings that formed an L, T, or cross plan; others had a dominant ell or bay projecting from the main facade; and still others had a central-passage arrangement in which the rooms on one side were shifted to front or rear along that axis in order to break up the rectangular plan.[14]

The French Style

The Second Empire or "French" style took a prominent place in the first big building projects after the war. Strongly identified with the industrial fortunes of the North, the style was favored by bustling entrepreneurs and appeared most often as an expression of new, urban money. It combined elements of symmetry and classicism with the assertively novel mansard or French roof. Boldly modeled decorations included brackets and bosses, chamfered posts and turned balustrades, and heavily framed, arched openings in common with the Italianate mode.

Figure 4.9. Heck-Andrews House, Raleigh, 1869–70. G. S. H. Appleget, architect; John M. Wilson and John A. Waddell, contractors. (North Carolina Division of Archives and History)

The Heck-Andrews House (fig. 4.9), erected in 1869–70 for Jonathan and Mattie Heck, was probably the first big house built in Raleigh after the war. Heck had come down from West Virginia during the war, engaged in wartime manufacturing, and allied himself with established local families. Remembered as "the first man in Raleigh to endeavor to break up the business lethargy prevailing after the surrender," he embarked promptly in 1865 on the first of many ambitious land and mineral development schemes, and in 1869 he was ready to build a house that was "in its day celebrated as the most pretentious private residence in the state." The Hecks employed architect G. S. H. Appleget, recently arrived from New Jersey, to design an ornate, towered residence. From the foundation to the top of the "manshard" tower, Appleget specified a frame house of the first quality, from the traditional frame "mortised and tenanted and pinned together good and strong" (rather than a lighter balloon frame, which had only begun to appear among lesser structures) to materials comprising "the best that is made" and finish "in the latest style." The plan also linked present to past, for behind the tower and fancy porch lay a familiar central-passage plan with flanking parlors. The builders and suppliers were John A. Waddell and John M. Wilson, who had spent their antebellum careers in Warren County; immediately after the war they bought timberlands along the North Carolina Railroad in Johnston County and

Figure 4.10. Banker's House, Shelby, 1874–75.

opened a sawmill, sash and blind factory, and contracting business to meet customers' orders all along the line.[15]

A similar aura of solidity and prosperity informs the Banker's House (fig. 4.10) in Shelby, which may also have been designed by Appleget. It was built about 1875 for banker Jesse Jenkins in the midst of the town's erratic economic resurgence; although changing fortunes soon cost Jenkins the house, subsequent owners were also prominent Shelby bankers. The elegant brick house appears conventionally symmetrical at first glance, but the plan reveals the new asymmetry: the rooms on the right are slightly advanced along the passage, subtly enlivening the massing.[16]

Although the Second Empire style never became universally popular, examples dotted growing postwar towns. The Dodd-Hinsdale House in Raleigh, built about 1879 for Raleigh mayor and merchant William Dodd, has a central tower with an insouciant mansard-on-mansard roof. Jonathan Heck's development investments included construction of a trio of small, identical towered houses in Raleigh's Oakwood suburb; these, like a mansard-roof cottage built in Fayetteville, followed plates in the 1871 supplement to *Bicknell's Village Builder*.[17] Others remodeled their houses in the French style, including Samuel McDowell Tate, Morganton political and railroad leader, who about 1868 added a mansard roof and three-story octagonal tower to his big Greek Revival brick house.[18]

The Gothic Cottage Style

The Downingesque mode, which had only begun to gain adherents in North Carolina before the war, attained its greatest popularity in the postwar era. In contrast to the French style, the Gothic cottage mode appealed to many established town and country families reclaiming prosperity and gentility. Examples sprang up in areas ranging from Edenton, Wilson, and Hamilton in the east to Greensboro, Mount Pleasant, and Morganton in the west.

The epitome of the Gothic cottage was built about 1866 for Thomas and Amelia Capehart near the railroad village of Kittrell on the Raleigh and Gaston Railroad (fig. 4.11). The children of eastern planter families, the Capeharts had come to start a mercantile business and a small farm on land bought from a wartime friend, planter George Kittrell.[19] The stylish house deviates strikingly from local norms in its L-plan, its steep-gabled front ell and matching dormers, and its full ensemble of board and batten, tracery-filled lancet windows, and trefoil-patterned bargeboards.

In and around Tarboro, recovering planters and merchants continued to demonstrate the taste for the picturesque that had appeared in the 1850s. Near Calvary Church, on which construction began again with money from a good cotton crop in 1867, the rector built a stylish brick cottage for his daughter. A rare rural example of the cottage mode in brick is Chosumneeda (fig. 4.13), probably erected in the late 1860s for physician and planter A. B. Nobles. The crosswing plan, steep roof, and peaked dormers feature a cheery assortment of pointed and segmental arches and corbeled brickwork, and the floral-patterned slate roof is flounced with sawn bargeboards. Continuing a familiar linkage between architectural and agricultural innovation, Nobles was a local leader in progressive farming who even held the county agricultural fair at his farm.[20]

The genteel picturesque ideal was not restricted to a single building but was part of an "artistic" whole that integrated the residence into an artfully naturalistic landscape, including suitable garden structures. A fine example of such ephemeral structures survives in the garden of Rachel and William Moore in Mount Airy. William ran a textile factory, a sawmill, and a tanyard near his residence. Rachel, a great gardener who owned copies of Downing's works, probably copied her gazebo (fig. 4.12) from the "rustic seat" of entwined branches—"the more irregular the better"—in Downing's *Treatise on Landscape Gardening*; it was made of twelve poles set in the ground, as he instructed, and was fashioned of laurel branches, which Rachel draped with a fragrant pink rambling rose.[21]

Figure 4.11. Capehart House, Vance County, ca. 1866.

Figure 4.12. Moore Gazebo, Mount Airy, late 19th century.

Figure 4.13. Chosumneeda, Edgecombe County, late 1860s.

Figure 4.14. Fourth Street House, Wilmington, late 19th century.

The other familiar face of the picturesque, the Italianate style, gained universal popularity after the war. In Wilmington, citizens continued their preference for the mode. Typical of many is a frame, side-hall-plan house on Fourth Street (fig. 4.14). It repeats the city's familiar low hip roof, vented and bracketed cornice, and canopied porch, but its porch posts and brackets, glass-paneled doors, and other millwork are characteristic of postwar manufacture.

In Goldsboro, where business was rebounding at the junction of the Wilmington and Weldon and the North Carolina railroads, two young merchants, brothers Henry and Solomon Weil, chose the Italianate style for their twin residences (figs. 4.15, 4.16). An elder brother, Herman, had come to Goldsboro from Baltimore in 1858 as a peddler and begun working for a local merchant. No sooner had Sherman's troops departed Goldsboro in 1865 than he brought his younger brothers to town and established H. Weil and Brothers, a mercantile business that

Figure 4.15. Henry Weil House, Goldsboro, 1875.

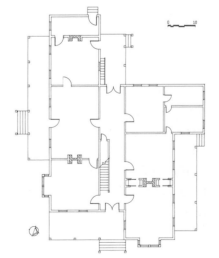

Figure 4.16. Henry Weil House. Plan. One of many versions of the L and T plans that became popular in the 1870s and 1880s. (Partin and Hobbs, Architects, Goldsboro)

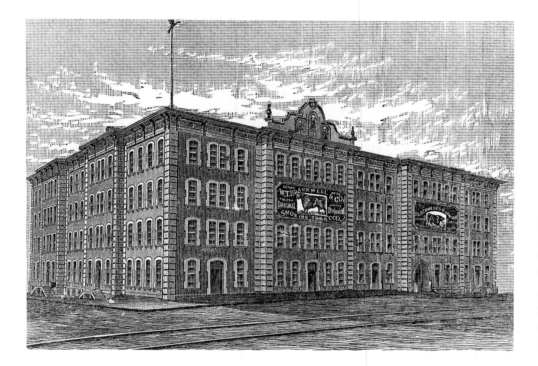

Figure 4.17. W. T. Blackwell Company (Bull Durham) Tobacco Factory, Durham, 1874. This factory still stands within a complex that expanded steadily throughout the 19th and 20th centuries. (North Carolina Division of Archives and History)

traded with farmers throughout the coastal plain. In 1874 Henry went to Raleigh to see "various homes that have lately been built. I wanted to look for one such as I might fancy for a dwelling house." He saw one that gave "a better idea of a house than I ever had before, a house of comfort," and obtained plans from the architect. In September 1875, Henry and Solomon and their new brides moved into their side-by-side houses. Typifying the postwar Italianate style, each richly decorated dwelling is tall and asymmetrical, with the right-hand rooms advanced along the central passage to form the gabled front ell.[22]

Scores of tall and ornate Italianate houses sprang up in the busy little cities of the 1870s and 1880s. Next door to Heck's French-style mansion in Raleigh, railroad magnate A. B. Andrews erected a massive Italianate house with a symmetrical, cross-gabled roof, probably likewise designed by Appleget and built by Wilson and Waddell. On the next street, political leader A. S. Merrimon built a tall crosswing Italianate house with millwork displaying motifs replicating bolts, rivets, and modern machinery. In Durham, where the first generation of tobacco entrepreneurs was building factories and houses fast and furious, Wilson and Waddell built for tobacconist W. T. Blackwell a similar house with a cupola atop the symmetrical cross-gabled roof; they probably also built the elaborate T-plan residence erected for Blackwell's partner, Julian Carr. Typical of the era, these two industrialists' new mansions stood convenient to their factory. In 1874 the W. T. Blackwell Company, whose manufacture of Bull Durham Tobacco was booming, erected a big brick factory in ornate Italian style (fig. 4.17). The factory was painted with a "colossal" image of the trademark Durham Bull, "rampant and triumphant," and it featured a calliopelike instrument that imitated the bellowing of a bull: "As it sometimes exercises quite early in the morning, the effect on strangers . . . is remarkable."[23]

Popular Houses

The new crosswing plans and asymmetrical facades, along with fashionable decorative motifs, permeated popular building throughout the rural and small-town landscape. Ells and wings, once added as secondary rear rooms, became prominent elements in postwar homes. Although L and T plans were most common, cruciform crosswing plans were also popular. At Fairfield, a trading village in Hyde County where buildings under construction in 1877 gained attention for their "tasteful ornamentations," Eliza and Patrick Simmons built a "large, convenient beautiful residence" (fig. 4.18) with a cruciform plan, dominated by a front center pavilion and emphasized by millwork that was probably adapted from *Bicknell's Village Builder*.[24] Crosswing plans also

Figure 4.18. Simmons House, Hyde County, 1877.

allowed builders to remake old buildings in new forms. About 1890 carpenter Will Waldrop, working in the Sandy Mush Valley near Asheville, transformed Malinda Payne's small hall-parlor-plan house into an L-plan cottage by adding an ell to the front (fig. 4.19). He gave the ell a bay window and a fancy gable ornament, built an L-shaped porch enriched with sawnwork, and embellished the roofs of both sections with peaked cross gables and bracketed cornices.[25]

Such novel designs did not replace customary forms and plans, however. Many new houses assumed old forms even as their builders took advantage of new mass-produced materials. With plentiful lumber and nails, such houses could be built faster and cheaper than ever before, neatly finished with factory-made boards and flooring, doors and windows, and tongue-and-groove sheathing. A staunchly rectangular and symmetrical dwelling, one or two stories tall, with a porch and a rear ell or shed containing a kitchen, remained the classic choice. Such houses dominated the rural landscape from the 1860s throughout the rest of the century and into the 1910s and 1920s.

The minimal dwelling remained the one-room-plan house, now often built with balloon framing and factory-sawn lumber. Typical of countless small dwellings that once dotted the landscape is a late-nineteenth-century tenant house in Franklin County (fig. 4.20); it is a 16-foot-square dwelling with a stone chimney and a rear shed extension, in form and plan little different from houses built for a century and more before it. The old two-room plan also continued in common use. The Lassiter Tenant House (fig. 4.21) in Gates County, one of many such houses, was built about 1890, soon after John and Missouri Lassiter acquired their hundred-acre farm.

Figure 4.19. Payne House, Buncombe County, ca. 1890. Will Waldrop, carpenter.

Figure 4.20. Tenant House, Franklin County, late 19th century. At that time, one-room dwellings were still common, mainly as rental, tenant, and small farmers' houses.

Figure 4.21. Lassiter Tenant House, Gates County, ca. 1890.

The Lassiters enlarged an existing house for themselves and built a second, smaller house to enable them to employ one family of tenants. Neatly finished with factory-made weatherboards, narrow beaded boarding, and a tin roof, the 24-by-14-foot house has a kitchen wing to the rear. Behind its firmly symmetrical facade, its two main rooms repeat the familiar asymmetry and direct intimacy of a hall-parlor plan.[26]

The two-story house, one room deep, also proliferated in rural areas. A fine example appears in the handsome dwelling (fig. 4.22) built for Sarah and Benjamin Hamilton Harris on their fifty-five-acre farm in Burke County. The Harrises employed carpenter Job Hicks to build their new house on a gentle slope between a steep hillside and the bottomlands of Irish Creek. Although built in 1902, the house exemplifies a form in common use from the 1860s through the 1920s. It is a symmetrical, rectangular dwelling with a gable roof, center-hall plan, and brick end chimneys. There is a kitchen ell in back and a shed porch across the front. In keeping with the times, carpenter Hicks finished the house with stout, chamfered porch posts and a handsome glass-paneled front door, and he ceiled the rooms nicely with tongue-and-groove matchboarding.[27]

To these familiar forms, builders could add as much or as little in the way of "artistic" trim as the budget and taste of the client permitted. Both carpenters and clients seemed to revel in the new possibilities. A vivid example is the Worrell House (fig. 4.23) in Murfreesboro, built by a sawmill owner for his daughter and her husband. The small, symmetrical dwelling drips with luxuriant millwork, and the porch displays an artisan's personal stamp: simple board posts feature bold jigsawed images in outline—spiky stars and vigorous, tautly stylized male figures. This house, like many more, exemplifies builders' traditional response to changing fashions— they retained a familiar form and updated the most obvious and easily changed elements, such as

Figure 4.22. Harris House, Burke County, 1902. Job Hicks, carpenter.

porches, roofline, and trim. This tried-and-true approach appears in the David A. Barnes House (fig. 4.24), also in Murfreesboro, built about 1875 for a prominent political figure by the veteran contractor Jacob Holt, who had left Warrenton after the war and resumed business in Virginia. Holt still built his standard house with center passage and four main rooms per floor, but he had adopted decorative eave gables, spiral brackets, finials, and pendants from *Bicknell's Village Builder* to assure postwar customers that they were getting "the best and most modern styles."[28]

Similar patterns followed the advance of the railroad and the sawmill into the timberlands of the mountains. Farmers in the valleys there replaced their log dwellings with frame houses garnished with newly available millwork. The Jeff White House in Madison County (fig. 4.25), built in 1881, is a conservative frame house with lacy sawn and turned ornament lavished on the bay windows and double porch, including a Masonic emblem set into the pediment. In Watauga County, the Baird family expanded an old house into a handsome two-story, central-passage dwelling with a rear kitchen wing and built a front porch dressed with decorative millwork (fig. 4.26). And in Ashe County beside the New River, Andrew and Delia Weaver expanded his father's two-room-plan dwelling and built a deep front porch adorned with sawnwork and taking the form of the double piazza that by this time had appeared in the mountains as well as in the coastal plain (fig. 4.27). Meanwhile, in Edenton and Beaufort and throughout the coastal area, builders continued to build double piazzas as they always had, but they now enlivened this old form with exuberant millwork that became plentiful as woodworking factories opened up in northeastern North Carolina.

In addition to the porch, the most noticeable touch of modernity added to familiar house

Figure 4.23. Worrell House, Murfreesboro, ca. 1880.

Figure 4.24. Barnes House, Murfreesboro, ca. 1875. Jacob W. Holt, builder. (North Carolina Division of Archives and History)

forms was the central front gable rising from the eaves to give an up-to-date and vertical demeanor to the facade. Will Waldrop in Sandy Mush, Jacob Holt in Murfreesboro, Wilson and Waddell in Durham, and hundreds of other builders across the country employed this easily constructed motif. Adapted from the Downingesque cottage mode and built either as a superficial wall dormer or as a cross-gable roof structure, the peaked front gable entered the popular idiom by the 1870s and proved a hardy favorite throughout the rest of the century, appearing in large and small, plain and fancy houses. At the Allen-Mangum House (fig. 4.28) in Granville County, the cross gable is part of a program of elaborate Gothic and Italianate–style carpentry. The same motif was equally effective in much simpler houses. Late in the 1890s, Nash County farmer James Wiley Matthews built a small frame house (fig. 4.29) for himself and his wife,

Figure 4.25. White House, Madison County, ca. 1881.

Figure 4.26. Baird House, Watauga County, late 19th century.

Figure 4.27. Weaver House, Ashe County, ca. 1848, expanded ca. 1895.

Figure 4.28. Allen-Mangum House, Granville County, ca. 1880.

Figure 4.29. Matthews House, Nash County, ca. 1899.

Loutouria Vester, doing most of the construction himself with factory-produced lumber and millwork. He built a T-shaped house with two main front rooms and a central passage, and he gave the front facing the road an air of serene modernity with a broad, lightly ornamented porch and a central gable rising gently from the roof.[29]

Thus, within a few years after the Civil War, popular housing had incorporated a few profound and interwoven changes that shaped building through the end of the century. Mass production of construction materials and ornate millwork went hand in hand with the movement of the picturesque modes into the popular mainstream, both in the wide acceptance of crosswing plans and in the standardization of decorative trim and roofline treatments. From the new range of possibilities offered by the industrial age, North Carolinians built thousands of houses, large and small, simple and elaborate, on main streets and in suburbs, in mill villages and on farms.

Log Construction in the Industrial Age

Not all North Carolinians adopted new methods of building. In many areas, log construction remained strong well into the twentieth century. As farmers continued to rely on familiar plans and notching methods, the most noticeable changes appeared in shifts in the uses of familiar building types. Log house construction declined in status as frame construction became cheaper and more accessible. Some late log dwellings were stoutly built and well crafted, but

Figure 4.30. Boyd House, Buncombe County, 1870s and after.

many were minimal houses, built quickly and often crudely. It was not so much that the standard of construction declined—rudimentary log houses had been part of the rural landscape from early settlement onward. Rather, the upper levels of log construction tapered off as more and more farmers who wanted and could afford large houses built them of frame or brick, leaving log construction to small farmers and landless families. The modest log dwellings of the late nineteenth and early twentieth centuries represent the last generations of an ancient and resilient tradition.[30]

Log construction was critical to cash-short farm families who wanted to build without spending much money or going into debt. A farmer could fell and hew the logs himself and raise the house with the aid of family, neighbors, or a hired workman. This method also offered the important advantage of phased building. One could build first a single pen with a sleeping loft. Then, depending on what time brought in the way of children and prosperity, the house might continue to suffice; if not, it could be expanded in an established way. In addition to single-pen houses, the saddlebag, double-pen, and dogtrot plans continued in common use.

In 1874 Erwin Boyd bought fifty acres in the Sandy Mush Valley of Buncombe County for $81.00, and soon he had built a dwelling of half-dovetailed logs, measuring about 16 by 18 feet and containing a single dirt-floored room and a loft above (figs. 4.30, 4.31). A decade before, Boyd had been a slave, unable to own property or even himself. Now he joined the thousands of

Figure 4.31. Boyd House. Plan by Carl R. Lounsbury after Douglas Swaim.

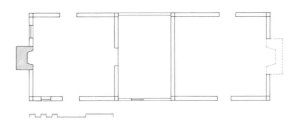

freed slaves and white farmers who depended on log building traditions to establish a measure of independence. Later in the century, Erwin's son Thad Boyd expanded the house by erecting a second pen about 16 feet square on the side toward the road, with a dry-laid stone chimney heating both the lower room and the loft. A covered passageway ran between the two sections, creating the familiar "dogtrot" form. Within a few years, Boyd weatherboarded over the passage to form an enclosed link between the two sections.[31]

Farther up the valley, in a meadow at the head of Sugar Creek, tradition holds that Cy Jones built in about 1890 a single-pen log house, 17 by 20 feet (fig. 4.32), with a dry-laid stone chimney. He used unusually large logs—almost planks—5 or 6 inches by 14 to 18 inches, of good poplar, well joined in the standard half-dovetail notch (fig. 4.33). The interior has two rooms, a boxed corner stair, and batten doors. As the family grew, Jones built a front porch and a frame rear shed 12 feet deep, perched on tall stone piers, and he covered the house with a roof of wooden shingles.[32]

Figure 4.32. Jones House, Buncombe County, ca. 1890s.

Figure 4.33. Jones House. Detail of half-dovetail notching.

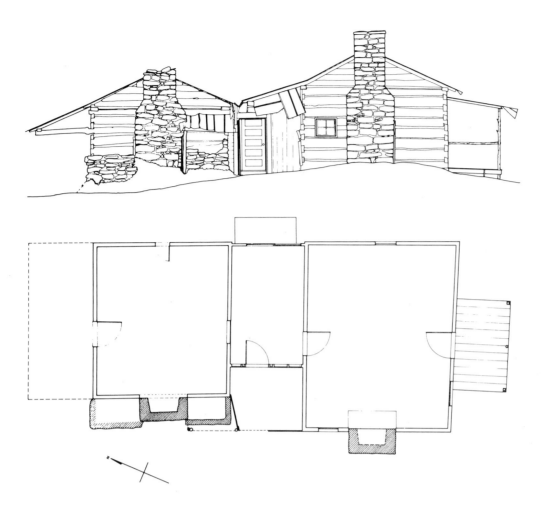

Figure 4.34. Baumgarner House, Burke County, ca. 1880. Plan and side elevation by Tom McGimsey. (Historic Burke Foundation)

It was in the mountains that log houses dominated the landscape the longest, usually in the form of small houses with fieldstone chimneys and often built in more than one construction phase.[33] But these familiar mountain dwellings were not the only prevalent type in late-nineteenth-century log architecture. Although the side-by-side plan of the Boyds' dogtrot dwelling was common, in some areas front-to-back expansion was also prevalent. Such was the case in Burke County, where, about 1880, Thomas and Margaret Baumgarner built a half-dovetail log dwelling, 16 by 18 feet, and within a few years erected a second 17-by-22-foot structure in front, linked to the old house—which became the kitchen—with a breezeway (fig. 4.34).[34]

Far from being restricted to the mountain region, log houses also continued to be built in other sections of the state. Throughout the Piedmont, even in areas near booming cities and factories, farm families relied on log construction. Near Durham, for example, black and white farmers erected log dwellings on their small farmsteads until well into the twentieth century. Not far from Greensboro, the Clapp family built a one-room log house in the 1880s or 1890s, then built another similar one about 1900 and made the old house into the kitchen. Diversity of form and method in Piedmont counties likewise continued, as, for example, in Caswell County, where black and white farmers built their dwellings with diamond, square, V, and half-dovetail notches and arranged them as single-pen, saddlebag, and dogtrot houses.[35]

In eastern North Carolina, where thousands of log dwellings once housed tenant and small farming families, such structures are now scattered and few. The Charles White Farm on the edge of the Dismal Swamp in Perquimans County exemplifies the pattern. Here, about 1870, a former slave built his two-room house, corncribs, shed, chickenhouse, and smokehouse, each of saddle-notched logs set on stump piers, with walls and roofs covered by riven shakes 3 to 4 feet long. Such buildings differed little from those described by William Byrd as the homes of the first settlers along the Carolina borderlands.[36]

In Onslow County's piney woods section, with its small farms and woodland economy, the lowland log construction tradition also persisted throughout the century. David and Rachel

Figure 4.35. Futral House, Onslow County, ca. 1885, expanded ca. 1904.

Futral, part of a family who had farmed along Back Swamp since the early nineteenth century, engaged in woodland agriculture on a hundred-acre farm, raising corn, rice, and sweet potatoes on about ten acres of improved land, letting their pigs, sheep, and cattle range free in the forest, and selling timber from their woodlands. About 1885 they built a house along customary lines—a one-room dwelling of saddle-notched logs, set on the trapezoidal lightwood blocks standard in the region, with roof plate extensions that may originally have sheltered a wooden chimney (fig. 4.35). About 1904 Futral deeded the farm to his son Amos, who framed up additional rooms to one side and shed rooms in back and built a long front porch; he covered the enlarged house with a new roof in the region's familiar coastal cottage form.[37]

Outbuildings and Farmsteads

Log construction continued for a longer period and among higher economic brackets in farm buildings than in dwellings. Especially in the western Piedmont and mountains, even families who erected large frame and brick houses still built log smokehouses with tightly chinked walls, the gable end sheltering the door; nestled log springhouses into hillsides; left the log walls of corncribs unchinked for ventilation; and erected the massive log barns that were powerful and handsome symbols of successful farming throughout the western counties.[38]

There was considerable variety in log barn construction. The double-crib barn continued in common usage, but four-crib barns also became prevalent, especially in the mountains. There were two main plans for four-crib barns. One arrangement had crossing runways that separated the cribs into four quadrants; one such barn, which still remains on the Young Farm in Mitchell

County, has an additional pair of log cribs at the second level, and the whole is draped with sheds on all sides.[39] In the transverse-crib plan, adjoining pairs of cribs faced a long central runway under the ridge of the roof. The early twentieth-century Morris Barn in Cherokee County exemplifies this form; it is made of V-notched logs, and its gables are airy with latticework. The Joe Spivey Barn in Buncombe County, built by farmer and carpenter Spivey for himself, is also a transverse four-crib barn, topped by a gabled loft with diagonal ventilating slats.[40]

In erecting these slatted barns, farmers throughout the mountains were adopting a form associated with the expansion of Burley tobacco culture. In the 1870s and 1880s, some mountain farmers participated in the bright leaf tobacco boom that overtook the Piedmont and eastern North Carolina, but this died out in the 1890s and was replaced in some sections by Burley tobacco. Burley is air-cured by hanging it in open, well-ventilated spaces—often in a barn used for many other purposes. A farmer who grew Burley tobacco along with other crops could hang his tobacco high in the well-vented rafters, hoist his hay into the loft, pile his ears of corn into a lower crib, and lead his cows into their stalls beside the runway.[41]

Toward the end of the nineteenth century, frame construction began to compete with log building among outbuildings in western Carolina, though often the plans were much the same. Large frame barns grew more numerous as some farmers adopted models published by agricultural journals. Many had the familiar gable roof, others the new and more spacious gambrel roof. Ventilated haylofts, to prevent rot or spontaneous combustion, and slatted corncribs were standard features. In many western North Carolina barns, vents took the form of decorative diagonal

Figure 4.36. White Barn, Madison County, late 19th or early 20th century.

slats or lattices. This, along with diagonal or chevron-patterned siding, gives the otherwise plain barns of the region a distinctive character. At the barn on the White Farm (fig. 4.36), for example, diagonal boarding is combined with a slatted corncrib set into the slope of the land.

A handsome example of a frame transverse-crib barn can be seen at the Baird Farm in Watauga County (fig. 4.37). Said to have been built by a Mr. Woodring, the barn features a clipped gable roof that extends in front as a wagon shelter, diagonally slatted eaves venting the hayloft, and slatted doors and walls to air the stalls. In the same valley, Woodring is also thought to have built the barn at the Mast Farm (fig. 4.38). There, an older structure is incorporated beneath a dramatic gambrel roof whose rounded form echoes the shapes of the hills beyond. Dormers and cupolas ventilate the loft, and a typical slatted corncrib is attached on one side.[42]

An interest in good ventilation and efficient use of space likewise shaped the design of the imposing "round" mule barn (fig. 4.39) built about 1895 for Lincoln County farmer William A. Graham, Jr. Graham, a prominent political figure who was devoted to progressive agriculture and the improvement of farming in the state, doubtless intended his barn as a model of innovative husbandry. Round, octagonal, and other polygonal barns were promoted in national agricultural literature as innovative and efficient building types for the modern farmer. Graham's mule barn, measuring some 64 feet in diameter, has sixteen sides, with opposing entry bays and a central court surrounded by fourteen stalls. Ingeniously arranged sliding doors and shutters ventilate and light the stalls, the boarding of the second story is spaced so as to vent the hayloft, and the central cupola is designed to pull air up through the entire building.[43]

Figure 4.37. Baird Barn, Watauga County, late 19th or early 20th century.

Figure 4.38. Mast Barn, Watauga County, late 19th or early 20th century.

Figure 4.39. Graham Barn, Lincoln County, ca. 1895.

In the late nineteenth century, a new building form appeared on Piedmont and eastern North Carolina farmsteads: the flue-cured tobacco barn (fig. 4.40). From the "Old Bright Belt" in the northern Piedmont along the Virginia border—where growing and curing techniques advanced rapidly in the late nineteenth century—eastward and southward to the coastal plain toward the end of the century, the spread of bright leaf tobacco spurred the creation of the barns necessary to its curing. In contrast to the mountains, where bright leaf tobacco was grown for only a brief period, the crop dominated the economy of many other areas of the state through the twentieth century.[44]

The "bright leaf" method of curing tobacco was discovered in 1839 and gradually refined over the years. It required delicate, fine-grained tobacco—best grown on thin, "starved" soil—that could be cured to a bright yellow color and mild flavor. Bright leaf curing involved a laborious, carefully regulated heating process, which required a precisely timed sequence of different temperatures to give the tobacco its desired color and quality. Each farmer grew his crop and prepared it for market through a process that demanded knowledge, skill, patience, and constant work. The curing could make or ruin the year's crop.

Until the third quarter of the nineteenth century, farmers commonly used wood or charcoal fires to cure their tobacco. Though stoves and flues had been tried, it was not until the 1870s that they became sufficiently reliable that farmers widely adopted flue curing. Flues carried the heat from a wood-fired furnace (outside the barn) into and through the barn without smoking up the tobacco; this method also reduced the amount of fuel consumed. There were two main ways of hanging tobacco in the barn. Until about 1900, workers usually cut the stalks of tobacco whole, split them, and hung them over sticks, which were placed on the tier poles in the barns. After the turn of the century, most farmers shifted to the "priming" method, in which workers "primed"

Figure 4.40. Tobacco barns, Caswell County, late 19th or early 20th century.

leaves individually as the plants ripened from the bottom up, tied the leaves into "hands," and attached them to sticks for hanging. Many farmers considered this method more efficient, and it also produced a leaf suited to the expanding cigarette market.

Tobacco-curing barns needed to be tight to hold in the heat and strong to support the weight of the tobacco. They needed to stand close enough together for convenience, but far enough apart that a fire would not spread from barn to barn. Within a barn, the horizontal space between poles, usually measuring about 4 feet, was called a "room," and the vertical dimension between poles a "tier." Barns were built so many "rooms" wide and so many "tiers" high. Barns ranged from 16 to over 20 feet square. In a modest-sized barn, about four hundred sticks of tobacco, each with thirty "hands" of tobacco, would fill a barn. Some tobacco barns were built of frame, others of tile, but log construction was frequently preferred for its insulating qualities.

Although they shared essential features, tobacco barns took various forms from region to region. In the "old belt" counties along the Virginia border, tobacco barns were almost always of log, as were many of the other outbuildings of the area. In Caswell, Person, and Rockingham counties, barns of fairly heavy logs are joined with a variety of notches—square, half-dovetail, diamond, or V—and daubed with red clay. Multiple layers of shallow pent roofs on slim struts skirt the barns, protecting the chinking from the weather and sheltering workers or equipment beneath. In the coastal plain, where late in the nineteenth century tobacco replaced cotton as the ruling staple, both frame and log tobacco barns appear grouped in long rows or neat clusters (fig. 4.41). Along the South Carolina border, builders of tobacco barns pushed shed construction to a virtuoso level of cantilevering, sometimes extending great tin sheds 11 or 12 feet on all four sides without visible supports (fig. 4.42).

Throughout eastern North Carolina, the tobacco barn took its place in the landscape of rural change. Working within an established tradition of small, separate, quickly built structures, farmers and builders accommodated the changing theories and technologies of tobacco curing. In raising a crop for a vast international business, rural builders created a starkly functional architecture replete with local and individual variety.

The tobacco barn was not an isolated element in the rural landscape, but part of a farmstead. The Puckett Farm (figs. 4.43, 4.44) in Granville County typifies the scale and relationships of many late-nineteenth and early twentieth-century farmsteads centered on tobacco. Joseph and Delia Puckett built the present house around 1899 on a 135-acre farm they had bought about ten years earlier. Like so many farm families, the Pucketts created an informal but ordered landscape for overlapping realms of work.[45]

The frame house stands at the center of the complex, facing south toward an old roadbed. It is a typical, gable-roofed dwelling with end chimneys and a compact central-passage plan. The original separate kitchen was replaced by a kitchen and dining wing that extends at the rear. Domestic outbuildings, the purview mainly of Delia Puckett, frame the house to the east and north. She drew water from the well beside the house, heated iron pots of water and laundered clothes and linen in the log wash house, and raised chickens in the log brooder house. To the east of these buildings stands the log corncrib and beyond it the frame stable for the Pucketts' mules and cows. Discreetly placed behind the barn is the frame privy. On the west side of the house, alongside the lane, stand a log smokehouse, a second corncrib, and a garage.

To the west, the buildings devoted to tobacco are arranged in a facing pair of courtyards. On the north side of the lane stand four flue-curing barns, each about 19 or 20 feet square. On the south is the log packhouse, which contains an "ordering room" where the cured tobacco was allowed to hang and regain pliability from moist air or steam. The last step in the process took place in the striphouse at the west end of the complex. When the tobacco was "in order," it was removed from the stick and the leaves were meticulously sorted by color, size, and quality—a task demanding knowledge and accuracy—before being retied into hands and readied for the market. In and around these small, specialized buildings, the Puckett family and their neighbors and hired workers—men, women, and children, black and white—gathered for the demanding, sociable labor of "working tobacco" each year.[46]

Figure 4.41. Tobacco barns, Martin County, early 20th century.

Figure 4.42. Tobacco barn, Robeson County, early 20th century.

Figure 4.43. Puckett Farm, Granville County, ca. 1899 and after.

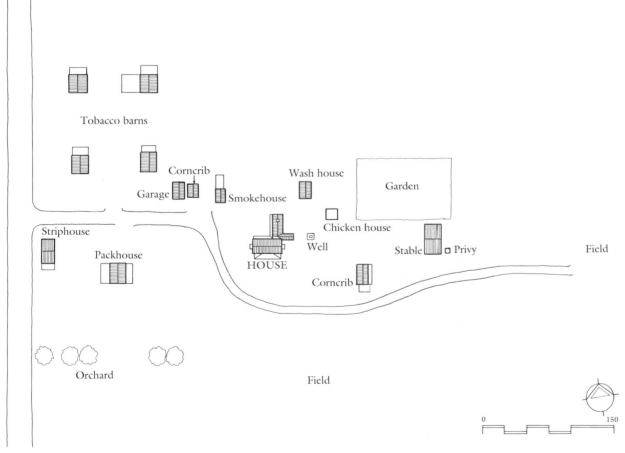

Tobacco barns

Corncrib

Wash house

Garage

Garden

Smokehouse

Chicken house

Striphouse

Well

Stable

Privy

Field

Packhouse

HOUSE

Corncrib

Orchard

Field

0   150

Figure 4.44. Puckett Farm. Site plan by Carl R. Lounsbury.

Waldensian Traditional Architecture

At the same time that families like the Pucketts were building their farmsteads within an established pattern of small, separate buildings, across the state in the foothills of the Blue Ridge a different strain of traditional rural building was making its own place in the landscape. North Carolina, like most southern states, received relatively few immigrants during the late-nineteenth-century influx from Europe. Its population was almost exclusively native-born. But a few Carolina investors sponsored colonies of "desirable" European immigrants, whom they typically identified as Protestant, northern European, and agrarian. In contrast to their contemporaries in other states, few of these immigrants re-created the traditional architecture of their homelands in buildings that survive to the present.

The exception is the Waldensian colony at Valdese in Burke County. The Waldensians were members of a Reformed religious group that began in the twelfth century and concentrated in the Cottian Alps in northwestern Italy. After surviving centuries of persecution, they were finally permitted freedom of worship in 1848. In the late nineteenth century, as the alpine valleys became overcrowded, outmigration began. A meeting between a Pennsylvania industrialist with investments in western North Carolina and a pastor of the Waldensian church led to a group of Waldensians leaving their home for Burke County in 1893. Waldensian architecture forms a unique chapter in North Carolina's heritage—traditional immigrant architecture that replicated the age-old customs of the land left behind, and buildings that combined traditional techniques with popular building forms of the early twentieth century, all within a single generation.[47]

Throughout Europe farmers customarily joined houses and barns into farmstead units. In the steep and rocky valleys of the Cottian Alps, where the Waldenians had farmed tiny terraced tracts since the Middle Ages, the traditional form was a stone house and barn set into the steep slope of the land. Typically, the family quarters stood above the barn, with a balconied porch overlooking the valley. When Waldensian farmers left their home valleys for North Carolina in 1893, they brought with them this farmhouse design, of which one remarkable example still stands.

The Refour House, a unique example of this European farm building type, possesses an ageless quality shared with the hillside farmsteads of the Waldensians' home valleys. When the Refour family settled on their land, they lived in a "sawmill shack" while preparing to build their farmhouse (figs. 4.45, 4.46). Refour chose the sloping site carefully and constructed the house of stone collected from the land. The lower story, backed into the hillside, contains stables for cattle. Above it, the main story is a single family living area with exposed beams, simple wooden lintels, and batten doors. A corner stair mounts to the sleeping loft above. At the back of the living area, Refour built a stone storage room, and in front he extended a cantilevered balcony that looks down toward the gentle valley below.

Other Waldensian colonists also built stone houses and outbuildings into their hillsides, though many eventually stuccoed their dwellings. Fieldstone was typical of small upland farmhouses in the alpine homeland, whereas the better dwellings of the villages and lower farms were typically stuccoed. Frank Refour, who had grown up in his father's hillside rock house, built a stuccoed stone house nearby when he began housekeeping. In the early twentieth century, too, Waldensian stonemasons began to accommodate the trends of their adopted nation, erecting handsome fieldstone versions of the American bungalow style as well as individualized dwellings for residents of Valdese.[48]

At the center of Valdese, the settlers set aside a hilltop site for the church that was the heart of their community life. They built a temporary church, decided to ally themselves with the Presbyterian denomination in America because of similarities in their methods of governance, and, after a period of great economic hardship, in 1895 began collecting money and materials for a permanent church. The congregation obtained a design from a Mr. Munsch in New York in 1896, began construction in 1897, and completed the church in 1899, with most of the work done by members of the church. In contrast to disparate farmhouse traditions, American and Euro-

Figure 4.45. Refour House, Burke County, ca. 1894.

Lower floor

Main floor

Upper floor

Figure 4.46. Refour House. Plans by Tom McGimsey. (Historic Burke Foundation)

pean nineteenth-century church architecture shared in the popular use of Gothic and Roman-esque Revival styles. The Waldensian Presbyterian Church (fig. 4.47) is a starkly handsome structure of stuccoed masonry. Its boldly sculptural forms, clean-cut arched openings, emphatic pilasters, and tall corner tower echo the churches left behind in Italy, yet it is as compatible in form and style with the churches in surrounding communities as it is with the Waldensians' memories of their homeland.[49]

Figure 4.47. Waldensian Presbyterian Church, Valdese, 1897–99. Mr. Munsch, architect; James H. Tron, Eli Bertalot, and Henry J. Long, head stonemasons; Henry Vinay, head carpenter.

Public and Commercial Buildings

Churches

As denominational groups reorganized amid the social changes brought by Civil War and Reconstruction, church building began on an unprecedented scale. As with domestic architecture, churches built in the 1870s and early 1880s tended to follow styles and forms established before the war, particularly the popularized Gothic Revival style. The mid-1880s brought innovations in plan and a greater scale and elaboration.

Social changes—country to city migration, emancipation, and the establishment of separate black and white congregations and denominations—had a profound effect. There had been a few independent black churches before the war, but many churches were racially mixed. Different denominations handled the new social order in various ways. The Methodist Episcopal Church, South, formed in 1845 because of sectional differences over slavery, continued after the war. After emancipation, black Methodists established their own congregations, most affiliating with the African Methodist Episcopal (A.M.E.) or African Methodist Episcopal Zion (A.M.E. Zion) churches, which had been formed in Philadelphia and New York, respectively, in the late eighteenth century. The Southern Baptist Convention had also been organized in 1845 and it, too, continued after the war; as black congregations became more numerous, they formed the National Baptist Convention. In 1861 Southern Presbyterians created the Presbyterian Church in the United States (originally "in the Confederate States of America"), which remained separate from the parent church until 1983. By contrast, although northern and southern Episcopalians had broken during the Civil War, the national church reunified promptly in 1865, and, within the state, church leaders maintained a single diocese in which they established a number of new black parishes.[50]

A powerful influence on church building was the growing supply of official denominational publications on church architecture. The Methodists' Board of Church Extension was one of several sources of designs for efficient, attractive, and practical church buildings suited to the worship and ideals of the denomination. These ranged from elaborate towered and domed monuments of brick or stone for prosperous urban congregations to the simple gable-end form for country and village churches. The ready availability of mass-produced building materials enabled scores of congregations to build neat frame or even brick churches for the first time. Large churches rose in towns, and in the countryside small congregations, whether their members were black or white, rich or poor, erected buildings that became landmarks of rural life.[51]

Gilboa Methodist Church (fig. 4.48) in Burke County exemplifies the plain beauty of the country church. When the congregation, which had met in log buildings for generations, dedicated their new frame church in 1879, the preacher cited it as "a splendid building [which] will compare favorably with many village churches." His words reflected prevalent opinions concerning appropriate rural and urban types. Set on a gentle hillside, the one-story, weatherboarded building has neither steeple nor Gothic windows; its gable-end orientation alone signifies its purpose. Within, quiet simplicity continues (fig. 4.49). Planed boards ceil the walls and ceiling,

Figure 4.48. Gilboa Methodist Church, Burke County, 1879.

Figure 4.49. Gilboa Methodist Church. Interior.

Figure 4.50. Paynes Chapel, Sandy Mush, Buncombe County, ca. 1889. Will Waldrop, carpenter.

and handmade plank pews face a raised pulpit. Behind the pulpit rises a single, elegant ogee arch suggesting the outline of a chancel, on which perches a dove, symbol of the Holy Spirit.[52]

In 1889, when Will Waldrop of Sandy Mush Valley in Buncombe County constructed Paynes Chapel (fig. 4.50), he too built a plain, gable-end frame structure, to which he added a few decorative touches. Crisp, thick moldings atop the tall windows, a boxed cornice, and precisely aligned doors and windows create a strong and orderly design embellished by kingpost gable decorations and an open belfry.[53] Waldrop's sense of proportion and the restraint and precision with which he used tokens of style and function made the little church both timeless and of its time.

Although plain buildings remained the norm for many small congregations, during the late nineteenth century the Gothic Revival style entered mainstream small-town and rural church architecture and became the most popular style for churches of all denominations. So universal was its acceptance, in fact, that the most stylized renditions of its elements—a pointed arch, a triangular headed door or window, a tower—became standard indicators of a church.

Some small congregations built elaborate renditions of the Gothic style such as the Fairfield Methodist Church (fig. 4.51) in Hyde County, built in 1877 and "finished in elegant modern style." Local reports claimed it was "a house of worship that will not suffer in comparison with nine-tenths of the churches in the State, taking both city and country"—quite a boast for a tiny village. The builder, William Walling, blended Gothic motifs with classical and Italianate ones.

Figure 4.51. Fairfield Methodist Church, Hyde County, 1877. William Walling, builder.

Dark, delicate Gothic trim enriches the lancet-framed chancel, and airy trusswork fills a roof bordered by ornamental sawnwork (fig. 4.52).[54] Episcopalians maintained their preference for the Gothic Revival style, and new editions of *Upjohn's Rural Architecture*, with its wooden chapel and church designs, continued to serve many small black and white congregations. Grace Church (fig. 4.53), built among Trenton's moss-hung live oaks in 1885, epitomizes the picturesque Upjohn mode in the industrial age. Skillfully deployed millwork includes battens that create an arcade beneath the eaves, complemented by the reverse motif of scalloped boards on the cornice, belfry, and triangular door and window hoods.

Figure 4.52. Fairfield Methodist Church. Interior.

Among the most elegant of the late Gothic Revival churches built for Episcopalian congregations is St. Joseph's Episcopal Church (fig. 4.54), built in Fayetteville in 1896. Like many black congregations in the postwar era, St. Joseph's was aided by a northern benefactor, in this case Eva Cochran of Yonkers, New York. At the dedication service in 1897, the distinguished crowd of black and white participants included the donor and her daughters. The novel form and richness of the church, the "tastefulness and appropriateness" of its every detail, attracted enthusiastic admiration. The local newspaper claimed that "with the exception of Mr. Vanderbilt's church at Biltmore, there is no church interior in the State so beautiful as that of St. Joseph's."

Figure 4.53. Grace Episcopal Church, Trenton, 1885.

Construction was supervised by Robert Strange, and the builder was W. C. Bain, a prominent Piedmont contractor. Whoever its architect—some reports cite a Boston firm—the church is a sophisticated rendition of the Gothic Revival, rendered with the gentle, organic forms and textured surfaces of the shingle style, while the dark gleaming interior presents a High Church arrangement in opulent Eastlake mode.[55]

Builders' boldly stylized versions of the Gothic Revival distinguished many churches of the late nineteenth century. The small frame building of Poplar Run A.M.E. Zion Church (fig. 4.55) in Perquimans County, probably built in the mid-1890s, epitomizes the monumentality attained through the confident handling of utterly simple forms.[56] Two strong towers flanking a broad

Figure 4.54. St. Joseph's Episcopal Church, Fayetteville, 1896. Robert Strange, superintendent of construction; W. C. Bain, builder.

gable dominate the facade, while subtle differences in the roofs prevent the towers from being identical. Combinations of two unequal towers were familiar throughout nineteenth-century Gothic Revival church architecture, but the form was especially strong among black congregations, especially the A.M.E. and A.M.E. Zion churches.

Urban congregations frequently built in brick or stone, often in stylish and even opulent fashion. Wilmington, the largest city in the state until 1910, was preeminent in its fine religious architecture. Samuel Sloan's First Baptist Church, begun before the war, was completed by 1870, as was St. Paul's Lutheran Church, both in Gothic Revival style. St. Mark's Episcopal Church (1871), the first black parish church consecrated in the diocese, was designed by the Boston architectural firm of William Emerson and Carl Fehmer in a "church-like" form: "The roof is sharp, the chancel recessed, the windows pointed Gothic."[57]

Especially striking was Wilmington's Temple of Israel (fig. 4.56). Organized in 1872 as a Reformed congregation, it was the first permanent Jewish congregation in the state. To build its temple, the new congregation contracted with Abbott's Building Company, also known as the Cape Fear Building Company, a versatile manufacturing and contracting firm that stayed busy in the city's postwar recovery. Alex Strausz of that firm is cited as architect. At the dedication of the temple in 1876, the invited public was "dazzled" by the light that streamed through stained glass windows onto the flowered emerald-green carpet, the chandeliers hung with roses and evergreens, the bronze columns carrying seven-branched candlestands, and the ark of marble with the Ten Commandments inscribed in gold. The stuccoed masonry building features a bold twin-tower facade, but with Moorish themes rather than Gothic—a common nineteenth-century device for Jewish religious architecture. Horseshoe arches and arabesque triplets and onion domes atop the towers create an exotic presence between the two Gothic Revival churches nearby, Walter's St. James Church and Sloan's First Baptist.[58]

Figure 4.55. Poplar Run A.M.E. Zion Church, Perquimans County, 1890s.

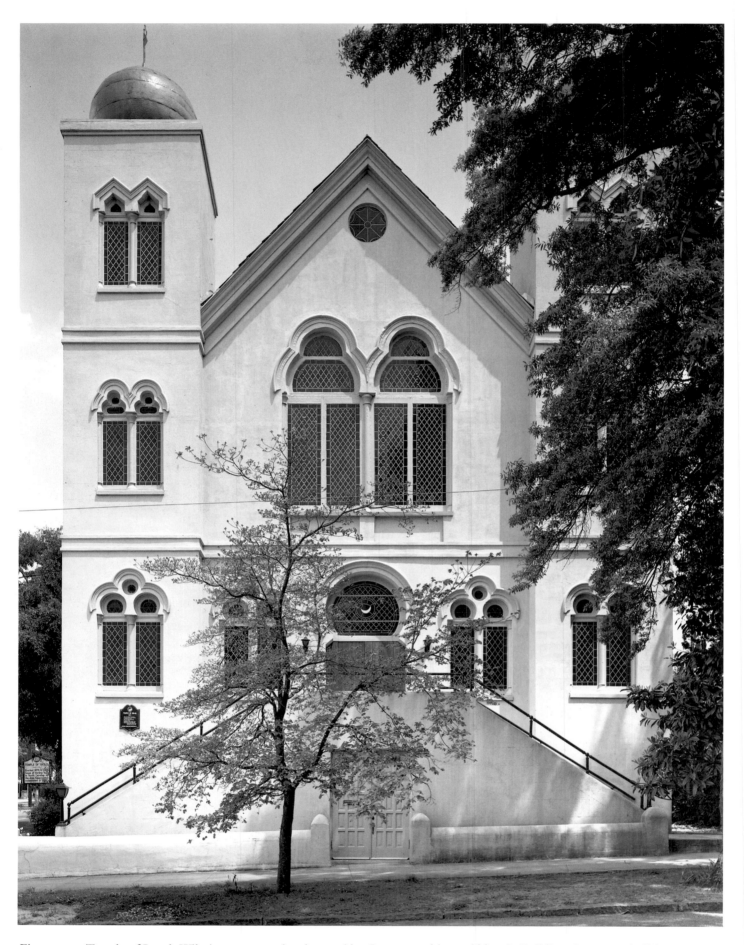

Figure 4.56. Temple of Israel, Wilmington, completed 1876. Alex Strausz, architect; Abbott's Building Company, builders.

Figure 4.57. St. Stephen A.M.E. Church, Wilmington, 1880–88. Lewis Hollingsworth, builder.

Among the major examples of postwar Gothic Revival in the city is St. Stephen A.M.E. Church (fig. 4.57), built 1880–88. The church began as Front Street Methodist, founded in the late eighteenth century with the "penny collections" of the predominantly slave congregation. The separate history of St. Stephen's began in February 1865, on the Sunday after federal troops occupied the city after the fall of Fort Fisher. When the white minister arrived to begin the early morning service customarily held for slave members, he found that a black church member and the black Union chaplain had already begun the service. "The whole congregation was wild with excitement, and extravagant beyond all precedent." The black church members prepared a docu-

Figure 4.58. St. Stephen A.M.E. Church. Interior.

ment asserting that "the church property was theirs, and was an African church," sought a "minister from the North," and strove to transfer the church "in a body" to the African Methodist Episcopal Church of the United States. This effort failed. On May 2, 1865, 642 black members withdrew and formed their own congregation, built a small church, and allied themselves with the A.M.E. denomination.[59]

In 1880 the congregation began work on a large new church, with most of the work being done by the members—a common practice among black congregations, which ordinarily included many skilled artisans. Lewis Hollingsworth, a builder, drew up the plans. By 1881, with the brick walls and the roof built, money ran out, and for four years the congregation worshiped in shifts in the basement. In 1885, however, the local newspaper reported that workmen were finishing the interior, including the "very handsome" galleries and "beautiful scroll work," which, it was predicted, would "set off the interior arrangement of the edifice to a great advantage." The church was ready for services in 1886, and the tower was built two years later.[60] Hollingsworth's simple and forceful design has a gabled facade that rises as a sheer wall to a parapeted roofline, pierced by clean-cut arched doorways and windows. Simple buttresses mark the bays and accentuate the corner tower. The robust energy of the late Gothic Revival fills the large sanctuary, where much of the woodwork was fashioned by church members (fig. 4.58). A high, vaulted ceiling focuses on the altar, and massive, hand-planed columns support the Gothic paneled galleries with their arcades of open quatrefoils.[61]

Although the established plans and styles of religious architecture enjoyed continued vitality, important changes had begun to appear as well. Mainstream Protestant churches adopted a new church plan drawn from their own history and designed to accommodate their worship: the theater or auditorium plan. Mid-nineteenth-century English and American evangelists preaching in cities had often rented theaters to accommodate the throngs they attracted. The arrangement of theaters, with their sloping floors, provided an excellent model for evangelical Protestant churches, for it offered a maximum number of good seats from which to see and hear the preacher. Sanctuaries with sloping floors, curving rows of seats, and aisles radiating out from the pulpit became widely popular in the late nineteenth century as denominational publications presented designs for auditorium or theater-plan churches in large and small sizes.[62]

In North Carolina, this new arrangement appeared in many churches, especially in the 1890s. Methodist architect Benjamin D. Price provided such a design for the Fifth Avenue Methodist Church in Wilmington, which was built in 1889–90 and was also featured in Price's book of plans for the Methodist Episcopal Church. Behind a facade with towers flanking a broad gable, the diagonally oriented sanctuary has the characteristic sloping floor and aisles that radiate from the pulpit, altar, and choir in the corner. Typical of the period's emphasis on maximum inclusion and efficiency, an adjoining lecture room has a rolling partition and reversible seats that permit it to become an extension of the sanctuary.[63]

Figure 4.59. First Methodist Church, Washington, 1899. Charles E. Hartge, architect.

Local architects, too, incorporated the new plan. The First Methodist Church (fig. 4.59) in Washington is a beautifully executed example, designed and built in 1899 by Charles E. Hartge, a German-born architect prominent in eastern North Carolina. Its cruciform sanctuary features a sloped floor and radiating blocks of pews beneath a coffered ceiling. The handsome exterior of deep red brick and granite trim is dominated by an imposing tower with elegant polygonal and cylindrical forms culminating in a dramatic belfry. In Charlotte, Grace A.M.E. Zion Church (figs. 4.60, 4.61) was built by one of its founding members, William W. Smith, Charlotte's leading black architect and builder, who executed the brickwork with a wealth of corbeled bands, pilasters, pinnacles, and parapets, typical of many churches at the end of the century. In the sanctuary, a complex, coffered ceiling dramatizes the auditorium plan with its concentric arcs of pews focusing on the altar, pulpit, and chancel choir.[64]

The auditorium plan was not restricted to large urban churches, however. Both in denominational publications and in actual practice, small churches also embodied the new plan; many of

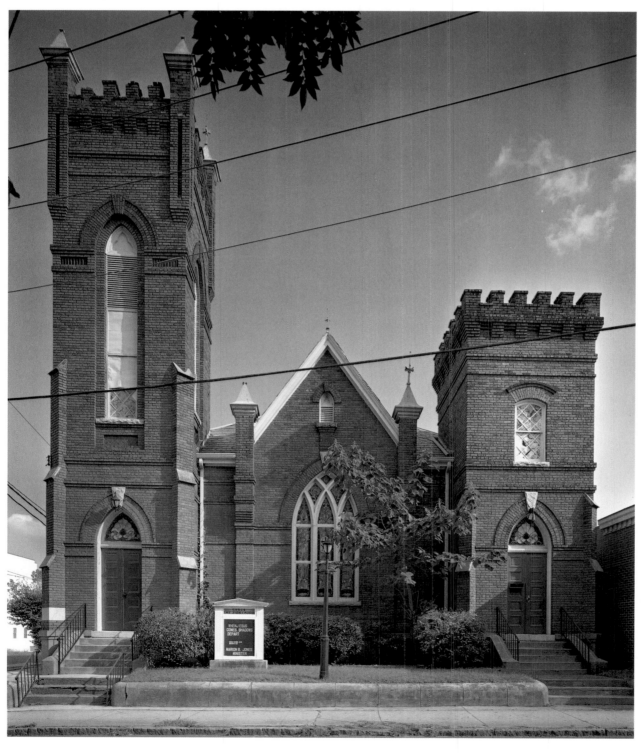

Figure 4.60. Grace A.M.E. Zion Church, Charlotte, begun 1900. William W. Smith, architect-builder.

Figure 4.61. Grace A.M.E. Zion Church. Interior.

Figure 4.62. Grassy Creek Methodist Church, Ashe County, 1904.

these were frame country churches built by local carpenters who emphasized their towers and broad gables with decorative shingling and millwork. The radiating pews and sloping floor might be oriented sideways within the church, as at Grassy Creek Methodist Church (fig. 4.62), built in 1904 and typical of scores of fine turn-of-the-century country churches. Or the entrance and the pulpit might occupy opposing corners of a diagonally oriented sanctuary, an arrangement executed in dramatic form at Cleveland Presbyterian Church (figs. 4.63, 4.64) in Rowan County, built about 1890, which has a tall corner entrance tower that accentuates the meeting of two broad gables.[65]

Although the Gothic Revival remained the prevalent style for church architecture, the Romanesque Revival took on new importance in large churches. For the 1893 First Presbyterian Church in Salisbury (fig. 4.65), Philadelphia architect Charles W. Bolton combined the massive forms, rough stone and pressed brick, round arches, and bands of windows first popularized in America during the 1870s and 1880s by New York architect Henry Hobson Richardson. The sweeping curves and broad arches of the Richardsonian Romanesque gave powerful expression to the theater-plan sanctuary and to an equally important element of new church planning—the Akron-plan Sunday school—used in this church and several others. From a central lecture room radiated a series of small classrooms; this permitted age-grouped Sunday school classes to hear the superintendent read a common lesson from the "uniform lesson" system used throughout the country each Sunday. Then, remaining in their seats in their own classrooms, the children

Figure 4.63. Cleveland Presbyterian Church, Rowan County, ca. 1890.

could participate in small group lessons for the rest of the Sunday school hour. A movable partition separated the Sunday school section from the sanctuary and allowed additional seating for large services. This efficient and orderly design was invented by an Akron, Ohio, Sunday school teacher and businessman in the 1860s. His idea, which found ready acceptance in mainstream Protestant church architecture, perfectly embodied the late nineteenth century's interweaving of evangelism and popular morality with rationalized efficiency. Greensboro's West Market Street Methodist Church, designed by S. W. Foulk of New Castle, Pennsylvania, and also built in 1893, is a monumental example of the Romanesque Revival–style church; its theater-plan sanctuary combines with an Akron-plan Sunday school, which could be joined to form a "vast auditorium" to hold 2,000 people.[66]

Figure 4.64. Cleveland Presbyterian Church. Interior.

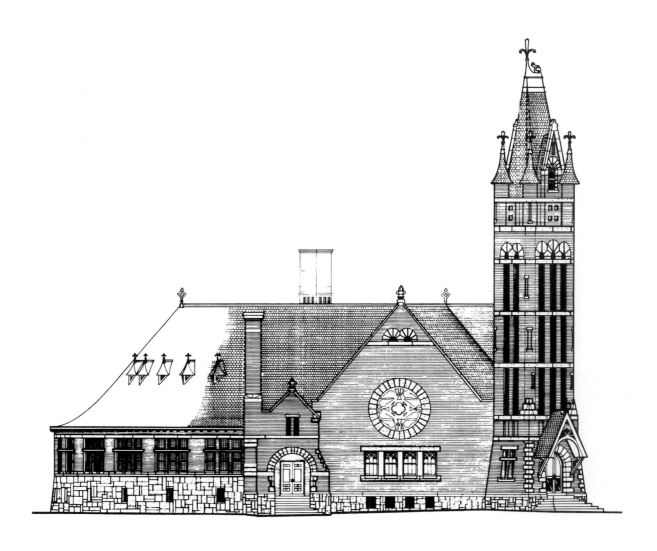

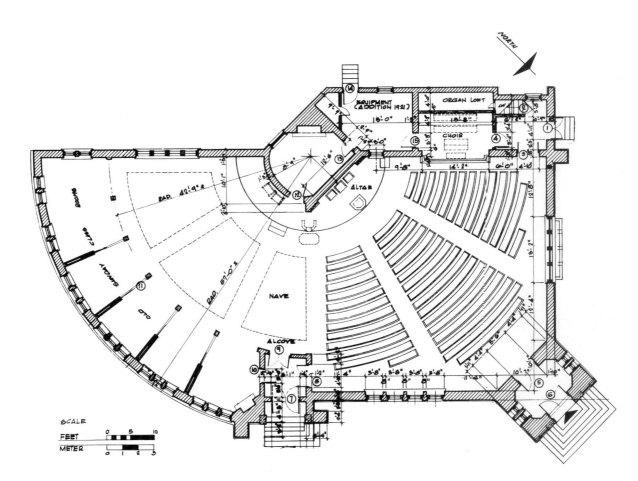

Figure 4.65. First Presbyterian Church, Salisbury, 1893. Charles W. Bolton, architect. Elevation and plan by Gus R. Anastes and Edward Mills. Destroyed; only the tower still stands. (Historic American Buildings Survey)

As contrasts between rural and urban churches suggest, the largest and most stylish buildings concentrated in the cities. The sequence of development seen in church architecture recurred in commercial and public buildings: the popularization of familiar picturesque styles in the 1870s and early 1880s, followed by the proliferation of new forms and styles in the 1880s and especially in the 1890s.

In commercial architecture, postwar expediencies and the first flurry of rebuilding produced hastily constructed frame commercial and industrial buildings, especially in the tobacco boomtowns of Winston and Durham. Fires regularly eliminated these, however, and as they were replaced, insurance requirements and business leaders' concern for a respectable and stable image promoted the construction of sturdy, often elaborate buildings of metal and masonry. Buildings with iron fronts or other manufactured metal trim became emblems of commercial prosperity. Italianate and classical motifs—columns, arcades, cornices, and quoins—predominated. The MacRae-Otterbourg Building (fig. 4.66) on Front Street in Wilmington is among the most elegant examples. Sedate colonnades frame large plate-glass windows, and classically detailed pilasters carry a paneled and bracketed cornice. It was built for merchant Donald MacRae in 1878–79, and by 1881 Louis Otterbourg, tailor and clothier, was advertising it as "Otterbourg's Iron Front Men's Wear Depot"—the "Handsomest Building in the South." The George R.

Figure 4.66. MacRae-Otterbourg Building, Wilmington, 1878–79.

French Store on the same street was built in 1873 and in 1884 was cited as the first full iron front in Wilmington. In Raleigh in 1874, builder Thomas Briggs erected a brick building with metal quoins, window hoods, and a dated parapet. Prominent among the national manufacturers of metal fronts was the Mesker Company of St. Louis and Evansville, who gained wide sales throughout North Carolina. The company sold entire storefronts in single, double, and triple sizes, or lower shopfronts only, all of which were sent by rail from their factory and assembled on site, complete with a company emblem.[67]

Commercial buildings of handsome brick construction were an enduring source of civic pride. Although there were a few stone facades, brick was the material of the new cities. Brick was cheaper than ever before because of the proliferation of railroads and brick manufacturing plants; it presented a powerful image of stability and fire resistance, and it offered the capacity for ornamental expression that sprang directly from the nature of the materials and the bricklayer's skill.

In Wilmington in 1899, architect Charles McMillen designed the new offices of the *Messenger* (fig. 4.67), which L. H. Vollers built of the city's favored Philadelphia pressed brick with brownstone trim.[68] The restrained design—which continued in two subsequent additions to house the Southern Bell Telephone and Telegraph offices—features heavy pilasters framing the broad plate-glass shop windows, an arcade of windows at the second level underlined by a continuous sill of rough stone, and a deep corbeled cornice.

There were infinite variations on such themes. The Brittain Store (fig. 4.68), built in the 1870s in the village of Summerfield, Guilford County, is a tour-de-force display of decorative bricklaying applied to a standard three-bay store, from the heavy molded labels around the door and windows to the quoined corners and the broad band of triangular-headed corbeling that makes a Gothic effect across the roof.[69] By contrast, in the Drhumor Building (fig. 4.69), built in Asheville in 1895, architect A. L. Melton repeated standard commercial elements in a sophisticated composition that earned local praise for its "artistic" character. He skillfully combined

Figure 4.67. Messenger and Southern Bell Telephone and Telegraph Building, Wilmington, 1899–1906. Charles McMillen, architect; L. H. Vollers, builder.

Figure 4.68. Brittain Store, Summerfield, Guilford County, 1870s. George J. Smith and Son, contractors.

Figure 4.69. Drhumor Building, Asheville, 1895. A. L. Melton, architect; Fred Miles, stonecarver.

Figure 4.70. Worth Manufacturing Company, Randleman, late 19th century.

openings topped by rough stone arches with bands of rectangular windows that proceed along the two street facades and swell out in a pavilion that rounds the corner. The glory of the building, though, is the extraordinary carved work by Fred Miles. At the street level, classical colonnettes rise to a cornice spectacularly alive with mythological creatures, classical figures, shells, and the faces of local personages.[70] On the streets of every growing town, architects and builders created these proud new brick buildings that were lauded as "modern," "artistic," and "city-like." They fully exploited the qualities of masonry—pilasters, corbeling, and paneling in brick and the rough and smooth textures of stone—and combined these with the rhythms and contrasts of arched and square openings to create a rich and lively commercial architecture.

The industrial architecture that housed the engines of prosperity generally took a similar form. For their textile mills and tobacco factories, industrialists first built simple frame or brick structures, then gradually expanded their operations with larger, more substantial, and more elaborate buildings. Most of these, following the New England models that shaped form as well as function, featured thick brick walls, rhythmic arched windows, and bracketed cornices of the Italianate style. One of scores of late-nineteenth-century examples is the Worth Manufacturing Company mill (fig. 4.70) on the Deep River at Randleman. It is typical of its era in many ways. It was built in the heart of the Piedmont on a rural, water-powered site; such small streams as the Deep and the Haw had powered the birth and rebirth of the textile industry. And, like most of its contemporaries, the Worth Mill began as a small building that, as the industry expanded, took on additions in various forms. Although the North Carolina industrial revolution began during the antebellum period, it developed rapidly in the late nineteenth century. Growth continued at such a pace that most of the intact landmarks of industrial architecture date from the turn of the century (see Chapter 5).

Civic and collegiate architecture provided the symbolic landmarks of growing towns. Though hard times slowed public construction, by the late 1870s a number of projects were underway. The Second Empire, neoclassical, and Romanesque styles prevailed throughout the 1870s and 1880s, and, beginning in the 1880s, several state projects introduced the Queen Anne style.

During Reconstruction and afterward, the U.S. government expanded its program of post office and federal courthouse construction. Designs provided by the supervising architect of the U.S. Treasury and contracts let through a national bidding process to contractors and materials suppliers brought to many North Carolina towns their first—and sometimes only—monumental examples of current national styles of architecture.[71]

A. B. Mullett, the supervising architect of the Treasury Department immediately after the war, was responsible for a generation of federal buildings in the Second Empire style, which expressed the aggressive confidence of the postwar age and appeared at its most bombastic in his State, War, and Navy Building in Washington, D.C. A simpler version of Mullett's national style is Raleigh's U.S. Post Office and Courthouse. First considered in 1857 but delayed by the war, the project was resumed in 1874–79. Originally planned to be of brick, the building was constructed of granite from a quarry near Goldsboro. Its mansard roof capped a composed and symmetrical building of strongly classical cast.[72]

Most other federal building projects in North Carolina waited until the 1880s and 1890s, when a series of U.S. courthouses and post offices were built in North Carolina towns. Designed under Mullett's successor, Willoughby J. Edbrooke, they were standard versions of the nationally popular Richardsonian Romanesque mode, sometimes accented with the design motifs and polychrome effects of the High Victorian Gothic style.[73] Although such styles had become standard fare in European and American cities by the 1880s, they were remarkable ventures in small towns, especially in the South. Wilmington's towered stone federal building was a massive, asymmetrical structure with great round-arched openings, built of Sanford sandstone. Less costly projects in smaller towns were usually of brick, such as the red-and-yellow brick federal building erected in New Bern in 1889–91. (Its clock tower was added a few years later at the behest of the local citizenry.)

The 1890–92 federal building in Statesville, now the Statesville City Hall (fig. 4.71), embodies Edbrooke's Romanesque monumentality at its most handsome and restrained. The contract for the building was given in June 1889 to Peter Demens, a colorful, Russian-born entrepreneur and sometime builder who had the Asheville federal building to his credit. Despite problems resulting from local workmen's unfamiliarity with federal construction standards, the departure of Demens's erratic and drunken partner, and other troubles, the building was completed quickly and well. Built of rich, red pressed brick, it has a simple, asymmetrical composition with a low, swelling tower, deep arched entry, and judiciously applied stone and foliated terra-cotta ornament.[74]

County and municipal building projects tended to favor classically oriented styles and symmetrical compositions; a central tower, rather than the earlier heroic portico, served as the chief indicator of public status. The Second Empire style was especially popular, for it combined obvious modernity with familiar classical dignity. When the Cabarrus County Courthouse in Concord burned in 1875, architect G. S. H. Appleget designed its replacement, a composition akin to his stylish mansions, with a mansard-roofed clock tower front and center.[75] Several other counties followed Appleget's example in the 1870s and 1880s. The Craven County Courthouse (fig. 4.72) in New Bern was designed by Philadelphia architect Samuel Sloan and built by New Bern contractor John B. Lane in 1882–83. The early nineteenth-century courthouse had burned in 1861, and for the next twenty years the court and county functions were housed in private buildings; when the jail also burned in 1879, the county moved at last toward a new building. Sloan produced a dignified, conservative design for the first major public building erected in

Figure 4.71. U.S. Post Office (Statesville City Hall), Statesville, 1888–91. Willoughby J. Edbrooke, supervising architect of the Treasury; Peter Demens, contractor.

New Bern since the war—a handsome structure in dark red brick, adorned with a vividly patterned slate roof, ornate iron trim, and stylish iron cresting atop the high mansard roof.[76] Across the state in Monroe, the blossoming railroad town, Thomas J. Holt, brother of the prolific antebellum builder Jacob Holt, provided a design for the new Union County Courthouse (fig. 4.73), which was built in 1886. Like Appleget, Holt combined verticality and a bulbous tower with a familiar and symmetrical classical formula.

The grandest of the late-nineteenth-century courthouses was the New Hanover County Courthouse (fig. 4.74), built in Wilmington in 1891–92. In keeping with Wilmington custom, it was designed by a Savannah architect, A. S. Eichberg, who won the commission over several competitors and was touted as "one of the leading architects of the United States," one who was "not only known in the South, but has a national reputation in his business, and has designed many of the most modern buildings in the Southern and Western states." Local supervision was provided by James F. Post. Construction was contracted to Valentine-Brown and Company of Brunswick, Georgia, and the materials arrived from dozens of distant suppliers. The 72-by-101-foot building boasted nearly fireproof construction—a brick structure faced with pressed brick and granite, with locally cast iron stairs, iron cornices, and a slate roof. Only the floors were of wood. The plan was arranged around intersecting corridors intended to "enhance its comfort in securing all the draught necessary at all seasons of the year." The whole was to be "ornamented in the most elaborate style." Eichberg combined the prominent towers, round arches, and textured granite of the Romanesque style—newly displayed at the city's U.S. post office—with the verti-

Figure 4.72. Craven County Courthouse, New Bern, 1882–83. Samuel Sloan (Sloan and Balderston), architect; John B. Lane, builder.

Figure 4.73. Union County Courthouse, Monroe, 1886; additions, 1922. Thomas J. Holt, architect; J. T. Hart, builder; C. C. Hook, architect (additions).

Figure 4.74. New Hanover County Courthouse, Wilmington, 1891–92. A. S. Eichberg, architect;
James F. Post, supervising architect; Valentine-Brown and Company, builders.

Figure 4.75. Main Building, Biddle Institute (Biddle Memorial Hall, Johnson C. Smith University), Charlotte, 1883.

cality and contrasting colors of the High Victorian Gothic. He arranged these in a symmetrical composition with a 130-foot clock tower; shorter flanking towers anchor the corners, and horizontal bands of light stone counter the vertical thrusts of the towers and tall arched windows.[77]

Collegiate architecture also rebounded after a long period of bare maintenance. Newly established state and denominational colleges for blacks and whites, men and women, required large main buildings. The functional, almost industrialized Romanesque Revival, executed in sturdy brick, met their needs with directness, substance, and economy. At Biddle Institute (fig. 4.75), a Presbyterian-sponsored school for blacks in Charlotte, a now-unknown architect or builder designed a towering brick main building, which was constructed with student and faculty labor. Typical of "Old Main" buildings on many campuses, it was a large, multiple-use structure designed to communicate an air of stability, success, and importance to the community. Although it displays the same symmetrical, towered composition and generally Romanesque themes as the New Hanover County Courthouse, these are executed in a starkly simple form, articulated only by the bricklayers' decorative techniques that became a hallmark of institutional and industrial architecture throughout the state. A contrasting face of academic architecture appears in Lea Laboratory (fig. 4.76), built in 1887–88 as a chemistry building for the Baptist-affiliated Wake Forest College. Fitting into the antebellum red-brick Palladian architecture of the campus, it was designed by Baltimore architect John Appleton Wilson in a remarkably early rendition of the Colonial Revival style—a prim yet vigorous tripartite composition with pedimented block, hyphens, and pedimented flankers. The characteristic late-nineteenth-century brickwork is rendered in Flemish bond, and unconventional pilasters and pediment adorn the entrance.[78]

Figure 4.76. Lea Laboratory, Wake Forest College (Southeastern Baptist Theological Seminary), Wake Forest, 1887–88. John Appleton Wilson, architect; Ellington and Royster, builders.

The state government also embarked on ambitious building projects. Although strapped for funds, aware of widespread poverty, and cautious amid controversies over extravagance and corruption, state leaders authorized a series of major institutional buildings. Like private clients of the time, rather than continuing the antebellum policy of patronizing some of the nation's foremost architects, they commissioned designs from the middle ranks of national and regional practitioners.

The first big state building to be completed was one that had been proposed repeatedly before the war but seemed newly pressing in the postwar era: the State Penitentiary. It was authorized in 1868 and designed by architect Levi Scofield of Ohio. Its castellated Gothic style combined the aspects of both a fortification and a community monument, and it was executed in intricately varied brickwork and stone. Employing a practice then in common use, the prison was built by its inmates. William J. Hicks was appointed director and architect of the prison, and under his direction the inmates, living at first in temporary quarters, made thousands of bricks and constructed the big, elaborately corbeled and towered building. Additional bricks and workmen also came from private firms in Durham and elsewhere. Work began in 1870 and the first block of cells was finished by the mid-seventies, but construction continued into the 1880s.[79]

With its competence established and its economic advantages obvious to a state in need of inexpensive brick buildings, the prison continued to make bricks and supply workmen on contract to state and private building projects. The Supreme Court Building, built near the Capitol in 1885–88, was supervised by Hicks and constructed of penitentiary brick. And when the State College of Agricultural and Mechanic Arts was established in Raleigh in 1887, the location of the campus made it convenient to use bricks from the prison. The Main Building (fig. 4.77), designed by Baltimore architect Charles L. Carson in a bold and simple Romanesque Revival style, was erected in 1889 of penitentiary brick and North Carolina sandstone.[80]

The principal architect for the state's major buildings of the 1870s and early 1880s was Samuel Sloan of Philadelphia. After the Civil War, Sloan, like A. J. Davis, had found himself bypassed by the urban architectural trends of the North, but unlike Davis, who retreated to his office, Sloan turned to the South in hopes of finding work.[81] Sloan's first commission was for a huge hospital for the white insane of western North Carolina, to be located near Morganton. Population growth—and, some said, the psychological impact of war and its aftermath—had

Figure 4.77. Main Building, State College (Holladay Hall, North Carolina State University), Raleigh, 1889. Charles L. Carson, architect. (North Carolina Division of Archives and History).

increased the demand for treatment of the insane beyond the capacity of A. J. Davis's antebellum asylum in Raleigh. North Carolina leaders, following a path blazed by Governor Morehead in 1849–50, visited Dr. Thomas Kirkbride in Philadelphia to consult with him on hospital planning. Kirkbride promptly recommended Sloan, who had been building hospitals from his plans, and the state commissioned Sloan to design an expansion of the Raleigh facility and a huge new asylum near Morganton to serve residents of western North Carolina. Thus began a final, productive chapter in Sloan's career.

For the Morganton hospital, located like the Raleigh asylum on a prominent hilltop site outside the town but accessible to the newly completed Western North Carolina Railroad, Sloan used Kirkbride's familiar E-shaped plan (fig. 4.78). He treated the huge structure with a high mansard roof, eclectic detail, and a central, domed administrative pavilion dominated by a

Figure 4.78. Western Insane Asylum (Broughton Hospital), Morganton, 1875–83, 1890s. Samuel Sloan and Adolphus Gustavus Bauer, architects; James Walker, contractor. (North Carolina Collection, University of North Carolina at Chapel Hill)

Figure 4.79. Memorial Hall, University of North Carolina at Chapel Hill, 1883–85. Samuel Sloan, architect. Destroyed. (North Carolina Collection, University of North Carolina at Chapel Hill)

towering, three-tier Corinthian portico. A contract was let in 1875 to James Walker of Wilmington, and work began. But when the money ran short, the project was stopped in 1883 with only the center section and one wing finished.[82]

When Sloan visited Raleigh during the course of the project to promote support for the hospital, he gained other state commissions. One was for an auditorium, Memorial Hall (fig. 4.79), for commencement exercises at the University of North Carolina. This was the first major postwar construction project at the university, which had closed from 1871 to 1875 and was still struggling to recover. Sloan designed an extraordinary, hexagonal brick building that measured 134 feet by 128 feet and stood 52 feet tall. Its adventurous form and eclectic motifs deviated radically from the conservative norms of the university. Two great semicircular wooden arches and eighteen arched rafters carried a tentlike slate roof that swept down to Gothic gables and buttresses. The churchlike impression continued in the gabled, twin-towered entry facade with its polychromed Romanesque arches. Planned to accommodate four thousand people, it was surely the largest hall in the state. Construction was difficult: the huge timber arches fell the first time the builders tried to raise them, and cost overruns temporarily stopped construction and required a desperate fund-raising campaign. Complaints over the costs grew loud. At its completion in 1885 the building had cost some $45,000, which the financially shaky institution could ill afford for a single-purpose building. But the spectacular building, which resembled nothing else on the campus, was much admired in its time—university president Kemp Battle hailed it as a "model to the students of architecture in the institution." It was the only major building erected on campus from the Civil War until the late 1890s.[83]

Figure 4.80. Executive Mansion, Raleigh, 1883–91. Samuel Sloan, architect; W. J. Hicks, contractor.

Controversy and cost overruns also beset Sloan's other major state project, the Executive Mansion in Raleigh (fig. 4.80). Sloan had gained the confidence of Gov. Thomas Jarvis during his work on the hospital in Morganton. The legislature authorized a new governor's residence in 1883 and directed the governor to save money by using convict labor and penitentiary-manufactured materials. Sloan arrived in Raleigh in the spring of 1883 with designs in hand for a sandstone mansion, adjudged to be "very artistic," "ornate," and "in modern style . . . with the ample porches, hallways and windows which every house built in this climate should have." But after Raleigh stonemasons refused to work with the convicts, the specifications were altered to produce a brick building with sandstone trimmings. Other cost-cutting measures eliminated expensive hardwood interior finish and altered the roofline. A contract for construction was let to prison architect W. J. Hicks for some $25,000. In a familiar tale, despite all these economies, costs ran high and appropriations were stopped. In 1888 a political attack on Jarvis claimed that Sloan was "superannuated and retired for a quarter century in his native town, and could not draw the plans of a dog kennel that would not cost 300 per cent more than his estimate."[84]

Finally, in 1891, the residence was ready for occupancy. In typically rapturous prose, the Raleigh newspapers assured readers that the "mansion" was "a source of pride . . . a veritable palace . . . spacious and elegant." But Sloan never saw any of his last major works completed. He died in Raleigh from the effects of sunstroke in 1884. His young assistant, Adolphus Gustavus Bauer, took over the work on the hospital, the auditorium, and the governor's mansion.[85]

The Executive Mansion was among the first North Carolina examples of the Queen Anne style. This eclectic style, which originated in England, first entered popular American architecture in the 1870s and gained acceptance in the 1880s. It featured complex and irregular forms, varied textures, dramatic rooflines, strong asymmetry, and projecting and receding elements that created extravagantly picturesque compositions. The "ornate" and "artistic" Executive Mansion featured characteristic Queen Anne elements in its complex roofline, its bevy of pavilions, balconies, and porches, and its contrasting materials. But Sloan tailored the composition to his clients' conservative bent. At its core the mansion was essentially symmetrical, restrained in outline, and reassuringly familiar in plan. Political cronies and visiting dignitaries mounted the front steps to a porch set in a central entrance pavilion and then stepped through a big double door into a broad central entrance hall flanked by pairs of spacious rooms, all aligned in a customary procession.

The Reign of the Queen Anne Style

By the time the Executive Mansion was completed, it was not as venturesome as it had been when Sloan drew up the plans in 1883. In the mid-1880s, the Queen Anne style entered the mainstream of North Carolina urban architecture. Literature of the period assured readers that the style promised new embodiments of "modern," "elaborate," and "artistic" taste. In 1881 William Comstock (formerly associated with A. J. Bicknell) published *Modern Architectural Designs and Details . . . in the Queen Anne, Eastlake, Elizabethan, and Other Modernized Styles*, in which he commented that "a great change has taken place in the style of Architecture," from the predominantly "French" to the "'Queen Anne,' 'Elizabethan,' 'Jacobean,' or 'Colonial' [which] while bearing many characteristics of their prototypes, do not adhere strictly to any of them." From this panoply of past motifs and modern forms, Comstock offered readers a selection of "low-priced, yet picturesque, designs of good character." The architectural journals that proliferated from the late 1870s through the 1880s and 1890s, such as the *American Architect and Building News*, *Carpentry and Building*, and the *Southern Architect*, likewise promoted the Queen Anne style.[86]

The Queen Anne style displayed the technological potential of the industrial age at its most extravagant and unabashed. The popularization of the style in North Carolina corresponded with the rise in urban and industrial wealth and, particularly, with the dizzying rise in the fortunes of industrialists. With its energetic forms and extravagant displays of mass-produced ornament, the Queen Anne mode perfectly suited the frenetic progress, urgent expansionism, and ebullient individualism of the period.

Rather than composing a simple L or T shape, the form of a Queen Anne building was usually a rectangle made irregular by bays, towers, wings, and balconies. Tall hipped roofs sprouted endless gables, dormers, and towers. The number and diversity of rooms multiplied. In the most elaborate plans, vestibules opened into central stair halls—often fitted with fireplaces— and thence into a flowing series of formal rooms. In simpler examples, an off-center passage had two, three, or four rooms on either side, often shifted to project one side forward. In still others, a basic square or rectangular plan gained sufficient appearance of irregularity through a projecting bay here or a wing there. Porches ran in and out, often billowing into a tower or gazebolike pavilion at a corner. Tall plate-glass windows were often bordered with square panes, called in catalogs of the time "Queen Anne windows." Such elements could be designed by local architects or copied or adapted from architectural books by competent local builders. The protean style made the Italianate and Gothic cottage forms appear simple by contrast.

Adolphus Gustavus Bauer, Samuel Sloan's assistant, created a constellation of Queen Anne–style buildings during his brief tenure in North Carolina. When Sloan died in 1884, Bauer completed designs for the Executive Mansion and the university's Memorial Hall. He left Raleigh in 1887 but returned in 1891 after peregrinations in Europe and America. He took commissions for the completion of Sloan's Morganton hospital and for a new project—the North Carolina School for the Deaf, to be located on a neighboring hillside site near Morganton. In his design for the school, Bauer translated the familiar E-shaped institutional plan into a majestic Queen Anne composition, its long skyline bristling with bartizans and spires, the sweeping double porches lending a domestic aura.

Bauer's masterpiece, though, was the Baptist Female University building (fig. 4.81) erected next door to Sloan's Executive Mansion in Raleigh. Bauer adapted the E-shaped plan to the needs of a multipurpose college building that was executed in full-blown Queen Anne style. The energetic forms coalesced in a great mass of projecting and receding towers and gables, pediments and turrets. Double and triple porches, the favorite promenade for gentle Baptist maid-

Figure 4.81. Baptist Female University, Raleigh, 1895–99. Adolphus Gustavus Bauer, architect. Destroyed. (North Carolina Division of Archives and History)

Figure 4.82. Battery Park Hotel, Asheville, 1886. Destroyed. (North Carolina Division of Archives and History)

ens, swirled across the front and around the towered corners. Work began on the building in 1895 and was completed in 1899; when opened, it was praised as convenient, attractive, comfortable, healthful, and homelike, "a delight to the eye, being the most handsome school building in the South." But Bauer, like Sloan, did not see his work completed. In May 1898, despondent following the death of his wife in 1897 and lasting trauma from an 1896 train accident, he shut himself in his room in Raleigh and shot himself. By that time, he had produced a body of work in North Carolina that captured his own romantic and restless spirit and that of the age in which he worked.[87]

Coeval with the Baptist Female University, and sharing its exuberant form and spreading piazzas, were the great resort hotels of the 1880s and 1890s. Some of the grandest were built in Asheville, where completion of the Western North Carolina Railroad inaugurated a boom era for the cool and picturesque mountain community in "the Land of the Sky." The Battery Park Hotel (fig. 4.82)—"the finest hotel in the South"—was built in 1886 on the old Battery Porter eminence overlooking the city. Its vividly modern outline presided over the community, and its lively procession of pavilions and towers, its roofline busy with dormers, turrets, and chimneys, and its balconies, piazzas, and gazebos conveyed an image at once grandiose and homelike. The Kenilworth Inn, completed in 1890 from a design by architects F. L. and W. L. Price of Philadelphia, was a splendid confabulation of balconied towers, half-timbered jettied gables, castellated entries, and clustered chimneys, suggesting an entire European village massed in one great picturesque pile.[88]

The most spectacular private residences in the Queen Anne style were built by North Carolina's fast-rising industrialists. In Durham, the town that epitomized the astonishing speed of industrial growth and moneymaking, tobacco barons quickly replaced their once remarkable Italianate residences with Queen Anne–style mansions, which, like their previous houses, were located in sight of their factories and facing the railroad. In 1887 Julian Carr, president of the Durham Tobacco Company, various banks, and electric companies, removed his Italianate-style Waverly Honor and erected Somerset Villa (fig. 4.83), a brick, stone, and marble concoction designed by architect John B. Halcott of Albany, New York, and built by W. C. Bain of Greensboro. Carr's "palace home" gleamed with carved paneling and imported fittings. The ceilings were painted with clouds and cupids by Jule Korner, alias "Reuben Rink," a North Carolina man who had developed Blackwell's fabulously successful Bull Durham advertising campaign. A Richmond newspaper praised Somerset Villa as "*the* conspicuous landmark [of Durham] upon which the eye first falls and upon which it loves to linger." Others, however, viewed this newfound splendor with skepticism. Retired professor Charles Phillips wrote to architect A. J. Davis from Chapel Hill that, though the South was still poor, "There is lately finished and occupied, in Durham, a private residence that cost $75000, a wooden building decorated lavishly, with

Figure 4.83. Somerset Villa, Durham, 1887. John B. Halcott, architect; W. C. Bain, builder. Destroyed. (Collection of Albert G. Carr)

Figure 4.84. Fairview, Durham, late 1880s. Washington Duke House and Duke Tobacco Factory. Until the 20th century, many North Carolina industrialists built their residences near their factories. The house has been destroyed; the factory, though altered, still stands. (North Carolina Collection, University of North Carolina at Chapel Hill)

mantelpieces of onyx, &c. This is because folks will smoke & chew and spit—even Chapel Hill boys and professors will do so."[89]

The trend toward elaborate residences continued as Washington Duke, patriarch of the booming tobacco firm of W. Duke and Sons, built in about 1888 a Queen Anne mansion called Fairview near his tobacco factory (fig. 4.84). In the 1890s, tobacco businessman George W. Watts built a towered stone-and-brick mansion from designs by architect C. H. Norton. Dozens of other houses went up throughout the city as tobacco manufacturing thrived.[90] But the grandest Queen Anne buildings in North Carolina reigned only briefly. The sprawling hotels, the college buildings, and the principal mansions are all lost. Some quickly succumbed to fires that spread through their endless wooden corridors; others' locations at the hearts of growing cities stood in the path of urban growth; still others fell victim to the twentieth century's antipathy for the extremes of Victorian aesthetic and attitudes—a joint attack from traditionalists and modernists alike.

Figure 4.85. Hylehurst, Winston-Salem, 1884. Henry Hudson Holly, architect; Fogle Brothers, contractors.

Beyond the great "palace homes," more modest versions of the Queen Anne style appealed to dozens of successful businessmen who, by the 1880s, had entered a new age of prosperity. They obtained designs from a wide range of sources—urban architects, architectural books, and local builders. Salem industrialist John W. Fries commissioned a design from New York architect Henry Hudson Holly, author of several popular patternbooks. Hylehurst (fig. 4.85), built in 1884 by Winston's Fogle Brothers, characterizes the popular midlevel Queen Anne style. Half-timbering, decorative shingling, paneled chimneys, and an inset balcony enliven the exterior. The plan is organized around a central stair hall with fireplace and has a parlor, sitting room, and library as well as a dining room, kitchen, and butler's pantry on the main floor. Each room features a different variety of wood. The parlor mantel (fig. 4.86), typical of the period, features glass-enclosed cabinetry for displaying a collection of bric-a-brac, revealing the residents' informed and artistic taste.[91]

In 1886 Wilmington businessman William McKoy and his wife, Katherine Bacon, considered several designs for their house offered by her brother, young architect Henry Bacon. But instead of his compositions in the shingled and colonial styles then coming into vogue, the couple decided on a Queen Anne–style residence (fig. 4.87) from *Carpentry and Building* (October 1886) and hired Wilmington architect James F. Post to adapt the design to their needs. An irregular but generally symmetrical plan ranges out from an entry hall, and the projecting gables, bays, and dormers of the house are enriched with brackets and grids of bosses, while the asymmetrical roof reaches out to shade a small, private upper porch.[92]

The Queen Anne style also lent itself to the remodeling of old buildings; many magazines of the period illustrated how one might modernize an old-fashioned house. Henderson businessman Ike Young reportedly employed Samuel Sloan, the architect of the Executive Mansion, to expand his antebellum house about 1883. Mistletoe Villa's symmetrical plan assumed a Queen Anne air with the addition of balconies, gables, and intricate porches (plate 14). The exterior

Figure 4.86. Hylehurst. Mantel. Elaborate wooden, slate, and marble mantels, often embellished with tile, cabinets, and inserts, appeared in most handsomely finished late-19th-century residences.

paint scheme specified colors to pick out all the elements that display the rich, bold coloristic effects of the age—the walls were to be "light and dark Olive, relieved with Maroon on the chamfers and small reeds," the shingling light red and slate colors, and the doors stained a mahogany color.[93]

In Asheville, where the tourist and invalid trade was growing, Julia Wolfe gradually expanded her boardinghouse, the Old Kentucky Home (called Dixieland in her son Thomas's *Look Homeward, Angel*), with room after room added to the rear, while the front presented the public with a fashionable gabled bay, inset balcony, and broad porch (figs. 4.88, 4.89). In the country-

Figure 4.87. McKoy House, Wilmington, 1887. James F. Post, architect; Alfred Howe, chief carpenter.

Figure 4.88. Old Kentucky Home (Wolfe House), Asheville, 1883, expanded early 20th century. The residence and boardinghouse was the setting for Thomas Wolfe's novel *Look Homeward, Angel*.

Figure 4.89. Old Kentucky Home. Dining room.

side, where few farmers had the interest in or extra cash for investing in elaborate dwellings, it was rare to see a farmhouse such as W. L. McGhee's in Franklin County (fig. 4.90). He, in fact, was a Franklinton crop-lien merchant who acquired a farm with an early nineteenth-century house already standing and erected in front of it a Queen Anne–style residence with octagonal bays, big front gables, and spindles, sunbursts, and arches trimming the porch and gables (fig. 4.91).

The Queen Anne style also proliferated among smaller houses. In such one-and-a-half-story dwellings as the Meares House in Monroe (fig. 4.92), the high roofline, expansive bays, and concentrated ornament of the Queen Anne style conveyed a cottagelike charm quite different from the imposing dignity of larger residences. Family tradition recalls that railroad agent Gaston Meares and his wife, Juanita, obtained a design for their house while attending a world's fair shortly before they built their house in Monroe about 1898. It appears likely that they obtained their plans from the popular Knoxville architect George F. Barber, perhaps while attending the Tennessee Centennial Exposition of 1897.[94]

Barber was a favorite source for North Carolinians who wanted Queen Anne–style dwellings. One of several architects tapping the national market for house plans, Barber had begun his career as a builder in Kansas and Illinois and in 1888 moved to Knoxville. The 1890 edition of Barber's *Cottage Souvenir* initiated a nationwide mail-order business that soon employed some thirty draftsmen and twenty secretaries. Barber advertised in popular trade and women's magazines: "You . . . want to build something convenient yet HANDSOME AND ARTISTIC. Write to us."

Figure 4.90. Person-McGhee House, Franklin County, ca. 1890.

Figure 4.91. Person-McGhee House. Porch.

The prospective client could either order stock plans from plates and price lists or describe specific desires and needs on Barber's printed form to obtain a customized design; in either case, plans and specifications were intended for ready execution by a local builder. More than two dozen commissions in North Carolina encompass a range of Barber's evolving style.[95]

Busy industrial leaders delighted in the stylishness and practicality of Barber's designs. In Elkin, shoe manufacturer Alexander Smith obtained plans for a magnificent residence built in 1893–97 by contractor T. A. Dean of Salem (fig. 4.93). The massing of the house is characteristic of Barber's Queen Anne style—high hip roof, front-facing gable bay, inset balcony, and corner towers. The exterior displays resplendent ornamentation, including half-timbering that glitters with pebbles, fish-scale shingling, sawnwork, spindles, and iron cresting.[96] A quite different image is projected in the mansion Barber designed for Richard J. Reynolds. Built in 1895 near his booming tobacco factories in Winston, Reynolds's residence featured gently rounded forms, shingled surfaces, bulbous towers, and the classical details then regaining popularity.[97]

In 1897 industrialist Charles T. Holt erected a Barber-designed residence (fig. 4.94) on a hill overlooking the family textile factories at Haw River. Charles's grandfather Edwin Holt, founder of the textile dynasty, had built his simple villa from an A. J. Davis design in 1849; his sons and sons-in-law, who rebuilt and expanded the business after the war, had erected L- and T-shaped Italianate houses and towered Second Empire–style dwellings. Charles, the third generation, commissioned a Queen Anne–style residence from Barber. The complex form and flowing plan

Figure 4.92. Meares House, Monroe, ca. 1898. Attributed to George F. Barber, architect.

Figure 4.93. Smith House, Elkin, 1893–97. George F. Barber, architect; T. A. Dean, contractor. (North Carolina Division of Archives and History)

Figure 4.94. Holt House, Haw River, 1897. George F. Barber, architect.

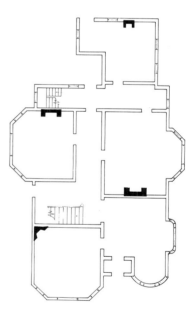

Figure 4.95. Holt House. Plan by Carl R. Lounsbury.

(fig. 4.95) are combined with classical themes, but polygonal shapes and angular pediments predominate, along with freely handled Palladian motifs and squatty Corinthian colonnettes.[98]

   Such exuberant frame houses expressed their owners' position and success frankly and proudly. Each prospering industrialist built his big house in the midst of the town or village he was creating, near the factories that were his life. Within a few years, this pattern would change as first the leading industrialists and then the expanding urban upper and middle classes moved out of town to suburban enclaves. In the 1880s and 1890s, however, the creators of new fortunes built mansions that were public landmarks of their hard-won wealth and their stature as catalysts of prosperity. The unembarrassed presentation of individual wealth, the use of architectural forms directly expressive of their industrialized production, and the display of mainstream "artistic" tastes as evidence of cultural stature—all were part of the ethos of the age.

Artistic Individualism of the Industrial Age

A few individuals participated more intensely in the ideal of architecture as personal artistic expression. The idea of the home as an individualized statement that included the assembly of collected art works and architectural elements into an artistic and unique ensemble had gained prominence in the later years of the nineteenth century. Surely the most eccentric expression of architectural individualism is Korner's Folly (fig. 4.96) in Kernersville. The house was the personal creation of Jule Gilmer Korner, whose father, a German clockmaker, had settled in the rural Moravian tract. The artistically talented Jule studied art in Philadelphia, returned home to work as a sign and portrait painter, and embarked on a career that brought artistic inventiveness into harness with booming industrialization. It was Korner, under the pseudonym Reuben Rink, who in 1883 created for Julian Carr the international advertising campaign that made Bull Durham tobacco a household word and left the handpainted bull trademark emblazoned on buildings and billboards—some as large as 80 by 100 feet—throughout the nation. Korner also painted and decorated the tobacco barons' mansions, such as Carr's Somerset Villa.[99]

In 1878 Korner began a building intended to combine his studio, office, and reception rooms, but, as his son recalled, "Pygmalion-like he became so attached to his first creation that

Figure 4.96. Korner's Folly, Kernersville, ca. 1878–86.

Figure 4.97. Korner's Folly. Interior.

he transformed it eventually into his home." A cousin dubbed it "the Folly." In 1880 Korner "christened" the house and, upon his marriage in 1886, he had much of the decoration installed. The house combined Jule's artistic bent and unorthodox ebullience with something of a German clockmaker's soul. The brick exterior with its high-peaked, cross-gable roof gives little hint of the interior, where the plan and ornament defy all categorization. Twenty-two rooms at seven different levels range from grandiose reception rooms to crowded little chambers, passages, and nooks that continually mystify the visitor. The strangeness of the rooms is intensified by the extravagant, often bizarre decoration—paneling, molded plaster, heads of demons, cupids, and animals, and ceilings painted with idyllic scenes (fig. 4.97).

Not far from Korner's Folly, another aspect of Germanic artistic expression appeared in the construction of Cedarhyrst (fig. 4.98), a stone mansion in the old Moravian town of Salem. Dr. Nathaniel Siewers, who grew up in Salem, had studied medicine in Germany, where he fell under the spell of German culture and the romantic nationalism that celebrated folk art, medieval castles, and revivalist architecture. Upon returning to Salem to establish his medical practice, Siewers employed architect Max Schroff of New York to design his house and office, Cedarhyrst, in a romantic restatement of Germanic themes. Built by the local Fogle Brothers firm, Cedarhyrst added a rich new layer to the architecture and culture of the old German community. In contrast to the playful pastiche of Korner's Folly, Cedarhyrst was a serious and studied composition. Rough limestone blocks face the walls and rise to castellated battlements, and shields and other medieval-inspired motifs adorn the porte cochere. Carved woodwork and stained glass fill

Figure 4.98. Cedarhyrst, Winston-Salem, 1893–95. Max Schroff, architect; Fogle Brothers, builders. The house now serves as the offices of the Moravian Church in America, Southern Province, and Salem Congregation.

Figure 4.99. Cedarhyrst. Stair hall. Peter Regennas, Paul Regennas, and Nat Peterson of Fogle Brothers, carvers.

the stair hall (fig. 4.99) and flanking rooms. Mottoes appear in German script: "Strongly built, trusting in God" inscribed in stone outside; "Make us well" in stained glass over the doctor's office, and so on.[100]

The epitome of European-inspired artistic expression was Biltmore. This great American mansion, the grandest of private dwellings in an era of great private palace building, was constructed for George Washington Vanderbilt near Asheville in the 1890s (figs. 4.100, 4.101). On a visit to Asheville in the mid-1880s, New Yorker Vanderbilt had decided to build a mountain lodge there, but his vision soon expanded. In 1885 he had inherited $10 million from his father, William Henry Vanderbilt. Artistic and bookish in his interests, the young man soon devoted his full energies—and eventually all of his fortune—to developing Biltmore.[101]

Vanderbilt employed as architect Richard Morris Hunt, who had served the Vanderbilt family previously in designing an opulent New York townhouse and several mansions in Newport, where a spirit of family competition produced ever more luxurious and monumental residences. Hunt had been the first American to train at the École des Beaux Arts in Paris; by the 1880s he was the dean of the American architectural profession. He brought to Biltmore his seasoned mastery of Beaux Arts principles, the imaginative and scholarly use of the architecture of the heroic past, and the use of space, form, and detail to create a carefully ordered sequence of arrival, movement, and aesthetic experience. In 1889 Vanderbilt and Hunt journeyed through Europe to develop ideas for the estate, and they found in the chateaus of the Loire Valley the ideal they sought. Hunt had an established preference for the Early Renaissance style of François I, which he had used in several other American mansions.[102]

Vanderbilt also hired Frederick Law Olmsted, the landscape designer who, like Hunt, was at the end of a long career as the head of his profession in the nation. As the plans took shape, Olmsted and Hunt collaborated to create a fully integrated design. Olmsted planned a naturalistic, picturesque park with curving roadways that led the visitor to the sudden vision of the house, seemingly remote from the world amid its formal gardens. Olmsted also pushed Vanderbilt toward large-scale reforestation and the establishment of a scientific forestry program on the 125,000-acre estate.

Construction began in 1890. The house and the landscaping proceeded simultaneously, as several hundred workmen were engaged in the grading, excavating, and, eventually, the construction and elaborate carving. A three-mile railroad spur was built to the site to transport materials, including Indiana limestone and steel beams and rafters. In 1892 the understory was completed; by 1893 the second story was done; in 1894 the roof was under construction; and at Christmas in 1895, Vanderbilt, his mother, and many friends celebrated the formal opening of the house.

Hunt's composition displayed his skillful adaptation of French Renaissance architecture to the needs of a modern palace. The tall roof with steep towers and dormers, the confident interplay between balance and subtle asymmetry, and the open and closed forms of arcades, loggias, conservatory, and spiral stair (copied in reverse spiral from that at Blois) combine to create an intensely romantic house. It is at once picturesque and palatial, vividly French yet perfectly attuned to its site in the Blue Ridge Mountains. The flowing plan of oval, polygonal, and rectangular rooms extending from the entrance hall and winter garden accommodated the purpose of private entertainment and recreation with friends, while displaying to best advantage Vanderbilt's—and the era's—penchant for European art works and architectural elements.[103] Different decorative schemes reigned as guests moved from the intimate, glass-roofed winter garden to the vast heraldic banquet hall. In the basement, modern technological efficiency and the complex operation of the fully staffed house are evident in the amazing scale of kitchens, storage, and laundry rooms. Here, too, guests could engage in the recreational luxury of a tiled indoor swimming pool (see fig. 4.1). The upper stories contained abundant bedrooms and servants' quarters.

Vanderbilt's favorite room was the library, approached by a 90-foot-long tapestry gallery with an adjacent loggia overlooking the mountains to the west. The walnut-paneled library (plate 15), lined with over 20,000 books, is dominated by an Italian black-marble mantel and an

Figure 4.100. Biltmore House, Asheville, 1890–95. Richard Morris Hunt, architect; Frederick Law Olmsted, landscape architect.

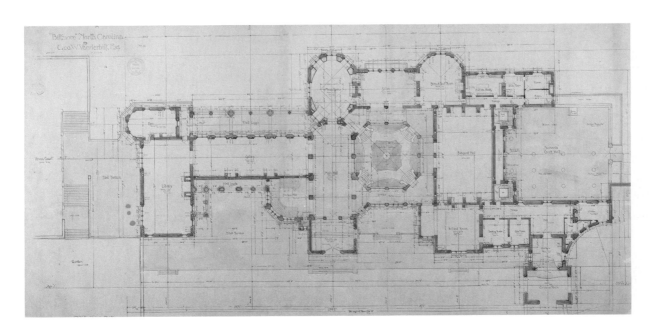

Figure 4.101. Biltmore House. Plan by Richard Morris Hunt. (Biltmore Estate)

overmantel by Karl Bitter that features large female figures; Bitter also created the steel Venus and Vulcan andirons. Nymphs and clouds swirl across the ceiling in an Italian allegorical painting, one of Vanderbilt's European purchases.

The architectural impact of the Biltmore project extended beyond the estate gates. Hunt and his talented assistant architect, Richard Sharp Smith, designed a remarkable series of masonry buildings in a severely elegant, richly coloristic style characteristic of northern European architecture of the late nineteenth century. Pebbledashed stucco, red tile roofs, and red brick trim provided a functional, handsome medium for a wide range of building types. In Asheville, Vanderbilt sponsored the construction in 1892–93 of the Young Men's Institute (fig. 4.102), a community facility paralleling the YMCA but meant to serve black citizens in the segregated city, including the several hundred black construction workers at Biltmore. R. S. Smith used the dark pebbledash and red brick and tile in a handsome and artfully organized multipurpose building containing a gymnasium, meeting rooms, and stores; the building accommodates a sloping site and many different entrances and imparts an urbane presence to its prominent corner site.[104]

The principal concentration of the estate style, for such it became, was in Biltmore Village itself. For the manorial village laid out at the entrance to the estate, Olmsted had lobbied successfully for an English rather than French style. Here the pebbledash, brick, and tile, plus a suitably fanciful dressing of half-timbering, were used in the village houses, offices, and railroad station.

Figure 4.102. Young Men's Institute, Asheville, 1892–93. Richard Sharp Smith, architect.

Figure 4.103. All Souls' Episcopal Church, Biltmore Village, 1895. Richard Morris Hunt, architect.

A late Hunt work of extraordinary power and beauty is the small but monumental All Souls' Episcopal Church (fig. 4.103), designed shortly before Hunt's death in 1895 as the centerpiece of the estate village. The church embodied Hunt's belief that the "Byzantine" church form, following the short-naved Greek cross plan rather than the elongated Latin cross, was the most functional ideal for Protestant worship; it embodied "dignity" and "repose" and was arranged so that all the congregation might hear and see the service.[105] At All Souls' Hunt concentrated the ideal elements of the parish church into powerful volumetric forms: a Greek cross plan dominated by the great square tower at the crossing; the nave reduced to an entry of the same depth as the transepts; and the apsidal chancel given equal prominence as an expansive cylindrical form under a sweeping conical roof. The dark pebbledash is accented by the red brick quoins, the crisply laid brick buttresses of the tower, and the richly textured red tile of the flowing roofs.

Begun during the prosperity of the late 1880s but completed amid the nationwide depression of the 1890s, Biltmore evoked a wide range of reactions that convey the conflicting currents of the Gilded Age. In Asheville, its construction boosted the local economy and gave the town unrivaled social and architectural panache. Some of the most talented men associated with its design and construction, as will be discussed in the next chapter, remained in Asheville and created buildings of a sophistication far beyond what the town or region had seen before. In the national press, however, such lavish expenditure generated a "torrent of condemnation": a writer in 1896 blasted American millionaires' unjustified engagement in "the most conspicuous European mode of asserting social supremacy, the building of great houses," while another insisted that the great houses were "out of harmony with the spirit of American institutions." Thorstein Veblen's *Theory of the Leisure Class* (1899) cited the Hunt palaces as examples of his new term, "conspicuous consumption."[106]

But while critics attacked its callous extravagance, other writers marveled at Biltmore's cost, scale, and luxuriousness. *Southern Architect*, a journal quick to publish any sign of magnificence in the still economically backward South, regaled readers with a detailed description of Biltmore's wonders—its twenty bathrooms, "invisible" electric lights, "wonderful system of storage batteries," elaborate gardens, stables for forty head of saddle and carriage horses, and the expenditure of $3 million on the house and another million on the gardens. Another observer saw the chateau as "one long tale of delight. . . . The proportions and scale, combined with the details, fill one with the kind of peace which comes from artistic perfection."[107]

The issues and innovations presented at Biltmore marked the end of one era and the beginning of another. In the century to come, the redefinition of "artistic" taste, the development of an architectural profession in a Beaux Arts tradition, the movement of the upper classes from the city to protected sylvan precincts, the proliferation of sanitation measures and electricity, and the concentration and display of wealth and power in new terms would create a new chapter in the architecture of the nation and of North Carolina.

CHAPTER 5

The Early Twentieth Century, 1900–1941

On all sides he heard talk, talk, talk—terrific and incessant. And the tumult of voices was united in variations of a single theme—speculation and real estate. People were gathered in earnestly chattering groups before the drug stores, before the post office, before the Court House and the City Hall. . . . The real estate men were everywhere. Their motors and buses roared through the streets of the town and out into the country, carrying crowds of prospective clients. One could see them on the porches of houses unfolding blueprints and prospectuses as they shouted enticements and promises of sudden wealth into the ears of deaf old women. . . . It was fantastic. Along all the streets in town the ownership of the land was constantly changing; and when the supply of streets was exhausted, new streets were feverishly created in the surrounding wilderness; and even before these streets were paved or a house had been built upon them, the land was being sold, and then resold, by the acre, by the lot, by the foot, for hundreds of thousands of dollars.
—Thomas Wolfe, *You Can't Go Home Again*

As the people of the conservative rural state navigated the transition to an urban, industrialized, corporate society, architecture—like the expanding networks of communication and transportation and the control of the economy—was increasingly shaped by national influences.[1] To be sure, regional building forms persisted, as they had in the late nineteenth century, in small rural houses and some types of farm buildings; thousands of black and white North Carolinians continued to live in simple frame and log dwellings that differed little from those of their parents and grandparents. By and large, however, national architectural forms became ever more prevalent, from the skyscraper to the millworker's house.

A pervasive sense of urgency to improve North Carolina's place in the national mainstream took architectural expression as leaders looked to national sources of professional expertise in seeking to establish new institutions and strengthen old ones, to expand cities, and to enhance the cultural identity of the state. In North Carolina, as elsewhere in America, the early twentieth century was the golden age of the architect and the planner, members of expanding professions who, influenced directly or indirectly by Beaux Arts precepts, offered the public the architecture of a new order. In the early twentieth century, North Carolina clients returned to their antebellum pattern of employing prominent national architects for especially large and venturesome projects as such projects became more numerous and more elaborate in this period of progressive economic development. Knowledgeable North Carolinians kept abreast of national advances in architecture, and they took pride in commissioning designs from leading professionals who provided both specialized expertise and urban panache, whether for their university campuses, churches, skyscrapers, hotels, or suburban developments.

Beaux Arts architects dominated practice through the 1920s, and in the 1930s a scattering of progressive clients commissioned from leading immigrant European architects some early and adventurous examples of the International style. At the same time, North Carolina's resident

Figure 5.1. R. J. Reynolds Tobacco Company Office Building, Winston-Salem, 1927–29. Richard H. Shreve and William Lamb, architects; James Baird Company, contractors. Elevator lobby.

architects—including native-born men and several who moved to the state to establish practices—attained new prominence. Every little city had its cluster of prolific architects, whose regional practices overlapped with those of architects in other southern states. Their work covered a broader spectrum of building than in times past or times to come, from public monuments to a wide range of residential work. Furthermore, a growing spate of popular magazines and standardized building components enabled national trends to permeate even ordinary housing to a greater extent than ever before.

Within this context, regional architectural identity began to dissipate. Regional preferences appeared not so much in specific local building forms, but rather in the selections North Carolinians made from the national spectrum of possibilities: economic limitations, climate, and deep-rooted attitudes undergirded a familiar bent for restrained rather than extravagant styles, for building types that were consonant with familiar forms and materials, and for the spacious, individualized use of land in keeping with old patterns of rural life.

Social and Economic Changes

The first four decades of the twentieth century brought sweeping social and economic changes. In the state election of 1900, after a bitter fight, white Democrats' effective "white supremacy crusade" ended the political challenge from blacks, Republicans, and Populists. The Democrats returned to power and inaugurated a long era of political stability and economic progress tied to racial segregation and social conservatism. State and local governments and expenditures expanded; the state devoted heroic efforts to expanding and improving public schools, colleges, and the state university; and, as the automobile became part of American life, a bond issue for highway construction in the 1920s countered the age-old problem of transportation and helped transform North Carolina into a "good roads state."

Yet, at the same time, agricultural problems persisted and farmers continued to suffer, the numbers of farm tenants kept rising, and erratic prices brought bouts of prosperity followed by deeper plunges into debt. The configuration of business and transportation networks changed as corporations consolidated on a national scale. The Southern, the Seaboard, and the Atlantic Coast Line railroad companies subsumed hundreds of small lines that crossed North Carolina. The American Tobacco Company, created by James B. Duke of Durham, swallowed up other tobacco companies. The scale and productivity of factories—mainly tobacco, textiles, and furniture—grew as North Carolina's industrialization continued to expand. Increasingly after World War I, factories participated in the "rationalized" segmentation of time, space, and workers to maximize output and profits, and labor conflicts erupted throughout the state.[2]

Cities and towns grew rapidly, for although the state remained predominantly rural, the population and its proportion of urban dwellers increased. In 1900, less than 10 percent of the total population of 1.8 million people lived in urban areas; by 1940 there were 3.5 million North Carolina residents, of whom about 975,000 lived in urban places. No dominant metropolis emerged, but rather a string of small cities and towns blossomed along the railroad lines and highways, and the Piedmont cities of Charlotte (1910) and Winston-Salem (1920) emerged as the largest in the state. Hydroelectric power was harnessed on the great rivers of the Piedmont, bringing new efficiency to manufacturing and convenience to town dwellers. Such changes brought new opportunities and prosperity to many, but they also came hard among a rural people who clung to a sense of individual independence and the small-town social economy. With the stock market crash of 1929 and the long years of the Great Depression, the economic and social framework changed forever as Americans and North Carolinians struggled to attain a new balance among the individual, business, and government.

Architecture of the New Order

The 1893 World's Columbian Exposition in Chicago, visited by some twenty-seven million Americans, had promoted the ideal of the White City—a European-inspired Beaux Arts vision of order, cleanliness, and control, cast in the imagery of a heroic past.[3] It encouraged the American City Beautiful movement and a city planning concept that separated communities into functional zones with ceremonial axes and focal monuments. Its grandiose columned and domed buildings depicting America as the new Rome influenced public architecture throughout the nation. The individual state buildings at the exposition, on the other hand, were renditions of a wide range of "colonial" models. These popularized the Colonial Revival as a movement that drew upon the whole span of preindustrial American architecture, from seventeenth-century New England to the antebellum era.

In North Carolina and throughout the South, this emphasis on efficient and orderly planning and on classical and colonial styles meshed conveniently with white Democrats' triumphant return to the old political order. The newly reentrenched leaders linked the ideal of progress and prosperity with the reestablishment of a hierarchical, predictable social order. Rejecting as "bumptious" and "callow" the ebullient ornament and restless designs of the preceding era, they sought an architecture that combined modern convenience and efficiency with the forms and symbols of continuity from antebellum and colonial times. In keeping with Beaux Arts ideals, planners and developers promoted the segmentation of communities. Electricity provided power quietly and from distant sources, and street paving and sanitation measures removed some of life's unpleasant realities from view and scent. First the streetcar and then the automobile made it convenient for the upper and middle classes to live at a distance from their workplaces, while the political and social climate also encouraged greater geographic separation among classes and races. City growth patterns—mill village, workers' neighborhood, or suburban enclave—combined developers' and planners' concepts of efficiency and profit with a rural flavor in keeping with the roots of their residents.

Several trends mark the architecture of this period. Industrial buildings grew ever larger, directly expressing their function and materials, first in a turn-of-the-century culmination of the nineteenth century's industrial Romanesque Revival style and then in more streamlined versions in the 1910s and 1920s. A vivid contrast to these buildings appears in the organic forms and natural materials, such as wood shingles and fieldstone, used for intentionally informal resort architecture and in the simplified house forms that were promoted as a domestic antidote to industrial pressures. Simultaneously, symbolic historicism regained its preeminence: classicism supplanted the Queen Anne and other eclectic and picturesque styles in public architecture, Gothic Revival continued in church and school buildings, and Colonial and other revival styles took the lead in domestic architecture. Only in a few instances in the late 1920s and the 1930s did some venturesome clients commission works in antihistorical Art Deco, Moderne, and International styles. By and large, North Carolinians, like many Americans, preferred an architecture that couched modernity in terms of continuity.

Industrial Architecture

Trends in factory architecture and industrial housing that had begun in the 1870s or 1880s and continued through the 1920s reached their fullest development during the period from about 1890 to 1910. Many of the best-preserved and most illustrative industrial landmarks date from the turn of the century. Huge complexes outstripped the small, isolated mills of the pioneer era. Gastonia, Spray (in present Eden), Roanoke Rapids, and Kannapolis were among the old and new textile sites that expanded into vast centers of industry.

In the new factories, form and function combined in massive brick buildings in the round-arched industrial style based on Romanesque German and Northern Italian architecture.[4] These boldly expressive buildings partook of an international industrial style that encompassed the manufacturing centers of Europe and America and blended the demands of factory organization with European antecedents and virtuoso displays of the bricklayer's art. In the post–Civil War era, as textile manufacturing recovered and developed steadily in the North Carolina Piedmont, industrialists drew heavily on New England architectural models. They built mill after mill, at first modest in size, but steadily increasing through additions to old mills and construction of larger new ones. The use of ornate brickwork peaked around the turn of the century, and a trend toward simpler forms appeared in the 1910s and 1920s.

The Durham Hosiery Mill (fig. 5.2) exemplifies textile mill architecture at the turn of the century. It was built in 1902 for Durham tobacco magnate Julian S. Carr, who had branched out into textile manufacturing. The towered Romanesque factory form satisfied demands of strength, fire resistance, natural lighting, and symbolic stature. Massive, tapering brick walls and massive structural timbers supported wooden floors that carried heavy loads and vibrating machinery.[5]

The thick plank floors and stout timbers were also part of the "slow burn" construction promoted by the New England Mutual fire insurance companies. In a fire, such bearing members would char but retain their structural strength instead of collapsing as iron did in high heat. Fire walls isolated such areas as the picker rooms and boiler rooms that were especially susceptible to fire. The tower allowed the stair (through which a fire could spread) to be closed off from

Figure 5.2. Durham Hosiery Mill, Durham, 1902.

Figure 5.3. Cliffside Mill, Rutherford County, begun 1900.

the main structure, and it typically supported a water tank for a sprinkler system. Such measures were crucial in a factory that processed highly combustible cotton and where workers and machinery operated in lint-filled air. The long, regular rows of great, arched windows created a rhythmic arcade along the long walls and provided air and natural light for the men, women, and children at work inside, a feature that remained important even after electricity was introduced.[6] The inherent decorative capacities of brick combined well with the Romanesque style in familiar bricklayers' techniques. Corbeled, turned, and tilted brick courses dramatize the walls, doorways, and windows and concentrate on the ornate and dominant tower.

As textile manufacturing expanded, some mills grew to a vast scale. Cliffside Mill (fig. 5.3) in Rutherford County, begun in 1900, was one of the last and largest water-powered textile mills. It was founded by western Carolina industrialist R. Rutherford Hayes, who operated mills all along the Second Broad River near the South Carolina border. As Hayes's operation expanded, Cliffside Mill repeated its prevailing architecture in a series of blocks stacked up on the steep riverside, their unifying brick and rhythmic arched windows creating a powerful image of continuing corporate growth.[7]

The monolithic power of factory architecture appears at its most imposing in the vast, steam-powered Loray Mills in Gastonia. The first big brick section was erected in 1900–1902 by the Flynt Construction Company of Palmer, Massachusetts—a massive, five-story building 504 by 130 feet, with room for nearly 1,000 workers. In 1920 the factory was sold to the Manville-Jenckes Company of Pawtucket, Rhode Island, which expanded the mill with a six-story, 100-by-140-foot wing. Touted as the world's largest textile mill under one roof, the complex, built by leading New England construction firms, combined modern technology with powerful forms and superb workmanship in brickwork and stone trim.[8]

At Cliffside and Loray, as at nearly every mill, the factory was part of a larger unit, the mill village. As mills were established on rural waterpower sites, housing had to be provided in order

Figure 5.4. Cedar Falls Cotton Mill Village, Randolph County, 1890s.

to attract and keep workers. The mill-village system, which strengthened the employer's control over his work force, continued as the industry developed. In contrast to the New England–influenced factory buildings themselves, the mill villages of the South developed along lines adapted from regional house forms and rural living patterns. The characteristic village included rows of small individual houses built of log or frame. The village usually ranged up beside the stream along a road leading from the factory, and it included such buildings as a church, lodge hall, and store. Usually workers were assigned to houses based on the number of family members—including the wife and children—who worked in the mill. Most nineteenth-century mill villages were small, as exemplified by Glencoe in Alamance County; established about 1880 on the Haw River by James and William Holt, members of one the Piedmont's pioneering textile families, Glencoe has now become almost a ghost town, and it is falling rapidly into ruin.[9]

While few of the pre-1885 villages survive in good condition, many of those built around the turn of the century still display the continuity of the village form. Some villages are isolated communities, such as Cedar Falls in Randolph County (fig. 5.4), where the houses stand along a ridgeline overlooking Sapona Mills on the Deep River below. Other rural villages, like Henrietta and Caroleen near Cliffside, expanded and coalesced to create larger communities.

As steam power came into widespread use after 1890, mills could be located in cities and on rail lines rather than along rivers and streams. The number and sizes of villages expanded rapidly in the new century, as the number of textile workers skyrocketed from 32,000 in 1900 to 125,000 in 1930. Such towns as Gastonia and Roanoke Rapids took shape as conglomerations of adjoining mill villages, while in Charlotte and Greensboro mill villages formed major new sectors of the existing cities. In other towns, a mill village might constitute a self-contained unit that was part of a diverse community. The Reidsville Cotton Mill, for example, was established in 1889 in a town whose economy was dominated by tobacco. In 1896 a new company bought the factory and, following a customary pattern of honoring the female relatives of industrialists, renamed it Edna Cotton Mill after the daughter of a major stockholder. The factory was expanded and new houses built in the village. "Paradise Alley" (fig. 5.5) is one of several streets of six-room duplexes built by Reidsville contractor Joe Husband for the Edna Cotton Mill in 1897. It typifies the urban mill village with its grid of streets reaching out from the railroad and the mill.[10]

Figure 5.5. Edna Cotton Mill Village, Reidsville, 1897.

Figure 5.6. China Grove Mill Village, Rowan County, 1890s.

Whatever the setting, certain house types recur in most mill villages. An especially prevalent plan is the center-chimney-plan house, similar to the saddlebag form, built either as a single-family house or as a duplex. This plan might be built one or two stories tall. The houses at Cedar Falls and Edna Cotton Mill illustrate the central-chimney duplex with dual entries opening from the front porch, plus a rear ell.[11] One-story dwellings often repeated the central-passage plan and two-room plan familiar in small rural houses. Another standard type was the L- or T-plan cottage exemplified in the houses (fig. 5.6) built for the Patterson Manufacturing Company in China Grove, Rowan County.[12]

In 1899, Daniel Augustus Tompkins, an engineer and mill operator in Charlotte, codified common wisdom in his book, *Cotton Mill: Commercial Features*, which he published for "the use of textile schools and investors." A South Carolina planter's son who had trained in engineering at Rensselaer Polytechnic Institute, Tompkins personified the New South's blend of a hierarchical rural culture with rationalized efficiency. He provided plans for a typical range of mill houses and urged mill owners to provide each house with a half-acre lot for a home garden. As he explained: "The whole matter of providing attractive and comfortable habitations for cotton operatives may be summarized in the statement that they are essentially a rural people. They have been accustomed to farm life, where there is plenty of room. While their condition is in most cases decidedly bettered by going to the factory, the old instincts cling to them. The ideal arrangement is to preserve the general conditions of rural life."[13] The southern mill village thus represented a careful and pragmatic architectural balance between the paternalism of the southern industrialist and the vestigial rural independence that the mill owner knew to be essential to maintaining a "contented" and stable work force.

After World War I, changes occurred in both mill operation and mill-village development. Along with a "less personal management style of the new generation of mill owners" came a new "self-consciousness" in village design that reflected the nationwide development of city planning. There was a movement not toward greater concentration but toward a suburblike development within the existing concept of individual space and a semirural atmosphere. Planner Earle Draper laid out landscaped villages such as Spindale (1920) in Rutherford County, with its curving streets, parks, and other amenities for workers at the huge Stonecutter Mill. And, even as village size continued to grow with the scale of the factories, and as such textile men as Stuart Cramer in Cramerton and James W. Cannon in Kannapolis strove to establish "model" villages, small individual houses remained the basic unit of the southern mill village.[14]

Figure 5.7. Hicks and Toms Tobacco Storage Warehouses, Durham, 1900, 1903.

Tobacco architecture created its own synthesis of functionalism, exuberant brickwork, and medieval-inspired historicism. The tobacco industry required many specialized types of buildings: sales warehouses in which skylights permitted purchasers to examine the tobacco farmers brought to sell; storage warehouses where tobacco was aged; and factories in which workers manufactured plug and smoking tobacco and cigarettes. In late-nineteenth-century Durham, Winston, and Reidsville—and in the coastal plain market towns such as Greenville and Wilson after 1890—small independent companies had built and operated various individual facilities.

But in 1890, the thirty-three-year-old Durham industrialist James B. Duke formed the American Tobacco Company, which combined the five major competing tobacco firms into one enormous trust that produced more than 90 percent of the cigarettes made in the United States. In the interests of control and efficiency, American stopped buying aged leaf from middlemen and began to buy tobacco direct from farmers at the auction houses; the company then redried, packed, and aged the tobacco in its own buildings. Between 1897 and 1911, the firm erected in Durham the specialized buildings this new procedure required, buildings intended to protect tobacco from fire—arson was a recognized threat—and to provide the natural ventilation necessary for aging. New warehouses were built year after year as needed.[15]

The Hicks and Toms Warehouses (fig. 5.7) of 1900 and 1903 are representative of the group. The thick walls, tin-covered shutters, fire walls, and heavy internal timber structures are typical of industrial architecture; these buildings were, in fact, insured by the New England Mutual Company. Their purpose—to store hogsheads of tobacco for periods of three to five years—defined their form still further. The tobacco was "prized" into hogsheads, each weighing about a thousand pounds. Workmen used freight elevators and rolling platforms ("johns") to lift and stack the hogsheads in three layers. The height of each story, the division of the long buildings into sections by fire walls, and the placement of supports were all determined by the size and arrangements of hogsheads. In order to regulate temperatures throughout the year to age the tobacco properly, the buildings incorporated a system of vents, chutes, windows, and chimney stacks. From these requirements and from the vigorous display of the brickmason's art and medieval-

Figure 5.8. Edenton Peanut Factory, Edenton, ca. 1909.

inspired forms, the Duke firm created a powerfully symbolic architecture. Belt courses, pilasters, arcades, and cornices of corbeled brickwork articulate each wall. The end and fire walls rise in castellated steps, and the roofs bristle with Gothic-paneled vent stacks and chimneys, row after row, roof after roof, block after block. Castlelike indeed, these warehouses announced the success and expanding domain of the American Tobacco Company and kept safe the treasury of aging leaf on which the firm's life depended.[16]

In the early twentieth century, industrial architecture took on increasingly simplified, almost abstract forms that stripped away most superficial elements of medieval-inspired ornament and emphasized forthright expression of structure. A severely handsome example is the Edenton Peanut Factory (fig. 5.8). It was built about 1909 by local investors who were making Edenton into a regional peanut market and processing center. The factory produced as many as 1,500 hundred-pound bags of shelled, cleaned peanuts a day, and these were loaded onto railroad cars on the track beside the building.[17] The mass of the 66-foot square building is dramatized through the subtle manipulation of brickwork. The tall base slopes inward, its buttresslike piers expressing the weight they bear. From the piers spring pilasters that rise through three stories to a continuous corbeled cornice, creating great vertical panels in the walls. Segmental-arched windows are placed in accord with internal needs. Capping the building and the campanile-like elevator tower are simple, broad-brimmed roofs of stylized Italianate form.

Railroad Architecture

The spectacular growth of factories depended on the expanding network of rail transportation. Railroad mileage in North Carolina had more than doubled between 1880 and 1890, and between 1890 and 1910 ownership of railroad lines was consolidated into huge corporations controlled from outside the state. The Atlantic Coast Line (1900) extended along the coast and encompassed the old Wilmington and Weldon line; the Seaboard Air Line (1900) included more

Figure 5.9. Hamlet Railroad Depot, Hamlet, 1900.

than a hundred smaller lines running through the inner coastal plain; and the Southern Railroad Company (1892) dominated the Piedmont. These tied North Carolina's rail connections into national north-south lines and countered the state's original concept of an east-west route to encourage in-state trade.[18]

The new corporate railroad giants spawned a new generation of handsome depots that were erected around the turn of the century, supplanting most of the smaller depots of former times. In small towns these depots, built in brick or frame, followed a characteristic one-story form and had a linear plan with waiting rooms—usually two to accommodate racial segregation—a ticket office, and freight rooms; a deep roof stretched out on angular brackets to shelter passengers. The Hamlet Railroad Depot (fig. 5.9), built for the newly formed Seaboard Air Line in 1900, exemplifies the picturesque functionality of this era of national railroad architecture. Its L-shaped form accommodates its site and purpose at the junction of the Charlotte to Wilmington route and the major line from the North to the Deep South. The rounded corner pavilion, which provides views of both lines, and the tiers of sweeping roofs emphasize the focal position of the station. Despite Hamlet's small size, the station was a major one, where trains stopped for as long as they did in Richmond and Philadelphia, and where train crews were often changed.[19]

The Southern Railway Company, which dominated the Piedmont, was formed in 1894 under the leadership of president Samuel Spencer and New York financier J. P. Morgan; in 1895 it leased the state-owned North Carolina Railroad for ninety-nine years, and it continued to absorb small lines. In 1902 architect Frank Pierce Milburn became the official architect for the firm, working out of its headquarters in Washington, D.C. His Southern Railway Station in Salisbury (fig. 5.10), built in 1907–8, is among his finest stations. Into the boldly geometric forms of the buff brick building, Milburn incorporated the curved gables and dominant central tower of the popular Spanish Mission style, creating a heady blend of modernity with the romantic aura of exotic places at the distant ends of the national rail system.[20]

Spencer Shops, the Southern Railway's vast repair facility located a few miles from Salisbury, is a monument to the new age of corporate capitalism, rationalized efficiency, and work accomplished on an unprecedented scale. Needing a major repair shop between Washington and Atlanta, the company enlisted the aid of prominent Salisbury landowners and attorneys and quietly purchased 168 acres nearby. Construction began in the spring of 1896 and by fall the shops opened: a machine shop, roundhouse, storehouse, and offices. Steel-frame buildings stood on masonry foundations with corrugated steel siding and slate roofs. Electric lights and hot-air heat made them among the most modern facilities of their time, as well as the largest. A new town, Spencer, was created to house the families of a work force that grew to more than 2,000.[21]

Figure 5.10. Salisbury Southern Railway Station, Salisbury, 1907–8. Frank P. Milburn, architect. Drawing by Frank P. Milburn. (North Carolina Collection, University of North Carolina at Chapel Hill)

Figure 5.11. Spencer Shops, Spencer. Back Shop, 1904–5.

Figure 5.12. Spencer Shops. Roundhouse, 1924.

New buildings followed steadily. The Back Shop (fig. 5.11) was built in 1904–5, a 600-by-150-foot building of steel columns and trusses enclosed with brick and glass walls. Beneath the skylit web of steel, tracks carried engines and cars to the areas where the knowing, oil-begrimed hands of skilled mechanics tore them down, repaired them, and reassembled them every day. The boiler shop, train sheds, and a planing mill were built by 1910. In 1924 a $500,000 roundhouse (fig. 5.12) replaced the original one: a concrete arcade of thirty-seven stalls held engines waiting to emerge onto the precisely balanced hundred-foot turntable. In its heyday, workers at Spencer Shops could do light repairs on seventy-five engines a day and completely rebuild an engine a day. As many as three hundred cars of freight could be handled daily at the switching yards. Passenger and freight cars were serviced, assembled into trains, and dispatched throughout the Southern system. At Spencer Shops, as nowhere else in North Carolina, the extent and power of the new corporate America appear in a single vast complex built by and for modern engineering.[22]

Industrial Classicism: Public Buildings

As the taste for classicism returned to the popular scene, one important current was a rationalized, stripped-down blend of industrial architectural themes with Romanesque, Italianate, classical, or colonial motifs. The Henderson Fire Station (fig. 5.13), built in 1908 by Robert Bunn, features a geometricized Romanesque style with simple, sculpted forms and tall, clean-cut arches. The gabled main block contains firemen's rooms in the second story and broad doorways at ground level, behind which fire trucks stand ready to roll. The tall, square tower presiding over the main street contains the town clock, its four faces visible for blocks around. The open belfry originally held a bullhorn that, connected to call boxes all around town, blared in code the location of fires to residents and volunteer firemen. A pulley system inside the tower enabled

Figure 5.13. Henderson Fire Station, Henderson, 1908. Robert Bunn, builder.

Figure 5.14. Ayden Town Hall, Ayden, 1915.

firemen to hang fifty-foot fire hoses straight to dry before rolling them up in readiness for the next fire.[23]

Architects and builders often combined the Romanesque industrial style with freely handled classical motifs. The Ayden Town Hall (fig. 5.14) of 1915 is a striking example, its individuality reminiscent of the work of Philadelphia architect Frank Furness. The central tower rises through a trio of elongated window slits to a bold cap. But instead of corbeled brickwork to define the walls and tower projections, there are arcades of dwarf pilasters, and the roofline is finished with a stylized classical cornice.

Similar themes appeared in turn-of-the-century school architecture. Charlotte architect Louis Asbury's Stonewall Jackson Training School near Concord and C. C. Hook's Queens College in Charlotte were sturdy red brick buildings with stylized classical details. And at the North Carolina College of Agriculture and Mechanic Arts in Raleigh, early twentieth-century buildings designed by H. P. S. Keller and others established a campus architecture that combined terra cotta and cream brick trim in eccentric, even mannerist columns, keystones, and cornices. Leazar Hall and the 1911 Building are among the many vigorous buildings that combined classical themes with an air of industrial practicality.

The "Anti-Industrial" Picturesque: Shingle and Resort Styles

Just as the cottage style, touted as an escape from the industrial age, had been favored for resorts and facilities in remote locations in the mid-nineteenth century, so the shingle style assumed a similar role later in the century. Introduced in the 1870s in New England as part of a growing sentiment for that region's colonial architecture, shingle-style architecture gained popularity in North Carolina in the 1890s and the early years of the twentieth century. Its organic forms, naturalistically textured surfaces, and informal plans suited a variety of clients and purposes, but a common thread was an association with locations remote from the increasing complexity of urban industrial life. Such buildings did not arise from local traditions but rather from the conscious selection of nationally popular styles for a particular use and setting.

Along the coast, the U.S. Life-Saving Service built a new generation of lifesaving stations that replaced the 1874 cottage-style stations with larger facilities in the shingle style. The wood-shingled walls and roofs were both up-to-date and well suited to the rigorous weather of the Outer Banks. In 1892 the Life-Saving Service adopted a standard plan for a shingled and towered station—the Quonochontaug type, after a Rhode Island model from which many copies and variations were built, including a display station at the Chicago World's Columbian Exposition in 1893. After 1900 the service also established prototypes specifically for southern locations, mainly for North Carolina. One type was built at Little Kinnakeet in 1904—a hip-roofed bungalow shaded by deep eaves and attached to a tall, square tower. Another southern model, the Chicamacomico type, erected at the Chicamacomico Life-Saving Station in 1910 (fig. 5.15), repeated elements from the Quonochontaug model, including the tall, sloping roof, simple lookout tower, and shingled roof and walls, but the columned front porch and double dormers were new. This was the last generation of such stations, for after 1915, when the Life-Saving Service

Figure 5.15. Chicamacomico Life-Saving Station, Dare County, 1910–11. Victor Mendlehoff, U.S. Life-Saving Service architect; Theodore S. Meekins, builder.

Figure 5.16. Nags Head beach cottages, early 20th century. Stephen J. Twine, builder.

was absorbed into the Coast Guard, motor-powered boats eliminated the need for the close network of small, self-sufficient stations on their remote sites.[24]

On those same remote Outer Banks, there developed an architecture of summer cottage life, an intentionally informal architecture adapted to both the pleasures of genteel socializing and the destructive forces of the sea. Nags Head retains a row of extraordinary beach cottages (fig. 5.16) from its early twentieth-century heyday. Like Flat Rock in the mountains, Nags Head was a place where families from a specific region built summer cottages, to which they repaired season after season. Nags Head drew its clientele mainly from the plantations and towns of northeastern North Carolina. Summer at Nags Head, wrote an Elizabeth City resident, "brought us together and made us one people. . . . It intertwined our children in the happy days of childhood," so that the children "grew up together and ma[r]ital relations followed." At Nags Head, families from throughout the region "built cottages, originated new business enterprises, revived old memories, gossiped on current events, and enjoyed the happiness of their families." Development at Nags Head had begun during the antebellum period on the sound side, but after the Civil War, families began to build cottages on the ocean side, "strung along the edge of the surf, above high water within 300 feet of the breakers," spaced so that "next door neighbors were not within 'speaking distance.' "[25]

Between about 1910 and 1940, builder Stephen J. Twine of Elizabeth City remodeled and expanded old cottages and erected spacious new ones in a mile-long row beside the sea. The cottages are of simple, inexpensive materials, with walls and roofs of natural wood shingles. The plain, spacious cottages stand high on wooden pilings, allowing low waves to move freely beneath the house in time of storm. "You could sometimes look through the floor and see the sand fiddlers," remembered one visitor fondly. Their footing on the shifting sands is meant to be severed: three times the row has been moved back from the encroaching sea.[26]

Plans of the foursquare and bungalow-style cottages are informal and open. One common arrangement—akin to plans long familiar in the coastal area—has two large front rooms, a small back passage through secondary rear rooms, and low-ceilinged bedrooms above. Typically a breezeway leads to the service wing with its kitchen and servants' rooms. Porches on two, three, or four sides expand the living space, and "lean-out" benches built into the railings slant out over

Figure 5.17. Nags Head. Porch of beach cottage.

thin air (fig. 5.17). Shutters are propped up on sticks to give shade from the summer sun or battened down tight to protect against the fury of storms: when open, their repeated diagonals lend a sleepy sense of leisure and complement the sweep of roofs and the opposing diagonals of the lean-out benches. Although hints of modernity appeared in the 1920s—a telephone at the Coast Guard station, a few automobiles, electric generators at a few cottages—most maintained that "the fascination of Nags Head is its absolute lack of any pretense to formality. Its beauty is its very primitiveness that has not been touched by the hand of man."[27]

This yearning for the simple life amidst unspoiled nature informed resort architecture in many communities as modernization swept across the landscape; many of the foremost patrons of naturalistic architecture were the leaders of industrial and commercial development. The work of architect Henry Bacon presents the period's most sophisticated use of naturalistic forms and textures in the service of modern needs. In the 1880s and 1890s Bacon had worked in the offices of McKim, Mead, and White in New York, and he had served as McKim's representative at the World's Columbian Exposition in Chicago. As a member of that prolific and influential firm, he

Figure 5.18. Lumina Pavilion, Wrightsville Beach, 1904. Henry Bonitz, architect. (New Hanover County Museum)

gained fluency in a range of styles. Bacon had lived in Wilmington as a boy and maintained warm connections with friends there. He attained a national reputation primarily for his institutional and commemorative work, his most famous commission being the Lincoln Memorial in Washington, D.C. He generally restricted his residential work to houses for friends and family, and in these he expressed a fluidity and delight in texture and surface that contrasted with his more formal public works.[28]

Most of Bacon's private commissions came from childhood friends in Wilmington, principally Hugh and Donald MacRae and their sister, Agnes MacRae Parsley.[29] The MacRaes were leading developers in Wilmington and its environs, and for them, as for many businessmen of their time, real-estate development and electric power went hand in hand. Hugh MacRae was president of the Consolidated Railways, Light, and Power Company, which ran an electric streetcar line from the city's center through its suburbs to Wrightsville Beach, where the family was developing a commuter seaside resort. In 1904 the power company built at the end of the line the famous Lumina Pavilion (fig. 5.18), a big, shingled dance and beach pavilion designed by Wilmington architect Henry Bonitz and named in honor of the wonders of electric power. Here the conductor's call, "Station Seven—Loooooomina!" signaled the streetcar's last stop. Beginning in 1911, Lumina was outlined in six hundred incandescent lights, which transformed it into a celebration of the il-lumina-ting power of electricity.[30]

Donald MacRae persuaded Bacon to design his house in Wilmington, which he built in 1901 (fig. 5.19). Bacon combined Queen Anne– and shingle-style elements in the dormered and towered roofline, wood-shingled walls, and lean, oriental-like joinery of the porch. The interior is finished in natural hardwoods with generally classical detailing. Suitable for a forward-looking businessman, the house was fitted with every modern convenience, from the combined gas and electric light fixtures to the tiled bathroom (fig. 5.20).[31] Although bathrooms had appeared in the homes of the wealthy in the nineteenth century, they became increasingly common around the turn of the century, their gleaming tile, porcelain, and metal fixtures representing the era's concern for comfort, sanitation, and cleanliness.

Figure 5.19. MacRae House, Wilmington, 1901. Henry Bacon, architect.

Figure 5.20. MacRae House. Bathroom.

The Donald MacRae House was built amidst a larger chapter in Bacon's work for the family—his chestnut bark–shingled architecture in the mountain resort of Linville, a community born of the era's ambivalent attitudes toward industrialization and nature. In 1899, when exploitation of western North Carolina's forests and minerals was booming, Donald and Hugh MacRae had organized the Linville Improvement Company and purchased sixteen thousand acres for mining and timber development. They laid out a site for a town to serve as the center of operations—"cleared and stumped so clean that it looked like a desert bordered with trees"—and built a rambling, shingled wooden hotel for housing, which "sprang up . . . like a mirage on the sands of the East." When the directors, accompanied by their wives, held a meeting at the inn, the women, it is said, were immediately captivated by the beauty of the area and persuaded the men to change their proposed development to a mountain resort. Under the guidance of the MacRaes, with Hugh as president of the venture, the resort in the shadow of Grandfather Mountain quickly took shape. In 1891 a visitor from Harvard University called it "the most peculiar and one of the most poetic places I have ever seen," located on "the premises of a land speculation and would-be boom." The company, he observed, "just planted a couple hundred thousand dollars in pure esthetics—a most high-toned proceeding in 'this degenerate age.' Later, doubtless, a railroad, stores and general sordidness will creep in. . . . This peculiar combination of virgin wilderness with perfectly planned roads, Queen Anne Cottages, and a sweet little modern hotel, has never been realized until our day."[32]

Bacon designed several of Linville's many shingled structures. In the mid-1890s he remodeled a farmhouse for Donald MacRae and designed a cottage called the Studio for an artist client, and in about 1900 he designed a cottage for the VanLandingham family. He combined indigenous materials in artful fashion: the exposed structural elements are natural logs and saplings with their bark intact, and the walls are covered with large, rough chestnut-bark shingles that unify outside and inside spaces. Bacon's beautiful All Saints Church (fig. 5.21) was built in 1913 with donations from Agnes MacRae Parsley. The outside is covered with chestnut bark, includ-

Figure 5.21. All Saints Episcopal Church, Linville, 1913. Henry Bacon, architect.

Figure 5.22. All Saints Episcopal Church. Interior.

ing the tower topped with a sapling cross. Within, the imagery and materials become richer and more complex (fig. 5.22). Against the bark-sheathed walls and ceiling, the elements of High Church Episcopalianism are wrought in branches, twigs, and bark—a roof truss of slender saplings beneath the hutlike bark ceiling, a rood screen of arcaded branches, and chancel furnishings of split and woven wood and bark and gleaming smooth-barked twigs. In this small, quiet space Bacon created a gentle aura of rustic elegance, a place that summons memories at once of summer camp and familiar home parish, of Gothic church and ancient brush arbor—a church both in and of the wildwood.[33]

Figure 5.23. Grove Park Inn, Asheville, 1912–13. Fred Seely, designer.

Naturalistic architecture appears on a grand scale at the Grove Park Inn (fig. 5.23) near Asheville. Like Linville, Asheville was thriving amid the railroad-based western Carolina land boom; the panache of the Vanderbilt era, good rail connections, and a salubrious climate attracted a hustling, cosmopolitan population. Pacing the fast development was E. W. Grove, a St. Louis pharmaceutical manufacturer who came to Asheville about 1900 to establish a factory but soon became involved in real-estate projects. In the 1920s he would level the old Battery Park Hotel and redefine the topography of an entire section of the city, create a series of luxurious suburbs, and see the population of the city more than double.

The story goes that Grove envisioned a great rustic hotel like the mountain lodges he had seen in Yellowstone Park. When Asheville architects rejected his concept, he turned to his son-in-law Fred Seely (a journalist) to plan the building, which represented a dramatic departure from the ornate Queen Anne–style hotels of the previous era.[34] Built in just under a year and opened on July 1, 1913, the Grove Park Inn emerges naturally from its mountainside site, presenting a long, simple form composed of boulders dragged down from the nearby hillsides with their moss intact and set densely into reinforced concrete. Broad, irregular stones form huge lintels over the paired windows. The roof is an undulating, rolling landscape of red tile that creeps up over the little hillocks of the dormer windows. The inn centers on a cavernous lobby, dominated by huge stone fireplaces and chimneys that contain the elevators. Continuing the rustic scheme, the lamps, hardware, and some of the lobby furniture were crafted by the Roycrofters, the colony of socialist artisans in East Aurora, New York. The rest of the sturdy wooden furnishings of the dining room and small, spartanly healthful bedrooms were adapted from Stickley and Roycrofter designs and manufactured in Mebane, North Carolina. Thus Grove, exponent of industrialism and booming development, created a landmark to the virtues of handicrafts and naturalism to offer respite to such prominent Americans as Thomas Alva Edison, Harvey Firestone, and Henry Ford.[35]

The Revival of Historicism: Beaux Arts, Gothic, Colonial

Influenced by the Beaux Arts classicism of the World's Columbian Exposition in Chicago, public buildings displayed the dominant symbolism of heroic portico and dome. Ranging from the inspired to the pedestrian and from the free classicism of the turn of the century to the soberly academic work of the post–World War I era, they share a common sense of proportion and propriety. Classically organized but functionally modern government buildings were part of the repertoire of every competently trained architect of the period.

County after county employed architects to design courthouses in the classical mode, as the idea of the "temple of justice," so popular in the antebellum boom era, regained strength. One of the most prolific firms in the courthouse business was that of Oliver Wheeler of Charlotte and his various associates. At least eight of the Wheeler courthouses were almost identical. They were economical, ranging in cost from about $20,000 to $70,000, and their materials and workmanship lay within the capabilities of local contractors.[36] The Randolph County Courthouse (fig. 5.24) in Asheboro, built in 1908 from designs by Wheeler, Runge, and Dickey, epitomizes the firm's work. The Randolph County commissioners reportedly admired the newly completed (1899) Iredell County Courthouse in Statesville, which had been designed by Hayden, Wheeler, and Schwend, so much that they asked for duplicate plans. Behind the conventional Corinthian portico, Wheeler's lively composition has a flurry of cornices and pilasters at different heights, projecting and receding pavilions, and a shallow mansardlike dome. On axis with the portico and dome rises the Confederate monument, a soldier standing at ease atop an obelisk. It was one of scores of such monuments built on prime public spots in the early twentieth century, a memorial at once to the Lost Cause and to the continuity and legitimacy of the New South.[37]

Many other courthouses also featured the projecting portico and dome, a formula that

Figure 5.24. Randolph County Courthouse, Asheboro, 1908–9. Wheeler, Runge, and Dickey, architects.

Figure 5.25. Jackson County Courthouse, Sylva, 1914. Smith and Carrier, architects.

could be rendered in many different versions. For the Jackson County Courthouse (fig. 5.25), architects Smith and Carrier—a prolific Asheville firm established by Richard Sharp Smith after he completed his work at Biltmore—took full advantage of the mountain topography in good Beaux Arts fashion: they designed a straightforward classical courthouse but used the hilltop site to create an extraordinary drama of approach. For the Cherokee County Courthouse (fig. 5.26), built in Murphy in 1926–27, architect James J. Baldwin used gorgeous, blue-toned local Regal marble to face the elegant building on its corner site. The Corinthian portico dominates a facade that steps back in measured stages from the center beneath a tall, imperial dome.

Another way of organizing a classical public building was to place the portico in antis, recessing it within the block of the building as a functioning porch space or stylizing it as an engaged colonnade.[38] Among the best and earliest examples of the latter treatment is the State Administration Building (fig. 5.27), built in Raleigh in 1913. Atlanta architect P. Thornton Marye designed a dignified, four-story building of Indiana limestone that embodies Beaux Arts precepts accommodated to a tight urban site facing Union Square. Slight projections and recesses create a rich and subtle effect. Setting a fortunate precedent, Marye took his cues from the Capitol in the height and materials of his building and in the use of a first-story base and pilasters rising through the upper stories.[39] Subsequent state buildings around Union Square have continued the conventions he established.

In 1901 the supervising architect of the U.S. Treasury Department, James Knox Taylor, proclaimed a return to the "classic style of architecture" in federal government buildings. Taylor's Beaux Arts–inspired architecture was intended to symbolize the power of the United States and

Figure 5.26. Cherokee County Courthouse, Murphy, 1926–27. James J. Baldwin, architect.

Figure 5.27. State Administration Building, Raleigh, 1913. P. Thornton Marye, architect.

its democratic ideals, inspire patriotism, and elevate public taste. Many federal buildings were individually designed, though usually from fairly standard models, and their scale and grandeur more often reflected the power of a community's congressman than the demands of government functions in a particular locale. Taylor's successor, Oscar Wenderoth, continued similar policies, but the office style moved from Roman-inspired neoclassicism toward a Renaissance Revival style characterized by arcaded loggias.[40]

The U.S. Post Office (fig. 5.28) built in Greenville in 1913–14 typifies Wenderoth's Renaissance Revival style. Leaders in the eastern North Carolina tobacco sales center campaigned hard for the facility, which the local newspaper predicted would "present an aspect of prosperity and solidarity of which all Greenvillians should feel proud."[41] Beneath a low red tile roof, the stuccoed, stone-trimmed building features large Italian-type windows at the first story and diminished windows above; a deep, arcaded loggia opens into a marbled and tiled lobby. Wenderoth's successors continued the established preference for classicism. The U.S. Custom House in Wilmington, designed under acting supervising architect James A. Wetmore and built in 1916–19, was among the largest federal projects in the state. Extending a full block along the Cape Fear riverfront, it replaced John Norris's antebellum Custom House, but it replicated Norris's temple facade in the end pavilions.[42] As many imposing federal buildings rose in towns throughout the state, they consistently expressed the spirit of the times, a contained, classical image of the "prosperity and solidarity" that local, state, and national leaders strove to achieve and maintain.

Figure 5.28. U.S. Post Office, Greenville, 1913–14. Oscar Wenderoth, supervising architect of the Treasury.

In planning new church buildings, architects and congregations could choose between the renewed emphasis on classicism and the abiding appeal of the Gothic Revival. In contrast to the simple temple-form churches of the antebellum era, however, urban churches often boasted grand pediments or porticoes fronting domed sanctuaries.

The most powerful examples were the great Spanish baroque churches built for Roman Catholic congregations by Rafael Guastavino, father and son. The elder Guastavino was a Spanish artisan who developed a unique "cohesive construction" method of erecting great domes of self-supporting tile. He worked in New York and other American cities before coming to work at Biltmore. He became a permanent resident of the area and took steps to provide the city with a larger Catholic church. At the Church of St. Lawrence (fig. 5.29), the vigorously composed facade with its twin, tile-domed towers stands before a domed sanctuary, their forms silhouetted against the rounded mountain ranges beyond. In the towers, rough brick stairs mount in self-supporting spirals. The oval sanctuary rises to a splendid dome of Guastavino's self-supporting tile, and the walls and ceilings gleam with an array of glazed ceramic tilework (fig. 5.30)—warm hues in the sanctuary and, in the lady chapel, the blue of the Virgin. The elder Guastavino died in 1908 before the church was completed, and his son finished the work. The younger man also completed in Wilmington the St. Mary Church, a domed, cruciform-plan Catholic church of similar Spanish baroque character, which he and his father had begun in 1908.[43]

Classically derived forms also accommodated Protestant congregations. The Southern Baptist Convention's *Complete Guide to Church Building* (1923), for example, presented designs for large and small churches in "Classic" style, which would "worthily express the mission and dignity of Christianity" and provide an auditorium well suited to preaching as "the central feature." First Baptist Church in Winston-Salem, designed by Tennessee architects Dougherty and Gardner and built in 1925, was offered as an ideal model for a large urban church; the eclectic, richly detailed composition, inspired by English baroque models, presents a heroic portico, dramatic steeple, and, beneath its broad dome, a spectacular circular version of the theater-plan sanctuary. Many smaller Protestant churches also featured porticoes and domed sanctuaries; especially prolific in this mode was architect J. M. McMichael of Charlotte, who designed such churches for congregations in small and large towns throughout the state.[44]

Still other churches combined classical motifs with a familiar linear plan. Many of these incorporated elements from American colonial church architecture. An early example is Howard Memorial Presbyterian Church (1907) in Tarboro, a red brick structure with motifs perhaps inspired by the colonial Christ Church in Philadelphia. Prominent among the architects who employed American colonial motifs in church and institutional architecture in the 1920s was Hobart Upjohn of New York, grandson of Richard Upjohn. Fluent in a wide range of revival modes, he designed for North Carolina congregations a series of handsome churches that combined red brick walls and colonial-derived classical elements, including his Village Chapel in Pinehurst and the Presbyterian Church in Chapel Hill. Characteristic of his work is the First Presbyterian Church in the growing textile town of Concord (fig. 5.31). The Flemish-bond brick walls, simple forms, and handsome classical detailing tie the building to the "colonial" past of the community; yet the church is part of a complex designed as an ensemble of facilities, including Sunday school, meeting rooms, and offices considered necessary for modern, growing congregations.[45]

The Gothic Revival, however, never lost its hold on church architecture. Hobart Upjohn's North Carolina work, for example, also included such imposing Gothic Revival churches as First Presbyterian Church in Wilmington and a new Chapel of the Cross in Chapel Hill, built alongside Thomas U. Walter's small antebellum church. Urban and rural congregations of every denomination built brick, frame, and stone churches in the Gothic style, and Episcopal parishes seldom deviated from the mode. One of the boldest among many twin-towered churches from the early twentieth century is New Chapel Baptist Church (fig. 5.32) in Plymouth, built in 1924.

Figure 5.29. Church of St. Lawrence, Asheville, 1907. Rafael Guastavino (father and son), architects.

Figure 5.30. Church of St. Lawrence. Detail of tilework.

Figure 5.31. First Presbyterian Church, Concord, 1927. Hobart Upjohn, architect.

Figure 5.32. New Chapel Baptist Church, Plymouth, 1924. S. C. Copeland, architect and pastor.

Figure 5.33. St. Paul's Episcopal Church, Winston-Salem, 1928. Ralph Adams Cram, architect.

The Rev. S. C. Copeland of Marion, South Carolina, was "architect and pastor." The raised entrance through a pair of tall columns introduces a classical element into a powerful composition of subtly different Gothic-inspired towers.[46]

The chief American proponent of the twentieth-century Gothic Revival in its most self-conscious phase was architect Ralph Adams Cram of New York. Like the ecclesiologists before him, Cram stressed the importance of neomedieval forms in "the creation of spiritual emotion through the ministry of all possible beauty of environment." A passionate, antimodern medievalist who was influenced by Ruskin, Morris, and Wagner, he found his principal clients among the nation's leading industrialists and business leaders. His North Carolina clients concentrated in Durham, Winston-Salem, and Asheville. St. Paul's Episcopal Church (fig. 5.33), built in 1928 in Winston-Salem's West End neighborhood, is a majestic late Gothic Revival building whose location exemplifies the trend toward building important churches in prestigious suburbs. The church was executed by the firm of Jacobs and Young, who also built Cram's celebrated St. John the Divine in New York City. Delighted with the steep hillside site, Cram took full advantage of its dramatic possibilities. Smooth Massachusetts granite walls rise from the slope like buttressed outcroppings and mount to a massive, blocky tower. Monumentality continues in the stout piers and elaborate millwork of the choir stalls, screens, and altar.[47]

Schools

During the 1910s and 1920s, North Carolina invested unprecedented sums in public education, including consolidated high schools and grade schools. Like churches, large schools were becoming multiuse complexes, with gymnasiums, auditoriums, and other spaces that made them into important community facilities. A few major school buildings displayed stylistic diversity: in Winston-Salem, Charles Barton Keen of Philadelphia designed the R. J. Reynolds High School in red-brick Jeffersonian classical style, with the large auditorium (1924) modeled on the rotunda at the University of Virginia; and in Raleigh, local architect William Dietrick's handsome, award-winning Needham B. Broughton High School (1929) was a towered, native stone building in Lombard Italianate style. Generally, however, associations with medieval English universities bolstered a longstanding preference for Scholastic or Collegiate Gothic in academic buildings.

Two of the state's finest Collegiate Gothic high schools were built by civic and industrial leaders to assert the status of public education in major textile cities. The Roanoke Rapids High School, designed by Hobart Upjohn and completed in 1921, is an ambitious and superbly appointed facility, commissioned and supported by textile company president Samuel Patterson. Its auditorium was claimed to be the best between Washington and Atlanta. The Gastonia High School (fig. 5.34) was designed by local architect Hugh White and built in 1922–24 at a cost of

Figure 5.34. Gastonia High School, Gastonia, 1922–24. Hugh White, architect.

Figure 5.35. Louis Round Wilson Library, University of North Carolina at Chapel Hill, 1928–29. W. M. Kendall (McKim, Mead, and White), consulting architect; Arthur C. Nash (Atwood and Nash), superintending architect. (North Carolina Collection, University of North Carolina at Chapel Hill)

$500,000. Local newspapers touted the modern plan and amenities of the twenty-nine-class-room facility: a swimming pool, auditorium, gymnasium, 1,100-volume library, and telephones in every classroom. Typical of Tudor-inspired high school architecture of the era, the brick walls are trimmed in stone, with ornamentation concentrated at the entry pavilion and crenellated parapets of the roofline.[48]

As college campuses developed in the 1910s and 1920s, architects and collegiate leaders shifted gradually away from the sturdy industrial classicism of the turn of the century toward more sophisticated classical and Gothic Revival architecture. Campus planning took on new sophistication as well, as Beaux Arts planning concepts redefined college campuses throughout the state and the nation, and as school leaders employed national architectural and planning firms with special expertise in campus design.

At the University of North Carolina, where little had been built for many years after the construction of Samuel Sloan's Memorial Hall in 1885, the turn of the century inaugurated what became an almost continuous building campaign. Beginning in 1898, Frank Milburn and other architects designed buildings in Collegiate Gothic and classical styles, most of which were pragmatic brick structures that filled in or extended from the original north quadrangle. After World War I, however, the university launched a major program of unified development that combined a Beaux Arts plan with a "renaissance of Southern Colonial at Chapel Hill." This campaign was part of a broader effort to expand the school into a major graduate university. As early as 1913, university president Edward Kidder Graham had appointed a faculty buildings and grounds committee. In 1917, in keeping with the national trend toward creating campuses in the City Beautiful image of order and unity, he invited the well-known urban planner and landscape architect John Nolen—already involved in planning suburbs in Charlotte—to advise the committee on campus development. Nolen surveyed the campus and proposed the simple and inspired idea of extending the campus beyond South Building as a complement to the original north quadrangle.[49]

In 1920, following delays due to the war, Graham's death in the influenza epidemic of 1918, and shortages of funds, the building program proceeded under president Harry Woodward Chase. The university employed the prestigious New York firm of McKim, Mead, and White as consulting architects to develop the plan in permanent form, the Aberthaw engineering firm from Atlanta to advise on the specifics of large-scale buildings, and the T. C. Atwood Company to design buildings in coordination with the consulting architect and to supervise construction. Building on Nolen's concept, the new south quadrangle, Polk Place, was laid out behind South Building, together with an additional cross-axis and lateral secondary quads. State funding for a multimillion-dollar building program began in 1921 and continued through the decade.[50]

Taking prominent roles in planning and architectural design were W. M. Kendall of McKim, Mead, and White and Arthur C. Nash, an architect trained at Harvard and the École des Beaux Arts who joined forces with T. C. Atwood in 1922. A decision was made to retain the "pioneer" buildings of the campus and plan new ones around them. As Nash recalled later, certain "out of key" buildings were to be "scrapped," and for the first time, "the University consciously adopted an 'official' style of architecture." A broadly defined "colonial" style unified the red brick dormitories and classroom buildings of the new quadrangle.[51] South Building was given a monumental portico to face Polk Place. Opposite it, the south end of the new quad was reserved for an "extraordinarily important" building—the library (fig. 5.35), built in 1928–29. Plans were developed according to the most advanced concepts of modern library operations. Working closely with Kendall in conscious emulation of McKim, Mead, and White's famous Low Library at Columbia University, Nash introduced a different mood with the monumental classical building of pale Indiana limestone. The serenely confident composition, with its Corinthian portico and Roman dome, evokes the full grandeur of Beaux Arts neoclassicism and asserts the stature of the library as the heart and symbol of a school emerging into a major modern university.[52]

A few miles away in Durham, another university was coming into being. At Duke University, born in 1924 from Trinity College and the Duke family fortune, Philadelphia architect Julian Abele of the firm of Horace Trumbauer planned two complementary Beaux Arts campuses—one a colonial-classical quadrangle in the spirit of the University of Virginia, the other a Gothic Revival campus in the tradition of the University of Chicago, Princeton, Oxford, and Cambridge (fig. 5.36). The philanthropy of James B. Duke combined with the broad vision of university president William Preston Few to create a major new university within a few short years.

Figure 5.36. Duke University, Durham. Plan of West Campus. (Duke University Archives)

Figure 5.37. Duke University. Chapel, 1930–32. Julian Abele (Horace Trumbauer), architects.

In 1892 the small Methodist school, Trinity College, had moved from rural Randolph County to Durham, encouraged by tobacco industrialists Julian Carr and the Duke family. Few, who became president of the college in 1910, convinced the Duke family to support his concept of making Trinity into a major southern university. The Duke Endowment, established in 1924, provided for a substantial annual income plus $6 million in construction funds—which Duke soon raised to $12 million.[53]

By the end of 1924, planning for the new university had already begun. Duke, who had previously employed Trumbauer to design his New York mansion on Fifth Avenue, had picked the architectural firm. Few's visits to several campuses, including Princeton and the University of Chicago, confirmed his preference for the Collegiate Gothic style. In March 1925, Duke, Few, and members of Trumbauer's firm walked the undeveloped tract to settle on the plan, and decided to shift the location of the proposed chapel to the highest ground. Duke also took an active role in choosing the stone (he was delighted with the economy of choosing the variegated,

Figure 5.38. Duke Chapel. Interior.

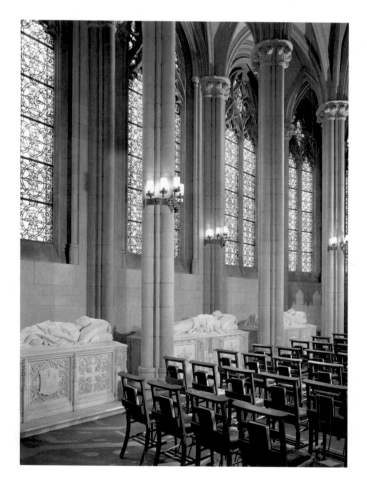

Figure 5.39. Duke Chapel. Memorial Chapel.
From left: Benjamin Duke, Washington Duke,
James Buchanan Duke.

warm-hued stone from a nearby Hillsborough quarry) and in selecting the landscape design firm of Olmsted Brothers. The architects first completed the plans for the rebuilding of the old Trinity College, which became the East Campus. An axial plan incorporated some of the existing classical buildings and was lined by new buildings in a dignified blend of Georgian Revival and Jeffersonian classicism. They then began designs for the new Gothic Revival–style West Campus. Duke became ill in July 1925 and died in October, leaving another $7 million for the university. By the fall of 1927, the new red brick buildings on the East Campus were occupied, and work had begun on the West Campus.[54]

The entire ensemble was designed by Abele, Trumbauer's chief designer and the first black to graduate from the Architecture Department at the University of Pennsylvania. For the West Campus he created a harmonious marriage of seemingly incongruous elements—the regular Beaux Arts plan of intersecting axes and open and closed quadrangles, and the irregular forms and varied motifs of the late Gothic Revival style. Oriels, towers, and parapets break up the masses of the large buildings, and each building or quadrangle displays subtly different variations on the Gothic theme. Intricate stone carvings, including witty neomedieval motifs symbolizing a building's function or department, express Abele's bent for artistically rich detail.[55]

By 1930 the library, medical school, and several other structures on the West Campus were essentially completed. That fall, despite the onset of the Great Depression, work began on the chapel (fig. 5.37). Duke had insisted, "I want the central building to be a church, a great towering church which will dominate all of the surrounding buildings, because such an edifice would be bound to have a profound influence on the spiritual life of the young men and women who come here." Construction continued for two years.[56]

The chapel is built in Gothic fashion, with self-supporting vaults rising from high stone walls, though in the roof steel is used instead of timber. The 210-foot tower, inspired by the Bell Harry Tower at Canterbury Cathedral, does not rise over the crossing but stands at the front, presiding over the campus as Duke intended.[57] Instead of kings and saints, the main portal is peopled with heroes of the Protestant tradition—Luther, Savonarola, and Wycliffe, Francis Asbury and George Whitefield, and John Wesley atop the entrance; and of the South—Thomas Jefferson, Sidney Lanier, and Robert E. Lee.[58] The walls are built of varicolored Orange County stone, the interior walls and ceiling are covered with Guastavino tile, and the carved trim is of Indiana limestone (fig. 5.38). In the small chapel planned by Few, recumbent likenesses of Benjamin Duke, Washington Duke, and James B. Duke are carved in marble atop richly worked sarcophagi. Not far away from the tobacco farm where they began and the huge factories they created, in a vast Gothic cathedral they never saw begun, they lie like medieval kings of old (fig. 5.39).[59]

By 1930, the two university campuses—one old, one new, one public, one private—had taken on the carefully ordered monumentality of the Beaux Arts tradition. At both campuses, leaders used the powerful imagery of a revered past to give form to dreams of a heroic future.[60]

Main Street: Architecture of Commerce and Progress

Main Street, North Carolina, developed rapidly in the period from 1900 to 1930, assuming a character it retained throughout most of the century. The small towns and small cities of the state depended on sales and manufacturing of local staples, cotton and tobacco, and forest products; their buildings and their businesses provided the link between the still agrarian society and the national marketplace. Each little city proudly boasted how its new building compared with those in distant urban centers—New York being the ultimate standard. Skyscrapers and elaborate commercial facades that might be commonplace in big cities came as exciting novelties to smaller communities. Automobile salesrooms and gas stations replaced old livery stables. Cafeterias invaded the territory of boardinghouse and tavern. Towering office buildings superseded the over-the-store office or the single-room office tucked beside the courthouse square.

Figure 5.40. Latta Arcade, Charlotte, 1915. William Peeps, architect.

Much commercial architecture continued the workaday simplicity of the plain brick box or the direct expression of functional engineering. At the Latta Arcade (fig. 5.40) in Charlotte, architect William Peeps designed for entrepreneur Edward Dilworth Latta an office building for small businesses; it was part of Latta's energetic campaign to transform Charlotte from "a cross-roads town into a city of office buildings, factories, and handsome suburbs." The skylit roof above a metal truss system casts natural light on the two-story arcade below. The office fronts and arcade fittings combine the straightforward modernity of plate glass and metal with the stylized classical detail of polished wood and marble. After viewing this "marvel of beauty and

Figure 5.41. Masonic Temple,
Rocky Mount, 1927.

Figure 5.42. Shell Service Station,
Winston-Salem, ca. 1930.

elegance," a writer for the *Charlotte Daily Observer* crowed that "the ornate quarters of steel brokers in Pittsburg or Wall Street geniuses in New York have little to outdo the splendor of the Latta Arcade."[61]

Many downtown buildings expressed their newness in the language of familiar stylistic devices. Colonial doorways and Grecian urns framed showrooms containing the latest models of automobiles. Skyscrapers rose to crowns of Gothic tracery or classical cornices. A few motifs invoked the ideal of modernity in the sweeping geometry of the Moderne or the jazzy exoticism and machine-inspired elegance of the Art Deco style.

In some cases, symbolic elements were geared to specific purposes. A number of prominent downtown Masonic buildings, for example, referred to the brotherhood's use of Egyptian history and symbolism. In Rocky Mount, the Masonic Temple (fig. 5.41), dedicated in 1927, presents a boldly tapered Egyptian temple facade with massive lotus-order columns and a sweeping flutter of wings beneath the cornice. A lighter and more literal corporate symbolism appeared in a series of gas stations built in Winston-Salem about 1930 to introduce Shell Oil products (fig. 5.42). In contrast to the standard filling-station architecture of the period—which ranged from brick boxes with canopies detailed in harmony with prevailing domestic styles to streamlined, gleaming tile exhibitions of the Moderne style—Joseph Glenn and Burt Bennett decided to advertise their new Shell dealership by building filling stations of molded concrete made in the shape of a shell, thus making each building into an attention-getting advertisement.[62]

Banks

In mainstream commercial architecture, the bank and the skyscraper exemplify the change toward specialized forms and the symbolic use of architectural themes. Previously, banks in North Carolina had reflected standard commercial styles of building. The renewal of classicism

Figure 5.43. Branch Banking Company Building, Wilson, 1903.

Figure 5.44. Patterson Building (Bank of Robeson), Maxton, 1911. Attributed to Cliff Parrish, architect.

and the proliferation of financial institutions created a bank architecture whose imagery of temples and vaults invited the confidence of a public only beginning to entrust their money to banking institutions.[63] Banks were typically located on prominent downtown sites, often at major intersections. Such buildings were planned to take good advantage of their sites, with architectural emphasis on the side as well as front elevations. For the Branch Banking Company Building (fig. 5.43), built in Wilson amid a tobacco sales boom in 1903, the builder used Renaissance Revival themes executed in boldly coursed yellow brick to assert an up-to-date image of "prosperity and solidarity."[64] The Patterson Building (fig. 5.44), built in Maxton in 1911 to house

Figure 5.45. Bank of Lumberton, Lumberton, 1914.

the Bank of Robeson, stands on a prominent triangular lot pointed toward the railroad. The flatiron-shaped building takes full possession of its site, and its columned entry, bold pilasters and cornice, and domed clock tower make the bank into the community landmark.[65]

The most distinctive early twentieth-century bank type took the literal form of a classical vault. The Bank of Lumberton (fig. 5.45), built by banker Angus McLean in 1914, is a handsomely detailed example with a terra cotta facade of paired Corinthian columns supporting a broad cornice and parapet.[66] Here, as in town after town throughout the state and nation, customers proceeded through tall columns or beneath a great arch to deposit their money or seek loans.

Skyscrapers were the new American building form. They had first appeared in New York and Chicago in the late nineteenth century, and by the early twentieth century, skyscrapers were rising in every small city in America. Whether they stood six stories or twenty stories high, they were the chief icons of prosperity, modernity, and progress. The introduction of steel construction and subsequently of steel-reinforced concrete, along with efficient elevators, freed buildings from old limitations on height. Skyscrapers were built ever taller, the stylized skin of their walls expressing height, elegance, and a sense of adventure in brick or stone, terra cotta, or glass. Like their fellow Americans, urban North Carolinians pointed with pride at each tall building. Newspapers gave special attention to the state's first examples of reinforced-concrete skyscrapers, the Independence Building in Charlotte (1908–9) and the Masonic Temple in Raleigh (1907–9).[67]

Most skyscrapers, however innovative their structures, were clothed in sedately classical skins. A three-part composition, paralleling the classical column's base, shaft, and capital, was widely used for both office buildings and hotels. Durham's First National Bank Building (fig.

Figure 5.46. First National Bank, Durham, 1913–15. Frank P. Milburn, architect.

Figure 5.47. Jackson Building, Asheville, 1923. Ronald Green, architect.

5.46), designed by Frank Milburn and built in 1913–15, is a well-detailed and representative example. The two-story base defines a formal street level with stone pilasters and cornices and indicates the public spaces within. The "shaft," rising through the middle five stories, is of buff brick laid in quoining patterns to emphasize the vertical dimension. The greatest elaboration appears in the "capital" of carved limestone, which asserts the building's place in the skyline and contains formal rooms or high-status offices.[68]

The verticality of the Gothic Revival made it an attractive alternative for skyscraper facades. P. Thornton Marye, the Atlanta architect who had designed the classical State Administration

Figure 5.48. Jefferson Standard Building, Greensboro, 1922–23. Charles C. Hartmann, architect; George A. Fuller Company, contractors.

Building, skillfully applied Gothic ornament in his tripartite scheme for the elegant Commercial National Bank Building (1912) in Raleigh. Above a base of Gothic arches and a vaulted lobby, he carried composite piers up through nine stories to a cap of corbeling and Gothic arches. In Asheville, architect Ronald Green used the Gothic Revival style in 1923 to dramatize western North Carolina's first skyscraper: twenty-seven-year-old entrepreneur L. B. Jackson's slender steel-framed office building (fig. 5.47), which rises thirteen stories on a tiny 27-by-60-foot lot. Attenuated buttresses pull the eye quickly up the brick and terra cotta walls to a traceried crown jutting with gargoyles and topped by a cathedral-like tower.[69]

Business leaders competed eagerly for superior height in skyscrapers. In 1923 the newly completed seventeen-story Jefferson Standard Building (fig. 5.48) in Greensboro laid claim to the title for tallest office building in the South. Built as headquarters for a North Carolina insurance firm, it contained six stories of company offices, plus rental offices and shops that made it "a city within a city" for 1,000 employees and 129 businesses. Charles C. Hartmann, a New York architect, was supervising construction of the O. Henry Hotel in Greensboro when Julian Price, president of Jefferson Standard, offered him the commission if he would set up practice in Greensboro.[70] Hartmann accepted and produced a splendid and skillfully designed Beaux Arts skyscraper. Twin towers flanking a light well rise from a unified three-story base sheathed in Mount Airy granite; the shafts of gleaming, cream-colored terra cotta feature clustered composite columns that divide the bays and rise to an opulent arcaded cap.

When the R. J. Reynolds Tobacco Company Office Building (fig. 5.49) in Winston-Salem was built in 1927–29, it surpassed all others as the tallest in the state. After the death of company founder R. J. Reynolds in 1918, and building on the fabulous success of the company's Camel cigarette, a new generation of leaders in the late 1920s developed the firm into a modernized, international business. By this time, Winston-Salem's "race to the sky" had been running since the 1911 construction of the seven-story Wachovia Bank Building. After the O'Hanlon Building rose to eight stories in 1915, Wachovia added a competitive eighth story in 1917. The Hotel Robert E. Lee was built to twelve stories in 1921, and W. M. Nissen began his office building of eighteen stories in 1926. Moving beyond the established classical norm, the Reynolds Company turned to the New York architectural firm of Shreve and Lamb for a boldly new design.[71]

A revolutionary image of the skyscraper had just appeared on the national scene in Eero Saarinen's 1922 entry for the Chicago Tribune Tower; though the Gothic-detailed design came in second in that competition, its mountainlike form and Mayan-inspired stepbacks exerted a powerful influence. This was soon evident in New York's American Radiator Building (1924), the fantasies depicted in Hugh Ferriss's book, *Metropolis of Tomorrow* (1929), and new ways of thinking about the American skyscraper.[72] At the same time, another new element in urban architecture appeared in the exotically modern Art Deco style, which had captured the popular imagination at the Paris Exposition des Arts Décoratifs et Industriels in 1925.

The Art Deco–style ziggurat skyscraper thus brought to Winston-Salem an American architectural form that, still adventurous even in New York, created a powerful image for the ambitious and forward-looking R. J. Reynolds Company. It was built by the James Baird Company on a bid of $1,900,000. Constructed of steel and reinforced concrete and faced with Indiana limestone, the twenty-two-story tower rises to a height of 315 feet. The vividly vertical design lifts the eye from street to sky in soaring strips to the narrow observation tower. Art Deco ornament of carved stone and Benedict metalwork accents the setbacks and enriches the lobby story. A tobacco-leaf theme, executed in copper and bronze hues, frames the deepset street entrances (fig. 5.50) and makes the elevator lobby into a gleaming treasury (see fig. 5.1). As the building neared completion in 1929, company pride swelled when their architectural firm gained worldwide fame as designers of the Empire State Building (1929–31), the symbol of the age.[73]

Figure 5.49. R. J. Reynolds Tobacco Company Office Building, Winston-Salem, 1927–29. Richard H. Shreve and William Lamb, architects; James Baird Company, contractors.

Figure 5.50. Reynolds
Building. Entrance.

The Art Deco Style: Kress and Asheville

The vivid geometry and sinuous forms of the Art Deco style captured the excitement of the 1920s urban boom. Inspired by glamorous images from the Exposition des Arts Décoratifs et Industriels, the style appeared throughout America as an expression of modernity. Motifs were borrowed from the world of art—from Futurism, Cubism, Art Nouveau; from the wonders of new technology—radio waves, airplane flight, and electricity; and from exotic cultures—Mayan, Mesopotamian, Egyptian, and American Indian. The Art Deco style also made its way into buildings in smaller towns, where it was often associated with such novel enterprises as movie theaters, dime stores, gas stations, and telephone companies. Some were designed by state or local architects, including the quietly sculptural, bas-relief Art Deco facade of Durham's Snow Building by Northup and O'Brien of Winston-Salem and George Watts Carr of Durham. Others were erected in various locales by regional or national corporations for whom an image of modernity was particularly apt: the Southern Bell Company, for example, erected a series of handsome Art Deco buildings in Greensboro, Charlotte, Salisbury, and Winston-Salem.[74]

The S. H. Kress Company of New York City, a nationwide chain of variety stores, put colorful Art Deco–style stores on main streets throughout America from the 1920s through the

1940s. Emblazoned with the Kress name, the gleaming terra cotta–fronted stores asserted themselves instantly as downtown landmarks, each conveying the distinctive image of the firm. Edward F. Sibbert, the firm's "vice-president for architecture," was in charge of Kress architecture from 1929 to 1954, during which time at least a dozen stores were built or rebuilt in North Carolina.[75]

The Greensboro Kress Store (plate 16), built in 1930, typifies Sibbert's work. The street facade displays a simple tripartite scheme, sheathed in creamy terra cotta and dark metal and accented with bright, molded panels in citrus yellow, orange, and green. Bulls-heads and garlands flank the central "Kress" sign. For each store, Sibbert would "make a very rough thumb nail sketch . . . and the Arch[itectural] designer would develop the set of sketches which we would play with until the right effect was found." As Sibbert remembered, "No specific style was followed. We did lean toward simplified modern (not modernistic). Tried to have our buildings stand out in the community but not too much. Avoided classical styles." Details came from published sources: "Some from Bauhaus Germany, some Mayan Temples plus Egyptian, etc." The facade material was usually supplied by the Atlantic Terra Cotta Company of Tottenville, Staten Island, New York. "We used Terra Cotta because it was durable, easy to clean, and liked by Mr. C. W. Kress, President." Sibbert "never used the term art-deco. If that was a style we knew it not. We tried to use good composition, simple ornamentation and coloring which we thought was significant of a Kress store, in average American towns."[76]

In the booming mountain resort city of Asheville, the architectural energy and crosscurrents of the early twentieth century appeared at their most ebullient. The town, which had grown explosively in the 1880s and rebuilt itself around the turn of the century, entered in the 1920s a third era of building that surpassed all others. The local *Asheville Citizen* declared in 1922 that "Asheville public affairs make a regular picture show, with the city hall as the chief stage set."[77] Fast growth, an increasingly wealthy and cosmopolitan clientele, and ambitious entrepreneurs with a sense of unlimited prospects for profit offered a fertile environment for architecture—and for architects. Asheville attracted and supported a diverse and talented group of architects remarkable for a city of its size.

Classical, Gothic, Renaissance, Tudor, and naturalistic styles all flourished. At Pack Square (fig. 5.51), the city center, Biltmore architect Richard Sharp Smith's lean and elegant reinforced-concrete Legal Building (1909), built in Renaissance Revival style, Edward Tilton's fine classical Pack Library (1925–26), and Ronald Green's Gothic Revival–style Jackson Building (1923) represented the city's urbane diversity. A few blocks away, E. W. Grove leveled the old Battery Park Hotel and the hill on which it stood. On its site, he built a new downtown skyscraper hotel with the same name (1923–24), designed by New York hotel architect William Stoddart. In 1926, on the newly filled plaza in front of it, architect Charles Parker planned for Grove a huge, Gothic-detailed, terra cotta–sheathed arcade building that occupied an entire city block and was intended as the base for a skyscraper office tower.[78]

Amidst such activity, Asheville also produced the state's finest collection of Art Deco–style architecture. This was principally the work of architect Douglas D. Ellington. A native of Clayton, North Carolina, Ellington had trained at Drexel Institute, the University of Pennsylvania, and the École des Beaux Arts and had taught architecture at Columbia University and the Carnegie Institute of Technology. He arrived in Asheville at the height of its greatest building boom. He continually articulated his ideas in articles in the local press and obtained national coverage of his Asheville work. Though he used a style that was novel and festive, he consciously grounded his work in Beaux Arts principles and a keen sensitivity to the landscape around him—its rounded mountains, its history, and its rich color palette—to create a highly personalized body of work deeply rooted in place.

His first major work in Asheville was the First Baptist Church (plate 18) of 1925–27, a domed brick building that presents a highly individualized marriage of geometric Art Deco ornament and a Beaux Arts form evoking the spirit of early Renaissance churches. Characteristic of large urban Protestant churches, it was planned as a multiuse complex, a group of five buildings that

Figure 5.51. Pack Square, Asheville. From left: Akzona (Biltmore) Building, completed 1980, I. M. Pei, architect; Vance Monument, 1896, Richard Sharp Smith, architect; Buncombe County Courthouse, 1927–28, Milburn and Heister, architects; Asheville City Building, 1926–28, Douglas D. Ellington, architect; Jackson Building, 1923, Ronald Green, architect; Legal Building, 1909, Richard Sharp Smith, architect; Pack Memorial Library, 1925–26, Edward L. Tilton, architect.

pyramid into a single structure, dominated by the domed sanctuary. The 90-foot dome is made, explained Ellington in the dedication booklet, of "nail and crete [which] combine to make it a unit which rests like an inverted bowl on the octagonal walls of the auditorium. The form is similar to the dome of the Cathedral of Florence, Italy." The subtle, vibrant coloristic effect of the roof tile was to become an Ellington hallmark; the *Architectural Record* described how the tile "graduates in tone from a fire-flash purple through brown and red and ochre to green, finally blending into the rusty green of the copper cupola." In the sanctuary, Ellington created the ultimate in worship space as theater auditorium, where he designed every detail of pulpit, choir, baptistry, and encircling seats in an Art Deco ensemble (fig. 5.52).[79]

The Asheville City Building (fig. 5.53), begun in 1926, is Ellington's principal monument, an extraordinary eight-story building that glows pink against the blue-green mountains. Ellington explained that he planned the "contours of the building [to] reflect the mountain background" and to "emerge from the ground in fortress-like strength and ascend to its full height with a sense of verticality and inevitability." The prevailing feather motif he described as "lightly remi-

Figure 5.52. First Baptist Church, Asheville, 1925–27. Interior. Douglas D. Ellington, architect.

niscent of the Indian era." The base of creamy pink marble is classical in inspiration, with stylized frieze and pilasters and a vaulted loggia and lobby lined with marble and mosaic. Warm brick walls rise to stepbacks accented by jagged feather motifs. The stepped roof of luscious raspberry tile is topped by a cupola ringed by brilliant blue, green, and yellow tile (plate 17). The *Asheville Citizen* assured residents that the building was in "the style of architecture now being used by Metropolitan architects in the new school of buildings which are refashioning the whole face of the large cities of the land." Others were less enthusiastic. Ellington had planned the City Building to stand beside a matching courthouse at the end of the square, a concept he presented in a plaster model. But the county commissioners vetoed the idea and instead employed Milburn and Heister of Washington, D.C., to design the tallest courthouse in the state, a seventeen-story, classically detailed block that rose slightly higher than Ellington's stepped-back pink tower.[80]

In the S & W Cafeteria (fig. 5.54) of 1929, Ellington applied his studied and inventive aesthetic to a small commercial facade intended to attract interest in cafeteria dining, still a novelty in the state. The facade scintillates with Mayan scrolls, chevrons, fountains, and abstracted classical elements in blue, gold, green, cream, and black beneath a spiky, bright blue roof. As Ellington explained in July 1929, he sought a "note of gaiety," a "cheerful or semi-festive

Figure 5.53. City Building, Asheville, 1926–28. Douglas D. Ellington, architect.

Figure 5.54. S & W Cafeteria, Asheville, 1929. Douglas D. Ellington, architect.

quality" befitting to the building's purpose and "in keeping with the life of a community where recreation is an important activity." Three months later, when the stock market crash came, Frank Sherrill (the S of S & W) recalled, "The building was about five-sixths finished, and we didn't know anything to do but go ahead."[81]

In Asheville, where frenzied development was grounded on a web of civic debt, the crash hit hard. Fortunes vanished. The principal bank failed and defaulted on the city's unsecured loans. Construction soon ground to a halt. The commercial boom of the 1920s ended, leaving a body of glamorous urban architecture that remained unchanged for years to come.

Residential Architecture

A host of new domestic styles and forms appeared in North Carolina between 1890 and the beginning of World War I; then, in the postwar period, there came an era of solidification and refinement, especially in the form of more scholarly and opulent renditions of historical revival styles. To an extent unrivaled before or since in North Carolina, the design of substantial residences—the houses of the upper and upper-middle classes—was dominated by professional architects.

In residential architecture the reaction against the extravagance of the late nineteenth century was especially strong. Housing reformers pressed for simplification of dwellings to improve health, family life, and efficiency.[82] Specific revival styles, particularly the Colonial Revival, supplanted picturesque eclecticism; new types became standard in the middle and lower ranks of housing, including the simple rectilinear or "foursquare" house, the bungalow, and the shotgun.

Frame construction continued to dominate in all but the grandest houses, though brick-veneered construction became more usual in the 1920s. And, as cities grew, residential settlement patterns turned outward toward suburban and country house sites. All these were part of national trends in housing. But although specific regional house forms were replaced by national types, North Carolinians continued to make their own regionally informed choices from the possibilities offered by a national domestic architecture.

The Colonial Revival

The Colonial Revival entered North Carolina residential architecture at the turn of the century, first through classicized adornments grafted onto houses of Queen Anne form—seen in the 1890s, for example, in the "colonial" details of George F. Barber's houses—and subsequently in a renewed emphasis on symmetry and a central portico. There were two main phases of the Colonial Revival. The first, broadly eclectic phase was part of the great era of American expositions. Though rooted in earlier trends, this phase began in North Carolina in the 1890s, flourished until World War I, and continued until the early 1920s. A second, overlapping phase began in the mid-teens with the more literal replication of Georgian and occasionally Federal themes. (The Tudor and Spanish revivals of the same era never offered serious competition in North Carolina.) This Georgian-Federal phase thrived in the 1920s and 1930s and, nourished by the model of Colonial Williamsburg, has continued to dominate architecture to the present.[83]

The early Colonial Revival permeated America through the usual routes of books, magazines, and architects, but it was particularly a style of the expositions, those great American fairs that showed Americans what their culture was becoming—and what American architecture should be. The 1876 Centennial Exposition generated a burst of patriotic enthusiasm for the American past and for Old Colonial, especially New England, architecture. At the World's Columbian Exposition of 1893, where the principal buildings exhibited Beaux Arts classicism, the individual states' buildings were more residential in character, and most of them highlighted each state's "typical"—usually "colonial"—architecture. Virginia, for example, built a replica of Mount Vernon; several other states erected free interpretations of "colonial" themes, with an array of gambrel and gable roofs and columned porticoes. Although North Carolina could not raise the funds for a state building, her leaders originally had planned to erect a replica of Tryon Palace.[84]

The passion for colonial architecture was part of a larger concern for stabilizing the identity of American culture in the face of massive immigration, class turbulence, and ever expanding industrialization. The Colonial Revival was extolled as the architecture of Americanness, of patriotism and longevity, and specifically as "the architecture of our Anglo-Saxon heritage." For many, the term "colonial" encompassed architecture not only from the seventeenth and eighteenth centuries but also from the early nineteenth century; for others, the meaningful "colonial" past embraced everything up to the age of industrialization.

In the South, the Colonial Revival carried the same meanings, but with an added dimension. In the wake of the bitter political conflict of the 1890s and the Democrats' successful "white supremacy crusade," the rebuilding of a hierarchical, biracial, economically progressive society was closely linked with the "Anglo-Saxon" colonial architecture. Tying the newly stabilized present with the South's own past, the Colonial Revival expanded to encompass the architecture of an idealized antebellum civilization and the values it had come to represent. White-columned monuments assured that the entire continuum of pre–Civil War culture was part of the powerful rubric of "colonial."[85]

Local and regional architects eagerly adopted the style. As they advertised their practice through promotional books and articles, the magic word "colonial" replaced "artistic" as the accompaniment to "modern." Charles Barrett of Raleigh, for example, published *Colonial Southern Homes* (1903), which repeated several designs from his associate William P. Rose's *That House*

Figure 5.55. Blades House, New Bern, 1903. Herbert Woodley Simpson, architect.

Figure 5.56. Blades House. Plan by
Herbert Woodley Simpson. (North Carolina
Division of Archives and History)

of 1901. Their so-called colonial residences were a diverse lot that included both towered Queen Anne houses and more symmetrical dwellings with porticoes and quiet rooflines—all decked in columns, pediments, and Palladian motifs.

When Charlotte architect C. C. Hook introduced the mode to his bustling New South community, he published newspaper articles that put the operative myth into plain language. "The civil war marked the change from good to bad architecture in the South," he explained.

Whereas antebellum gentlemen "familiar with the classics and having other colonial work as models . . . took pains to preserve the proper proportions," after the war, with "*things being reversed in general*," new money replaced old, and architecture was handed over to "the most ignorant class of men. . . . All colonial details and proportions were discarded as being 'old timey' [and] *the jack-leg carpenter with the deadly jig-saw ran riot in the land*." But now, "out of all this chaos we again have a revival of the colonial," which in its "purity expresses more real refined sentiment and more intimate associations with our history." Hook proffered therewith a design for a "colonial" residence, symmetrical and pure white, with a "stately portico."[86]

New Bern architect Herbert Woodley Simpson displayed special flair in his residences for eastern North Carolina's new industrialists. A magnificent example is the Blades House (figs. 5.55, 5.56), built in 1903 in New Bern for lumberman William B. Blades, who had come from Maryland in the 1880s and with his brothers established plants at Elizabeth City and New Bern to exploit local timber, water and rail transportation, and cheap labor.[87] In this house, Simpson blended the animated form of the Queen Anne with the classical themes of the Colonial Revival to create a design of extraordinary energy and richness. His plan took full advantage of the prominent corner lot, having the principal entrance in a corner tower and two boldly different street facades. On the south, main front, a pedimented center pavilion and flanking end towers suggest symmetry, which is countered by making one tower open and polygonal, the other rounded and closed. The one-story porch of clustered Corinthian columns moves in and out with the bays and towers. Hundreds of acanthus consoles nestle beneath the eaves of porch and roof. The rooms within sweep out from the corner "reception hall" into an open stair hall, sitting room, dining room, parlor, and library opulent with columned mantels, dark paneling, and heavy cornices. Rather than using standard millwork, Simpson incorporated specific themes from New Bern's Federal-period heyday, as seen in its early nineteenth-century townhouses and in the Masonic temple, of which Simpson was a member.[88]

Throughout the state, houses combined Queen Anne massing and classical details in a fashion almost always called colonial.[89] In many communities where conservative taste and economic conditions had limited acceptance of earlier, more extravagant versions of the Queen Anne style, these restrained, classicized houses represented the main expression of the Queen Anne aesthetic—tall, dignified houses built for substantial middling citizens. Typical of many is

Figure 5.57. Berry House, Burke County, 1906.

the Berry House (fig. 5.57), located near the railroad and furniture manufacturing town of Drexel and built in 1906 for Lillie and Charles Berry; he was a local grocer and town postmaster. Their house has the standard high roof with a tower on one side and a front-facing gable wing on the other, but in contrast to the multiple textures and intricate decorations of the previous era, the restrained detailing consists of Palladian window motifs, pediments, and simple, turned columns.[90]

There were many one-story renditions of the new style as well. An individualized example is the house (fig. 5.58) built about 1899 for Sam and Melissa Oliver in Marietta near the South Carolina line. The Queen Anne cottage form is executed with simple columns and strong symmetry. Sam Oliver planned the house himself, had the millwork cut at his sawmill, and built the house with help from local workmen. He arranged the rooms and passages to accommodate long-standing customs. Two doors open from the front porch into passages that flank the central living room and carry the breeze alongside the dining room and kitchen and through to the back porches. Doors from the front porch also open into two projecting front bedrooms that originally had no other access to the house: family accounts repeat a familiar story of reserving these rooms for preachers and doctors visiting the village.[91]

One of the most popular and powerful versions of the Colonial Revival in North Carolina was the type called in the literature of the times "Southern Colonial," which gained prominence about 1900. The principal feature of the symmetrical Southern Colonial residence was a central portico of colossal order and one-story porches extending out to the sides. The plan displayed a grand return to the familiar central-passage, double-pile plan never long absent from the conser-

Figure 5.58. Oliver House, Marietta, Robeson County, ca. 1899.

Figure 5.59. Robinson House, Elizabeth City, 1914. Herbert Woodley Simpson, architect; Kramer Brothers, builders.

vative architecture of the region. Nearly every architect working in the state incorporated the Southern Colonial model into his repertoire. Frank Milburn, for example, designed such a house as the residence for the president of the University of North Carolina in Chapel Hill.[92]

The style was so popular that it was selected as the form for the North Carolina Building erected at the 1907 Jamestown Ter-centennial Exposition in Norfolk. This exposition celebrated the South's claim as the first imprint of Anglo-Saxon culture in America. The sponsors erected a "Colonial acropolis restful to the eye and satisfying to sentiment," which they hoped would "result in a revival of interest in Colonial architecture, which is really the only distinctive American order of building." Designed by Zimmerman and Lester of Winston-Salem and built by J. E. Elliott of Hickory, the North Carolina Building was described as "a fine permanent colonial home . . . of large colonial design with immense columns and porches." The popularity of this type of house was enhanced by its presentation at the exposition. Lumber merchant Kenneth L. Howard in fact copied the Jamestown example for his own residence in Dunn. That the Southern Colonial house was built as often in town, as the residence of a cotton-mill owner or banker, as on the plantation of a cotton planter only strengthened the sense of continuity and the power of the image.[93]

New Bern's Herbert Simpson mastered the style in grand fashion. For William Blades's brother, James, he designed in New Bern a big brick version, which, when completed in 1913, was lauded as "one of the most imposing mansions in the state . . . of colonial style," notable for its "spacious verandah . . . supported by massive columns of the Corinthian style."[94] William Blades commissioned Simpson to design a similar house in Elizabeth City as a wedding gift for his daughter Ivy and her husband, Elizabeth City businessman Charles Robinson. The house was completed in 1914 by the leading local contractors, Kramer Brothers. Looming over the county courthouse across the street, the Robinson House (fig. 5.59) displays the energy Simpson

Figure 5.60. Lee House, Monroe, 1912–14. Wheeler and Stern, architects; William Ervin Wallace, builder.

Figure 5.61. Lee House. Interior.

brought from Queen Anne precedents. Although the composed rectangular mass and towering portico dominate, the gabled bays, myriad dormers, receding and projecting verandas, curvaceous balustrades bristling with urns, and the thickets of Corinthian columns—fifty-two of them—give the mansion irrepressible vitality as well as grandeur.[95]

If the Robinson House presented the "Southern Colonial" at its most exuberant, the Lee House (fig. 5.60), built in Monroe in 1912–14, typifies the quieter versions that graced residential sectors of every growing town. Monroe was blossoming as a railroad and cotton commercial center, where the infant chamber of commerce assured potential investors of a stable future run by civic leaders who had recently triumphed over the Populist challenge. James H. Lee, the epitome of the native-born businessman who energized local commerce, had moved to Monroe in 1892 from the little town of Marshville, opened a drugstore and a dry-goods business, and soon assumed leading roles in Monroe's bank, telephone company, and cotton mill. The successful entrepreneur soon commissioned a house design from Charlotte architects Wheeler and Stern. As in their courthouse work, Wheeler and Stern adapted a standard formula to suit their client. They built a symmetrical house with a broad central passage, pedimented side bays, a colossal portico, and a veranda that extends into a porte cochere. Fine workmanship and an air of simplicity inform the Ionic order of the porches, turned balustrades, and classically detailed mantels, stairs, and paneling characteristic of the period (fig. 5.61).[96]

Other Revivals

The architects who introduced the Colonial Revival also offered their clients myriad other possibilities. C. C. Hook of Charlotte typifies such architects' pragmatic fluency in a range of styles; his work displays his own bold flair for the dramatic. His designs encompassed shingled, gambrel-roofed cottages as well as big columned mansions, Gothic and Romanesque Revival churches, Jacobean and Richardsonian Romanesque commercial and civic buildings, and red brick neoclassical collegiate structures. His practice radiated from Charlotte into the thriving industrial towns of the Piedmont, where he found patronage among the new magnates of textiles, mining, and railroading.[97] Two examples suggest the diversity of Hook's approach.

For the Salisbury residence (fig. 5.62) of mining engineer and developer Egbert Barry Cornwall Hambley, Hook designed a highly individualized manorial mansion. Hambley, a native of Penzance, Cornwall, had first come to the region as a mining engineer for the Gold Hill Mines in Rowan County, then returned to promote ambitious projects in mining and quarrying, industrial development, and hydroelectric power. With a Pittsburgh investor, he established the Whitney Company. Its chief project was the construction of a dam at the narrows of the Yadkin River—"a giant scheme to grapple with and subdue elemental nature, forcing her with many inventions to lend her untamed energy, . . . that much good may result," including a "revolution in manufacturing" intended to transform the Piedmont into "the New England of the South."[98]

Hambley wanted a house in which to entertain potential investors in his company, a purpose Hook met with a castlelike residence that displayed the local granite and perhaps evoked its owner's English origins. Built in 1902–3 in an intimate, grid-plan neighborhood, the house sits back on its huge lot, walled in stone and approached through stone gateposts. The walls are of buff brick, the high roof is patterned slate, and native stone is lavishly bestowed on the dominant tower, chateauesque dormers, and massive porch. Soon after the house was completed, however, construction of the dam was slowed by accidents and typhoid. Hambley died of typhoid in 1906 at age forty-four; the Whitney Company folded; and a decade later the Aluminum Company of America implemented Hambley's concept with a dam at the narrows that powered their manufacturing complex at Badin.[99]

For textile magnate Abel Caleb Lineberger of Belmont, Hook designed another house (fig. 5.63) on a large scale, made of buff brick and located on a spacious, landscaped lot. Lineberger came from a local family, long settled in the Piedmont, who had led Gaston County's rapid

Figure 5.62. Hambley House, Salisbury, 1902–3. C. C. Hook, architect.

Figure 5.63. Lineberger House, Belmont, 1919–21. C. C. Hook, architect.

nineteenth-century development as a textile manufacturing center.[100] Perhaps his local roots and preferences, as well as the shifting tides of taste, shaped the design of a house that, although large and luxurious, had nothing of the castlelike grandeur of the Hambley House. Instead, Hook produced a horizontal composition with a comfortably domestic aura. Built in 1919–21 in a free adaptation of the Renaissance Revival style, the house has nine bays opening across the facade beneath a low tile roof that extends to shelter a porch at one end and a porte cochere at the other. The balustraded porch, arched French doors, and deep, bracketed cornice emphasize the sense of openness and horizontality.

Simple Living: The Foursquare and the Bungalow

Contemporaneously with the revival of classical and colonial themes came house forms and styles that emphasized the virtues of simplicity, unpretentiousness, and efficiency. One such form that gained extraordinarily wide use throughout the nation was the plain, hip-roofed, two-story square-plan house. The simplifying influence of the Prairie School of architects in the Midwest coincided with the boxy shape beneath the bays and towers of many late-nineteenth-century houses. Today identified variously as the foursquare and rectilinear style, at the time such houses were one type among many labeled in advertisements and promotional literature as "comfortable," "substantial," or "a simple, straightforward house of the block shape."[101] These houses usually followed either central-passage plans or four-room plans. A handsome example is the Livesay House (fig. 5.64), superbly sited in the rolling farmland of the Grassy Creek community. It was built in 1914 for Robert Livesay and his wife, who was a member the Greer family, long established as dairy farmers in the Grassy Creek community. The clean, square form, wide front porch, and symmetrical hip roof with dominant front dormer present a plain, substantial image suitable to a successful farming family.[102]

Figure 5.64. Livesay House, Grassy Creek, Ashe County, 1914.

At the same time, and reflecting a shared concern for simplicity and practicality, another popular house type, the bungalow, appeared in North Carolina. The bungalow was both a house type and a style. The name derived from the deep-roofed, informal cottage or *bangla* in India. California and New York architects designed finely wrought bungalows for wealthy clients seeking modern, natural, healthful living. But the essential elements of the bungalow—a low-slung silhouette dominated by a broad roof, an open, informal plan incorporating a porch, and simple, geometricized detailing and use of natural materials—also permitted its successful translation into simpler, mass-produced houses. By the 1910s, bungalow magazines appeared regularly, and mail-order firms supplied builders and prospective homeowners with plans for bungalows of all types.[103]

Bungalows suited North Carolina's needs and habits. They were cheaply and easily built. They ranged in size and elaboration to accommodate all economic levels, and they communicated a message of simplicity, unpretentious coziness, and modernity. Their characteristic broad eaves and deep porch fit the climate—indeed, in profile many bungalows resembled coastal cottages in their integration of porch and house. In the typical bungalow plan (fig. 5.65), which emphasized informality and openness, one entered directly from the porch into the living room, and the living room and dining room—whether side by side or front to back—opened into one another. Little if any space was devoted to formal hallways, and rooms were usually arranged either in two parallel rows or in a rough square. This plan melded easily into communities in which the hall-parlor plan and one- or two-room log dwellings were still in current use or memory.[104] From the turn of the century until the depression, North Carolinians—from farm to mill village to suburb, rich or poor, landowner or tenant, black or white, conservative or adventurous—built, bought, and rented bungalows.

The "true" bungalow, according to contemporary popular literature, was one story tall and usually had one or more wide, front-facing gables that integrated the porch and house. Detailing ranged from the geometric "craftsman" style to oriental to colonial; heavy tapered posts, angular brackets, and exposed rafter ends were standard components. On Seaman Street in Durham (fig. 5.66), three bungalows of the 1920s display a typical range of rooflines and porch treatments. One has a continuous, front-facing gable roof with an oriental flair, another a hip roof and gabled front dormer; one has clustered porch posts, another heavy tapered ones, and so on.

A few bungalow types took their places in the landscape as the early twentieth-century successors to common small and large house types. An especially popular small version of the bungalow had a front-facing gable roof and a plain shed or gabled porch. Standard brackets,

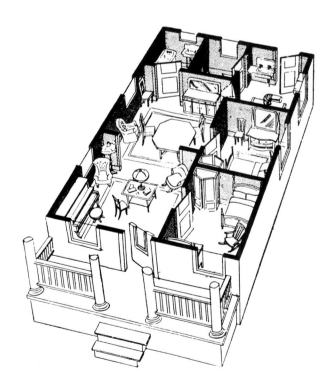

Figure 5.65. A typical bungalow plan, from *Aladdin Plan of Industrial Housing*, 1918.

Figure 5.66. Seaman Street houses, Durham, 1920s.

rafter ends, and tapered porch posts emphasized its bungalow character. A house in the small town of Ayden (fig. 5.67) exemplifies the type, though this one has a special feature in its porte cochere or carport—evidence of the proud possession of an automobile. This bungalow form, further simplified, became a standard, cheap, up-to-date dwelling for small farms, working-class neighborhoods, and mill villages.

At the same time, larger bungalows became a standard middle- and upper-middle-class house for farmers, merchants, and professional men's families. An especially prevalent form was the so-called "semi-bungalow," a spacious house with a second story treated as a half-story with large dormers. Exemplary of the many substantial rural as well as suburban bungalows of the period is the Lipe House (fig. 5.68), built for Jane and Levi Lipe on their Stanly County farm. Part of an established rural community of German-descended farmers, Levi Lipe was the first county farm agent; the family's spacious bungalow, together with agricultural buildings and a windmill, exemplified the model of progressive rural living. Its weatherboarded walls, deep porch, and respectable but unpretentious character give the large bungalow, like the foursquare house, a comfortable place among the region's sequence of substantial farmhouses.[105]

Many North Carolina bungalows were precut manufactured houses sent to the buyer by rail for assembly on the site. This practice was the logical extension of the mail-order architectural services of George F. Barber and others. The North American Construction Company of Bay City, Michigan, which manufactured Aladdin Readi-Cut houses, and its competitor, Sears, Roebuck and Company, with its "honor built" homes, were among the largest firms. They produced houses of every popular type, bungalows being among their cheapest and most popular items. Efficiency, standardization, and reliability—the virtues of rationalized mass production—were their watchwords. Their houses, they claimed, could be built in a day. The customer who obtained a house "direct from the forest to the home" avoided middlemen and was assured of the lowest price and a reliably high quality. Aladdin bungalows combined standard shapes and plans

Figure 5.67. McLawhorn House, Ayden, ca. 1920.

Figure 5.68. Lipe House, Stanly County, early 1920s.

with distinctive details: doors with eight small glass panes over three long panels; porch balustrades with a central horizontal solid band; and, sometimes, hardware marked with the firm's name. Lyrically written catalogs kept readers abreast of the language of popular architectural ideals.[106]

Roanoke Rapids is a showcase of Aladdin houses. Textile-mill development had begun at the falls of the Roanoke River in the 1890s when textile investor John Chaloner of New York commissioned Stanford White of McKim, Mead, and White to design a mill, community buildings, and several houses. In the 1910s and early 1920s, as the mills multiplied and grew under the direction of Samuel F. Patterson, the Roanoke Mill Company turned to the Aladdin firm, which had a fully developed program for industrial housing. *The Aladdin Plan of Industrial Housing* (1918), asserting that "a housed labor supply is a controlled labor supply," offered a range of houses for all grades of workers. The models suggested for foremen and executives were identical to those the Aladdin firm also promoted for suburban residences in their other catalogs, though with texts varied to suit the purpose.[107]

Roanoke Rapids presents a full selection of Aladdin models. Along Jackson Street, for example, several different models were built about 1919–21. At 512 stands "the Pomona" (figs. 5.69, 5.70), an "ever popular California type" suited to "factory executives"; in the residential catalog this was praised as a "snugly compact" design in which each element "blends naturally into the whole." On the same street, at 417, stands "the Marsden," a "semi-bungalow" with upstairs bedrooms: "suitable especially for executives and plant superintendents . . . it has the quaint California bungalow atmosphere." Next door, at 419 Jackson, stands "the Plaza," cited in the Aladdin residential catalog and said to be inspired by "one of the best known bungalows in Pasadena, California," with the low roofline of the "true California bungalow." Entering through a "true craftsman front door," one had "a view through the living room and dining room for thirty feet." The quantity of manufactured housing in early twentieth-century North Carolina is not yet known, but, from all indications, it appears likely that hundreds, if not thousands, of Carolina dwellings arrived by rail.[108]

The bungalow also permitted individualized and elaborate expression, especially when built for prosperous town dwellers. The neighborhoods around Wilson's West Nash Street and the suburbs of Asheville, for example, boast sophisticated bungalows that were costly, often architect-designed residences. In Mount Airy, a handsomely detailed bungalow of local stone was built for the president of the local North Carolina Granite Corporation. J. D. Sargent had come from Vermont in 1910 to superintend work at the quarry. In 1918 he bought out the company and began developing it into a national granite supplier. The next year he completed his new house (fig. 5.71), an artistically appointed and spacious—but perhaps intentionally unpretentious—dwelling emphasizing the beauty of his quarry's pale granite. Craftsman-style geometry blends with such Tudor motifs as half-timbering in the gables. The garage (fig. 5.72), typical of the times, was built to match the house, and yard ornaments completed the granite ensemble.[109]

El Nido (fig. 5.73), a Spanish Mission–style bungalow in Shelby, shows how a house might satisfy an owner's romantic vision. Maude Sams Gibbs and her husband, physician E. W. Gibbs, had both grown up in the rural mountains. Maude Gibbs possessed an artistic bent, yearned for a warmer climate, and dreamt of a life beyond the mountains. After a time in Asheville, the couple moved to Mooresboro, in Cleveland County in the North Carolina foothills, so that Gibbs could develop his medical practice, with the promise that they would move to California in ten years' time. But this was not to be, and they moved instead to Shelby, the county seat. With plans obtained from a California architect friend, Aurelia Swanson, Maude Gibbs built in 1920–21 El Nido (the Nest), an exotic oasis of California, complete with a terraced yard planted with yucca and cactus. The tile structure is covered with stucco embedded with crushed pink granite, and molded metal tiles imitate a red tile roof. Within the open bungalow plan, Maude created a Spanish interior (fig. 5.74) using tile and painted canvas, furnishings, and art works and built independent second stories for the master bedroom and her studio.[110] El Nido epitomizes many ideals of its era: the nest as woman's domestic space; the feminine persona as artist in her own right; and the exotic aura of Spain coupled with the compelling American dream of California.

Figure 5.69. Jackson Street House, Roanoke Rapids, 1919–21.

Figure 5.70. "The Pomona," *Aladdin Plan of Industrial Housing*, 1918.

Figure 5.71. Sargent House, Mount Airy, 1919.

Figure 5.72. Sargent House.
Garage.

Figure 5.73. El Nido, Shelby, 1920–21.

Figure 5.74. El Nido. Living
room and dining room.

Residential Patterns

The people who filled North Carolina's burgeoning towns and cities were, by and large, native North Carolinians venturing in from the countryside and small towns. When textile developer D. A. Tompkins spoke of textile workers as "essentially a rural people," his words were equally true of himself and most of those around him. This rural bent and background combined with the general trend toward separation and segmentation in American towns and the South's Jim Crow laws of racial segregation to create distinctive urban patterns.

Leaders in North Carolina city development drew selectively upon northern urban models. Small apartment houses—four, five, or six stories tall—were hailed as indications of progress and urbanity. In 1906, when Wilmington investors prepared to build the Carolina Apartments (fig. 5.75), the New York pedigree of the design was a strong selling point in a city eagerly renewing its urban ambiance. The architect, Robert Louis Shape, it was reported, was "one of the leading architects of New York city, having charge with Mr. George B. Post, of the erection of the New York Stock Exchange building, which will cost five and one half million dollars." The Carolina Apartments shouldered up prominently at the high-status intersection of Fifth and Market streets, asserting itself as an equal neighbor to the Bellamy Mansion on one corner and Samuel Sloan's First Baptist Church on another. The two streets had been made into landscaped boulevards, and Fifth Street was soon to be renamed Fifth Avenue. Civic leaders also aggrandized the plaza of Market Street in good Beaux Arts fashion with a series of commemorative monuments by well-known urban designers: Revolutionary War hero Cornelius Harnett (1906); Confederate leader George Davis (1909); and—at the crossing of Market and Fifth Avenue—the Kenan Memorial Fountain (1921). These were subsequently joined by a Confederate monument on Third Street designed by Henry Bacon (1924).[111]

The six-story Carolina Apartments is built of dark brick in Flemish-bond pattern, accented with classically influenced stone sills, lintels, keystones, and belt courses. The arched, five-story light wells on three sides are both functional and decorative. Consistent with Wilmington's

Figure 5.75. Carolina Apartments, Wilmington, 1906. Robert L. Shape and L. K. Motz, architects; Henry Bonitz, supervising architect; Central Carolina Construction Company, contractors.

piazza tradition, balconies grace the upper apartments. Although most of the apartments were housekeeping units of various plans, those on the sixth floor were studio apartments without kitchens. A dining room occupied the ground floor, and residents customarily dressed for dinner, took the elevator to the mezzanine floor, and descended the grand staircase to the formal dining room.[112]

Most twentieth-century residential development moved expansively outward rather than creating denser urban neighborhoods. Cities emerged as collections of many different types of neighborhoods that stretched out from small commercial centers and along main roads and streetcar lines into the old fields. Developers partook of national trends but selected those aspects that fit the regional and local market. Patterns of development, particularly the trend toward greater social and geographical segregation and the emphasis on individual dwellings with separate lots, no matter how large or small, shaped and were shaped by the social conditions of the times. Subtle social, topographic, geographic, and architectural distinctions were readily understood by residents, if not necessarily by strangers. Two city subdivisions—East Wilson and Charlotte's Myers Park—illustrate two of many types of southern urban neighborhoods.

In contrast to many northern cities, where rural blacks often moved into row houses or tenements formerly occupied by whites, small, fast-growing southern towns did not have enough existing housing to meet the demand. The waves of inmigration required construction of hundreds of cheap, quickly built houses. Development usually occurred in small units, ranging from a single house or a cluster of three or four houses to entire blocks. Although the land was platted in thin slices to maximize profits, multifamily units were rare. Like mill owners, most developers constructed small, one- or two-family houses suited to the rural background of the occupants, each on its own narrow lot, with room for a garden and a front porch addressing the street. Some such neighborhoods were racially mixed until the 1920s or later; others were mainly white; others were mainly or exclusively black. East Wilson contains one of the best-kept of these neighborhoods.

The 1910s and especially the 1920s were a time when East Wilson grew rapidly as a predominantly black community on the east side of the railroad track that bisects the tobacco town of Wilson. East Green and nearby streets were the most prestigious avenues, where black business and professional men, dentists, physicians, merchants, real-estate developers, and teachers erected handsome residences that were standard versions of Queen Anne, foursquare, and bungalow styles. Other areas of East Wilson consisted mainly of rental houses, which black and white developers built near the major employers, the large tobacco warehouses and factories near the railroad tracks.[113]

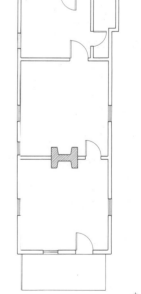

Figure 5.76. Roberson Street House, Wilson, 1910s. Plan by Carl R. Lounsbury after Richard Mattson and Suzanne Pickens.

Figure 5.77. Carroll Street House, Wilson, ca. 1910.

One predominant house type in the neighborhood is the shotgun house (fig. 5.77). This form, which began to appear in great numbers in North Carolina towns during the early twentieth-century inmigration, is a narrow, linear house with its gable end facing the street. It is one room wide, with two, three, or more rooms extending back from the street. This house type traces back to early nineteenth-century New Orleans and Haiti, where it developed from African, Indian, and French traditions.[114] A typical Wilson example on Roberson Street (fig. 5.76) is 15 feet wide and 45 feet deep and contains three rooms—living room-bedroom, bedroom, and kitchen. Usually the front door and a window open onto the front porch, though some houses have only a door in front.

Though the basic plan of the shotgun remained constant, some details changed subtly as builders responded to shifts in popular house styles and standard millwork. The house on North Carroll Street, erected about 1910 as rental property, probably by J. C. Hadley, a white real-estate developer and tobacconist, exemplifies the pre–World War I shotgun in its steep roofline, boxed cornice returning into the gable, louvered vent decoration, and turned porch posts. The row of houses Hadley built on Roberson Street between 1900 and 1910 repeats similar elements. Changes in the 1920s are evident in the Vick Street houses (fig. 5.78), built by black developer Samuel Vick, which have a shallower roofline, wide eaves, and exposed rafter ends.

The small bungalow and the shotgun house of the 1920s shared many common features of plan and execution. The house at 206 North East Street (fig. 5.79), built about 1925, has a shotgun plan executed with a full complement of bungalow detail. Another widely used arrangement, seen in one good example on East Nash Street (fig. 5.80), followed a bungalow format but had two front doors entering two parallel rows of rooms, a plan that allowed the house to be used by one family or as a duplex.[115]

Although some developers built rows of uniform dwellings, many did not. South Reid Street (fig. 5.81), for example, has houses of many different types and plans: a gable-front bungalow with inset porch, three slightly different shotgun houses, and an L-shaped cottage. Located close together on their narrow lots, these houses, like many others of their era, compose a neighborhood of porches and front yards oriented to the street, where a clean-swept yard, a neatly hedged lawn, or a luxuriantly blossoming garden reveal individual ways of treating the social spaces in front of each dwelling.

The creation of suburbs in North Carolina, where every class had rural roots, represented the confluence of national trends and regional customs. In the urbanized North, upper and middle classes sought relief from disease and crowding, the noises and smells of factories, and the immigrant poor and turbulent working classes. In North Carolina, urban growth had come so slowly and on such a small scale that, even in 1900, towns were still striving to become "city-like," and few cities were large enough to warrant escape.

Figure 5.78. Vick Street houses, Wilson, 1920s.

Figure 5.79. North East Street House, Wilson, ca. 1925.

Figure 5.80. East Nash Street House, Wilson, 1920s.

Figure 5.81. South Reid Street, Wilson, ca. 1910–20.

Antebellum North Carolina cities exhibited a pattern of residential development that dominated town life long enough to provide continuity with suburban growth patterns. In such antebellum towns as Greensboro and Raleigh, for example, the estates of the leading planter-lawyers lay within easy walking distance from the courthouse or capitol; each large house was surrounded by domestic outbuildings, perhaps the owner's law office, a stable, and a garden. Many such establishments were still standing in the early twentieth century.[116] The ideal of the American suburb thus converged with an established local and regional model: it reinforced the sense of continuity with the antebellum past, and it put into physical terms the social segregation of race and class, in keeping with the political climate of the times. In many ways the suburb suggested an idealized plantation moved into convenient proximity to the factory, the bank, and the store.

In one typical North Carolina promotional brochure, developers made the suburban vision explicit, describing their neighborhood as "an ideal place of residence," where "you may have the conveniences and advantages of both country and city combined": "open air, abundant sunshine, freedom from dust and noise," along with gas, electricity, water, and streetcars equivalent to "uptown service" and "twenty acres of beautiful parks." But there were more persuasive arguments: "The home . . . is the visible expression of yourself"; "This house and land is his, and he is master of it"; "Each home owner prides himself on his grass and flowers"; "The premises shall not be occupied by negroes or persons of negro blood"; "Each dwelling . . . shall cost not less than $3,000"; "There are no poor sections"; "It is pre-eminently desirable as a home place for those who wish to put themselves in touch with the best social conditions."[117]

The first suburbs in North Carolina cities were grid-plan neighborhoods built near major arteries; these proliferated in the 1890s and early 1900s as streetcar lines extended the edges of towns. By about 1910, reflecting national trends, North Carolina developers began to favor naturalistically platted suburbs geared to the automobile as well as the streetcar. They employed professional planners to lay out curvilinear street plans graced with open parks. The houses that lined these streets composed ever more costly and exclusive residential districts, and many of them were designed by national, regional, and local architects.[118]

Myers Park in Charlotte represents this second generation of North Carolina suburbs at its grandest. By 1910 Charlotte had become the largest city in the state, with a population of 34,000; in the next two decades it would grow to 83,000. The business-oriented city lay at the center of the booming Piedmont cotton-manufacturing region, which by 1927 surpassed New England as the center of the nation's textile industry. It was also headquarters to James B. Duke's Southern Power Company, the hydroelectric firm that caused Charlotte to call itself "the City of Electrical Energy, the Bright Spot on the Map." There in 1891 Edward Dilworth Latta had established a grid-plan streetcar suburb, Dilworth, and in 1911 he was planning a curvilinear extension designed by the Olmsted brothers. In that year, competing developer George Stephens inaugurated a still more ambitious suburb, Myers Park, which he laid out on the 700-acre cotton plantation of his father-in-law John Myers and later expanded to some 1,100 acres.[119]

To create a model suburb for Charlotte's growing elite, Stephens hired Boston landscape architect and city planner John Nolen. Nolen planned the whole ensemble, from its looping streets and boulevards to landscape designs for individual lots. Stone portals announced the entrance to the enclave, which became sylvan with remarkable speed as developers transplanted mature trees in an effort to provide "shade to order." Such street names as Amherst, Dartmouth, Harvard, and Wellesley, and eventually Cambridge, Oxford, and Stanford, provided attractive associations, and from the outset, Stephens's effective marketing drew the city's top textile and utility company executives to establish residences there.[120]

The phalanx of residences on Sherwood Road (fig. 5.82) characterizes the powerful sense of group membership the neighborhood conveys. Standing in even ranks beneath their great trees,

Figure 5.82. Sherwood Road, Myers Park, Charlotte, 1920s and 1930s.

they recall individually the architecture of the great Virginia planter or the English squire; as an ensemble, they evoke a shared set of tastes, values, and ambitions. Here, it seems, whole counties' worth of plantation houses are lined up in genteel, assured presence in a setting at once rural in its sylvan spaciousness and urban in its concentration of wealth and power.

The houses of Myers Park illustrate the range of forms and styles preferred by prosperous urban North Carolinians after World War I. Colonial styles dominate. They most often take the form of a symmetrical brick or frame residence, two stories tall, with proportions and details adapted from Georgian or Federal models. A frame house built about 1915 on Queens Road (fig. 5.83) is a restrained and handsome example of the conventional Georgian Revival style that remained popular for years to come. A broader, foursquare version appears in a spacious brick house built on Hermitage Road (fig. 5.84) about 1921. The Snyder House (fig. 5.85), built in 1922 on Queens Road for a Coca-Cola businessman, displays Charlotte architect Martin Boyer's skill in dramatic effects: from the swirling streetside approach to the upward diminution of the roof tiles, every detail emphasizes the grandeur of the opulent brick residence.[121]

Myers Park also has several gambrel-roofed Dutch Colonial–style houses and a few stuccoed Spanish Revival houses, whose tile roofs, curved gables, and occasional towers and balconies evoke the lush life of California or Florida. Anglophilic businessmen also admired the half-timbered Tudor Revival style. An especially fine example is the Queens Road residence of Earle Sumner Draper (fig. 5.86), the planner who was Nolen's assistant and who, in 1917, took over supervision of the work in Myers Park. In Draper's house, brick and stucco combine with elaborate half-timbered detail, glittering diamond-paned windows, and a complex plan extending back from the projecting entry porch. Smaller houses also incorporated touches of the English or period cottage style: a brick house on Brandon Road (fig. 5.87) features the characteristically quaint overlapping gables, diamond panes, and steep roofline curving out over a garden gateway.

Figure 5.83. Queens Road House, Myers Park, Charlotte, ca. 1915.

Figure 5.84. Hermitage Road House, Myers Park, Charlotte, ca. 1921.

Figure 5.85. Snyder House, Myers Park, Charlotte, 1922. Martin Boyer, architect.

Figure 5.86. Draper House, Myers Park, Charlotte, 1923. Franklin Gordon, architect.

Figure 5.87. Brandon Road House, Myers Park, Charlotte, ca. 1925.

These revival styles, like the curvilinear street plan, soon reappeared in every prosperous city in the state, often in suburbs laid out by Nolen's associate Draper. Greensboro's Fisher Park and Winston-Salem's western suburbs, for example, abound with imposing residences in Colonial, Georgian, Italianate, Tudor, and other revival modes, and Raleigh's Hayes-Barton contains a body of restrained, well-detailed Georgian Revival work.[122]

Expanding resort communities supported similar architectural trends. Pinehurst—laid out by the Olmsted brothers late in the nineteenth century as a health resort amid the pines of the Sandhills—and nearby Southern Pines developed as golf and hunting centers in the early twentieth century. In the 1920s, as wealthy and cosmopolitan residents built houses in Tudor and Colonial Revival styles, a high standard was set by the work of Aymar Embury II, a prolific New York country house architect and a widely published writer on early American architecture and the Colonial Revival style. Embury's design for novelist James Boyd's residence, Weymouth (1922), is characteristic in its scholarly yet imaginative use of Georgian and Federal precedents.[123] And, as the mountain resort town of Asheville boomed and its deluxe suburbs multiplied, clients enjoyed an exotic diversity of styles: "They are building so much that they can play at it," commented one resident, "build one type house here and another there; . . . decide one morning that what they want is a Mexican adobe house, and remember the next morning that it is not that at all—what they really want is a medieval German castle."[124]

The hunting lodge and the country house represented the luxurious extreme of the outward movement of the elite. A number of such residences were erected in North Carolina in the early twentieth century; though located in rural areas, they were all part of a national urban sphere of architectural patronage and design. Among the most opulent were hunting lodges built for wealthy businessmen around the turn of the century—now long lost except in local lore. In the central Piedmont, northern businessmen, including members of the Gould, Morgan, and Lorillard families, established private quail-shooting reserves, where they built lodges convenient to rail connections north. W. Gould Brokaw's Fairview Park near High Point was the most extravagant—a 160-foot-long lodge supposedly designed by architect Stanford White. Near Wilmington, on Wrightsville Sound, stood Airlie Lodge, a fabulous villa built about 1902–3 for Pembroke and Sarah Jones. Pembroke Jones, born in Wilmington, had become a leading New York financier, and the couple had become part of the Gilded Age society of New York and Newport. Jones built Airlie Lodge as a seaside villa in which to entertain his friends, including both the local elite and a stream of visitors from New York, Newport, and elsewhere who arrived by rail to partake of lavish hospitality, as well as hunting and fishing. The lodge was designed by Jones's son-in-law John Russell Pope, one of the nation's leading Beaux Arts architects. Sited on a bluff overlooking the sound, the lodge was a concrete structure in an Italian villa mode, with great two-story arched windows lighting a single immense room in the main block; wings held guest rooms, servants' quarters, and a glass-domed dining room.[125]

The glamorous and remote Whalehead Club (fig. 5.88) on the Currituck Banks still stands from this era of luxurious private leisure. It was built in the early 1920s for Edward C. Knight, Jr., a Philadelphia businessman and heir to a manufacturing, railroad, and publishing fortune, and his French wife, Amanda Marie Louise Lebel. Local legend reports that the Knights built the clubhouse after one of the local shooting clubs operated by northern businessmen refused to allow Amanda, an avid hunter, to accompany her husband on a visit. Knight purchased some two thousand acres on the banks, and the couple spent the hunting seasons of 1922–25 supervising construction of their $383,000 private lodge. No architect has been identified.[126]

The stunning house presents contrasting facades to the land and water sides of a picturesquely landscaped setting. The high gable roof sweeps down to dormers, banks of windows, and porches that stress the horizontal line, while the massing expresses public, private, and service zones. Amanda's taste pervades the opulent Arts and Crafts and Art Nouveau detail (fig. 5.89), sleek natural wood fittings, and Tiffany light fixtures; her favorite waterlily motif unifies the formal rooms' furnishings, woodwork, and even the silverware. Whalehead was built for private enjoyment, with its functional zones containing few public rooms but very large master bedrooms and many servants' quarters; the log book noted only occasional guests.[127]

Figure 5.88. Whalehead Club, Currituck County, 1922–25.

Figure 5.89. Whalehead Club. Entry hall.

Country houses and hunting lodges had somewhat different purposes but shared common elements of planning: they were spacious residences designed to accommodate leisurely recreation and elaborate entertainment, a staff of servants, abundant technological conveniences, and a unified design of house and landscape to display the owner's tastes and assure privacy.[128] Country house architecture in North Carolina likewise developed largely within a national, urban framework, specifically the Philadelphia country house movement. A country house was usually conceived as a family's principal residence, located on a transportation line that allowed the man of the house to commute to his office while maintaining his family in a healthful, spacious estate suitable to elaborate entertaining. Key examples, the creations of wives of wealthy industrialists, express personal ideals on a grand scale.

At Reynolda (fig. 5.90) near Winston-Salem, Katharine Smith Reynolds, wife of tobacco industrialist Richard J. Reynolds, created a country estate that blended private luxury with a concern for progressive paternalism and agricultural and social reform. A native of Mount Airy, Katharine Reynolds was educated at the State Normal and Industrial School for Women in

Figure 5.90. Reynolda House, Winston-Salem, 1914–17. Charles Barton Keen, architect; Thomas Sears, landscape architect.

Figure 5.91. Reynolda House. Plan by Edwin Bouldin after Charles Barton Keen. (Reynolda House, Museum of American Art)

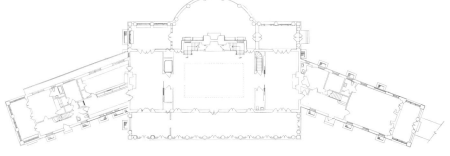

Figure 5.92. Reynolda House. Porch.

Greensboro, where the "influence toward reform and improvement was extremely strong." In 1905 she married Richard Joshua Reynolds and moved into Reynolds's big downtown residence. She had four children and by 1912 had plans underway for a one-thousand-acre estate.[129]

Conceived and executed in the midst of the American Progressive movement, "the farm" expressed Katharine Reynolds's idea of "a model, producing country estate" to provide a healthful family home; a working farm to demonstrate modern agriculture and domestic science to rural men and women; an ideal "village" with a school, church, and housing; and landscaped gardens accessible to the community. Like other well-informed North Carolina clients, she turned to established specialists for the expertise required to realize her vision. For advice on farm management she consulted experts from the state agricultural college in Raleigh. To design the estate she employed leaders in the Philadelphia country house movement—landscape architect Thomas Sears and architect Charles Barton Keen—whose published work accorded with her ideas.

In keeping with his own and his client's preferences, Keen skillfully underplayed the bulk and costliness of the sixty-room, $200,000 mansion, settling its 195-foot length into the gently sloping terrain. He combined smooth, stuccoed walls with rough fieldstone chimneys and foundations and stout, stylized Tuscan columns. Bands of windows and the Ludowici-Celadon tile roof and pent eaves stress the horizontal line. The rooms and porch areas are elegantly appointed with paneling, carving, tile, and ironwork by Philadelphia artisans. Beaux Arts principles underlie a clear ordering of procession and functional zones, but the plan is developed with remarkable openness and informality (fig. 5.91). The main entrance originally gave directly into the large two-story living room, from which proceed the dining room, sitting room, and library. On every side, sun porches, sleeping porches, and, originally, a rounded porte cochere opened much of the house to the outdoors (fig. 5.92).[130]

Figure 5.93. Graylyn, Winston-Salem, 1929–32. Luther Lashmit, architect.

Graylyn (fig. 5.93), constructed in 1929–32 across the road from Reynolda, is the product of a quite different time in social and corporate history. It was the youthful work of Winston-Salem architect Luther Lashmit, who was commissioned by Bowman Gray, president of the R. J. Reynolds Tobacco Company, and his wife, Nathalie Lyons Gray, to design a private family residence that would express her artistic tastes and world travels.[131] The Grays hired Philadelphian Thomas Sears, the landscape designer for Reynolda, and turned for architectural services to Lashmit, of the local firm of Northup and O'Brien. Schooled in a Beaux Arts–influenced curriculum at the Carnegie Institute of Technology in Pittsburgh, Lashmit had just returned from travel and study in France. He began drawings in 1927. At the ground breaking for the main house in January 1929, a family member pronounced Graylyn "a monument to success."[132]

Influenced by the widely published Norman Revival country houses of Philadelphia, and in accord with Mrs. Gray's fondness for the architecture of Normandy and Brittany, Lashmit combined simple forms with richly textured stone from Gray's native Randolph County and a high roof of multihued slate.[133] The severity of the main facade emphasizes the 240-foot length; a zoned plan bends in an obtuse L with a stair tower in the elbow. Aided by a Baltimore decorating firm, Nathalie Gray "told us room-by-room what she wanted," recalled Lashmit. "She had a set of blueprints made a certain size so she could take them on trips with her."[134] The decors of the principal rooms vary from medieval to English Georgian to Turkish. The swimming pool has an ocean-liner theme in tile and metal, and the men's dressing room is tiled with a border of Camel brand images.[135]

Construction had only begun when the crash of 1929 came. But with millions of unemployed Americans smoking cigarettes, Reynolds and other tobacco companies thrived. In 1931 *Fortune* magazine celebrated the firm's status as "America's most profitable tobacco concern," with profits of some $300 million a year. The journal noted that Bowman Gray "will now and then lay down his tools for an European trip, and by way of importing European culture, he and Mrs. Gray have removed whole rooms from Touraine chateaux across the Atlantic for their enormous new house outside of Winston-Salem. . . . This house is talked about throughout the Carolinas." Not all the talk was so favorable. Impoverished farmers resented tobacco manufacturers' profits, which Graylyn symbolized. In 1931, after receiving threats to harm the family and to blow up the house, the Grays temporarily stopped construction. Guardhouses and the ornamental iron gate between tall walls now became functional. The house was completed in 1932.[136]

Depression and Recovery

The Great Depression soon curtailed construction nearly everywhere. With the completion of Duke Chapel in 1932, that campus expansion program stopped. At the University of North Carolina, work was finished on a dorm under construction and a bell tower designed by McKim, Mead, and White was built in 1930–31, but then construction stopped.[137] Builders and architects went without work, some recent graduates of architectural school never entered their profession, and it was estimated that nearly half of the nation's architectural firms failed in 1930. The bottom came in 1933. Slowly at first, and increasingly after 1935, relief funds for public works reinvigorated the construction industry. By the late 1930s private construction had begun to recover.[138]

The architecture of the 1930s followed several trends of patronage and stylistic development. The principal private clients were a few individuals whose fortunes had weathered the crash and its aftermath and who, in a buyer's market, could obtain fine work at low cost. The principal public patron was government—mainly federal, state, and local projects assisted by the Public Works Administration (PWA) and Works Progress Administration (WPA). In stylistic terms, two main threads emerged from the many that had woven the rich fabric of the 1920s: one was the revival styles—mainly the Georgian, with its emphasis on an orderly American past; the other the modernist—whether in the streamlined Moderne and Art Deco or the new International style brought directly from Europe by recent immigrants—that focused on technology and the future as the source of hope and progress.

Tatton Hall (fig. 5.94), built in 1935–36 on the outskirts of Raleigh, best exemplifies the 1930s Georgian Revival. Norman and Mishew Edgerton had roots in Raleigh and eastern North Carolina; they also possessed business holdings that survived the crash. Friends in Winston-Salem urged them to hire landscape architect Charles Gillette, who in turn suggested New York architect William Bottomley. Norman Edgerton visited Richmond to see Bottomley's work there and found that the architect "had time, it being the Depression."[139] Trained at Columbia University and the École des Beaux Arts, Bottomley possessed a sure sense of form and proportion, an inventive approach to plan, and admirable knowledge of American Georgian and Federal architecture. At Tatton Hall, Bottomley combined Georgian motifs in a fluent and original composition. The main facade centers on a pedimented pavilion with flanking wings. The garden facade, by contrast, extends in gentle curves to suggest a rear courtyard. The plan flows asymmetrically from a lateral entry hall dominated by a spiral stair; rooms are lavishly finished with locally manufactured paneling and eclectic appointments in Georgian, restrained Art Deco, and Chinese themes.[140]

While a few luxurious houses were being built in revival styles, modernism was gaining strength. In 1933, the U.S. Post Office in Greensboro (fig. 5.95) neared completion. The project, begun in 1931, had brought work and pride to a community mired in the depths of the depression. The massive stone building presented the still unfamiliar modernist aspect of public architecture. Though classical in its symmetrical composition, central pavilion, and dominant pilasters

Figure 5.94. Tatton Hall, Raleigh, 1935–36. William Lawrence Bottomley, architect; John F. Danielson, contractor.

and frieze, it displays the sleek, incised detail and abstract motifs of the Moderne and Art Deco styles. Mount Airy granite, Indiana limestone, and aluminum sheathe the exterior; inside, the public areas continue the theme of modernized classicism in marble, Virginia greenstone, and aluminum. At its dedication in July 1933, some five thousand people gathered to see dignitaries and hear speeches, a military band played, and army airplanes "zoomed noisily through the summer sky."[141]

Local reaction to the building expressed widely shared ambivalence about current architectural trends. A writer for the *Greensboro Daily News* was troubled by "the extreme of its departure from enduring canons of the art." Contrasting the post office with Harry Barton's classical courthouse nearby, he wrote:

> The monumental architects of the 1930's are presumed to be trying to express the era, which is, God wot, hard and graceless enough; although we trust these qualified interpreters of it, exaggerate. In the spirit-entrancing curves of the courthouse's embellishments, no doubt there is something of the worship of all the heathen gods of Mount Olympus; the other seems to be trying to proclaim, if any god at all, a *deus ex machina*. Still, if this mode in monumental building does indeed express our day and generation, it may be at least accorded the high merit of honesty; however its glimpses may fail to make us less forlorn. After all, we are a pragmatic people, little disposed and having little time, to ponder the classics or contemplate the esoteric cosmos. . . . What we are looking for in post offices is a suitable place for postal public servants to work.[142]

Figure 5.95. U.S. Post Office, Greensboro, 1931–33. James A. Wetmore, acting supervising architect of the Treasury.

The writer also put his finger on changes in federal building policies. During the 1920s, the Office of the Supervising Architect of the Treasury had adopted policies of standardization, efficiency, and economy; these values replaced the ideal of individualized Beaux Arts monumentality, a concept too often associated with pork-barrel patronage, waste, and architectural bombast. Based on an idea introduced in 1915, four classes of buildings were defined within "a rational system of uniformity and business economy." Put into effect in the 1920s, the system meant that the architecture of each building—use of stone or brick facing, fireproof construction, and the interior use of marble, metal, ornament, and art—was calibrated to the community and the amount of receipts the facility generated. Plans and types were standardized, and classical details were kept to a minimum. In 1926–27, attempting to shift from congressional patronage to a systematic plan, the Public Buildings Act authorized a survey of public building needs and a plan for future construction projects. This Public Buildings Program formed the basis for allocation when, in 1930, Congress began to pour money into public works to combat unemployment.[143] The Greensboro U.S. Post Office exemplifies this first, critical generation of depression relief work.

In 1933, after the election of Franklin Delano Roosevelt, the Treasury Department was reorganized, and the supervising architect's office was relocated in the Division of Public Works, which oversaw design and construction of scores of new post offices. Few of these continued the Greensboro building's modernist approach. Most post offices were built in simplified revival styles intended to be "a credit to the communities and in accord with the traditions of the localities." Policy dictated maximum use of local materials to encourage local employment. In North Carolina small towns, most of these structures are one- or one-and-a-half-story buildings with colonial and classical motifs, usually executed in red brick or local stone. Many of their lobbies contain murals—a break with the predepression convention that restricted murals to major post offices. The Public Works of Art Program (1933) and then the Treasury Relief Art Project (1935), funded by the Works Progress Administration, provided work to artists and placed these murals in communities in which, perhaps, no public work of art had ever been displayed before.[144]

At the same time, the National Industrial Recovery Act (NIRA) established the Public Works Administration, which funded construction of scores of community centers, armories, and other facilities built throughout North Carolina. Several PWA community buildings used pole-log construction or rough local stonework. Such buildings as armories took modernist, sometimes militaristic forms, and many buildings displayed a streamlined, stripped-down classicism. In Raleigh, federal funds aided construction of the state's Education Building and Justice Building, whose stone facades featured stylized bases, pilasters, and entablatures following P. Thornton Marye's precedent on Union Square. The administration of the University of North Carolina obtained relief funds to help build dormitories and a medical building in a streamlined continuation of the red-brick Georgian Revival campus style.[145]

During the 1930s, a few individuals began to build in boldly modernist terms. Important early examples of the International style appeared in the mountains of North Carolina. Although the native population and architecture of the mountains were rural and conservative, the climate and landscape attracted a diverse set of forward-looking individuals. The International style, developed at the Bauhaus in Weimar, Germany, emphasized forms that stressed pure volume and clean, horizontally composed geometry; flat roofs, flush walls, cantilevered elements, and windows continuous with the walls combined to achieve the severe, elegant geometry intended to transcend national, historical, or regional traditions.

One of the earliest International-style buildings in America was the Weyman Memorial Laboratory of the Highlands Museum and Biological Laboratory (fig. 5.96), designed by Oskar Stonorov of Philadelphia. The facility in Highlands was a new, innovative national center for biological study, located there because of the area's varied fauna and flora. Stonorov had recently emigrated from Germany; the laboratory was apparently his first American commission. Planning began in 1930, and the building was finished in 1931 for only $2,868. It was a small but adventurous frame structure; its flat roof, smooth matchboard walls, bands of windows, and utter simplicity typify Stonorov's use of the International style for cheap, practical buildings. The laboratory gained fame when it was illustrated in Henry-Russell Hitchcock and Philip Johnson's *The International Style* (1932), the book that advanced and defined the new mode for Americans. But the idealized geometry was ill suited to the locale: Highlands receives heavy winter snows and the highest annual rainfall in America outside the Pacific Northwest. The building rotted and the flat roof leaked, no matter how many times it was replaced. In 1958 the building was totally remodeled with a pitched roof and asbestos shingles. "It was a pity," said the president of the corporation. "It was a handsome building and everybody liked it."[146]

Later in the 1930s, as important proponents of the International style left Europe to become leaders in American architectural education and practice, like-minded clients in North Carolina turned to them for advanced designs. Architect Walter Gropius came to teach at Harvard and, with Marcel Breuer and others, brought advanced European ideas to America. In North Carolina in 1933, a group of intellectuals and artists led by John Andrew Rice had begun Black Mountain College on the campus of the Blue Ridge Assembly, a summer YMCA facility near Asheville. Through Philip Johnson, Rice brought Bauhaus refugees Josef and Anni Albers from Germany to join the faculty. In 1937 the college leaders decided to establish their own campus. At Albers's suggestion, Gropius and his associate Breuer were asked to design a central multiuse complex, and they produced a plan and model. But when faced with estimates of some $500,000, rather than seeking a cheaper design from Gropius and Breuer, the college turned to A. Lawrence Kocher, former professor at the University of Virginia and Carnegie Institute of Technology. Kocher put into effect his interest in economical International-style architecture: he designed a Studies Building as the first of a series of campus structures, using simple forms and

Figure 5.96. Weyman Memorial Laboratory, Highlands Museum and Biological Laboratory, 1930–31. Oskar Stonorov, architect. (Highlands Biological Station)

Figure 5.97. Weizenblatt House, Asheville, 1940–41. Marcel Breuer, architect. Anthony Lord, supervising architect.

inexpensive materials and student workmen. He moved to Black Mountain to teach and supervise. Only the Studies Building—begun in 1940 and requiring more than two years to finish—was erected.[147]

Not far away, another client of cosmopolitan tastes commissioned and completed a handsome residence designed by Marcel Breuer (fig. 5.97). Sprinza Weizenblatt, a Viennese ophthalmologist, had settled in Asheville in the 1930s. She met Breuer at Black Mountain College, where interesting activities frequently attracted sophisticated Asheville residents. Asheville architect Anthony Lord was engaged to write specifications and supervise construction. Dr. Weizenblatt, Lord recalled, was a lively woman with a wide range of interests, who "wanted the new thing." Breuer designed a modest duplex residence, which he set into the sloping terrain so as to provide privacy from the street while opening up the rear elevation with windows looking down the hillside. The house was begun in the fall of 1940 and finished in 1941. Two massive blocks of rough native stone are accented by simple bands of wood and expanses of glass. The flat roof and linear, asymmetrical forms contrast with the various revival-style residences of the neighborhood, as do the natural materials and quiet design that integrate the house into the landscape.[148]

By the end of the 1930s, as building began again in earnest, the bifurcation of popular taste renewed itself. Many clients wanted the red-brick colonial style encouraged by Williamsburg, the restored Virginia capital that provided a permanent exposition of colonial America. In addition to its influence on houses, the Williamsburg style was introduced as a suitable model for creating an idyllic village image—a model adopted in Chapel Hill, long considered a village but now a

Figure 5.98. Merry Acres, Winston-Salem, 1940. Luther Lashmit, architect. Destroyed.
(Wake Forest University Library)

growing university town, and in Kannapolis, the center of a vast and modern textile-village empire.[149]

A wider variety of clients also wanted modernist buildings. In Asheville the Citizen-Times Building (1939), designed by Anthony Lord, showed stark forms accented by bands of glass block windows. Simplified Art Deco and Moderne themes reappeared in such postdepression sky-scrapers as the Durham Life Building in Raleigh (1940), designed by Northup and O'Brien and boasting one of the nation's first air-conditioning systems for a tall building.[150] Gas stations, bus depots, automobile dealerships, and a few houses also display the adventurous motifs of the recovery era's optimistic modernism. Paradoxically, the grandest house in the style was built for R. J. Reynolds, Jr., and designed by Luther Lashmit, who only a few years earlier had designed Graylyn. Merry Acres (fig. 5.98), built in 1940, was a huge and luxurious residence with sleek planes and volumes of white stuccoed elegance stepping down a gentle slope. Lashmit, like many of his contemporaries whose practices spanned the depression, incorporated modernist ideas in much the same fashion as he had used revival modes. The plan repeated the zoned layout of Graylyn but had wings projecting at right angles and a curving pavilion rounding the corner.[151]

World War II brought full recovery from the depression and demanded fast, large-scale construction. Contractors and architects who had managed to keep enough work in the 1930s now faced opportunities for vast projects that required a scale of organization and efficiency hitherto unknown. The Airship Docks (fig. 5.99), built at Weeksville near Elizabeth City at the beginning of the war, are among the state's most spectacular monuments of wartime building. Lighter Than Air (LTA) ships played an essential role in protecting American ships. In 1940 Weeksville was chosen as the site for an LTA base midway between Florida and the main base at Lakehurst, New Jersey. The helium-filled airships required huge docks, and the U.S. Navy required fast construction. The contract went to the J. A. Jones Construction Company of

Figure 5.99. Air Ship Dock No. One, U.S. Naval Air Station (LTA), Weeksville, Pasquotank County, 1940–41. J. A. Jones, contractor.

Charlotte, which had survived the depression with the aid of post office work. The firm completed the job in under nine months. Dock One is 960 feet long and six stories high, with room for six airships. The huge building looms like a vision of the future from the flat landscape, its quonset form resembling a giant barracks, its clamshell doors opening eerily to expose three tiers of airships tethered within. Dock Two is a frame structure with vast timber trusses and flat, accordian-type doors.[152]

The world war brought the end of an era and laid the foundation for the beginning of a new age in architecture. Civilian construction stopped for nearly five years. When construction began again in 1946 and 1947, the seeds of change planted during the depression and war quickly grew into vast new patterns in the American landscape. The pent-up demand for construction brought boom times for the building industry. The divergence of taste widened as a new generation of modernists took up the banner against Beaux Arts–trained traditionalists. The automobile and a host of technological advances combined with unprecedented prosperity, exodus from the farm, and sweeping social changes to remake the landscape throughout most of the state.[153] In 1940, however, all this lay beyond anyone's view. North Carolinians had begun to build again. If some built with an eye to a future in which the promise of technology loomed large while others found reassurance in the architecture of a familiar past, those differences seemed less important than economic stability and new hope for the state and nation. What many knew, then as now, was that the future was full of unforeseeable events that would, yet again, remake the state, its people, and its architecture.

Color Plates

Plate 1. Rose Hill, Caswell County. Parlor wing added ca. 1829.

Plate 2. Edwards-Franklin House, Surry County, ca. 1799.
Painted wainscot and door in second-story room,
probably 1820s.

Plate 3. Bynum-Sugg House, Edgecombe County,
early 19th century. Door in second-story room.

Plate 4. Savage House, Edgecombe County, early 19th
century. Wainscot.

Plate 5. Reich-Strupe-Butner House, Bethania. Parlor wall
painting by Naaman Reich, mid-19th century.

Plate 6. City Hall-Thalian Hall, Wilmington, 1854–58. John M. Trimble, architect; James F. Post, superintending architect; John C. Wood and Robert B. Wood, masonry contractors; G. W. Rose, carpenter. Interior of Thalian Hall.

Plate 7. Cherry Hill, Warren County, ca. 1859. John A. Waddell, builder, school of Jacob W. Holt. Parlor.

Plate 8. Watson House, Warren County, 1850s. Attributed to Jacob W. Holt, builder. Front passage.

Plate 9. Archibald Taylor House, Franklin County, 1850s. Attributed to Jacob W. Holt, builder. Front passage.

Plate 10. Coolmore, Edgecombe County, 1859–60. E. G. Lind, architect; N. A. Sherman, builder; Mr. Dreyer, fresco painter. Entry vestibule.

Plate 11. Coolmore. Stair in rotunda.

Plate 12. Coolmore. Gentlemen's parlor.

Plate 13. Redmond-Shackleford House, Tarboro, 1880s. The paint scheme is attributed to Bavarian fresco painter Edward Zoeller, a resident of Tarboro from about 1850 until 1897.

Plate 14. Mistletoe Villa, Henderson, expanded 1883. Attributed to Samuel Sloan, architect. The paint colors are based on paint research and construction specifications.

Plate 15. Biltmore House, Asheville, 1890–95. Richard Morris Hunt, architect. Library.

Plate 16. S. H. Kress Building, Greensboro, 1930.
Edward F. Sibbert, architect.

Plate 17. City Building, Asheville, 1926–28.
Douglas D. Ellington, architect.

Plate 18. First Baptist Church, Asheville, 1925–27. Douglas D. Ellington, architect.

Notes

Abbreviations

Frequently cited books, journals, and repositories have been identified by the following abbreviations in notes.

Manuscript Repositories

A&H   North Carolina Division of Archives and History, Department of Cultural Resources, Raleigh
MMA   Metropolitan Museum of Art, New York, N.Y.
NA   National Archives, Washington, D.C.
NCC   North Carolina Collection, University of North Carolina Library, Chapel Hill
NYPL New York Public Library, New York, N.Y.
SHC   Southern Historical Collection, University of North Carolina Library, Chapel Hill
YU   Yale University Manuscripts and Archives, Sterling Library, New Haven, Conn.

Publications and Unpublished Documents

ABNC   Catherine W. Bishir, Charlotte V. Brown, Carl R. Lounsbury, and Ernest H. Wood III, *Architects and Builders in North Carolina*
CRNC   William L. Saunders, ed., *Colonial Records of North Carolina*
DNCB   William S. Powell, ed., *Dictionary of North Carolina Biography*
EANC   Frances Benjamin Johnston and Thomas Tileston Waterman, *The Early Architecture of North Carolina*
JSAH   *Journal of the Society of Architectural Historians*
NCHR   *North Carolina Historical Review*
NR form   National Register of Historic Places Nomination Forms, Archives and History, Raleigh
RM   Adelaide L. Fries et al., eds., *Records of the Moravians in North Carolina*
SRNC   Walter Clark, ed., *The State Records of North Carolina*

Chapter 1

1. Schoepf, *Travels in the Confederation*, 2:103. Although the German visitor's account dates from the 1780s, by which time North Carolina's forests had been diminished, his description of farms and forests puts in vivid terms the same conditions reported by travelers throughout the colonial period. See, for example, Lawson, *New Voyage*; William Byrd, in Boyd, *William Byrd's Histories*; "William Logan's Journal"; Andrews, *Journal of a Lady of Quality*, 145–95. On the reduction of the forests, see Merrens, *Colonial North Carolina*, 107. The idea of the forest society appears in Charles F. Carroll, "The Forest Society of New England," in Hindle, *America's Wooden Age*, 13–36.

2. On the natural landscape, see Louis B. Wright and Marion Tinling, eds., *Quebec to Carolina in 1785–1786, Being the Travel Diary and Observations of Robert Hunter, Jr., a Young Merchant of London* (San Marino, Calif.: Huntington Library, 1943), 274 (quote), 272–79; Schoepf, *Travels in the Confederation*, 2:104–8, 121–23, 136–37; Ezell, *New Democracy*, 9.

3. My discussion in this section draws upon Cary Carson, "English," in Upton, *America's Architectural Roots*, 54–61; John B. Jackson, *Discovering the Vernacular Landscape* (New Haven, Conn.: Yale University Press, 1984); Stilgoe, *Common Landscape of America*, esp. chaps. 1 and 2; Upton, "Early Vernacular Architecture." For North Carolina, I have used mainly Ekirch, "*Poor Carolina*"; Fenn and Wood, *Natives and Newcomers*; Parramore, "Tuscarora Ascendancy"; Merrens, *Colonial North Carolina*; and, esp., Lounsbury, "Development of Domestic Architecture"; *ABNC*, 9–47.

4. John MacDowell to Secretary of the Society for the Propagation of the Gospel, Apr. 17, 1760, *CRNC*, 6:236–38.

5. Boyd, *William Byrd's Histories*, 52. Ekirch, "*Poor Carolina*," 20–25, 222–27 (on property holding in the colony).

6. The description of English settlers in Virginia adopting Indians' agricultural practices, ca. 1717, comes from Hugh Jones, *The Present State of Virginia*, edited by Richard L. Morton (Chapel Hill: University of North Carolina Press for the Virginia Historical Society, 1956), 55. On crop production in North Carolina, see Merrens, *Colonial North Carolina*, 108–41. Principal products for the market were corn, wheat, tobacco (mainly in the north), rice and indigo (mainly in the southeast), livestock, and forest products.

7. William Byrd, in Louis B. Wright, ed., *The Prose Works of William Byrd of Westover* (Cambridge, Mass.: Harvard University Press, 1966), 204, and Alexander McAllister to Cousin, [1770?], in Alexander McAllister Papers, SHC, quoted in Ekirch, "*Poor Carolina*," 30–31, 29. On views of time and work, see David Bertelson, *The Lazy South* (New York: Oxford University Press, 1967); Sobel, *The World They Made Together*, 15–67.

8. It is known that white southerners learned agricultural techniques and other lessons from Indians and Africans. On Virginians, see Jones, *Present State of Virginia*, 55; on African influence on rice growing, see Peter Wood, *Black Majority: Negroes in Colonial South Carolina* (New York: Alfred A. Knopf, 1974), esp. 35–91. Whether the new settlers also learned building techniques suitable to the locale has not yet been established. On continued interaction with Indians, see Carson et al., "Impermanent Architecture"; Upton, "Early Vernacular Architecture," 121; Parramore, "Tuscarora Ascendancy." On black-white cultural interaction, including architecture, see Sobel, *The World They Made Together*, 100–153; Carl Lounsbury's review of Sobel in *Winterthur Portfolio* 24, nos. 2/3 (Summer/Autumn 1989): 187–89.

9. See, for example, *SRNC*, 23:234–43, 680–85, 808–11. In Corbinton (later named Hillsborough) in 1755, for example, the minimum house built to "save" a lot had to be of stone, brick, or frame, or of squared and dovetailed logs, and it had to measure at least 20 by 16 feet (William Churton, Gent., to Herman Husband, Nov. 4, 1755, Orange County Deed Book I,

122–23, Orange County Records, A&H, courtesy of Mary Claire Engstrom). By 1767 town law required that the minimum house be of brick, stone, or frame, the same size as above but with at least 9 feet pitch and with a brick or stone chimney. The laws also enabled the town trustees to prevent construction of mortar, clay, or wooden chimneys and to pull down any that were considered hazardous (*SRNC*, 25:500–503).

10. See Lounsbury, "Development of Domestic Architecture," 23, and "Building Process," 435; *CRNC*, 1:300, cited in Lounsbury, "Development of Domestic Architecture," 22; John Lawson, *Lawson's History of North Carolina* (1714; reprint, Richmond, Va.: Garrett and Massie, 1951), 228. Lawson said that the log house had belonged to Gov. Seth Sothel (governor of Carolina, 1682–89). At the time of the incident related by Lawson, the structure was in use as a secure storage house for goods to be traded to the Indians, but an Indian had burrowed beneath it to steal the contents (Boyd, *William Byrd's Histories*, 94). For a summary of the debate over the antecedents of American log construction, see Stephen G. Del Sordo, review of *American Log Buildings: An Old World Heritage*, by Terry G. Jordan, *Winterthur Portfolio* 21, nos. 2/3 (Summer/Autumn, 1986): 201–2.

11. Log construction is treated at greater length in Chapter 2.

12. Newsome, "Twelve North Carolina Counties," *NCHR*, 5:440; *Fayetteville Observer*, Sept. 1, 1856. A rare example extant in the Albemarle is the Cullen Jones House (ca. 1810) in Chowan County: a one-room log house later incorporated into a frame dwelling (Brad Barker, "Cullen Jones House," Chowan County survey file, Survey and Planning Branch, A&H). On "lowland" log construction in the coastal South, see Patricia Irvin Cooper, "Toward a Revised Understanding of American Log Building," in Wells, *Perspectives in Vernacular Architecture, II*, 227–28. For various construction methods and their regional distribution, see Kniffen and Glassie, "Building in Wood."

13. The history of this house has not been established, but it has been connected with the O'Quinn family (longtime residents in the region) during the present century and possibly longer. The house was pointed out to Michael Southern and me by Ted Lawrence of Sanford. The Sandhills region, which lies on the western edge of the lower coastal plain and remained rural and isolated for many years, contains many key examples of log buildings, most of them still unstudied.

14. John Lawson reported in 1709 the durability of the pitch pine, "replete with abundance of Bitumen," which "seems to suffer no Decay, though exposed to all weathers, for many Ages; and is used in several Domestic and Plantation Uses" (*Lawson's History*, 100). The Wayne County Poor House Specifications (Wayne County Records, 1836, A&H) typify several usages of lightwood blocks: the building was to be a frame house with a brick chimney and was to sit 1½ feet above the ground on "Good lightwood Blocks to go under the house five under each side and one at each end the blocks all to be laid on there side." An "old log house" was to be renovated for reuse and "a good dirt chimney" built to it. The use of lightwood blocks continued in some areas into the early twentieth century and in some areas was discontinued only after the advent of concrete blocks.

15. "William Logan's Journal," 9.

16. In 1981 the house was stabilized and the chimney was repaired (David R. Black, "Rehabilitation of the Boyette Slave House and Its Stick Chimney," in Wells, *Perspectives in Vernacular Architecture, II*, 211). Another example was the Ebenezer Log Church in Chatham County, with a dovetailed log chimney; the building was lost in the 1970s ("Ebenezer Log Church," NR form, 1974).

17. Wynette Parks Haun, *Johnston County, North Carolina, Court Minutes 1759 thru 1766* (Durham: privately printed, 1974), 3. That the logs were to be hewed or sawed 4 inches thick indicates that they may well have been of the type now usually called planks (meaning sawed to a uniform thickness considerably smaller than the height of the plank), whereas "plank" was

the term used for thinner planks applied inside. For other specifications for dovetailed log jails, see Pasquotank County Accounts, 1809, A&H. The Wayne County Gaol Records (Wayne County Records, 1813, A&H) specify a jail 36 by 20 feet, with timbers hewn to 6 inches thick and 8 to 12 inches high, made of post oak or pine, "the two walls to be dufftailed and good Inch Trunnells 6 Inches long to be put at the distance of 4 feet in each log." On dovetailed, squared-log buildings in early New England, see Cummings, *Framed Houses of Massachusetts Bay*, 89–94, and Richard M. Candee, "Wooden Buildings in Early Maine and New Hampshire: A Technological and Cultural History, 1600–1720," Ph.D. diss., University of Pennsylvania, 1976. Cummings cites Candee's suggestion that late-medieval Scottish log buildings may be precedents for New England work (*Framed Houses of Massachusetts Bay*, 89). On similar dovetailed plank buildings in the mid-Atlantic, see, for example, Herman, *Architecture and Rural Life*, 89.

18. Haley and Winslow, *Perquimans County*, 54, 209.

19. Ibid., 16, 114. The Pasquotank Log House was moved to Perquimans County and then dismantled and taken to Winston-Salem. The rafters of the gable roof rested on a tilted false plate—that is, the timber atop the uppermost plank was set at an angle rather than flat.

20. Ibid., 30, 115.

21. See Upton, "Traditional Timber Framing," esp. 51–61; *ABNC*, 14–18.

22. *CRNC*, 1:711–12, quoted in *ABNC*, 42. Construction of this church is discussed in ibid., 41–43. In 1708 the vestry sought to have a brick floor laid, but they later gave up this plan and decided to have a plank floor, which was cheaper and easier to install (Vestry Records of St. Paul's Church, Edenton, transcript by Elizabeth V. Moore, in possession of author). See also Lawson, *Lawson's History*, 98, 100.

23. Vestry Records of St. Paul's Church (Moore transcript).

24. Thomas Pollock, Will, July 20, 1722, in Grimes, *North Carolina Wills and Inventories*, 346–47. The carpenter was identified as Mr. West, the bricklayer as Mr. Coke [Thomas Cooke] (Thomas Pollock Letterbook, May 2, 1721, 43, A&H, quoted in *ABNC*, 9, 43). Pollock wrote to agents in Boston that he was "ingaged with the plague of Building" for his sons and complained that carpenters in Carolina were "very indefferent, Lasy and Slow." He urged his agents to recruit among tradesmen arriving from Europe a house carpenter for him, whom he would be willing to pay "20: 30: nay Even at 40: for a year if Good at his trade," and he was also willing to buy tools for the worker if necessary. He also requested his agents to find him indentured servants who were bricklayers and carpenters (ibid., 254, 256). Whether Coke and West were among these immigrants is not certain.

25. John Urmston, July 7, 1711, in *CRNC*, 1:764; John Brickell, *The Natural History of North-Carolina* (1737; reprint, Murfreesboro: Johnson Publishing Co., 1968), 275. On the building trades, see *ABNC*, chaps. 1–2; Bishir, "Black Builders in Antebellum North Carolina."

26. On the social function of architectural finish, see esp. Upton, *Holy Things and Profane*, 101–18, and Herman, *Architecture and Rural Life*, 42–60.

27. Haley and Winslow, *Perquimans County*, 113; Thomas C. Parramore, "The Newbold-White House: A Documentary History of the Property and Its Inhabitants," research report, 1973, copy in Restoration Branch, A&H. The property was patented in 1684 by Joseph Scott, a Quaker, who died in 1685; it passed through various owners during the eighteenth century. The name comes from late owners. No certain construction date has been established even after extensive archaeological and historical research. Al Honeycutt believes the house dates from the last quarter of the seventeenth century or first quarter of the eighteenth; Carl Lounsbury, based on comparisons with Virginia examples, suggests the first or second quarter of the eighteenth century (personal communications from Honeycutt

and Lounsbury, 1988–89).

28. Common room names used in the eighteenth century were *hall* for a large room, *passage* for what is now usually considered a hall or hallway, *parlor* for a private principal room, and *chamber* for a variety of rooms, including bedchambers. See Lounsbury, "Development of Domestic Architecture"; Upton, "Vernacular Domestic Architecture."

29. In the Newbold-White House, as in most colonial work, the mason used queen closers (small brick bats), one toward the end of each course, to make his bonding pattern work out. In the nineteenth century, bricklayers usually employed king closers (bricks about two-thirds the size of a normal brick), which they placed at the ends of the brick courses. For comparison with Virginia brickwork, see Loth, "Notes on Virginia Brickwork," 87–89.

30. See ibid., 102.

31. The interiors of the Jordan House were destroyed by fire in 1928 ("Jordan House," NR form, 1971). A pamphlet published ca. 1684, *Information and Direction to Such Persons as Are Inclined to America, More Especially Those Related to the Province of Pennsylvania*, described a three-room house of an established type and recommended it for beginners: 30 by 18 feet, with one partition near the middle and another that divided one end of the house into two rooms. T. T. Waterman attributes this document to William Penn, but Cary Carson and his coauthors question the attribution (*EANC*, 173; Carson et al., "Impermanent Architecture").

32. *EANC*, 31–32, 65.

33. Haley and Winslow, *Perquimans County*, 17–18; Thomas Butchko, "Historic Architecture of Gates County," typescript report, 1988, copy in Survey and Planning Branch, A&H, 16–17. In each case, only a single brick end survives.

34. The date of Milford is given as 1746, based on a dated brick found in the north chimney. Although altered inside, the plan had an off-center passage flanked by two large rooms (*EANC*, 32; "Milford," NR form, 1971).

35. The Palmer-Marsh House is known by the names of subsequent owners. Interiors of the first story of the house were changed in the nineteenth century and restored or reconstructed in the twentieth century. The second-story work is more nearly original. For discussion of exposed and decorated framing members, see Cummings, *Framed Houses of Massachusetts Bay*, 158–62; Allcott, *Colonial Homes in North Carolina*, 22, 84–87 (for Palmer-Marsh House).

36. See Cheeseman, "History of the Cupola House"; Bivins et al., "Cupola House"; *EANC*, 29–30; Pierce and Alswang, *American Interiors*, 41–44. Despite extensive research, the construction history of the house is not yet fully established. Prices paid for the property by owners from Sanderson to Francis Corbin were all £100 or less, which seems low for such a house (cf. Thomas Pollock, above, and St. Paul's Church, below). In *Robert Kirshaw* v. *Francis Corbin's Adm.*, carpenter Kirshaw sued Corbin's estate for £600 but was awarded £211.6.0; there is no evidence as to the nature of the debt (Cheeseman, "History of the Cupola House," 43–44). Several writers have suggested that the house was built for Sanderson but substantially remodeled in 1758 for Corbin. John Bivins and his coauthors give evidence that the house reflects a single main building campaign and suggest that it probably dates from 1724–40 ("Cupola House," 130). In the absence of compelling documentary or archaeological evidence, or of comparable buildings in the region, I believe that a date in the 1740s or even the 1750s is also possible.

37. Justices of Currituck Precinct took action against Robert Peyton for not building the courthouse according to agreement; in 1726 he claimed he had complied (Colonial Court Records, 107:86, 163, A&H, courtesy of Robert Cain).

38. Bivins et al., "Cupola House," 73–79. On early New England framing methods, see Cummings, *Framed Houses of Massachusetts Bay*, esp. 52–93. Evidence suggests that the roof structure is a single ensemble. It may reflect a cautious carpenter's

method of dealing with the unfamiliar dual problem of cupola and overhang, in which he avoided putting the stress of the cupola and the massive roof trusses on the spiked jetty and false girt.

39. Salmon, *Palladio Londinensis*, 1734, 1738. Helen Park notes that the two most popular builders' guides in the colonies were Salmon's *Palladio Londinensis* and Francis Price's *British Carpenter* (*List of Architectural Books*, 118–19). Although the principal mantels in the Cupola House are not exact copies of Salmon's plate H (added in the 1738 edition), their composition, with compressed pediment and rectangular panels and consoles flanking the central panel, is similar and distinctive. When the similarities of the house's pedimented and triangular doorways, scrolled pediments, and astral paneled doors to plates XX–XXIII and XXVI are also considered, the presence of so many elements in common between Salmon's 1738 edition and the Cupola House woodwork suggests the book's possible influence on an artisan who followed a common practice of adapting and recombining motifs. Bivins et al. see other influences as being more likely ("Cupola House," 117–19). On carving techniques, see ibid., 84–97.

40. See Herman, *Architecture and Rural Life*, 15.

41. Old Town Plantation House is believed to have been built in 1742 for Samuel Holloman and bought by Elisha Battle, a prominent planter and political figure, in 1747; the construction date is tied to a dated brick ("Old Town Plantation," NR form, 1972). Such separate porch chambers are often called "preacher rooms" by residents of eastern Carolina; it is unclear how far back this tradition goes.

42. Anastatia Sims, "The King House of Bertie County," research report, 1976, 5–14, copy in Restoration Branch, A&H; William King inventory, 1778, Bertie County Estate Records, A&H, cited in ibid., app. C. A dated brick is marked with the year, 1763, and the initials W E K.

43. For further discussion and illustrations, see Lounsbury, "Development of Domestic Architecture"; Haley and Winslow, *Perquimans County*, 18–20; *EANC*, 26–31, 45, 65; Butchko, "Historic Architecture of Gates County" and *On the Shores of the Pasquotank*; Lane, *North Carolina*, 24–42.

44. Sandbeck, *New Bern and Craven County*, 458, 551–52. Cf. plans of the Hawks House (ca. 1760–70) and Palmer-Tisdale House (ca. 1767) in ibid., 13–19, 256–57, 386–88. Like some contemporary New Bern houses and the Palmer-Marsh House in Bath, the Gordon House has a finished basement with a cooking fireplace.

45. Brad Barker, site visit and personal communication with author, June 17, 1989.

46. Ruth Little, Catherine Bishir, and Jerry Cross, "Lane-Bennett House," NR form, 1983.

47. Peter DuBois to Samuel Johnston, Jr., Feb. 8, 1757, Hayes Collection, SHC, quoted in Wrenn, *Wilmington*, 234; SRNC, 23:867–68.

48. William Luten Account Book, Oct. 4, 1773, 29, A&H. On North Carolina porches, see Little-Stokes, "North Carolina Porch." My thanks to Jay Edwards for sharing his manuscript, "The Complex Origins of the American Domestic Piazza-Veranda-Gallery" (1989). See also Roger G. Kennedy on the Caribbean trade connections of what he describes as the "Caribbean cottage" (*Architecture*, 61–72). In eighteenth- and nineteenth-century North Carolina, *piazza* was the most common term for a functional porch extending across all or most of the front, rear, or side of a house. Here, I use *porch* broadly and *piazza* only for porches intended for use and extending across all or most of a building.

Another dimension of architectural crosscurrents between North Carolina and the Caribbean islands appears in the frequent shipment of prefabricated house frames from North Carolina ports to the islands. For instance, many ships clearing Port Brunswick (Cape Fear) in the 1760s carried one, two, three, or four house frames bound for Caribbean ports—Barbados, St. Christopher's, Jamaica, Granada (Shipping Register, Exports, 1765–75, Treasurer's and Comptroller's Papers, Port Records, Port Brunswick, A&H, courtesy of Robert Cain). This practice continued in the 1780s; see Carl Lounsbury's mention of this in *ABNC*, 473 (n. 97).

49. Wrenn, *Wilmington*, 234. The plan had a central passage with two rooms on one side and a large room and porch on the other.

50. Powell, *Correspondence of William Tryon*, 1:138. Tryon also noted that the parlor floor stood about five feet above ground level and that the ceilings of the rooms were low. Russellborough was built for John Russell near Brunswick, Gov. Arthur Dobbs occupied it after 1758, and Tryon moved into it in 1765 (ibid., 1:143). Other houses in Brunswick had similar piazzas, some raised over subporches floored in brick (Stanley A. South, "Russellborough," 360–72).

51. "The Burgwin-Wright House," *Lower Cape Fear Historical Society Bulletin* 22 (1979): 1, 4. The columns of the portico were added in the mid-nineteenth century; H. G. Jones shows an 1846 daguerreotype of the house with plain columns (*North Carolina Illustrated*, title p.). Similarly elaborate paneled and carved work graced the lost plantation houses along the Cape Fear, including Burgwin's country house, the Hermitage, and Cornelius Harnett's Maynard. See Henry J. MacMillan, "Colonial Plantations of the Lower Cape Fear," *Lower Cape Fear Historical Society Bulletin* 12 (Feb. 1969): 1, 3–6.

52. Higginbotham, *Papers of James Iredell*, 1:173, 178, 183, 188, 205, 207, 211. These men were prominent among North Carolina's leadership in the Revolutionary and post-Revolutionary eras: Iredell, who married Hannah Johnston in 1773, was a leading proponent of federalism and the adoption of the Constitution and served as a justice of the U.S. Supreme Court; Samuel Johnston was later governor of North Carolina; and Hewes, the leading merchant, was a signer of the Declaration of Independence.

53. *Connecticut Courant*, Nov. 30, 1767, reporting from Williamsburg, Va., and quoted in Merrens, *Colonial North Carolina*, 54. See also Ramsey, *Carolina Cradle*.

54. See Thorp, "Assimilation," 37–42, for a commentary on adaptation to frontier farming even among the Moravians.

55. Herzog, "Early Architecture of New Bern," 14–15; Todd and Goebel, *Christoph Von Graffenried's Account*, 377, 296–97, 316.

56. Ramsey, *Carolina Cradle*, 146–51; Merrens, *Colonial North Carolina*, 57–62 (quote, 1789, from Pastor Roschen, 59; estimate of numbers, 61).

57. Carl Hammer, Jr., *Rhinelanders on the Yadkin: The Story of the Pennsylvania Germans in Rowan and Cabarrus* (Salisbury: Rowan Printing Co., 1943), 96–97. Concerning German and English language use in the antebellum Piedmont, see Rev. Samuel Rothrock Diary, 1834–93, A&H; on tombstones, see Ruth Little, "Folk Art in Stone," in Touart, *Building the Back Country*, 267–81. See also Edward A. Chappell, "Germans and Swiss," in Upton, *America's Architectural Roots*, 68–73, and "Acculturation in the Shenandoah Valley"; Glassie, *Pattern in the Material Folk Culture*; William Woys Weaver, "The Pennsylvania German House: European Antecedents and New World Forms," *Winterthur Portfolio* 21, no. 4 (Winter 1986): 243–64. See esp. Touart, "Acculturation."

58. A brief account of the Moravians appears in *RM*, 1:11–15. For a fuller treatment, see Daniel B. Thorp, *The Moravian Community in Colonial North Carolina: Pluralism on the Southern Frontier* (Knoxville: University of Tennessee Press, 1989). For their assistance on Moravian architecture and history, I am grateful to John Larson and John Compton.

The Moravian leadership sent thirteen men to make the trip to Wachovia; two more who planned to go only partway continued the journey with the group. These and two others soon returned to Bethlehem, leaving eleven to settle the colony. Ten stayed at Bethabara; one settled a farm outside the village (*RM*, 1:73–74, 484).

59. In writing of construction work, the Moravian diarist made a distinction between the familiar term *aufgeschlagen*, meaning raising as in a frame house, and a coined word, *aufgeblockt*, for laying up logs (*RM*, 1:287, translator's note). On fachwerk in America, see William H. Tishler, "Fachwerk Construction in the German Settlements of Wisconsin," *Winterthur Portfolio* 21, no. 4 (Winter 1986): 275–92.

60. *RM*, 1:313, 2:589; Thorp, "City That Never Was."

61. Campbell, "Buildings of Salem," 79–100, 121–25, 131; *RM*, 2:604; John Larson, "Old Salem," booklet produced for Vernacular Architecture Forum Annual Meeting, Winston-Salem, 1982.

62. *RM*, 2:770.

63. Touart, *Building the Back Country*, 5–6; *RM*, 1:109, 2:782, 834, 838–39.

64. J. C. Leonard, "Valentin Leonardt, the Revolutionary War Patriot of North Carolina," *Pennsylvania-German* (1910), quoted in Touart, "Acculturation," 73.

65. See Upton, "Traditional Timber Framing," 79–80. A similar structure was planned for Home Church in Salem but not built (John Larson to author, July 6, 1989). See photograph collection, neg. no. S102, Old Salem, Inc., Winston-Salem, for a drawing of that proposed roof truss.

66. Jo White Linn, "Michael Braun," in *DNCB*, 1:220–21; Hood, *Rowan County*, 274–75.

67. Norris W. Preyer, "Hezekiah Alexander," in *DNCB*, 1:14–15. Data on plan of house courtesy of Bruce Harvey, curator, Hezekiah Alexander Homesite and History Museum, Charlotte.

68. Personal communications on Maryland architectural comparisons from Paul Touart, Orlando Ridout V, and Al Honeycutt, July–Oct. 1989.

69. See Park, *List of Architectural Books*; Schimmelman, *Architectural Treatises*.

70. Richard L. Bushman, "American High-Style and Vernacular Culture," in Greene and Pole, *Colonial British America*, 345–83. See, for example, Andrews, *Journal of a Lady of Quality*, 147, 154, 160, 185.

71. Patricia Bunomi asserts that "North Carolina's church establishment was the least effective of any in the colonies" (*Under the Cope of Heaven*, 50). See Paul Conkin, "The Church Establishment in North Carolina, 1765–1776," *NCHR* 32, no. 1 (Jan. 1955): 1–30; Sarah M. Lemmon, "The Genesis of the Protestant Episcopal Diocese in North Carolina, 1701–1823," *NCHR* 28, no. 4 (Oct. 1951): 426–62.

72. Letters from churchwardens and vestry of St. Thomas Parish on Pamlico River, N.C., Oct. 10, 1734, and John Garzia, St. Thomas Parish, N.C., May 8, 1735, Fulham Papers, Lambeth Palace, England, transcript of microfilm courtesy of Carl Lounsbury.

73. Elizabeth V. Moore, "St. Paul's Episcopal Church, Edenton, N.C.," undated [ca. 1970s] typescript history, copy in "St. Paul's Episcopal Church" survey file, Survey and Planning Branch, A&H; Society for the Propagation of the Gospel, Letter Books, Series B, 1701–86 (microfilm), transcript courtesy of Carl Lounsbury; *Virginia Gazette*, Oct. 15, 1736. On April 14, 1729, Richard Everard reported that the church was not built, nor was it likely to be, for the commissioners appointed to build it "who have 600 pounds in their hands are now the only Opposers of Building one. . . . We had several meetings to consult about building it but could not agree" (letter from Richard Everard, Apr. 14, 1729, Fulham Papers). The total expenditure in the 1730s campaign was £1,240.17.4, the largest single item being £561 to the bricklayers ("Money disbursed on Acct. of the Church [1736–1737]," Robert B. Drane Papers, SHC).

74. *SRNC*, 23:144; *CRNC*, 4:793; Vestry Records of St. Paul's Church (Moore transcription), May 19, 1750, Oct. 9, 1761, Oct. 28, 1765, Oct. 31, 1772, Aug. 28, 1773, May 18, Aug. 20, 1774, May 7, 1775; Bill (1762) to "Enable the Commissioners of the Church of Edenton to discharge the Contracts by them made with the Workmen Employed in finishing the inside of the said Church,"

in *CRNC*, 6:945; drawing of church steeple, Edenton, in John Hawks Papers, SHC.

75. On Virginia churches, see Upton, *Holy Things and Profane*, 47–98. At St. Paul's, the original interior work decayed after the Revolution and was replaced in 1806–7 when the church was restored by English architect and carpenter William Nichols, who also built the spire. In 1948 another restoration of the church was begun, detailed drawings were made, and much of the woodwork was removed temporarily. On June 1, 1949, the church burned, and the gallery, roof, and spire were destroyed. The walls remained standing, however, and the interior was restored using elements that had been removed, including floors, pews, doors, and windows; the columns, paneling, and cornices were rebuilt. The oak woodwork, chancel, and sanctuary furniture and stained glass date from 1848–49 and memorial tablets from 1868 to the present (Moore, "St. Paul's").

76. *CRNC*, 5:158, 6:237, 235. The church was under construction by 1754, but it was still incomplete when it was severely damaged by a storm in the summer of 1760. By June 15, 1762, the timber for the roof had been provided, and "Mr. Dick a carpenter who wrought at his excellency the Governor's has undertaken the roofing of it" (*CRNC*, 6:730). St. Philip's was burned during the Revolution and is now a stabilized ruin at Brunswick Town State Historic Site. See Jerry Cross, "St. Philip's Church, Brunswick County, North Carolina," research report, 1975, Restoration Branch, A&H; *CRNC*, 8:514–15.

77. Richard Beale Davis, "Arthur Dobbs," in *DNCB*, 2:83; Inventory of Estate, Arthur Dobbs Papers, SHC. On George City, see *SRNC*, 25:373–78; *CRNC*, 6:xxiii–xxiv, 1–4, 834–35, 932–34.

78. William Tryon to SPG, July 31, 1765, in Powell, *Correspondence of William Tryon*, 1:143–46 (quote, 145).

79. *Virginia Gazette* (Williamsburg), Oct. 25, 1770, quoted in Butler and Watson, *North Carolina Experience*, 117. In 1778, James Iredell wrote that the town of Hillsborough had exceeded his expectations: "It is far from being a disagreeable town, as to appearance, and there is a remarkable handsome church in it" (G. J. McRee, *Life and Correspondence of James Iredell* [New York: D. Appleton, 1857–58], 1:379, courtesy of Mary Claire Engstrom). An unsigned drawing of the Hillsborough church, placed in the John Hawks Collection, SHC, can be feasibly, though not certainly, attributed to Hawks. It is illustrated in *ABNC*, 84.

80. Herzog, "Early Architecture of New Bern," 108. See *CRNC*, 9:95–97, 115, 146, 168 (quotes, 95). The petition sought to relieve the vestry from its engagements with builders—to which the builders had agreed. Person's bill to this effect passed the assembly but was rejected by the council of state. The protest may have prevented construction of one of the two buildings, the Tabbs Creek Chapel. McCartney, the priest of the parish, served as chaplain to Tryon's troops. Henderson narrowly escaped injury when Regulators broke up his court in Hillsborough, had his house near Williamsboro burned by Regulators in 1770, and, in June 1771, was among the justices who sentenced twelve Regulators to be hanged as traitors (Powell, *Correspondence of William Tryon*, 2:637, 774, 816; Mark E. Miller, "Richard Henderson," in *DNCB*, 3:105–6).

81. Indenture, John Taylor et al. and John Linch, Oct. 2, 1771, Francis Lister Hawks Collection, A&H. See also *ABNC*, 85–87. The church was modified late in the nineteenth century and extensively restored in the mid-twentieth century.

82. See Dill, *Governor Tryon* and "Tryon's Palace," for a chronology of the design development. See also William Tryon to Sewallis Shirley, July 26, 1765, in Powell, *Correspondence of William Tryon*, 1:140, on "Mr. Hawks the Master Builder I took over with me from England." On Hawks as a professional architect, see *ABNC*, 121–25.

83. William Tryon to Earl of Shelburne, Jan. 31, 1767, in *CRNC*, 7:430–31 (see ibid., 7:542–43, for Hawks's estimate of costs); ibid., 7:442; Herzog, "Early Architecture of New Bern," 70–73.

84. Powell, *Correspondence of William Tryon*, 2:289–92; *EANC*, 32–33, 83–86; Sandbeck, *New Bern and Craven County*, 21–25.

85. John Whiting of Rhode Island and Francisco de Miranda of South America, quoted in Dill, *Governor Tryon*, 114, 118.

86. Sandbeck, *New Bern and Craven County*, 24–34, 335–36.

87. On Bellair, see Sandbeck, *New Bern and Craven County*, 453–61, 540–41. Sandbeck relates that the house is believed to have been built for Richard Dobbs Spaight, who inherited the property in 1765 but was sent to Scotland to be educated and did not return until 1778; the house may have been built during this time, though it is possible that it was built after the Revolution. In 1781 Hawks had power of attorney for Spaight, evidence of the close connection between the two men. In 1787 Spaight sold the house to Wilson Blount, who occupied it until 1799.

88. On the Nathaniel Duckenfield House in Bertie County, see Audit Office Papers, 1765–90, British Public Records Office, Loyalist Claims (xerox copies at A&H); William S. Price, Jr., "Nathaniel Duckenfield," in *DNCB*, 2:111. See also a letter from Henry E. McCulloh to James Iredell mentioning a plan drawn by William Churton, cartographer, "for me of Duckinfield. . . . I am sure the plan will be worth much more to him" (Higginbotham, *Papers of James Iredell*, 1:51).

89. *Virginia Gazette*, June 4, 1767. Money was to be paid to Cullen Pollock, Joseph Hewes, Thomas Nash, Edward Vail, or William Souther (*SRNC*, 23:929–30; John Hawks, plan and specification of prison, June 1, 1773, John Hawks Papers, SHC; John Hawks to Joseph Hewes, Sept. 29, 1773, ibid.). In sending the papers to Chapel Hill on Nov. 12, 1857, Robert T. Paine of Edenton stated that they concerned the jail, the church, and the courthouse. There are no other records of the construction of the courthouse, so its date of completion is uncertain. In 1768 joiner Gilbert Leigh was instructed to make benches for attorneys and jurors, and in 1770 Leigh and John Green were paid about £15 for carpentry work on the clerk's office (see Marc Brodsky, "An Historical Report on the Chowan County Courthouse, Edenton, North Carolina," 1986, 29–31, copy in Restoration Branch, A&H). It is not clear whether the courthouse was still in some way unfinished as late as 1773.

90. In June 1774 the walls were whitewashed, and a court order instructed the sheriff to prevent people from playing games in the courthouse and "daubing the walls thereof" (Brodsky, "Chowan County Courthouse," 29).

91. Ibid., 39–40, 26.

Chapter 2

1. On this period, see Watson, *An Independent People*; Robert M. Calhoon, "An Agrarian and Evangelical Culture," in Butler and Watson, *North Carolina Experience*, 171–91. On architecture, see *EANC*; Lounsbury, "Building Process" and "Development of Domestic Architecture"; Lane, *North Carolina*; *ABNC*, 52–60. See also Juliana Margaret Conner Diary, June 10–Oct. 17, 1827, typescript, Brevard Collection, A&H. The courthouse Conner described had recently been erected from a design by English architect and builder William Nichols and was subsequently replaced by another columned courthouse in the late 1850s (see chap. 3 below). The reference to Sleepy Hollow ties in with the reputation of North Carolina as the Rip Van Winkle state in this period. The reference to "dutch" people apparently confuses the Dutch inhabitants of Washington Irving's New York communities with the German residents of Piedmont North Carolina; "Deutsch" (German) was often erroneously repeated as "Dutch."

2. County reports, 1810, quoted in Newsome, "Twelve North Carolina Counties." See also *ABNC*, 54.

3. In the 1770s and thereafter, American publishers printed editions of Abraham Swan's *British Architect* (Philadelphia, 1775), Batty Langley's *Builder's Jewel* (Boston, 1800), William Pain's *Practical Builder* (Boston, 1792), and others, editions of which had been published in England earlier in the century. See

Hamlin, *Greek Revival Architecture*; Hitchcock, *Architecture Books*.

4. Benjamin, *American Builder's Companion*, vii–viii. Benjamin's first book, *The Country Builder's Assistant* (1797), the first original American builder's book, combined late Palladian themes with touches of Adamesque in a mode influenced by Pain and other English sources.

5. See Dell Upton, "Vernacular Architecture," in Wilson and Ferris, *Encyclopedia of Southern Culture*, 110–15, on similar patterns elsewhere.

6. Stick, *Outer Banks of North Carolina*, 74–77, and *North Carolina Lighthouses*, 11–14. See Stilgoe, *Common Landscape of America*, 109–11, on lighthouses as the first instances of national architecture beyond the control of local authorities.

7. *Daily National Intelligencer* (Washington, D.C.), May 24, 1816, quoted in John B. Flowers, Janet Seapker, and Mary Alice Hinson, "Bald Head Island Lighthouse," NR form, 1975.

8. Personal communications from David Keough, U.S. Military History Institute, Carlisle Barracks, Pa., and Dale Floyd, Office of Chief of Engineers, Aug. 24, 1989, notes in files of author; Robinson, *American Forts*, 85–132.

9. Personal communication from Paul Branch, Historic Site Manager, Fort Macon, Aug. 29, 1989; Branch, "Report on Fort Macon, 1834–1984," typescript report, 1986, Fort Macon Research File; Richard Shriver Berry, "Fort Macon: Its History," *NCHR* 27, no. 2 (Apr. 1950): 163–77; Tony P. Wrenn, "Fort Macon," NR form, 1972; "The Fortification Drawn by Capt. Wm. Tell Poussin," Drawer 61, sheets 4 and 6, and "Plan and Sections Shewing the Condition of Frot [*sic*] Macon," Sept. 30, 1829, by William A. Eliason, RG 77, Drawer 61, sheet 13, NA, photocopies in Fort Macon Research File, A&H.

10. Specifications for "A State House 110 by 52 feet," undated, Cameron Family Papers, SHC; House Resolution, Dec. 5, 1792, quoted in Murray, *Wake*, 88. The contractor for the State House was Rhodham Atkins of Wake County. William S. Powell points out, further, that the plan of the new capital was influenced by the town plan intended for George City in 1758 (*North Carolina through Four Centuries*, 212–13).

11. Agreement, James Patterson et al. and President and Trustees of the University, July 19, 1793, University Papers, University of North Carolina Library, Chapel Hill; Allcott, *Campus at Chapel Hill*, 13–14 (plan of Old East compared to Yale dormitories by John Trumbull); Turner, *Campus*, 55–57.

12. Henderson, *Campus of the First State University*, 72–81; Turner, *Campus*, 47–52.

13. The stone is inscribed ZUR EHRE GOTTES: IST GEBAUT: / DIE KIRCH WELCHE IHR HIR AN SAUT: / VON EINEM VOLCK SO GOTT ER KENDT: / UND SICH NACH IESUM CHRISTUM NENT: / DIE AUCH MIT IHM SIND EIN VERLEIBET: / UND SICH DIE REFORMRTEN SCHREIBET: / 1795: GNADEN KIRCH ENDE. This has been translated as "To the glory of God has been built the Church which you behold, by a people who God confess and name themselves after Jesus Christ, who are also incorporated with him, and they call themselves The Reformed. 1795 Grace Church Completed" (Hood, *Rowan County*, 245). Subsequently both congregations added bell towers and remodeled their worship spaces.

14. "St. Paul's Lutheran Church," NR form, 1971. The building housed Lutheran and Reformed congregations until 1901, when the Reformed group built their own church. There are similarities in decorative work with Holly Bend (fig. 2.68) in Mecklenburg County and the Perkins House (fig. 2.112) in Catawba County.

15. A chalk inscription on the ceiling reads "Thos. Sheridan, 1828," and the church was dedicated Dec. 13, 1828 (Ruth Little-Stokes and Robert Topkins, "Brown Marsh Presbyterian Church," NR form, 1975). On Sheridan, see Bishir, "Black Builders," 452.

16. Bruce S. Cheeseman, "Kerr Mill" and "Mill Bridge," in Hood, *Rowan County*, 148–49, 175–76; Hood, *Rowan County*, 166–68; Joe Mobley, "Kerr Mill," NR form, 1976. Joseph Kerr

(1762–1829) owned the land until his death. However, local tradition assigns the mill to Samuel (1799–1865), and it is not unlikely that he took responsibility for such a project upon his return to the family plantation.

17. Little-Stokes, *Caswell County*, 209–10.

18. Later the Union Tavern was the residence and cabinet shop of Thomas Day (see chap. 3 below). The first-story arches were later filled in with solid partitions (Little-Stokes, *Caswell County*, 209–10).

19. John G. Zehmer and Sherry Ingram, "Wright Tavern," NR form, 1970.

20. This discussion derives largely from Peter Sandbeck's *New Bern and Craven County*; John B. Green III's *New Bern Album*; Lynda Vestal Herzog's "Early Architecture of New Bern"; fieldwork and research by Janet K. Seapker and Tony P. Wrenn; and Francisco de Miranda (1784) and Bishop Francis Asbury (1802), quoted in Herzog, "Early Architecture of New Bern," 28, 33.

21. Ann Pettigrew to Ebenezer Pettigrew, Dec. 30, 1824, Ebenezer Pettigrew to James C. Johnston, Apr. 9, 1819, and Ann Pettigrew to Mary Williams Bryan, Feb. 12, 1827, in Lemmon, *Pettigrew Papers*, 2:51, 8, 80. See also Ann Pettigrew to Ebenezer Pettigrew, Jan. 31, 1825, ibid., 2:58.

22. On New Bern artisans, see Sandbeck, *New Bern and Craven County*, 89–94; Herzog, "Early Architecture of New Bern," 290–372; Bishir, "Black Builders," 442–43.

23. Rodman, *Journal of a Tour*, 16–17. The £8,400 purchase price has suggested to some writers that the house was at least partially completed when Stanly bought the half-block lot in 1779. But see Sandbeck, *New Bern and Craven County*, 415, on wartime inflation and the likelihood that Stanly built the house, consistent with Attmore's comment.

24. Abraham Swan's *British Architect* was published first in London in 1745 and had many English editions. An American edition, published in Philadelphia in 1775, was the first architectural pattern book published in this country. Swan's other works, like those of William Pain, Batty Langley, Isaac Ware, and others, also remained in widespread use for many years after they were first published. There are especially strong similarities between the "Philadelphia character" of the work at the Stanly House and that at the Powell House in Philadelphia and the Corbit House in Odessa, Delaware (*EANC*, 34; Sandbeck, *New Bern and Craven County*, 29–30). Whether Philadelphia-trained artisans were involved in the building of the Stanly House, either as on-site workers or by fabricating woodwork sent to New Bern, is not known (see, however, note 25 below). For other usages of Swan's plates in the 1780s, see Brock W. Jobe and Marianne Moulton, "Governor John Langdon Mansion Memorial, Portsmouth, New Hampshire," *Antiques*, Mar. 1986, 638–41. Flush-boarded walls accented with quoins, as at the Stanly House, appeared in mid-Atlantic and New England houses of the period. For comparisons, see Herzog, "Early Architecture of New Bern," 135. In New Bern, flush boarding also appeared in the earlier Patrick Gordon House (Sandbeck, *New Bern and Craven County*, 14).

25. John Bivins asserts that the brackets are Philadelphia work and contrasts them with the "elaborate but naive" brackets at the Coor-Bishop House (ca. 1767), also in New Bern (*Furniture of Coastal North Carolina*, 397).

26. John Wright Stanly Estate Papers, 1789, Craven County Records, A&H, lists Stanly's possessions with remarkable specificity. For the dinner party, see Rodman, *Journal of a Tour*, 20–21.

27. Herzog, "Early Architecture of New Bern," 115–21, 178–221.

28. Sandbeck, *New Bern and Craven County*, 54–57, 327–28, 175–76.

29. One room-by-room inventory from Federal-period New Bern (the only example for this period in the state known to the author) illustrates how the family of bank president and ship owner James McKinlay used their townhouse (James McKinlay

Estate Papers, Craven County Estates Papers, 1819, A&H, courtesy of John Green). The McKinlay House was a three-story building plus attic, with three main rooms and a front stair passage on each floor. The entry hall was floored with oilcloth, furnished with two dining tables and a settee, and adorned with eleven prints, a thermometer, and a spyglass. On the first floor, the dining room and the parlor were fitted with Venetian blinds and carpets and had fireplaces with andirons, tongs, fender, and "mantel ornaments." The parlor, remarkably, also contained furniture for dining: a set of mahogany dining tables, twelve chairs, a sideboard, a closet full of china and glassware, waiters, and candlesticks. The dining room contained an additional sideboard, knifeboxes, and a buffet with china and glassware, plus furnishings for genteel pastimes: a piano, a lady's workstand, twelve chairs, two writing desks, two tea tables, a tea chest, and a backgammon box. On the second floor, the drawing room on the south was furnished with two sofas, twelve chairs and three tea tables, a carpet and rug, fireplace tools, eight prints, mantel ornaments, and window curtains. On both the first and second floors were carpeted and curtained "bedrooms" with mahogany furniture. Less elaborately furnished bedrooms occupied the third floor; these were fitted with "paper window hangings." Also on the first floor, perhaps in wings or separate structures, were the kitchen and pantry and McKinlay's counting room, which contained desks and "other countingroom furniture" and a bed.

30. Donnell Account Book, 1816–19, Bryan Papers, SHC.

31. "Mr. King is a Superior workman having built Mr. Smallwoods, Judge Donnell & Several other Houses and the State Bank in this place—and is a very pleasant man when sober. . . . Mr. Deweys Jack now in your employ worked a Considerable time with Mr King" (John M. Roberts to Duncan Cameron, Feb. 20, 1833, Cameron Family Papers, SHC, courtesy of Ford Peatross).

32. See Herzog, "Early Architecture of New Bern," 67–68, for possible sources for these moldings. Peter Sandbeck identifies Pain's *Practical House Carpenter*, plates 72, 73, and 75, as the source of New Bern's characteristic step-end wave brackets (*New Bern and Craven County*, 67–68).

33. Sandbeck, *New Bern and Craven County*, 74–83; Green, *New Bern Album*.

34. Sandbeck, *New Bern and Craven County*, 74–77, 373–74. The plan may be compared to the earlier Patrick Gordon House and Clear Springs Plantation House, both of which have two main rooms and three rear chambers encompassed under a single roofline. The Nimocks House in Fayetteville is another important example of a center-chimney-plan house; it is one-and-a-half stories with a rear engaged porch. A barrel stair rises at the rear behind the chimney.

35. Tisdale inherited the lot in 1797 from his father William, likewise a silversmith (Sandbeck, *New Bern and Craven County*, 74–83, 215–23).

36. Ibid., 46–47; Bishir, "Philadelphia Bricks."

37. Sandbeck, *New Bern and Craven County*, 45–46; Peatross, *William Nichols*, 10–11; Mary Ellen Gadski, "The History of the New Bern Academy," research report, 1977, 55–57, copy in Restoration Branch, A&H.

38. Sandy was paid $500 as "installment on contract" on each of four occasions—Nov. 5, 1819, Jan. 11, 1820, Sept. 18, 1820, and Oct. 22, 1821—plus $6.80 for "extra work" on Dec. 22, 1821. (If Sandy's contract was typical, these payments were probably keyed to completion of phases of the work.) The payments were apparently for Sandy's workmanship, for the accounts also list many payments to suppliers of materials (Tony P. Wrenn, notes from William Hollister Account Books, 1819–24, "First Presbyterian Church [New Bern]" survey file, Survey and Planning Branch, A&H; William Hollister Account Books, 1801–83 [microfilm], A&H). Uriah Sandy was trained in New Bern as the apprentice of carpenter Benjamin Good, who was in turn trained by John Dewey. Sandy may have been the son of James Sandy and Mary Hawks Sandy and was possibly related,

through his mother, to John Hawks (Herzog, "Early Architecture of New Bern," 329).

39. The pulpit was replaced after the Civil War; a restoration of the church (1934–37) reinstated the original pulpit, which had been found in the basement. A curved niche behind the pulpit was eliminated and arched trim applied to the wall. See Sandbeck, *New Bern and Craven County*, 49–51; T. T. Waterman, "Presbyterian Church, New Bern, Craven County, North Carolina," Historic American Buildings Survey, 1940, copy in Survey and Planning Branch, A&H; *EANC*, 248; L. C. Vass, *History of the Presbyterian Church in New Bern* [Richmond: Whittet and Shepperson, 1886]).

40. *Carolina Centinel* (New Bern), Nov. 18, 1820, July 14, 1821. The church was gutted by fire in 1871 and was rebuilt with the old walls but a new tower (Sandbeck, *New Bern and Craven County*, 52–53, 191–92). No Nichols connection has been documented, but his patronage among Episcopalians elsewhere and his Gothic motifs at St. Matthew's Church in Hillsborough and at Hayes suggest a possible link.

41. Ebenezer Pettigrew to Ann Blount Pettigrew, Jan. 5, 1830, in Lemmon, *Pettigrew Papers*, 2:130.

42. These volumes were among the books listed in Stone's personal estate. Abraham Swan commented that the exterior end chimneys in his plan (plate 61) were unusual for England but assured readers that the idea was "taken from *Palladio*, who seldom failed placing his Chimneys betwixt the Windows." The exterior chimney placement was a common regional trait in eastern North Carolina. Timbers in the attic are dated 1803. Information on Hope Plantation courtesy of James Jordan and John E. Tyler. See also Melonie Johnson Taylor, "David A. Stone: A Political Biography," master's thesis, East Carolina University, 1968.

43. *Raleigh Register*, Oct. 9, 1818, quoted in Taylor, "David A. Stone," 13; David Stone Estate Papers, Bertie County Records, A&H, inventory of personal estate reproduced in Taylor, app.

44. Deed of Gift from Samuel Johnston to James C. Johnston, Dec. 29, 1814, Will of Samuel Johnston [Nov. 9, 1814], and Samuel Johnston to James C. Johnston, Nov. 14, 1814, Hayes Collection, SHC; Martha M. Smith, "James Cathcart Johnston," in *DNCB*, 3:302–4. On the family's attitudes toward extravagance, see also *ABNC*, 56–58.

45. James Cathcart Johnston, Personal and Plantation Expense Memorandum Book, 1813–16, 74:80–104, and 1816–18, 75:4–64. Hayes Collection, SHC. James E. Johnston, account with Josiah Collins, May 10, 1817, and William Nichols to James C. Johnston, undated [1814?], ibid.; Bishir, "Black Builders," 433–34, 459–61. Joe Welcome and Jim Millen belonged to planter Josiah Collins.

46. See Peatross, *William Nichols*; John Sanders, "William Nichols," in *DNCB*, vol. 4 (forthcoming); *ABNC*, 126–29.

47. John Hawks's 1773 letter to Joseph Hewes in Edenton asked Hewes to deliver an enclosure to a Mr. Johnston, doubtless Samuel Johnston (Hawks to Hewes, Sept. 29, 1773, John Hawks Papers, SHC). Could Hawks have provided a design for Johnston, either for an earlier building at Hayes, for an unbuilt project, or for his Bertie County plantation, the Hermitage? See Lane, *North Carolina*, 146–48. Samuel Johnston's will and James Johnston's construction records suggest that Hayes was a new building, but it may have been influenced by a predecessor.

48. Quotation from Hall, "Architecture," 119. Peatross, *William Nichols*, 5, 10–11, cites vol. 1, plate 56, of George Richardson's *New Vitruvius Britannicus* (London, 1802) as the source of the curved portico and the order from *Antiquities of Athens*. See Herzog, "Early Architecture of New Bern," 107, on possible sources for the plan, including Benjamin's *Country Builder's Assistant* (1798). Hayes reverses the orientation of Tryon Palace, which had the courtyard toward the land and town.

49. The room names—passage, drawing room, dining room, back parlor, and chambers—are drawn from James Johnston to Joseph Blount, July 15, 1817, and Nichols to Johnston, May 1, 1817, Hayes Collection, SHC.

50. A memo enumerating books in the library records 175 folio volumes, 83 quarto, 540 octavo, and 181 duodecimo (Johnston Plantation Memorandum Book, 1816–18, Hayes Collection, SHC). Samuel Johnston's large library composed much of his son's collection. On the busts from New York, see Nichols to Johnston, May 1, 1817, Hayes Collection, SHC. The following busts adorn the library, beginning over the door and proceeding to the right: Chancellor Kent, Sir Walter Scott, empty niche (which formerly contained a bust of Daniel Webster), DeWitt Clinton, Zachary Taylor, Henry Clay, George Washington, James L. Pettigrew; over the mantel are John Jay, John Marshall, and Alexander Hamilton. This list was provided to author by Annette Wood, Hayes Farm, June 28, 1989.

51. Blackwell P. Robinson, "Willie Jones," in *DNCB*, 3:330–31.

52. A brick dated 1793 suggests that the house may have been standing when Hill bought the property from John Ricks, but family tradition has associated the construction with the Hills, who bought the place about 1808–10 (John B. Flowers and Catherine Cockshutt [Bishir], "The Hermitage," NR form, 1975). Possibly Hill installed the parlor mantel (apparently of the same school as the main mantel at Mulberry Hill) and the hall mantel, copying similar motifs, ca. 1810. A doorway treatment similar to the Hermitage appears at Mowfield in Northampton County, indicating overlapping patterns of regional artisans in this period.

53. On the development of pediment-front and related forms, see *EANC*, 36–41; Lane, *North Carolina*, 111–25.

54. On Little Manor, see description and photographs in *EANC*, 38–40, 105–10; Lane, *North Carolina*, 122–26. New Bern memoirist John D. Whitford attributes this house to Thomas Bragg, a Craven County artisan who moved to Warren County, but this assertion has not been documented ("A History of the Walking Stick," undated typescript, John D. Whitford Papers, A&H).

55. Elizabeth V. Moore, "Mulberry Hill," Chowan County survey file, Survey and Planning Branch, A&H; Elizabeth V. Moore, John B. Flowers, Bruce MacDougal, and Catherine Cockshutt [Bishir], "Mulberry Hill," NR form, 1975; Lemmon, *Pettigrew Papers*, 1:xiii, 389, 458, 467–74. *EANC*, 68–69, shows the house before the stair was repaired and the present portico built copying a New Bern model.

56. See Bishir, "Montmorenci–Prospect Hill School." Edgar Thorne has provided invaluable assistance in my study of these families and houses.

57. Ibid., 85–95; *EANC*, 39–40, 113–29. T. T. Waterman observed, during removal of the Montmorenci stair for the Winterthur Museum, that the "not inconsiderable" structural feat of building a freestanding spiral staircase was the product of "trial and error, as during demolition it could be seen that the carriages had been reinforced again and again, until the stair became steady" (*EANC*, 40). The stair did not fit the space for which it was intended, and its elements were copied in another stair of different height and a different spiral (author's examination of stair with Kenneth Ames, Winterthur Museum, June 1987; Montmorenci files, Winterthur Museum).

58. *EANC*, 40–41, 113–22; Bishir, "Montmorenci–Prospect Hill School." Family tradition attributed the house to a Mr. Burgess, who was probably carpenter James Burgess (J. Marshall Bullock, "James Burgess," typescript biographical sketch, 1982, in possession of author).

59. See Bishir, "Montmorenci–Prospect Hill School." Recent examination of the house by the author and by contractor Todd Dickinson during restoration shows that the rear portion was built after the front, evidently quite soon. Use of an "old" form in this way provided an acceptable method of adding rooms for a growing family without altering the formal appearance of the house from the front. For a reminiscence about Elizabeth Person Mitchel and life at Elgin Plantation, see Peter Mitchel Wilson, *Southern Exposure* (Chapel Hill: University of North Carolina Press, 1927), 13–22.

60. The French wallpaper appears to date from 1820–30, the carpet and furnishings from the 1850s or 1860s, and the chandelier from the 1870s or 1880s (Richard C. Nylander to author, Sept. 7, 1988).

61. Hamlin, *Greek Revival Architecture*, 194–96; Peatross, *William Nichols*, 10–12.

62. The date of the ballroom is variously put at the 1818 wedding of John A. Cameron and Catherine McQueen Halliday, widow of merchant Robert Halliday, or the 1830 wedding of Margaret Halliday (Robert's daughter) to banker John Sandford. The Halliday House was subsequently destroyed, but the ballroom was moved to its present location at the Woman's Club of Fayetteville. This house, by coincidence, was John A. Cameron's residence; its portico (ca. 1820) is attributed to Nichols as well (Peatross, *William Nichols*, 10–11).

63. *Raleigh Register*, quoted in Murray, *Wake*, 209–10; Ithiel Town to Roger S. Baldwin, Dec. 9, 1822, Baldwin Family Papers, YU (notes courtesy of Dell Upton); Peatross, *William Nichols*, 12. See the discussion of Nichols's practices as architect in *ABNC*, 126–28.

64. Hamlin, *Greek Revival Architecture*, 194–95; Peatross, *William Nichols*, 14–15.

65. Quote, William Anderson to Duncan Cameron, Feb. 14, 1825, Cameron Family Papers, SHC, courtesy of Marshall Bullock. In 1806–9 Nichols had repaired and remodeled St. Paul's Church in Edenton, and in 1826 he designed a small frame building for Christ Church in Raleigh.

66. Seldom built before the Revolution, the two-story house, one room deep and more than one room wide, remained a common choice for substantial dwellings well into the twentieth century. Some had central passages, though many followed a hall-parlor plan, and most had tall exterior end chimneys. It was this form, too, that emigrants carried west from the Upper South as they settled and built in the territory beyond the Appalachians. This prevalent type has been dubbed the I-house (Fred B. Kniffen, "Folk Housing: Key to Diffusion," *Annals of the Association of American Geographers* 55, no. 4 [Dec. 1965]: 549–77). On its use in North Carolina, see Michael T. Southern, "The I-House as a Carrier of Style," in Swaim, *Carolina Dwelling*, 70–83.

67. Jeremiah Battle, "Edgecombe County," Thomas Henderson Letterbook, Archives and Records Section, A&H.

68. The house is believed to have been built in the 1790s for Gideon Edwards, longtime state senator and one of the county's wealthiest planters, who owned 2,333 acres and 50 slaves at his death in 1810. It was then the home of his daughter Mildred and her husband, Meshack Franklin, son of planter and governor Jesse Franklin. In several areas of the house there are two layers (and periods) of decorative painting (Phillips, *Simple Treasures*, 12–13, 108–9).

69. Laura Phillips, "Grand Illusions: Decorative Interior Painting in North Carolina," paper delivered at the Vernacular Architecture Forum Annual Meeting, 1988, forthcoming in Thomas Carter and Bernard Herman, eds., *Perspectives in Vernacular Architecture, IV* (Columbia: University of Missouri Press, 1991).

70. See the entry for Elmwood, in Brown, *Heritage and Homestead*, 322. For descriptions of Locust Grove, the Battle-Malone House, and the Robideaux House, see Pearce, *Franklin County*, 24–37. A related mantel exists at Prestwould in nearby Mecklenburg County, Virginia (author's observation). Prestwould was built between 1788 and 1795 (Calder Loth, ed., *The Virginia Landmarks Register* [Charlottesville: University Press of Virginia for the Virginia Historic Landmarks Board, 1986], 272). Another such mantel was photographed by Frances Benjamin Johnston at Cascine but has since been removed. Plans with two main front rooms plus smaller rear ones divided by a stair passage also appeared in pre-Revolutionary houses such as Clear Springs Plantation and the Patrick Gordon House in Craven County (see chap. 1 above). In Franklin County, a simi-

lar plan occurs in the one-and-a-half-story late-eighteenth-century houses Cascine and Green Hill (Pearce, *Franklin County*, 9–15).

71. Charles Richard Sanders, "Duncan Cameron," in *DNCB*, 1:311; Anderson, *Piedmont Plantation*, 17–31. The plasterer's bill of 1812 names the rooms (Henry Gorman, bill, 1812, Cameron Papers, SHC, courtesy of Jean Anderson). The Bennehan and Cameron influence on building was considerable: Richard Bennehan chaired the building committee for the State House of the 1790s, Duncan Cameron chaired the board of commissioners first appointed to build the Capitol in the 1830s, and Duncan's son Paul took a prominent role in the antebellum and postwar affairs and building projects of the university.

72. Anderson, *Piedmont Plantation*, 31. The porch may be by William Nichols, with whom Duncan Cameron was acquainted.

73. Cameron Papers, vol. 55, May 3, 1811, cited in Anderson, *Piedmont Plantation*, 29; *Raleigh Star*, June 21, 1811. In 1809 William Jones, Henry Gorman, John J. Briggs, and Elhannon Nutt were involved in work on John Haywood's house, Haywood Hall (Linda Griggs, "Haywood Hall," 17, research report, copy in Restoration Branch, A&H; "House in the Horseshoe," survey file, Survey and Planning Branch, A&H). Similar work also appears at Sans Souci in Hillsborough (*EANC*, 138).

74. Sanders, "Ayr Mount." The portico is a reconstruction, based on surviving evidence, accomplished during a recent restoration of the house.

75. Thomas B. Littleton to Duncan Cameron, Aug. 7, 1817, Cameron Papers, SHC, courtesy of Jean Anderson. See also William Kirkland to Thomas Ruffin, Dec. 13, 1815, Thomas Ruffin Papers, SHC, courtesy of John Sanders. Kirkland described his brick house in some detail and complained, "I think Mr. Collier charges me with the laying of a great many more Bricks than he ought to do."

76. Petitions, 1790, Legislative Papers, A&H, courtesy of George Stevenson; Rodman, *Journal of a Tour*, 45–46.

77. Little-Stokes, "North Carolina Porch."

78. The date of the Church Street house remains uncertain. Architectural features suggest a date between 1760 and 1790, but archaeological investigation indicates use only after 1790 (Stanley A. South, "Examination of the George Hooper House," archaeological report, 1962, copy in possession of author, courtesy of Peter Sandbeck). The basement kitchen is seen in New Bern and other coastal houses.

79. The house was moved to Tarboro in 1969 and restored, and the chimney was reconstructed. See "The Pender Museum, Tarboro, North Carolina," undated leaflet [1970s?], which dates the house at ca. 1810. In later years, the hall-parlor coastal cottage moved down the social ladder, but the form continued in use through the nineteenth century. In Onslow County, for example, houses with front piazzas and rear shed rooms account for over half the surviving antebellum dwellings and remained common into the twentieth century (Dan Pezzoni, Onslow County Survey, 1987–88; conversation with author, June 1988; Onslow County Survey Report, unpublished typescript, 1988, Survey and Planning Branch, A&H).

80. Allcott, *Colonial Homes*, 68–74; personal inspection by Al Honeycutt, Peter Sandbeck, and author, 1988.

81. Thomas Butchko, Davyd Foard Hood, and Jim Sumner, "Mag Blue House," NR form, 1982. A local carpentry touch appears in the design of the porch posts, which are turned and chamfered, with the bottoms of the solid wooden posts being carved out in a small arch to allow water to drain away; the survival of such posts here and at other local houses such as Mill Prong Plantation in Scotland County testifies to the effectiveness of this technique.

82. "Ellerslie," NR form, 1974.

83. *Guide Book: Historic Edenton and Chowan County* (Edenton: Edenton Woman's Club, 1984), 11. The house was probably built just before the Revolution by Robert Smith, but it could

have been built or expanded by Josiah Collins, who bought it in 1786.

84. Ruth Little, typescript report on Bladen County Survey, Survey and Planning Branch, A&H; "Oakland," NR form, 1971.

85. Ruth Little-Stokes and Joe Mobley, "Purdie Place," NR form, [1976]. Here, as at Oakland, elements of the porch structure have been replaced over the years, but the doorways in both stories suggest the original presence of porches of similar forms.

86. Personal communication from Peter Sandbeck, 1988, based on architectural investigation of Lavender House; Rodman, *Journal of a Tour*, 45–46.

87. For this concept, I am indebted to Dan Pezzoni (personal communication, June 1988, based on his 1987–88 survey of Onslow County) and to Jay Edwards ("The Evolution of Vernacular Traditions," paper delivered at the Vernacular Architecture Forum Annual Meeting, 1988).

88. Tony P. Wrenn and Janet K. Seapker, "Jacob Henry House," NR form, 1971. Some formal definitions of house types treat porches and sheds as secondary rather than primary plan elements. Visually, structurally, and, perhaps above all, functionally, however, the coastal Carolina porches and sheds are primary elements of the house form and plan; that they may be added, changed, filled in, or subtracted is, paradoxically, part of that essentialness.

89. John Bivins, Jr., "Restoration of the Potter's House (Krause-Butner House), Bethabara," unpublished research report, 1974, copy in Survey and Planning Branch, A&H.

90. A brewery and brewer's house, built in 1777–78 by Salem artisans Melchior Rasp and Christian Triebel, burned in 1802, but the rebuilding of the house the next year may have reused elements from the dwelling section (Frank L. Horton, "Bethabara Parsonage [Brewer's House]," Historic American Buildings Survey, 1962, copy in Survey and Planning Branch, A&H; telephone conversations with Rod Meyer, Historic Bethabara, June 21, 1989, and John Clauser, June 1989).

91. This discussion derives mainly from John Larson, "The Moravian Architecture of Salem, N.C.: From Congregational Consensus to Individual Expression," paper given at Winterthur Conference, 1983, and "Johann Gottlob Krause," typescript biography, 1982, copy in possession of author.

92. Frank L. Horton, "Bethabara Church and *Gemeinhaus*," Research Report for Restoration, 1969–70, copy in Survey and Planning Branch, A&H. Abraham Loesch, master mason of Salem, quarried the stone and did the mason's work. "Stranger" workmen included Abraham Meyer and Stephen Muller. The total cost was about £475. The building was consecrated November 26, 1788, with trombone music, choruses of hallelujahs, songs, and prayers (Horton, "Bethabara Church," 13).

93. On Craig, see Aufseher Collegium Minutes, Apr. 24, May 6, 1794, cited by S. Scott Rohrer, "Gottlob Krause: Master Builder," typescript research report, Old Salem, Inc., Winston-Salem, 1989, courtesy of John Compton. Deeds, wills, and tax and census records show only that Craig was present in the area and did not own extensive property (Jim Sumner, research notes, 1989, copy in possession of author). This flowering of patterned brickwork was a part of a broader Piedmont trend. See, for example, the spectacular diapered, glazed header work at the Alexander-Withrow House and store (ca. 1789) in Lexington, Va. (Royster Lyle, Jr., and Pamela Hemenway Simpson, *The Architecture of Historic Lexington* [Charlottesville: University Press of Virginia for the Historic Lexington Foundation, 1977], 13–14).

94. This discussion is drawn principally from Larson, "Moravian Architecture of Salem."

95. John F. Bivins, Jr., "Restoration of the John Haley House," research report, 1970, copy in Survey and Planning Branch, A&H. The Matthew Moore House, north of Salem in Stokes County, is similar to the Haley House.

96. Brown, *Our Enduring Past*, 125. See also the descriptions

of Oak Grove (1782) in Gaston County, with its glazed header Flemish bond and lozenges, and the Somers House in Guilford County (both lost), in *EANC*, 198–200; Touart, *Building the Back Country*, 106, on the Alexander Caldcleugh House (ca. 1800–1810), with glazed headers and heart pattern in the Flemish-bond brick chimney; Brengle, *Gaston County*, 6, on Oak Grove and the Thomas Rhyne House (1799 date in headers).

97. See Hood, *Rowan County*, 347–48.

98. Bernard Herman, "Continuity and Change in Traditional Architecture: The Continental Plan Farmhouse in Middle North Carolina," in Swaim, *Carolina Dwelling*, 160–71.

99. H. McKelden Smith notes an even division between three-room and hall-parlor plans in Guilford County's early brick houses ("Guilford County: The Architectural Traditions in an Exclusively Vernacular Landscape," in Swaim, *Carolina Dwelling*, 153–54). See also published surveys cited for other Piedmont counties.

100. The woodwork from the Perkins House is installed as the Catawba Room at the Museum of Early Southern Decorative Arts in Winston-Salem. The Perkins House features lozenge patterning on the chimney ("Perkins House," NR form, 1974; "Rosedale," NR form, 1972).

101. Cotton, *Historic Burke*, 165–66, 168, 171–72, 174.

102. The Forney, Brevard, Davidson, and Graham families of Lincoln and nearby Mecklenburg counties were linked by marriage and by involvement in iron manufacturing, and they occupied positions of economic and political leadership in the region. See Louise C. Smith, "Daniel Munroe Forney," in *DNCB*, 2:221; Laura Page Frech, "Peter Forney," ibid., 2:222–23; Max Williams, "Alexander Brevard," ibid., 1:218–19; "Ingleside," NR form, 1971. Forney is said to have obtained a plan for his house from Benjamin Latrobe while in Washington during either his father's or his own recent terms in Congress; though circumstantially possible, this is undocumented, and the character of the house does not suggest Latrobe's involvement. On the practice of obtaining plans from Washington, D.C., workmen at this time, see Bishir and Bullock, "Mr. Jones Goes to Richmond," 73. The house seems more akin to the work of William Nichols, especially the heroic Ionic portico. Could the architect celebrated in the family tradition have been the architect of the North Carolina State House remodeling rather than of the U.S. Capitol? *EANC*, 214–18; Hood, *Rowan County*, 38–53, 298.

104. David Smith (1787–1874) was the son of Peter Smith/Schmidt and Elizabeth Arends (1783–1870), the daughter of immigrant Lutheran minister Johann Arends (Brown, *Our Enduring Past*, 199; Austin Allran, "John Godfrey Arends," in *DNCB*, 1:39–40).

105. Brown, *Our Enduring Past*, 152. The date "1826" appears on the metal gutter box.

106. Thaddeus Mason Harris, *Journal of a Tour into the Northwest Territory of the Alleghany Mountains* (Boston: Manning and Loring, 1805), 15, quoted in Lounsbury, "Building Process," 435. On early nineteenth-century views of log houses, see *ABNC*, 54. This discussion draws extensively on fieldwork and analysis by others, as illustrated—roughly from east to west—in Pearce, *Franklin County*; Little-Stokes, *Caswell County* and *Iredell County*; Lounsbury, *Alamance County*; Smith, *Guilford County*; Hood, *Rowan County*; Kaplan, *Cabarrus County*; Brown, *Our Enduring Past*; Phillips, *Simple Treasures*; Taylor, *Frontier to Factory*; Touart, *Building the Back Country*; Mohney, *Davie County*; Cotton, *Historic Burke*; Swaim, *Cabins and Castles*; and Williams, *Marble and Log*. Especially useful analyses appear in Ruth Little-Stokes, "Thirty-six Early Log Houses in Caswell County, North Carolina: A Typology," in *Caswell County*, 9–20; Swaim, *Cabins and Castles*.

107. As early as 1776, a traveler found that the Cherokee were living "mostly, in log-cabins" comparable to those of white settlers (William Bartram, quoted in Williams, *Marble and Log*, 14; concerning Cherokee log building, see 12–15).

108. Little-Stokes, *Caswell County*.

109. Phillips, *Simple Treasures*, 7–9, 255. The first known owner was Robert James Hill (1786–1844), a farmer and Primitive Baptist minister, who in 1807 married Elizabeth Vest (1787–1869); they had eight children, including Robert James Hill, whose granddaughter still owns the place.

110. Butchko, *Sampson County*, 13, 47. In this region, as an 1810 account recalled, "the first Inhabitants of Duplin and Sampson counties built and lived in log Cabbins, and as they became more Wealthy, some of them Built framed Clapboard Houses with Clay Chimneys. . . . The greatest Number of the Citizens yet build in the old Stile" (Newsome, "Twelve North Carolina Counties," *NCHR*, 5:440). See also the Hollingsworth-Hines House (ca. 1800), a dovetailed log house, in Butchko, *Sampson County*, 14, 77. For a remarkable incident related to log building in the early Cape Fear region, see George Barrington's account of the "Affair of the Logg House" erected and razed on his property in 1733. Barrington remembered, too, an incident fifty years earlier concerning a log house: "Seth Southwell Esqr who being surprized on his own Plantation and clap't into a Logg House." He feared people "in this Country might have the same intentions to me, if I would have suffered the Logg House to have remained uncovered" (*CRNC*, 3:618–19).

111. Touart, *Building the Back Country*, 6; Pearce, *Franklin County*, 4; Taylor, *Frontier to Factory*, 22–23, 111; Brown, *Our Enduring Past*, 2–3. See also the Setzer House in Little-Stokes, *Iredell County*, 5–8, and the Pfifer House in Hood, *Rowan County*, 23.

112. [Bernard Herman and Jim Sumner], "Daniel Stone House," NR form, 1982. Edward Yancey of Vance County called the author and Michael Southern's attention to the house in 1975; he said the house was called "the blockhouse" in the county, but whether this name is an old one or was given after a later comparison with New England examples is not clear. It seems unlikely that the building is old enough to have actually served as a blockhouse for defense against Indians, hostilities in this section having ended by the 1740s or before. It is also noteworthy that the German word for log house is *blockhaus*. See also the log Hodges House in Surry County, with a cantilevered overhang front and rear, in Phillips, *Simple Treasures*, 8–9.

113. Mast family history, typescript in possession of Francis and Sybil Pressly, Valle Crucis; the history is drawn from C. Z. Mast, *A Brief History of Bishop Jacob Mast and Other Mast Pioneers* (Scottsdale, Pa.: Mennonite Publishing House, 1911).

114. Robert Beverley, *The History and Present State of Virginia*, edited by Louis B. Wright (Chapel Hill: University of North Carolina Press, 1957), 290. Scholars of the Chesapeake region offer various explanations for the separation of functions. See Upton, "Early Vernacular Architecture," and Carson et al., "Impermanent Architecture," concerning the changing family patterns and planter-servant relationships both in England and the Chesapeake in the seventeenth century.

115. Anderson, *Piedmont Plantation*, 27–34. In 1814, bills were presented for the materials and labor of building a schoolhouse, dairy, "Jim's house," two small buildings the size of the dairy (outhouses perhaps), and a stable well. In 1814, too, the kitchen was built, for Rebecca Cameron wrote to her husband, "Mr. Colyer requested me to ask you if you wished the walls of the kitchen filled in with brick, he says you talked of it some time ago. I am afraid I shall hardley get an answer before he has finished the work he has on hand" (Rebecca Cameron to Duncan Cameron, Mar. 15, 1814, Cameron Papers, SHC, quoted in ibid., 30). The columned porticoes were added in the antebellum period.

116. Clauser, "Front Yard—Back Yard."

117. Ibid., 77; Hood, *Rowan County*, 28.

118. The house was built in stages between 1815 and the 1830s on a plantation that had 2,700 acres and 16 slaves in 1860 (Thomas Butchko, "Historic Architecture of Gates County,"

typescript report, 1988, copy in Survey and Planning Branch, A&H; idem, "Gatling Farm," Gates County survey file, Survey and Planning Branch, A&H).

119. Butchko, *On the Shores of the Pasquotank*, 28–30, 122.

120. The study of farm buildings in eastern North Carolina is still in its early stages. See Brad Barker, Chowan County survey files; Thomas Butchko, Gates County survey files and report; and Pasquotank County survey files; all in Survey and Planning Branch, A&H.

121. Halifax County report, Thomas Henderson Letterbook, 1810–11, A&H; George P. Rawick, ed., *The American Slave: A Composite Autobiography*, ser. 2, 14:39, quoted in Lounsbury, "Building Process," 438.

122. William Shepard letter, undated, Collins Papers, A&H, quoted in Lounsbury, "Building Process," 437.

123. Smith, *Guilford County*, 13.

124. Touart, *Building the Back Country*, 23–25. Henry Glassie analyzes patterns of double-crib barns in "The Pennsylvania Barn in the South, Part 1," *Pennsylvania Folklife* 15, no. 2 (1965–66): 12–17. See also idem, "The Double-Crib Barn in South Central Pennsylvania, Part 4," *Pioneer America* 2, no. 2 (1970): 23–28.

Chapter 3

1. Olmsted, *Journey in the Seaboard Slave States*, 305–76 (quotes, 314–15, 325, 321, 348, 349–51). Although wealth and slaveownership were less concentrated in North Carolina than in neighboring states, Olmsted found similar landscapes in Virginia and South Carolina. On the Rip Van Winkle nickname, see Lefler and Newsome, *North Carolina*, 314, 326, 352.

2. Olmsted, *Journey in the Seaboard Slave States*, 366.

3. Ibid., 363, 365.

4. Ibid., 318–19. Free-ranging livestock still wandered many town streets during this period.

5. On this period, see Lefler and Newsome, *North Carolina*; Clayton, *Close to the Land*.

6. For further development of these themes, see *ABNC*, 162–82.

7. See Murray, *Wake*, 245–456, on this era in Raleigh.

8. *Raleigh Register*, Dec. 31, 1833; *Report of the Commissioners for Rebuilding the Capitol* (Raleigh: T. Loring, 1836). This discussion draws mainly on research by John Sanders and Cecil Elliot. See Sanders, "North Carolina State House," "North Carolina State Capitol," and "'This Political Temple'"; Elliot, "North Carolina State Capitol." See also each year's *Report of the Commissioners*, 1834–40 (titles vary slightly); State Capitol file, Capital Buildings Papers, Treasurer's and Comptroller's Papers, A&H, including references supplied by Elizabeth Reid Murray.

9. Murray, *Wake*, 227–44; *Raleigh Register*, Dec. 28, 1832, quoted in Murray, 235; Elliot, "North Carolina State Capitol," *Southern Architect*, 5:20.

10. *Raleigh Register*, Jan. 18, 1833; *Fayetteville Observer*, Apr. 16, 1833; Elliot, "North Carolina State Capitol," *Southern Architect*, 5:20, 23; *Report of the Commissioners*, 1834, 5. On February 24, 1833, William Gaston wrote to Susan (Gaston) Donaldson: "The commissioners for rebuilding the state capital have before them Mr. Towne's several plans . . . [including one] which is without dome, surrounded by columns. I wish Mr. D[onaldson] would correspond with the Governor on the subject, the Governor has a high opinion of his taste" (quoted in Allcott, "Robert Donaldson," 354). In May it was reported that there were "some things yet to be settled in relation to the Building. Mr. Nichols, in drawing his Plan, has found it necessary to deviate a little in the size of the Wings, and there exists some difference of opinion whether the rusticated Rock of the first Story ought to have a bevil or square edge" (Joseph Gales to Duncan Cameron, May 2, 1833, Cameron Family Papers, SHC). William Nichols, Jr., complained that after having been em-

ployed "to design the Capitol," he had "produced a set of plans which were entirely approved of and adopted by the commissioners. . . . They voted me a *pittance* not sufficient to defray my personal expenses—rejected my services, and confided the execution of my plans to incompetent hands" (W. Nichols [Jr.] to David L. Swain, Dec. 22, 1833, Epistolary Correspondence, David L. Swain Papers, University Archives, University of North Carolina, Chapel Hill).

11. John Cameron of Fayetteville, a business associate of Town's in the Clarendon toll bridge project, was the brother of Duncan Cameron, chairman of the building commission. William Gaston, who represented Town in legal matters, was also the father-in-law of Robert Donaldson—a New York client and friend of Town's and a native of Fayetteville; Gaston was probably the principal influence in getting Town the job (Sanders, "North Carolina State Capitol," 476; Allcott, "Robert Donaldson," 345–55; Elliot, "North Carolina State Capitol," *Southern Architect*, 5:23).

12. *Report of the Commissioners*, 1834, 5; Elliot, "North Carolina State Capitol," *Southern Architect*, 5:23–24.

13. On the vicissitudes of the fire-damaged statue and the 1970 installation of a copy from the original Canova model, see Murray, *Wake*, 231–32.

14. Scott, "David Paton"; Elliot, "North Carolina State Capitol," *Southern Architect*, 5:24; John Sanders, "David Paton," in *DNCB*, vol. 5 (forthcoming).

15. Ithiel Town to David Paton, Mar. 2, 1835, David Paton Papers, A&H; Sanders, "'This Political Temple,'" 4. On Paton's role, see also *ABNC*, 163–66.

16. On changes in the basement and the shifting of rooms and addition of galleries, see *Report of the Commissioners*, 1838; on Soanesque elements, see Sanders, "North Carolina State Capitol," 477, 481–83; and, for comparisons with Edinburgh neoclassicism, see Scott, "David Paton."

17. William Strickland to David Paton, Nov. 4, 1836, David Paton Papers, A&H; *Report of the Commissioners*, 1836; Beverly Daniel to William Strickland, Oct. 30, 1837, and Strickland to Daniel, Nov. 10, 1837, David Paton Papers, A&H.

18. On similarities between the Senate chamber and the banking room in Soane's Bank of England, see Sanders, "North Carolina State Capitol," 481–83.

19. *Report of the Commissioners*, 1835, 1836, 1838.

20. *Senate Report of the Joint Select Committee on Public Buildings*, Legislative Report no. 14 (Raleigh: State of North Carolina, 1838).

21. *Report of the Commissioners*, 1840, quoted in Elliot, "North Carolina State Capitol," *Southern Architect*, 5:22; *Raleigh Register*, June 19, 1840 (headed, apparently in error, July 19). See also Murray, *Wake*, 250–55.

22. *Raleigh Rasp*, Sept. 10, 1842, quoted in Murray, *Wake*, 255.

23. *Raleigh Register*, Oct. 28, 1845 (reprint of article from *Richmond Religious Herald*), quoted in Murray, *Wake*, 255; *Raleigh Register*, June 19, 1840; *Senate Report of the Joint Select Committee on Public Buildings and Rebuilding the Capitol, 1840–1841* (Raleigh: State of North Carolina, 1841), quoted in Sanders, "'This Political Temple,'" 1.

24. Oates, *Story of Fayetteville*, 257–60, 188 (for 1817 ordinance establishing the rules of the market).

25. *Fayetteville Observer*, May 29, 1832, quoted in Roy Parker, Jr., "Setting the Record Straight," *Fayetteville Observer-Times*, Sept. 2, 1984. Parker also cites traveler Mortimer DeMott's description (Feb. 1837) of a "fine looking courthouse situated in the center of the place and built of square brick pillars with arches in the intervening spaces. The lower part or what would be the first story is used as a market. The houses are so arranged as to form a public square around it." Recent architectural and archaeological investigations indicate reuse of the previous stone foundations (personal communication from John Larson, Apr.–May 1989).

26. Similar pinnacles and Gothic arches appeared nearby at

St. John's Episcopal Church, rebuilt after the fire by William Drummond.

27. Oates, *Story of Fayetteville*, 188, cites the hours chimed: breakfast at 7:30, dinner at 1:00, curfew at 9:00. On the function of the town bell for free and slave residents, see *Carolina Watchman* (Salisbury), Apr. 6, 1858, courtesy of James Brawley.

28. See, for example, the Perquimans County Courthouse (1823–24) in Haley and Winslow, *Perquimans County*, 159; specifications for the Person County Courthouse (1824–25), Person County Building Records, A&H, calling for a building 52 by 34 feet, with courtroom and jury room on one floor. In Virginia's early nineteenth-century, two-story, temple-form courthouses, the courtroom was often two stories high (personal communication from Carl Lounsbury, Feb. 18, 1989).

29. Mary Claire Engstrom, "John Berry," in *DNCB*, 1:146–47; Eva Ingersoll Gatling, "John Berry of Hillsboro."

30. Specifications for Courthouse, Jackson, 1858, Miscellaneous Records, Northampton County Records, A&H. A. J. Riggs of Goldsboro contracted to build the courthouse for $10,000 and completed the job in 1859 (ibid.). Tradition holds that planter Henry K. Burgwyn designed the building; he was trained at West Point and took an interest in architecture, and he was on the building committee, but as yet his role as designer is not documented. The specifications follow a professional format and refer to plan and elevation drawings.

31. *Carolina Watchman*, Oct. 20, 1854, Aug. 23, 1855, courtesy of James Brawley.

32. Ibid., Aug. 4, 1857, courtesy of James Brawley. George A. Dudley and William D. Ashley were contractors for carpentry at the Company Shops of the North Carolina Railroad in present-day Burlington (Black, *Burlington*, 14).

33. *Greensboro Patriot*, Oct. 15, 1858.

34. Johnson, *Ante-Bellum North Carolina*, 369–409; Joseph Brevard to Alexander Brevard, Dec. 16, 1802, *Raleigh Register*, Oct. 1, 1804, and *North Carolina Standard* (Raleigh), Apr. 22, 1857, all quoted in Johnson, *Ante-Bellum North Carolina*, 371.

35. Of 2,117 congregations and 157,014 church members, the breakdown was as follows: 966 (61,000) Methodist; 780 (65,000) Baptist; 182 (15,053) Presbyterian; 53 (3,036) Episcopalian; 38 (3,942) Lutheran; 44 (3,000) Christian; 22 (2,000) Society of Friends; 10 (2,000) Moravian; 15 (1,633) German Reformed; 7 (350) Roman Catholic (ibid., 369). The total population in 1860 was 992,622, of whom 331,059 were slaves.

36. Robert M. Calhoon, "An Agrarian and Evangelical Culture," in Butler and Watson, *North Carolina Experience*, 172–79; Johnson, *Ante-Bellum North Carolina*, 371–409; Scott Strickland, "The Great Revival and Insurrectionary Fears in North Carolina: An Examination of Antebellum Southern Society and Slave Revolt Panics," in Robert C. McMath and Orville V. Burton, eds., *Class, Conflict, and Consensus: Antebellum Southern Community Studies* (Westport, Conn.: Greenwood Press, 1982), 57–95; Weiss, *City in the Woods*.

37. "Rock Springs Camp Meeting Ground," NR form, 1972; Mrs. Gabriel Sigmon, "History and Tradition of Rock Springs Camp Ground," undated booklet, copy in "Rock Springs Camp Meeting Ground" survey file, Survey and Planning Branch, A&H; Lincoln County Deeds, A&H. The inner section of lots—squares of twenty-two lots apiece on each side—were sold in 1830 for about $1.25 per lot. See also NR and survey forms for Pleasant Grove Camp Meeting Ground, Union County; Balls Creek Camp Meeting Ground, Catawba County; and Tucker's Grove Camp Meeting Ground, Lincoln County. Although Methodists normally promulgated precise instructions for church institutions, their camp-meeting grounds apparently operated on a local, autonomous basis (Weiss, *City in the Woods*, 3–4). While northern camp-meeting grounds evolved in stylish directions, the southern camp-meeting ground continued along these primeval lines.

38. Many of the tents appear to date from the late nineteenth or early twentieth century, while others have been rebuilt lately. See D. Sullins, *Recollections of an Old Man* (Bristol, Tenn.: King Printing Co., 1910), 31–39, for recollections of a similar campground that had log huts with sawdust or straw floors and a large arbor where seating by gender was observed.

39. Strickland, "Great Revival" (on interracial activity); Sobel, *The World They Made Together*. Like several camp-meeting ground histories, Mrs. Sigmon's "History and Traditions of Rock Springs Camp Ground" states that slaves helped build the arbor; but this may simply have been part of a pattern of black involvement in all types of construction (see Bishir, "Black Builders"). Weiss suggests no source for the early plans of camp meetings and observes that "by any standards of Western tradition, this is eccentric place-making, clearly implying an unusual relationship between family and community" (*City in the Woods*, xii). For village and compound types, see, for example, Susan Denyer, *African Traditional Architecture: An Historical and Geographical Perspective* (New York: Africana Publishing Co., 1978), 75, 81, 90, 112–13, 123, 147–48. Of course, many village and city planning traditions throughout the world use similar concentric forms.

40. Mathews, *Religion in the Old South*, 81–93. See Patrick, *Architecture in Tennessee*, 105–7, on Methodist and Presbyterian preferences for plain churches.

41. Joshua Leigh, "On Church Building," 1834 manuscript circular, Methodist Episcopal Church, South, North Carolina, Salisbury District, Iredell Circuit, Church Records, 1834–50, Duke University Manuscript Collection, Perkins Library, Durham, courtesy of Carl Lounsbury. The gallery was to rest on columns 7′10″ tall and rise 15″ to the sides of the house. The ceiling was to be 15′ high. Seats were to be 2′6″ center to center and 18″ above the floor. The altar was to be on a platform 9″ high with an altar rail, and the floor of the pulpit was to be 2′ above the altar floor.

42. The seats at Bethesda Presbyterian Church, for example, were to have "legs . . . 13 inches wide and 1½ thick—one inch slope at bottom and 3 in the back. The back 16 inches high with a strip of molding on top. Seat 13 inches wide and 1½ thick the back 16 inches thick, the ends next to the aisles closed with 16 inch plank 1 inch thick, with 2 aisles lengthwise 4 feet wide and aisles leading from the side doors 3 feet wide, each seat to occupy 2½ feet space, seats in the gallery as below, the back ones raised if necessary, with a neat pulpit raised 2 feet from the floor and a neat table." Specifications, Mar. 31, 1860, Bethesda Presbyterian Church Records, Aberdeen, N.C., quoted in Davyd Foard Hood and Jerry Cross, "Bethesda Presbyterian Church," NR form, 1979.

43. Johnson, *Ante-Bellum North Carolina*, 337–43; Timothy Mattimoe, "The Primitive Baptists in Eastern North Carolina: Some Historical Survivals in American Protestant Culture," paper given at the annual meeting of the Southern Historical Association, 1989. Church records and traditions indicate that the Bear Grass Church was established in 1829 and built soon after; alterations in the later nineteenth or early twentieth century include the broadened roof overhang and narrow sheathing inside (Timothy Mattimoe to author, Sept. 28, 1988).

44. See untitled, handwritten historical sketch and W. A. Cade, "William Meredith, the Founder of Methodism in Wilmington," typescript history of Front Street Methodist Church, in Grace Methodist Church Records (Wilmington, N.C.), microfilm copy in A&H.

45. When the Goldsboro Presbyterian Church building committee advertised for proposals for the construction of a brick church 55 by 40 feet, they already had plans and specifications on hand (*Wilmington Tri-Weekly Commercial*, Dec. 2, 1854, courtesy William Reaves, Wilmington). See Lafever's similar design for St. James's Catholic Church in New York (1835–37) and in *Beauties of Modern Architecture* (1835) and Benjamin's Ionic version of this form in his *Builder's Guide* (1838). See also Hamlin, *Greek Revival Architecture*, 147, plate XLIX.

46. Back Creek Presbyterian Church was established in 1805, when families caught up in the revival of 1802 withdrew from the old Thyatira Presbyterian Church and employed a minis-

ter—shared with Third Creek—who had been an active revivalist. The congregation met for years in a log building before erecting their brick church (Hood, *Rowan County*, 79, 127–28, 119–20; Hollis and Julien, *Look to the Rock*, 40–53; Davyd Foard Hood, *Third Creek Church* [Statesville: Brady Printing Co., 1985]).

47. The Rehoboth congregation, which had its roots in an eighteenth-century Anglican chapel, affiliated in 1828 with the Methodist denomination. J. S. Norman deeded the trustees the land for $5.00 in 1850, and his and his brother's slaves are credited with the construction of the church (Sharlene P. Nelson, "117 Year History of Rehoboth," undated typescript, copy in Rehoboth Church survey file, Survey and Planning Branch, A&H; Janet Seapker and Robert Topkins, "Rehoboth Methodist Church," NR form, 1976).

48. Johnson, *Ante-Bellum North Carolina*, 348–53; Harry L. Watson, *Jacksonian Politics and Community Conflict* (Baton Rouge: Louisiana State University Press, 1981), 30–31.

49. It is cited as the congregation's third building, following a log meeting house (ca. 1765) and a small nineteenth-century frame building (Rev. R. A. McLeod, *Historical Sketch of Long Street Presbyterian Church* [Sanford: privately printed, 1923], 14).

50. *A Centennial Historical Address Delivered before the Presbytery at the Bluff Church, the 18th Day of October, 1858, by James Banks, Esq.* (Fayetteville: Printed at the Presbytery Office, 1858); Bluff Presbyterian Church records, microfilm, A&H; [Ruth Little], "Old Bluff Presbyterian Church," NR form, 1974. Beside the church stands a marker commemorating a century of Scots Presbyterianism in the region, carved by Scots immigrant stonecutter George Lauder (who came to North Carolina to work on the Capitol and then moved to Fayetteville).

51. Turner, *Campus*, 90; Mathews, *Religion in the Old South*, 87–97. Presbyterians, especially the Piedmont Scotch-Irish, had traditionally emphasized education and had established a number of academies in the eighteenth century. The Quakers, Moravians, and Anglicans had also established early schools. These efforts now expanded and were joined by those of Baptists, Methodists, and others. See William S. Powell, *Higher Education in North Carolina* (Raleigh: Archives and History, 1970), for a listing of colleges.

52. This building is lost, but one of two contemporary faculty houses still stands: "South Brick," built by Berry with Greek Revival trim adapted from Benjamin's *Practical House Carpenter* (Murray, *Wake*, 300–302; Paschal, *History of Wake Forest College*, 1:71–73, 104–19).

53. Proceedings of the Building Committee, Feb. 12, 1835, Episcopal School of North Carolina Papers, A&H; Murray, *Wake*, 309–10. The school had two flanking buildings erected in 1835 of stone from the Capitol quarry. Duncan Cameron, first chairman of the Capitol building commission, was principal benefactor and probably brought Drummond into the project.

54. J. Marshall Bullock, "Albert Gamaliel Jones," typescript biography, ca. 1983, in possession of author; E. Frank Stephenson, *Renaissance in Carolina* (Murfreesboro: Murfreesboro Historical Association, 1971–73), 1:11, 161, 2:131. On college building contracts, see *ABNC*, 160–61. Other college buildings of the era include Judson College in Hendersonville, built by Henry T. Farmer; the Lutheran Western Carolina Male Academy in Mount Pleasant; Main Building at Salem Academy in Winston-Salem, built by Francis Fries; the Presbyterian-sponsored Peace Institute in Raleigh, built by Thomas and Jacob Holt; and plans for a main building at Methodist Trinity College in Randolph County, contracted by Jacob Holt but not built because of the Civil War.

55. Minutes and Annual Reports of the Concord Presbyterian Female College Board of Trustees, 1852–61 (Mitchell College, Statesville), quoted in William C. Moose, "History of Mitchell College Main Building," typescript, 1985 (copy in possession of author), and idem, "Many Trials Endured as College Constructed," *Statesville Record and Landmark*, June 9, 1985; *Carolina*

Watchman, June 14, 1855. By 1855, the Conrad firm, doubtless expecting to have the college finished, also had other projects underway, including the Rowan County Courthouse in Salisbury and Cooleemee in Davie County; the firm had previously built Blandwood and the North Carolina Hospital for the Insane, both designed by A. J. Davis (see below).

56. Turner, *Campus*, 90–91. See, for example, Whig and Cliosophic Halls at Princeton (1837–38), which may have influenced the buildings at Davidson.

57. Allcott, *Campus at Chapel Hill*, 35–43, and "Scholarly Books and Frolicksome Blades"; Henderson, *Campus of the First State University*, 133–45; A. J. Davis to David L. Swain, May 31, 1850, David L. Swain Papers, SHC, quoted in ibid., 141. Originally, Davis thought of including tobacco leaves as well (ibid., 142–43).

58. C. Reed Wingate, *Beaufort County: Two Centuries of History* (Raleigh: Edwards and Broughton, 1962), xx.

59. The structure may have been built in the 1850s for Connecticut-born Hamilton merchant Joseph Waldo, perhaps as a combination residence and store (Robert Topkins, Charles Blume, and Catherine Cockshutt [Bishir], "Darden Hotel," NR form, 1975).

60. Little-Stokes, *Caswell County*, 42, 57, 70, 198.

61. See Lane, *North Carolina*, 186–88.

62. David R. Black to Richard Barentine, Aug. 1, 1988, Homestead File, Restoration Branch, A&H; Touart, *Building the Back Country*, 58–60.

63. Day books and account books of James G. Torrence, Torrence Family Papers, microfilm, Atkins Library, University of North Carolina at Charlotte; Richard Banks, typescript annotated guide to Torrence Family Papers and typescript history of house, courtesy of Richard Banks and Suzanne Pickens. Plasterer Gorman may have been the same man who worked for Duncan Cameron at Fairntosh.

64. Carpenter Hampton may have bought "Nicholson's Architecture" to help with the structural challenge of such a stair, for Englishman Peter Nicholson's works were considered the chief authority for building spiral staircases. Many builders used Biddle's stair in combination with Greek and Roman Revival motifs from Benjamin. John Haviland's *Improved and Enlarged Edition of Biddle's Young Carpenter's Assistant* (1837) replicated Biddle's old plates along with Haviland's new Grecian mantels and doorways.

65. Cotton, *Historic Burke*, 25–27, 152–53.

66. Haley and Winslow, *Perquimans County*, 38–43; Raymond A. Winslow, Jr., and Catherine Cockshutt [Bishir], "Cove Grove" and "Land's End," NR forms, 1974, 1973; additional research was conducted by Jim Sumner in 1989. By 1830 Leigh had acquired some 1,740 acres and, with fifty-nine slaves, had become the county's third largest slaveholder.

67. For examples of Nichols's similar work in Alabama, see Peatross, *William Nichols*, 15–22. Also of interest are comparisons with Hayes: the arcaded porch base, a lozenge-pattern mantel, and some resemblance between the scallop-shell newels at Cove Grove and Land's End (and others) and the applied pineapple motif of the dining-room mantel at Hayes. Measurements courtesy of Raymond Winslow, "Cove Grove" survey file, Survey and Planning Branch, A&H.

68. House measurements by Raymond Winslow, "Land's End" survey file, Survey and Planning Branch, A&H. Family tradition asserts that Leigh began Land's End in about 1825, the year he married his second wife, Susan Banks. Although he might have begun the house then, the extensive use of Benjamin's *Practical House Carpenter* indicates a completion date in the 1830s. An attic door is said to bear the date 1837. In 1847 Leigh was sued for usury; in 1851 a local black barber, while shaving him, was said to have stolen his pocketbook, which contained $400 in cash and over $30,000 in notes and other papers. When Leigh died intestate in 1854, the administrators of his estate posted bond in the sum of $500,000. Six of his twelve children survived him and divided property that amounted to

$392,500 in land, a hotel in Elizabeth City, slaves, stocks, a schooner, and other possessions ("Land's End," undated, unsigned typescript [1970s], Leigh and Winslow Papers, SHC). For examples of other related, probably later, houses, see the discussion of Ashland, the Jonathan Hill Jacocks House, and the Edmund Blount Skinner House, in Haley and Winslow, *Perquimans County*, 40–42, and the treatment of Athol, Ashland, and Sandy Point in *EANC*, 42–43, 160–61.

69. William S. Tarlton, *Somerset Place and Its Restoration* (Raleigh: Archives and History, 1954). On Josiah Collins I, II, and III, see *DNCB*, 1:404–6. Bills dated in the late 1830s indicate the house's likely construction date. In 1838, there were bills for bricklaying and brickmaking by Davy and John, who were evidently slaves, and a brick contract was negotiated with Dempsey Spruill. In 1839 Jesse Sawyer was paid $355.78 for 258¾ days of carpentry work. Sawyer also worked at Somerset for 239½ days in 1842 and 112 days in 1844. On a plantation of Somerset's scale, carpentry work might be needed on an almost continuous basis, so it is not certain which of the above work was done on the house itself. In the 1850s, the house was freshened up. Painter Richard Barfield painted the woodwork with woodgraining and marbleizing in 1856, and in 1859 imported marble mantels were installed ("Architectural Evidence," typescript report in Historic Sites Section, A&H, which draws upon Collins Letter Book and Ledger B, Collins Family Papers, SHC, courtesy of William McCrea).

70. Henrietta and Mary Matilda Collins were the daughters of planter and merchant Josiah Collins II of Edenton, and the house was erected on Collins family property (Elizabeth V. Moore, *Guidebook to Historic Edenton and Chowan County* [Edenton: Edenton Woman's Club, 1984], 24; John G. Zehmer, "Pembroke Hall," NR form, 1976; personal communication from Elizabeth V. Moore, Dec. 1989, on Collins and Page family history).

71. John G. Zehmer and Sherry Ingram, "Midway Plantation," NR form, 1970; Lala Carr Steelman, "The Life-Style of an Eastern North Carolina Planter: Elias Carr of Bracebridge Hall," *NCHR* 57, no. 1 (Jan. 1980): 21–22.

72. Bishir, "Jacob W. Holt."

73. Ibid.

74. See Tony P. Wrenn, "Thomas Day," in *DNCB*, 2:45–46; Barfield, *Thomas Day*; Little-Stokes, *Caswell County*, 35–38.

75. See, for example, Benjamin, *American Builder's Companion*, plates 33, 37; Robert Farris Thompson, *Flash of the Spirit: African and Afro-American Art and Philosophy* (New York: Vintage Books, 1984).

76. See Little-Stokes, "North Carolina Porch," 109. Robert Doares, notes from R. B. Humphrey Journal, private collection, copy provided to author; R. L. Godfrey, "Humphrey-Williams House," *The Robesonian*, Apr. 26, 1987; "Humphrey-Williams House," NR form, 1973.

77. The composite map in Figure 3.68 is based on archaeological evidence (1952–54, 1981, 1982), documentary sources, and maps. The bathhouse has been reconstructed, and the storehouse was moved to its present site (William McCrea, notes to author, Jan. 1989). For a vivid account of the lives of slave and white families at Somerset, see Dorothy Spruill Redford, *Somerset Homecoming: Recovering a Lost Heritage* (New York: Anchor Books, 1988).

78. Brad Barker, "Elliott Farm," Chowan County survey file, Survey and Planning Branch, A&H, and personal communication to author, June 17, 1989.

79. Robert Topkins and Ruth Little-Stokes, "Walnut Grove," NR form, 1975; additional research by Jim Sumner, 1989.

80. Robert Topkins and Greer Suttlemyre, "Andrew Seagle Farm," NR form, 1975; Brown, *Our Enduring Past*, 117; additional research by Jim Sumner, 1989. The chimney is dated 1860. It is not entirely clear whether the house was built earlier and expanded in 1860 or built in 1860 and expanded later. Family tradition claims that Andrew Seagle built the addition when his

son married. For a concrete description of life on a small North Carolina Piedmont farm in this period, see Arthur Menius III, "James Bennitt: Portrait of an Antebellum Yeoman," *NCHR* 58, no. 4 (Oct. 1981): 305–26.

81. Michael R. Hill, "The Carson House of Marion, North Carolina," research report, 1982, copy in Restoration Branch, A&H.

82. Not until the early twentieth century did a later generation install doors at the ends to enclose the passage at the Carson House. Comparison with Wright Tavern, also with a central passage open to the porch, may supply the reason for leaving the dogtrot open.

83. Thorp, "Assimilation." Despite development around it, the village plan survives virtually intact. See Michael O. Hartley and Martha Brown Boxley, "Bethania in Wachovia," preservation planning report, 1989, copy in Survey and Planning Branch, A&H; Ruth Little-Stokes, "Bethania Historic District," NR form, 1975; Taylor, *Frontier to Factory*, 7–8.

84. Emma Lehman, "Houses in Bethania," typescript memoir, 2–3, copy in Bethania survey file, Survey and Planning Branch, A&H.

85. *RM*, 10:5344–45.

86. Gwynne S. Taylor, "Francis Levin Fries," typescript biography, ca. 1982, copy in possession of author. In 1853 Fries proposed construction of a new main building for the Salem Academy and, while visiting New York, obtained a design from A. J. Davis. Davis promptly made a "Design for Francis Fries, Salem, North Carolina, 2 elevations for a female Seminary, 4 stories high." Fries supervised construction (1854–56). As built, the structure indicates modifications or a departure from Davis's plan (A. J. Davis Diary, Oct. 29–31, 1853, A. J. Davis Collection, Avery Architectural and Fine Arts Library, Columbia University, New York, N.Y., quoted in Lane, *North Carolina*, 261).

87. *RM*, 11:5980, 5982. John Larson, "The Moravian Architecture of Salem, N.C.: From Congregational Consensus to Individual Expression," paper presented at Winterthur Conference, 1983. Also a factor at the time was the knowledge that the lease system was legally indefensible.

88. Council minutes, Nov. 22, 1859, Belo House file, Old Salem, Inc.

89. See Upton, "Pattern Books and Professionalism."

90. *Wilmington Herald*, Nov. 17, 1857. For Wilmington architecture and history, I have depended on Wrenn, *Wilmington*; on William Reaves of Wilmington, who provided Wilmington newspaper references from his research files; and on Janet K. Seapker and Edward Turberg.

91. *Wilmington Chronicle*, May 17, 1843, Sept. 2, 1840, Aug. 26, 1846 (reprinted from *Providence Journal*). See also Mar. 31, Oct. 20, and Dec. 29, 1841.

92. See *ABNC*, 184–85, 466 (nn. 147, 148), on builders in Wilmington; see Mattison and Thomas advertisement (boasting of their architectural experience in "the North"), *Wilmington Chronicle*, Jan. 28, 1846, quoted in *ABNC*, 184.

93. Wrenn, *Wilmington*, 79–82; *Wilmington Advertiser*, Nov. 17, 1837, Feb. 1, 1839; letter from W. C. Lord, Thomas H. Wright, A. J. DeRosset, and R. B. Drane, Mar. 25, 1845, Letters Received Relating to the Construction of Customhouses and Other Structures, K Series, 1833–49, no. 328, NA; Janet K. Seapker, "John C. and Robert B. Wood," typescript biography, 1989, copy in possession of author.

94. Letter from John Hill, Thomas H. Wright, and P. K. Dickinson, Mar. 31, 1845, Letters Received Relating to the Construction of Customhouses and Other Structures, K Series, 1833–49, no. 332, NA. Upon completion of the job, the bank directors presented Norris with a silver pitcher, which he treasured throughout his lifetime and in his will singled out as a bequest, "the silver pitcher presented to me by the Bank of Cape Fear, North Carolina" (Morrison, *John S. Norris*, 55).

95. *Wilmington Chronicle*, Aug. 20, 1845. Norris also designed

other private buildings in Wilmington—so many during the Custom House project that complaints were registered with the Treasury Department. One likely attribution is the A. J. DeRosset, Jr., House (1841), a large frame house with classical porch, built by C. H. Dahl, carpenter at St. James. See Mary Ellen Gadski, "The History of the DeRosset House," research report, 1978, copy in Restoration Branch, A&H.

96. Wrenn, *Wilmington*, 224; *Wilmington Chronicle*, July 14, 21, 1847.

97. *Wilmington Chronicle*, Aug. 18, 1847, Feb. 9, 1848. In 1845 Benjamin Gardner of Wilmington was "architect and superintendent" of a jail in Savannah, and in 1847 he advertised that he had "resumed his profession in Wilmington" (*Wilmington Chronicle*, Apr. 2, 1847). In 1848 he provided plans and specifications for a courthouse and jail in Goldsboro. He was probably influenced by Norris (J. Marshall Bullock, "Benjamin Gardner," typescript biography, 1982, copy in possession of author).

98. Wrenn, *Wilmington*, 206–7. In 1896 an article praising Post (who was still alive) cited as two of the city's finest buildings the Bellamy House, "planned and superintended" by Post, and the John A. Taylor House, "planned by Benjamin Gardner, a Wilmingtonian" (*Wilmington Dispatch*, July 7, 1896, courtesy of William Reaves).

99. Seapker, "James F. Post"; *ABNC*, 149–53. Among the patternbooks advertised in Wilmington newspapers were *Wightwick's Hints to Young Architects*, *The American House Carpenter*, Edward Shaw's *Rural Architecture*, and Asher Benjamin's *The Architect and Practical House Carpenter* (*Wilmington Chronicle*, Mar. 20, 1850); Samuel Sloan's *The Carpenter's New Guide* (*Wilmington Tri-Weekly Commercial*, Dec. 24, 1853); Gervase Wheeler's *Homes for the People* (ibid., May 22, 1855); [Samuel Sloan's] *The City Architect* (ibid., Feb. 26, 1856); and the *Architects and Mechanics Journal* (*Daily Herald*, Jan. 3, 1860).

100. Wrenn, *Wilmington*, 89–90; James F. Post Account Book, microfilm, A&H; Janet K. Seapker, "Wilmington Historic District," NR form, 1974 (on iron versions of the trellis foliage). See also the similar MacRae-Dix House of 1851–52 (Wrenn, *Wilmington*, 87).

101. "Specifications of a Brick House . . . for Mr. Z. Latimer," 1851, Lower Cape Fear Historical Society, Inc., Wilmington. The Woods subcontracted carpentry to Post for $3,135. Dr. James H. Dickson's house (ca. 1849) stood on East Front Street, and Edward Kidder's house (completed ca. 1852) stood at the northeast corner of Second and Church streets. They, like the house of Dr. DeRossett, Sr., are all lost (Edward Turberg to author, Apr. 11, 1989). See Wrenn, *Wilmington*, 132–35, 142. Reference to existing buildings in a contract and evolution of design during construction were standard (*ABNC*, 82–83; Bishir, "Jacob W. Holt"; idem, "Good and Sufficient Language for Building," forthcoming in Thomas Carter and Bernard Herman, *Perspectives in Vernacular Culture, IV* [Columbia: University of Missouri Press, 1991]).

102. Wrenn, *Wilmington*, 76–78; *Wilmington Daily Journal*, Oct. 12, 1858, cited in Isabel M. Williams, "Thalian Hall Historical Research Report," undated research report, copy in Restoration Branch, A&H. A linen drawing of the elevation, found in the cornerstone, was signed by R. B. Wood and is illustrated in Lane, *North Carolina*, 220. Wood was paid $40 on Dec. 8, 1855, for "drawing plans and specifications for the city hall," and Post's contract as superintending architect stated that he would make working plans as needed.

103. Letters Received, Public Buildings Services, 1843–1910, RG 121, Box 1644, Entry 26, NA. The Presbyterian Church and Marine Hospital are lost; the Baptist Church still stands (Wrenn, *Wilmington*, 209–13, 90–91).

104. John D. Bellamy, *Memoirs of an Octogenarian* (N.p.: privately printed, 1942), 8; Seapker, "James F. Post"; James F. Post Account Book, microfilm, A&H; Journal of Rufus Bunnell, Bunnell Family Papers, YU. Bunnell mentioned using Post's architectural books but did not cite specific titles. Edward

Shaw's *Modern Architect* (Boston: Dayton and Wentworth, 1855) contains plates (9–10, 37–38) that may have been resources.

105. Journal of Rufus Bunnell, Mar.–Aug. 1860, Bunnell Family Papers, YU.

106. Mullin, *Episcopal Vision/American Reality*; Rankin, "Bishop Levi S. Ives."

107. John Henry Hobart, *The Worship of the Church on Earth* (Philadelphia, 1823), 15, quoted in Mullin, *Episcopal Vision*, 77. See Stanton, *Gothic Revival*; Patrick, "Ecclesiological Gothic"; Pierson, *American Buildings*, 2:149–73.

108. Patrick, "Ecclesiological Gothic"; Malone, "Levi Silliman Ives"; Rankin, "Bishop Levi S. Ives"; Blackwell P. Robinson, "The Episcopate of Levi Silliman Ives," in London and Lemmon, *Episcopal Church in North Carolina*. Ives had attended the New York Theological Seminary, studied under High Church leader Bishop John Henry Hobart, and married Hobart's daughter. Bishops in Virginia, by contrast, resisted High Church Gothic Revivalism. See James L. McAllister, Jr., "Architecture and Change in the Diocese of Virginia," *Historical Magazine of the Protestant Episcopal Church* 45 (1976): 297–323; Del. Upton, "New Views of the Virginia Landscape," *The Virginia Magazine of History and Biography* 96, no. 4 (Oct. 1988): 403–70.

109. Philip A. Rees, "Chapel of the Cross, an Architectural History," master's thesis, University of North Carolina, 1979; idem, "Thomas U. Walter," typescript biography, 1981, copy in possession of author; Ida Brooks Kellam and Elizabeth Francenia McKoy, "St. James Church, Wilmington, North Carolina: Historical Records, 1737–1852," mimeographed typescript, Wilmington, 1965, copy in "St. James Church" survey file, Survey and Planning Branch, A&H. Quote from *Sketch of St. James's Parish* (New York: E. J. Hale and Son, 1874), 50.

110. Patrick, "Ecclesiological Gothic"; Stanton, *Gothic Revival*.

111. Rankin, "Bishop Levi S. Ives"; Levi Silliman Ives, *The Address at the Laying of the Corner Stone, St. Mary's Church, Burlington, New Jersey* (Burlington, N.J.: E. Morris, 1847), quoted in Patrick, "Ecclesiological Gothic," 138; Malone, "Levi Silliman Ives," 185. Ives was one of four American bishops listed as patrons of the Cambridge Ecclesiologists' journal, *The Ecclesiologist*, and his sermon at the 1846 cornerstone laying of Richard Upjohn's St. Mary's Church in Burlington, New Jersey—one of the first great American examples of the English parish church type—was published as a key statement of ecclesiological tenets (Patrick, "Ecclesiological Gothic," 121).

112. Phoebe B. Stanton, "Richard Upjohn," in Placzek, *Macmillan Encyclopedia of Architects*, 4:236–43. Having outgrown William Nichols's 1820s wooden church, the vestry wanted a new church with seating for five hundred people on the main floor plus galleries at sides and front, for a cost of $10,000 to $12,000. In a knowledgeable aside, Mason noted, "We should prefer the arrangement of the chancel which you have offered in the Church of the Ascension but of course you will be the best judge" (Richard Sharp Mason to Richard Upjohn, Dec. 30, 1842, Richard Upjohn Papers, NYPL).

113. L. S. Ives to Richard Upjohn, Jan. 12, 1846, and Mason to Upjohn, Nov. 15, 1847, Richard Upjohn Papers, NYPL. Upjohn to Mason, Oct. 14, 1846, and Memorandum of Agreement, June 7, 1848, Christ Church Records, A&H. Mason later reported, "Our church is universally admired. The oiled and varnished Southern pine makes a beautiful interior equal I think to oak" (Mason to Upjohn, July 10, 1856, Richard Upjohn Papers, NYPL). See also Marshall Delancey Haywood, "History of Parish of Christ Church," 29.

114. Olmsted, *Journey in the Seaboard Slave States*, 319.

115. Rankin, "Bishop Levi S. Ives"; Robinson, "The Episcopate of Levi Silliman Ives." Valle Crucis was seen as a monastic order disturbingly akin to "the Romish Church" (see George E. Badger, *An Examination of the Doctrines Declared and Powers Claimed by the Right Reverend Bishop Ives* [1849], quoted in

Marshall Delancey Haywood, *Lives of the Bishops of North Carolina* [Raleigh: Alfred Williams and Co., 1910], 113). *Puseyite Developments, or Notices of the New-York Ecclesiologists Dedicated to Their Patron, the Right Reverend Bishop Ives of North Carolina* (1850), an anonymous pamphlet widely circulated in the diocese, complained about ecclesiological policies.

116. Laura A. W. Phillips, "St. Paul's Episcopal Church and Cemetery," NR form, 1980; "New Churches," *New York Ecclesiologist* (1851, 1849), cited in Patrick, "Ecclesiological Gothic," 132.

117. William Horn Battle to Lucy Martin Battle, Mar. 22, 1851, Battle Family Papers, SHC.

118. Malone, "Levi Silliman Ives," 314–17.

119. Lawrence Wodehouse, "'Upjohn's Rural Architecture' in North Carolina," *North Carolina Architect* 15, no. 11 (Nov. 1968): 13–22; Aldert Smedes to Richard Upjohn, May 1–Oct. 7, 1856, Richard Upjohn Papers, NYPL.

120. Bishop Atkinson's Address, Annual Convention of Diocese of North Carolina, 1858, quoted in Stuart Hall Smith and Claiborne T. Smith, Jr., *The History of Trinity Parish, Scotland Neck Edgecombe Parish, Halifax County* (Scotland Neck: privately printed, 1955), 57.

121. See discussion of First Baptist of New Bern in Sandbeck, *New Bern and Craven County*, 120, 360–61; discussion of St. Anne's in Stephen C. Worsley, "Catholicism in Antebellum North Carolina," *NCHR* 60, no. 4 (Oct. 1983): 426–27. On the associations of the round-arched style, see Kathleen Curran, "The German *Rundbogenstil* and Reflections on the American Round-Arched Style," *JSAH* 47, no. 4 (Dec. 1988): 351–73; William H. Pierson, Jr., "Richard Upjohn and the American *Rundbogenstil*," *Winterthur Portfolio* 21, no. 4 (Winter 1986): 223–42; Gwen W. Steege, "The *Book of Plans* and the Early Romanesque in the United States: A Study in Architectural Patronage," *JSAH* 46, no. 3 (Sept. 1987): 215–27.

122. This discussion comes mainly from Allcott, "Architect A. J. Davis in North Carolina," "Robert Donaldson," and *Campus at Chapel Hill*; Lane, *North Carolina*, 234–57; Donoghue, "Alexander Jackson Davis." See also Jane Davies, "Alexander Jackson Davis," in Placzek, *Macmillan Encyclopedia of Architects*, 1:505–15.

123. Donoghue, "Alexander Jackson Davis," 232–84.

124. Allcott, "Robert Donaldson," 354–58. John Cornelius Donoghue describes Donaldson as "mediary in bringing together the artist without an audience [Davis] and the author-publisher without an artist [Downing]" ("Alexander Jackson Davis," 284–86).

125. Allcott, "Robert Donaldson," 350–66, and "Architect A. J. Davis in North Carolina," 14. On plans for a literary society library in North Carolina for Donaldson that was "found too expensive," see Davis Diary, Oct. 1832, p. 141, A. J. Davis Collection, NYPL. Davis intended to visit Gaston in Raleigh on his 1844 trip to North Carolina, but Gaston died the day Davis left New York, and Davis later designed his gravestone, a handsome classical monument still in New Bern's cemetery (Allcott, "Robert Donaldson," 361–62). Town and Davis also donated plans to rebuild the Presbyterian Church in Fayetteville after the 1831 city fire.

126. Allcott, "Architect A. J. Davis in North Carolina," 10–11; Donaldson to Davis, Jan. 14, 1844, A. J. Davis Papers, NYPL. On his journey, Davis kept notes about the people he met, such as "Persons at Raleigh with whom I became somewhat acquainted—Ex. Gov. James Iredell, Bishop Ives, and lady, Mrs. John Taylor, George E. Badger, late Secy of Navy, Mr. Gales, Editor of Register," and "Pedigree of Morehead," "Pedigree of Lindsey," and so on (Davis Daybook, 1844, A. J. Davis Papers, NYPL).

127. Jane Davies cites Blandwood as "one of the first towered Italianate villas built in the United States . . . perhaps the earliest still standing" and "probably the prototype for one of the most popular American house patterns in the Italianate mode" ("Blandwood and the Italian Villa Style," 11, 13). A. J. Davis later listed Blandwood as an "Italian tower residence" (Davis vol-

umes, 8:13, A. J. Davis Collection, MMA). On the Conrads, see J. Marshall Bullock, "Conrad Family," typescript biography, ca. 1982, copy in possession of author. In 1849, when the Conrads took the bid to complete the library at the Capitol, a local builder was annoyed that the work had gone to "Governor Morehead's upcountry carpenters" (*Raleigh Star*, Jan. 24, 1849).

128. Allcott, *Campus at Chapel Hill*, 32–35, and "Architect A. J. Davis in North Carolina," 10–14; Swain to Davis, Mar. 10, 1845, A. J. Davis Papers, NYPL; Davis to Swain, Mar. 24, 1845, University Papers, University of North Carolina Library, Chapel Hill, quoted in Allcott, "Architect A. J. Davis in North Carolina," 12. Interior woodwork and the furnishings of the halls were executed by Thomas Day of Milton (Swain to Thomas Day, Nov. 24, 1847, Philanthropic Papers, SHC, quoted in Barfield, *Thomas Day*, 11).

129. A. J. Davis to Gov. Swain, n.d. [probably 1847], A. J. Davis Collection, NYPL.

130. Allcott, "Architect A. J. Davis in North Carolina"; idem, "Architectural Developments at 'Montrose.'"

131. E. M. Holt to A. J. Davis, Mar. 2, 1849, Davis Letterbook, A. J. Davis Collection, NYPL, 152–53. Holt sketched his existing 18-by-23-foot house, which he wanted to incorporate into a larger dwelling. Other sketches on the page appear to be Davis's. On Holt, see Rachel Y. Holt, "Edwin Michael Holt," in *DNCB*, 3:182–83; Bess Beatty, "The Edwin Holt Family: Nineteenth-Century Capitalists in North Carolina," *NCHR* 63, no. 4 (Oct. 1986): 511–35. Holt's textile mill on Alamance Creek began operation in 1837. Holt and Fries were close friends who alternated trips north to get ideas and machinery, and Holt was also a stockholder and director of the North Carolina Railroad. Edwin Holt's brother, William Raney Holt, built the Homestead in Lexington (see above). See Donoghue, "Alexander Jackson Davis," 302–5, for other far-flung clients who contacted Davis as a result of Downing's publications.

132. Lounsbury, *Alamance County*, 34–35; idem, "Building Process," 453–55; Occasional Diary of E. M. Holt, 1849, E. M. Holt Papers, SHC. The carpenter was Eli Denny, a local man.

133. Downing, *The Architecture of Country Houses*, 313.

134. Davis's innovative asylum plan for Blackwell's Island in New York City was not completed as he conceived it (Donoghue, "Alexander Jackson Davis," 160–65). See Davis's drawings comparing the North Carolina asylum, the Blackwell Island asylum, and Middlesex Asylum, London, in his "Index to Some of the Most Important Works of Alex. J. Davis, 1830–1880," vol. 2, A. J. Davis Collection, MMA.

135. Morehead to Davis, Dec. 16, 1849, Davis Letterbook, 1850, A. J. Davis Collection, NYPL. Davis's diary notes his visits according to Morehead's directions, including a long consultation with Kirkbride. On the New Jersey Hospital, designed by architect John Notman from a plan suggested by Dr. Kirkbride, see Constance M. Greiff, *John Notman, Architect* (Philadelphia: The Athenaeum of Philadelphia, 1979), 103–7.

136. *North Carolina Standard*, Nov. 18, 1854; Murray, *Wake*, 428–29. Observations on the evolution of asylum design courtesy of Edward Chappell, personal communication, Feb. 1989.

137. A. J. Davis, "Index," vol. 2, A. J. Davis Collection, MMA. In the twentieth century the hospital was named after Dorothea Dix, the proponent of treatment of the insane who had persuaded the North Carolina legislature to build the hospital. A fire in 1926 damaged the building, and mid- and late-twentieth-century structures have replaced the central pavilion. The wings remain, altered but structurally recognizable (Murray, *Wake*, 429).

138. Paul V. Turner cites Davis's design for Davidson as exemplary of "the ambitious mid-nineteenth-century spirit of American college building" (*Campus*, 124–25). See also Donoghue, "Alexander Jackson Davis," 318; Hamlin, *Greek Revival Architecture*, 212; Davis, "Vitruvian Tuscan," in Davis volumes, 8:19, A. J. Davis Collection, MMA. In the latter work, Davis states that the building was to be 500 by 600 feet; in other versions it was to be 600 feet square. On the Chambers bequest, see James S.

Brawley, "Maxwell Chambers," in *DNCB*, 1:351–52. The college emerged from the war impoverished, and Chambers Hall, as it was called, subsequently burned.

139. See *ABNC*, 142; Lounsbury, "Building Process," 445–47.

140. Peter W. Hairston, *The Cooleemee Plantation and Its People* (Winston-Salem: Hunter Publishing Co. for Davidson County Community College, 1986), 33–44; Peter Hairston to George Hairston, Sept. 1850, J. E. B. Stuart to George Hairston, Apr. 1852, quoted in ibid., 35, 38. At Cooleemee, agricultural production and slaveownership rose rapidly between 1850 and 1860, a trend that coincides with completion of the railroad and plank road. The number of swine increased from 204 to 400, with similar increases in the production of corn and cloth; tobacco brought about $3,600 in 1853 and nearly $9,000 in 1858. There were 57 slaves on the plantation in 1850, 201 by 1857, and 400 in 1861 (Hairston, *Cooleemee Plantation*, 35). Other plantations brought Hairston's holdings to many thousands of acres.

141. Hairston, *Cooleemee Plantation*, 41–44. The contract was for $9,000, but additional items brought the cost to over $10,400 by the time of the project's completion in 1855 (Peter W. Hairston to author, Aug. 4, 1985; copies of accounts from Conrad and Williams, Peter W. Hairston Papers, SHC). After completing Blandwood and contracting for the lunatic asylum, William Conrad had died in 1850, and his brother John and father Joseph engaged John Wilson Williams as partner (Bullock, "Conrad Family").

142. Brown, *Our Enduring Past*, 127. Typical of many such houses, this one has a conventional central-passage plan and restrained Greek Revival–type finish inside.

143. *Tarboro Southerner*, Dec. 12, 1865.

144. Sadie Smathers Patton, *A Condensed History of Flat Rock: The Little Charleston of the Mountains* (1961; 3d ed., Flat Rock: privately printed, n.d.), 33–34; Swaim, *Cabins and Castles*, 68.

145. Patton, *Condensed History of Flat Rock*, 59–62. An initial plan for the hotel was rejected as too costly and was reduced to keep the cost under $7,000. Patton quotes construction costs as follows: "To amount paid by 10 subscribers, $10,000; By purchase of land, $4,500; By building house, to H. T. Farmer, $7,000; To E. C. Jones for plans, $230.00; J. & J. Hilderan (This for furniture), $678.00; By cash to Farmer on outbuildings contracted for at $1,200" (ibid., 61).

146. Ibid., 62; personal communications from John Wesley Jones and Langdon Oppermann, 1988, on date of Many Pines. Beaumont was originally an L-shaped cottage of stone with bargeboards and dormers, while Rutledge Cottage is a simple frame cottage. The stone rectory of St. John in the Wilderness suggests an inspiration from the rectory in *Upjohn's Rural Architecture*. Others, such as Kenmure, were square frame or stone houses adorned with bracket cornices in the Italianate mode. Several houses, including Argyle, Teneriffe, Saluda Cottages, and Mountain Lodge, were screened with porches of sawnwork and arcaded lattices similar to the hotel.

147. Sybil Bowers, "Rugby Grange," NR form, 1986; Swaim, *Cabins and Castles*, 72–73, 140, 68.

148. Bishir, "Jacob W. Holt."

149. Ibid. John A. Waddell was working and living with Holt as a journeyman carpenter in 1850; in 1860 he was head of his own household. Waddell continued to work in association with Holt through the 1850s, probably as a foreman on key projects. Cherry Hill was built for the widow and children of George Alston; Alston family tradition recalls Waddell on-site as builder, and a payment to Waddell of $4,774.69 on January 1, 1859, from the Alston estate confirms this (Catherine W. Bishir, "John A. Waddell," typescript biography, 1980, in possession of author; "Cherry Hill," NR form, 1974).

150. Vine Hill contract between J. W. Holt and A. D. Williams, Sept. 5, 1856, Archibald D. Williams ledger, microfilm, A&H. Holt's extra costs for Sylva Sonora, a plantation house now lost, included "extra graining in back rooms of house, $25.00," indicating that graining in the principal (front) rooms was part of the original agreement (Sylva Sonora bills, J. W.

Holt and John E. Boyd, 1857–58, copy in possession of author).

151. John B. Flowers and Catherine Cockshutt [Bishir], "The Hermitage," NR form, 1975. In 1853 Thomas Blount Hill, Jr., then residing in Hillsborough, deeded 2,290 acres to John Tilery, who probably built the outbuildings.

152. Anderson, *Piedmont Plantation*, 49–76; Paul Carrington Cameron, *Address before the Orange County Agricultural Society, 1854*, quoted in *ABNC*, 142.

153. Paul C. Cameron to Thomas Ruffin, Sept. 28, 1860, Ruffin Papers, SHC, quoted in Anderson, *Piedmont Plantation*, 57–58.

154. Paul Cameron, Account with Nichols, Rogers, and Company, Durham, June 1860–Jan. 1862, Accounts and Statements, Cameron Family Papers, SHC, copy courtesy of Ken McFarland, Stagville Plantation. This structure echoes a pattern also notable in other regions: the move toward innovative agricultural buildings that consolidated many functions was accompanied by increasingly elaborate structural systems, including virtuoso framing displays (Herman, *Architecture and Rural Life*, 224–28). Similarities in the massing of the barn with Percival's New East and New West may be only coincidental, but possibly there is a connection, for Cameron was prominent in the committee that worked with Percival on the project (see below).

155. The engine house may date from the original 1832 construction or possibly from the rebuilding campaign under W. J. Hicks for the McCulloch Gold Mine in 1852, after the North Carolina Railroad arrived (Smith, *Guilford County*, 17, 136; John Leonard Rigsbee, "William J. Hicks," in *DNCB*, 3:128–29).

156. Black, *Burlington*, 16, 51. The architect of the Company Shops buildings is not known. However, on August 6, 1858, W. S. Andrews, an architect from Columbus, Ohio, advertised in the *Greensboro Patriot* his willingness to provide plans for public buildings, villas, and cottages; among his references was Cyrus P. Mendenhall of Greensboro, an officer of the North Carolina Railroad.

157. Sandbeck, *New Bern and Craven County*, 121–22.

158. *Carolina Watchman*, Nov. 2, 1858. On Hendren's work on the building, see *Carolina Watchman*, Oct. 2, 1855; *Salisbury Herald*, Mar. 11, 1857; *Carolina Watchman*, Mar. 17, 1857, Apr. 20, 1858, courtesy of James Brawley; and Davyd Foard Hood, "A. B. Hendren," biographical sketch, in possession of author.

159. *North Carolina Standard*, Nov. 16, 1859.

160. Bushong, "William Percival." See also Lawrence Wodehouse, "The Elusive William Percival, Architect, and Pre–Civil War Follower of Upjohn, Downing, and Town and Davis," typescript, ca. 1970, copy in Historical Publications Section, A&H; William B. Bushong, "Montfort Hall and Its Architect, William Percival," master's thesis, Appalachian State University, 1979.

161. *North Carolina Standard*, Nov. 16, 1859.

162. *The Struggles and Fruits of Faith: First Baptist Church, Raleigh, North Carolina* (Raleigh: privately published, 1962), 18–31; *North Carolina Standard*, Nov. 16, 1859. In a characteristic pattern, the church began in 1812 with 9 white and 14 black members; by 1826 there were 224 members, of whom two-thirds were blacks. After troubled times in the 1830s, growth resumed in the 1840s, and a new emphasis on decorum put aside such old forms as "shouting" and public footwashing. In 1856 the congregation obtained a new pastor, Thomas E. Skinner, a graduate of the University of North Carolina and holder of a doctorate in theology. The church history notes, "The year 1856 can justly be called the most important single year in the history of the church since its founding in 1812. In that year The Raleigh Baptist Church ceased to be a struggling institution, frequently dependent upon outside support and sometimes with its very existence in serious doubt. It became instead, and has remained, an institution worthy of the capital city of a growing state" (*Struggles and Fruits of Faith*, 28).

163. Allcott, *Campus at Chapel Hill*, 44–49; Henderson, *Campus of the First State University*, 148–53. The building committee consisted of David L. Swain, William H. Battle of

Chapel Hill, and William A. Graham of Hillsborough. Paul Cameron was added in 1859 and provided money to complete the buildings (Bushong, "William Percival," 323–25).

164. *North Carolina Standard*, Nov. 16, 1859 (from a conversation with Percival), quoted in Bushong, "William Percival," 323. See also ibid., 319; Allcott, *Campus at Chapel Hill*, 48–49.

165. Elizabeth Dancy Battle, "James Smith Battle" and "William Smith Battle," in *DNCB*, 1:112, 118–19.

166. William Bushong ("William Percival," 327–33) and Lawrence Wodehouse ("Elusive William Percival") compare the rotundas of the Battle and Montfort houses with the Capitol. Also see Bushong on Percival's work on the Capitol, which acquainted him intimately with the building. On William Montfort Boylan, a leisure-loving playboy, and his father, William Boylan, a New Jersey native who became a rich planter, journalist, president of the Raleigh and Gaston Railroad, and supporter of the North Carolina Railroad, see Sarah McCulloh Lemmon, "William Boylan," in *DNCB*, 1:205; Bushong, "Montfort Hall." The rotunda columns in Montfort Hall feature capitals with squirrels and doves, surely a reference to its resident's penchant for hunting. Harrison was a landowner and railroad entrepreneur who built the house in anticipation of his marriage to Margaret Jeffreys of Franklin County (Bushong, "William Percival," 331–33).

167. *North Carolina Standard*, Nov. 16, 1859; Bushong, "William Percival," 317, 338.

168. Powell Family Papers, 1859–61, private collection, photocopies in possession of author. The Powells also traded by rail and water with other markets, including Wilmington, North Carolina, and Norfolk, Richmond, and Petersburg, Virginia.

169. J. D. Hufham, *Memoir of Rev. John L. Prichard* (Raleigh: Hufham and Hughes, 1867), 117–25, quoted in Wrenn, *Wilmington*, 211–12.

Chapter 4

1. On developments in this period, see Dwight B. Billings, Jr., *Planters and the Making of the "New South": Class, Politics, and Development in North Carolina, 1865–1900* (Chapel Hill: University of North Carolina Press, 1979); Escott, *Many Excellent People*; Hall et al., *Like a Family*; Nathans, *Quest for Progress*; Tullos, *Habits of Industry*.

2. *Tarboro Southerner*, Mar. 15, 1883.

3. *Union Republican* (Winston), Jan. 14, 1886, Jan. 6, 1887, quoted in Taylor, *Frontier to Factory*, 37.

4. See Charlotte V. Brown's discussion of architectural change in this period in *ABNC*, 247–57. On Victorian-era architecture in North Carolina, see Schumann et al., *Grand Old Ladies*.

5. *Union Republican*, Jan. 14, 1886, quoted in Taylor, *Frontier to Factory*, 37. See Carl Lounsbury's analysis of the industrialization of building in *ABNC*, 193–239, and "From Craft to Industry."

6. Stick, *Outer Banks*, 288–91; *North Carolina Lighthouses*, 63–67 (quote, 63); Ronald G. Warfield, "Cape Hatteras Light Station," NR form, 1977. On Fresnel lenses, see *North Carolina Lighthouses*, 49–50. The other day marks are: Cape Lookout in checkers (diamonds), Bodie Island in horizontal bands, and Currituck, in natural red brick (Stick, *North Carolina Lighthouses*, 68–69). In recent years Cape Hatteras Lighthouse has been threatened with erosion and several alternatives have been suggested for its preservation, including moving it.

7. Stick, *Outer Banks*, 259.

8. Personal communication from John Wilson, Apr. 10, 1989, based on interviews with longtime local residents and children of former lighthouse keepers; copy of published drawing of Keepers Dwelling, 1875, NA; photograph of an inscription in attic, where W. C. Horner, a German house builder from Baltimore, wrote that he had finished the job on May 8, 1876 (courtesy of John Wilson, June 1989).

9. This account is drawn from York, "Architecture of the United States Life-Saving Stations" (thesis) and "Architecture

of the U.S. Life-Saving Stations" (article); Stick, *Outer Banks*, 168–79, which gives a concise history of North Carolina's life-saving stations.

10. W. D. O'Connor, "The United States Life-Saving Service," in *Appleton's Annual Encyclopedia of the Year 1878* (New York: D. Appleton and Co., 1889), 759, quoted in York, "Architecture of the U.S. Life-Saving Stations," 7.

11. York, "Architecture of the U.S. Life-Saving Stations," 6–7.

12. Touart, *Building the Back Country*, 55. In 1978 the depot was moved across the tracks from the south to the north side and restored for community use; as a result, the ticket bay that once faced the tracks now faces the main street.

13. Woodward began publishing regularly in the late 1860s: *Woodward's Country Homes* (1865), *Woodward's Architecture* (1867), *Woodward's Cottages and Farm Houses* (1867), and *Woodward's National Architect* (1868), as well as a quarterly magazine. A. J. Bicknell published *Bicknell's Village Builder* (1870), *Supplement to Bicknell's Village Builder* (1871), *Detail, Cottage and Constructive Architecture* (1873), *Wooden and Brick Buildings with Details* (1875), and *Specimen Book of One Hundred Architectural Designs* (1879). See Garvin, "Mail-Order House Plans," 310–12.

14. Upton, "Pattern Books and Professionalism," 144–45.

15. Catherine W. Bishir, "Jonathan McGee Heck," in *DNCB*, 3:92–94; Kemp Battle, quoted in Bishir, "Jonathan McGee Heck," and Lizzie Wilson Montgomery, *Sketches of Old Warrenton* (Raleigh: Edwards and Broughton, 1924), 262; Specification for a House for Mrs. J. M. Heck [1869], and Contract, Mrs. J. M. Heck with Wilson & Waddell, July 22, 1869, J. M. Heck Collection, A&H; "Heck-Andrews House," NR form, 1971. John A. Waddell had worked with Jacob Holt before the war and had erected Cherry Hill in Warren County (Catherine W. Bishir, "John A. Waddell," typescript biography, 1980, in possession of author).

16. Appleget had moved to Charlotte and was advertising for work (*Charlotte Daily Observer*, May 26, 1875).

17. *Supplement to Bicknell's Village Builder* (New York: A. J. Bicknell and Co., 1871).

18. Cotton, *Historic Burke*, 150.

19. Catherine Cockshutt [Bishir] and Jim Sumner, "Thomas Capehart House," NR form, 1977.

20. Catherine Bishir and Joe Mobley, "Chosumneeda," NR form, 1979. Thomas Coates, who worked with Percival as contractor before the war, may have built these houses and also completed the church.

21. Patricia S. Dickinson, "William Alfred Moore House," NR form, 1985; Downing, *Treatise on . . . Landscape Gardening*, 423–32, quoted in ibid. See also Downing, *Cottage Residences*, 123, 171. Both Rachel and William Moore came from families long prominent in the northwestern Piedmont.

22. Davyd Foard Hood and Joe Mobley, "The Solomon and Henry Weil Houses," NR form, 1976. Henry Weil to Mina Rosenthal, July 1874, quoted in Moses Roundtree, *Strangers in the Land: The Story of Jacob Weil's Tribe* (Philadelphia: Dorrance and Company, 1969), 29, 33. Appleget might have designed these houses as well: he claimed to have designed "all the best buildings, with only a few exceptions in Raleigh, Goldsboro, and Greensboro" (*Charlotte Daily Observer*, May 26, 1875).

23. Mena Webb, *Jule Carr: General without an Army* (Chapel Hill: University of North Carolina Press, 1987), 47–50, 67–69, 105; *Tobacco Plant* (Durham), Mar. 8, 1876. The *Raleigh Daily Sentinel*, Oct. 6, 1875, noted that the "well-known building firm of Wilson and Waddill [sic], who put up Col. Heck's elegant residence" in Raleigh, was building a cotton factory on the Haw River in Alamance County and a hotel and "handsome residence" for W. T. Blackwell in Durham. According to W. G. Wilson, Jr., grandson of John M. Wilson, the firm also built the Julian Carr residence in Durham (W. G. Wilson, Jr., letter to the editor, *Raleigh News and Observer*, Oct. 27, 1980).

24. *Tarboro Southerner*, Nov. 15, 1877. Carpenter William Walling was building the Methodist Church nearby and may have been involved in the Simmons House; local carpenter Cason

Emery Swindell is also identified as probable builder.

25. Swaim, *Cabins and Castles*, 86, 100, 131.

26. Interviews with Princess Polson and Forrest and Joyce White, longtime neighbors of the Lassiters, and Mary Lee Lassiter Taylor, granddaughter of John R. Lassiter, conducted by Brad Barker, Gates County, Apr. 1989. Polson, the Whites, and Taylor remembered the names only of recent tenants: Sam and Gladys Jones in the 1940s and John and Eva Blanchard in the 1950s. For a firsthand account of rural housing and living conditions in one eastern North Carolina county, see Boyce, *Economic and Social History of Chowan County*.

27. Cotton, *Historic Burke*, 195.

28. Personal communication from Margaret Long Stephenson, Murfreesboro, Nov. 1989; Bishir, "Jacob W. Holt," 6, 19. In the Jan. 11, 1877, *Murfreesboro Enquirer*, J. P. Phillips advertised that having served his apprenticeship under the "well-known Contractor and Builder Jacob W. Holt, Esq.," he was prepared to build "in the best and most modern styles."

29. Richard Mattson to author, Aug. 8, 1988 (reporting his interview with Annie Pearl Brantley of Spring Hope, N.C., on the Matthews family).

30. This discussion is based on several survey publications, including Swaim, *Cabins and Castles*, 62–63; Cotton, *Historic Burke*, 17–19; Little-Stokes, *Caswell County*, 9–20; Smith, *Guilford County*; Williams, *Marble and Log*, 36. For a study of the use of small, mainly log houses in one region during this period, see Michael Ann Williams, "The Little 'Big House': The Use and Meaning of the Single-Pen Dwelling," in Wells, *Perspectives in Vernacular Architecture, II*, 130–36. See also Williams, "Homeplace." For perspectives on similar houses in Kentucky, see Charles E. Martin, *Hollybush: Folk Building and Social Change in an Appalachian Community* (Knoxville: University of Tennessee Press, 1984).

Our picture of various periods of log construction, as with all other types of construction, is skewed by surviving evidence. Time and change have erased from the landscape all but the sturdiest buildings from the more distant past, so that of the thousands of crude log and frame houses of the eighteenth and early nineteenth centuries, none now survive; hence our image of early houses draws disproportionately from the best examples. In early twentieth-century photographs and a few extant buildings from the late nineteenth and early twentieth centuries we can see the last vestiges, the final generations, of age-old traditions of handmade minimal housing. Even this last generation of minimal housing has all but vanished, and most of those that still stand are vacant and decaying. Within the last half-century, mass production has halted that tradition and transformed the production of minimal housing, for the mobile home and prefabricated house serve a somewhat comparable market today.

31. Swaim, *Cabins and Castles*, 133; subsequent fieldwork by Douglas Swaim, 1988.

32. See Swaim, *Cabins and Castles*, 62.

33. The remote location of these two houses is also typical of extant log structures—not so much of the patterns that once existed, for log buildings were formerly more widespread in the landscape, but of those structures that have survived recent decades of change and development.

34. Cotton, *Historic Burke*, 200.

35. Carl Lounsbury and George W. McDaniel, "Recording Plantation Communities: Report on the Architectural and Historical Resources at Stagville," typescript research report, 1980, copy in "Stagville" survey file, Survey and Planning Branch, A&H; Little-Stokes, *Caswell County*, 9–20; Smith, *Guilford County*, 94; interview with Clapp family, conducted by author, Guilford County, Spring 1988. Although a few years later the Clapp family expanded their quarters more dramatically by building a spacious frame house, a daughter still remembers that, for her mother, the big change was the second log house that gave her a separate kitchen.

36. Haley and Winslow, *Perquimans County*, 61–62.

37. Dan Pezzoni, "Futral Family Farm," NR form, 1989.

38. See, for example, Hood, *Rowan County*, 32–38; Kaplan, *Cabarrus County*, 20–21; Cotton, *Historic Burke*, 181; Swaim, *Cabins and Castles*, 61, 115.

39. Examination of building and interview with Norman Young, conducted by author, Mitchell County, May 1988.

40. See, for example, the early twentieth-century Chastain and Robinson double-crib barns in Cherokee County, described in Williams, *Marble and Log*, 37, 103, 113. On the four-crib barns, see Williams, *Marble and Log*, 106; Swaim, *Cabins and Castles*, 61, 125; Glassie, *Pattern in Material Folk Culture*, 89. Over the border in Tennessee, a dramatic variation evolved wherein cantilevered second levels were built atop double-crib barns, but this form is not common in North Carolina.

41. Personal communications from Douglas Swaim and Michael Southern, 1986–89.

42. Interviews with Frank Baird (Baird Farm) and Francis Pressly (Mast Farm), conducted by author, Valle Crucis, Watauga County, May 1988.

43. Greer Suttlemyre and Joe Mobley, "William A. Graham, Jr., Farm," NR form, 1977; interview with Walter Clark, Graham Farm, Mar. 25, 1989, conducted by author. Graham was the son of Gov. William A. Graham of Hillsborough. See also Lowell J. Soike, *Without Right Angles: The Round Barns of Iowa* (Des Moines: Iowa State Historical Department, 1983).

44. This discussion is drawn from Tilley, *Bright-Tobacco Industry*, 37–82; Jim Sumner, "North Carolina Tobacco Barns," *North Carolina Historic Preservation Office Newsletter* (Summer 1989): 12–16; Ligon Flynn and Roman Stankus, "Carolina Tobacco Barns: Form and Significance," in Swaim, *Carolina Dwelling*, 112–17; Laura Scism, "North Carolina Tobacco Barns: History and Function," in ibid., 118–27.

45. Marvin A. Brown and Patricia Esperon, "Puckett Family Farm," NR form, 1987. See also Brown, *Heritage and Homestead*.

46. Tilley, *Bright-Tobacco Industry*, 83–88.

47. Cotton, *Historic Burke*, 95; Dana E. Mintzer, "Waldensian Presbyterian Church," NR form, 1984. See also the recollections of Frank Refour, who came to Valdese in 1893 as a small child, in Judy Barlow, "He Remembers Early Waldensia," *Morganton News-Herald*, Aug. 25, 1971. For information on Waldensian architecture, I am indebted to J. Randall Cotton, Millie Barbee, and Ethel Bonnet, who guided me on an informative tour of Waldensian communities in the Cottian Alps in May 1985. See also Corrado Gavanelli, "Architettura Valdese," unpublished report, Politecnico Di Milano, 1985, courtesy of Millie Barbee; John Pons, *A History of the Waldenses* (Valdese: privately published, 1968); George B. Watts, *The Waldenses in the New World* (Durham: Duke University Press, 1941); idem, *The Waldenses of Valdese* (Charlotte: Heritage Printers, 1965).

48. Cotton, *Historic Burke*, 90–100. Especially notable is the Dalmas House (1929), with Waldensian symbols executed in stonework. Waldensian stonemasons worked not only in their own community but in distant North Carolina locations where their skills were in demand. Gimghoul Castle in Chapel Hill and some of the stonework along the Blue Ridge Parkway, for example, are said to be the work of Waldensian stonemasons.

49. Lead stonemasons were James H. Tron, Eli Bertalot, and Henry J. Long; John Garrou contracted to slake lime; John Guigou was in charge of hauling rock; and Henry Vinay took charge of carpentry (Mintzer, "Waldensian Presbyterian Church"). See Mrs. Louis Philip Guigou, "Historical Sketch of the Waldenses and the Waldensian Presbyterian Church, Valdese, N.C.," and "History of the Waldensian Presbyterian Church—Valdese, N.C., 1883–1960," typescript church histories, copies at Waldensian Presbyterian Church, Valdese. The Waldenses of Valdese maintain a strong sense of their heritage, manifest in continuing contact with their home valleys and in their festivals, religious observances, and an outdoor drama tracing their story.

50. See the following articles in Wilson and Ferris, *Encyclopedia of Southern Culture*: James F. White, "Church Architecture," 1276–77; Charles Reagan Wilson, "African Methodist

Episcopal Churches," 1311; F. Joseph Mitchell, "Methodist Episcopal Church, South," 1321–22; Charles Reagan Wilson, "National Baptists," 1324; James H. Smylie, "Presbyterian Church in the United States," 1325–26; Lawrence L. Brown, "Protestant Episcopal Church," 1327; Bill J. Leonard, "Southern Baptist Convention," 1330–31. When congregations split along racial lines, the predominantly white group usually retained the original church property and building; sometimes they aided the black congregation in building a new church. For an analysis of different denominational developments among black and white congregations, see Roberta Sue Alexander, *North Carolina Faces the Freedmen: Race Relations during Presidential Reconstruction, 1865–67* (Durham: Duke University Press, 1985), 66–67.

51. On symbolism and space in country churches (focusing on fieldwork in Alleghany and Hyde counties), see Eliza Davidson, "North Carolina Country Churches: Explorations in the Mountains and the Tidewater," in Swaim, *Carolina Dwelling*, 184–95.

52. Cotton, *Historic Burke*, 115–16; "New Church Dedication," *Blue Ridge Blade*, Oct. 25, 1879, quoted in Dana E. Mintzer, "Gilboa Methodist Church," NR form, 1984. Church members are reported by tradition to have made most of the furniture. Church member Taylor Duckworth is credited with carving the dove, which was installed about 1900.

53. Swaim, *Cabins and Castles*, 131. Malinda Payne gave the land and money for the chapel.

54. *Tarboro Southerner*, Nov. 15, 1877; "Fairfield," Hyde County survey file, Survey and Planning Branch, A&H.

55. *Fayetteville Observer*, Mar. 27, 29, 1897, courtesy of Jim Sumner; Edward Turberg and Walter Best, "St. Joseph's Episcopal Church," NR form, 1980. Eva Cochran, daughter of a Yonkers rug manufacturer, Alexander Smith, also gave a somewhat similar, shingled Gothic Revival church to Sorrento, Maine, a summer colony community. Whether the two churches share a single (yet unidentified) Boston architect is unknown (Roy Parker, Jr., "Setting the Record Straight," *Fayetteville Times*, Aug. 14, 1983; personal communication from Richard Chafee, July 26, 1989).

56. Haley and Winslow, *Perquimans County*, 233.

57. *Spirit of Missions*, Sept. 1875, quoted in Wrenn, *Wilmington*, 152. St. Mark's was organized in 1858 as a racially mixed congregation but became a black mission in 1866. Emerson and Fehmer of Boston were partners from 1870 to 1885, and Emerson was an early and influential proponent of the shingle and Colonial Revival styles.

58. Wrenn, *Wilmington*, 117–19; *Wilmington Star*, May 13, 1876, and *American Israelite*, n.s. 4, no. 21, quoted in *Seventy-fifth Anniversary, Temple of Israel, Wilmington, North Carolina, May 12, 1951* (Wilmington: Temple of Israel, 1951), 9; *Wilmington Star*, Dec. 16, 1869, Aug. 15, 1875.

59. Rev. L. S. Burkehead, "History of the Difficulties of the Pastorate of the Front Street Methodist Church, Wilmington, N.C., for the Year 1865," in *Historical Papers of Trinity College*, ser. 8 (Durham: Trinity College Historical Society, 1909), 33–118, cited in W. McKee Evans, *Ballots and Fence Rails: Reconstruction on the Lower Cape Fear* (New York: Norton, 1974), 24–25; W. A. Cade, "William Meredith, the Founder of Methodism in Wilmington," typescript history of Front Street Methodist Church, in Grace Methodist Church Records (Wilmington, N.C.), microfilm copy in A&H. Methodism in Wilmington, as in many other communities, had begun primarily among blacks. As early as 1803, Francis Asbury recorded in his diary of his visit to Wilmington: "I met the people of color, leaders and stewards; we have eight hundred and seventy-eight Africans, and a few whites in fellowship" (quoted in Wrenn, *Wilmington*, 136). See also Nathans, *Quest for Progress*, 72–73.

60. *Wilmington Star*, Jan. 7, 1885, quoted in Wrenn, *Wilmington*, 137.

61. In 1913 the church built a handsome annex with important community facilities: classrooms for teaching of domestic sci-ence, a swimming pool, and a doctor's office (Wrenn, *Wilmington*, 137–38).

62. See A. Robert Jaeger, "The Auditorium and Akron Plans—Reflections of a Half Century of American Protestantism," master's thesis, Cornell University, 1984.

63. Wrenn, *Wilmington*, 149–50.

64. William H. Huffman, "Grace A.M.E. Zion Church, Survey and Research Report," Charlotte-Mecklenburg Historic Properties Commission, 1980, copy in Survey and Planning Branch, A&H; Thomas W. Hanchett, "W. W. Smith, Black 'Designer and Builder,'" *North Carolina Preservation*, no. 67 (Spring 1987): 7–9. Hanchett notes that Smith and his wife were founding members of the church in 1886: Smith is said to have promised to supply the men if the congregation would provide the materials. The congregation, established as a temperance congregation in 1886, worshiped in a frame church from 1887 to 1898 and by 1900 had begun "a handsome brick church 55 by 90 and ornamented with three towers . . . the largest negro church in Charlotte" (*The Star of Zion*, Nov. 1, 1900).

65. Davyd Foard Hood, "The Architecture of the New River Valley," in Swaim, *Carolina Dwelling*, 214–15; Hood, *Rowan County*, 82–84, 122–23.

66. Gayle Hicks Fripp, "West Market Street Methodist Episcopal Church, South," NR form, 1985. Stained-glass windows for the church are said to have come from the German Pavilion at the 1893 World's Columbian Exposition in Chicago. Brick was made locally at the Kirkpatrick Brick Yard; granite trim was from Mount Airy, North Carolina. The Bain Building Company, later the Cape Fear Manufacturing Company, produced the original woodwork. The sanctuary was remodeled in 1957.

67. Wrenn, *Wilmington*, 31. See Charlotte V. Brown's analysis of trends in urban commercial architecture in *ABNC*, 248–51.

68. Wrenn, *Wilmington*, 183–84. McMillen was a Minnesota architect who came to Wilmington to design the Masonic Temple and took several additional commissions in the state.

69. The Brittain Store was built in the 1870s for Henry Clay Brittain by George J. Smith and his son, who were contractors, carpenters, and coffin makers. Across the intersection, Brittain's cousin Noah Webster Ogburn built a store of similar scale and competing detail (Smith, *Guilford County*, 164).

70. "Art in Business Blocks," *Asheville Daily Citizen*, Aug. 16, 1895, cited in Black, *Downtown Asheville*, 22, 46.

71. See *History of Public Buildings*; *ABNC*, 273–74.

72. Wodehouse, "Alfred B. Mullett"; Correspondence and Reports, 1857–74, Wake County Post Office and Courthouse, Letters Received, Public Buildings Services, 1843–1910, RG 121, NA.

73. *History of Public Buildings*, 438–57, lists the projects as follows: Asheville—authorized and appropriated 1888, built 1890–93, cost $99,255.13; Charlotte—authorized 1888, appropriated 1888–90, built 1889–91, cost not stated; Greensboro—authorized 1882, built 1883–86, cost $52,683.23; New Bern—authorized 1889, appropriated 1889–91, built 1895–97, cost $68,746.60; Raleigh—appropriated 1857, built 1874–79, cost $341,496.87; Reidsville—authorized 1891, appropriated 1891, built 1893–94, cost $20,935.89; Statesville—authorized 1888, appropriated 1888–92, built 1890–91, cost $72,972.27; Wilmington—built 1888–91, cost $156,513.36.

74. Charlotte V. Brown treats this project in detail in *ABNC*, 274–77; Michael T. Southern, "Peter Demens," *North Carolina Preservation* 65 (Oct./Nov. 1986): 7–9.

75. Kaplan, *Cabarrus County*, 38.

76. Sandbeck, *New Bern and Craven County*, 227.

77. Wrenn, *Wilmington*, 73–74.

78. Ruth Little-Stokes and Robert Topkins, "Lea Laboratory," NR form, 1975. Ellington, Royster, and Company of Raleigh reportedly built the structure of penitentiary brick.

79. Murray, *Wake*, 598–99. See also William J. Hicks obituary, undated newspaper clipping [1913], William J. Hicks Collec-

tion, A&H; various reports and accounts in Central Prison Collection, A&H.

80. Waugh, *North Carolina's Capital*, 144–45. The Supreme Court Building is now the Labor Building. Main Building of the State College of Agricultural and Mechanic Arts is now Holladay Hall at North Carolina State University.

81. This account is drawn mainly from Cooledge, *Samuel Sloan*, and Bushong, "A. G. Bauer."

82. Cooledge, *Samuel Sloan*, 103–4; Bushong, "A. G. Bauer," 308–9. By this time in the North, competing architectural philosophies, such as the "Cottage System" of small units, were in favor for hospitals for the insane (Cooledge, *Samuel Sloan*, 106–7). James Walker was the Scots-born Wilmington builder who built Sloan's antebellum First Presbyterian Church; he was the brother of John Walker, contractor for the Wilmington Marine Hospital.

83. Bushong, "A. G. Bauer," 311–13 (Bushong notes that this building also was to be built of penitentiary bricks); Kemp Battle, *Sketches of the History of the University of North Carolina* (1889), quoted in Cooledge, *Samuel Sloan*, 112. Paul Cameron, chairman of the building committee for the university after the war, bailed the project out by supplying $8,000 to complete the building, and he gave the dedication address at the opening (Anderson, *Piedmont Plantation*, 127). Another $10,000 was raised by selling marble memorial tablets to families of alumni and setting the inscribed tablets into the walls of the hall; Swain's name was thus removed from the title. In the 1910s and 1920s its extreme form and inconvenient arrangements attracted growing disfavor, and it was razed in 1930, one of very few major campus buildings to be destroyed. Archibald Henderson describes it as "a huge antediluvian monster of the turtle variety . . . an architectural monstrosity . . . execrable" (*Campus of the First State University*, 198–99, 200).

84. *The Executive Mansion, Raleigh, North Carolina*, 5th ed. (Raleigh: North Carolina Department of Cultural Resources, 1985), 10–11; Thomas J. Jarvis to William L. Saunders, Sept. 20, 1877, William Laurence Saunders Papers, A&H, cited in Bushong, "A. G. Bauer," 310; *Raleigh Sentinel*, Mar. 29, 1888, quoted in ibid., 310; Jack Zehmer and Sherry Ingram, "Executive Mansion," NR form, 1970. The letter from Jarvis to Saunders is a crucial, detailed account of the problems with the mansion, written by Jarvis while he was serving as minister to Brazil. See also "William J. Hicks, Architect and Warden: North Carolina State Penitentiary," undated [1880s] bills and receipts for materials for the mansion, Central Prison Collection, A&H.

85. *Raleigh News and Observer*, Jan. 14, 1891, quoted in Bushong, "A. G. Bauer," 311.

86. William T. Comstock, *Modern Architectural Designs and Details* (New York: William T. Comstock, 1881), preface. For a chronology and analysis of architectural journals, especially in the late nineteenth century, see Mary Woods, "The First American Architectural Journals: The Profession's Voice," *JSAH* 48, no. 2 (June 1989): 117–38.

87. On May 2, 1896, Bauer was in a train accident that resulted in permanent medical problems. And on Jan. 9, 1897, his wife Rachel died a few days after giving birth to a son. Bauer continued to work and also focused his attention on erecting a monument for Rachel in Raleigh's Oakwood Cemetery in the spring of 1897. See Bushong, "A. G. Bauer"; Carmen Andrew Prioli, "The Indian 'Princess' and the Architect," *NCHR* 60, no. 3 (July 1983): 283–303.

88. Swaim, *Cabins and Castles*, 79–80, 40. The *American Architect and Building News* issue dated August 22, 1891, illustrated the Kenilworth Inn. The Kenilworth burned in 1909, and the Battery Park was razed in the 1920s to make way for a new Battery Park Hotel, in whose lobby is a tile image of its predecessor. The Zinzendorf Hotel in Winston was built from designs by Wheelwright and Haven of Boston; it burned in 1892 (*American Architect and Building News*, July 25, 1891; Taylor, *Frontier to Factory*, 38–39).

39. Webb, *Jule Carr*, 104–12; Charles Phillips to A. J. Davis, Nov. 28, 1888, A. J. Davis Collection, Avery Architectural and Fine Arts Library, Columbia University.

90. Durden, *Dukes of Durham*, 152; Roberts et al., *Durham*, 233–34.

91. Gwynne S. Taylor, "Hylehurst," NR form, 1983. Fries, son of antebellum Salem industrial modernizer Francis Fries, had with his brothers rebuilt the family business after the war and was now expanding it rapidly. See Anna Withers Bair, "John William Fries," in *DNCB*, 2:245.

92. Seapker, "James F. Post," 1, 3–4.

93. "Specifications of the Workmanship and Materials to Be Used in Alterations, Additions, and Remodeling of a Dwelling House for Colonel I. Young at Henderson, North Carolina," unsigned, undated [ca. 1883] manuscript in Ike Young Estate Papers, Granville County Records, A&H; Michael T. Southern, Jerry Cross, and Catherine Bishir, "Mistletoe Villa," NR form, 1978. The colors specified are similar to those that once enriched the Executive Mansion in Raleigh. Family tradition claims that the house was remodeled from a design by Sloan, though the architect may also have been Bauer.

94. See Allison H. Black and David R. Black, "Monroe Residential Historic District," NR form, 1987. Two versions of the story claim that the Meareses were attending either the Chicago World's Columbian Exposition of 1893 or a St. Louis fair in 1896 (none is known); the house is said to have been built in 1898. It seems more likely that the couple attended the Tennessee Centennial Exposition of 1897 in Nashville, which Knoxville architect Barber is believed to have attended regularly (telephone conversation with Michael A. Tomlan, Sept. 1989). Tomlan asserts that the house follows a popular Barber format.

95. This discussion is drawn from Tomlan, "Toward the Growth of an Artistic Taste," 5–19. See also Charlotte V. Brown's discussion of Barber's impact in North Carolina in *ABNC*, 277–79. In addition to Barber, George and Charles Palliser and Robert W. Shoppell published plan books and supplied plans and specifications by mail. Among their books were *Palliser's Model Homes for the People* (1876, 1878); *Palliser's American Cottage Homes* (1878); and Shoppell's *Artistic Modern Houses of Low Cost* (1881), *How to Build, Furnish and Decorate* (1883), and *Shoppell's Building Plans for Modern Low-Cost Houses* (1884); there were others throughout the century (see Garvin, "Mail-Order House Plans"). How extensively Palliser's and Shoppell's books or mail-order designs were used in North Carolina has not been determined.

96. Phillips, *Simple Treasures*, 36–37, 95.

97. Plans from George F. Barber for R. J. Reynolds residence, Reynolds Family Papers, Archives, Z. Smith Reynolds Library, Wake Forest University, Winston-Salem. The R. J. Reynolds House is pictured in Taylor, *Frontier to Factory*, 74.

98. Charles T. Holt was the son of former governor Thomas Michael Holt, who was the second son of Edwin's ten children. On the Holt houses, see Lounsbury, *Alamance County*, 34–61 (esp. 54, on the evolution of family tastes). Lounsbury notes some elements that Barber may have taken from William T. Comstock's *Modern Architectural Designs and Details* (1881). Tomlan reports that Barber owned several architectural books of the period, perhaps including works by Comstock and Bicknell, and certainly by Palliser ("Toward the Growth of an Artistic Taste," 6). See also Bess Beatty, "The Edwin Holt Family: Nineteenth-Century Capitalists in North Carolina," *NCHR* 63, no. 4 (Oct. 1986): 511–35; Linda Marquez-Freeze, Jerry L. Cross, and Davyd Foard Hood, "Charles T. Holt House," NR form, 1982. See Michael A. Tomlan to Davyd Foard Hood, Dec. 17, 1981 (copy in "C. T. Holt House" survey file, Survey and Planning Branch, A&H), which cites Barber references to the Holt house: the residence of "Charles T. Holt, son of ex-governor Holt," in "Some of Our Clients and Their Homes," an undated booklet by Barber (p. 3); Barber, *Modern Dwellings* (1898), 268–69; and Barber's *American Home* magazine, Oct. 1896, 116.

99. Webb, *Jule Carr*, 74–75; "Korner's Folly," NR form, 1972.

100. *Winston-Salem Journal and Sentinel*, Jan. 3, 1971. Max Schroff was listed with offices in New York from 1881 to 1900 (Dennis Steadman Francis, *Architects in Practice, New York City, 1840–1900* [New York: Committee for the Preservation of Architectural Records, 1980], 68).

101. The name combined the family's ancestral town of Bildt, Holland, with the English word "more," meaning rolling countryside (*Biltmore House and Gardens*, 2).

102. This discussion is drawn from Baker, *Richard Morris Hunt*, 412–32; David Chase, "Superb Privacies," in Stein, *Architecture of Richard Morris Hunt*, 151–71; *Biltmore House and Gardens* (Asheville: The Biltmore Company, 1976). Extensive original papers are collected at Biltmore and are analyzed in Susanne Brendel, "Documentation of the Construction of Biltmore House through Drawings, Correspondence, and Photographs," master's thesis, Columbia University, 1978.

103. For an analysis of Hunt's inventive planning, see Chase, "Superb Privacies." On the romanticism of Biltmore, see Baker, *Richard Morris Hunt*, 421.

104. Johnny Baxter, Betty Bettz, and Catherine Bishir, "Young Men's Institute," NR form, 1977; H. McKelden Smith and Susanne Brendel, "Biltmore Village," NR form, 1977; Swaim, *Cabins and Castles*, 184. Richard Sharp Smith was born in Yorkshire in 1852, trained in London, and at age twenty came to New York, where he worked for B. L. Gilbert and then for Hunt and Hunt. He was sent to superintend construction of Biltmore and remained in Asheville, where he had a prolific and illustrious architectural practice; he died in 1924.

105. Richard Morris Hunt, "The Church Architecture That We Need," address delivered to the Fourth Church Congress of the Protestant Episcopal Church, Oct. 30, 1877, and published in *American Architect and Building News*, Nov. 24, 1877, 374–76, and Dec. 1, 1877, 384–85. Quoted in Baker, *Richard Morris Hunt*, 257–58. Montgomery Schuyler has discussed Hunt's use of the "Byzantine type" for the "modern Protestant church" ("The Works of the Late Richard M. Hunt," *Architectural Record* 5 [Oct.–Dec. 1895]: 120–22).

106. E. L. Godkin, "The Expenditure of Rich Men," *Scribner's Magazine* 20, no. 4 (Oct. 1896): 497–500, and Joseph Lee, "Expensive Living, the Blight on America," *New England Magazine* 18 (Mar. 1890): 54, quoted in Chase, "Superb Privacies," 167–68.

107. T. H. Lindsay, "Biltmore House," *Southern Architect* 9, no. 1 (Nov. 1897): 318; Catherine Clinton Howell Hunt (Hunt's widow), quoted in Baker, *Richard Morris Hunt*, 431.

Chapter 5

1. *You Can't Go Home Again* (1934), Thomas Wolfe's account of change in "Libya Hill," describes the novelist's return from New York to his native Asheville during the booming growth of the late 1920s. On this period, see also David R. Goldfield, "North Carolina's Early Twentieth-Century Suburbs and the Urbanizing South," in Bishir and Earley, *Early Twentieth-Century Suburbs*, 9–19; Goldfield, *Cotton Fields and Skyscrapers*; Hobbs, *North Carolina: Economic and Social*; Lears, *No Place of Grace*; Nathans, *Quest for Progress*; Roth, *Concise History of American Architecture*; Tindall, *Emergence of the New South*; Wiebe, *Search for Order*; Woodward, *Origins of the New South*. See also Charlotte V. Brown's and Ernest Wood's analyses of architecture and building practices in *ABNC*, 290–428.

2. On the impact of rationalized management techniques, based on Frederick Taylor's time-motion studies, on textile workers after World War I, see Hall et al., *Like a Family*, 183–236.

3. Beaux Arts precepts, like the City Beautiful movement, stressed an order based on historical, mainly classical precedents; formal symmetry focusing on ceremonial axes for approach, entries, and movement within a city or a building; ornament designed to express a clear hierarchy of importance and the relationship of parts to the whole; and clearly expressed definitions of separate functional zones, whether these were public, private, and service spaces within a house or industrial, ceremonial, and residential sectors within a community. These ideas were in sharp contrast to the rampant, often uncontrolled, commercial and residential growth of the late nineteenth century. For a good, brief overview of this architecture and planning, see Roth, *Concise History of American Architecture*, 172–227. For an analysis of the City Beautiful movement in a social and cultural as well as an aesthetic context, see Daniel M. Bluestone, "Detroit's City Beautiful and the Problem of Commerce," *JSAH* 47, no. 3 (Sept. 1988): 245–62.

4. See William H. Pierson, Jr., "Richard Upjohn and the American *Rundbogenstil*," *Winterthur Portfolio* 21, no. 4 (Winter 1986): 223–42. As early as the 1840s, Rhode Island architect Thomas Tefft had employed the Romanesque style, with its towers, broad roofs, corbeled brickwork, and endless rows of arched windows, as a handsome and suitable model for America's factory architecture.

5. By 1907 the Durham Hosiery Mill had 11,000 spindles, 1,000 knitting machines, and 1,000 employees (see Barry Jacobs, "Durham Hosiery Mill Number One," NR form, 1978). The advent of silk hosiery reduced the demand for cotton hosiery, and after 1922 the structure was used for storage and other purposes; recently it has been converted to housing.

6. See Kaplan, *Cabarrus County*, 28–30; Brengle, *Gaston County*, 13–22. D. A. Tompkins (*Cotton Mill*, 158–70) describes the New England Factory Mutuals and the expansion of their insurance to "outside" mills built and equipped to their standards; he notes that "practically all" cotton mill insurance was written under this system. He lists general requirements, including: (1) automatic sprinkler systems: (2) outside water protection; (3) two separate sources of water supply; (4) "slow-burning" or "mill" construction; (5) continuous maintenance of steam pressure (in steam mills); (6) watchman with approved time detector clock; (7) fire organization of workers in mill. Tompkins also outlines features of slow-burning construction, including brick walls, heavy timbers, and thick floors, and defines the sections to be separated by fire walls.

7. The average number of spindles per factory rose from 1,885 in 1880 to 6,400 in 1900 and 10,000 in 1927. In 1900 eleven North Carolina mills had more than 20,000 spindles. This expansion after 1890 was caused in part by the flow of northern capital and the beginnings of the "exodus of northern mills to the South." The total value of textile manufacturing increased from about $30 million in 1900 to $450 million in 1930. The number of mills rose from 177 in 1900 to 579 in 1927. In 1900 the work force in the textile industry was made up of men (42 percent), women (34 percent), and children (24 percent). Steam-powered mills composed 16 percent of the total in 1880, 48 percent in 1890, and 64 percent in 1900 (Lefler and Newsome, *North Carolina*, 508–9, 581–82).

8. Brengle, *Gaston County*, 180.

9. Brent Glass, "Southern Mill Hills: Design in a 'Public' Place," in Swaim, *Carolina Dwelling*, 138–49; Hall et al., *Like a Family*, 114–20; Tullos, *Habits of Industry*, 18–24. See also Holland Thompson, *From Cotton Field to Cotton Mill* (New York: Macmillan, 1906); Brengle, *Gaston County*; Kaplan, *Cabarrus County*; Lounsbury, *Alamance County*; and Whatley, *Randolph County*.

10. Phillips, *Reidsville*, 32–33. Paradise Alley is now Landcaster Street.

11. Whatley, *Randolph County*, 111.

12. The Patterson Manufacturing Company was organized in China Grove, a village that grew up after a rail line was completed (Hood, *Rowan County*, 217, 222).

13. Tompkins, *Cotton Mill*, 117, 145.

14. On changes in management and labor relations after World War I, see Hall et al., *Like a Family*, 183–236; on the move toward professionally planned villages, see Glass, "Southern Mill Hills," 145–49 (quote, 148). E. S. Draper, "Southern Mill

Village Developments," *Textile World*, Apr. 2, 1921; (?) Thomas W. Hanchett, "Earle Sumner Draper," in Bishir and Earley, *Early Twentieth-Century Suburbs*, 79.

15. Mansell, "American Tobacco Company Brick Storage Warehouses," 12–17; Claudia Roberts Brown, "Smith Warehouse," "Watts and Yuille Warehouses," and "Bright Leaf District," NR forms, 1983; Roberts et al., *Durham*. The first American Tobacco Company warehouse was the one-story Walker Warehouse of 1897. W. J. Hicks, architect and warden of Central Prison in Raleigh, was involved in the project in some capacity, certainly as supplier of penitentiary brick, possibly as designer. He wrote Benjamin N. Duke that after consulting with Mr. Walker of the company, he had "made the figures for the brick considering the building would be 126 x 220 feet" but would adjust the amount if plans changed. "If you decide to make these or other changes will you please notify me, otherwise I will make the sketch as you have directed" (W. J. Hicks to B. N. Duke, Oct. 28, 1897, Letters to Benjamin Duke, 1891–98, Manuscripts Department, Duke University Library, quoted in Mansell, "American Tobacco Company Brick Storage Warehouses," 35).

16. Mansell, "American Tobacco Company Warehouses," 16–47.

17. The first floor of the Edenton Peanut Factory was for storage, the second for picking, the third and fourth floors for polishing, and the fifth floor contained hoppers. Most of the roughly 100 workers were blacks, and many were women. Originally the factory was powered by a steam engine fueled by peanut hulls (Barry Jacobs, "Peanut Factory/Edenton Peanut Company," NR form, 1978).

18. Lefler and Newsome, *North Carolina*, 517–18.

19. Nancy Roberts, "The Hamlet Station," *The State*, July 1, 1972, 8–9; Brent D. Glass, "Seaboard Coast Line Passenger Depot, Hamlet," Historic American Engineering Record Inventory Form, copy in Survey and Planning Branch, A&H; Lefler and Newsome, *North Carolina*, 517.

20. See Wodehouse, "Architecture in North Carolina," 29; idem, "Frank Pierce Milburn," 291–93, 301. Milburn's Union Station in Durham (1904–5) was of similar type but is no longer standing.

21. Allen Paul, "Southern Railway Spencer Shops," NR form, 1977. John Steele Henderson, part of Rowan County's industrializing, modernizing old elite, served as purchasing agent for the Southern (see John J. Beck, "Building the New South: A Revolution from Above in a Piedmont County," *Journal of Southern History* 53, no. 3 (Aug. 1987): 441–70.

22. Allen Paul, "Southern Railway Spencer Shops."

23. Telephone conversation with Richard Rogers, assistant fire chief, Henderson, Sept. 14, 1988. Rogers remembered using the tower for these purposes when he began to work there in 1957. Since then the horn and call box system has been discontinued, with telephones now used instead, and the firemen dry their hoses outdoors on racks.

24. See York, "Architecture of the United States Life-Saving Stations" and "Architecture of the U.S. Life-Saving Stations." The first shingled stations were remodelings of earlier stations, designed by service architect Albert B. Bibb. The influential Quonochontaug station was designed by Bibb's successor, George Russell Tolman (York, "Architecture of U.S. Life-Saving Stations," 11–18, and "Architecture of United States Life-Saving Stations," 58–59). North Carolina examples of the Quonochontaug type included Core Bank (1895), Oregon Inlet (1897–98), and Currituck Beach (1903). "Southern Pattern" stations included Little Kinnakeet, Ocracoke, Fort Macon, and Bogue Inlet, all built in 1904. Chicamacomico-type stations included Chicamacomico (1911), Kitty Hawk (1911), Nags Head (1912), and Poyners Hill (1913). The old Chicamacomico station was converted to use as a boathouse.

25. Bishir, "Unpainted Aristocracy"; *Elizabeth City Economist*, July 6, 1900; Edward R. Outlaw, Jr., *Old Nag's Head*, 2d ed. (Norfolk, Va.: privately printed, 1956), 21.

26. Jonathan Daniels to author, Oct. 1, 1976, quoted in Bishir, "Unpainted Aristocracy," 367.

27. *Raleigh News and Observer*, Sept. 8, 1929.

28. On Bacon, see Tony P. Wrenn, "Henry Bacon, Jr.," in *DNCB*, 1:77–79; Leslie Boney, "Henry Bacon, Jr.," typescript biography, 1987, copy in possession of author; Jan Avgikos, "Henry Bacon," in Placzek, *Macmillan Encyclopedia of Architects*, 1:123–24. Bacon was born in Illinois in 1866 but moved with his family to Southport, North Carolina, in 1876 when his father, an engineer, took charge of a major project at nearby New Inlet; in 1880 the family moved to Wilmington. Except for a year at school in Boston, Henry Bacon, Jr., attended school in Wilmington and was graduated from Tileston High School in 1884. Though he later lived mainly in New York, he maintained contact with Wilmington friends. He was buried in the Bacon family plot at Oakdale Cemetery, Wilmington.

29. Claudia P. Roberts [Brown], "Linville Historic District," NR form, 1978. Bacon designed Chesterwood for sculptor and friend Daniel Chester French, houses in Wilmington for MacRae's three children, and Live Oaks (1912) on Masonboro Sound near Wilmington for Walter and Agnes MacRae Parsley; she was Donald MacRae's sister. Live Oaks is an imposing residence built of local oystershell concrete called coquina. See Hood et al., *New Hanover County*, 22–23.

30. Hood et al., *New Hanover County*, 45–47; "Lumina Shone as Hub of Beach Life," *Wilmington Star-News*, Wilmington's 250th anniversary edition, July 23, 1989, 53. Lumina survived Hurricane Hazel in 1954 but was razed in 1973. In 1907 the Tidewater Power Company became the successor of the Consolidated Railways, Light, and Power Company (personal communications from Leslie Boney, Jr., May 1989, and Harry Warren and Janet K. Seapker, Oct. 6, 1989).

31. Wrenn, *Wilmington*, 83–84. See *Wilmington Messenger*, Feb. 7, 1901, quoted in ibid., 84.

32. Roberts, "Linville Historic District"; Linville Golf Club, *Yearbook 1978*, 6–7, quoted in ibid.

33. In "Linville Historic District," Claudia Roberts notes the similarity of the branch and bark work with motifs seen in *Palliser's New Cottage Homes and Details* (New York: Palliser, Palliser and Co., 1887). See also Ashton Chapman, "Chestnut Bark and Baronial Castles," *The State*, May 15, 1969, 13.

34. Swaim, *Cabins and Castles*, 87–88, 202.

35. Ibid., 88. See also William O. Moore, "Resort Asheville," *North Carolina Architect* 25, no. 4 (July/Aug. 1978): 21–25.

36. Little-Stokes, *Iredell County*, 73.

37. The buff-colored, "hydrolic-pressed" facing bricks (700,000 of them) came from Washington, D.C., while 1,000,000 common bricks came from the Glenola Brick Works. The entire building cost about $34,000, compared with a range among the other, similar courthouses from $20,000 for Ashe County to $70,000 for Stokes County (Whatley, *Randolph County*, 208). See also the courthouses in Scotland (1901), Ashe, Stokes, Wilkes, Watauga (all 1904), and Avery (1912) counties in Burns, *100 Courthouses*.

38. Frank Milburn's Durham County Courthouse, Greensboro architect Harry Barton's Johnston County Courthouse in Smithfield, C. C. Hook's Mecklenburg County Courthouse, and Louis Asbury's City Hall in Charlotte are among the many examples of the form.

39. In 1905, requiring more space for state government, state leaders had considered enlarging the Capitol; Frank Milburn submitted a design that essentially would have destroyed the antebellum building. This disaster was averted, however, and instead plans were made to erect a new building to accommodate the supreme court, library, and various offices (Wodehouse, "Frank Pierce Milburn," 294; Waugh, *North Carolina's Capital*, 176).

40. U.S. Postal Service, *History of Post Office Construction*, 3–7; James Knox Taylor, Annual Report of the Office of the Supervising Architect, 1901, quoted in Craig et al., *Federal Presence*, 232. With its Congressional influence strengthened after

the turn of the century, North Carolina obtained its share of Beaux Arts patronage architecture, including handsome federal buildings in Henderson, Salisbury, Washington, Durham, and Charlotte.

41. *Greenville Daily Reflector*, Mar. 20, 1912, quoted in Stanley Little and Maurice C. York, "United States Post Office/Federal Building," NR form, 1984.

42. Wrenn, *Wilmington*, 15–16.

43. Robert Topkins and Mary Alice Hinson, "Church of St. Lawrence," NR form, 1976; George R. Collins, "The Transfer of Thin Masonry Vaulting from Spain to America," *JSAH* 27, no. 3 (Oct. 1968): 176–201; "Listing of Guastavino Buildings in the State of North Carolina," list and letter from Collins to Bishir, Feb. 9, 1978, copies in "St. Lawrence" survey file, Survey and Planning Branch, A&H; Wrenn, *Wilmington*, 145–46. The elder Guastavino is buried in a vault within St. Lawrence, his name and work cited in a tablet of glazed tile. It is not entirely clear what Guastavino's role was in the design of St. Lawrence, for the firm of Smith and Carrier may have been involved in an important way—the firm's papers have recently been discovered and analysis of them is not yet complete (Douglas Swaim to author, Sept. 1988, telephone conversation).

44. Burroughs, *Complete Guide to Church Building*, 11–16, 27–29, 97–103. For a typical McMichael church, see First United Methodist Church in Elizabeth City, in Butchko, *On the Shores of the Pasquotank*, 174, 301.

45. Kaplan, *Cabarrus County*, 49, 122. The church was featured in *Southern Architect* 58 (Mar. 1932): 17–25. Grandson of Richard Upjohn, Hobart Upjohn of New York was one of the country's best-known church architects and worked in Gothic and colonial styles. In contrast to many of his contemporaries, who rejected Victorian-era architecture, Hobart Upjohn believed that "all ages of style and design have their beautiful spots" ("Chapel of the Cross," *American Architect*, Apr. 5, 1926, 410). Descriptions of Upjohn's projects in North Carolina were published in journals of the times: the Junior-Senior High School in Roanoke Rapids (*American Architect*, July 18, 1923, 62); Sprunt Presbyterian Church in Chapel Hill (*Architectural Record* 55 [Mar. 1924]: 253); Village Chapel in Pinehurst (*American Architect*, Feb. 20, 1926, 302); First Presbyterian in Wilmington (*American Architect*, Mar. 20, 1928, 358). He also designed several other buildings in North Carolina, including the library (1927, now Brooks Hall) at North Carolina State University (see *ABNC*, 322).

46. Cornerstone inscription, New Chapel Baptist Church, Plymouth.

47. Winston-Salem Section, NCAIA, *Architectural Guide to Winston-Salem, Forsyth County* (Winston-Salem: NCAIA, n.d.), 90.

48. Lauren-Brook Taves and Maurice C. York, "Roanoke Rapids High School," NR form, 1988; Mary Alice Hinson, Tony L. Gray, and Jerry Cross, "Gastonia High School," NR form, 1983; *Gastonia Daily Gazette*, May 22, 1924.

49. Wilson, *University of North Carolina*, 358–65; Allcott, *Campus at Chapel Hill*, 66. Nolen was engaged in planning Myers Park in Charlotte for developer George Stephens, a University of North Carolina alumnus; it was through Stephens that Nolen was invited by Graham to visit the university (Henderson, *Campus of the First State University*, 235–36). In his youth, Stephens had attended the World's Columbian Exposition in Chicago, which is believed to have influenced his ideas of planning (personal communication from George Stephens [grandson], Jan. 1990).

50. Wilson, *University of North Carolina*, 365–74; Allcott, *Campus at Chapel Hill*, 66.

51. Henderson, *Campus of the First State University*, 234–44, 271–84 (on design and construction), 341–52 (a commentary on the "architectural salvation" of the campus under McKim, Mead, and White), 363–69 (specific authorship of campus buildings). Quotes are from Arthur C. Nash, "Campus Architecture: Survey and Prospect," in ibid., 326–28. Nash stated his own sense of "Colonial" architecture (329):

One generally accepted definition of "Colonial" is: "Architecture such as prevailed in the British settlements of North America previous to the Revolution. It was chiefly a modification of the English Georgian style." There is still another way in which the term "Colonial Architecture" currently is used by architects and by the general public; that is, to make it include not only exact replicas of original buildings dating from that period, but, also, to have it include buildings whose only claim to the "Colonial" label is that they have their roots, so to speak, in Colonial soil; or, are carried out, with more or less success, in the Colonial tradition. This latter definition is one that I make use of in the present discussion. I make it inclusive, not only of buildings constructed within the strictly Colonial time-bracket, but, also, of post-Revolution buildings of the so-called "Late Colonial" or "Greek Revival" period; and even of modern buildings carried out in a Colonial manner.

Charlotte V. Brown describes the organization of this complex construction campaign in *ABNC*, 325–30.

52. Allcott, *Campus at Chapel Hill*, 51–54; Aberthaw Construction Company Report, Apr. 28, 1921, University Papers, University of North Carolina Library, Chapel Hill, quoted in ibid., 69; Henderson, *Campus of the First State University*, 346.

53. Durden, *Dukes of Durham*, 199–260. Some tales claim that Duke "bought" the university after unsuccessfully trying to "buy" Princeton and Yale, but see ibid., 235–37. The Duke Endowment, which continued established charitable interests of the family, assigned the income from an initial endowment of securities worth about $40,000,000 to benefit several schools, hospitals, orphanages, and the Methodist church—and Duke University, which was to receive 32 percent of the income. In addition, $6,000,000 was to go to establish the university; James B. Duke later added $2,000,000 to the building fund and $4,000,000 for a medical school. The Duke family were strong Methodists and evidently took to heart John Wesley's advice on money—to "make all you can, save all you can, give all you can."

54. Durden, *Dukes of Durham*, esp. 226–27. "We walked all over those grounds," recalled one participant, "jumping ditches and crossing wagon roads and going through shrubbery and all that kind of thing, with Mr. Duke always in the lead" (Dr. Watson Rankin, interview quoted in ibid., 239).

55. William King, "The Architecture of Duke University," slide lecture given at the annual meeting of the Historical Society of North Carolina, 1989. King notes that stonemasons were drawn from within the region, while the carvers came from northern cities and from Italy and Scotland. On the relation of Beaux Arts planning and Gothic architecture, see Turner, *Campus*, 245; William Maxwell Blackburn, *The Architecture of Duke University* (Durham: Duke University Press, 1939), 7–8.

56. The woodwork was executed by Irving and Casson/A. H. Davenport, Inc., of Boston. The ironwork was by William H. Jackson Company of New York (information from conversation with William King, Duke University Archivist, Sept. 6, 1988).

57. *The Duke University Chapel*, booklet produced by the Office of University Publications, Duke University, ca. 1987–88.

58. William King relates that the stonecutters' sheds stood near the chapel, and as the carvers produced the figures, students passing by took a keen interest in their work. The story is told that when the stonecutters completed each figure, they would bring it out for the students to admire. But when the Robert E. Lee figure was presented, the students began to snicker: the artisans had mistakenly inscribed Lee's belt buckle with "U.S."; corrected, they chiseled out the error (telephone conversation with William King, spring 1988).

59. Charles Keck of New York carved the recumbent figures.

Left to right, they are Benjamin Newton Duke (1855–1929), Washington Duke (1820–1905), and James Buchanan Duke (1856–1925) ("Duke University Chapel, Durham, North Carolina," undated brochure, ca. 1988; *Duke University Chapel*).

60. At Chapel Hill, Samuel Sloan's Memorial Hall, much castigated by the leaders of the new "colonial" school of building, was razed in 1930.

61. *Charlotte Daily Observer*, Jan. 16, 22, June 16, 1915; Mary Alice Hinson and Robert Topkins, "Latta Arcade," NR form, 1975.

62. Mary Alice Hinson, "Shell Service Station," NR form, 1975.

63. Earlier temple and vault banks had appeared in the neoclassical architecture of the antebellum period in major American cities, including William Strickland's Second Bank of the United States. But the widespread popularity of the vault and temple bank came to most American towns in the early twentieth century. On temple and vault forms and other types of commercial facades, see Richard Longstreth, "Compositional Types in American Commercial Architecture," in Wells, *Perspectives in Vernacular Architecture, II*, 12–23, esp. 17–18.

64. A banking firm organized by Alpheus Branch and partners in 1872 was reorganized in 1900 after Branch's death in 1893, and the new company, the Branch Banking Company, soon erected this building as the headquarters of an expanding operation. It evolved into today's large BB&T corporation (Mary Shoemaker and Vicki Craft, "Branch Banking and Trust Company Building," NR form, 1978). The rear three-bay extension of the building, designed in harmony with the original section, was added in 1934.

65. Letsinger, *Maxton*, 41. The architect is identified as Cliff Parrish of Rockingham. The clock tower is said to have been added shortly after the building was completed and funded with private subscriptions. The bank was named for its location in Robeson County.

66. Lea and Roberts, *Central Lumberton*, 18. The architect, said to have been named either Blue or Bethune, has not been identified further.

67. Condit, *American Building*, 241; Dan Morrill and Ruth Little-Stokes, "Independence Building," NR form, 1987; Janet Silber, "(Old) Masonic Temple Building," NR form, 1979.

68. Roberts et al., *Durham*, 40.

69. Black, *Downtown Asheville*, 27, 37.

70. Ruth Little-Stokes and H. McKelden Smith, "Jefferson Standard Building," NR form, 1975, which incorporates data from the authors' interview with architect Hartmann (Greensboro, Oct. 23, 1975). The George A. Fuller Company of Washington and New York took the construction contract, and work began on the $2,500,000 building in the summer of 1922. According to Hartmann, North Carolina suppliers united to raise their prices for materials, so that, except for the Mount Airy granite of the base, all materials were purchased outside the state.

71. Taylor, *Frontier to Factory*, 58; Tilley, *R. J. Reynolds Tobacco Company*, 322–70. In 1924 William N. Reynolds handed the presidency of the company to Bowman Gray and became chairman of the board. The firm moved away from "the dominance of its founder into the less personal sphere of corporate life" (ibid., 322). Richard H. Shreve and William F. Lamb worked with Carrère and Hastings before beginning their own firm in 1924. Arthur Harmon joined the firm in 1929 during planning for the Empire State Building (Christopher S. Gray, "Shreve, Lamb, and Harmon," in Placzek, *Macmillan Encyclopedia of Architects*, 4:54).

72. Roth, *Concise History of American Architecture*, 240.

73. Tilley, *R. J. Reynolds Tobacco Company*, 329; *R. J. Reynolds Tobacco Company Office Building*, undated promotional leaflet, ca. 1929, copy in possession of author. The R. J. Reynolds Building was featured along with the Empire State Building (under construction) in R. H. Shreve, "The Economic Design

of Office Buildings," *Architectural Record* 67 (Apr. 1930): 340–59. At the Reynolds Building, lower sections extend to the side and rear to form a U-shaped plan. Like the Jefferson Standard Building, the Reynolds Building was built to house not only company offices but also income-producing shops in the first story, a public arcade, and rental office space (telephone conversation with James A. Gray, Sept. 20, 1988). Mr. Gray recalled that the Reynolds Building began construction when the Nissen office tower was still underway. The crash of 1929 hurt rentals, but the Reynolds Building attracted tenants while the Nissen Building stood partly vacant and incomplete throughout the Great Depression, and only leases by federal government agencies during World War II permitted its completion. Although the Reynolds Building's promotional brochure stated that the fourth, fourteenth, and fifteenth floors were to be reserved for doctors and dentists, Mr. Gray does not recall such tenants; many of them had offices in the Nissen Building, and the Reynolds tenants tended to be lawyers, railroad and insurance companies, and other businesses with direct or indirect links to the tobacco business.

74. Roberts et al., *Durham*, 41. These Southern Bell buildings (1928–31) were designed by Oliver J. Vinour, partner of P. Thornton Marye of Atlanta in the firm of Marye, Alger, and Vinour (Harry W. Howell [successor firm] to T. S. Cates of Southern Bell, Feb. 25, 1977, and T. S. Cates to author, Mar. 2, 1977).

75. Edward Sibbert, notes, Feb. 28, 1977, and Mar. 27, 1979, provided to H. McKelden Smith and Catherine W. Bishir, with assistance of Hobart E. Lias and F. Edgar Kerby of Kress Company, copies in possession of author. Based on Sibbert's notes, his North Carolina stores are as follows (in Sibbert's notation, MR = Major Rebuilding): Charlotte, 101 S. Tryon St., 1941; Durham, 101 W. Main St., 1929; Fayetteville, 113 Maxwell St., 1929 (MR); Gastonia, 111 W. Main St., 1930; Goldsboro, 112 N. Center St., 1936; Greensboro, 108 S. Elm St., 1930; High Point, 141 S. Main St., 1940; New Bern, 307 Middle St., 1951 (MR); Raleigh, 102–4 Fayetteville St., 1953; Rocky Mount, 162 S. Main St., 1934 (MR); Salisbury, 300 S. Main St., 1936 (MR); Wilmington, 11 N. Front St., 1930 (MR). Sibbert had studied architecture at the Pratt Institute in Brooklyn and Cornell University, then worked in Miami Beach and New York City, where the Art Deco style was blossoming, before joining Kress in 1929. During his tenure as director, the firm's architectural division had from twenty to a hundred employees, depending on demand.

76. Sibbert notes.

77. *Asheville Citizen*, Jan. 31, 1922, quoted in Black, *Downtown Asheville*, 12.

78. Black, *Downtown Asheville*, 12–16, 23–30. After Grove died in 1927, construction stopped, and though the Grove Arcade was completed in 1929, the tower was never built (ibid., 14, 52).

79. Elma Towe, *Dedication of the First Baptist Church, Asheville, N.C.* (Asheville: First Baptist Church, 1927), 4; "First Baptist Church, Asheville," *Architectural Record* 68 (Aug. 1930): 107–18 (quote, 114); Mary Alice Hinson, H. McKelden Smith, and Robert Topkins, "First Baptist Church [Asheville]," NR form, 1976.

80. *Asheville Citizen*, Mar. 18, 1928, quoted in Black, *Downtown Asheville*, 29; Douglas D. Ellington, "The Architecture of the City Building, Asheville, North Carolina," *Architectural Record* 64 (Aug. 1928): 89–93, 125–36; Swaim, *Cabins and Castles*, 93–94; Susanne Brendel, "Urban Asheville," *North Carolina Architect* 25, no. 4 (July/Aug. 1978): 10–15.

81. *Asheville Citizen*, July 15, 1929. Frank O. Sherrill and Fred R. Webber, natives of western North Carolina, had served as mess sergeants in World War I and operated a lunch counter together in the Ivey's Department Store in Charlotte. They opened North Carolina's first cafeteria in Charlotte on July 14, 1920 (Mary Alice Hinson and Robert Topkins, "S & W Cafeteria," NR form, 1976).

82. See Gowans, *Comfortable House*; Clark, *American Family Home*, 131–92; Bishir and Earley, *Early Twentieth-Century Suburbs*, esp. Margaret Supplee Smith, "The American Idyll in North Carolina's First Suburbs: Landscape and Architecture," 21–30.

83. On the Colonial Revival in America, see Rhoads, *Colonial Revival* and "Colonial Revival and American Nationalism," upon which this discussion draws. See also Mardges Bacon, "Toward a National Style of Architecture: The Beaux-Arts Interpretation of the Colonial Revival," in Axelrod, *Colonial Revival in America*, 91–121.

84. See Rhoads, *Colonial Revival*, 125–42; Susan Prendergast Schoelwer, "Curious Relics and Quaint Scenes: The Colonial Revival at Chicago's Great Fair," in Axelrod, *Colonial Revival in America*, 184–216. On North Carolina women's unsuccessful efforts to replicate Tryon Palace, see *ABNC*, 294; William Stephenson, "How Sallie Southall Freeman Brought North Carolina to the Chicago World's Fair of 1893," *NCHR* 57, no. 4 (Oct. 1981): 372–76.

85. Catherine W. Bishir, "Building the Myth," paper delivered at annual meeting of the Organization of American Historians, 1987.

86. *Charlotte Observer*, Dec. 20, 1903, quoted in *ABNC*, 300–301. See Charlotte V. Brown's discussion of architects' promotional publications in ibid., 300–302, 478 (n. 22).

87. Gertrude S. Carraway, "James Bishop Blades," in *DNCB*, 1:170.

88. Janet K. Seapker, "Blades House," NR form, 1971; Sandbeck, *New Bern and Craven County*, 162–65, 377–78. See also plans and photographs of Simpson's work in Herbert Woodley Simpson Collection, A&H.

89. The Queen Anne style had frequently included classical elements such as Palladian windows and columns as part of the eclectic blend of motifs and forms. Thus, technically, the movement toward the classicized or "Colonial" Queen Anne house was not so much a radical change as a shift in emphasis within existing possibilities. However, among the mainstream of popular Queen Anne–style houses in North Carolina, the change was more noticeable. Earlier Queen Anne–style houses had tended to have turned, bracketed, occasionally half-timbered, and generally nonsymbolic millwork trim. The program of *predominantly* classical motifs appeared around the turn of the century.

90. Cotton, *Historic Burke*, 58. The house was designed by a Mr. Hillsinger, an architect who is said to have come from New York to Burke County in search of gold; he found none but stayed to design the Berrys' house. The timber and clay for the residence are said to have come from the Berrys' ninety-one-acre farm.

91. Telephone conversation with Mrs. J. S. Oliver, Marietta, Mar. 17, 1989.

92. [Milburn], *Examples*. See also the R. B. Raney House in Raleigh, in Barrett, *Colonial Southern Homes*. Advertisements in Barrett's book included one for the American Column Company of Battle Creek, Michigan, which had supplied "14 immense columns" for the Raney House: "Making colonial columns has been our specialty for more than 15 years; this work is under the personal supervision of our Mr. F. R. Angell, who is recognized authority on all matters pertaining to colonial architecture."

93. *The Official Blue Book of the Jamestown Ter-Centennial Exposition, A. D. 1907* (Norfolk: Colonial Publishing Co., 1909), 367–68; Davyd Foard Hood, "Kenneth L. Howard House," NR form, 1982.

94. *New Bern Sun*, May 2, 1913, quoted in Sandbeck, *New Bern and Craven County*, 164. The house has been destroyed.

95. Butchko, *On the Shores of the Pasquotank*, 194–95, 249–50. Ivy Blades married Charles O. Robinson in 1913. He was the son of Charles H. Robinson, who had come from New York to Elizabeth City via Norfolk after the Civil War, and Mary Leigh, descendant of the James Leigh who had built Land's End in Perquimans County. The Blades family operated a planing mill in Elizabeth City, to which rough lumber was carried from New Bern sawmills; among the family ships was the "Ivy Blades," which carried above its sails three pennants labeled I, V, Y (interviews with Charles O. Robinson, Jr., conducted by author, Elizabeth City, Nov. 1988, Apr. 27, 1989).

96. Allison H. Black and David R. Black, "Monroe Residential Historic District," NR form, 1987; [?] Stack and [?] Beasley, *Sketches of Monroe and Union County* (Charlotte: News and Times Printers, 1902). The Lee House was built by carpenter William Ervin Wallace. Prominent among Monroe's many other examples of the type is the Belk Mansion. Red Springs in Robeson County has an imposing collection of early Southern Colonial houses. Other notable examples include the Cannon-Guille House (1906) in Salisbury, designed by Charlotte architect J. M. McMichael, and the Boyd-Kerr House in Warrenton. Both Wilson and Raleigh once had monumental versions, now lost.

97. See, for example, C. C. Hook and F. M. Sawyer, *Some Designs by Hook and Sawyer* (Charlotte: Queen City Printing and Paper Co., 1902).

98. Brent D. Glass, "Egbert Barry Cornwall Hambley," in *DNCB*, 3:14–15; Hood, *Rowan County*, 70, 303–4.

99. Glass, "Egbert Barry Cornwall Hambley," 15.

100. Brengle, *Gaston County*, 242. Caleb John Lineberger (1818–1914) established a mill about 1850, and his son, Abel Caleb (1858–1948), began his own textile career working in his father's mill in 1880. Within a few decades he became one of the principal leaders in the county's textile boom.

101. Hanchett, "Four Square House" and "Four Square House Type," 51–53; Gowans, *Comfortable Home*, 84–89. Quote from Aymar Embury II, 1911, in Hanchett, "Four Square House," 59.

102. Davyd Foard Hood, "Grassy Creek," NR form, 1976. The house has two main rooms in front, plus the inset porch and three rear rooms; it is finished in tongue-and-groove sheathing inside.

103. Standard works on the bungalow are Lancaster, "American Bungalow" and *American Bungalow*, and King, *Bungalow*. See also Clark, *American Family Home*, 74–83, 171–92.

104. For analysis of the small bungalow as an extension of traditional two-room-plan usages in southwestern North Carolina, see Williams, "Homeplace."

105. Interviews with Thomas Lipe, Nov. 30, 1989, and Vernon Honeycutt, Dec. 3, 1989, conducted by Donna Dodenhoff, Stanly County, notes provided to author.

106. Personal communication from Henry Taves, 1988; *Aladdin Homes* (Bay City, Mich.: North American Construction Co., 1916), 9; Stevenson and Jandl, *Houses by Mail*; Gowans, *Comfortable House*, 41–65. The Aladdin Company's headquarters were in Bay City, Michigan, but mills were located near timber sites. In 1915 seven mills operated in Michigan, Louisiana, Oregon, Florida, and Canada, and in 1922 an Aladdin factory was established in Wilmington, North Carolina. The factory stood in the community of Love's Grove on the Atlantic Coastline Railroad, with direct connections to New Bern on the Seaboard line and to Weldon via Goldsboro on the old Wilmington and Weldon track (information on Wilmington courtesy of Edward Turberg, Wilmington). This would have permitted many North Carolinians to obtain Aladdin houses at low freight costs. Carl Lounsbury discusses the production of prefabricated buildings by North Carolina companies in the postwar era in *ABNC*, 227–31.

107. Quote from *Aladdin Plan of Industrial Housing* (Bay City, Mich.: North American Construction Co., 1918), 31. See Roth, "McKim, Mead, and White." Most of the Stanford White buildings have been greatly overbuilt (the mill) or razed. Several "turtleback" mill houses are believed to date from this era, but it is possible that they are of the subsequent period.

108. *Aladdin Plan of Industrial Housing*, 68, 72; *Aladdin Homes*, 86, 50, 87. Henry Taves introduced me to the Aladdin houses of Roanoke Rapids, and A. Edwin Akers of Roanoke Rapids provided historical data (Akers to author, Oct. 6, 1988).

Roanoke Rapids also contains many other Aladdin models that are not bungalows. On Jackson Street is a foursquare house that may be "the Rochester" ("the strong, substantial, American type"). Workers' houses along Madison and Monroe streets probably include the narrow, two-story "Herford" (a living room in front, with a stair, dining room, and kitchen behind and four tiny bedrooms and a bath upstairs) and "the Edison" (two bedrooms, a living-dining room, kitchen, and bath all on one floor, in "one of the prettiest little bungalows ever built"). More elaborate residences represented on the broad main street include "the Brentwood," with an English air, and "the Villa" ("a Bit of Old Italy").

109. Phillips, *Simple Treasures*, 158.

110. Interview with Ray Gibbs, daughter of Dr. and Mrs. Gibbs, conducted by author, Feb. 1988. A local contractor, Mr. Branton, built the dwelling, and James Catierres came from California to paint the interior ceiling and decorations.

111. Wrenn, *Wilmington*, 132, 208–9, 203–4, 212–13, 85–86.

112. Conversation with Claude Howell, Wilmington, Mar. 10, 1989. Howell has lived in the building all his life; his parents were among the original tenants.

113. Richard Mattson, "East Wilson Historic District," NR form, 1988. Data on the neighborhood and its houses comes from the NR form and from subsequent interviews conducted by Mattson.

114. John Michael Vlach, "The Shotgun House: An African Architectural Legacy," *Pioneer American* 8 (Jan.–July 1976): 47–70, reprinted in Upton and Vlach, *Common Places*, 58–78; Vlach, "Afro-Americans," in Upton, *America's Architectural Roots*, 43–45. In Wilson this type of house typically is called an "endway" house, its end facing toward the street (Mattson, "East Wilson Historic District").

115. This plan, like the shotgun, is common throughout the South.

116. Gail Williams O'Brien, *The Legal Fraternity and the Making of a New South Community, 1848–1882* (Athens: University of Georgia Press, 1986), 87–88. In Raleigh see, for example, the Hogg-Dortch House at Jones and Blount streets and the (still surviving) Haywood House on New Bern Avenue. Within about a mile of the Capitol stood the suburban estates or nearby plantations of the Boylan, Cameron, Devereux, Harrison, Mordecai, and Taylor families, among others (Waugh, *North Carolina's Capital*).

117. *Cameron Park: Its Purpose, Its Attainments, and Its Future Outlook* (Raleigh: Edwards and Broughton, n.d.).

118. See Smith, "American Idyll," in Bishir and Earley, *Early Twentieth-Century Suburbs*, 21–28; see also treatments of specific cities and neighborhoods, such as Raleigh's Glenwood, Charlotte's Dilworth, and others, in ibid.

119. Thomas W. Hanchett, "Charlotte: Suburban Development in the Textile and Trade Center of the Carolinas," in Bishir and Earley, *Early Twentieth-Century Suburbs*, 69–76; Kratt and Hanchett, *Legacy*, 33–34.

120. Hanchett, "Charlotte"; Kratt and Hanchett, *Legacy*. In 1919 James B. Duke purchased the 1915 residence of Southern Power Company executive Z. V. Taylor and had its architect, C. C. Hook, expand it into a fifty-two-room, columned colonial mansion. It was Duke who had told the Stephens Company that they needed to plant larger trees; thereafter the firm began moving in thirty- and forty-foot trees (ibid., 164, 76–78).

121. Data on houses comes from Thomas Hanchett, "Myers Park Historic District," NR form, 1987.

122. See Gayle Hicks Fripp, "Greensboro's Early Suburbs," and Davyd Foard Hood, "Winston-Salem's Suburbs: West End to Reynolda Park," in Bishir and Earley, *Early Twentieth-Century Suburbs*, 49–57, 59–67.

123. Alexander, *Resort Community*, 45–57. See, for example, Aymar Embury II, *The Livable House* (New York: Moffat Yard and Co., 1917); idem, "Current Tendencies in Country House Design in the East," *Architectural Record* 52 (Oct. 1922): 251–345. A devoted student of southern "colonial" architecture, Embury also contributed to the White Pine series that presented mea-

sured drawings, photographs, and essays on early American landmarks.

124. *Asheville Citizen*, Sept. 5, 1926, quoted in Swaim, *Cabins and Castles*, 91.

125. Lawrence S. Earley, "Quail Paradise in the Piedmont," *Wildlife in North Carolina* 50 (Dec. 1986): 18–23. A description of Airlie Lodge appears in Lewis Philip Hall, *Land of the Golden River* (Wilmington: privately printed, 1975), 24–30. Pope trained at Columbia University and the École des Beaux Arts; he gained financial security from his marriage to Sadie Jones. His best-known designs include the Jefferson Memorial, the National Archives Building, and the National Gallery of Art, all in Washington, D.C. (Richard Chafee, "John Russell Pope," in Placzek, *Macmillan Encyclopedia of Architects*, 3:450–51).

126. Claudia P. Roberts [Brown], "Whalehead Club," NR form, 1979. Many local residents were involved in construction and subsequent work at the Whalehead Club, and there are abundant local stories about the place. Roberts and John Wilson of Manteo, architect of the current renovation, interviewed several local residents. Roberts notes that for his Newport house, Clarendon Court (1904), Knight employed Philadelphia architect Horace Trumbauer, who also designed Knight's 1928 house, Stonybrook, in Middletown, Rhode Island. See Claus von Bulow, "Clarendon Court, Newport, R.I., a House and Its Ghosts," *Bulletin of the Newport Historical Society* 47, no. 156 (Fall 1974): 218–26; "E. C. Knight Dies," *New York Times*, July 24, 1936.

127. Roberts, "Whalehead Club"; plans (unsigned and undated), Whalehead Club, photocopies courtesy of John Wilson.

128. Smith, "Reynolda." See also Russell G. Whitehead, "The American Country House," *Architectural Record* 54 (Nov. 1923): 393–489; Roth, *Concise History of American Architecture*, 232–36.

129. This discussion is based on Smith, "Reynolda"; Peggy S. LaRochelle and Helen Moses, "Reynolda Historic District," NR form, 1980; conversations with Margaret Supplee Smith and with Nick Bragg and Elizabeth Morgan, Reynolda House, 1983. Although dwarfed in scale by Biltmore, Reynolda shared the ideas of a manorial village and the progressive modeling of scientific techniques (forestry and mountain crafts at Biltmore, farming and domestic science at Reynolda).

130. See Charles Barton Keen's plans for "Country Residence near Winston-Salem, N.C., for R. J. Reynolds, Esq.," Archives, Z. Smith Reynolds Library, Wake Forest University, Winston-Salem. Philadelphia metalworker Samuel Yellin executed the elaborate ironwork. Henry Mercer produced the decorative ceramic tile. Finish work is by Irving and Casson/A. H. Davenport. In "Reynolda: A Rural Vision," Margaret Supplee Smith quotes present-day architectural historian and theater critic Brendan Gill on Reynolda: "This structure, completed in 1917, is perhaps the first of an entirely new genre—a house on a grand scale that yet assumes an exterior demeanor almost as modest as that of a bungalow. We are in the presence not of wealth made formidably manifest, according to the practice of earlier generations, in a mock-chateau like Biltmore House or a mock-palazzo like The Breakers but in the circumstances charmingly of the family; the intention here is plainly not to show off but to be happy among friends—a pleasing novelty in the first decades of the twentieth century." Keen designed a number of fine residences, some in a style related to Reynolda, both in Winston-Salem and in Charlotte (See Hood, "Winston-Salem's Suburbs").

131. Gray, "Graylyn"; *The Story of Graylyn* (Winston-Salem: Graylyn Conference Center, [1984]).

132. *Winston-Salem Journal*, Jan. 8, 1929, quoted in Gray, "Graylyn," 37, 39. The construction contract went to the North-Eastern Construction Company of New York, which had a branch office in Winston-Salem and had undertaken several projects in the city.

133. Gray, "Graylyn," 31–32, cites the influence of *A Monograph on the Work of Mellor, Meigs, and Howe* (1923) and *An American Country House, the Property of Arthur E. Newbold, Jr., Esq., Laverock, Pa.* (1925).

134. Roy Thompson, interview with Luther Lashmit, *Winston-Salem Journal*, June 29, 1980, quoted in *Story of Graylyn*, 30; Thompson, quoted in ibid., 1.

135. The paneling and doors of the library came from the Hotel d'Estrades in Paris; the French government tried to stop the removal but the French Supreme Court ruled in the Grays' favor (Gray, "Graylyn," 62, 73–74; *Story of Graylyn*, 19). Recalling Gray's tobacco connections in the Middle East, the card room contains paneling removed from a small mosque in Istanbul, while the "tent room" incorporates an embroidered tent Gray brought back from Egypt. Tile came from the Enfield Pottery and Tile Works of Enfield, Pennsylvania; ironwork was designed and crafted by Joseph Barton Benson of Philadelphia (*Story of Graylyn*, 12).

136. *Fortune* 3 (Jan. 1931): 45–55; telephone conversation with Thomas A. Gray, Winston-Salem, May 1, 1989. The Valiant decorating firm of Baltimore, which had depended on the Gray commission to weather the depression, folded.

137. Henderson, *Campus of the First State University*, 221–24, 368.

138. See John L. Bell, Jr., *Hard Times: Beginnings of the Great Depression in North Carolina, 1929–1933* (Raleigh: Archives and History, 1982); Anthony J. Badger, *North Carolina and the New Deal* (Raleigh: Archives and History, 1981). Among the most visible and monumental products of public works were the Wright Brothers Memorial in Dare County and the Blue Ridge Parkway in western North Carolina.

139. Interview with Norman Edgerton, Raleigh, Jan. 1989. The contractor was John F. Danielson, a Swede. John J. Blair, a Winston-Salem businessman, recommended Gillette.

140. Davyd Foard Hood, "Tatton Hall" survey file, 1977, Survey and Planning Branch, A&H; idem, "William Lawrence Bottomley's Role in the Design of the Twentieth-Century Country House and *Great Georgian Houses of America*," paper presented at the annual meeting of the Society of Architectural Historians, 1986; Waugh, *North Carolina's Capital*, 178. As Hood points out, contemporaneously with construction of Tatton Hall, Bottomley chaired the editorial committee of the Architects' Emergency Committee that published *Great Georgian Houses of America* (2 vols., 1933, 1937). For Bottomley, as for Aymar Embury and the architects employed in the Historic American Buildings Survey during the depression, study of American architecture led to a more sophisticated revival architecture.

141. *Greensboro Daily News*, July 7, 1933. The building was contracted by George H. Rommel of Louisville, Kentucky, for $585,000. Components were supplied by firms in North Carolina, Chicago, Milwaukee, Atlanta, and New York (ibid., May 28, 1933). See "United States Post Office and Courthouse, Architectural and Historical Survey," U.S. Postal Service Report, Dec. 1977, copy in Survey and Planning Branch file, A&H.

142. *Greensboro Daily News*, May 31, 1933.

143. Craig et al., *Federal Presence*, 210–350. See U.S. Postal Service, *History of Post Office Construction*, 9–10, for classifications of federal architecture according to locations, drawn from Secretary of the U.S. Treasury Department, *Annual Report on the Finances: 1915* (Washington, D.C.: Government Printing Office, 1915). In 1930, more members were added to the supervising architect's staff, 133 architectural firms were commissioned to design federal buildings, and scores of new buildings began.

144. U.S. Postal Service, *History of Post Office Construction*, 14–25 (quote, 18, from *Architectural Forum*, Sept. 1933).

145. Ibid., 14–25; Harris and Lee, *Raleigh Architectural Inventory*, 52–53; Henderson, *Campus of the First State University*, 287–94.

146. Ernest Wood, "An Early Modernist Building Succumbs to North Carolina's Mountain Climate," *North Carolina Architect* 25, no. 1 (Jan./Feb. 1978): 35–37 (quote, 36, from Ralph M. Sargent, former president of the corporation). See also Ralph

M. Sargent, *Biology in the Blue Ridge: 50 Years of the Highlands Biological Station, 1927–1977* (Highlands: Highlands Biological Foundation, 1977), 11–16; Jan Schall, "Oskar Stonorov," in Placzek, *Macmillan Encyclopedia of Architects*, 4:134–35; Henry-Russell Hitchcock and Philip Johnson, *The International Style*, enl. ed. (1932; reprint, New York: Norton, 1966), 223. The laboratory was featured in *Architectural Record* 72 (Oct. 1932): 243–46.

147. Duberman, *Black Mountain*, esp. 55–56, 155–59; Wodehouse, "Kocher at Black Mountain"; Page Pless, "Black Mountain Historic District," NR form, 1981. See also Reginald R. Isaacs, "Marcel Breuer" and "Walter Gropius," in Placzek, *Macmillan Encyclopedia of Architects*, 1:286–87, 2:251–63. On Robert E. Lee Hall at the Blue Ridge Assembly campus (designed by architect Louis E. Jallade of New York and completed in 1912), see Michael T. Southern and Betty Lawrence, "Blue Ridge Assembly Historic District," NR form, 1979. For a photograph of the Breuer-Gropius model for Black Mountain College, see Peter Blake, *Marcel Breuer: Architect and Designer* (New York: Museum of Modern Art, 1949), 74.

148. Telephone conversation with Hertha Horwitz, niece of Dr. Weizenblatt, Aug. 29, 1989; telephone conversation with Anthony Lord, Mar. 13, 1989; building permit no. 7236, Sept. 21, 1940, Asheville Planning Department (estimated cost, $21,000), courtesy of Douglas Swaim. Lord recalled that the stone came principally from a quarry near Fletcher, but when the quarry closed down during the winter, Dr. Weizenblatt, an avid hiker who had become acquainted with foresters at neighboring Mount Pisgah Forest, was able to get the rest of the stone from a quarry on Mount Pisgah. Lord remembered that despite the unusual design of the house, there was "nothing unusual" in terms of its construction. The contractor was Dion Roberts of Asheville. Lord also recalled that Breuer gave a lecture at a meeting of the Asheville AIA chapter: "He was a nice guy . . . a youngish man . . . came down [to North Carolina] a good many times." See also Swaim, *Cabins and Castles*, 205; Blake, *Marcel Breuer*, 117.

149. Diane Lea notes that the "Williamsburg idea" for downtown Chapel Hill was promoted by university alumnus John L. Morehead in 1940 and was encouraged by the local newspaper. The first major downtown building in the Williamsburg style was the Town Hall, designed by Atwood and Weeks in 1938; it served as a catalyst for the town's subsequent planned development in the style in the 1940s and 1950s ("'Williamsburg' Style"; Mary Reeb, "Chapel Hill Town Hall," NR form, 1989). Peter Kaplan describes Charles and Ruth Coltrane Cannon's interest in the 1930s in planning a Williamsburg-style downtown for Kannapolis, which was executed mainly in the 1940s and 1950s (*Cabarrus County*, 156–57).

150. Raymond Arsenault, "The End of the Long Hot Summer: The Air Conditioner and Southern Culture," *Journal of Southern History* 50, no. 4 (Nov. 1984): 598–628. In 1939 Willis Carrier invented the Conduit Weathermaster System, which employed high-velocity air propelled through narrow tubes to cool tall buildings; the Bankers Life Building in Macon, Georgia, the Durham Life Building in Raleigh, and the United Carbon Building in Charleston, West Virginia, were the first buildings to use the new system (ibid., 606–7).

151. Winston-Salem NCAIA, *Architectural Guide to Winston-Salem*, 104. The grounds were landscaped by Thomas Sears. "Merry Acres" or "the Ship," as it was known locally for its streamlined form, was destroyed in 1978 (Taylor, *Frontier to Factory*, 70–78). See Northup and O'Brien, "Residence for R. J. Reynolds, Winston-Salem," plans, 1939, Archives, Z. Smith Reynolds Library, Wake Forest University, Winston-Salem.

152. Butchko, *On the Shores of the Pasquotank*, 50–51.

153. See Ernest Wood's account of postwar developments in *ABNC*, 349–428.

Selected Bibliography

This bibliography contains frequently cited sources and works of general interest.

Manuscripts and Archival Material

Chapel Hill, North Carolina

Southern Historical Collection, Wilson Library, University
of North Carolina
  Bryan Family Papers
  Cameron Family Papers
  Cupola House Papers, microfilm
  Arthur Dobbs Papers, microfilm
  Robert B. Drane Papers
  W. A. Graham Papers
  Peter W. Hairston Papers
  John Hawks Papers
  Hayes Collection
  Ernest Haywood Papers
  E. M. Holt Papers
  Mordecai Family Papers
  David L. Swain Papers
University Archives, Wilson Library, University of North
  Carolina
  University Papers

New Haven, Connecticut

Yale University Manuscripts and Archives, Sterling Library
  Journal of Rufus Bunnell, Bunnell Family Papers

New York, New York

Avery Architectural and Fine Arts Library, Columbia
  University
  A. J. Davis Collection
  Richard Upjohn Collection
Metropolitan Museum of Art
  A. J. Davis Collection
New York Public Library
  A. J. Davis Collection
  Richard Upjohn Collection

Raleigh, North Carolina

North Carolina Division of Archives and History, Department of Cultural Resources
  Archaeology and Historic Preservation Section
    National Register of Historic Places Nomination
      Forms (originals at National Park Service, Wash-
      ington, D.C.)

    Research reports, Restoration Branch
    Survey files of historic properties, Survey and Plan-
      ning Branch
  Archives and Records Section
    Church Records
    Colonial Court Records
    County Records
    North Carolina State Government Records
      Capital Buildings Papers
      General Assembly Records: Petitions
      Legislative Papers
      Prison Department Papers, Central Prison
      Treasurer's and Comptroller's Papers
    Private Collections
      Brevard Family Papers
      Francis Lister Hawks Collection, microfilm
      Jonathan M. Heck Papers
      William J. Hicks Papers
      David Paton Papers
      Thomas Pollock Letter Book
      James F. Post Ledger, microfilm
      William Laurence Saunders Papers
      John D. Whitford Papers

Washington, D.C.

National Archives
  General Correspondence, 1910–39
  Letters Received, Public Buildings Services, Record
    Group 121, 1843–1939
  Letters Received Relating to the Construction of Cus-
    tomhouses and Other Structures, Record Group 56, K
    Series, 1833–49

Winston-Salem, North Carolina

Museum of Early Southern Decorative Arts
  Research files
Old Salem, Incorporated
  Research files
Z. Smith Reynolds Library, Archives, Wake Forest
  University
  Reynolds Family Papers

Private Collections

James Brawley research files, Salisbury
Elizabeth Reid Murray research files, Raleigh
Powell Family Papers, Tarboro
William Reaves research files, Wilmington

Books, Articles, and Unpublished Sources

Alexander, Ann C. *Perspective on a Resort Community: Historic Buildings Inventory, Southern Pines, North Carolina*. Raleigh: Archives and History, 1981.

Allcott, John V. "Architect A. J. Davis in North Carolina . . . His Launching at the University." *North Carolina Architect*, Nov./Dec. 1973, 10–15.

———. "Architectural Developments at 'Montrose' in the 1850s." *North Carolina Historical Review* 42, no. 1 (Jan. 1965): 85–95.

———. *The Campus at Chapel Hill: Two Hundred Years of Architecture*. Chapel Hill: Chapel Hill Historical Society, 1986.

———. *Colonial Homes in North Carolina*. Raleigh: Carolina Tercentenary Commission, 1963. Reprint. Raleigh: Archives and History, 1975.

———. "Robert Donaldson, the First North Carolinian to Become Prominent in the Arts." *North Carolina Historical Review* 52, no. 4 (Oct. 1975): 333–66.

———. "Scholarly Books and Frolicsome Blades: A. J. Davis Designs a Library-Ballroom." *Journal of the Society of Architectural Historians* 33, no. 2 (May 1974): 145–54.

Anderson, Jean B. *Piedmont Plantation: The Bennehan-Cameron Family and Lands in North Carolina*. Durham: Historic Preservation Society of Durham, 1985.

Andrews, Evangeline Walker, ed. *Journal of a Lady of Quality*. New Haven, Conn.: Yale University Press, 1922.

Ashe, Samuel A. *David Paton, Architect of the State Capitol, an Address by Samuel A. Ashe*. Raleigh: North Carolina Historical Commission, 1909.

Axelrod, Alan, ed. *The Colonial Revival in America*. New York: W. W. Norton and Co. for the Henry Francis du Pont Winterthur Museum, 1985.

Baker, Paul R. *Richard Morris Hunt*. Cambridge, Mass.: MIT Press, 1980.

Barfield, Rodney. *Thomas Day, Cabinetmaker*. Raleigh: North Carolina Museum of History, 1975.

Barrett, Charles W. *Colonial Southern Homes*. Raleigh: Edwards and Broughton, 1903.

Benjamin, Asher. *The American Builder's Companion*. Boston: Etheridge and Bliss, 1806.

———. *The Country Builder's Assistant*. Greenfield, Mass.: Thomas Dickman, 1797.

———. *The Practical House Carpenter*. Boston: R. P. and C. Williams, Annin and Smith, 1830.

Bicknell, Amos Jackson. *Bicknell's Cottage and Village Architecture*. New York: A. J. Bicknell and Co., 1878.

———. *Bicknell's Village Builder*. New York: A. J. Bicknell and Co., 1870.

———. *Supplement to Bicknell's Village Builder*. New York: A. J. Bicknell and Co., [1871].

Biddle, Owen. *The Young Carpenter's Assistant*. Philadelphia: Benjamin Johnson, 1805.

Bishir, Catherine W. "Asher Benjamin's *Practical House Carpenter* in North Carolina." *Carolina Comments* 27, no. 3 (May 1979): 66–74.

———. "Black Builders in Antebellum North Carolina." *North Carolina Historical Review* 61, no. 4 (Oct. 1984): 423–61.

———. "Jacob W. Holt, an American Builder." *Winterthur Portfolio* 16, no. 1 (Spring 1981): 1–32. Reprinted in *Common Places*, edited by Dell Upton and John Vlach.

———. "The Montmorenci–Prospect Hill School: A Study of High-Style Vernacular Architecture in the Roanoke Valley." In *Carolina Dwelling*, edited by Douglas Swaim, 84–103. Raleigh: North Carolina State University School of Design Student Publication, 1978.

———. "Philadelphia Bricks and the New Bern Jail." *Association for Preservation Technology* 9, no. 4 (1977): 62–66.

———. "The 'Unpainted Aristocracy': The Beach Cottages of Old Nags Head." *North Carolina Historical Review* 54, no. 4 (Oct. 1977): 367–92. Reissued as *The "Unpainted Aristocracy": The Beach Cottages of Old Nags Head*. Raleigh: Archives and History, 1983.

Bishir, Catherine W., and J. Marshall Bullock. "Mr. Jones Goes to Richmond: A Note on the Influence of Alexander Parris' Wickham House." *Journal of the Society of Architectural Historians* 43, no. 1 (Mar. 1984): 71–74.

Bishir, Catherine W., Charlotte V. Brown, Carl R. Lounsbury, and Ernest H. Wood III. *Architects and Builders in North Carolina: A History of the Practice of Building*. Chapel Hill: University of North Carolina Press, 1990.

Bishir, Catherine W., and Lawrence S. Earley, eds. *Early Twentieth-Century Suburbs in North Carolina*. Raleigh: Archives and History, 1985.

Bivins, John, Jr. *The Furniture of Coastal North Carolina*. Winston-Salem: Museum of Early Southern Decorative Arts, 1988.

Bivins, John, Jr., James Melchor, Marilyn Melchor, and Richard Parsons. "The Cupola House: An Anachronism of Style and Technology." *Journal of Early Southern Decorative Arts* 25, no. 1 (May 1989): 57–132.

Black, Allison Harris. *An Architectural History of Burlington, North Carolina*. Burlington: City of Burlington, 1987.

Black, David R. *Historic Architectural Resources of Downtown Asheville, North Carolina*. Asheville: City of Asheville, 1979.

Boyce, W. Scott. *An Economic and Social History of Chowan County, North Carolina, 1880–1915*. 1917. Reprint. New York: AMS Press, 1973.

Boyd, William K., ed. *William Byrd's Histories of the Dividing Line betwixt Virginia and North Carolina*. Raleigh: North Carolina Historical Commission, 1929. Reprint. New York: Dover Publications, 1967.

Brendel, Susanne. "Urban Asheville." *North Carolina Architect*, July/Aug. 1978, 10–15.

Brengle, Kim Withers. *The Architectural Heritage of Gaston County, North Carolina*. Gastonia: Gaston County, 1982.

Brown, Marvin A. *Heritage and Homestead: The History and Architecture of Granville County, North Carolina*. Oxford: Granville County Historical Society, Inc., 1988.

———. *Our Enduring Past: A Survey of 235 Years of Life and Architecture in Lincoln County, North Carolina*. Lincolnton: Lincoln County Historic Properties Commission, 1986.

Buchanan, Paul E. "The Eighteenth-Century Frame Houses of Tidewater Virginia." In *Building Early America*, edited by Charles E. Peterson, 54–73. Radnor, Pa.: Chilton Book Co. for the Carpenter's Co. of Pennsylvania, 1976.

Bullock, James Marshall. "The Enterprising Contractor, Mr. Cosby." Master's thesis, University of North Carolina, 1982.

Bunomi, Patricia U. *Under the Cope of Heaven: Religion, Society, and Politics in Colonial America*. New York: Oxford University Press, 1986.

Burns, Robert, ed. *100 Courthouses: A Report on North Carolina Judicial Facilities*. 2 vols. Raleigh: Administrative Office of the Courts, 1978.

Burroughs, P. E. *A Complete Guide to Church Building*. New York: George H. Doran Co. for the Sunday School Board of the Southern Baptist Convention, 1923.

Bushong, William B. "A. G. Bauer, Architect for the State of North Carolina, 1883–1893." *North Carolina Historical Review* 59, no. 3 (July 1983): 304–31.

———. "William Percival, an English Architect in the Old North State, 1857–1860." *North Carolina Historical Review* 57, no. 3 (July 1980): 310–39.

Butchko, Tom. *An Inventory of Historic Architecture, Sampson County, North Carolina*. Clinton: City of Clinton, [1981].

———. *On the Shores of the Pasquotank: The Architectural Heritage of Elizabeth City and Pasquotank County, North Carolina*. Elizabeth City: Museum of the Albemarle, 1989.

Butler, Lindley S., and Alan D. Watson, eds. *The North Carolina Experience: An Interpretive and Documentary History*. Chapel Hill: University of North Carolina Press, 1984.

Campbell, Betty Jean. "The Buildings of Salem, North Carolina, 1766–1856." Ph.D. diss., Florida State University, 1975.

Carson, Cary. "The 'Virginia House' in Maryland." *Maryland Historical Magazine* 69, no. 2 (Summer 1974): 185–96.

Carson, Cary, Norman F. Barker, William M. Kelso, Garry Wheeler Stone, and Dell Upton. "Impermanent Architecture in the Southern American Colonies." *Winterthur Portfolio* 16, nos. 2/3 (Summer/Autumn 1981): 135–96.

Chappell, Edward A. "Acculturation in the Shenandoah Valley." *Proceedings of the American Philosophical Society* 124, no. 1 (1980): 55–89.

Cheeseman, Bruce S. "The Cupola House of Edenton, Chowan County." Research report, 1980, copy in Restoration Branch, Archives and History, Raleigh.

———. "The History of the Cupola House, 1724–1777." *Journal of Early Southern Decorative Arts* 25, no. 1 (May 1989): 1–56.

———. "The Survival of the Cupola House: 'A Venerable Old Mansion.'" *North Carolina Historical Review* 63, no. 1 (Jan. 1986): 40–73.

Clark, Clifford Edward, Jr. *The American Family Home, 1800–1960*. Chapel Hill: University of North Carolina Press, 1986.

Clark, Walter, ed. *The State Records of North Carolina*. 16 vols. (numbered 11–26). Winston and Goldsboro: State of North Carolina, 1895–1906.

Clauser, John, Jr. "Front Yard—Back Yard: Everything in Its Place." In *Indians, Colonists, and Slaves*. Special Publication no. 4, *Florida Journal of Anthropology* (1985): 71–84.

Clayton, Thomas H. *Close to the Land: The Way We Lived in North Carolina, 1820–1870*. Series edited by Sydney Nathans. Chapel Hill: University of North Carolina Press, 1983.

Comstock, William. *American Cottages*. New York: William T. Comstock, 1883.

———. *Modern Architectural Designs*. New York: William T. Comstock, 1881.

Condit, Carl W. *American Building*. Chicago: University of Chicago Press, 1968.

Cooledge, Harold N., Jr. *Samuel Sloan: Architect of Philadelphia, 1815–1884*. Philadelphia: University of Pennsylvania Press, 1986.

Cotton, J. Randall. *Historic Burke: An Architectural Inventory of Burke County, North Carolina*. Morganton: Historic Burke Foundation, 1987.

Craig, James H. *The Arts and Crafts in North Carolina, 1699–1840*. Winston-Salem: Museum of Early Southern Decorative Arts, 1965.

Craig, Lois, and the staff of the Federal Architecture Project. *The Federal Presence: Architecture, Politics, and Symbols in United States Government Building*. Cambridge, Mass.: MIT Press, 1979.

Cummings, Abbott Lowell. *The Framed Houses of Massachusetts Bay, 1625–1725*. Cambridge, Mass.: Harvard University Press, 1979.

Davies, Jane. "Blandwood and the Italian Villa Style in America." *Nineteenth Century* 1, no. 3 (Sept. 1975): 11–14.

Dill, Alonzo Thomas, Jr. *Governor Tryon and His Palace*. Chapel Hill: University of North Carolina Press, 1955.

———. "Public Buildings in Craven County." *North Carolina Historical Review* 20, no. 4 (Oct. 1943): 301–26.

———. "Tryon's Palace: A Neglected Niche of North Carolina History." *North Carolina Historical Review* 19, no. 2 (Apr. 1942): 119–67.

Donoghue, John Cornelius. "Alexander Jackson Davis, Romantic Architect, 1803–1892." Ph.D. diss., New York University, 1977.

Downing, Andrew Jackson. *The Architecture of Country Houses*. New York: D. Appleton, 1850.

———. *Cottage Residences*. New York: Wiley and Putnam, 1842.

———. *A Treatise on the Theory and Practice of Landscape Gardening Adapted to North America*. New York: Wiley and Putnam, 1841.

Duberman, Martin. *Black Mountain: An Exploration in Community*. New York: E. P. Dutton, 1972.

Durden, Robert F. *The Dukes of Durham: 1865–1929*. Durham: Duke University Press, 1975.

Edmunds, Mary Lewis Rucker. *Governor Morehead's Blandwood and the Family Who Lived There*. Greensboro: privately printed, 1976.

Ekirch, A. Roger. *"Poor Carolina": Politics and Society in Colonial North Carolina, 1729–1776*. Chapel Hill: University of North Carolina Press, 1981.

Elliot, Cecil D. "The North Carolina State Capitol." *The Southern Architect* 5, no. 5 (May 1958): 19–22; 5, no. 6 (June 1958): 23–26; 5, no. 7 (July 1958): 24–27.

Escott, Paul D. *Many Excellent People: Power and Privilege in North Carolina, 1850–1900*. Chapel Hill: University of North Carolina Press, 1985.

Ezell, John S., ed. *The New Democracy in America: Travels of Francisco de Miranda in the United States, 1783–84*. Translated by Judson P. Wood. Norman: University of Oklahoma Press, 1963.

Fenn, Elizabeth A., and Peter H. Wood. *Natives and Newcomers: The Way We Lived in North Carolina before 1770*. Series edited by Sydney Nathans. Chapel Hill: University of North Carolina Press, 1983.

Flowers, John Baxton III, and Marguerite Schumann. *Bull Durham and Beyond*. Durham: The Durham Bicentennial Commission, 1976.

"A French Traveler in America." *American Historical Review*

26, no. 4 (1920–21): 726–47.

Fries, Adelaide L., Douglas LeTell Rights, Minnie J. Smith, and Kenneth G. Hamilton, eds. *Records of the Moravians in North Carolina*. 11 vols. Raleigh: North Carolina Historical Commission, 1922–69.

Garvin, James L. "Mail-Order House Plans and American Victorian Architecture." *Winterthur Portfolio* 16, no. 4 (Winter 1981): 309–34.

Gatling, Eva Ingersoll. "John Berry of Hillsboro, North Carolina." *Journal of the Society of Architectural Historians* 10, no. 1 (Mar. 1951): 18–22.

Gebhard, David. "The American Colonial Revival in the 1930s." *Winterthur Portfolio* 22, nos. 2/3 (Summer/Autumn 1987): 109–48.

Gibbs, James. *A Book of Architecture, Containing Designs of Buildings and Ornaments*. London: n.p., 1728.

Glass, Brent. "Southern Mill Hills: Design in a 'Public' Place." In *Carolina Dwelling*, edited by Douglas Swaim, 138–49. Raleigh: North Carolina State University School of Design Student Publication, 1978.

Glassie, Henry. "Eighteenth-Century Cultural Process in Delaware Valley Folk Building." *Winterthur Portfolio* 7 (1972): 29–57.

———. *Folk Housing in Middle Virginia: A Structural Analysis of Historic Artifacts*. Knoxville: University of Tennessee Press, 1975.

———. *Pattern in the Material Folk Culture of the Eastern United States*. Philadelphia: University of Pennsylvania Press, 1968.

Goldfield, David R. *Cotton Fields and Skyscrapers: Southern Region and City*. Baton Rouge: Louisiana State University Press, 1982.

Gowans, Alan. *The Comfortable House: North American Suburban Architecture, 1890–1930*. Cambridge, Mass.: MIT Press, 1986.

———. *Images of American Living*. Philadelphia: J. P. Lippincott, 1964.

Gray, Thomas Alexander. "Graylyn: A Norman Revival Estate in North Carolina." Master's thesis, University of Delaware, 1974.

Greene, Jack P., and J. R. Pole. *Colonial British America: Essays in the New History of the Early Modern Era*. Baltimore, Md.: Johns Hopkins University Press, 1984.

Grimes, J. Bryan. *North Carolina Wills and Inventories*. Raleigh: Edwards and Broughton for the Trustees of the Public Libraries, 1912.

Gunter, S. Carol. *Carolina Heights, Wilmington*. Wilmington: City of Wilmington Planning Department, 1982.

Haley, Dru Gatewood, and Raymond A. Winslow, Jr. *The Historic Architecture of Perquimans County, North Carolina*. Hertford: Town of Hertford, 1982.

Hall, Jacquelyn Dowd, James Leloudis, Robert Korstad, Mary Murphy, Lu Ann Jones, and Christopher B. Daly. *Like a Family: The Making of a Southern Cotton Mill World*. Chapel Hill: University of North Carolina Press, 1987.

Hall, Louise. "Architecture." In *The North Carolina Guide*, edited by Blackwell P. Robinson, 107–27. Chapel Hill: University of North Carolina Press, 1955.

Hamlin, Talbot. *Greek Revival Architecture in America*. 1940. Reprint. New York: Dover Publications, 1964.

Hanchett, Thomas W. "The Four Square House in the United States." Master's thesis, University of Chicago, 1986.

———. "The Four Square House Type in the United States." In *Perspectives in Vernacular Architecture*, edited by Camille Wells, 51–54. Annapolis, Md.: Vernacular Architecture Forum, 1982.

Harris, Linda L., and Mary Ann Lee. *Raleigh Architectural Inventory*. Raleigh: City of Raleigh Planning Department and Archives and History, 1978.

Henderson, Archibald. *The Campus of the First State University*. Chapel Hill: University of North Carolina Press, 1949.

Herman, Bernard L. *Architecture and Rural Life in Central Delaware, 1700–1900*. Knoxville: University of Tennessee Press, 1987.

Herzog, Lynda Vestal. "The Early Architecture of New Bern, North Carolina, 1750–1850." Ph.D. diss., University of California at Los Angeles, 1977.

Higginbotham, Don, ed. *The Papers of James Iredell*. 2 vols. Raleigh: Archives and History, 1976.

Hindle, Brooke, ed. *America's Wooden Age: Aspects of Its Early Technology*. Tarrytown, N.Y.: Sleepy Hollow Press, 1976.

———. *Material Culture of the Wooden Age*. Tarrytown, N.Y.: Sleepy Hollow Press, 1981.

A History of Public Buildings under the Control of the Treasury Department. Washington, D.C.: Government Printing Office, 1901.

Hitchcock, Henry-Russell. *Architecture Books: A List of Books, Portfolios, and Pamphlets on Architecture and Related Subjects Published in America before 1895*. Enl. ed. New York: DaCapo Press, 1976.

Hobbs, Samuel Huntington, Jr. *North Carolina: Economic and Social*. Chapel Hill: University of North Carolina Press, 1930.

Hood, Davyd Foard. *The Architecture of Rowan County*. Salisbury: Rowan County Historic Properties Commission, 1983.

Hook, C. C., and F. M. Sawyer. *Some Designs by Hook and Sawyer*. Charlotte: Queen City Printing and Paper Co., 1902.

Hopkins, John Henry. *Essay on Gothic Architecture*. Burlington, Vt.: Smith and Harrington, 1836.

Jaeger, A. Robert. "The Auditorium and Akron Plans—Reflections of a Half Century of American Protestantism." Master's thesis, Cornell University, 1984.

Johnson, Guion Griffis. *Ante-Bellum North Carolina: A Social History*. Chapel Hill: University of North Carolina Press, 1937.

Johnston, Frances Benjamin, and Thomas Tileston Waterman. *The Early Architecture of North Carolina*. Chapel Hill: University of North Carolina Press, 1947.

Jones, H. G. *North Carolina Illustrated, 1524–1984*. Chapel Hill: University of North Carolina Press, 1983.

Kaplan, Peter R. *The Historic Architecture of Cabarrus County, North Carolina*. Concord: Historic Cabarrus, 1981.

Kennedy, Roger G. *Architecture, Men, Women, and Money in America, 1600–1860*. New York: Random House, 1985.

Kimball, Fiske, and Gertrude Carraway. "Tryon's Palace." *New-York Historical Society Quarterly Bulletin* 24, no. 1 (Jan. 1940): 20–21.

King, Anthony D. *The Bungalow: The Production of a Global Culture*. London: Routledge and Kegan Paul, 1984.

Kniffen, Fred. "Folk Housing: Key to Diffusion." *Annals of the Association of American Geographers* 55, no. 4 (Dec. 1965): 549–77.

Kniffen, Fred, and Henry Glassie. "Building in Wood in

the Eastern United States: A Time-Place Perspective." *Geographical Review* 56, no. 1 (Jan. 1966): 40–66.

Kratt, Mary Norton, and Thomas W. Hanchett. *Legacy: The Myers Park Story*. Charlotte: Myers Park Foundation, 1986.

Lafever, Minard. *The Architectural Instructor*. New York: George P. Putnam, 1856.

———. *The Beauties of Modern Architecture*. New York: D. Appleton, 1835.

———. *The Modern Builder's Guide*. New York: Henry C. Sleight, Collins and Hannay, 1833.

Lancaster, Clay. "The American Bungalow." *Art Bulletin* 40 (Sept. 1958). Reprinted in *Common Places*, edited by Dell Upton and John Vlach, 79–106.

———. *The American Bungalow, 1880–1930*. New York: Abbeville Press, 1985.

Lane, Mills. *Architecture of the Old South: North Carolina*. Savannah, Ga.: Beehive Press, 1985.

Langley, Batty. *The Builder's Jewel*. 1741. Reprint. Charlestown and Boston: S. Ethridge for Samuel Hill [Hall], 1800.

———. *The City and Country Builder's and Workman's Treasury of Designs*. London: S. Harding, 1745.

Lawson, John. *A New Voyage to Carolina*. 1709. Reprint edited by Hugh Talmage Lefler. Chapel Hill: University of North Carolina Press, 1967.

Lea, Diane E. "'Williamsburg' Style Creates a 'Village' Atmosphere." *North Carolina Architect* 26, no. 1 (Jan./Feb. 1979): 14–19.

Lea, Diane E., and Claudia P. Roberts. *An Architectural and Historical Survey, Central Lumberton, North Carolina*. Raleigh: Department of Cultural Resources, 1980.

Lears, T. J. Jackson. *No Place of Grace: Antimodernism and the Transformation of American Culture, 1880–1920*. New York: Pantheon, 1981

Lefler, Hugh Talmage, and Albert Ray Newsome. *North Carolina: The History of a Southern State*. Chapel Hill: University of North Carolina Press, 1963.

Lemmon, Sarah McCulloh, ed. *The Pettigrew Papers*. 2 vols. Raleigh: Archives and History, 1971, 1988.

Letsinger, Philip S. *Inventory of Historic Architecture of Maxton, North Carolina*. Maxton: Town of Maxton, 1982.

Lewis, Emanuel Raymond. *Seacoast Fortifications of the United States*. Washington, D.C.: Smithsonian Institution Press, 1970.

Little-Stokes, Ruth. *An Inventory of Historic Architecture: Caswell County, North Carolina*. Yanceyville: Caswell County Historical Association and Archives and History, 1979.

———. *An Inventory of Historic Architecture, Greensboro, N.C.* Greensboro: City of Greensboro and Archives and History, 1976.

———. *An Inventory of Historic Architecture: Iredell County, North Carolina*. Statesville: City of Statesville, Town of Mooresville, Iredell County, and Archives and History, 1978.

———. "The North Carolina Porch: A Climatic and Cultural Buffer." In *Carolina Dwelling*, edited by Douglas Swaim, 104–11. Raleigh: North Carolina State University School of Design Student Publication, 1978.

London, Lawrence Foushee, and Sarah McCulloh Lemmon. *The Episcopal Church in North Carolina, 1701–1959*. Raleigh: The Episcopal Diocese of North Carolina, 1987.

Loth, Calder. "Notes on the Evolution of Virginia Brickwork from the Seventeenth Century to the Late Nineteenth Century." *Association for Preservation Technology* 6, no. 2 (1974): 82–120.

Lounsbury, Carl R. *Alamance County Architectural Heritage*. Graham: Alamance County Historical Properties Commission, 1980.

———. "The Building Process in Antebellum North Carolina." *North Carolina Historical Review* 60, no. 4 (Oct. 1983): 431–56.

———. "The Development of Domestic Architecture in the Albemarle Region." *North Carolina Historical Review* 54, no. 1 (Jan. 1977): 17–48. Reprinted in *Carolina Dwelling*, edited by Douglas Swaim, 46–61.

———. "From Craft to Industry: The Building Process in North Carolina in the Nineteenth Century." Ph.D. diss., George Washington University, 1983.

McKim, Mead, and White. *Recent Buildings Designed for Educational Institutions*. New York: Beck Engineering Co., 1936.

Malone, Michael Taylor. "Levi Silliman Ives: Priest, Bishop, Tractarian, and Roman Catholic Convert." Ph.D. diss., Duke University, 1970.

Mansell, Elizabeth Lloyd Meihack. "American Tobacco Company Brick Storage Warehouses in Durham, North Carolina: 1897–1906." Master's thesis, University of North Carolina, 1980.

Mathews, Donald G. *Religion in the Old South*. Chicago: University of Chicago Press, 1977.

Mattson, Richard L. *The History and Architecture of Nash County, North Carolina*. Nashville: Nash County Planning Department, 1987.

Meeks, Carroll L. V. *The Railroad Station: An Architectural History*. New Haven, Conn.: Yale University Press, 1956.

Merrens, H. Roy. *Colonial North Carolina in the Eighteenth Century: A Study in Historical Geography*. Chapel Hill: University of North Carolina Press, 1964.

[Milburn, Frank P.] *Examples from the Work of Frank P. Milburn and Company*. Washington, D.C.: National Publishing Co., n.d.

Milburn, Frank P., and Michael Heister. *Selections from the Work of Milburn, Heister & Co.* Columbia, S.C.: State Co., 1907.

Mohney, Kirk Franklin. *The Historic Architecture of Davie County, North Carolina*. Mocksville: Davie County Historical Society, 1986.

Morrill, Dan. "Edward Dilworth Latta: The Charlotte Consolidated Construction Company (1890–1925): Builders of a New South City." *North Carolina Historical Review* 62, no. 3 (July 1985): 293–316.

Morrison, Mary Lane. *John S. Norris, Architect in Savannah, 1846–1860*. Savannah, Ga.: Beehive Press, 1980.

Mullin, Robert Bruce. *Episcopal Vision/American Reality: High Church Theology and Social Thought in Evangelical America*. New Haven, Conn.: Yale University Press, 1986.

Murray, Elizabeth Reid. *Wake: Capital County of North Carolina*. Raleigh: Capital County Publishing Co., 1983.

Murtagh, William J. *Moravian Architecture and Town Planning*. Chapel Hill: University of North Carolina Press, 1967.

Nathans, Sydney. *The Quest for Progress: The Way We Lived in North Carolina, 1870–1920*. Series edited by Sydney Nathans. Chapel Hill: University of North Carolina Press, 1983.

Newsome, Albert Ray. "Twelve North Carolina Counties in 1810–1811." *North Carolina Historical Review* 5, no. 4 (Oct. 1928): 413–46; 6, no. 1 (Jan. 1929): 67–99; 6, no. 2 (Apr. 1979): 171–89; 6, no. 3 (July 1929): 281–309.

Newton, Roger Hale. *Town and Davis, Architects.* New York: Columbia University Press, 1942.

Nicholson, Peter. *The Carpenter's New Guide.* 1793. Reprint. Philadelphia: M. Carey and Son, 1818.

Oates, John A. *The Story of Fayetteville.* 2d ed. Fayetteville: Fayetteville Woman's Club, 1972.

Olmsted, Frederick Law. *Journey in the Seaboard Slave States.* New York: Dix and Edwards, 1856.

Pain, William. *The Builder's Companion.* London: n.p., 1758.

———. *The Builder's Pocket Treasure, or, Palladio Delineated and Explained.* London: W. Owen, 1766.

———. *The Practical Builder.* London: I. Taylor, 1774.

Pain, William, and James Pain. *Pain's British Palladio or, the Builder's General Assistant.* London: I. and J. Taylor, 1790.

Palliser's New Cottage Homes. New York: Palliser, Palliser, and Co., 1887.

Park, Helen. *A List of Architectural Books Available in America before the Revolution.* Los Angeles: Hennessey and Ingalls, 1973.

Parramore, Thomas. *Express Lanes and Country Roads: The Way We Lived in North Carolina, 1920–1970.* Series edited by Sydney Nathans. Chapel Hill: University of North Carolina Press, 1983.

———. "The Tuscarora Ascendancy." *North Carolina Historical Review* 59, no. 4 (Oct. 1982): 307–86.

Paschal, George Washington. *History of Wake Forest College.* 3 vols. Raleigh: Edwards and Broughton, 1935–43.

Patrick, James. *Architecture in Tennessee, 1768–1897.* Knoxville: University of Tennessee Press, 1981.

———. "Ecclesiological Gothic in the Antebellum South." *Winterthur Portfolio* 15, no. 2 (Summer 1980): 117–38.

Pearce, Thilbert H. *Early Architecture of Franklin County.* Freeman, S.D.: privately printed, 1977.

Peatross, C. Ford. *William Nichols, Architect.* Birmingham: University of Alabama Art Gallery, 1979.

Phillips, Laura A. W. *Reidsville, North Carolina: An Inventory of Historic and Architectural Resources.* Reidsville: Archives and History and Reidsville Historic Properties Commission, 1981.

———. *Simple Treasures: The Architectural Legacy of Surry County.* Winston-Salem: Surry County Historical Society, 1987.

Pierce, Donald C., and Hope Alswang. *American Interiors: New England and the South, Period Rooms at the Brooklyn Museum.* New York: Brooklyn Museum, 1983.

Pierson, William H., Jr. *American Buildings and Their Architects.* Vol. 1, *The Colonial and Neoclassical Styles*; vol. 2, *Technology and the Picturesque, the Corporate, and Early Gothic Styles.* Garden City, N.Y.: Anchor Press, Doubleday, 1976, 1980.

Placzek, Adolf K., ed. *The Macmillan Encyclopedia of Architects.* 4 vols. New York: Macmillan, 1982.

Powell, William S. *The First State University: A Pictorial History of the University of North Carolina.* Chapel Hill: University of North Carolina Press, 1972.

———. *North Carolina through Four Centuries.* Chapel Hill: University of North Carolina Press, 1989.

———, ed. *The Correspondence of William Tryon and Other Selected Papers.* 2 vols. Raleigh: Archives and History, 1980.

———. *Dictionary of North Carolina Biography.* 3 vols. to date. Chapel Hill: University of North Carolina Press, 1979–.

Ramsey, Robert W. *Carolina Cradle: Settlement of the Northwest Carolina Frontier, 1747–1762.* Chapel Hill: University of North Carolina Press, 1964.

Rankin, Robert. "Bishop Levi S. Ives and High Church Reform in North Carolina: Tractarianism as an Instrument to Elevate Clerical and Lay Piety." *Anglican and Episcopal History* 57, no. 3 (Sept. 1988): 298–319.

Ranlett, William. *The Architect.* 2 vols. 1847–49. Reprint. New York: DeWitt and Davenport, 1851.

Rapoport, Amos. *House Form and Culture.* Englewood Cliffs, N.J.: Prentice-Hall, 1969.

Rhoads, William B. *The Colonial Revival.* 2 vols. New York: Garland Publishing Co., 1977.

———. "The Colonial Revival and American Nationalism." *Journal of the Society of Architectural Historians* 35, no. 4 (Dec. 1976): 239–54.

Roberts, Claudia, Diane Lea, and Robert M. Leary. *The Durham Architectural and Historic Inventory.* Durham: City of Durham, 1981.

Robinson, Willard B. *American Forts: Architectural Form and Function.* Urbana: University of Illinois Press for the Amon Carter Museum of Western Art, 1977.

Rodman, Lida Tunstall, ed. *Journal of a Tour to North Carolina by William Attmore, 1787.* James Sprunt Studies in History and Political Science, vol. 17, no. 2. Chapel Hill: University of North Carolina Press, 1922.

Rose, W. P. *That House.* Raleigh: Edwards and Broughton, 1900.

Roth, Leland M. *A Concise History of American Architecture.* New York: Harper and Row, 1979.

———. "Three Industrial Towns by McKim, Mead & White." *Journal of the Society of Architectural Historians* 38, no. 4 (Dec. 1979): 317–47.

Salmon, William. *Palladio Londinensis: Or, the London Art of Building.* London: Ward and Wicksteed, 1734; A. Ward, 1738.

Sandbeck, Peter B. *The Historic Architecture of New Bern and Craven County, North Carolina.* New Bern: Tryon Palace Commission, 1988.

Sanders, John L. "Ayr Mount on the Eno River, near Hillsborough, North Carolina." *The Magazine Antiques,* May 1989, 1190–1201.

———. "The North Carolina State Capitol of 1840." *The Magazine Antiques,* Sept. 1985, 474–84.

———. "The North Carolina State House and Capitol, 1792–1872." Research report, 1972, copy in Restoration Branch, Archives and History, Raleigh.

———. "'This Political Temple, the Capitol of North Carolina.'" *Popular Government* 43, no. 2 (Fall 1977): 1–10.

Saunders, William L., ed. *The Colonial Records of North Carolina.* 10 vols. Raleigh: State of North Carolina, 1886–90.

Schimmelman, Janice G. *Architectural Treatises and Building Handbooks Available in American Libraries and Bookstores through 1800.* Worcester, Mass.: American Antiquarian Society, 1986.

Schoepf, Johann David. *Travels in the Confederation, 1783–1784.* 2 vols. New York: Burt Franklin, 1968.

Schumann, Marguerite, Sterling Boyd, and JoAnn Sieburg-Baker. *Grand Old Ladies: North Carolina Architecture during the Victorian Era.* Charlotte: East Woods Press, 1984.

Seapker, Janet K. "James F. Post, Builder-Architect: The Legend and the Ledger." *Lower Cape Fear Historical Society Bulletin* 30, no. 3 (May 1987): 1–7.

Severens, Kenneth. *Southern Architecture: 350 Years of Distinctive American Buildings.* New York: E. P. Dutton, 1981.

Sloan, Samuel. *The Model Architect.* Philadelphia: E. G. Jones and Co., 1852.

Smith, H. McKelden. *Architectural Resources: An Inventory of Historic Architecture: High Point, Jamestown, Gibsonville, Guilford County.* Raleigh: Archives and History, 1979.

Smith, Margaret Supplee. "Reynolda: A Rural Vision in an Industrializing South." *North Carolina Historical Review* 65, no. 3 (July 1988): 287–314.

Sobel, Mechal. *The World They Made Together: Black and White Values in Eighteenth-Century Virginia.* Princeton, N.J.: Princeton University Press, 1987.

South, Stanley A. "Russellborough: Two Royal Governors' Mansion at Brunswick Town." *North Carolina Historical Review* 44, no. 4 (Oct. 1967): 367.

Southern, Michael T. "The I-House as a Carrier of Style." In *Carolina Dwelling*, edited by Douglas Swaim, 72–83.

Stanton, Phoebe B. *The Gothic Revival and American Church Architecture: An Episode in Taste, 1804–1856.* Baltimore, Md.: Johns Hopkins University Press, 1969.

Stein, Susan R., ed. *The Architecture of Richard Morris Hunt.* Chicago: University of Chicago Press, 1986.

Stevenson, Katherine Cole, and H. Ward Jandl. *Houses by Mail: A Guide to Houses from Sears, Roebuck and Company.* Washington, D.C.: Preservation Press, 1986.

Stick, David. *North Carolina Lighthouses.* Raleigh: North Carolina Department of Cultural Resources, 1981.

———. *The Outer Banks of North Carolina, 1584–1958.* Chapel Hill: University of North Carolina Press, 1958.

Stilgoe, John R. *Common Landscape of America, 1580 to 1845.* New Haven, Conn.: Yale University Press, 1982.

Summerson, John. *Architecture in Britain, 1530 to 1830.* 6th rev. ed. New York: Penguin Books, 1977.

Swaim, Douglas, ed. *Cabins and Castles: The History and Architecture of Buncombe County, North Carolina.* Asheville: City of Asheville, County of Buncombe, and Archives and History, 1981.

———. *Carolina Dwelling.* Raleigh: North Carolina State University School of Design Student Publication, 1978.

Swan, Abraham. *The British Architect, or, the Builder's Treasury of Staircases.* London: n.p., 1758.

———. *A Collection of Designs in Architecture.* 2 vols. London: n.p., 1757.

Taylor, Gwynne Stephens. *From Frontier to Factory: An Architectural History of Forsyth County.* Winston-Salem: Winston-Salem/Forsyth County Historic Properties Commission and Archives and History, 1981.

Thorp, Daniel B. "Assimilation in North Carolina's Moravian Community." *Journal of Southern History* 52, no. 1 (Feb. 1986): 19–42.

———. "The City That Never Was." *North Carolina Historical Review* 61, no. 1 (Jan. 1984): 36–58.

———. *The Moravian Community in Colonial North Carolina: Pluralism on the Southern Frontier.* Knoxville: University of Tennessee Press, 1989.

Tilley, Nannie May. *The Bright-Tobacco Industry, 1860–1929.* Chapel Hill: University of North Carolina Press, 1948.

———. *The R. J. Reynolds Tobacco Company.* Chapel Hill: University of North Carolina Press, 1985.

Tindall, George Brown. *The Emergence of the New South, 1913–1945.* Baton Rouge: Louisiana State University Press, 1967.

Todd, V. H., and J. Goebel, eds. *Christoph Von Graffenried's Account of the Founding of New Bern.* Raleigh: North Carolina Historical Commission, 1920.

Tomlan, Michael A. "Toward the Growth of an Artistic Taste." Introduction to George F. Barber, *Cottage Souvenir Number Two.* Watkins Glen, N.Y.: American Life Foundation and Study Institute, 1982.

Tompkins, D. A. *Cotton Mill: Commercial Features.* Charlotte: Observer Printing House, 1899.

Touart, Paul Baker. "The Acculturation of German-American Building Practices of Davidson County, North Carolina." In *Perspectives in Vernacular Architecture, II*, edited by Camille Wells, 72–80. Columbia: University of Missouri Press for the Vernacular Architecture Forum, 1986.

———. *Building the Back Country: An Architectural History of Davidson County, North Carolina.* Lexington: Davidson County Historical Society, 1987.

Tullos, Allen. *Habits of Industry: White Culture and the Transformation of the Carolina Piedmont.* Chapel Hill: University of North Carolina Press, 1989.

Turner, Paul Venable. *Campus: An American Planning Tradition.* Cambridge, Mass.: MIT Press, 1984.

U.S. Postal Service. *History of Post Office Construction, 1900–1940.* Washington, D.C.: U.S. Postal Service, 1982.

Upjohn, Richard. *Upjohn's Rural Architecture.* New York: George P. Putnam, 1852.

Upton, Dell. "Early Vernacular Architecture in Southeastern Virginia." Ph.D. diss., Brown University, 1980.

———. *Holy Things and Profane: Anglican Parish Churches in Colonial Virginia.* Cambridge, Mass.: MIT Press, 1986.

———. "Pattern Books and Professionalism: Aspects of the Transformation of Domestic Architecture in America, 1800–1860." *Winterthur Portfolio* 19, nos. 2/3 (Summer/Autumn 1984): 107–50.

———. "Traditional Timber Framing." In *Material Culture of the Wooden Age*, edited by Brooke Hindle, 35–93. Tarrytown, N.Y.: Sleepy Hollow Press, 1981.

———. "Vernacular Domestic Architecture in Eighteenth-Century Virginia." *Winterthur Portfolio* 17, nos. 2/3 (Summer/Autumn 1982): 95–119.

———, ed. *America's Architectural Roots: Ethnic Groups That Built America.* Washington, D.C.: Preservation Press, 1986.

Upton, Dell, and John Michael Vlach, eds. *Common Places: Readings in American Vernacular Architecture.* Athens: University of Georgia Press, 1986.

Watson, Harry. *An Independent People: The Way We Lived in North Carolina, 1770–1820.* Series edited by Sydney Nathans. Chapel Hill: University of North Carolina Press, 1983.

Waugh, Elizabeth Culbertson. *North Carolina's Capital, Raleigh.* Chapel Hill: University of North Carolina Press, 1967.

Weaver, William Woys. "The Pennsylvania German House: European Antecedents and New World Forms." *Winterthur Portfolio* 21, no. 4 (Winter 1986): 243–65.

Weiss, Ellen. *City in the Woods: The Life and Design of an American Camp Meeting on Martha's Vineyard.* New York: Oxford University Press, 1987.

Wells, Camille, ed. *Perspectives in Vernacular Architecture, I.*

Annapolis, Md.: Vernacular Architecture Forum, 1982.

———. *Perspectives in Vernacular Architecture, II.* Columbia: University of Missouri Press for the Vernacular Architecture Forum, 1986.

Whatley, Lowell McKay, Jr. *The Architectural History of Randolph County, North Carolina.* Asheboro: City of Asheboro and County of Randolph, 1985.

White, James F. *Protestant Worship and Church Architecture: Theological and Historical Considerations.* New York: Oxford University Press, 1964.

Whitehead, Russell F. "Some Work of Aymar Embury II in the Sandhills of North Carolina." *Architectural Record* 55 (June 1924): 505–68.

Whitworth, Henry P., ed. *Carolina Architecture and Allied Arts.* Miami: Frederick Findiesen, 1939.

Wiebe, Robert H. *The Search for Order, 1877–1920.* New York: Hill and Wang, 1967.

"William Logan's Journal of a Journey to Georgia, 1745." *Pennsylvania Magazine of History and Biography* 36 (1912): 1–16, 162–86.

Williams, Isabel M. "Thalian Hall." Research report, copy in Restoration Branch, Archives and History, Raleigh.

Williams, Michael Ann. "Homeplace: The Social Use and Meaning of the Folk Dwelling in Southwestern North Carolina." Ph.D. diss., University of Pennsylvania, 1985.

———. *Marble and Log: The History and Architecture of Cherokee County, North Carolina.* Murphy: Cherokee County Historical Museum, 1984.

Wilson, Charles Reagan, and William Ferris, eds. *Encyclopedia of Southern Culture.* Chapel Hill: University of North Carolina Press, 1989.

Wilson, Louis R. *The University of North Carolina, 1900–1930.* Chapel Hill: University of North Carolina Press, 1957.

Winston-Salem Section, NCAIA. *Architectural Guide: Winston-Salem, Forsyth County.* Winston-Salem: Winston-Salem Section, NCAIA, 1978.

Wodehouse, Lawrence. "Alfred B. Mullett's Court Room and Post Office at Raleigh, North Carolina." *Journal of the Society of Architectural Historians* 26, no. 4 (Dec. 1967): 301–5.

———. "Architecture in North Carolina." *North Carolina Architect,* Nov./Dec. 1969, Jan./Feb. 1970.

———. "Frank Pierce Milburn (1868–1926), a Major Southern Architect." *North Carolina Historical Review* 50, no. 3 (July 1973): 289–303.

———. "Kocher at Black Mountain." *Journal of the Society of Architectural Historians* 41, no. 4 (Dec. 1982): 328–32.

Wood, Ernest. "A Look at an Early Modernist Building in North Carolina." *North Carolina Architect,* Jan./Feb. 1978, 35–37.

Woodward, C. Vann. *Origins of the New South.* Baton Rouge: Louisiana State University Press, 1951.

Worsley, Stephen C. "Catholicism in Antebellum North Carolina." *North Carolina Historical Review* 60, no. 4 (Oct. 1983): 399–430.

Wrenn, Tony P. *Wilmington, North Carolina: An Architectural and Historical Portrait.* Charlottesville: University Press of Virginia, 1984.

York, Eugene V. "The Architecture of the United States Life-Saving Stations." Master's thesis, Boston University, 1983.

———. "The Architecture of the U.S. Life-Saving Stations." *The Log of Mystic Seaport* 34, no. 1 (Spring 1982): 3–20.

The Historic Preservation
Foundation of North Carolina, Inc.

Created in 1939 as the North Carolina Society for the Preservation of Antiquities, the Historic Preservation Foundation of North Carolina, Inc., is the state's only private, nonprofit statewide preservation organization. Its purpose can be simply stated: The Preservation Foundation seeks to build a society in which all North Carolinians are aware of and concerned about the state's built heritage so that future generations may enjoy it.

The national reputation of the Preservation Foundation has rested largely on the work of its revolving fund, the first of its kind in the nation and still the most active by far. The revolving fund, which acquires endangered historic properties until sympathetic new owners can be found, has in its first decade directly generated more than $25 million in private investment in historic preservation.

The Preservation Foundation also promotes historic preservation through workshops, seminars, technical briefings, and development of preservation leadership. The foundation sponsors special events throughout North Carolina and gives annual awards for outstanding achievements in historic preservation.

The Preservation Foundation was the 1987 recipient of the Southeast Regional Preservation Award from the National Park Service. The first organization to receive this award, the Preservation Foundation was cited as "the premier statewide preservation organization of the South, if not the Nation."

The Preservation Foundation is supported by the contributions of its members. For more information, contact The Historic Preservation Foundation of North Carolina, Inc., Post Office Box 27644, Raleigh, North Carolina 27611-7644.

Index

References to illustrations appear in italic type.

Abbott's Building Company, 317
Abele, Julian, 396–97, 399
Aberthaw (engineering firm), 397
Adam, Robert and James, 52
Adamesque neoclassicism, 52, 67–73, 96, 97, 196
Advertising: by builders, 111; tobacco, 344, 354; for house plans, 350
Africa: immigrants from, 1, 2; influence on architecture, 180, 207, 465 (n. 8), 476 (n. 39), 478 (n. 75)
African Methodist Episcopal Church, 310, 317, 321
African Methodist Episcopal Zion Church, 310, 317
Agriculture: geography and, 1, 2; and state economy, 51–52; commercial, 161–62; farm outbuildings, 213–17; books on, 214; plantation architecture, 257–60; single-crop farming, 273; production, 364, 465 (n. 6), 481 (n. 140). *See also* Barns; Farms; Outbuildings; Plantations
Air conditioning, 492 (n. 150)
Airlie Lodge (near Wilmington), 443
Airship Docks (Weeksville), *454*, 455
Akron-plan Sunday schools, 325–27
Akzona (Biltmore) Building (Asheville), *413*
Aladdin Plan of Industrial Housing, *426*, 429, *429*
Aladdin Readi-Cut houses, 427–29, 490 (n. 106), 490–91 (n. 108)
Alamance County, 185, 243, 368
Albemarle Sound, 1–2
Albers, Josef and Anni, 452
Alexander, Hezekiah and Mary Sample, 36
Alexander House (Mecklenburg Co.), 36, *36*, 124
Allen-Mangum House (Granville Co.), 292, *294*
All Saints Episcopal Church (Linville), *382*, 382–83, *383*
All Soul's Episcopal Church (Asheville), *360*, 361
Alston, George, 481 (n. 149)
Aluminum Company of America, 423
American Architect and Building News, 342
American Indians, 2, 465 (nn. 6, 8). *See also* Cherokee Indians; Tuscarora Indians
American Revolution, 49, 51, 468 (n. 52)

American Tobacco Company, 364, 371–72, 487 (n. 15)
Andrews, A. B., 287
Andrews, W. S., 481 (n. 156)
Anglican churches, 9, 37, 41, 42, 57, 58, 78
Appleget, G. S. H., 282, 283, 287, 333, 482 (n. 22)
Architects, 43–44, 85–86, 96–101, 162–63, 223–24, 363–64; and courthouses, 385; industrial age and, 275; Great Depression and, 448. *See also* individual architects
Architectural books, 19, 37, 41, 45, 52, 82, 88, 223, 245, 281. *See also* individual titles at authors
Architectural Record, 412
Art Deco, 365, 409, 411–16, 448
Artis, Elvin, 231–34
Asbury, Francis, 400, 434 (n. 59)
Asbury, Louis, 376
Asheboro, N.C., 385
Ashe County, 292, 325, 425
Asheville, N.C., 219, 242, 254; commercial buildings in, 330, 405; hotels in, 344, 384; houses in, 347, 357, 361, 429–30; public buildings in, 359, 413; church in, 390; Gothic Revival in, 394; Art Deco in, 412–16, *413*; resorts, 443; modernist style in, 455
Asheville City Building (Asheville), *plate 17*, *413*, 413–14, *415*
Ashley, William D., 175–77, 476 (n. 32)
Atkins, Rhodham, 470 (n. 10)
Atkinson, Thomas, 240
Atlantic and North Carolina Railroad, 261
Atlantic Coast Line Railroad, 364, 372
Atlantic Terra Cotta Company, 412
Attmore, William, 66, 121
Atwood, T. C., Company, 396
Atwood and Weeks, 492 (n. 149)
Aust, Gottfried, 30
Ayden, N.C., 376, 427
Ayden City Hall (Ayden), *375*, *376*
Ayr Mount (Hillsborough), 109, *112*, 112–13, *113*, 473 (n. 74)

Back Creek Presbyterian Church (Rowan Co.), 185–87, *186*, 476–77 (n. 46)
Bacon, Henry, Jr., 346, 379–80, 382, 433, 487 (nn. 28, 29)

Badin, N.C., 423
Bain, W. C., 316, 344
Bain Building Company, 484 (n. 66)
Baird, James, Company, 363, 409
Baird Barn (Watauga Co.), 301, *301*
Baird House (Watauga Co.), 292, *293*
Bald Head Island Lighthouse (Brunswick Co.), 53, *54*
Baldwin, James J., 386
Balloon framing, 275
Baltimore, Md.: workmen from, 265–67; building materials from, 266
Banker's House (Shelby), *282*, 283
Bank of Lumberton (Lumberton), 403, *405*
Bank of New Bern (New Bern), 76
Bank of Robeson (Maxton), 403, 489 (n. 65)
Bank of the Cape Fear (Wilmington), *224*, 224–26, 478 (n. 94)
Bank of Washington (Washington), *193*, *193*
Banks, 403–5, 489 (n. 63). *See also* individual banks
Bannerman House (Sampson Co.), 142, 143, *144*
Baptist Female University (Raleigh), *343*, 343–44
Baptists, 37, 57–58, 78; evangelism of, 177, 178, 180; churches of, 183–84, 224, 230–31, 240, 262, 390, 391, 412–13, 481 (n. 162); growth among black congregations, 310–11
Barber, George F., 350–51, 417, 427, 485 (n. 94); *Cottage Souvenir*, 350
Barfield, Richard, 478 (n. 69)
Barnes, David A., House (Murfreesboro), 292, *292*
Barns, 149, 152; log, 158, 299–300, 483 (n. 40); English, 152; double-crib, 158, 299; frame, 214, 258–60, *259*, 271, 300–301; four-crib, 299–300; "round," 301; tobacco curing, *303*, 303–4, *305*
Barracks, The (Tarboro), 263–65, *265*
Barrett, Charles: *Colonial Southern Homes*, 417–18, 490 (n. 92)
Barrington, George, 474 (n. 110)
Barton, Harry, 449
Bath, N.C., 2; house in, 16; churches in, 37–38, 41
Battery Park Hotel (Asheville), 344, *344*, 384, 412, 485 (n. 88)